The Story of Secret Service

Also from Westphalia Press
westphaliapress.org

The Idea of the Digital University

Masonic Tombstones and Masonic Secrets

Eight Decades in Syria

Avant-Garde Politician

L'Enfant and the Freemasons

Baronial Bedrooms

Conflicts in Health Policy

Material History and Ritual Objects

Paddle Your Own Canoe

Opportunity and Horatio Alger

Careers in the Face of Challenge

Bookplates of the Kings

Collecting American Presidential Autographs

Misunderstood Children

Original Cables from the Pearl Harbor Attack

Social Satire and the Modern Novel

The Amenities of Book Collecting

The Genius of Freemasonry

A Definitive Commentary on Bookplates

James Martineau and Rebuilding Theology

No Bird Lacks Feathers

Earthworms, Horses, and Living Things

The Man Who Killed President Garfield

Anti-Masonry and the Murder of Morgan

Understanding Art

Homeopathy

Ancient Masonic Mysteries

Collecting Old Books

The Boy Chums Cruising in Florida Waters

The Thomas Starr King Dispute

Ivanhoe Masonic Quartettes

Lariats and Lassos

Mr. Garfield of Ohio

The Wisdom of Thomas Starr King

The French Foreign Legion

War in Syria

Naturism Comes to the United States

New Sources on Women and Freemasonry

Designing, Adapting, Strategizing in Online Education

Gunboat and Gun-runner

Meeting Minutes of Naval Lodge No. 4 F.A.A.M

The Story of Secret Service

by Richard Wilmer Rowan

with a new introduction by Rahima Schwenkbeck

WESTPHALIA PRESS
An imprint of Policy Studies Organization

The Story of Secret Service
All Rights Reserved © 2013 by Policy Studies Organization

Westphalia Press
An imprint of Policy Studies Organization
1527 New Hampshire Ave., NW
Washington, D.C. 20036
dgutierrezs@ipsonet.org

ISBN-13: 978-1935907473
ISBN-10: 1935907476

Cover design by Taillefer Long at Illuminated Stories:
www.illuminatedstories.com

Updated material and comments on this edition
can be found at the Westphalia Press website:
www.westphaliapress.org

Introduction

Since the issuance of the Monroe Doctrine, the United States has adopted a stance colloquially known as the "policeman of the world." The United States has actively participated in several wars, military actions, and extensive covert operations worldwide, typically pursued in the name of preserving democracy, financial interests, preventing the spread of Communism, and, on occasion, peace. Richard Wilmer Rowan's work, *The Story of Secret Service*, a review of "thirty-three centuries of secret service" worldwide, starts far earlier than the issuance of the Doctrine. It helps to remind us of the very short impact that the United States has had on world affairs and of the surprising and sometimes diabolical actions governments have taken over time to ensure their interests over the course of world history. Rowan actually finds that the United States had lagged behind in developing undercover techniques because of long standing isolationist policies (526). Such a widely encompassing work as Rowan's helps one gain a better perspective on world history, and spices it up with sordid tales of espionage.

Perhaps the largest grievance that can be taken with a work on such a subject is that so many stories—of a field filled with anonymity, silence and deception—have been forgotten to history. This allows Rowan a great deal of room for speculation, of which he admits while detailing a "highly unstatistical chart" with "no supporting scientific evidence" but which he uses to explain that the amount of spies has multiplied sevenfold over the course of the past 33 centuries (7). Despite this open admission to writing of the unknown and all of the perils it entails, Rowan's dense work is well aware that it offers just a small chunk of the long history of covert service throughout history. There are a few, general parameters that guide *The Story of Secret Service*. Rowan focuses on the development of espionage as it relates to the needs and interests of a government, rather than industrial espionage, which involves corporations. This work is also Eurocentric. While stories of Mogolian and Feudal Japanese spies dot the landscape, the primary focus is on European lore. Thus, Roman tales of espionage are captured instead of the well-known strategies of subversion penned by Sun-Tzu, or the use of pochteca by the Aztecs.

Making one's way through Rowan's work, one must command an equal knowledge of sprawling kingdoms, empires, lesser known figures, new developments in technology and the continual changing of the guard over the centuries. Stories of well-known figures and events, such as Cleopatra, the Inquisition, Ghengis Khan and the Dreyfus Affair help to keep pace with the dizzying speed at which Rowan barrels through centuries. The rewards are tidbits of information about organizations and figures not often considered to be spies. For example, Rowan details the "militant fathers of the Society of Jesus...a secret service corps d'élite" (66). Here Rowan uses several illustrations to explain that Jesuits often found themselves "religious fugitives" and crept their way into the walls and floors of homes to avoid detection. This was made possible by Father Oven, who traveled across England in order to help develop a mass of false ceilings, trap doors, revolving panels and other trickery to aid in hiding the wanted Jesuits (69).

Changes in available technology operate in the background as the centuries fly by in this work. The introduction of photography, for example, played a new and significant role in the development of undercover actions. Rowan details the experiences of Lafayette C. Baker, who served as a Union spy during the Civil War. The camera was a novelty at the time, so it did not matter that the large one Baker carried around was broken. It proved to be the perfect guise and through it Baker was able to secure so much valuable information on Confederate movements that upon his return and report to Union soldiers he was on the quick path to promotion, escalating to the rank of brigadier general (287). We also see a broad swath of weaponry develop, from the introduction of gunpowder and its discontents, to muskets, knives, poison gas, smoke clouds, Krupp rifles and Skoda howitzers and spy planes, to mention a few. Rowan's work shows how developments towards new, larger, and more powerful weapons as well as innovative combinations of simple materials alike can turn the tide. Sometimes a show of force is all that is needed, while other, desperate times can spur on surprising inventiveness with astonishing results.

The Story of Secret Service illustrates how deeply religious differences have sadly divided the world's population for countless centuries. Rowan begins his work with the story of Delilah operating as "a secret agent of the Philistines" (9), citing the Torah's story of the twelve spies mandated by God and directed by Moses (12) to set the stage for covert service as being ingrained in the human experience and of divine inspiration. Later, Rowan details the many military and covert operations that Mohammed faced (38). Perhaps this religious foundation of spying that Rowan develops is necessary to help assuage concerns about the moral ambiguity that spying often raises.[1] Espionage often calls for relationships to develop under false pretenses, and at worst, incite violence and mass deaths. This says nothing of the laws that espionage violates and creeping concerns about what the "right" side actually is.

Rowan ends with "Epilogue or Prologue?" not entirely aware that in a few years the world would be embattled in the Second World War. *Secret Service* offers a helpful look at the worldwide circumstances that led into the outbreak of World War II. Writing in 1937, Rowan details the murkiness of relationships between countries in the aftermath of World War I and the rise of fascism. He is well versed in the particular atrocities committed by Italian Fascists and German Nazis, noting that "the political police of Italy have a blunt instrument which they use to break a suspect's jaw, laying him up for a long painful period without fracturing the skull or otherwise gravely endangering his life," among other instruments of torture (669). He concludes that "[t]he world...has marched almost heedlessly into a twilight zone of war preparations and perpetual alarm" (6). As Dwight Eisenhower would later caution the United States from developing a military industrial complex, Rowan, along with others such as Daniel Guérin, wrote of similar danger that developed alongside the rise of fascism. This long history of secret service shows the perils of a world that has advanced itself on secrecy, coercion and lies.

Rahima Schwenkbeck

---

1. Klehr, Harvey. "Reflections on Espionage." *Social Philosophy & Policy* 21.1 (Winter 2004): 141-166; 143.

THE STORY OF SECRET SERVICE

THE STORY OF
SECRET SERVICE

RICHARD WILMER ROWAN

 *With linecut illustrations*

PRINTED AT THE *Country Life Press*, GARDEN CITY, N. Y., U. S. A.

To
RUTH GERRARD

CONTENTS

CHAPTER		PAGE
1	Thirty-Three Centuries of Secret Service	1
2	In the Shadows of Adventure	9
3	The Cunning of Antiquity	18
4	Spies, Slaves and a Fire Brigade	23
5	Byzantium to Bagdad	33
6	The Sect of the Assassins	42
7	Modern Spies from Medieval Asia	48
8	Treacheries, Sacred and Profane	54
9	Church and State	57
10	The Arts and Craft of the Jesuits	66
11	Police Espials, or the Kings' Evil	73
12	Walsingham Sights the Armada	76
13	The Scavenger Spies of Mogul India	83
14	Father Joseph and the Cardinal's Spies	87
15	Espionage and the Honors of War	92
16	Mr Thurloe and Mr Pepys	103
17	Espionne of the Bedchamber	108
18	Defoe and the Jacobites	112
19	Bourbon Police Espionage	120
20	The Bewitching Chevalier	128
21	Caron de Beaumarchais, alias Norac	138
22	The Furtive Practice of Doctor Bancroft	143
23	Clandestine Spirit of '76	149
24	Liberty, Equality, Fraternity—Intrigue	159

CONTENTS

CHAPTER		PAGE
25	DE BATZ, THE GASCON WIZARD	163
26	FOUCHÉ FACING FOUR WAYS	168
27	MONTGAILLARD THE UNMITIGATED	173
28	IMPERIAL SECRET POLICE	184
29	DUBLIN CASTLE'S CORPS OF DOUBLE-DEALERS	194
30	BRITAIN LEADS WITH A CUCKOLD	198
31	THE CONTINENTAL BLOCKADE	202
32	THE POWERFUL IMPACT OF POUNDS STERLING	212
33	A CRACKPOT'S COUP	216
34	AN EMPEROR OF ESPIONS	226
35	NAPOLEONIC ADVERSARIES	235
36	HIGH PRIESTESS OF HOLY PEACE	240
37	CARBONARI AND CAMORRA	247
38	PROLOGUE TO SECESSION	252
39	THE BALTIMORE CONSPIRATORS	265
40	AGENTS BLUE AND GRAY	274
41	LAFAYETTE BAKER AND BELLE BOYD	284
42	CRAZY BET AND OTHER LADIES	296
43	REBELS OF THE NORTH	310
44	BEFORE THE DELUGE	317
45	STIEBER THE SPY-MASTER	326
46	KING OF SLEUTHHOUNDS	336
47	LESSONS FROM A SCHOOL OF HARD KNOCKS	346
48	PRIVATE PATRONS OF INTELLIGENCE	354
49	DE BLOWITZ AT BERLIN	364
50	THE OCHRANA	368
51	AGENT PROVOCATEUR	374
52	THE DEGRADATION OF ALFRED DREYFUS	386

CONTENTS

CHAPTER		PAGE
53	PICQUART AND ZOLA: THE COUNTER-DETECTION	395
54	THE FRENCH REACTION	408
55	THE ACCREDITED SPIES	413
56	MESSENGERS TO GARCIA AND AGUINALDO	416
57	THE SOUTH AFRICAN WAR	426
58	SPIES OF THE RISING SUN	432
59	WATCHDOGS OF DICTATORDOM	441
60	TRAPPING AN ARCHTRAITOR	445
61	THE COSTLY TREASON OF ALFRED REDL	453
62	SECRET COMMITTEES OF MACEDONIA	462
63	BLACK HAND IN THE BALKANS	473
64	THE COMING OF WORLD CATASTROPHE	482
65	THE SHEEP'S CLOTHING OF WILHELM STIEBER	486
66	THE DRAMA BEGINS: DOWN WITH THE CURTAIN	496
67	INTELLIGENCE AND SECRET SERVICE	502
68	THE QUICKSANDS OF TSARDOM	512
69	SABOTAGE	518
70	SPECIAL MISSIONS	526
71	GENIUS IN THE NEAR EAST	533
72	ADVENTURES IN ESPIONAGE	544
73	THE MARTYRDOM OF EDITH CAVELL	548
74	THE REAL FRÄULEIN DOKTOR	557
75	RIGORS OF THE ANTWERP SCHOOL	565
76	THE SPY "SCHOOL" OF ALICE DUBOIS	574
77	LIQUIDATION OF A LUXURY	584
78	WHO WAS GUILTY?	596
79	STRATAGEMS AFLOAT	601
80	STRATAGEMS AFIELD	610

CONTENTS

CHAPTER		PAGE
81	Caporetto: The Perfect Surprise Attack	620
82	French Operatives in the Secret War	626
83	The Censor in Secret Service	636
84	The Bluff Barrage	643
85	Silber and Zievert, the Censor Spies	647
86	The Reservoir of Victory	656
87	An American Secret-Service Story	660
88	A World Made Safe for Deaths of Democracy	664
Notes		671

ILLUSTRATIONS

	PAGE
The Expanding "Shadow" of World-Wide Espionage	7
A System Mithridates and Delilah Never Dreamed of	11
The Roman Empire at Its Maximum Extent	30
The Ingenious Hiding Place of Jesuit Agents	68
Concealed Entrance to Staircase, Hardwick Hall	69
Authentic Secret-Service Drawing: the "Insect"	134
Design of Fortifications Concealed by the "Insect"	135
The V-Shaped Notch	190
Entomologist Sketch Enclosing the Design of an Enemy Fortress	229
The Private Cipher of Miss Elizabeth van Lew	302
An Authentic Diagram of Modern Military Espionage	350
The Handwriting of Alfred Dreyfus	396
The Handwriting of Ferdinand Walsin Esterhazy	397
The Evidence of the "Bordereau"	398
For Smoking and Concealing	427
In Time of Danger	427
Location of German Agents Arrested in England, August 4, 1914	493
Interior Design of the Incendiary "Crayon" Pencil	517
The Sabotage "Cigar"	522
Espionage System of the British Secret Service at the Time of the World War	546
Spy Sketch in Chemical Ink Underneath the Postage Stamp	577

ILLUSTRATIONS

	PAGE
A Q-boat Navigating the War Zone in Shabby Disguise	606
The Decoy Ship of Q-boat Cleared for Action	607
A German Interpretation of the French Intelligence in War Time	628
Key to Design of French Intelligence Organization	629
Secret Agent's Sketch of a Naval Base	650
Espionage Drawing of the Naval Base after Transmission of the Sketch	651
Political Police Supervision Espionage and Censorship, Europe, in January 1937	665
Political Police, Censorship and Military Secret Service in the Far East, January 1937	667

THE STORY OF SECRET SERVICE

Chapter One

THIRTY-THREE CENTURIES OF SECRET SERVICE

SPIES AND SPECULATORS for thirty-three centuries have exerted more influence on history than on historians. There are various moral, ethical and optical explanations of this phenomenon of scholarship; but perhaps the most plausible is to be found in the character of spies, the nature of their work, and the often unsavory motives of those who have been the chief beneficiaries of espionage and the intrigues of political secret agents. Spies, in short, are a veritable insecticide upon the Great-Man treatment of history, which of all treatments is the most romantic and most palatable. And the great men themselves, when composing memoirs or correcting the grade of their eminence, have been disposed to protect their spies and secret emissaries—even those safely deceased—by preserving their anonymity and resisting the temptation to divide with them the credit which otherwise must burden the narrator alone. Concern for the ultimate security of the spy is never so acute, it appears, as when the time comes to save him from his reckless, mercenary inclination to share in the public acclaim.

Voltaire observed that the sound of history is the tread of sabots going upstairs and the patter of satin slippers coming down. Behind this evolutionary "sabotage" of polite society we may catch another sound, the faintest creaking, perhaps, the stealthy steps of intriguers going up and down the backstairs of history, century after century, affecting the future of great and small nations and the lives and happiness of multitudes. The tremor of their steps might not register upon the most delicate seismograph, but the influence of their acts can accumulate hurricane force. If we look sharp we may see the conspirators and spies at their work, but we must watch them with a very careful, insulating vigilance. Their triumphs come unexpectedly, their blunders are innumerable—and both carry a terrific bystander-recoil.

In this program of study the kings and queens, the emperors and empresses, shall only be known by the company of spies that they keep. The artful employers of spies have been legion. We could never count them all; but let us observe as many as we can—from the days of happy partnership between Moses and Jehovah in a certain affair of espionage to the ultra-imperial modernistic dictators, who frankly avoid the contaminations of divine guidance and only submit to the limitations of Divine Right in order to assure themselves that they can do no wrong.

Tyrannies from the earliest dawn of history have been established in power by a thrilling show of force, but tyrants have had to maintain their power by a special form of stealth which is called secret service. Now every activity of the spy, amateur, hireling or professional, in peace or in war, is a form of secret service; and every mission or clandestine enterprise carried out by an agent of government may belong to secret service. While in process of compounding this record we shall have to touch upon all of its forms; yet the *organization* of spies, the calculated teamwork of secret agents and their systematic military or political employment, represents the kind of secret service whose story has waited long to be told in a unified manner. Direction and management of such organizations are an integral part of government and in themselves a form of secret service, moving through a very gradual development to their present state of specialization and complexity. Secret service is not only the weapon of tyrannies or the safeguard of governments and armies; in its own right it has become a subterranean method of international combat. Many famous collisions of rival secret services might be compared to warfare; yet the difference between a conflict of secret agents and the actual conflict of soldiers is the difference between an operating room and an abattoir. And in secret service, too, the operation is a success even though the patient dies.

With a record of thirty-three centuries of secret service to unfold it is surprising to detect so few symptoms of evolution. The changes of time and experience, if any, have been largely for the worse. Governments fall, great empires decline, the very peoples of the earth decay and vanish; but the degeneration of government as evinced in the more subtle forms of repression and secret service endures like sex perversion or recurs like cancer and influenza. The spies that hovered in a cloud around Jesus of Nazareth were just as repellent in character and clumsy in technique as the agents of political police in half-a-dozen European states today, but by comparison with the modern informers and *agents provocateurs* they seem rather less malign.

The operations of spies or secret police are invariable abridgments of the rights of the individual and of the decent conduct of the affairs of state. However deeply rooted and inherent the *government trait* of secret service, no thoroughly respectable world would tolerate it.

It is an ironic era in which to speculate upon political utopia or the millennium; but, when it comes, we shall instantly recognize the gates of pearl—not because they are pearl, but rather because they have no keyholes or other conveniences for spies and secret police.

There will always be more agents of intrigue and more activities of espionage under a despotism than under a democracy. Yet with democracies thrown upon the defensive, where is the first- or second-class Power today that manages to get along without secret service? As if perversely countering the splendid progress of science and the arts, governments—and especially the autocratic governments—seem eager to accelerate their own descending spiral of consummate treacheries. Is man, with the potential blessings of all this progress inviting him, bent on becoming a political monster? It has begun to seem so; and the sinister work of military or political secret service and police espionage offers a congenial refuge to all the barbarians lost in an unappreciated civilization. "A spy or modern plumbing in every home" is the choice to be bravely made; and "a spy in every home" is the actual program now arranged to appease the gangster heirs of the Neanderthalers, who also seem to have been a race that preferred to exist or perish as a pure Nordic strain.

Long ago an Austrian political police administration became singularly exercised about, and set a close watch upon, certain of its charges —the inmates of the autocratic state—who were persons suspected of *philanthropy*. According to the directing brain of the imperial secret police, compassion mingling with openhanded liberality would only "shake to its foundations the Christian religion." That sounds very comical in this enlightened age. An age, however, in which perhaps 50,000 persons are regularly employed to spy upon those suspected of liberal thought!

Fact Finding and Foul Play

Closely allied to the science of foul play which we call secret service there is that scientific accumulating of facts, near facts, suspicions and reformed falsehoods which governments and army and naval bureaus recommend as Intelligence—one of those thoroughly modern innovations that turn up disconcertingly in the Bible and Shakespeare. In *Macbeth* there is the device ordered by Malcolm:[1]

> *Let every soldier hew him down a bough,*
> *And bear 't before him; thereby shall we shadow*
> *The numbers of our host, and make discovery*
> *Err in report of us.*

That "erring" in report of the enemy is one of the things Intelligence was designed to prevent. On the night before the battle of Arbela a notion prevailed upon the Persian high command that Alexander of Macedon would overcome his handicap of fighting a vastly superior force by launching a night attack. The same idea had been urged upon the young conqueror-king, and he had rejected it with a very up-to-date and Grecian understanding of something which our thirty-three centuries have seen repeatedly invented—propaganda. Alexander told his veteran adviser, Parmenio, that he did not want to "filch a victory" whose value would have been impaired, as Arrian remarks, if gained under circumstances allowing Darius an excuse for his defeat and justification for renewing the contest. Whereupon the army of Alexander lay down and had a good night's sleep; while the Persians continued awake, entertaining the most restless apprehensions. "Darius . . . formed his troops at evening in order of battle, and kept them under arms all night,"[2] the very worst physical preparation for soldiers destined to suffer an historic reverse and exhaust themselves fighting or fleeing throughout the whole of the following day. Darius, whose very name suggests conquest and Persian military power, had no proper system of Intelligence and such inadequate espionage, he virtually threw away his chances of beating Alexander before a single phalanx moved against him.

The potential value of the spy or secret agent to Intelligence is best illustrated by these lost opportunities of celebrated commanders. If we describe nearly a full turn around our circumference of centuries we come to the same quarter of the world again and to the Allies' first naval attack upon the then ill-fortified Dardanelles. This attack occurred months before the tragic misadventure of Gallipoli and might easily have prevented it. A powerful Anglo-French Mediterranean fleet under the British admiral, De Robeck, bombarded the fortifications of the Dardanelles with immediate and splendid results—which remained deplorably unappreciated. Though mounting a few of the best Krupp guns served by German artillerists, the Turkish defenses of the strait were soon battered to dust. On the authority of the American ambassador, Henry Morgenthau,[3] the Allies were to learn too late that the Turkish Government—including the Turko-German high command—had become so sure that De Robeck's fleet would take Constantinople, they were already moving in panic across to Asia Minor and had loaded the official archives aboard a train that would presently depart for Anatolia—when the all but victorious attacking fleet steamed away and did not return.

One more day of that effective shelling and the precious strait would have been opened; which would have meant the opening of the Black Sea and a warm-water route to Russia, letting in the desperately needed equipment, munitions and hospital stores, letting out the hungrily desired surplus of the granary of Europe. It would have meant, too, the saving of that futile slaughter at Gallipoli, of thousands of other casualties in Mesopotamia and Palestine, and probably more than a million lives on the Russian, Serbian and Roumanian fronts, where inadequate armament turned so many attacks into massacres. All this surely, the Allies stood to win; but they cast it away when the fleet retired in error and did not resume its bombardment until an army was to be landed under fire and the Turkish defenses had been meanwhile enormously strengthened.

Want of intelligence disclosing how their success was so nearly attained, want of a spy able to communicate from Constantinople no more than Ambassador Morganthau had personally observed, cost the Allies every advantage that might have accrued to them. And this, be it noted, was primarily a defeat sustained by the British Secret Service whose continual achievements from the reign of Henry VII provide this record its truest framework of historic continuity. Rome, it is true, has been the Eternal City in nothing more acutely than in espionage, assassination and intrigue. But the secret agents of the Church or the spies of Fascism today have only an occupational kinship with the political police of the Caesars. France, like Britain, has had a virtually continuous installation of government espionage from the fifteenth century, but the turbulence of French history since 1789 has robbed its secret service of much external importance. Only during the Napoleonic Wars and during and directly after the World War has the French Secret Service achieved an international scope of inquisitiveness comparable to that of the British.

It has been the stellar role of the espionage organization of Great Britain to attain its most remarkable efficiency under Thurloe in the years of the English Civil War and the Cromwellian Protectorate, but to oppose thereafter the three other great revolutions of modern times. As we shall see, British agents risked every hazard to combat the American, the French and—until very recently—the Russian revolutions. With the curious result of achieving two defeats and one Bonaparte! Of the three, the British concentration upon the fluctuating fortunes of Russian authority was more specifically a matter of not minding one's own business and yet came actually closest to reactionary realization. For a spread of critical months, while Bruce Lockhart bewitched the ladies and Sidney Reilly bribed the Letts, it was touch and go whether the political philosophy of

Nikolai Lenin or the versatile interferences of His Majesty's Conservative government were to become historically responsible for the chaos descending upon Russia.

Tensions of the Truce

The war to end war and make the world safer for democracy ended with a pattern of peace that excluded international tranquillity and caused a veritable rash of revolutions, uprisings and violent repressions upon the face of the earth. And today it is appropriate that we review the crowded annals of secret service, inasmuch as we are—every one of us—living in an era of secret service, when the secret agent and spy have ceased to be necessary evils of belligerency and become a means of provocation, or instruments of neighborly repression, or sharply edged tools of not too well-masked hostility.

The world, in short, has marched almost heedlessly into a twilight zone of war preparations and perpetual alarm. Sixteen years of peace-worship, unending conferences, proposals of disarmament, limitations upon naval tonnage, and dove-bedecked propaganda have left Europe and half the world blistered, gassed and stricken. In this diplomatic shambles, moreover, there has been no peace, even while Great-Power spokesmen and ambassadors left roaming "at large" talked peace. Disarmament has been passed over conference tables like a bottomless decanter of port. The worthy and articulate League of Nations has suffered more setbacks than social justice in a Tory court. But there have been counter-revolutionary adventures all over Russia and Siberia, war in Asia Minor, war in north Morocco, war in Syria, war in China, in Manchuria, in parts of Mongolia. Palestine is having its share of armed insurrection. A peculiarly abominable small war was fought for the greater glory of munitions makers and oil-field concessionaires in the Chaco, between Bolivia and Paraguay. That struggle ran its sanguinary course, and then came the new or 1935-model of "undeclared" war upon Ethiopia. It seemed to redouble the tensions of Europe, but there was something far worse in store for what is still euphemistically known as "world peace", even though the very worst had overtaken undisciplined Ethiopians. The civil war in Spain has moved the focus of anxiety to the other end of the Mediterranean, while Herr Hitler continues his hilarious pastime of teasing and terrifying the old gentlemen and young geniuses of Downing Street and the Quai d'Orsay. The recent diplomatic invention of a "neutrality" that sponsors insurgents and grants rebels equality has shocked all who still cherished the delusion that the foreign policies of France

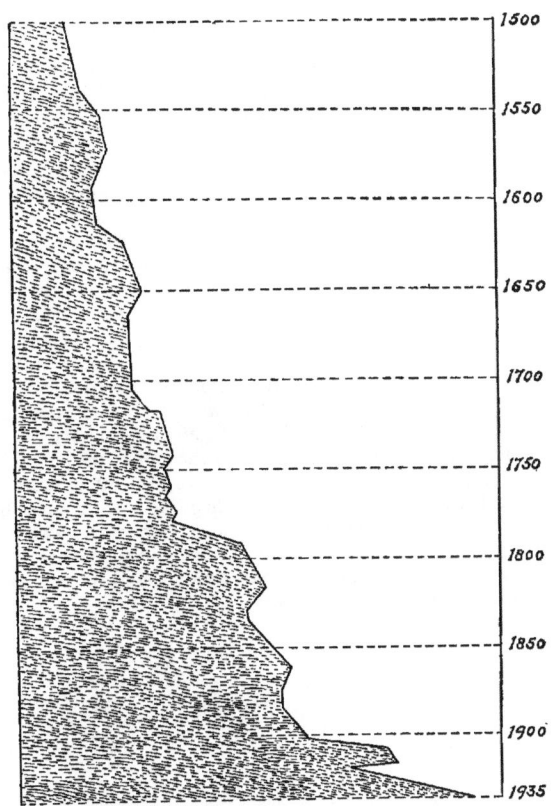

THE EXPANDING "SHADOW" OF WORLD-WIDE ESPIONAGE, POLITICAL POLICE REPRESSION AND MILITARY SECRET SERVICE

This highly unstatistical chart has no supporting scientific evidence other than the story of secret service itself, and the reader who pursues these centuries of intrigue down to the present will surely concede that there are at least seven trained professional spies, counter-spies or agents of secret police in action over the world today for every lurking amateur and hireling informer of four centuries ago.

and Great Britain are dictated by *democratic* principles of government. Thus far the Spanish struggle has been "localized" with the same disregard for human rights that distinguishes the subjugation of Ethiopia.

It was everywhere agreed that the outbreak of a general European war in the summer of 1914 had "ended an epoch." But the new epoch then presumably begun was exceptionally shortlived, for the Armistice of 1918 and the subsequent crop of treaties and agreements likewise have ended something which we may still hope was only an epoch and not civilization. It would be gratifying to promise a review of the events and operations of secret service, political police and international espionage during and directly following the World War as the final chapter of our story. But those operations and events only suggest an *introductory* chapter to the history of secret service in the great war—or wars—of our immediate future. Before some such horror descends upon us or our less belligerent neighbors, we had best pretend that it is the end, even if only the end of the past thirty-three centuries. And so let us navigate, if we can, the hitherto but vaguely charted seas of secret service. Perhaps we shall discover how the bellicose bankrupts and bullies of Fascism "got that way", and learn where the governments of peoples once again submitting to the discipline and living conditions of armed camps found the precedents which misguide them.

CHAPTER TWO

IN THE SHADOWS OF ADVENTURE

AS THE CHIEF END OF SECRET SERVICE down to comparatively recent times has been espionage, its most formidable and engrossing operatives have been spies. We shall meet in the pages which follow a great many of them, either extraordinary persons who ventured upon some form of espionage or rather ordinary persons who turned out to be remarkably adept as spies. But a number of adroit individuals have been enrolled as secret agents for purposes far removed from conventional spying; while still others we shall find have been agents of espionage without the advantages, hindrances or discipline of belonging to an organized system of secret service.

One of the first whose name is known, Delilah, was an impromptu secret agent of the Philistines. Apart from her tonsorial specialty, she allowed Philistine spies to hide in her house (Judges, 16:9) and used her sex to gain intelligence from a powerful enemy, playing the model confederate, resolved to earn the eleven hundred pieces of silver promised her by "the lords of the Philistines." She achieved what amounted to a complete espionage triumph, locating the largest effective force of her employers' adversaries and contriving the stroke which put that force out of action. For her conquest of the Goliath of dalliance she was not overpaid, excessive as the Philistines' fee may seem compared to the thirty silver pieces handed Judas Iscariot.

Another of the illustrious practitioners of ancient times proved so aggressive and efficient, he virtually invented an espionage service, which operated wholly for his private advantage and was staffed entirely by himself. It was not alone the flattery of contemporary historians that termed this spying conqueror-king, Mithridates VI of Pontus, "the Great." Uncommon as it was for a royal prince to train himself to act as his own secret agent, it was the normal thing for him to grow up to be suspicious and cruel; and the career of Mithridates may be accepted as a classic of tyrannical self-interest. He combined the cunning of the spy with the anxieties of the brutal despot whose intelligence he collected, and he appears to have been an interesting, successful, accomplished and frequently malodorous monarch. Ancient authorities, however, chose to invest him with a durable halo. His talents were so engaging that they saw in his unspeakable animosities merely a mild form of egotism.

He succeeded his father at the age of eleven and found the throne of Pontus immediately uncomfortable. It seems that his mother made several attempts upon his life, apparently because she considered his birth her own redeemable mistake. The boy king grew so afraid of his mother's ill will that he fled to the mountains, there accepting the hard lot of a fugitive and exile, but adding the amusements of a hunter and spy. When at length he felt bold enough to return to Sinope, he threw his mother into a dungeon and put his younger brother to death; and that was simply a minor demonstration of his greatness.

While in exile he had mastered twenty-two languages and dialects, traveling over Asia Minor—at the age of fourteen—disguised as a caravan boy. He visited many tribes, learned about their customs and spied upon their military strength. He was able to vanquish his mother and brother and to ascend the throne; and the years spent as an exile had given him an appetite for conquest. When next he set forth into Asia Minor he took with him a carefully trained and powerful army. No matter how far he might wander hereafter, he could conquer the land and continue to feel right at home.

Mithridates as a spy was so well informed that he was reluctant to put his trust in anybody.[1] Before he began his eighteen years' contest with such Roman generals as Sulla, Lucullus and Pompey, he had found time to murder his mother, his sons and his sister, whom he had married according to dynastic custom. Later, to prevent his enemies from enjoying his harem, which regal collectors acknowledged one of the most tasteful assortments of concubines in that quarter of the ancient world, he had every one of the coveted wenches slain. Like all masters of spies or secret service, like suspicious and sinister despots of every age and clime, Mithridates experienced black forebodings by day and flaming nightmares after dark. He could soothe his nerves with a Blood Purge in June, or whenever he felt the need of it, but still the pressure of envious rivals and imaginary malcontents kept him in a perpetual itch of ignoble expediency.

In Asia Minor he massacred over 100,000 subjects of Rome, thus magnifying his own hatred of Romans. Yet he escaped the consequences of that butchery when Sulla consented to a discreditable peace so that he might be free to hurry his legions back to Rome, beat Marius at the battle of the Colline Gate, and resume the massacring of Marians. In the last of the Mithridatic wars, the ruler of Pontus pitted his skill as a general against Lucullus and Pompey in turn, and, far

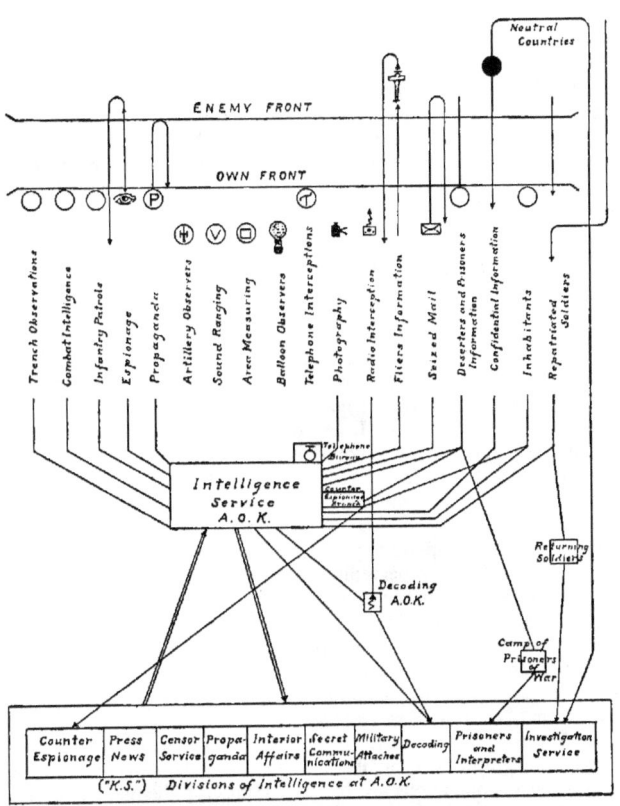

A SYSTEM MITHRIDATES AND DELILAH NEVER DREAMED OF

The organization of the *Kundschafts Stelle* or Austro-Hungarian Intelligence Service, according to the design published by General Maximilian Ronge, its former chief.

from being overthrown by those formidable commanders, he was able to plot against Rome to the end of his days, an end that came with long-anticipated suddenness. Mithridates was planning a great league of the warlike tribes of the Danube that would join him in invading Italy from the northeast, when one of his sons whom he had unaccountably neglected to murder brushed him from his throne with a powerful draught of poison.

Rahab the Harlot to "Fiddler" Foley

The necessities of compression and the complexities of more modern secret service will draw us rapidly down the earlier centuries, even while battles are being won, peoples subjugated and dynasties cast into oblivion by means of espionage and organized intrigue. Rahab, the harlot of Jericho (Joshua, 2:1-21), who sheltered and concealed the spies of Israel, made a covenant with them and duped their pursuers, was not only an impromptu confederate of immense value to the Jewish leaders of that far-distant day, but also established a "siren in secret service" plot-pattern which is still of periodic relief to motion-picture producers.

When advancing upon the promised land the long-overdue Hebrew fugitives from Egypt repeatedly made use of spies; and it is evident that their calling was held not unworthy of honor. For thirty centuries it is only the very occasional master of secret service whose name, together with his exploits, turns up on the pages of history. The Old Testament, however, names the twelve spies whom the Lord directed Moses to send into the land of Canaan (Numbers, 13:3-15) and records that "all those men were heads of the children of Israel." And when Moses sent them forth to spy out the land he did not propose a mere topographical expedition. After the usual consultation with Jehovah—who, one might say, has only Himself to blame if spies have persistently plagued mankind—Moses was equipped to lay down the law of offensive secret service.

The great seer told his tribesmen to go up into the mountain, to see the land and see the people dwelling therein—to discover whether they were few or many, whether strong or weak, and whether the land were good or bad, what cities were there, and if the people dwelt "in tents, or in strong holds." He further advised that they learn if the land were fat or lean and determine the extent of its wood supply; and finally they must be "of good courage, and bring of the fruit of the land." (Numbers, 13:17-20.) Stieber, the notorious Prussian spy-master whom we shall meet in the nineteenth century, added thousands of espions to the twelve instructed by Moses but had little that was new to add to those ancient Hebraic admonitions.

In the centuries between the espionage program of Moses and the equally overweening campaigns devised by Wilhelm Stieber, we are going to witness the gradual development of military and political secret service and observe the most famous spies of history engaged in their clandestine work. It is as impossible to determine the exact beginning of secret service as of espionage, though hundreds of years must have divided them. There is no record of any ancient war in which spies did not play some part. Spying, in its rudimentary form, resembles such "instinctive" pursuits as scouting and hunting. Scientists have noted that primitive, savage races, having only the simplest weapons and no perceptible sense of tactical discipline or group strategy, will yet display, when preparing to make or meet an attack, that essential wariness which results in effective reconnaissance and a kind of crude espionage. The beginning of organized secret service is no less obscured by time. Whoever elected to invent it as a by-product of some conflict or other failed to register either his name or the date. Had Moses distributed his twelve spies as a cross-country chain, with each one dependent upon the co-operation of his eleven comrades, we should be able to trace the origin of organized and systematic espionage to its earliest environment of bullrushes. The Biblical record, however, is clear; the instructions to the spies of Israel show that they formed an expedition of independent adventurers—an agent of offensive espionage duplicated a dozen times to allow for the probabilities of discovery and death.

Perhaps the best clue we have to the sources of primitive secret service is to be found, not in the methods pursued by any one man or woman, but in the subtleties and caste-consciousness of priestcraft in ancient times. When Cyrus and his Persian army defeated the Babylonians under Belshazzar, he lay siege to the city of Babylon; but then, with the connivance of the priests of Bel-Marduk, the "soldiers of Cyrus entered Babylon without fighting"—this hieratic transaction occurring in 539 B.C. Nabonidus, the father of Belshazzar and the last monarch of the Semitic Chaldeans, was overthrown and taken prisoner by Cyrus. Nabonidus was intelligent, highly educated and imaginative, and he had recognized the weakness of his empire induced by the powerful, wealthy priesthoods and their antagonistic cults. Venturing to interpose reforms and centralize religion in Babylon, he ordered many local gods introduced into the temple of Bel-Marduk, earning the instantaneous hostility of the priests of Bel, whose holy conservative horror of an innovator set them quickly to plotting against this Bolshevism. Cyrus entered Babylon, and Persian sentinels were posted at once to protect the sanctity of the great god Bel-Marduk. All the priesthood was craftily engaged in selling out Nabonidus; but Cyrus can only have dealt with a few ecclesiastic envoys, a committee of betrayers.

Many ancient kings were kept efficiently well informed by their spies, yet the endeavors of those agents were too furtive to be remembered, and the monarchs they served are themselves all but forgotten. The military and political espionage of the Roman and Byzantine empires were the product of systematic, highly organized secret service. Only a few names, however—Crassus, Commodus, the courtesan-empress, Theodora, whom we shall encounter presently —survive to distinguish these imperial operations in twenty centuries of incessant, anonymous intrigue. When civilization declined in the West with the fall of Rome, one of its least considered beneficences was the decline of military and—to large extent—political espionage. Politicians of the Holy Roman Empire and of the even holier Roman Catholic Church employed spies, disbursed bribes and fomented pretentious conspiracies; yet we shall have to wait until after the Crusades and the conquests of the Mongols for the great campaigns of ecclesiastical secret service managed by the Inquisition, the Jesuits and other instruments heated and sharpened to harry the infidel or heretic.

In military affairs the necessity of gaining intelligence was not forgotten, but it made no progress in method from the time of Mithridates. When Alfred the Great felt that he must acquire information concerning his enemies, he enlisted himself as the earliest agent of the English Secret Service. Disguised as a bard he visited the Danish encampment by stealth and there sized up the threat against his West Saxon kingdom. A great Norman leader, Robert Guiscard, though his army was ravaged by pestilence under the stoutly defended walls of Durazzo, warned its garrison that "his patience was at least equal to their obstinacy", having already fortified his patience by entering into a secret correspondence with a certain Venetian nobleman inside the beleaguered city. The Venetian, whose price was "a rich and honourable marriage", sold Durazzo to Guiscard. "At the dead of night several rope-ladders were dropped from the walls; the light Calabrians ascended in silence; and the Greeks were awakened by the name and trumpets of the conqueror." For three days, however, they "defended the streets . . . against an enemy already master of the rampart."[2] Nearly seven months had elapsed "between the first investment and the final surrender" of Durazzo, and its resistance had only then been overcome by a transaction of bribery and betrayal.

All over Europe in its endless wars there was neither nationalism nor patriotism, and the sharp outlines of duty or feudal allegiance were regularly dimmed by fluctuating market quotations of self-interest. What secret service there was that did not specialize in assassination related mainly to negotiations selling out hard-pressed friends to some more generous enemy. The hireling informers and betrayers, however, were seldom to be found festering under the cuticle of the middle or lower classes. Only the elegances of life at court attracted them; and there they found a market for any disreputable talent. The guild system, the cloistered economics of feudal and medieval times, left the labor spy to become the proud achievement of our modern industrial civilization. With many craftsmen and apprentices, but few large employers, there was even a century ago no provocation or malign excuse for labor espionage. By comparison industrial spying seems a veteran enterprise, a rare old profit-seeking brew. Its authentic origin is as obscurely hidden as that of any other of the more primitive espion practices; but at least one celebrated fortune was founded rather romantically by a pioneer industrial spy of England, who may even have been the first of his kind and who was certainly the most handsomely rewarded—that picturesque musician-adventurer known to the seventeenth century, and to his descendants of the British peerage, as "Fiddler" Foley.

Industrial Secret Service

This eminent borrower of foreign guild secrets was an already well-to-do ironmaster of Stourbridge in Worcestershire when he came to the conclusion that mere prosperity was not enough. He resolved to discover the secrets of superior Continental methods of treating iron and producing steel. And, in justice to Foley's grasping, hard-headed inquisitiveness, we may note that he did not try to send or bribe a renegade spy. What he wanted to know he meant to learn for himself. At the risk of his life he journeyed abroad, and, being an admirable violinist, he chose to disguise himself as a minstrel. Jointly employing his bluff good humor and musicianly verve, Foley wandered barefoot and ragged from town to town in Belgium, Germany, Bohemia, northern Italy and Spain, while endeavoring to steal the venerated secrets of steel from master craftsmen.

At length he believed that he had ferreted out all he needed to know about the foreign production of iron and steel. He returned to England, only to discover that something was still wanting. Again this indomitable deceiver went abroad on the tramp with his fiddle. This time he made sure that he had attained his object; and when his success as a spy leaked out, foreign ironmasters and their guilds became acutely resentful. Foley's acquisition of their old and jealously guarded secrets was destined not only to rob the Continent of English, Scotch and Irish customers but also to bring into operation a dangerous competitor in the Continental market. And so the guilds he had despoiled retaliated with secret service of their own. Believing that Foley, for reasons of personal profit, would not impart his knowledge to others in England, they made several attempts to assassinate him. Other guild agents came stealthily to Stourbridge to try to wreck his iron works; but neither the assassins nor the pioneer *sabotageurs* met with success. The personal espionage of "Fiddler" Foley introduced new processes of steel manufacture into England and made the fortune of the industrial spy and his immediate heirs.[3]

Whatever its ethical impact, industrial espionage never seems to attain that noisome ripeness we discover in labor espionage. Not even a big book has the modern plumbing or incinerating facilities to do justice to the subject of the labor spy, the "detective" agencies that investigate everything but criminal practices, including their own, and countless "up-to-date" employers' attitudes toward their workers as well as toward each other's trade secrets. Mountainous evidence of the growth of labor spying in democratic countries is available to anyone equipped with a gas mask and a long stick. We therefore only touch upon it incidentally, and for two reasons: (1) to prove that no pressure, persuasion or personal delusion of any kind has induced its abridgment or omission, and (2) to explain that anybody capable of helping to dig a sewer can rise and shine—and grow affluent—as a manipulator of labor espionage.

The use of the labor spy has stayed right where it started; it is not secret service in any subtle form but a primitive survival among highly organized intelligence and surveillant systems. "Fiddler" Foley's contest with the guilds was staged so long ago, its deceit and pecuniary gain seem like achievements, even as the profitable pillaging of Henry Morgan and other buccaneers have an ever increasing flavor of remote and swashbuckling romance. But the twentieth-century labor spy—who is even so new he has no ancestry to abuse—is no more of a romantic adventurer than any pickpocket or fraudulently "crippled" or "blinded" beggar. The factory owners desire espionage agents to invade their plant. What defenses keep them out?

As an employer the factory management can hire and fire, put any new man to work, a stranger—a spy; and so that introductory process —often so stealthy and nearly always so hazardous to the military espion—is as nothing in the practice of labor spying. Moreover, while communicating his information invariably endangers the patriot agent of secret service, the reports of the labor spy may be submitted after hours from a public telephone booth or forwarded in writing to an intermediate local address. How is that going to betray him?

Unless the labor spy is stupid as well as unscrupulous he runs no risk of being detected and is only exposed to hard work and possibly accidental injury. But many a naval agent in an alien shipyard has to work as hard, while incurring the real perils of steady communication with his chief overseas. Wherefore this record shall mainly confine itself hereafter to the effective operations of secret services, the exploits of their agents, or the intrigues of the masters directing them—and now begin with a brief backward glance at various antique ingenuities of pioneer military espionage.

CHAPTER THREE

THE CUNNING OF ANTIQUITY

THERE WERE MANY SPIES but very few secret-service organizations in ancient times, for the evident reason that, whatever limitations of comfort, communication or scientific comprehension the ancients suffered, they were spared administrative impedimenta and most of our virulent forms of red tape. Kings and commanders solved their own intelligence problems; and a chief or captain who led his followers into battle was not very likely to digest the reports of his spies through four or five bureaucratic intermediaries.

What the ancients lacked in system, moreover, was counterbalanced by their exceptional fertility of invention and instinctive cunning. Those stratagems and surprise onslaughts which the Bible and the *Iliad* prove to have been really the suggestion of Jehovah or the martial Greek gods were a form of impromptu secret service that, lacking sportsmanship but producing the results desired, had to be insured against the contempt of posterity by means of a firm religious origin.

When Alexander the Great was marching into Asia it is recorded there came to him hints and rumors of disaffection growing among his allies and mercenaries. The young conqueror thereupon sought the truth and got it by the simplest expedient. He announced that he was writing home and recommended to his officers that they do likewise. Then, when the couriers were ladened and had set out for Greece, he ordered them quietly recalled and proceeded to investigate all the letters that they carried. Malcontents were detected; legitimate causes of grievance exposed. This very system was employed in measuring the morale and combative spirit of American expeditionary troops in France through the decisive months of 1918. Thus the origin of military postal censorship blended with counterespionage.

Scipio Africanus, one of the few victorious captains of antiquity who seems wholly admirable to the modern mind,[1] was not ashamed to spare the lives of his combat forces—and, in some degree, the lives of his foes—by resorting to artifice before an engagement if that enabled him to make his battle strategy more flexible and conclusive.

Frontinus, a military writer of the time of Vespasian, in a work which he proudly entitled *Stratagems*—the key to all military and political success in ancient days—describes how Scipio Africanus entered into negotiations with Syphax, King of Numidia, ostensibly to arrange a treaty with the African monarch, but in reality to facilitate Roman espionage. Cornelius Lelius was the envoy Scipio appointed; and according to the preliminary agreement there were to be no military officers in his suite. Therefore a number of high-ranking officers accompanied Lelius in disguise.

It was the Roman envoy's ruse, when he had come and pitched his tents near the camp of Syphax, to allow a spirited horse to break loose from the picket line. At once the disguised officers, many of them posing as menials and attendants, set out in pursuit of the racing steed, and they ingeniously contrived to pursue it all over the camp of Syphax, until their combined observations made up a reliable intelligence summary of the strength of the Numidian army. Another day the stratagem of the disguised officers came near to being exposed when a Numidian general stopped one of the Romans and studied him suspiciously. He then blurted out the accusation that the Roman was a military officer of note, saying that he had known him years before when they were studying together at school in Greece. Cornelius Lelius, having observed the encounter, stepped forward instantly and raised his whip, striking his Roman colleague full in the face.

How dare a low creature, a dog of a slave, array himself so richly as to be mistaken for a Roman general?—he demanded, again raising the whip, while the other cringed. The Numidian stood confounded, for he knew the Roman code; and no man would dare strike a military leader of the Latin republic as Lelius had just struck him that he had thought to recognize. The cringing pose of the "slave" was especially convincing, and now he slunk away while Lelius apologized—to the Numidian—for having lost his temper.

In his long and grueling contest with Hannibal, Scipio Africanus was put to the gravest test a patriot commander may face. The Carthaginian military genius was inexorably bent upon weakening and ruining Rome, lest the no less implacable Roman politicians and speculators survive and grow strong enough—as they ultimately did—to obliterate Carthage. In winning the decisive battle of Zama, Scipio displayed a rare combination of mental flexibility and clearness of vision and actually changed his tactics in the midst of the battle. He had devised two ways to cope with the impact of Hannibal's shock troops, whose literal brute strength had to be met in the solid shape of eighty-five heavily armed Carthaginian war elephants. Scipio could not bombard the caterpillar treads or ignite the petrol supply of those lumbering ancient tanks, but he could get on their collective nerves. To do this he gathered all the trumpeters and hornblowers of his camp in one body, which greeted Hannibal's oncoming elephants with a terrific blast of sound. Dissonance then and there saved the day for the legions. Terrified, the elephants went out of control, introducing Scipio's second improvisation into the fabric of that illustrious battle. The Roman commander-in-chief had drawn up his troops at Zama so that they would present to the advancing enemy a broken front rather than the conventional solid ranks And with the Romans awaiting the shock in files, the madly charging elephants were offered lanes through which to pass—Scipio's novel formation expediting their panicky departure from the field of combat.

Scipio was not alone a brilliant military strategist but was extraordinarily generous and magnanimous compared to the average eminent Roman of his time. When his brother, Lucius Scipio, was sent in command of the first Roman army to cross into Asia, Africanus insisted upon accepting a subordinate command. It was, however, his veteran skill and foresight which brought to a triumphant termination the ensuing contest with Antiochus III, the Seleucid king, and Hannibal, a fugitive from Carthage after the Second Punic War and driven to seek refuge in Asia Minor. The brothers in this conflict appear to have been served by an uncommonly efficient intelligence corps, and, owing to its speedy system of communication, were warned in good time when Hannibal and Antiochus began preparing a surprise offensive. The immediate regrouping of Lucius Scipio's forces led to his crushing victory at Magnesia in Lydia over "a great composite army" under Antiochus.

How Rome Grew Invincible

The Roman Senate, that Tory club of grasping ingrates, found something peculiarly distasteful about Lucius Scipio's triumph in Asia Minor. After taking thought it was decided to ruin the younger brother of Africanus before his success had gone to his head; and so he was charged with misappropriating the tribute moneys he had exacted from Antiochus when that disillusioned dynast sued for peace. Scipio Africanus was infuriated by this outrage; and when his brother attempted to face the accusing senators, Africanus angrily interfered. He snatched from Lucius' hand the accounts he stood ready to submit, tore the documents to pieces and threw them in the face of the Senate. He reminded Rome that Lucius had brought the governmental treasury a vast sum—equivalent to nearly ten million dollars today.

Later, however, his opponents succeeded in having Lucius prosecuted and condemned; whereupon the victor of Zama came and rescued him by force. Scipio Africanus was himself impeached, and he asked his countrymen to recollect that it was the anniversary of the battle of Zama. He dared the rich equestrian order and his envious senatorial foes to proceed against him. And still later, when Africanus had "retired in disgust from Rome to his estates" and the conspirators nerved themselves to resume the attack upon his brother, the veto of one of the tribunes of the people was exercised to avoid the proceedings against Lucius Scipio.

Secret agents of the Roman Senate were more successful in their vengeful campaign against Hannibal. Terms dictated to Antiochus, like those given Carthage at the end of the Second Punic War, required that Hannibal be surrendered to the "justice" of his foes. The Carthaginian hero had left the court of Antiochus and fled to Bithynia; but even there Roman spies ran him to earth. The king of Bithynia was not disposed to risk offending the vindictive senators, and he arrested Hannibal to send him to Rome and certain condemnation. Against this very contingency Hannibal carried poison concealed in a ring, and upon taking that poison he died. Scipio Africanus, the only Roman who was his military peer and conqueror, died that same year—183 B.C.—at the age of fifty-four.

The ruling caste of Romans had learned how to jettison all mercy, all gratitude, all scruples, and so Rome inevitably became invincible. Force was the major instrument, but cunning ran like a slave beside its grinding chariot wheel. When Sertorius was the Roman commander in Spain he was, according to Polyaenus, the possessor of a white fawn that he had trained to follow him everywhere, "even to the steps of the tribunal." This little fawn was taught to approach at a given signal, and Sertorius himself gave the signal when about to pronounce his decision in judicial cases. The fawn appeared to convey information to the Roman general; and Sertorius allowed it to become widely known that he derived both secrets and guidance from the fawn. His spies, meanwhile, were everywhere active, and all that they learned was credited to the supernatural powers of the animal. Iberian tribesmen marveled at the intimate knowledge of Sertorius and were afraid of his compact with the uncanny fawn—a nicely exploited stratagem that did the tribes no harm and helped to pacify the country.

Frontinus describes the ancient use of carrier pigeons, while Justus

Lipsius tells of the education of swallows for use in military and political espionage. Among all nations of the East, according to this authority, it was customary to train birds as long-distance messengers, which tends to explain the seemingly modern speed of some communications of imperial Roman intelligence. Cipher was well known to the Greeks and, hence, to the Romans, the *skutate* of the former becoming the *skutala* of the marching legions, meaning a wooden cylinder around which an inscribed papyrus was rolled.

Hannibal's invasion of Italy—"the most brilliant and futile raid in history"—gained him many victories and nearly bled Rome to death, but the mere slaughter of Romans and a great city's despair would not have sustained him for fifteen years if he had not also made powerful allies. It will be remembered that in the World War the most notable triumphs, and certainly the most widely advertised, were those of diplomacy and secret service—the winning to one side or the other of new combatant partners. And so may we not assume that Hannibal's thorough preparations paved the way for the alliances resulting from each of his successes in the field? His army throughout those incredible expeditionary years was cut off from its base by P. Cornelius Scipio's artful counter-campaign[2] along his Iberian line of communications; and the Carthaginian's unrivaled all-time record of "living off the country" may be attributed in some measure to the long-time operations of his emissaries and his spies.

Chapter Four

SPIES, SLAVES AND A FIRE BRIGADE

IN THE ROMAN STATE, which did so much to "modernize" administrative tyranny, make the strong richer by impoverishing the weak, make swindling, bribery and speculation the chief end of politics and war the main instrument of policy, it was inevitable that among the many ambitious generals and scheming careerists there would be one to discover the profit he might gain from a private system of secret service. The man who made the discovery and put it into execution with striking—and grimly humorous—results was Marcus Lucinius Crassus.

The last century of the republic—from the murder of Caius Gracchus[1] in 121 B.C. to the defeat of Antony by Octavius—was an era of almost incessant turbulence and bloodshed. It was a shrewd man who could keep himself informed of the shifting focus of military suzerainty and manage to survive the periodic partisan massacres. The secret service of Crassus was well organized and skillfully operated; it not only excelled the espionage of its contemporaries but is by far the best of its kind to be found in the annals of antiquity.

Because he was more successful than anyone else in applying his systematic employment of spies and secret agents to the most popular of Roman sports, accumulation of stupendous wealth or autocratic power, Crassus has been spared no contempt; while Caesar, who dipped into the spy-master's gold and made equally excellent use of his channels of intelligence, is treated with the awe and respect that history accords the proven saint or established demigod. Crassus had precedents to guide him and unscrupulous competitors to spur him on. He improved many schemes which he did not originate and displayed fertile ingenuity in surviving misfortune to prey upon the misfortunes of his adversaries.

His father, Crassus the ex-consul, and his elder brother, Publius, perished in the terrible massacre of 87 B.C., when the gangs of Marius hunted down every adherent of Sulla. But Marcus Crassus escaped and made his way "through untold perils to Spain, where he lay hid for many months in a cave by the sea-shore."[2] When at length he dared to emerge from this refuge, he took up the only career which appeared congenial to him, a youth of distinguished family, who had lost everything in the market crash of civil war. He joined a small band of outlaws and became a freebooter on the high seas. From this beginning with a few reckless followers he was soon able to expand, until at length he joined Sulla as the commander of a well-trained body of troops.

Crassus was victorious in many actions of the civil war and came out of it with a highly promising military reputation. His principal opponent had been Spartacus, who in 73 B.C. led an uprising of slaves and gladiators. Spartacus himself was a gladiator from Thessaly, and with seventy companions he revolted and fled from a gladiatorial "farm" near Capua. Thereafter the Latin public was treated to a fierce gladiatorial display, the first in history to spread beyond the arena. And the Romans had no taste for it. Slaves and gladiators in great numbers rallied around the insurrectionary leader, who for a time developed a natural fortress in the then apparently extinct crater of Mount Vesuvius. The object of this miscellaneous force of rebels was never overthrow of the government but escape and dispersal to homelands at all points of the compass. Even so, against the military power of Rome, Spartacus held out in southern Italy for two years, Crassus finally overcoming him "by great payments and exertions after a prolonged and expensive campaign."[3] The fright which the Roman authorities had experienced was grimly exposed in the ensuing crucifixion of 6,000 of the captured followers of Spartacus.

Success, as might be expected, dilated three major flaws in the character of Marcus Crassus—pride, jealousy and greed. He even dared to show his jealousy of Pompey, and by offending the dictator produced an overnight eclipse of his own career as an army commander. But there still remained open to him the congenial project of accumulating wealth. He speculated in the properties of the proscribed, then very numerous, and otherwise enriched himself enormously. As a forestaller and moneylender he exacted high rates of interest, yet cunningly charged no interest if the borrower was a citizen whose influence he expected to use. Discovering a profit in education, he established a school for slaves; and the well-educated slaves "graduated" from this academy brought him the highest prices.

Crassus, employing both slaves and freemen, next organized a complicated enterprise which seems the only case on record wherein a millionaire became a multimillionaire by combining a private secret service with a private fire brigade. This fire-fighting contingent was perhaps the most ironically humorous of all the many "rackets" devised by Roman speculators. Five hundred workmen, equipped with ropes, buckets, ladders and other implements, were held in readiness until one of Crassus' roving agents tapped his widespread communicative system and reported a fire. The crowded, insanitary conditions of ancient cities made fires both frequent and dangerous. Crassus, given an alarm to answer, would sally forth at the head of his salvage corps, approach the neighborhood of the fire, see which way the wind was blowing, and begin interviewing householders whose property seemed most endangered. He would offer to buy their houses, as they stood, for an unreasonably low price. If the frightened owner agreed, the fire brigade was hurried into action and generally managed to save the property. If the owner kept his head and refused to be taken advantage of, Crassus trooped off with his firemen, leaving the blaze as a public responsibility. In time, according to Plutarch, he became master of a very considerable part of the house property of Rome.

Crassus and the Parthian Shots

The secret-intelligence operatives of Crassus, when not objectively looking for fires, were devoted in the main to gathering evidence for Crassus to use in the law courts. He defended all manner of clients and won his cases by coming prepared with the facts where many a more eminent opponent countered with nothing but eloquent declamation or personal abuse. Crassus thus became a kind of underworld power as well as a plutocrat. He pressed his loans upon the right people. He exerted an ever-expanding influence upon persons needing his legal services, his sources of information, or his solvents of gold. Having established his reputation in every shady quarter of Rome, he found it easier to recruit the spies, agents and renegade informers who helped to strengthen his intelligence system; and the more "inside" information they brought him, the richer his harvests of multiple gains.

We cannot undertake to follow the tortuous schemes that brought him back into politics and won him election as consul. Pompey was the other consul. He and Crassus were still bitterly antagonistic; and yet, much as they hated each other, they hated the constitution of Sulla even more and joined in a campaign to efface its principal features, without offering Rome anything new in its stead. It was a basic part of Crassus' political philosophy and political method to purchase popular support by lavish expenditures, preferably from the public purse, but, if necessary, from his own. In 67 B.C. the Gavinian law commissioned Pompey to exterminate the pirates then so numerous and bold, they were actually strangling Roman commerce. In consequence of his prompt success against these vermin, Pompey was transferred by the Manilian law to the command opposing our dangerous friend, Mithridates.

Crassus had intrigued against the diversion to his rival of two such pre-eminent assignments. But Pompey fought and campaigned and stayed away from Rome for nearly seven years. And Crassus discovered that a very ample stage had been swept and lighted for himself alone. It was at this period of his plutocratic progress that Julius Caesar joined him as lieutenant and then "managing partner"; and even the Great-Man histories concede that it was Crassus' money and Crassus' means of advancement, his spies, informers and claques of heavily subsidized riffraff that provided the dissolute, extravagant young patrician with the ladder on which he climbed to potential dictatorship.

Both Crassus and Caesar were charged with being implicated in the plots of Catiline. But what we know of those renowned conspiracies is rather too fragmentary to mark the spots where Crassus slithered in and out. It is certain that he was himself well informed, and that he volunteered some information to Cicero respecting the apparent designs of the insurgents. However, he made sure that his disclosures were belated and virtually worthless. It was alleged that he muffled himself in a cloak and called on Cicero at dead of night, presenting him with an anonymous letter he said he had just received, a letter warning him to be away from Rome on the day of the preconcerted outbreak.[4] If such a letter really passed from Crassus to Cicero, one of the former's agents probably wrote it. By his ostentatious vigilance Crassus sought to insure himself against capital charges if the plotters should fail; yet he did nothing that would seriously compromise his undercover relations with Catiline and his accomplices in the event of their succeeding.

Cicero, the consul of 63 B.C., displayed his customary prudence when he refrained from bringing a charge of high treason against Crassus, whose fingers pulled the most effectual strings and whose adroit subventions inflated every purse. The informer, Tarquinius, during his interrogation before the Roman Senate, began giving evidence which incriminated Crassus. But at once a pandemonium of debtors' indignation swept the chamber. Scores of senators owed Crassus money, and all of them commenced to shout "False witness" with vocal chords as strained as their credit. Whereupon Cicero remanded the informer to prison without permitting him to continue his testimony. It was thought that the famous orator had been taking the temperature of his own party by evoking such evidence, and that he drew back from an open attack upon Crassus when he counted up the disaffections.

The following year tormented the minds of the politicians with a new and livelier menace, for great Pompey announced that he was marching his legions home. "Neither Crassus nor Caesar on one side, nor Catulus and Cato on the other, felt their heads quite safe upon their shoulders." Every aspiring schemer and demagogue had been intriguing against Pompey in his absence. However, Crassus kept his head as usual and employed his wits to divorce Pompey from a friendly alliance with Cicero. This he accomplished personally, and without the aid of spies, by flattering Cicero while at the same time surfeiting Pompey with even more excessive laudation of the orator. Not even a Roman general believed in the importance of oratory; and so Pompey was gradually heated to a state of resentful acquiescence and joined forces with Crassus and Caesar, who then needed him far more than he needed them.

Caesar was up to his eyebrows in debt to Crassus. As the hero of the populace he threw around huge sums and provided festivals and entertainments on the most expensive scale. Collaborating with Pompey, he and Crassus arranged for the latter to bargain and buy himself at great cost the much-prized command in the East. Lucullus had gloriously penetrated Pontus, while Pompey had topped off his military fame by completing "the looting of Armenia." Crassus' remembrance of his skill as a general urged him to find some new and prosperous corner of Asia and transfer its movable assets to his own account. We come, therefore, to one of the queerest of the many ironies brightening this devious record of secret-service attainment. Crassus, despite his ponderous fortune, was still avaricious and eager to outbid Rome for a chance to risk his life far afield where another fortune might be made. He had literally founded his fortune upon espionage and resources of intelligence and on occasion had proved himself an adept agent of conspiracy and a master of political intrigue. Yet all of this experience he proceeded to discard the moment he wrapped himself in his conqueror's toga. Military intelligence meant less to him than the culverin or the flintlock, which would have to wait centuries to be invented.

Crossing the Euphrates, Crassus pushed on into Persia, expecting to find cities to besiege and sack and solid contingents of spearsmen to charge and destroy. Instead his plodding infantry met only an infuriating, fluid opposition, the Parthian "nation" of mobile tribes, daring horsemen and deadly bowmen, commanded by a monarch in

Median costume.[5] The "Parthian shot" was noisy, accurate and alarming, for the Parthian bow was the composite bow, made of five or more plates of horn "like the springs of a carriage." It discharged a high-speed arrow with a startling *twang*.

Marcus Crassus as a commander of the legions had neither the foresight to uncover his peril nor the hardihood to order a retreat in time to save his army at the expense of his glory at home. And so the end came in a two-day massacre that historians have called the "battle" of Carrhae. Staggering in the heat, starved, worn and thirsty, the Romans indomitably plodded through sand to charge a foe that could not be overtaken, but who circled around them and shot them down. Twenty thousand were slain, and half as many more made prisoner, to be "marched on eastward . . . into slavery in Iran." Crassus' exact fate was never authenticated. One legend submits that he was taken alive, but then executed by having molten gold poured down his throat. An unlikely compliment from the Parthians, who had never suffered his usuries!

Spies and the Roman Proscriptions

Nine years after Carrhae Julius Caesar was assassinated. A year later Lepidus, Octavius and Marcus Antonius met on a tiny island in a tributary of the river Po and after two days' deliberation announced themselves to ten legions as the triumvirs for the next five years. What they kept secret was a list of seventeen actual or potential antagonists who were to be murdered immediately. And even the three did not then suspect that their "little list" would grow and spread like a stain of blood until some three hundred senators and over two thousand capitalists would be added to the slaughter. The triumvirs' proscriptions ultimately "blacklisted . . . all the members of the older generation who had achieved something out of the ordinary."[6] With abominable guile this trio of military despots offered a large reward for betrayal of their opponents—often as much as half the property of the unfortunate citizen proscribed—and then protected their corps of informers by promising that no transfers of property following an execution would be recorded. Thus a sudden reversal of political fortune, as in the years of the sanguinary seesaw of Marius and Sulla, would not lead to vengeance upon the spy for his betrayal or necessarily result in restitution of the property. On a foundation of intrigue as debased as that, and by means of a mechanism as corrupt and cunning, the glory of imperial Rome was presented to the judgment of posterity.

The historian Velleius Paterculus wrote some years afterward: "Loyalty towards the proscribed was shown chiefly by wives, to a moderate extent by freedmen, very little by slaves, and not at all by sons." There were sons, in fact, among the self-made secret agents who peddled their informations to the triumvirate. And in that bull market of vindictive greed and calumny the imperial Roman secret service was born. Octavius, having overthrown Antonius, took warning from the overthrow of Julius Caesar and did not fall into the trap of kingly advertisement. Absolute power was his; but he assumed the title of "Augustus, the Blessed", an imposing camouflage suggested by a "dissolute rascal", Munatius Plancus, who had already distinguished himself by dancing naked before Cleopatra. Once that alien queen and her celebrated soldier-lover were out of the way and the Roman Senate debauched or emasculated, Augustus became appreciably "blessed", and the stealth and denunciations of his spies were toned down. It remained for some of his more monstrous successors to establish imperial police espionage as a malarial mist obscuring the throne from every impulse of enlightenment and decency.

It is an interesting fact—bearing acutely upon certain governments of our own day—that political police activities were horribly expanded in the reigns of emperors whom classical historians unite to condemn, while contracting or disappearing entirely under the rule of a Trajan or Marcus Aurelius. Both of those great monarchs were absolute; which refutes the contemporary belief that abominable police repressions are "inevitable" under any form of despotism. Many Caesars who were not too notorious relied upon a Roman secret service that covered the civilized world, even as Roman commerce, the Roman courier service and Roman legions watching the long frontiers encompassed it. But only in the reign of a Commodus or Caracalla will we discover the recognizable ancestor of yesterday's Russian *Ochrana* or *Cheka*, or of the German *Gestapo* and Italian *Ovra* of today.[7]

The delators or professional informers employed by Commodus were not only enemies of their country and "legal assassins", as Gibbon observes, but also unusually incompetent police spies and safeguards. The singular conspiracy of Maternus saw "a private soldier, of a daring boldness above his station" defy the authority of the empire in Spain and Gaul and, when the governors of the provinces were finally roused by the emperor's threats to take concerted action against him, move secretly to advance on Rome. Maternus led a growing force whose recruits were army deserters—like himself—fugitive slaves or men he liberated by opening the prisons in the course of his depredations. With the provincial governors, some of them hitherto

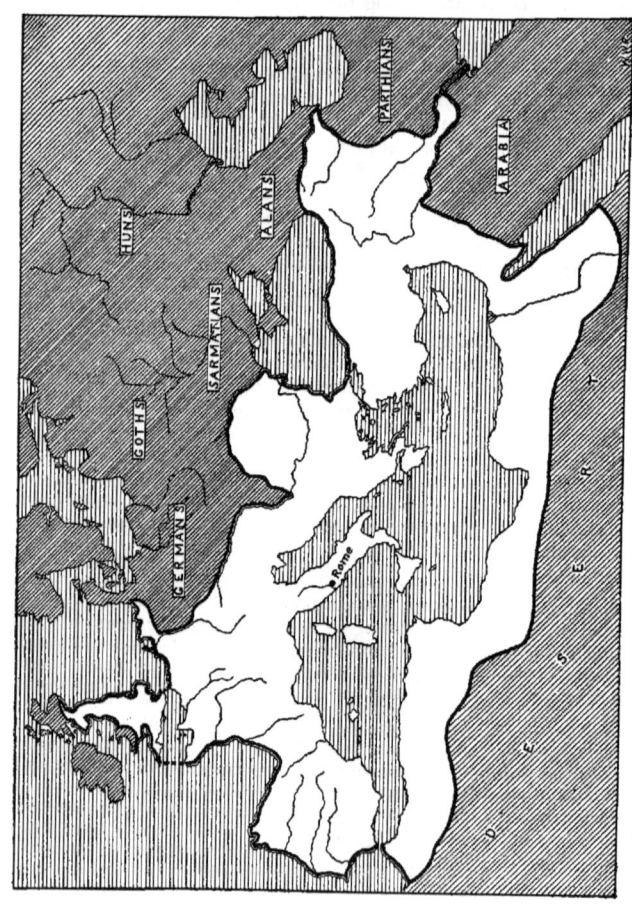

THE ROMAN EMPIRE AT ITS MAXIMUM EXTENT IN THE REIGN OF THE EMPEROR TRAJAN (98–117 A.D.)

The political secret service of Rome, like all other dictatorial administrative organizations, reached out to the farthest frontiers of this vast domain of Western civilization.

his silent partners, now spurred to attack him, seeing his band about to be surrounded and destroyed, he changed his program with extraordinary resourcefulness. In small parties his followers dispersed, passed over the Alps and trickled down into Italy, to reassemble in Rome during the licentious festival of Cybele. Maternus proposed to assassinate the hated son of Marcus Aurelius and ascend the vacant throne. His well-armed troops in various disguises were scattered over the city. Tomorrow would see Commodus stabbed and an incomparable hazard overcome. Only at the final hour the "envy of an accomplice" prevented the execution of Maternus' brazen plan; and none of Commodus' horde of spies helped to defeat this Robin Hood of antiquity.

Succeeding reigns contrived to dispense with delation; but the spirit of the born delator was willing, and his flesh was anything but weak. By outliving the occasional moderate and even distinguished men who donned the purple, the delator could always count on the passing of that respectable depression, and then some new mongrel sadist would arise to give him work again. The sons of Septimius Severus, Geta and Caracalla, attempted to manage Roman destinies in tandem, until Caracalla promoted the inevitable murder. And then, having slain his brother and threatened his mother, the young emperor ordered out the informers and assassin-prowlers to attend to all the "friends of Geta." It has been computed that, under this "vague appellation . . . about twenty thousand persons of both sexes suffered death." Helvius Pertinax was killed merely because of a pun. He had been overheard to say that Caracalla, who had assumed the names of several conquered nations, ought to make *Geticus* an addition, having "obtained some advantage of the Goths or Getae"; for which "unseasonable witticism" he was put to death. No wonder the imperial spies, bred on such nonsense and rewarded with the property of any luckless citizen they denounced, proved so ineffectual in dealing with genuine conspirators.

There is one tormenting inquiry that relates to the secret service of imperial Rome, some answer to which the writer has long pursued. Was Judas Iscariot simply the traditional unstable partisan turned informer, or was he a professional agent of the far-spread imperial organization? The "thirty pieces of silver" do not suggest those handsome emoluments which the attentive delators of Rome derived from each victim's property. But the almost timeless technique of vigilant governments—and Tiberius was very vigilant—in getting a spy "on the inside" to report upon every dangerous insurgency would argue that, if Jesus of Nazareth had created the impression in Judea that

Biblical literature implies, the Roman authorities would not have left information and betrayal to treacherous accident.

In his masterly study, *The Messiah Jesus and John the Baptist*, Robert Eisler has seemed to come as close to deciding this professional or amateur status of Judas as any scholar is ever likely to do. Eisler directs our attention to the significant fact that none of Christ's followers was immediately charged with any violation of the Roman law. No Apostle was arrested or even denounced to the authorities. "Judas, the paid agent of the hierarchy, or the Roman *speculators* represented the situation thus and no otherwise; the traitor may have had good reasons for sparing the twelve, to whose number he himself belonged."[8] But if Judas had been a trained Roman hireling or professional operative ordered to penetrate the seeming political conspiracy involving the "King of the Jews", he would have had nothing to dread—save at the hands of the Jews—and would not have feared involvement. In that case more than one Apostle might have shared the lowly death of crucifixion.

CHAPTER FIVE

BYZANTIUM TO BAGDAD

THE ADMINISTRATIVE WEAKNESS, dynastic fermentations and wavering frontiers of the Byzantine Empire are strangely belied by its thousand years of survival. Byzantium developed to a point of historic saturation the luxuries, treacheries and homicidal policies of the East; but we may make only a brief survey of these Eastern influences as they were manifested in perhaps the most formidable of all the secret-service regimes of the empire's turbulent millennium.

The courtesan-empress, Theodora, in her comely youth—some years before her elevation to the throne as consort of Justinian—had been a popular performer in those interludes of pantomime which added obscene buffoonery to the theatrical programs of the hippodrome. An ordinance forbade actresses to appear stark naked; and so Theodora was required to protect the management by wearing a "narrow girdle", of a bulk which seems to have impressed the contemporary historian, Procopius,[1] as a peak load for a carrier pigeon. Having gained this youthful experience in the presence of multitudes of spectators, Theodora on ascending to the dignity of the purple resolved that none of her subjects should ever conceal anything. Whereupon she discovered a unique aptitude for the mastery and manipulation of spies.

Theodora's secret service had the single large objective of silencing her critics and suppressing her past. Informers and spies of Justinian's empress were not required to concern themselves with the external enemies or internal problems of the state but hovered around those personages Theodora identified as rivals in capacity, influence or family connections, suspecting nearly every one and sparing no suspect. "Her numerous spies observed and zealously reported every action, or word, or look, injurious to their royal mistress."[2] To be accused by them meant arrest and virtual conviction, as is ever the way with the espionage of political police. On the word of one of her spies the most influential victim would be "cast into her peculiar prisons,[3] inaccessible to the inquiries of justice; and it was rumoured that the torture of the rack or scourge had been inflicted in the presence of a female tyrant, insensible to the voice of prayer or of pity."

Not a few of her "unhappy victims perished in deep unwholesome dungeons, while others were permitted, after the loss of their limbs, their reason, or their fortune, to appear in the world, the living monuments of her vengeance, which was commonly extended to the children of those whom she had suspected or injured. The senator or bishop whose death or exile Theodora had pronounced, was delivered to a trusty messenger, and his diligence was quickened by a menace from her own mouth. 'If you fail in the execution of my commands, I swear by him who liveth for ever that your skin shall be flayed from your body.'" By means of such savage injunctions zeal and dread seem to have been curiously combined.

The most devoted henchman of the empress was the prefect, Peter Barsyames; and whenever her supremacy as the favorite and strong right hand of Justinian appeared to be threatened, Peter was as eager as a fireman to answer the alarm. On one occasion he even took the offensive against a noble queen who was rich, beautiful, cultivated, a widow in some distress, younger than Theodora, and blonde.

Queen Amalasontha, regent of Italy, was the daughter and heiress of Theodoric, great leader of the Ostrogoths, and the niece of Clovis, warrior king of the Franks. But in spite of her militant ancestry she found herself sorely beset by the twin problems of ruling Italy and surviving the unruly impulses of the Goths. "Encompassed with domestic foes, she entered into a secret negotiation with the emperor Justinian," yet one not long kept secret from the agents of Theodora.[4] Having "obtained the assurance of a friendly reception", the unhappy Amalasontha "had actually deposited at Dyrrachium, in Epirus, a treasure of forty thousand pounds of gold" preparatory to retiring in safety "from barbarous faction to the peace and splendour of Constantinople." But it was not to be; for Theodora had been talking to Peter Barsyames about this impending visitor, twenty-eight years of age. Barsyames, like Edward Gibbon, may have heard that "the endowments of her mind and person had attained their perfect maturity", but as the agent of one ever ready to dispute "the conquest of an emperor" Peter hurried to Italy. And on the very day of Queen Amalasontha's embarkation for the sea voyage to Constantinople she suffered an attack which some records describe as "convulsions", resulting in her death in awful agony before night settled down. To others she was "strangled in her bath", another excruciating commonplace of Byzantine secret service. Whatever the form of her assassination, Justinian was moved to threaten furious reprisals upon her alleged assassins; yet who can doubt that their chief accessory before the fact still lay beside him in his bed?

Theodora's Ruling Passion

While Amalasontha's beauty, rank and youth had been an especial provocation, the Empress Theodora conceived a passion for inflicting some sort of convulsions upon every rival, male or female, whose talents or personality attracted Justinian. John of Cappadocia was a famous example of the able and avaricious official whom the emperor favored and his consort hated. He had earned the confidence of Justinian by his zestful plundering of the provinces for the dual purpose of lining the imperial coffers and his own privy purse. "Although he was suspected of magic and Pagan superstition, he appeared insensible to the fear of God or the reproaches of man; and his aspiring fortune was raised on the death of thousands, the poverty of millions, the ruin of cities, and the desolation of provinces." This Fascist proconsul from "the dawn of light to the moment of dinner ... laboured to enrich his master and himself at the expense of the Roman world; the remainder of the day was spent in sensual and obscene pleasures, and the silent hours of the night were interrupted by the perpetual dread of the justice of an assassin. His abilities, perhaps his vices, recommended him to the lasting friendship of Justinian",[5] who advanced him to the rank of praetorian prefect of the East, an office so close to the throne and so ideal for self-aggrandizement that Theodora's bitter enmity was bound to attend the promotion.

John of Cappadocia had his own palace spies and knew what imperial dangers threatened him. Peter Barsyames' poisoners, archers and poniard-wielders were kept at a safe distance; for John's guards hugged him even closer than his "obscene pleasures." The masses abominated him. But "their murmurs served only to fortify the resolution of Justinian"; and for ten years John's health escaped the consequences both of his excesses and his "oppressive administration."

The prefect's inflexible hold upon life, his job and Justinian's admiration baffled every dark design; and so Theodora turned with slight misgiving from violence to intrigue. It would be more expeditious to have John stabbed or to transfer the serpent's venom of her mind to the wine he was drinking. However, there was always a surplusage of accomplices and confederates on whom the empress could rely. She took counsel with her friend Antonina, the wife of Belisarius, and the plot which the two great ladies concocted was accurately aimed to strike at John through his daughter Euphemia. John, they knew, was devoted to the girl and readily swayed by her wishes or opinions. A noted soothsayer had also played into Theodora's hands by encouraging John to believe that he should one day seat himself upon the imperial throne.[6]

Antonina came to Euphemia and hinted that Belisarius, Justinian's conquering general, was dissatisfied with his rewards and inclined to turn against the emperor. Why should not Euphemia's father work in harmony with Belisarius, since together they might easily overthrow Justinian? "John, who might have known the value of oaths and promises, was tempted to accept a nocturnal and almost treasonable appointment with the wife of Belisarius. An ambuscade of eunuchs and guards had been posted by the command of Theodora." But "the guilty minister . . . was saved by the fidelity of his attendants."[7] John appears rather to have been saved by a warning received from Justinian himself or one of his spies who happened not to be answerable to Theodora. However, that implacable schemer had obtained enough evidence to persuade Justinian of his favorite's incipient treachery. John was "sacrificed to conjugal tenderness or domestic tranquility." He was forced to take deacon's orders, though the emperor's friendship "alleviated his disgrace, and he retained in the mild exile of Cyzicus an ample portion of his riches."

It was an appropriate irony that the wife of Belisarius should contrive John's undoing, since he had previously decimated one of the Byzantine general's proudest armies. According to Roman military practice, the bread or biscuit of the soldiers was twice prepared in the oven, and the "diminution of one-fourth was cheerfully allowed for the loss of weight." To gain a "miserable profit" and save the expense of wood, John as prefect had given orders that the flour for Belisarius' expedition "should be slightly baked by the same fire that warmed the baths of Constantinople." When "the sacks were opened, a soft and mouldly paste was distributed" to the troops, who, nourished upon that "unwholesome food, assisted by the heat of the climate," were soon ravaged by an epidemic and dying like flies. Small wonder that the vindictiveness of John's enemies was not readily appeased, and that Theodora's agents sought for and found "a decent pretext" in the murder of John's old enemy, the bishop of Cyzicus.

John of Cappadocia, who had "deserved a thousand deaths, was at last condemned for a crime of which he was innocent," being "ignominiously scourged like the vilest of malefactors . . . a tattered cloak the sole remnant of his fortunes." Banished to Antinopolis in Upper Egypt, the prefect of the East "begged his bread through the cities which had trembled at his name. During an exile of seven years, his life was protracted and threatened" by Theodora's persistent surveillance and "ingenious cruelty"; and only her death permitted the emperor to "recall a servant whom he had abandoned with regret."[8] But if her vindictiveness and her skill in affairs of espionage and intrigue were a burden to Justinian, it is also clear that on at least one very critical occasion the empress' courage and reliance upon clandestine measures saved Justinian's throne. At the height of the *Nika* turbulence all the imperial generals, including Belisarius, agreed with the emperor that immediate flight from Constantinople was their only recourse. Justinian's reign was at an end, "if the prostitute whom he raised from the theatre had not renounced the timidity as well as the virtues of her sex." Theodora dissuaded the emperor and his councilors from their despairing choice, suggesting instead a subterranean counter-revolt that saved them from their foes as well as from "unworthy fears."

The mutual hatred and transitory reconciliation of the rival factions of blues and greens had excited a sedition that all but "laid Constantinople in ashes." For five days the city was abandoned to the mob, whose watchword, *Nika*—vanquish!—gave a name to this devastating insurrection. "If flight were the only means of safety," Theodora cried, "yet I should disdain to fly. Death is the condition of our birth, but they who have reigned should never survive the loss of dignity and dominion." Her firmness restored courage to the palace, and her advice discovered the "resources of the most desperate situation." Justinian sent out secret agents with large sums of money to corrupt the leaders of the blues and the greens and reawaken the implacable animosity of the rival factions. Still loyal to Justinian were three thousand veterans of the Persian and Illyrian wars, under the command of Belisarius and Mundus. These Goths and Heruli, the fiercest barbarian mercenaries in the Byzantine service, marched silently in two columns from the palace, to force "their obscure way through narrow passages, expiring flames, and falling edifices." Both divisions attacked simultaneously, bursting open "the two opposite gates of the hippodrome" and surprising the mob of insurgents who were unable to resist their "firm and regular attack." About 30,000 persons were thereupon massacred, and the sedition dissolved in that niagara of blood.

The nephews of the Emperor Anastasius, Hypatius and Pompey, who had timidly accepted the acclaim of the rioters, upon being arrested implored Justinian's clemency. But the emperor "had been too much terrified to forgive", and they, together with "eighteen illustrious accomplices, of patrician or consular rank, were privately executed . . . their palaces razed, and their fortunes confiscated."[9] The hippodrome, that bourse of belligerent rivalry between the blues and greens, was "condemned, during several years, to a mournful silence." Many churches and palaces had been burned and a large hospital with all its sick patients consumed. However, the sums of gold disbursed by their secret agents had kept Theodora and her consort upon the throne to recoup their losses by confiscating the properties of those whom the factions had favored.

Greek Fire

Political rather than military intelligence has always preoccupied the Oriental mind. The East has excelled in what might be termed dynastic secret service, or the use of spies for the protection of the sovereign and the frustration of his relatives and rivals. Whereas the neglect of even rudimentary espionage in critical military campaigns has been repeatedly exposed. During Mohammed's early struggle for supremacy much skirmishing, sporadic raids and similar inconclusive hostilities at length inspired the leading combatants of Mecca to gather a force 10,000 strong—a formidable host at the time in that obscure corner of Asia. It was agreed in Mecca that the dangerously growing influence of Medina must be obliterated. But Mohammed with the aid of a Persian convert had entrenched himself at Medina. When his Bedouin enemies rode up to wipe the puny upstart from the face of the earth, they found themselves confronted by a trench and a wall. Obviously they had forgotten how Moses and other Semitic seers had relied upon espionage; no spies had been sent on ahead from Mecca who could warn the invaders against this unspeakable innovation.

They could ride around the trench and wall, shrieking intricate Arabic insults and discharging equally feeble flights of arrows, but they could not gallop over it. Encamping, they sought some means of appealing to high heaven—in lieu of a more immediately impotent league of nations—against the budding prophet's unsportsmanlike device. However, Mohammed's magic was the mightier, and heavy rains soon complicated the discomfort of his foes. All the advantages of a tactical surprise remained with the *defenders* of Medina; and the prophet's military conquests may really be dated from the day that this army of foes from his birthplace dispersed in drenched disgust.

The Arabian chronicles[10] reveal that at the crisis of the battle of Tours, which was one of the great crises of Christian civilization in Western Europe, the Moslems became "fearful for the safety of the spoil which they had stored in their tents." Then a "false cry" arose that the Franks were plundering the Saracenic camp. Several squaddrons of Abd er Rahman's best horsemen ventured to detach themselves from the savage engagement and gallop to the succor of the loot. "But it seemed as if they fled; and all the host was troubled. And while Abd er Rahman strove to check their tumult, and to lead them back to battle, the warriors of the Franks came around him, and he was pierced through with many spears, so that he died. Then all the host fled before the enemy"—and the pillaging of the glutted tents soon began in earnest. Was that fateful "false cry" raised by avaricious Moslems or by Frankish agents sent forward with that very design? We shall never know. The great Martel and his Christian victors were not disposed to proclaim that artifice enabled them to overthrow the infidel. While the Arabian chroniclers were uncommonly candid for any era in admitting as much as they did.

It took Mohammedan spies and investigators more than four hundred years to discover the secret of the celebrated "Greek fire", though, according to Gibbon, the process of "compounding and directing this artificial flame was imparted by Callinicus, a native of Heliopolis in Syria, who deserted from the service of the caliph to that of the emperor." Evidently a derivative of petroleum, or "the *naphtha*, or liquid bitumen, a light, tenacious, and inflammable oil, which springs from the earth", its other ingredients seem to have been sulphur and "the pitch that is extracted from evergreen firs." Safeguarding this "discovery or improvement of the military art" was the principal counter-espionage problem of Constantinople all through that cumulative "distressful period when the degenerate Romans of the East were incapable of contending with the warlike enthusiasm and youthful vigor of the Saracens." It "might occasionally be lent to the allies of Rome; but the composition . . . was concealed with the most jealous scruple, and the terror of the enemies was increased and prolonged by their ignorance and surprise." This formidable and shrewdly preserved secret could be "employed with equal effect by sea and land, in battles or in sieges." It produced a loud explosion, a thick smoke and a "fierce and obstinate flame, which not only rose in perpendicular ascent, but likewise burnt with equal vehemence in descent or lateral progress." It was not to be extinguished but "nourished and quickened by the element of water; and sand, urine, or vinegar, were the only remedies that could damp" its flagrant fury.

Thus the alchemist eminence of Byzantium's burning bulwark; and we are told that even "at the end of the eleventh century, the Pisans, to whom every sea and every art were familiar, suffered the effects, without understanding the composition, of the Greek fire." It finally came into the possession of the Mohammedans, and during the Crusades the knighthood of Christendom discovered that this terrible *feu Gregois* was "shot with a pile or javelin from an engine that acted like a sling." To an eyewitness, Joinville, it came flying through the air "like a winged long-tailed dragon, about the thickness of a hogshead, with the report of thunder and the velocity of lightning." But no sooner had the agents of Islam acquired this monstrous blessing than an even more destructive novelty came booming out of Asia. And with the concoction of gunpowder the elusive goals and receding horizons of scientific espionage signaled a chase that continues furiously down to this very hour.

The Arabian Nights' Spy

The cruelty, corruption or indifference of Christian despots, the brutalizing existence of the unprivileged masses, sent many a recruit in the sixteenth century to the roving galleys of the corsairs. Prisoners chained to the oars who agreed to embrace Mohammedanism often rose to high command at sea and undreamed of affluence ashore. And it was equally easy for the Moslem pirates of the Mediterranean to enlist their spies in every land and port. We have been diverted from a purely chronological survey of secret service in the Near East to the four-hundred-year mystery of Greek fire. Before proceeding to a sect of secret agents, a veritable clan of killers and spies, we must look backward for a moment to a sovereign of the East who is immortal in literature if not in history as a benign adventurer-spy. The Abbasid caliph, Haroun-al-Raschid, of the *Arabian Nights' Entertainments,* remains the ideal autocrat, disguising himself and walking humbly among his subjects to ascertain if the just and the unjust are being minced together by the vast machinery of the state. This caliph, though as sure of his immortality as any saint ever to be canonized, was evidently not the romantic investigator or histrionic artist that the classic legend describes.

Sir Marks Sykes has called the Bagdad of Haroun-al-Raschid "a gigantic mercantile city surrounding a huge administrative fortress, wherein every department of state had a properly regulated and well-ordered public office.... Christians, Pagans, Jews, as well as Moslems, were employed in the government service.... An army of clerks, scribes, writers, and accountants swarmed into these offices and gradually swept the whole power of the government into their own hands by separating the Commander of the Faithful from any direct intercourse with his subjects. The Imperial Palace and the entourage were equally based on Roman and Persian precedents. Eunuchs, closely veiled 'harems' of women, guards, spies, go-betweens, jesters, poets, and dwarfs clustered around the person of the Commander of the Faithful, each, in his degree, endeavouring to gain the royal favor and indirectly distracting the royal mind from affairs of business and state." [11]

CHAPTER SIX

THE SECT OF THE ASSASSINS

IF THE DOCTRINES of the Ismaelians or Assassins of Persia had spread over the world, secret service would have grown up to become a state religion instead of a political art. It has always been the fashion to refer to the Assassins as though they alone invented and perfected homicide as a crime, informal execution or governing convenience. But what was already a commonplace in the days of Greece and Rome can scarcely be attributed to an Asiatic sect contemporary with the Crusades.[1] The Assassins, as a departure from this commonplace, raised the intimidation or systematic removal of eminent obstacles to the dignity of a national policy.

Gibbon and others have condemned them as pestilential vermin for doing systematically, and almost painlessly, what popes, kings and every rank of ambitious adventurer did as a matter of course, with any amount of amateurish bungling. In writing of the conquests of the Mongols, Gibbon observes: "I shall not enumerate the crowd of sultans, emirs, and atabeks whom he [Holagou Khan] trampled into dust; but the extirpation of the *Assassins,* or Ismaelians of Persia, may be considered as a service to mankind." Applauding such wholesale butchers as the Mongols for this "extirpation" is rather like praising the Black Death for eliminating lepers or lunatics. Genghis Khan, his leading generals and immediate successors, on some of their best days, must have attained the startling maximum of 100,000 lives extinguished between sunrise and sunset; while no record suggests that the Ismaelians killed off that many of their neighbors and rivals in a decade or even in a century. Politically they were too subtle to resort to war and too artistic to emulate the blind wrath of a pestilence.

One turns the pages of Gibbon from assassin to assassin, until arriving at the Assassins seems more like an accumulation than a novelty. For countless centuries, up to and including the thirteen covered by Gibbon, the great thrones of the then known world had been regularly cleared and refurnished with an occupant by a routine of palace plots and violence. And somebody was bound at length to think of turning all these haphazard dagger thrusts, garrotings and poison drafts into a ritual of diplomacy and religion. What Gibbon and others were apparently unable to forgive was the Ismaelians' distillation of warfare until it spared the masses of mankind and picked off only the most important and solvent individuals. The founder of the sect of the Assassins had no respect for the esprit de corps of feudal times. He appears to have invented conquests which trampled into dust "sultans, emirs, and atabeks" without churning all their soldiers, scholars and merchants, women, children and slaves into mincemeat also.

The ultimate defeat and uprooting of the Assassins of Persia by the Mongol conquerors in 1256 proved that a brilliantly designed and directed military campaign can extinguish the most craftily organized "national" secret service[2]—for it is obvious that, of all political formations, the sect of the Assassins most nearly resembles the secret service of a modern Fascist state. The Assassins were a secret society disciplined and aggrandized to an unparalleled degree of communal power and security. They were a fraternal order that became an aggressive minority that became the dominant faction in their communities and soon thereafter usurped the functions of the state itself. Every member was a "soldier" among the Ismaelians, and every "soldier" was a spy, propagandist and counter-spy, but chiefly a clandestine combatant and killer. Sworn or cowed to an absolute obedience, subservient to a ruler whose very person was a despotic bureaucracy, the Assassins were the model storm troopers of a dictator-drugged Asiatic Fascism. In a comparatively limited area the Assassins strove for hegemony, and they went far uphill along that path, largely by assuring themselves that their leader was a unique and holy man whose meanest conceptions of self-interest larded racial or sectarian destiny with the very will of God.

We are told that in the ninth century, A.D., a man of Persian lineage, bearing the not uncommon name of Abdallah and residing at Ahwaz in the south of Persia, "conceived the design of overturning the empire of the khalifs by secretly introducing into Islam a system of atheism and impiety."[3] This was to be done very gradually; and Abdallah's son and grandson were subtly at work upon it when they made a convert who speedily brought the system into active operation. His name was Carmath, his followers the Carmathites; and a bloody war between these sectaries and the troops of the caliphs continued sporadically throughout an entire century. But at last the Carmathites were soundly beaten and driven underground; which is significant to us here only because it led straight on to the founding of the sect of the Assassins. A resident of Rei in Persia, anxious to conceal his religious opinions and clear himself of the charge of heresy entertained by the governor of his province, who was rigidly orthodox, sent his only son Hassan to Nishapur to be instructed by the celebrated imam, Mowafek. There the youth became intimate with two brilliant fellow students, Omar Khayyam and Nizam Ul Mulk. These three made an agreement, suggested by Hassan ben Sabah, that if one of them should succeed, the other two would share in his good fortune. And we shall see how this pact was respected by Nizam and Omar but violated by its originator.

The Talent for Treachery of Hassan ben Sabah

Nizam Ul Mulk became the first statesman of his time, vizier to Alp Arslan, famous sultan of the Seljuks; whereupon he remembered his promise and offered help both to Hassan and Omar. The latter, as a distinguished astronomer who also wrote poetry, would accept only an annual pension of 1200 ducats so that he might pursue his scientific studies and compose his enchanting verses unhampered by the necessity of having to earn a living. Hassan was far more calculating in his demands. He began rehearsing his predestined role as the first grand master of the Assassins by playing the treacherous friend to the man who had respected his pledge and introduced him at court. Hassan made himself an unofficial spy of the sultan, learning all he could about Nizam's transactions by insinuating himself into his confidence and encouraging him to discuss affairs of state. Whatever he found out he reported straightway to the sultan, and on each act or decision of his friend and patron, the vizier, he put the worst possible interpretation. Hints of the incapacity and flagrant dishonesty of Nizam Ul Mulk fell like a gentle rain upon the throne.

Hassan's innuendoes caused the ruler of the Seljuks to order Nizam Ul Mulk to prepare a balance sheet of his empire's assets and liabilities. The vizier said that such an accounting could not be made in less than a year's time. Hassan, who had been secretly preparing, offered to do it for the sultan and for "his old school friend, the vizier," in forty days. But by this time Nizam Ul Mulk, so shrewd in matters of statecraft, seems to have learned to put up his guard in an affair of friendship. Hassan was ready to submit his balance sheet at the end of the forty-day period, when he discovered certain documents were missing. He claimed that agents of the vizier had taken them, but this he was unable to prove, and the irritable sultan commanded Hassan to retire from court and leave the government to his appointed officials.

It was inevitable that a schemer who found himself humiliated and outwitted should hate those whom he held responsible. The names of Nizam Ul Mulk and his master, the sultan, went to the top of the incipient Assassin's first "black list", and there they stayed until he erased them with blood. It was in 1071 that Hassan ben Sabah became a convert to the Ismaelites, whose propagandists swarmed over a vast area extending from Morocco to China and Zanzibar. Hassan, who had experienced many adventures, must have learned from the Ismaelians, yet it was he alone who contributed a brand-new idea to the political science of his day. He invented a sanctimonious interpretation of murder and treated it as an avowed political weapon, very much after the fashion, as Freya Stark suggests,[4] of British suffragettes and their use of the hunger strike centuries later.

We cannot trace here the gradually accelerated growth of the sect which Hassan founded. Twenty years after his exile from the court of the Seljuks both the sultan and Nizam Ul Mulk were dead. Hassan's agents were the homicidal instruments in each case, while Hassan himself remained safe in his "secret garden." There he is reputed to have drugged and attached to his cause those murderous parasites, first made known to Western Europe in the Crusaders' chronicles, who give us the word *assassin* derived or corrupted by the French from the Arabic *hashshashin*, or hashish eaters. Hassan ben Sabah was feared and execrated by his contemporaries, who never forgave him for discovering that murder was no mere dynastic expedient or passionate accident but a fraternal exercise and proof of a religious education.

Sabotage of the Nerves

While some of the Assassins' exploits of homicide were performed to gain money or earn the favor of very influential persons, most of their victims were notable men whom they had reason to fear. Hassan's stealthy retainers were perhaps the first operatives who employed sabotage as a form of secret service, but they sought invariably to dynamite morale rather than buildings and bridges. In more than one celebrated instance their fear of an opponent was countered by fears that they managed to communicate to him; and if he proved befittingly afraid, they were ready to omit the lethal stroke.

Sindjar, sultan of the Seljuks, dispatched an army to recapture those castles of Kuhistan which the Ismaelian order had seized; whereupon Hassan ben Sabah diplomatically charged his agents to visit the sultan, not to kill, but to arrange for peace. Hassan even contrived to bribe or bring pressure to bear upon officers of the sultan's own household, who spoke in his favor, yet to no avail. Sindjar brushed every negotiator aside. Until at length the "Assassin" technique had to be resorted to, Hassan prevailing upon a servant to thrust a dagger into the floor beside Sindjar's bed while he slept. When the sultan awoke and saw the weapon, he decided to say nothing that might suggest fear and encourage his foes; but presently a slave entered with a message conveyed by emissaries of Hassan ben Sabah. The sultan broke the seals and read: "Were I not well inclined toward Sindjar, the man who planted that dagger in the floor would have fixed it in the Sultan's bosom. Let him know that I, from this rock, guide the hands of the men who surround him."

Sindjar, a sagacious mortal, was convinced. The co-ordination of the dagger and the delivery of the letter so impressed him that he ceased to combat the spreading power and influence of the Ismaelians. His reign thereafter was the period of greatest prosperity for Hassan who thus "founded a sect upon sophisms and a State upon murder."[5] Growing fear of the sect had the curious result of safeguarding individual Assassins when taken prisoner. Severe punishments were seldom meted out to them; and the bold prince or judge who condemned an Ismaelian to torture and death was almost certain to have signed away his own life as well. Their neighbors mostly attempted to placate and reason with the Assassins, none ever feeling sufficiently well organized to restrain them with blows as subtle and foul as those they had been trained to strike.

Foremost among the intimidated were certain princes controlling key fortresses which the lord of the Assassins commanded them to surrender to him. Afraid to refuse, they were no less fearful of lodging the Assassins in such strongholds. And so, as a desperate solution, they gathered all their people together and, practically as an overnight picnic, razed their coveted strongholds to the ground.

In his own lifetime Hassan ben Sabah made an idea work for him until his furtive authority spread like a chilling shadow from north Persia to the Mediterranean coast. His followers prospered not only in Persia but also took over Ismaelian and other strongholds in Syria, where they dominated as semi-independent Persian colonies and where they came into touch with and considerably influenced the armies of European Crusaders. Hassan had borrowed his teachings from Greece and Egypt, Persia and Palestine. His agents, like other Ismaelian apostles, were trained in the House of Science at Cairo. But his systems of government and discipline were peculiarly his own; and it was not until long after his death that the sect he had founded degenerated from zealots into professional murderers with a schedule of prices or retaining fees and payment exacted in advance.

It has been repeatedly urged that the Christian knightly orders owed a great deal to Hassan's unholy brotherhood. The Templars, even before their arrogance affronted and their riches tempted Philip the Fair and his creature, Pope Clement V, were alleged to have imitated the Ismaelian sect in many particulars; and, despite the false accusations and malicious rumors which helped to cause the Templars' downfall in 1313,[6] comparison of the general administration of the two orders—opponents though they were for a time in Syria—reveals much wherein they were virtually identical.

The Assassins, too, were destined to fall before the onset and stratagems of a greater power that coveted their wealth. The Mongol invaders of Persia in 1256 took the Ismaelian strongholds one by one until they came to impregnable Alamut, designed by the only omnipotent military engineer to withstand any form of human siege. Hassan ben Sabah—according to the legend—had acquired it by shrewd negotiation in 1091, after visiting it as his own private spy and determining "the matchless strength" of its position in a valley south of the Caspian. And henceforward he never had left it, remaining there enthroned and secure, cultivating his "secret garden", served and surrounded by his ever-faithful *hashshashin,* while mingling a natural selection of homicide with the liberal arts until he died thirty-four years later.

His ultimate successor at Alamut was one Rukneddin, who neglected to order the assassination of all of Mongolia's generals. He blundered again by falling into Mongol hands, and, as a terrified hostage, commanded his reluctant garrison to surrender. Soon after thus evacuating Alamut in exchange for his life, the Assassins' leader was slain by order of the Great Khan. And so we progress to the conquests of the Mongols and behold them amazingly well informed through their systematic employment of spies. Doubtless they had learned all about the invincibility of Alamut, yet discovered in the character of its last, unheroic lord the one abiding flaw.

CHAPTER SEVEN

MODERN SPIES FROM MEDIEVAL ASIA

AN ORDER issued by a Mongol ruler on the borders of China lowered the price of fish in the markets of England in the year 1238, until forty or fifty herring could be bought for a shilling. This was, in part at least, an authentic stroke of secret service. The Mongol conquerors made use not only of spies in a brilliantly effective intelligence system but of propagandists also and were pioneers in that "attack on the rear", that bluff-barrage of frightfulness aimed at civilian morale, which was reinvented after the outbreak of war in 1914. The inhabitants of Gothia—Sweden—and Fries, according to Matthew Paris, were prevented in 1238 by their growing fear of the oncoming Tartars from sending their ships as usual to the herring-fishery on the coast of England; and as there was no exportation, the English market was glutted. The fear spreading among the Swedes was justified, yet significantly premature. Since we now know something more of the Mongol methods of preparation for attack and conquest than was understood in Western Europe for six hundred years, it is clear that agents of the Asiatic army commanders were far out in front of the actual invasion, laying down a "smoke screen" of intimidating propaganda. The agents themselves are said to have been chiefly Russians. Not until 1241 was the Mongol general, Subutai,[1] ready to launch his attack upon Hungary, whose people were the only branch of the Turko-Mongol race still remaining outside the authority of the successors of Genghis Khan. And after being frightened for three years, the inhabitants of Gothia and Fries had probably grown tired of their own intimidation and gone fishing again.

The invasion of Central Europe had been Subutai's plan for nearly twenty years. In the spring of 1221, with the permission of their emperor, Genghis, Subutai and his equally successful companion-general, Chépé Noyon, had advanced into South Russia as far as the Donetz basin. "Everywhere they established a stable military and civil administration. Further, they organized an elaborate system of information to discover the weak points and rivalries of Europe. In this they found the Venetians quite willing to sacrifice the interests of Christian Europe in order to gain an advantage over their great trading rivals, the Genoese. In return for Mongol help in ousting the Genoese trade-centers in the Crimea, the Venetians acted as part of the intelligence service of the Mongols."² But two years later Genghis Khan was moved to recall both Subutai and Chépé. They returned to Asia by way of the northern end of the Caspian; and when Genghis died in 1227 the program of European conquest was indefinitely suspended.

A young statesman of the Kin Empire, after Genghis' armies had overrun that fertile dominion, said to him: "Thou hast conquered a great empire in the saddle. Thou canst not govern it so." Genghis had ordered the execution of all those self-seekers and rodent deserters who had abandoned the sinking Kin dynasty, holding that he would never be able to rely on them; but Ye Liu Chutsai was spared and invited by Genghis to join him in governing his immense newly gained realm. Thereafter the wise counsel of the Chinese statesman proved as vital to Mongol stability as the brilliant strategy of generals or the accuracy of military intelligence was necessary to Mongol victory.

Ogotai, Genghis' second son, whom he had designated his successor, heeded the advice of Ye Liu Chutsai,³ which gave a Chinese complexion to the policy of the empire and discouraged European expeditions. But Subutai was not to be restrained forever; "his network of spies and propagandists" had been preparing the ground for a spectacular invasion of the West; while the Pope was dissuaded from any timely proclamation of a Holy War by the extravagant hope of converting the Mongols *en masse* to the Roman Catholic faith, a hope based upon reports that a substantial number of the Asiatic invaders were already Nestorian Christians. Subutai had gathered together precisely the force which he estimated he would need and was so supremely well informed that he knew just how to pull "the wires on which danced the royal puppets of Western civilization."⁴ The Emperor Frederick II seems not to have cared to exert himself to help stay the engulfing Asian tide, while lesser princes of Central Europe remained importantly oblivious to the invincible blend of plan and method by which the Mongols meant to sweep them to destruction.

It has been estimated that the invading Mongols numbered little more than 100,000 fighting men. Perhaps 150,000 had set out, but they had suffered losses in battle, and various other subtractions had been made to protect the lines of communication with Asia; therefore, barely two thirds of Subutai's original army accompanied him on his sweep through Poland and Hungary. The Mongol spy system both reported the superior numbers of the Central Europeans and accurately judged their inferior powers of mobility, intelligence and generalship. Without which dependable estimate we may assume so able a commander as Subutai would never have hazarded the distance and physical odds.

The Mongols, however outnumbered, attacked the army of Duke Henry of Silesia on April 9, 1241, all but annihilating it and preventing its junction with the forces of Wenceslas of Bohemia, a day's march to the south. After Liegnitz, Gibbon relates, the Mongols filled nine sacks with the right ears of the slain. And on April 10—the very next day—Subutai and his nominal superior, Prince Batu, checked their strategic retreat, recrossed the Sajo River at night and fell upon King Bela IV and his Hungarians, Germans, Croats and French volunteers, front, flank and rear, and utterly routed them. Bela escaped, but 70,000 of his knights and men-at-arms were left dead upon the field. It is impossible to dismiss the superb timing of these devastating actions as a lucky accident.

The Observations of Carpini

The chronicler, Carpini, tells of the speed, silence and invincible perfection of the Mongols' squadron evolutions directed and controlled by black-and-white signal flags. We know of their peculiarly "modern" innovations of espionage and propaganda, reconnaissance and pony post. If, then, the unbeatable Subutai and his colleague, Kaidu, synchronized their annihilating strokes to fall upon successive days— April 9 and 10—we may safely assume that those Asiatic commanders of the thirteenth century were served by some unique system of intercommunication, undetected even by the more alert European observers and so lost to surviving annals of the Mongol triumphs in the field. As a kind of peace delegate and spiritual envoy Fra Carpini was sent to the court of the Mongol khan, soon after the terrifying invasion of 1239-42, to urge that the Asiatic conquerors stop slaughtering Christians. Carpini, a brave and zealous man, seems instinctively to have exercised the talents of a first-rate spy. He returned to the West with comprehensive reports upon the "Tartars" and their armed strength, and exhorted all the rulers of Europe to borrow the new and more effective military methods of the Mongols.

With a safe interval of seven centuries critics applaud the Mongol innovations that made Genghis and his army leaders invincible. The synchronized destruction of the armies led by Henry of Silesia and Bela of Hungary remains an enigma of military science, yet hardly more baffling than Subutai's ability to move his vanguard in three days —March 12 to 15^5—a distance of about 180 miles through hostile country still deep in snow. Their mobility was the unvarying characteristic of Mongol contingents and a decisive basis of strategy in nearly all Mongol campaigns. Genghis Khan seems to have been centuries ahead of his time in his provisions for rapid communication; and as a means of getting news of emergencies and important dispatches from the most distant points of his vast realm he developed the pony post or *yam*, which reached its state of most efficient operation in the reign of Kublai Khan. A journey of 1500 miles in ten days was the not uncommon record of a single postrider. The couriers rode at full gallop, changing their mounts every twenty-five or thirty miles. Marco Polo found the horse-post houses twenty-five miles apart, with four hundred horses at some posts and two hundred at others. "If even a king were to arrive at one of these houses, he would find himself well lodged."

With 10,000 such posts of the *yam* dotting the new military roads and old caravan routes of Asia, and with 300,000 fleet horses available, it is not surprising that the *Kha Khan* was kept well informed. A messenger with dispatches for the Khan covered his 150 miles a day without rest, had precedence over all other travelers, and commanded swift attention and the best horse of each station. There was a government clerk at every posthouse to note the time of the couriers' arrival and departure. Marco Polo came back to Europe with the belief that, "when there is a call for great haste," there were postriders who would cover 200 or 250 miles "in the day and as much in the night", which preserves the travel-stained lineaments of a physical impossibility.[6] "These couriers," the Venetian set forth, "are highly prized; and they could never do it did they not bind hard the stomach, head and chest with strong bands."

Mongol Secret Service

A demand for speed of communication, for accuracy and timeliness of information, led directly to the institution of secret service, to which the Mongols contributed with much instinctive cunning. We even find Subutai characteristically making his debut in the annals of Mongol conquest with an espion's ruse. He rode to an encampment of Tartars, explaining that he had deserted the Mongol khan and hoped to join their clan. He was so convincing that he made the Tartars believe their Mongol foes were not in the neighborhood; and so they were quite unprepared when the main body of Subutai's companions fell upon them. This dodge seems to have worked again and again, Mongol agents being sent on ahead to pose as deserters and complain of ill-treatment while laying down a "smoke screen" of false intelligence.

The Golden Emperor of Cathay unwisely asked Genghis for Mongol aid in his continual war upon the ancient house of Sung in South China. Chépé Noyon—"with his weakness for wearing sable boots"—was sent with a force of cavalry to fight beside the Cathayans while closely observing the riches of their land. Soon after the return of this spying expedition Genghis began preparing to invade Cathay, his first attempt upon a civilized power of superior defensive strength, and even now he launched his campaign by dispatching beyond the great wall a contingent of spies and scouts, who were "to capture and bring back informers." Espionage and artifice had a vital part in the Mongols' conquest of China. Chépé on one occasion pretended to abandon his baggage train but turned and rode back swiftly to overwhelm the Cathayan garrison that had swarmed out of an impregnably fortified city to plunder the carts, supplies and other lawful prizes of war.

In that year of 1214 Subutai was on detached service and ordered to study the situation in Northern China. For several months the talented young commander virtually disappeared, forwarding nothing but an occasional routine report as to the condition of his horses. Yet when he returned he brought with him the submission of Korea. Having met with no serious obstruction he had simply pressed on—as he was later to do in Europe—until he found and subdued a new country.[7] Wherever the Mongol army advanced it carried along interpreters, "mandarins to take over the administration of captured districts" and merchants who could be called upon to act as spies. These traders seem to have been a nondescript lot, chosen from many nationalities. As the mounted horde of Genghis swept toward Cathay or Islam, a screen of skirmishers and scouts was thrown out in front of each column; while ahead of them traveled the merchant-spies, two or three together, diligently hunting information of every kind.

In addition to the merchants who acted as spies—or the spies who posed as merchants—there was in the Mongol armies a great variety of mercenaries, drawn from every corner of Europe and Asia. The fame of the Mongol conquests steadily increased the number of adventurers eager to find fortune in the ranks of the ever victorious; and an intelligence system on a war footing was bound to acquire intimate facts about all lands and peoples from this polyglot stream of recruits. Foreigners of military distinction took service with the generals of Genghis or his successors. After their occupation of Hungary, Prince Batu and Subutai sent an expedition to ravage Austria, which was done with Mongol thoroughness. That expedition was under the command of an English Knight Templar who attained high rank in the army of the Asiatic emperor.

Genghis, as one habitually making use of military secret service, understood the value but also the menace of espionage and dealt harshly with those caught spying upon his forces. The *Yassa* was his code of Mongol laws, blending his own will with the more expedient of tribal customs; and the twenty-first of the twenty-two *Yassa* commandments which Pètis de la Croix derived from Persian and other chroniclers was:[8] "Spies, false witnesses, all men given to infamous vices, and black sorcerers are condemned to death." Even so, in that fixed plan of invasion which Mongol generals followed with unbroken success until 1270, when the Mamelukes halted their advance upon Egypt, the second prescribed duty was—the sending out of spies and the bringing in of captured informers, who must be questioned and made to give information that could be checked off against the reports of the spies.[9]

The Mongols are reputed to have first demonstrated to Europeans the deadly uses of gunpowder and to have popularized the Chinese invention of paper, which has ever since then made peace treaties so much easier to tear up. Their further introduction of efficient military secret service, intelligence and staff communication was an example not soon hammered into the thick, warlike skulls of Western captains and kings. But we shall later discover what extraordinary influence it exerted upon those Mongol descendants who governed with many spies and infinite splendor, as the Mogul emperors of India.

CHAPTER EIGHT

TREACHERIES, SACRED AND PROFANE

IT IS NOT NECESSARY to be too subtle or stealthy if one's adversaries are trusting and naïve; and some of the spiritual, military and even political magnificoes in the time of Niccolò Machiavelli owned a naïveté bordering on the supernatural. Marion Crawford in his *Sketches from Venetian History* has observed that it was an age in which the safe conduct seemed invariably a prelude to political assassination. And it struck him as extraordinary that men should have persisted in putting any faith in such promises. The safe conduct was a contribution from the age of chivalry to an age of unabashed chicaneries; its abuse was not peculiar to Venetian or Italian secret service, and at the beginning of the fifteenth century it was already as commonplace a mechanism of abduction or betrayal as the poniard and the poisoned cup were instruments of private vengeance or expedited inheritance.

John Huss, the learned Czech, rector of the university at Prague, was decoyed to the Council of Constance (1414–1418) under promise of a safe conduct. Since he was suspected of abominable heresies, his opponents were reassured from the start about breaking their word and being absolved from that sin if the obstinacy of the accused could only be corrected at the stake. The sin committed by Huss had originated in his venturing—about 1396—to deliver a series of lectures based upon the doctrines of the great Oxford teacher, Wycliffe.[1] He was put on trial at Constance and ordered to recant certain of his opinions. When he refused because he was not convinced of his error, he was warned that it was his duty to obey his superiors and recant whether he was convinced or not. And when he still refused, he was condemned, delivered to the secular arm—that useful device which saved the Church from committing its own judicial murders—and burned as a heretic.

Huss, a wise critic, who must have been suspicious of orthodox integrity—or he would not have required the safe conduct—none the less fell a victim to the elasticity of conscience then impoverishing the spirit of Christendom. The trap laid for him was especially edged with sharp teeth, as the safe conduct was promised by the Emperor Sigismund himself, and had Huss refused to take the monarch's word, he would have been guilty of lèse-majesté and, perhaps, of that heinous secular heresy called high treason.

Sigismund, the tyrannical ruler of the Holy Roman Empire, had things very much his own way at the Council of Constance. He forced Pope John XXIII to attend and did not even trouble to *promise* him safe conduct. The Holy Father proceeded reluctantly to his doom, accompanied, the record reveals, by one who had known him before he became pope, Cosimo de' Medici, grandfather of Lorenzo the Magnificent, who came to Constance "at the risk of his life to help to defend him; and had to fly in disguise when Pope John was deposed and imprisoned by the Council."[2] The following year (1416) the Council continued its appointed task of reuniting Christian peoples by burning a colleague of Huss, Jerome of Prague. And this outrage, coupled with the betrayal and martyrdom of Huss, provoked an insurrection in Bohemia, which is important here because it was the first of the terrible religious wars that invited Christians to practice espionage, assassination and every form of treachery, intolerance and desecration upon each other in all parts of the world for three centuries.

In this period one need not look for evidences of secret service and espionage intrigues. The spies and assassins, the double-dealers and feline deceivers march four abreast continuously down the long ramps of dynastic, religious or political machination. It is much more of a task to look for magnanimity and disinterested motives, for any sort of patriotism or traces of simple integrity. And to find these things often *would* be secret service. The thought and the writings of Machiavelli cover this period and give us a name that has erroneously stood for personal cunning and ruthless self-interest. But the worthy Florentine systematized all those crafty articles of faith after he had himself been crudely undone. The stupid plotting of two "harebrained young men", Boscoli and Capponi, led to Machiavelli's untimely political demise. He was even put to the torture and slightly crippled by the cruelties of the rack, whereupon he retired to the passive torments of literary composition and wrote a masterpiece—not about the abolition of torture, but about applying it more subtly to the right people.

His native Florence suffered a devastating plague in 1629 "which raged with great violence for many months" and which witnessed the innovation of a kind of sanitary secret service that we shall not meet with in this record again. Because a "board of health" was established in the emergency and because its members compelled even the inmates of monasteries and convents to observe sanitary rules, the Church was moved to denounce the health regulations as impious. Ultimately the members of the board were made to do penance; while Dominican friars took advantage of the pestilence to organize a form of house-to-house espionage, inquiring into all domestic matters and adding public indignation to the misery of a stricken city. Even some wise and devout Florentines found it difficult to distinguish plague from plague.

Chapter Nine

CHURCH AND STATE

MEDIEVAL CHURCHMEN, who had to keep their minds attuned to the pretentious trifles of doctrine and ritual, found a natural outlet for their excessive acuteness in the strategy and management of secret service. All through these centuries we shall discover ecclesiastics in skillful command of spies and temporal intriguers; until the unfrocked priests and other relapsed *religieux* come into their own as accomplished practitioners among the brigades of diplomatic agents, police spies and political conspirators of the French Revolutionary epoch. However, almost any individual having the muscular mentality to wriggle his conscience out of the straitjacket of religious vows, or enough independence of spirit to escape from conformity, can look to some branch of secret service in turbulent times for a more congenial, untrammeled vocation.

The medieval world was savage and ruthless beyond measure as well as steeped in dissimulation and bad faith. Kings and great nobles were violent, and unspeakably cruel and despotic; numbers of the lower clergy were stupid, faithless and corrupt, or else remote and ascetic, a dustbin of impractical erudition; while the bishops and princes of the Church were cunning and avaricious. The soldiers, trading classes and peasantry were uniformly stupid and cruel. Torture and exhibitions of capital punishment could be palmed off upon them as both bread and circuses. It remained for the medieval Church, however, to put cruelty and burnings and gruesome public executions on the firm, popular basis of exalting religious spectacle. Discovering holy excuses for sadism was one of the most characteristic achievements of medieval, as compared with simple pagan, times.

Even so, it was the churchmen and not the soldiers who kept alive that system of inquiry which we call the gathering of intelligence. And to the medieval mind the use of spies and informers must have seemed a dubiously humane substitute for the certainties of the hoist, hot pincers, or the excruciating *potro* or water-torture. Where formerly some defenseless underling had been put upon the rack, spies had to be paid, a costly fad in fathoming the privacies of neighbors, rivals and foes. The Church of Rome, divided at this time on so many issues, had two schools of opinion as to the relative merits of espionage and torture. But that rolling mill of faith, the Spanish Inquisition, being geared to annihilate doubt of every kind, settled the question for itself by relying abundantly upon both.

It would not be difficult to make out a case for the Roman Catholic Church as the progenitor and beneficiary of a system of intelligence, espionage and propaganda incomparably superior to any other found in these annals. But right here we come upon that test of "conflict" and "strength of opposition" which, by the standards we have set, distinguishes a notable secret-service organization from mere promiscuous snooping and spying. One does not speak of the "bravery" of the hunter who traps small game, or of the "marksmanship" of the sportsman who kills fish in a lake with a charge of dynamite. And there is little therefore to applaud about the cunning, subtlety or inquisitorial keenness of men who became feared and powerful because they could obtain signed "voluntary" confessions from helpless victims who had lately suffered upon the rack. There was some innovation of method but no greatness where every law, taboo, custom and condition was arranged to produce a one-sided outcome, and where the cards were often both marked and stacked against unwilling opponents who had to be bound, gagged and blindfolded before sitting down to play.

The secret service of the Church—with exceptions which shall be noted—was very largely like that, ubiquitous yet sporadic, always the parasite of some tyranny. It could gain all sorts of *private* ends; but did it check or foster Protestantism, retard the coming of the Reformation of Luther and Calvin by a year or by a day? Even when breaking up, and the broken parts concealed in a blue haze of controversy, the Church continued to send forth its protective screen of skirmishers and secret agents. The cracks, however, grew deeper, the broken edges more unmendable; and in spite of all the spying, the burnings and inquisitions by torture, the last defenses of dogma were shattered by the inquiries of troubled minds.

Torquemada and the Torture Chambers

Before the election of Pope Innocent III it had been only the occasional duty of the curial court to make inquests into cases of heresy. But Innocent III—who "raised the Papal power to the highest point" —saw in the new order of the Dominicans a formidable instrument for extirpating heretics and unbelievers, and so established the Inquisition as a perpetual system of inquiry and suppression throughout the Roman Catholic world. It was expected to light its cleansing piles of faggots in every quarter of Christendom; but it is the Holy Office or Inquisition in Spain to which we must turn for history's most appalling portrait of men of great talent and inflexible faith devoutly consummating evil in a perfervid endeavor to do good.

A virtually *Spanish* Inquisition was set up in England for a time during the reign of "Bloody Mary", whose consort, Philip II of Spain, must have convinced her of its efficacy. And effectual it was, for the "executions began in January, 1555" and continued until England's last Roman Catholic sovereign[1] was discredited for all time, most of the victims of the English Inquisition being ignorant, harmless folk who, as Burghley said, "had never heard of any other religion than that which they were called on to abjure." An inviting target for the most insistent and subtle of the Inquisitors was the heir to the throne, Mary's half-sister Elizabeth; but that harassed and suspected princess "went daily to mass" and, we learn, was not to be "trapped" by any of her questioners.[2] Possibly her intimidating encounters with the Catholic Inquisition explain the later severity of counter-espionage which began afflicting partisans of Rome throughout England soon after Elizabeth succeeded to the throne.

The Holy Office in Spain was not abolished until 1809, and, though its procedure was medieval, the years of its worst abuses of arbitrary power were in every sense modern. Frey Tomás de Torquemada, the Dominican monk who became grand inquisitor, was the principal architect of the hideous Spanish structure of the Inquisition. And this *Chekist* of Holy Church—whose authority came to him by royal edict, dated September 27, 1480—not only put his demonic imprint upon the life and religious thought of Spain for generations to come, but also bequeathed modern government a pattern which no master of political police need ever attempt to excel. Torquemada[3] came of a distinguished family and was the nephew of the learned Cardinal of San Sisto. Such was the austerity of character of the monk, Tomás, that he never ate meat and would permit the use of linen neither in his apparel nor upon his bed. He observed the rule of poverty imposed by his order without regard to family obligations, being unable to provide his only sister with more than a pittance to keep her from genteel starvation.[4]

The Spanish inquisitors whom Torquemada, as appointed collaborator of the Cardinal of Spain, Mendoza, selected to serve the Holy Office were not all of them "Torquemadas", but most of them were men of exceptional subtlety and disarming simplicity. They asked nothing for themselves save recognition as the sacred investigators of

God with absolute dominion over the lives and consciences of all persons living within the borders of Spain—living or dead, for the dead were regularly denounced, tried, condemned and appropriately dishonored by the canonical processes of the Inquisition. Implacable purpose and human will as unbending as the stones of a cathedral buttress were concealed in these inquisitors beneath a habit of sincerity which became corrupted to bigotry mainly because their age was bigoted and corrupt, and because in the intoxicating power which churchmen then habitually sought to usurp they were as excessive as drunkards. The inquisitors' fidelity was the kind that, if it could not move mountains, never recoiled from the duty of torturing and burning a whole community of supposed heretics. Like the conqueror in Tacitus who "made a desert and called it Peace", they made an austere reign of terror and called it a revival of faith. In Spain today they are suffering the long pent-up counter-terror—provoked by Torquemada, his creatures and imitators—in every mass attack upon the authorities and communicants, the wealth and edifices of the Church.

The records of the Inquisition are confused by the blatant apologies of its servants or admirers and the savage animosity of those who deemed it wholly malignant and vile.[5] Nothing conducted by men of private integrity could be wholly vile. The Inquisition was, in fact, like its operatives, deceptively sincere and good. But there is something both exasperating and ironic about the "secret-service" manifestation of that sincerity and that goodness. The underlying theory of procedure that made the Holy Office more infernal than holy was as direct and brutal as martial law. If we compel a nation to turn informer, the inquisitive friars decided, if we give credence to every trivial denunciation, and if, having subjected those denounced to exhaustive and recurrent torture, we accept their "voluntary" confessions, not many persons guilty of heresies are going to escape us.

That was, indeed, God's truth. But the net result was thousands of tortured suspects confessing to offenses against orthodoxy which they were not subtle enough to understand and had to be rigorously *taught* that they had committed. A hardly less appalling result was many more thousands of vicious or intimidated men, women and even children turned spies and informers, giving information against their own relatives and acquaintances—or getting even with an envied or despised neighbor or superior—by the self-protective process of confiding to the Holy Office secret information that was spiritually incriminating. Such a system of intelligence and espionage reflects no credit upon the Holy Office or the Church that gave it both its power and its administrators. It was a system as easy to manage—and to imagine—as the antique sanitary precautions which sought to detain an epidemic at the gates of palaces by burning down the infected hovels of the poor.

In its torturings and deceptive interrogations the Spanish Inquisition enjoyed every excuse that conscientious zealots can find for crime and chicaneries. The end, which was the faith of God, always justified the means, which happened to improve upon every known form of pagan sadism and cunning. Torture, bear in mind, was never in itself deemed a form of punishment. It was not even a judicial error if some obstinate fellow, from too much strain and dislocation and choking, should die before a death sentence could be legally passed upon him. Torture was unashamedly applied to victims with nothing more to admit, who had run their minds dry hastily and voluntarily confessing grievous sins. But the torture came upon them none the less because they had failed to incriminate others. Suffering, it was found, stimulated the memory—or the imagination. Another clerical dodge of the old school was that of promising some shrieking wretch God's mercy if he would but speak the truth. He spoke; and the promised "mercy" was interpreted as his swift execution, without any more torture.

Torquemada's "history"—according to Prescott—"may be thought to prove that of all human infirmities there is none productive of more extensive mischief to society than fanaticism." The Dominicans of Torquemada's mold might be the sort of ambulant bigots who could solemnly preach—in 1342—that the Black Death was a visitation upon the land because it harbored Jews. But once these deadly Black Friars were diverted to the holy work of the Inquisition they became more catholic and oppressed everybody. Proceedings were instituted threatful to the lives and property of men of the very first importance among Spaniards. One of these was the vice-chancellor of Aragon, Alonso de Caballeria, who had been a distinguished member of the council summoned by Torquemada to arrange details for the introduction of the Holy Office into Aragon. Another harshly dealt with was Don Jaime de Navarre—called the Infante of Navarre or the Infante of Tudela—who was the son of the queen of Navarre and a nephew of the Spanish king.

Police Espionage of the Holy Office

A fugitive from the Inquisition had come to Tudela in Navarre and found refuge there "for a few days" until he could make his escape into France. Spies of the inquisitors reported this act of hospitality and mercy; whereupon the Holy Office dared to arrest Infante Jaime in the very capital of his mother's independent kingdom. Taken to Zaragoza, he was actually thrown into prison. He was then subjected to the penance of being whipped in procession around a church by two priests in the presence of his bastard cousin, Alfonso of Aragon, an archbishop at the age of seventeen. Further to humiliate the Infante of Navarre he was compelled to stand as a penitent, candle in hand, in full view of the people during high mass. Only thus could he be absolved of sacerdotal censure.

Alonso de Caballeria, however, stands forth as no royal prince but one of the few men of his time who defied the Inquisition and yet survived and prospered. He was held in great esteem by the king and was a man of extraordinary accomplishments and courage. When the Holy Office, acting as usual upon the denunciations of anonymous informers, arrested him on the charge of having sheltered fugitives and also on the suspicion of being himself a Judaizer, Caballeria stoutly refused to recognize the jurisdiction of the ecclesiastical court or the authority of Torquemada. Going over their astonished tonsures, he appealed directly to the pope, and even lodged with the holy father an intrepid complaint against the inquisitors.

The heavens did not fall, though a lot of good people kept glancing up uneasily. The greatly daring vice-chancellor was the son of a rich Jewish nobleman, who, having been baptized, had changed his name from Bonafos to Caballeria. The character of the accused man and the strength of his position caused Pope Innocent VIII on a memorable day—August 28, 1488—to forward a brief prohibiting the Inquisition from proceeding further against Caballeria. The sun still crossed the heavens from east to west; but black spots danced before the tormented eyes of Frey Tomás de Torquemada. He elected to overrule the judgment of the pope, arguing that false allegations discredited Caballeria's appeal to Rome. The pope, however, felt in a mood to assert his supreme authority; and on October 20 the minutes of the case against the vice-chancellor were transmitted to the Vatican, where the persecution of Caballeria ebbed into the archivists' quiet oblivion. Alonso de Caballeria lived to gain many honors and rise in rank until he became chief judge of Aragon.

We may understand how seldom a designated victim escaped the poisoned pinpricks of inquisitorial genius by the attention which Llorente, the great Catholic historian and critic of the Spanish Inquisition, gives to Caballeria's case both in his *Memoria Historica* and *Historia Critica*. The Inquisition had been designed to extirpate heresy, and it was not going to fail in Spain through any want of energy, thoroughness or vigilance. The New-Christians were the gravest problem and had to be spied upon incessantly, thousands of prosperous and obedient subjects of the Spanish sovereign, Jews and Moors, who, obeying a royal edict, had embraced Christianity and been baptized, but who were envied, suspected and generally thought not to be sincere *conversos*. One must not be heard singing an Arab song or found with henna dye upon the fingernails. For the salvation of the soul of Spain everyone had to suffer the rack or the *potro* who had aroused suspicion "by indulging in too frequent baths, or even by too strict observance of the Sabbath."

To keep track of the numberless peccadilloes of this nationally suspected and potentially outlawed minority, the Inquisition honored itself by establishing "the most wonderful police system that the world has ever seen."[6] This superlative can hardly be disputed; for the most virulent political police and domestic espionage bureaus of modern dictatorships seem but light carbon copies of the bloodstained Spanish *Cheka* of the Church. We learn that a "vast civilian army was enrolled in the service of the Holy Office, as members of the tertiary Order of Saint Dominic." These lay brothers enjoyed many coveted advantages, such as immunity from taxation and the right to "plead benefit of clergy", which meant that no civil court could proceed against them, while every ecclesiastical court was privately disposed in their favor. It is not surprising, then, that so many Spaniards sought to be enrolled as lay brothers—guards or spies—that their number had to be very strictly limited.

Originally a penitential order, it soon became known as the Militia Christi, and its members as familiars of the Holy Office. They dressed in black and wore the white cross of Saint Dominic upon their cloaks and doublets, being also required to join the Confraternity of Saint Peter Martyr. Few inquisitors ventured to appear in public without an armed escort of these black-garbed familiars. Included in the pampered battalions of the Militia Christi were "men of all professions, dignities and callings" who liked the idea of paying no taxes and of being immune to civil lawsuits or prosecution. They provided the recruits for the secret service of the Inquisition; they were "the eyes and the ears of the Holy Office, ubiquitous in every stratum of society."[7]

The Inquisition not only relied upon espionage but also trained its corps of spies carefully and well, issuing a manual for their guidance which was as candid and unblushing about the technique of betrayal as the manuals issued to its inquisitors were disingenuous, diabolical and blandly barbarous. There is a "compendious tome" annotated by Francesco Pegna—first published in Rome, 1585—that preserves for us, among many stratagems, this classic admonition of church espionage:

> Be it noted that the spy, simulating friendship and seeking to draw from the accused a confession of his crime, may very well pretend to be of the sect of the accused, but he must not say so, because in saying so he would at least commit a venial sin, and we know that such must not be committed upon any grounds whatever.

Justification for spy-betrayals and torture was found by Eymericus, the author of a celebrated manual,[8] in these words: "For although in civil courts the confession of a crime does not suffice without proof, it suffices here"—at that G.H.Q. of sanctified duplicities, the Holy Office—for heresy "being a sin of the soul, confession may be the only evidence possible."

Where an advocate was permitted to speak in defense of one accused by the Inquisition, Torquemada in Article XVI of his notorious *Instructions* laid upon him the obligation to abandon his defense the instant he realized his client was guilty. By canon law no attorney was allowed to plead for a heretic in any court, civil or ecclesiastical, even in cases having nothing to do with heresy. Witnesses, generally spies, who "appeared" against one accused, actually did not have to appear at all and were never exposed to the rigors of interrogation by counsel for the defense. Witnesses appearing for those accused by the Inquisition were a rare and reckless lot. In most trials there simply were no defense witnesses. To testify in favor of any one charged with heresy might cause the witness himself to become a suspected heretic; and then the plaguelike shadow of the Holy Office would fall across his home, his family, his means of livelihood, and everything and everyone touching his life in any degree, and the spies would flock around, while he survived in awful dread, till the Militia Christi came and led him away to a dungeon, to deceitful ceremonies of examination and torture.

The sin of usury as well as heresy ultimately concerned the Inquisition. But in most ecclesiastical "crimes" the "heresy angle" could be made to emerge by any gifted inquisitor after only an hour or so of judicious inquiry. Torquemada, raised to great power as grand inquisitor and president of the Suprema, continually endeavored to expand the jurisdiction of the Holy Office. Bigamy, he ruled, was primarily "an offense against the laws of God and a defilement of the Sacrament of Marriage." Adultery he failed to interpret as a defilement of that same sacrament, but contrived that sodomy should for the first time be prosecuted as a sin rather than a crime, and that persons convicted of it by the Inquisition be burned at the stake.

Torquemada's chastity was as inflexible as his doctrines, and he seems to have been moved to wrath by the great numbers of the clergy whom his spies reported unchaste. The most dangerous form of this immorality was called "solicitation"—*solicitatio ad turpia*—or the abuse of the confessional in seducing female penitents. It was an offense that gravely wounded the Church, inasmuch as it loaded to the muzzle with choice ammunition all the enemies and calumniators of Rome. Torquemada managed to interpret "solicitation" as a form of heresy, since many persuasive priests assured their more timid penitents that the lady's consent would not be a sin. Giving false assurances of that nature was, indeed, a defilement of the sacrament; and the firm hand of the Holy Office fell upon the enterprising confessor who thus disguised his concupiscence as the will of God. But savage as Torquemada and his inquisitors appear to have been with all sorts of sinners and "self-delators", there is no evidence that they dealt too harshly with oversolicitous churchmen.[9] The rack and the fire, according to the best opinion prevailing at the Holy Office, must be reserved for infidel plotters and heretics, preferably Jews.

Chapter Ten

THE ARTS AND CRAFT OF THE JESUITS

THE CONSCIENCES OF MONARCHS were often imperceptible even to their own Catholic confessors, or they were as slippery as eels and only the Jesuits could maintain a hold upon them. When the popular Don Carlos, son of Philip II of Spain, confessed to a prior that he nourished a mortal hatred against his father—which must have made it unanimous—the prior violated a primary law of the priesthood and immediately reported the "sin" to Philip, who as promptly procured the murder of his heir. Jesuit fathers were celebrated or notorious—according to the point of view—as the chaplains and confessors of royalty and were even known as "the priests from Spain"; but none of them would have betrayed a confession to a temporal superior and none would have acted as a private spy for so despicable a king.

The militant fathers of the Society of Jesus were a secret-service corps d'élite, an incomparable and indispensable body of "shock troops", who were trusted and hated, loyally supported and savagely reviled, who stooped to persuasive deceits and frauds and even baser practices, but never stooped to serving two masters. They fought for two centuries with the same weapons men of their own times used and understood, but they fought always for the glory and power of the Church.

It is not inappropriate to call the Jesuits "shock troops" in their secret-service missions as well as in their better-known work as spiritual missionaries and teachers of the Catholic faith. Yet a frontal attack was seldom their characteristic strategy; and in many instances no such attack would have been possible by the time they were mobilized to deal with a virulent case of heresy or dissent. The Papal See always had at its disposal, as we know, its cohort of cardinals and a legion of legates and genuinely learned men. Yet wherever in Europe the interests of Rome necessitated some operation of diplomacy, counter-influence or intrigue—which today seem indistinguishable from the pressure-plots and conspiracies of temporal powers —the Jesuits proved themselves the cleverest and most energetic of workers for the Catholic cause.

THE ARTS AND CRAFT OF THE JESUITS   67

Perhaps the populace must be stirred up against a king of independent faith, or some natural exercise of secular powers seemed inconvenient to the politicians of the Church. Jesuit fathers were the agents for such an ecclesiastical emergency. A small company of them, having the moral stamina and unscrupulous fervor of an army of ten thousand, would launch the clandestine camisado, spreading propaganda, recruiting partisans, intriguing with potential insurgents and exhorting potential assassins.[1] In the prolonged "war" between Rome and the authorities of Protestant England there were times when the whole country seemed "overrun with Jesuits", though never more than a handful of these ingenious and resolute invaders were at large in the kingdom at any one round of the struggle. A priest with as many aliases as an ex-convict and habitual criminal of today may seem fantastic to the modern reader; but such was the industry and conspirant abilities of the Jesuit agents in England that some of them had ten and even twenty names in circulation to screen and disperse the activities of a single zealot.

The English police captured a Roman Catholic adversary whose real named proved to be Thomas Holland. He was also widely known as Saunderson and as Father Holland-Saunderson. He had contrived to emerge from the underground channels of his peculiar "parish" in many and various guises: as an elderly traveler with a flowing beard, as a young man athletic and clean shaven, as a nobleman's lackey, and as the haughty nobleman himself, as a wealthy merchant, roistering soldier, or abstracted scholar and pedant. All these agents of the papal secret service were Father Holland-Saunderson. An Englishman by birth, he could speak English with a Flemish, French or Spanish accent and was found to be fluent in all three of those tongues, with or without an *English* accent. At his principal place of refuge, provided him by Catholic adherents, all the accouterments of conspiracy and espionage were uncovered, including false beards, wigs, the materials of make-up known at that time, and quantities of apparel suitable to nearly every station in life.

Agents of the crown were spurred by Sir Francis Walsingham and other superiors to uncover the "headquarters" of what zealous Protestants termed the "Jesuit conspiracy." Presently a police informer called attention to the seat of the Abingtons, near Worcester. Known as Hindlip Hall, it might better have been called Castle Merlin, for such was the wizardry of its construction, the authorities entered there and searched it thoroughly—and though its residents had not departed—came away solemnly pronouncing it deserted. Where, oh, where had the Abingtons gone? Into the walls, into the wainscoting,

68   THE STORY OF SECRET SERVICE

through the floors, and up or down spiral staircases into padded inclosures, cellar havens, or obscure and airy attic roosts!

Not long after the first futile visitation a watchful Anglican noble told the police that the Abingtons were back. Living as they did in virtually a double dwelling, they had condescended to return to England from their private preserves of the hunted. A servant of the

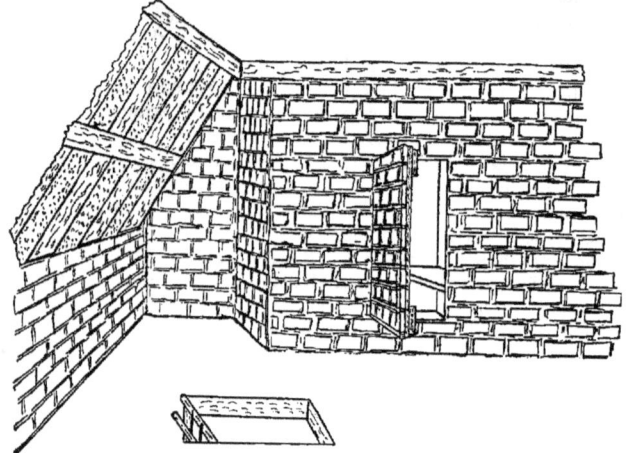

THE INGENIOUS HIDING PLACE OF JESUIT AGENTS ON HAZARDOUS HOLY SERVICE IN ELIZABETHAN ENGLAND

Hardwick Hall, County Durham, contains this cunningly walled-in room with the concealed "stone" entrance to be approached by means of ladder and trap door.

suspected family, being overtaken and rigorously questioned, was ultimately induced to give the show away. It was then discovered that the large hall of the castle concealed a number of spacious hiding places, that all the rooms were connected by secret staircases and trap doors with the cellars. There were even fireplaces that provided, alongside the flues, small cavities into which the religious fugitive might crawl.

Hindlip Hall was probably unique of its kind in all England; but there were many more residences of Roman Catholics which came to be conveniently equipped with revolving pictures, sliding panels, trap doors, false ceilings and other screening arrangements so cunningly fashioned that the government's agents, regardless of all they were engaged in learning about these devices, continued to be deceived by new ones. It appears that they were originated and clandestinely installed by a single Jesuit genius, Father Oven, who

A wall panel concealing entrance to spiral staircase, Hardwick Hall.

traveled about England in various guises, using the names Draper, Walton, Andrews and "Little John."

Parsons and Campion

It is not to be supposed that Father Oven's contrivances were the frail ingenuities of stage melodrama. When the sturdy Elizabethan police agent searched, he *searched,* a convert to anarchy and demolition. Father Aylworth, another of the wanted Jesuits, was cunningly able to lie hidden while the hunting instinct of his adversaries was visible and in full cry, and later described what he saw and heard: "They began by assailing the walls with hammers and pickaxes, probed into every corner and left no stone unturned. Not only were the walls demolished, but also the floors and even the outhouses and stables were not spared; they thrust their swords into the sacks of corn and other heaps of grain and dug into the unpaved parts of the garden and yard with staves."[2]

The more formidable agents of the Church of Rome were pursued no less relentlessly. Word came that two noted Jesuits, Robert Parsons and Edmund Campion, were on their way to England; at once the counter-spies hired by the English to watch French seaports were notified of this alarming invasion. A ship's captain was located soon afterward who admitted knowing a good deal about a pair of travelers whose descriptions—as willingly supplied by him—suggested Parsons and Campion. This amiable mariner provided other information and had his listeners gaping at the sensational nature of his disclosures. Before taking his leave he mentioned that a friend of his —"a merchant named Patrick"—would be along, and, saying that he had business with the man, he asked as a favor to have his journey expedited.

The merchant "Patrick" duly passed over into England, and nothing more was heard either of him or the thoughtful captain. Reports soon began pouring into London, however: the Jesuit fathers, Parsons and Campion, had arrived, were quietly moving about, preaching and hearing confessions. Parsons, it appears, had been the ship's captain; Edmund Campion, the merchant. Parsons had so cleverly distracted the port watchers and ship searchers on both sides of the Channel, they allowed him and his colleague to slip through their cordon. And what was the simple magic he employed? He professed to turn informer and affected to reveal the vividly "treasonable aims" of the two Jesuit emissaries, who, he confessed, had been his passengers.

English spies traced the pair to the attic of a Roman Catholic home, reporting to the Anglican authorities that they only emerged from this impromptu "priest's hole" between 2 and 4 A.M. The house, belonging to a man named Gilbert, was surrounded, raided and searched; but Parsons and Campion had escaped. A few days later a cleverly concocted libel upon Queen Elizabeth and the Church of England was being distributed to the students at Oxford. The Jesuits were subsequently found to have set up a secret printing press at Stonors Park near Henley. And this, be it noted, not much over a century after the introduction of printing into England, is the first of the secret-service presses discovered in this record. Clandestine publications have since then become a standard agency of offensive secret service; and we shall find them distributed by the Jansenists, the fanatic *Convulsionnaires*—whose poodle dog's "disguise" helped smuggle in "the papers"—Marat's *L'Ami du Peuple* will issue virtually from the sewers of Paris, and Russian revolutionary sheets pass the torch of discontent on to *La Libre Belgique* and other less celebrated underground broadsides discharged by the hidden presses of the World War.

The Jesuit leaders, Campion and Parsons, were never for a day inactive, and therefore regularly providing clues that the huntsmen on their trail were bound to utilize. They might change their place of refuge every night, but the successive searchings of these abodes within forty-eight hours of their flight warned them how narrow was their fugitive margin. "We shall not long be able to escape the hands of the heretics," Campion wrote from one hiding place to a colleague in Rome, "so many eyes are centered upon us, so many enemies beset us. I am constantly disguised, and am continually changing both my dress and my name."[3]

Parsons and Campion finally separated to divide their heroic labors in the vineyards of faith and to deny the English the likely chance of catching them both at a single stroke. Campion, sad to relate, was no false prophet, and fell into "the hands of the heretics" one day when he was in the act of celebrating Mass before a small Roman Catholic community. Having taken him at last, the English police put themselves out to humiliate him; and he was conducted to London with his hands tied behind his back, his feet bound by a rope passing under the belly of his horse, and on his hat a notice proclaiming: *Edmund Campion, the rebellious Jesuit.*

Crowds gathered to stare at him as though a Jesuit agent was something imported from Timbuktu. Being confined in the Tower and rigorously examined, Father Campion refused to reveal the names of his accomplices or give information tending to incriminate anyone; whereupon he was condemned to death for high treason and hanged and quartered in the barbaric fashion of that day. His bold collaborator, Robert Parsons, was never arrested but remained a zealous conspirator so long as he lived, making several other secret journeys into England and persevering in his contest with Walsingham and his successors of the English Protestant government.

We may not pursue this vain and bitter struggle any further. The Jesuits allowed themselves to hope that, with the death of the illegitimate heretic, Elizabeth, the English countryside would become less dangerous ground. Was not James I the son of the "martyred" Mary Queen of Scots? But James was soon happily occupied in injuring Roman Catholics, and the new Scots king of Britain even wrote and published a treatise debating religion with its leading authority, the pope. The Duc de Sully, great minister of King Henri IV of France, called the disputatious Stuart "Europe's most learned fool", which was a good deal milder than what the Jesuits called him.

Argument, intrigue and the "weapons of courtliness" had served them for a century, but after that they armed themselves with the "weapons of abuse" and joined in the Protestant fun. The Lutherans had virtually invented a vocabulary of slander to pour over their papal opponents. Prodded by such vituperative powers, the Jesuits replied in kind. It was alleged by the Lutherans that a certain Cardinal Bellarmine, whose controversial writings inflamed theologians of the opposite camp, "always kept in his stable four goats which he used for his pleasure," and which were brought to him "adorned with the most costly jewels, precious stones, silver and gold." Hearing that one, the Jesuits went to work upon Luther's private life, but reserved a few odds and ends of odium to fling at King James.

CHAPTER ELEVEN

POLICE ESPIALS, OR THE KINGS' EVIL

AS EARLY AS THE FOURTEENTH CENTURY it occurred to a king of France to establish a police system. Charles V, "the Wise," who administered justice anywhere, in the open field or under the first stately tree, sponsored the innovation of police "to increase the happiness and security"[1] of his subjects. This fatal beneficence increased everything except the happiness of generations of Frenchmen. Police serving as the personal agents, spies and truant officers of the sovereign soon became an instrument of oppression, a symbol of limitless despotism. While conveying the outward manifestation of the monarch's supreme will, the system provided the bars and fetters which checked and restrained all liberty. The French found themselves deprived by degrees of their commonest rights and privileges, the institution of police virtually forbidding them to work, live, travel from place to place, dress or nourish themselves without special permission.

While France and most other countries of the Continent were overpoliced, England had a population which stubbornly refused to surrender its own liberties. Good citizens acted together in self-defense; the duties of constable were incumbent upon all, though many avoided it by paying for a substitute. One of the earliest efforts to establish systematic police was the so-called Watch and Ward statute of Edward I in 1285, which recognized the principle that inhabitants of every district must combine for their own protection against the lawless.[2] By royal proclamation the profession of "State Informer" was created in 1434. What the informer was particularly enjoined to discover and expose was the writing, distributing or affixing of seditious bills. The reward of the informer in such cases —twenty pounds and one half of the goods of the convicted seditionist —was a substantial gain, which probably invited much trafficking in false information.

The prevalent industry of the king's espials, together with the lawful use of torture, were distinctions of the reign of Edward IV. But it was left to the first of the Tudors, Henry VII, to protect his throne and discourage the plots of rival claimants by means of a continuously improving system of secret service. This English ruler, while only the pretender, Henry of Richmond, had learned both the menace and the merits of spies. Richard of Gloucester—his implacable Plantagenet foe, Richard III—harried him from refuge to refuge with bribes to his hosts and the groping fingers of espionage. Henry felt safe in Brittany; but Richard's agents found him there and arranged to have him seized. Because of his own vigilant counter-spies, Henry was warned in time to escape.[3]

Christopher Urswick, recorder of London, was the chief Tudor agent; and it was to him that the pretender soon to be king chiefly owed his survival as a hunted fugitive. Another Tudor spy, Will Collingbourne—who was executed by Richard III—continued, as it were, to taunt his royal foe from the grave, since he had composed while imprisoned a mocking and much-quoted rhyme, "The Cat, the Rat and Lovel the Dog." Sir Roger Clifford, a Tudor adherent, was being dragged to his execution on a hurdle when a friendly friar attending him cut his bonds to set him free. The unfortunate knight tried to run for his life, but his legs were too numb from the cruel bonds to permit much of an effort and he was retaken and duly hanged.

High treason was the favorite crime of the age, and so conveniently vague in England as in all other monarchies, almost any difference of opinion affronting the king sent the bold offender to the horrors of Tyburn. Mere beheading or hanging was not deemed painful enough; unspeakable agonies were inflicted to warn the populace of the gravity of the traitor's "crime." Henry Tudor won the battle of Bosworth Field when Sir William Stanley crossed over to his side with three thousand men. And thereafter, like many another who picked up his crown on the point of a sword, Henry VII was mainly on guard against some succeeding "pretender" who might move against him with a weapon sharpened in secret. Penurious though he was, Henry maintained a multitude of active spies, intelligencers—those primitive journalists easily induced to spy for a king—and foreign informers.

Henry VIII, when he came to the throne, enjoyed more robust vices and left the espionage to his ministers of state. It was Cardinal Wolsey's agent, De Giglis, who poisoned Cardinal Christopher Bainbridge. The poisoner, though Italian, was titular bishop of Worcester, which kept the affair strictly under Church auspices. There was an incredible demand for poisons and lethal potations in the Eternal City; and it is of record that the night Pope Adrian VI died of a poison draught the Roman populace decorated his chief physician's house with garlands and added the inscription, so that even the dullest should be left in no doubt—"To the deliverer of his country!" This pope, "a man of humble birth risen to eminence solely through the great respect entertained for his profound theological learning", says G. F. Young, was obnoxious to all parties simply because he believed the Church needed to be reformed and was endeavoring to reform it. Something of the same cleric-carnival spirit that dispatched this honest old man put Savonarola to the torture daily for sixteen days, and once had him on the rack *fourteen times* in a single day. When nothing could be extorted from his anguish or proved against him, his enemies turned to the secondary resort of forgery.

It was a prolonged, bitter contest, whether the rack and the hoist or forgeries, deceits and espials produced the more wholesome results. In England spies seem to have been preferred. In Russia Tsar Ivan the Terrible might employ his primitive secret service—the *Opritchina* —to multiply the miseries of his subjects, but he invariably prescribed torture. When Ivan marched secretly to punish a city he fancied was growing rebellious he slaughtered every Russian met on the way— about sixty thousand, some have said—in order to keep his expedition secret. Compared to such efficiency the secret service of a Wolsey failed in its only objective: to win the cardinal his election as pope. The more widespread and ruthless espionage system of Thomas Cromwell was a purely dynastic affair, and Thomas himself aspired to be the dynast, but not all his whispering informers could save him from Tudor wrath and the block. After Henry VIII came young Edward and then Catholic Mary. To each troubled reign its ferment and intrigues! But now another queen ascends the English throne; and we have come to an age of spacious achievement, in Elizabethan secret service as in all the arts and in national prestige.

Chapter Twelve

WALSINGHAM SIGHTS THE ARMADA

THAT IDEAL CHIEF of English secret service, Sir Francis Walsingham, was slender and dark and looked like an Italian fencer; his mind had flashing rapier qualities of Italian subtlety, and his fine Italian hand gently stirred the broth of popes, kings and Catholic conspirators without seeming to touch it. The secret-service achievements of Walsingham were great because his adversaries were numerous, implacable and filled with murderous zeal. He fought the Jesuits, who visited England in disguise, not only to preach and spy, but also to destroy. He protected Queen Elizabeth from countless assassins, and if, as seems probable, he now and again invented these dangers, we must remember that she was obstinate and penurious and had to be frightened into defraying a third or a half of the actual cost of first-rate intelligence and counter-espionage services, the invaluable safeguard of her life and kingdom.

The queen appreciated his watchful industry and called him her "Moor", yet allowed him to beggar himself by conducting much necessary secret service of a continually threatened Protestant realm at his own expense. Walsingham was, however, so devoted to his devious craft and so loyal to Elizabeth, he seems scarcely to have noticed the handicaps which she inflicted upon him. When funds were denied him, he borrowed what England had to have, pledging his resources as a private citizen rather than as a principal secretary of the crown. Besides combatting the most artful and subterranean offensives of the Society of Jesus and other agents of Rome, he took upon himself the mighty chore of overmatching the designs of Spain. And we shall see how he helped to accomplish the discomfiture of His Most Catholic Majesty, Philip II, one of the dullest and least inspiring creatures who ever laid his blight upon the brotherhood of mankind. Walsingham it was who first sighted Philip's Invincible Armada, and Walsingham's agents who harried this argosy of hate before a single Spanish galleon spread its sails.

It was likewise his curiously unpleasant—though grimly congenial—duty to keep watch upon Mary Stuart. That hostile queen and incarcerated guest was not unnaturally bent on mischief. She wanted to escape, to see her enemies—both Scots and English—punished, and, if she was not personally intrigued by assassins' proposals, she was the one relative and rival of the Protestant queen to whom the secret crusaders of Catholic England all looked for encouragement. Walsingham called her "the Bosom Serpent", and with Puritan candor and foreboding advocated chopping off her head.

The distinguished scholar, Dr Conyers Read, who has done justice to Sir Francis Walsingham in three fascinating volumes,[1] considers that the extent and organization of his secret service has been widely exaggerated. It was so effective in operation, it was bound to seem "universal" both to those it saved and those it defeated; but the mocking hindrances of penury surrounded its performances like the net of a foreign foe, preventing most of the expenditures that England's peril dictated or the development national interests required. Apart from the counter-espionage directed at Mary Stuart and her partisans, Walsingham's best agents were English students residing in Italy. He treated them generously, granting a "pension" of one hundred pounds a year; and when these alert young men helped him gather vital intelligence concerning the Spanish Armada, they returned to Elizabeth a thousandfold the pensions she had grudged them.

It is peculiarly worthy of note that Walsingham gave England its first national secret service. He did not use his spies and shadows like Thomas Cromwell to enlarge his personal authority. Plot after plot—Babington, Ridolfi, Throgmorton—was frustrated and exposed in defense of the sovereign's life; but his greatest stroke helped to bulwark England against its alien enemies, and the end of purely dynastic secret service was at hand. In Venice Stephen Paule listened to the gossip of the Rialto and reported what was being said about Spain. But the best agent assigned to the problem of Philip's naval preparations was one of the two Antony Standens who had originally accompanied Darnley to Scotland and added nothing to his feeble fame. Wild and reckless young men, English Catholics when disposed to remember it, their unrestrained behavior is said to have cost Darnley much respect among the Scots. But now one of these two Standens was attending to a brilliant mission of anti-Spanish espionage.

He had contrived to become friendly with Giovanni Figliazzi, Tuscan ambassador to Spain. He was, too, on good terms with the government of Tuscany. Being acquainted with his exceptional opportunity, he borrowed a hundred crowns—and that "borrowed" gives us a glimpse of Walsingham's straitjacket—and dispatched a certain Fleming to Spain. Standen elected to use the name "Pompeo Pelligrini" to cover his intrigue; and now the English were being served by a wonderfully alien and mysterious combination—from Figliazzi or the Fleming to Pelligrini to Elizabeth's subtle Moor. The Fleming, it seems, was a jewel of an agent whose brother happened to be in the employ of the Marquis of Santa Cruz, grand admiral of the Spanish navy. Matters kept hidden from the obliging Figliazzi were penetrated by the Fleming spy at first hand. Communication must have been hazardous, intricate and slow; and yet it came to pass that in March 1587 Sir Francis was able to present his sovereign with an authentic copy of Santa Cruz' reports to *his* sovereign, giving the most detailed accounts of the Armada, its ships, equipment, armed forces and stores.

This was perfect espionage; it could not have been improved. At Standen's suggestion Walsingham began corresponding with Figliazzi when the envoy returned to Florence from Madrid. The Tuscan craved the good will of Queen Elizabeth; and the amiable and useful correspondence seems to have lasted. Largely guided by Walsingham, the English government made a shrewd attempt to retard the sailing of the Armada, whose exact condition of offensive readiness was so accurately divulged to London. Bankers of Genoa were induced to withhold loans to Philip II, so that in addition to the knowledge which is power, the power that was golden ducats came to be delicately manipulated by English secret service. In June 1587 Standen expressed his conviction that the Spaniards would muster up no great naval offensive against England that year, as accurate an historic observation as any spy ever made. This was evidently the report that Walsingham forwarded to Burghley with the comment: "Your Lordship by the enclosed from Florence may perceive how some stay is made of the foreign preparations." In a postscript the great chief of secret service added: "I humbly pray your Lordship that Pompey's letter may be reserved to yourself. I would be loathe the gentleman should have any harm through my default."[2]

Secret messages smuggled in to Mary Stuart in kegs of beer—the final device of her conspiring adherents—had all been intercepted. Walsingham could read at one sitting the coded correspondence of Mary's partisans. The captive queen was invited to hunt the deer in the neighboring park of Sir William Aston's estate and gratefully accepted this diversion. During her absence Walsingham's men arrested her secretaries and searched through all her papers, discovering that which was used to send Elizabeth's rival to the block.

As a young man Francis Walsingham had been allowed a five years' educational journey through Europe. He had studied in Italy and was a disciple of the Italians in his technique of counter-intrigue. He had been the English ambassador in Paris at the time of the Massacre of St Bartholomew and had protected many endangered English Protestants. His guest on that sanguinary occasion was young Philip Sidney, who became his son-in-law. From the difficult Paris embassy he had returned to England to become a responsible secretary of state. He had the right temperament and the right experience, and he was aided by powerful support from Leicester. It has been written that he stood back of Leicester, and that in back of Walsingham stood militant Puritanism. He was a leading spirit in the Puritan party, as well as the queen's fanatic defender, blunting all the weapons of her Roman Catholic foes. It is perchance significant that the secretary of state whose masterly management of English secret service has been thought to rival, or even to surpass, that talent of Sir Francis Walsingham's was the Puritan ally of Oliver Cromwell, John Thurloe.

Elizabethan Secret Service

Judging from the secret-intelligence reports and correspondence of foreign ambassadors going in and out of England during the latter half of the sixteenth century, there was no more agitating enigma than the virginity of the Virgin Queen. Elizabeth coquetted and vacillated diplomatically with Ivan the Terrible and other far less monstrous potentates who sought her hand in marriage. But neither the expectations of these distant suitors nor the reputation of the queen was impaired by the espionage of alien eyes.

Frederick Chamberlin has proved in a scholarly work[8] that envoys or agents who were genuinely neutral—such as those representing the king of Sweden and the Venetian Council of Ten—wrote as men convinced of the virtue and modesty of the English sovereign and respectful of her greatness and diplomatic skill. Even the spies of Philip of Spain, who were trained to believe the worst of any heretic, yet geographically far enough removed from Philip's blighting phobias to feed him a little truth, could invent nothing more damaging to Elizabeth than were the repeated Catholic plots which sought to take her life. The armor of her protection, like her private character, developed no serious flaw; a great queen and difficult lady well served by incomparably loyal and vigilant men.

Before Walsingham there had been a Cecil, and after him there was another Cecil, competent and persevering. The intelligence and counter-espionage service lost none of the vigor of Walsingham's day, though possibly its problems were growing more compact, since the

Jesuits' "invasion" was less aggressive, Philip of Spain was a dying man, and Mary Stuart was dead. One agent of Elizabethan secret service still commands the attention of scholars and the admiration of the discriminating, not for his political achievements or the dark conspiracies he fathomed, but because in a crowded life of twenty-nine years he found time to prove himself an inspired pioneer of English poetry and drama. And young Christopher Marlowe was not the only Cambridge student who accepted employment as a government spy.

Marlowe, it is believed, was most active as a secret agent between February and July, 1587, as he was absent from college at that time. He was accused of going abroad to Rheims, which came desperately close to a charge of having turned—or of intending to turn—Roman Catholic. In France the Duc de Guise, leader of orthodox Catholicism, ally of Philip II, bitter foe of England and striving to the last to rescue his niece, Mary Queen of Scots, made it a point to offer hospitality to English students and seminarists, intending if possible to use them in his plots against Elizabeth. Those plots broke down for a variety of reasons; and one was the number of students entertained by Guise or his lieutenants who had been sent to France by English spy-masters. If Marlowe went to Rheims with the permission of the authorities he can only have gone to spy upon the Catholic conspirators by professing to join them.

The emigration of students from Cambridge to Rheims had grown very brisk after 1580 and was at its height in 1587. Father Parsons, the celebrated Jesuit campaigner, escaping to Rouen after Father Campion's arrest, had submitted an account of his work to the Jesuit general headquarters in Rome on September 26, 1581. Included in Parsons' report we find—"at Cambridge I have at length insinuated a certain priest into the very university under the guise of a scholar or a gentleman commoner and have procured him help from a place not far from the town. Within a few months he has sent over to Rheims seven very fit youths."[4] Marlowe, if he followed the procedure of the other English agents sent to France, must have let it become known that he had a fondness for the Roman Catholic ritual. Thus commended to the attention of a Jesuit agent in Cambridge, he was presently smuggled over to Rheims as a promising sympathizer and potential convert, after which introduction his secret-service mission became relatively easy. And Marlowe, too—according to Tom Nashe —was a "Machiavellian" and allowed himself the right to "cloake bad accions with Commonwealthe pretences", a prevailing trait of all the "Machiavellians."[5]

James Welsh of Magdalene College, Cambridge, on leaving Cambridge was unable to find employment as a schoolmaster—and so became a spy upon the Catholics for Bishop Aylmer of London. The Scotch poet, William Fowler, was one of Walsingham's agents in Scotland; while Anthony Munday, player and playwright, went to Rome in 1578–79 to spy upon the English seminary there, as his *English Romayne Life* admits. Later he was an associate of that jolly chap, the rackmaster, Topcliffe, and helped to interrogate recusants; and success in the torture chamber seems to have won him employment with Archbishop Whitgift. Another literary man who found it possible to earn a living in secret service—which belles-lettres did not provide—was Marlowe's friend, Matthew Roydon, who had some mysterious link to the interests of James VI while that peculiar Scots monarch was awaiting the end of Elizabeth's reign. Even Ben Jonson, his biographers have thought, was a secret agent of the English government. Marlowe had talented rivals in espionage.

The circumstances of Marlowe's death were exceedingly suspicious. Evidence introduced has seemed to be fraudulent, and Frizer was granted a free pardon for killing the poet within a month of his death. Robert Poley, who was present at the time of Marlowe's death, was a plausible, efficient spy—"well educated, gentlemanly in demeanor"— once a member of the Sidney household and steward to Lady Sidney, Walsingham's daughter, after Sir Philip's death, from which position he came into the service of Walsingham himself. What was Poley doing in that upstairs room of the Deptford tavern when Christopher Marlowe was stabbed? Many scholars, profoundly uninterested in Elizabethan secret service, have tried to find the answer to that question. In an age that saw political espionage lead almost invariably to charges of high treason, strange consequences descended upon espionage agents. Poley was a fellow continually emerging from the shadows. He was in the pay of the vice-chamberlain, Sir Thomas Heneage, and known as "Pistol's Man"—he was linked with Walsingham's celebrated decipherer, Thomas Phelippes, who, after Walsingham's death, branched out with a kind of commercial spying agency and capitalized his experiences in the service of the government.

Dr William Parry, M.P., was a dangerous agent of the time—a fortune hunter and convicted criminal—known to Burghley and others as the double-dealer par excellence. He boasted that his machinations had "shaken the seminary at Rheims to its foundations." Finally Burghley saw his chance and got rid of him. Parry, acting as a *provocateur,* broached a plot for the assassination of Elizabeth to a well-known Roman Catholic, Edmund Neville. Neville, not to be taken in so antique a trap, spoke at once to Burghley, who affected to believe in the "plot" and had Parry executed. And we know of the tragedy that overtook Elizabeth's own physician, Doctor Lopez—the condemned spy who, some have thought, gave Shakespeare his inspiration for the character of *Shylock*. Lopez certainly never engaged in any plot against the queen who had honored him, a foreigner and a Jew, but prejudice was strong, and the faintest whisper of high treason could be fatal. The singular involvement and catastrophe of poor Lopez is retold so brilliantly by Lytton Strachey in his *Elizabeth and Essex* that it is needless and presumptuous to attempt to retell it here.

CHAPTER THIRTEEN

THE SCAVENGER SPIES OF MOGUL INDIA

IN THE ORIENT, even to this day, the "divine right" of a monarch is secondary to the popular—or coolie—belief in the living ruler's actual divinity. Of all divine gifts omniscience is generally preferred as the most useful politically; and often when its manifestation has seemed a bit indistinct, a first-rate spy system has proved a godlike assistant to the straining mortal on the throne.

By means of remarkably devised operations of secret service the Mogul emperors of India regulated a vast and populous realm having the utmost social and religious complexity. The lasting fame of Akbar, Jahangir, Shah Jahan and Aurangzeb rests not upon conquest or military exploits so much as upon the smoothly geared mechanism of their empire's government, "the solidarity of its internal affairs."[1] Even in the Occident we remember Akbar as the "Great Mogul" because of the enlightened self-interest of the sixteenth-century reign of Baber's grandson; and now we know that some of that enlightenment entered his palace every evening the year round in the summarized reports of a multitude of spies.

Akbar ascended the throne in 1556 and at once began developing his secret-intelligence and espionage service. With it he effectually governed his realm, in that he ruled as an absolute monarch according to his own strict conception of right and justice after having informed himself thoroughly by giving personal attention to the reports of his numerous spies. With no pressing anxiety about his neighbors or interest in espionage beyond his own frontiers, this sagacious master of Hindustan employed more than four thousand agents[2] for the sole purpose of bringing him the truth that his throne might rest upon it. Since more than one spy was bound to report upon the same local matter, the Great Mogul was as hard to deceive as a shrewd city editor.

Akbar's intimate friend and counselor, Abul Fazl, was the soldier, statesman and eminent organizer who, after him, had most to do with the perfection of the intelligence service as well as all other outstanding developments of unified rule in India. It was either Abul Fazl or his brother, Faizi, the celebrated scholar in Hindu literature,[3] who observed that spies "check the zeal" of officials. Evidently these wise men of the East long ago grasped a fact that is still gratuitously ignored in Germany and other autocratic areas—that a centralized tyranny first becomes abominable through the misuse of power by its numerous petty tyrants.

Reports upon travelers seem to have been especially prized in the secret-service design of the Mogul monarch. This may have denoted an experiment in counter-espionage; but there is little to indicate that the emperor feared or ever thought of enemy spies from foreign lands. There seems instead to have persisted a novel concept of the sovereign as a kind of royal innkeeper whose infallible knowledge of all arrivals and departures guarded the repute and welfare of the whole community.

Sir John Hawkins vs The Mocarrub Khan

Traveling in the Orient as envoy of Elizabeth of England, that sea rover extraordinary, Sir John Hawkins, landed in India at Surat and was most uncordially received by a local lordling, the Mocarrub Khan. Sir John, as Spaniards had discovered, was one not easily diverted from his purpose, and he stoutly pursued his journey to Agra, whither spies had preceded him with news. The English admiral, having experienced one bout of bad manners, approached the city unobtrusively, expecting a second repulse. But now he was welcomed with all due honor as a guest and ambassador. Being received in private audience, Hawkins was tactfully reserved on the score of his grievances; and ere he could mention them, Akbar confided to him all of which the visitor had right to complain, expressed august regret and assured him discipline already had been prescribed in Surat.

An intelligence system of that high efficiency was of first importance in overawing a people with their ruler's all-seeing eye and all-knowing mind. Criminals were discouraged, while rebels, malcontents and political plotters had to subside or suffer in a country policed from house to house by secret agents each and every day. This spying was performed in India by the companies of scavengers, who twice daily, according to the law, were required to enter dwellings and clear away the refuse.[4] While thus busily collecting whatever had been discarded, they gathered up also the cerebral rubbish of a garrulous population.

Here in an historic example we find the old Roman saying mens sana in corpore sano[5] applied by a blend of sanitary and secret service to the body politic. Archives of the Mogul intelligence system, had any been preserved to this day, might have even more to tell the modern psychologist than the Oriental scholar. The multitudinous banalities of people who gossiped with sweepers and cleaners and knight errants of the garbage cart would help perhaps to unveil some mystery of the human mind that is still a goal of scientific research. And what influence upon the lives of his subjects was exerted by the emperor's method of inquiry? Were loquacious people allowed to lapse into habitual shiftlessness and waste? Or were neatness and frugal housekeeping disapproved in the reticent as symptoms of opposition to the status quo?

The scavenger-spies were the news gatherers and gossip paragraphers of their age, and they seem to have devoted themselves in the main to the accumulation of unsavory trifles. As history discloses, military espionage was nearly always ineffectual or neglected and virtually unknown as one of the most ancient arts of war practiced by the native princes of India. The Moguls, in spite of their descent traced through Baber to the indomitable Genghis Khan, were no more gifted in this than the princes they had superseded; and their spy service, so perfect as an instrument of political police, lost all its range and utility when brought to bear upon anything more warlike than a bazaar riot.[6] Aurangzeb, who was Akbar's great-grandson, is said to have failed so dismally in his campaign in the Dekkan because of erroneous reports submitted by military spies.

Yet this same Aurangzeb was called "saintly" because of the diligent espionage of his scavengers and secret police. On one occasion a wall had collapsed, and while nothing whatever was being done about it in the fashion of the Orient, word came to the emperor of the accident. Three fakirs had last been seen conversing near the wall; now presumably their shattered bodies lay beneath its debris. Whereupon Aurangzeb, when he had come to the place in his progress through the city, gave orders that the broken wall be cleared away and the bodies underneath be taken up and given fitting burial. And his people were amazed that he should know of the three fatalities when they did not, and praised him for his great wisdom and respect for the dead.

The son of this Mogul sovereign, young Shah Alam, was somewhat less saintly but just as well served by a personal corps of spies. The emperor's spies kept watch upon this heir, and the agents of the heir protected him from falling into disfavor by watching the emperor and his agents. One evening the spies of Aurangzeb reported that Shah Alam in his own palace was disporting himself gaily and not alone. Aurangzeb's goodness was not a professional attitude, and he intensely disapproved of the licentious inclinations of Shah Alam. Acting at once upon the information, he prepared to call on his wayward son to reproach him for his sins. But here the son's spies intervened.

An emperor's visit, however urgent, must maintain the imperial dignity—and dignity is slow. Aurangzeb was just dropping in to surprise the revelers; but the prince's spies gave him ample warning of his father's approach. The spies helped servants transplant the feast and unceremoniously whisked off with the girls. Shah Alam meanwhile had posed himself with studious decorum; so that there were no young ladies present when Aurangzeb surged in on his first born. In fact, the well-advised young prince was discovered with a book, which would be the Koran.

Chapter Fourteen

FATHER JOSEPH AND THE CARDINAL'S SPIES

THERE WERE some French nobles and churchmen disinclined to take part in rebellions but very few who denied themselves the bracing recreation of political conspiracy. To destroy feudalism had been the joyous lifework of Louis XI; but the feudal spirit of aristocratic insurrection refused to perish. And so all the power and authority which would one day be consolidated in the splendors of Louis XIV had to be picked up a piece at a time, in strange ways and by not always honorable means, and fitted together like a huge national puzzle by men whose resourcefulness and patience were fortunately inexhaustible.

Armand Jean Duplessis, Cardinal Duc de Richelieu, was the most brilliant and successful of these builders of Bourbon majesty. It was truly said of him that he did too much good for men to speak evil of him, and too much evil for men to speak well of him. And it might be proved with little partisanship that most of the evil that he did was done with excellent accuracy of aim to those subjects of his king who continually planted themselves in the way of every good which he sought to accomplish. Having a pest of archplotters to exterminate, formidable dissensions within the kingdom, and powerful enemies beyond its borders, Richelieu—even though he never had heard of secret service—would have been shrewd and unscrupulous enough to invent it. In pursuing the nationalist program of Louis XI, it is not too much to say that the cardinal gave France its first unity as a kingdom with his espionage organization. When there were not yet police officers, judges, soldiers, postal servants, or even tax gatherers to obey the king in all quarters of his turbulent realm, there was a network of spies to send prompt and accurate intelligence to Paris. Being kept that well informed did much to promote Richelieu's versatile renown. Those who opposed him, who were blind to his patriotic greatness and administrative genius, were desperately afraid of his omniscience.

Two extraordinary persons stand in these annals to the left and right of the red-robed statesman. Richelieu's indispensable right hand was his director of secret service, the mild and subtle *l'éminence grise,* or gray cardinal, Father Joseph du Tremblay, a devoted, masterly technician whose habit of scoring at the expense of influential adversaries was to cost him his promised reward of a cardinal's hat. At Richelieu's left, when not otherwise hidden, disguised or detained, we find the most tormenting, romantic conspirator in a very paradise of intrigue, Marie de Rohan, Duchess of Luynes and of Chevreuse. Many have called her the "queen of cabals";[1] and Richelieu himself complained on his deathbed that Marie's addiction to politics had measurably shortened his days.

If the cardinal who could rule France but never completely curb Marie de Rohan speaks as our best proof of her infinite capacity to inflict pain and disturb the peace, we have another eminent witness and victim, the Emperor Ferdinand, whose denunciation of Father Joseph du Tremblay established for all time the clandestine merits of that talented Capuchin. Cried the monarch of the Holy Roman Empire: "a worthless friar has disarmed me with his rosary, and put six electoral hats into his narrow cowl." The emperor, though bitter, was recording an historic understatement. Father Joseph as the instrument of Richelieu had accomplished a good deal more. Cardinal Richelieu never permitted his fidelity to the Church to retard his genius for being a Frenchman. He had been intriguing to save the sorely intimidated princes of Protestant Germany and had lately concluded a secret treaty with the Lion of the North. Gustavus Adolphus, with a disciplined army of Swedes, Scots and other seasoned campaigners, had invaded Germany, landing on the island of Usedom near the mouth of the Oder. But the ravaging triumphs of the Imperial forces had so terrified the Protestant states that, eagerly as they had invited the Swedish king to hazard his life, throne and military reputation, none among his expected German allies dared venture to welcome the new champion. Richelieu and Father Joseph saw again the earthly advantages of not being Protestants and proceeded to aid Gustavus with an Olympian stroke. An air raid, a submarine attack, a Gettysburg and Marne were rolled together, the "worthless" Capuchin's contribution; for Father Joseph helped to sweep from the field the ablest Imperial general and all but scattered fragments of his undefeated army.

The general was Wallenstein and the army numbered 100,000 men, "owing no allegiance to any one but their commander . . . raised by personal contract as was the custom of the time, and so not bound by any ties of patriotism." The German Catholic princes, inflated with triumphs to which they had personally given little more than grudging support, were afraid of Wallenstein's arrogance and enormous wealth and power. They objected to his troops' exactions and urged that he be dismissed from his command. A soldier of boundless ambition, strange, somber and reserved, he had earned the enmity of Maximilian of Bavaria, the second prince of the empire, who was encouraged by the other electors and by Madrid. Richelieu as the secret ally of Gustavus was resolved to get rid of the most formidable obstacle to be encountered by the Swedes, "another little enemy" whom Ferdinand and his courtiers deemed weak and comic. Wallenstein alone perceived how the Swedish king menaced the Catholic cause; but the Catholic princes were jealous of Wallenstein, and Richelieu had sent Father Joseph to advise the emperor and attend to any mischief that might present itself. "It would be well to oblige the Electors in this trifling matter," said the agent of France. "It will help to secure the Roman crown for the King of Hungary, and when the storm shall have passed away, Wallenstein will be ready enough to resume his former station."

Ferdinand was not alone in wondering what a general with thousands of soldiers under arms would do when informed of his dismissal. Father Joseph, perhaps, counted upon creating an Imperial diversion of civil war. But Ferdinand accepted his counsel with a show of more reluctance than he probably felt; and Wallenstein received the envoys and their disagreeable news with astonishing amiability. Dignified and serene, he retired to his vast feudal estates, where sixty pages attended him and twelve patrols continuously circled around his palace grounds "to keep every noise at a distance." With his retirement the major part of his army vanished from the field, many of his veterans enlisting under the Protestant banner of Gustavus Adolphus. And what of Father Joseph? Did he quietly return to Richelieu and describe his coup? In time, but only when it was complete; for the Capuchin first busied himself making sure that Ferdinand suffered another reverse in the failure of the king of Hungary's election.

As a stroke of diplomatic secret service the affront to and removal of Wallenstein, the disappearance of his army, and the recruiting of some of his best troops to aid the Swedish king rank among the crown jewels of subtle intrigue. A noted military critic and historian has written: "It is difficult to overestimate the influence this tremendous weakening of the Imperial army exercised on the fortunes of the war, and of Europe, allowing the Swedish King to consolidate his position in Germany and widen his base for the far-reaching operations of the next year."[2] The great cardinal, convinced that the interests of France required a Protestant counterpoise in

Germany, did more than induce Gustavus to join in the terrible struggle that became the Thirty Years' War. He sent help in the form of a secret expedition that entrenched itself at the side of the Imperial throne and won what amounted to a long and arduous campaign—by getting rid of Wallenstein and a major part of his army.

Many of the cardinal's best agents are said to have been Englishmen. He found them intrepid, unprejudiced and generally reliable; and like Walsingham he had them living unobtrusively in most of the capitals and key cities of the Continent. Their names are unknown, and so are the rewards Richelieu promised them. Father Joseph is known to have been assured that he would be created a cardinal; but the strong opposition of Spain kept Pope Urban VIII from pronouncing the promotion. Years later Mazarin saw fit to reward his most useful spy, Ondedei, by nominating him to the bishopric of Fréjus; and there was a considerable uproar about appointing so notorious a schemer to high ecclesiastical office. Only with many private persuasions was Mazarin able to convince the pope that the nomination ought to be confirmed.

Mazarin was never the leader and statesman that Richelieu had proved to be; and he had in Ondedei and his hirelings no Father Joseph or espionage system as a whole that was the equal of Richelieu's. Where the latter cardinal broke up the Cinq-Mars conspiracy, terrified Gaston of Orleans, the king's brother, and preserved the integrity of France, Mazarin was best served by spies in avoiding Beaufort and other elegant assassins. By adroitly kidnapping the English agent Montague, Richelieu's secret service vanquished Buckingham and a great coalition. Marie de Rohan had encouraged Buckingham's attentions to the queen; and as a result the dazzling George Villiers, favorite of King Charles I, had been forbidden to return to France. With the arrogance of his type Buckingham now proposed returning with a powerful army. Three squadrons, each bearing 10,000 men, were to strike at La Rochelle, at Guienne and Normandy; on being disembarked these contingents were respectively to hold the mouths of the Garonne, the Loire and the Seine. Lorraine was to attack in the north; Savoy in the south; and Marie was to enlist her kinsman, Henri Duc de Rohan, leader of the Huguenots. But a few of the cardinal's agents captured Montague and conducted him to the Bastille. Matched against such a well-remembered triumph, Mazarin's spies could only stumble through the wars of the Fronde.

Montague's papers were all taken from him, and Richelieu and Father Joseph poured over them together. This was in 1628, and half of Europe seemed to be fusing in one annihilating attack upon the masterful French cardinal. Venice was in, and the Dutch were flirting with England, Lorraine, Savoy and the Huguenots. Even the emperor was expected to lend German aid. The queen and the Comte de Soissons were in the plot at court. But Montague's papers made a world of difference. The queen became mortally afraid, she afterward confessed; while Marie de Rohan, "queen of cabals", fled to Spain—assisted by every man she met; she won them all—and finally passed the frontier in an odd masculine disguise, wearing a blond wig, but with dark gypsy stain upon her skin. She was far more talented than that in plotting and seducing, yet her intrigues and seductions gave her a good deal of practice in running away.

The queen was not harmed, but her personal spy, La Porte, went into the Bastille, where he managed to keep open his lines of communication by having secret messages passed down to him through the floors and ceilings of two tiers of cells. Mazarin confronted chiefly a reckless internal opposition; but it was the superlative French and foreign opposition of his swollen torrent of enemies that made Richelieu's secret service invincible. The time came when all the players were growing old; and even Marie de Rohan could be allied to Father Joseph. Richelieu wanted this intriguing sorceress where he could watch her, and so he personally arranged for her pardon, her readmission to France and to the society of the queen whose dearest friend she formerly had been. Richelieu himself is reputed to have fallen under Marie's spell in 1631 when the two famous adversaries became allied against the queen mother, Marie de' Medici.

During the minority of Louis XIV the Italian cardinal-successor of Richelieu also dealt in a form of secret service involving, but not offending, a queen mother. Fair Anne of Austria, with Buckingham only a memory, was the royal dowager in Mazarin's life. They corresponded like the clandestine lovers many of their contemporaries supposed them to be; and all their numberless tender messages, mingling affairs of state with the most sublime compliments, were inscribed in code—a fascinating contrivance which the queen rather than the cardinal is believed to have originated.

CHAPTER FIFTEEN

ESPIONAGE AND THE HONORS OF WAR

THE MILITARY SECRET AGENT has suffered like the professional soldier as war-making down through vigorous and combative centuries has been allowed to degenerate from a pleasing and profitable gentlemen's sport to a repellent national enterprise, with even its few gains and revenues subject to public accounting. Once upon a time there were the gallant standards of chivalry, coupled with the ransoming of prisoners who could afford to pay, the sacking of cities, and frequent furloughs of looting and rapine. Spies of old were not expected to take part in the knightly commerce of ransoming captives; they were never encouraged to drop everything, as the men-at-arms would do, for the martial diversions of rapine.[1] But neither were they much exposed to the horrors of warfare, mutilation, famine, filth, disease and, lately, gas poisoning—now made available to all.

Among Asiatics, as we have seen, the crafty arts of military secret service appear always to have been more commonly accepted and congenial; while the great captains of Asia were intelligently disposed to act upon the findings of their own agents. In Western Europe, however, the age of chivalry brought espionage into disrepute, honorable commanders scorning to spy upon an adversary for the merely crude purpose of discovering what weight and perils of opposition beset them. The celebrated Chevalier de Bayard ordered prisoners of war executed for trying to score on a foul, inasmuch as they were musketeers and so caught experimenting with that imported abomination, gunpowder. And spies were thus similarly condemned, for the first time, it would seem, because they were spies, rather than because they were suspected enemies capable of bearing arms.

In the sixteenth century this attitude, at least toward military spies, seems to have moderated. In France, for example, all such spies were under the immediate orders of the high constable and "actually enjoyed a certain degree of esteem."[2] This is shown in a famous anecdote of the Duc d'Epernon, a persistent campaigner, if not one of the great commanders of his time. A man had been brought before him accused of behaving suspiciously. The duke ordered him searched and thus came to the conclusion that the fellow was a spy. "Devil take me if I did not suppose that you were only a thief," said D'Epernon. "I should have had you whipped till you went spinning like a top. . . . But I see now that you are really an honest spy. Here are two gold pieces for you. Be off—and tell those that sent you that, when we meet them, we shall see that their work is cut out for them."

It was a commonplace in the wars of that brutally religious era to encourage swift and even cowardly capitulations by hanging the bravest defenders of towns and fortresses that had failed yet failed gallantly to withstand a siege. This same D'Epernon, after reducing Antibes with its Savoyard garrison, hanged twenty-two of the defenders and sent the rest to the galleys. The "little city of Montauroux" was taken and saw "fourteen of its captains hanged, more than fifty soldiers strangled, and five hundred sent to the galleys." If victorious commanders dared display such unchivalrous rancor, the hazards of the spy were generally an improvement upon the ordinary fortunes of war.

A Dutch Carpenter Who Dropped His Dispatches

In a conflict even more insanely savage than the religious wars of France and Germany, the memorable siege of Alkmaar in 1573 was raised by means of a stratagem that adds the name of Peter van der Mey to these annals of secret service. Peter, a carpenter and patriot, contributed both ingeniously and heroically to the defense of Dutch liberties. "If I take Alkmaar, I am resolved not to leave a single creature alive; the knife shall be put to every throat." Thus wrote the Spanish general, Alva, to Philip II, who eagerly agreed that rope or knife was the ideal holy ornament for his Protestant subjects' throats. And yet, "with the dismantled and desolate Haarlem before their eyes, a prophetic phantom, perhaps, of their own imminent fate . . . the handful of people shut up within Alkmaar" prepared to meet the assault of Alva's Spanish veterans. "Their main hope lay in the friendly sea. The vast sluices called the Zyp . . . were but a few miles distant. By opening these gates, and by piercing a few dykes, the ocean might be made to fight for them. To obtain this result . . . consent of the inhabitants was requisite, as the destruction of all the standing crops would be inevitable." Alkmaar, however, "was so closely invested, that it was a matter of life and death to venture forth, and it was difficult, therefore, to find an envoy for this hazardous mission."[3]

Motley describes how Peter van der Mey volunteered to undertake the adventure and how bravely and skillfully he discharged his duties as an impromptu secret agent. As a result, Governor Sonoy "opened many of the dykes", so that the land in the vicinity of the Spaniards' camp "was becoming plashy."

The carpenter-envoy returned with dispatches containing an eloquent promise from William the Silent to flood the whole countryside and drown the Spanish army. Dutch crops and cattle would have gone down with the enemy; but Alva was disinclined to put the burghers to that economic test. And so "the stout men of Alkmaar, cheering and jeering, watched the Spaniards breaking camp." Peter van der Mey stood among them. In making his way back into the city he had contrived to lose his precious dispatches, so that they were read by Alva rather than by Alkmaar. The plashy land, the inundation threatened by the Prince of Orange, the ruse of the lost dispatches were the decisive results of his secret-service expedition.

This sort of military "secret service", the intermittent and impromptu employment of spies and clandestine emissaries, continued throughout the Thirty Years' War, the English Civil War, and all ensuing conflicts down to the eighteenth century. The political espionage of a Sir Francis Walsingham, or a Cardinal Richelieu or a Mazarin, was strikingly advanced and "modern", almost as effective as it is ever likely to be, and a century, therefore, ahead of its military counter-part. In the Thirty Years' War the genius of Gustavus Adolphus produced a primitive smoke screen, which waited until the World War for its scientific and tactical development. At the famous crossing of the river Lech, by setting fire to damp straw the Swedish king created a smoke cloud that concealed the passage of his infantry. But in spite of this—his defeat of the Imperialists under Count von Tilly at the Lech being considered Gustavus' tactical masterpiece—and other superlative military innovations, he seems to have neither neglected nor organized nor improved upon the espionage methods of his age. As a young king, traveling incognito as Captain Gars—*Gustavus Adolphus Rex Sueciae*—he had visited Germany and become familiar with its people and with the country over which he would fight his most illustrious campaigns; but these journeys can hardly be set down as a royal apprenticeship in the Mithridatic manner or a calculated program of espionage and reconnaissance after the fashion of Alfred the Great.

There was an equally surprising poverty of secret-service invention in the career of Gustavus' ablest competitor, Albrecht Wenzel Eusebius von Waldstein, whose name is best known to us as Wallenstein. This Protestant Czech, "the princes' scourge and soldiers' idol," lent his special brand of military genius to the Imperialist camp in the Thirty Years' War. He was created Duke of Friedland, Sagan and Mecklenburg, with the right of striking coin and granting patents of nobility. And it appears that he initiated military camouflage; but though his talents gained him, a man of humble origin, unparalleled wealth and power, he was the ultimate victim of intriguers and never a master of the implements of political conspiracy.

When he was inspired to invent camouflage, Wallenstein had fortified a bridgehead on the Elbe and was there attacked by Count Mansfeld, "one of the most remarkable of all soldiers of fortune." Having been beaten off, Mansfeld prepared to renew his attack; and Wallenstein, learning of this—from a spy, perhaps—ordered "the bridge hung over with sails, under the concealment of which he passed his whole army over unobserved, and fell upon Mansfeld, who was routed with a loss of some nine thousand men."[4] Now in his aspiring youth Wallenstein had set out to win a rich widow many years his senior and had so successfully masked the mercenary character of his honorable intentions that the deeply smitten mature heiress gave him a love potion. Inexpertly concocted, it made him dangerously ill and was near to causing his death. Such an artful fortune hunter was entitled to invent camouflage.

If Wallenstein appears to have neglected most of the advantages which others derived from the political espionage and military intelligence systems of his day, the explanation is perhaps to be found in this great commander's curious addiction to astrological readings of fate. Why employ spies and traitors when one is equipped to consult the stars? Wallenstein had a complete and cosmic spy service in Seni, his personal astrologer, who seems to have been brutally candid when reporting upon the eternal verities of the heavens. Seni is reputed to have foretold the very hour when Captain Devereux would drive home his assassin's halberd and Wallenstein, with the resignation of the true believer, without even drawing his sword, receive the foul blow of an historic ingratitude.

The "Conspiracy" of 20,000,000 Florins

Why was the most brilliant of Imperialist generals assassinated? The Emperor Ferdinand II envied him his success and power and was immeasurably indebted to him for military services; but also Ferdinand owed Wallenstein a more tangible debt that had mounted to astronomical figures—20,000,000 florins. The various negotiations and intrigues which culminated in the killing of Wallenstein are too numerous and intricate to follow here, but the principal maneuvers against him by his enemies of the Imperial court may be quickly scrutinized. Wallenstein had suffered at Lützen (1632) a shattering reverse, losing his artillery and baggage. And yet this defeat caused widespread Imperialist rejoicing. The *Te Deum* was sung in all Roman Catholic countries, for the price of the Protestant victory had been the death of Gustavus Adolphus. Wallenstein took the field in the spring of 1633 with a splendidly equipped force of 40,000 men and, "with his great rival removed," was expected to overwhelm the opposition. "Instead . . . another transformation of this extraordinary man" saw him enter upon "his last and grandest rôle—that of fathering German unity. . . . Negotiations with the Saxons were his first step, but beyond this his intentions remain one of the enigmas of history."[5]

They were not, however, accounted an enigma by Imperialist spies and agents of the Church; every rumor and innuendo was the subject of an urgent report, and a creeping barrage of these warnings and denunciations cut off the Emperor Ferdinand from whatever small sustenance of truth he required. It was alleged that Wallenstein had proposed to join with the Saxons in forcing peace upon the emperor. The Jesuits were then to be expelled from the empire, Protestants were to be guaranteed religious liberty and their confiscated property restored. Now it is known that the Saxon general, Arnheim, approached Oxenstierna, the great chancellor of Sweden, with an offer which he declared came from Wallenstein. But no record was ever produced which proved he had Wallenstein's consent to the negotiation; whereas it was Richelieu's opinion of Arnheim that "the court of Rome had lost in him the most perfect Jesuit that ever lived." At this very time, moreover, Wallenstein was urging as a "preliminary to peace" that the Swedes must be driven out of Germany; while agents of Richelieu were promising Wallenstein such tantalizing bribes as the crown of Bohemia and a million livres a year if he would join France against the emperor.

Wallenstein, apart from his private ambitions, had every provocation of base ingratitude, political hindrance and ecclesiastical meddling to urge him to change sides, yet there has never been disclosed convincing proofs either of his treacherous intriguing or intent. An avowed desire for peace and religious toleration multiplied his detractors at court, even as his efforts to improve discipline and curb pillaging caused the disaffection of many of the soldiers of fortune who were his subordinate officers. After accomplishing his "military masterpiece", the victory of Steinau, which forced the surrender of Count Thurn and a Swedish army, Wallenstein granted magnanimous terms to his Protestant opponents, an act which his enemies craftily exaggerated. He was following up his success at Steinau, was actually "on the verge of cutting off the Swedes from the Baltic", when that mystic blend of timidity and intrigue which reigned over all at Vienna devised a new checkmate, and he was recalled to protect Bavaria. Not long afterward Ferdinand, while keeping up his cordial correspondence, resolved once again to rid himself of the most formidable soldier in Europe.

The emperor was—in part, at least—misguided by a greedy cabal of Italians, Spaniards and Bavarians. Wallenstein had never hesitated to show his contempt for these officers, the Italians being especially obnoxious to him. He had characterized them as no better than brigands, with a minimum of courage and military capacity. And now they eagerly joined with the rest in working Ferdinand's fears up to such a melodramatic pitch that in January, 1634, he gave General Piccolomini and General Gallas a "secret commission . . . depriving Wallenstein of command" and proclaiming him an outlaw "to be taken 'dead or alive!'"

There was danger in handling this unprecedented warrant. Wallenstein was famous and victorious and still "at the head of a great and devoted army." But Piccolomini and Gallas were spurred to the hazard by a promise of sharing in the division of his immensely valuable estates. The Emperor Ferdinand's "share" would, of course, be the timely cancellation of a mere indebtedness of 20,000,000 florins. Rumors of the contemptible plot seem to have reached Wallenstein, who was too rich and influential not to have a few friends or agents lurking in Vienna; and thereupon calling all his officers together and "signing with them a joint declaration of their *'entire devotion to the Emperor'*", he appointed two aides to ride to Vienna with his own complete submission. It informed Ferdinand that he was willing to resign his command and that he would appear anywhere at any time to answer whatever charges had been brought against him. But this disarming offer never reached the emperor. Piccolomini's patrols intercepted both dispatch bearers; and when Wallenstein was presently informed that the proclamation of outlawry had been posted in Prague, he recognized his grave danger and the blasting triumph of his foes.

Only one refuge presented itself. He had received many flattering invitations from Cardinal Richelieu; and now in his extremity he turned to the very men who had opposed him as the leading Imperialist general. But the first appeal for aid that he sent the Duke of Weimar was mistaken for a ruse—which circumstance, as his defenders have ably suggested, rather discredits Vienna's claim that there existed a well-advanced "Wallenstein conspiracy" to betray the Catholic cause and go over to the allies. Taking only a small escort Wallenstein now journeyed to the frontier fortress of Eger, whence he intended to proceed to the meeting point Weimar's emissary would propose. Eger was held by two Scottish soldiers of fortune, Colonel Gordon and Major Leslie; and when Wallenstein revealed the emperor's latest triumph of ingratitude, both officers agreed to accompany him.

Wallenstein's escort, however, was commanded by a Colonel Walter Butler—a brave name to be further besmirched by a more infamous partisan of the border country in the American War of Independence —and this intriguing Irishman, having volunteered to protect his commander, had meanwhile sent his chaplain to General Piccolomini to acquaint him with Wallenstein's line of flight. Butler, now both a spy and a Judas, showed Gordon and Leslie the writtten orders from Piccolomini which the chaplain-agent had contrived to transmit; whereupon the three pledged themselves to oblige the Italian and the emperor. Into this appendix to the court conspiracy against Wallenstein, Butler brought seven other bold warriors, "five Irishmen and two Spaniards." Adherents of the man to be murdered were invited next evening to join Gordon at supper in the citadel. There they were locked in, with guards at every door, but nothing of their contingent plight was revealed to them until the dessert had been served and the lackeys dismissed. Then, at a given signal, eighteen dragoons sprang from rooms adjoining the dining hall and killed the unarmed guests.

There was a council held immediately, at which Gordon is said to have made a plea for clemency. Butler overruled him. Then Butler, with Captain Devereux and six Irish dragoons, invaded Wallenstein's quarters. Butler waited below. Seni, the astrologer, had just been dismissed for the night after warning his chief and ardent disciple that the planets "foretold impending danger." Devereux, as a messenger from Mars, broke into the bedroom; and Wallenstein, aroused by the sudden commotion and turning from the window, confronted him. Offering no resistance, no plea or word of prayer, the great Czech opened his arms to the blow, and Devereux's halberd cut him down.

Ferdinand and his avaricious henchmen, while gorging themselves upon the spoils, paused at intervals to invent and elaborate their account of Wallenstein's dire "plot" against church and state. He had negotiated with Gustavus, he had "not only employed Protestants in his army, but allowed them free exercise of their religion and estates." His generous attitude toward foes and "heretics", his whole untimely spirit of toleration, was true; but all the other charges were the basest fabrication[6]—and yet accepted even by German historians until Dr Förster gained access to the archives of Vienna only a little over a century ago. When Frederick the Great had asked Joseph II how "it really was with that story of Wallenstein", the Austrian answered evasively that he "could not possibly doubt the integrity" of his ancestor. For two hundred years the House of Habsburg thus rigidly maintained both the imperial fiction and *esprit de corps*.

Famous Champions of Military Espionage

Since Wallenstein did not even attempt to heed the warnings of Seni, whom he employed, consulted and trusted as a faithful aide, it is needless to argue that effective espionage, or army secret service, would have saved him from the imperceptibly clandestine plots of his enemies. The spying and counter-spying organization of another military master of the seventeenth century, Oliver Cromwell, was brilliantly effective in forefending assassination; so also were the secret services of Richelieu and his successor, Cardinal Mazarin. These systems, like that of the cardinals' successor, Louvois, the able war minister of Louis XIV, are elsewhere described. And so, in charting the almost glacial progress of military secret service in competition with its more enterprising political and diplomatic rivals, we come at last to four stars of the martial firmament who, each in his own way and in varying degrees, made some contribution to the professional employment of spies in time of war.

The careers of Marlborough and Prince Eugene, of Maurice de Saxe and Frederick the Great have few similarities beside their victorious mastery of the arts of war and their comprehension of the significance of military intelligence as one of those arts. Marlborough, in his most brilliant campaigns as depicted by his descendant and current biographer, Winston S. Churchill, seems to have had a marksman's unerring aim in finding the right spy or informer to bribe, while his great companion-in-arms, Prince Eugene of Savoy, a grandnephew of the devious Mazarin, paid a pension to the postmaster of Versailles who regularly opened the correspondence of the French commanders and copied out valuable military extracts. Another agent employed by Prince Eugene was that Abbé Lenglet-Dufresnoy—a notorious double spy—who, on coming from prison where his interlocking allegiances had lodged him, set to work with refreshed vigor and exposed the astonishing Cellamare conspiracy. It aimed, during the minority of King Louis XV, to overthrow the regent of France in the interests of Spain. Cellamare was the Spanish ambassador, and, under instructions from the notorious Cardinal Alberoni, he "concocted obscene tales about the regent for Alberoni to retail to the king and queen, not so much for the purpose of stimulating their marriage relations as to alarm their bigotry."[7]

Maurice de Saxe, the celebrated victor of Fontenoy, whom Louis XV honored by reviving for him Turenne's title of "Marshal-General of the King's camps and armies", not only made use of "spies and guides", but also wrote about them; and we find in the tenth chapter of his posthumously published military classic, *Reveries on the Art of War*:[8]

You cannot give too much attention to spies and guides. Monsieur de Montecuculli says, they are as useful as the eyes in your head, and, to a general, are quite as indispensable. He is right. You cannot spend too much money in order to obtain good ones. They must be obtained from the country in which war is being waged. Intelligent and skilful people must be employed. They must be distributed everywhere: among officers of the headquarters' staff, among sutlers, and especially among contractors for food-supplies; for the victualling depots and bread-bakeries afford an excellent means of judging the enemy's intentions.

These spies must not be known to each other and should be entrusted with various commissions. Some—those who are suited for the purpose—will smuggle themselves into the ranks; others, again, will accompany the army as buyers and sellers. Each member of the second group must know one of the first, so that he may acquire from him the information to be reported to the general who pays him. This particular task should be entrusted to a man who is intelligent and reliable. His trustworthiness must be checked daily, and you must make sure that he is not being bribed by the other side.

Frederick the Great soon afterward brought his own genius to bear upon the science of foul play, putting an end to espionage for all time as a gay or noble adventure. Frederick's aptitude for war was never more clearly displayed than in his shrewdly systematic use of spies. He has even been called the father of organized military espionage; and his royal necessity was the mother of the organization he invented. But primarily Frederick aspired to be a French wit. He esteemed Voltaire highly and corresponded with him and even flattered him with acid imitation. When the pope was endeavoring to extinguish the Jesuits—and might have succeeded, too, but for the society's survival in Protestant lands—he wrote Frederick, urging a Jesuit expulsion from Prussia. Whereat the king trotted out his best brand of Voltairean malice: "Since I am regarded as a heretic, the Holy Father can absolve me neither from keeping my promise nor from behaving as an honorable man and king."

Frederick called the Pompadour "Cotillon IV"; and his quips at the expense of Maria Theresa and the empress of Russia, if not always as witty as M. Arouet's might have been, carried the long-range impact of royal utterance. Secret agents and gossips carried them across Europe. The Prussian, already condemned as a land robber—his theft of Silesia from Maria Theresa having incensed the admirers of that illustrious lady—thus contrived to add humor and cynicism to his list of alien offenses. In very influential boudoirs it was being debated how to punish the upstart monarch. Frederick, like Voltaire, discovered that the friction of small words can start a volcanic conflagration.

Instead of a wit he had to try to become the greatest military commander of his time, else he would be obliterated forever by the prodigious alliance of France and Russia who were joining Austria with the possibility of Sweden and Saxony to follow. He surveyed his small, poor kingdom, his well-drilled army, his rich and towering foes. He had once beaten Austria, but then—who hadn't? To beat them all he realized now he must outguess them. Wherefore he organized his secret service so that he might nourish his guessing upon wide and substantial intelligence; and this service of his came to be the unique military innovation of the age, with such measures and methods of making war secretly as are still effective after more than a century and three quarters of change in every other branch of armed conflict. Frederick has been quoted as saying that he had, when in the field, one cook and a hundred spies. As to that, he needed but one cook, for he was frugal and often ailing. But he managed to afford many times a hundred spies; and he himself generally checked off their reports, one against another. It was his habit to divide his agents into four classes: (a) common spies, recruited among poor folk glad to earn a small sum or to accommodate a military officer; (b) double spies, the low informers and unreliable renegades, of value chiefly in spreading false information to the enemy; (c) spies of consequence—courtiers and noblemen, staff officers and kindred conspirators, invariably requiring a substantial bribe or bait; and (d) persons who are forced to undertake espionage against their will. And the energetic Prussian did more than classify, he established rules for obtaining and using every grade of spy or secret agent.

Under his fourth category he suggested that a rich burgher must be thoroughly intimidated, which might best be done with threats to burn down his home, destroy his fortune, or injure or even kill his wife and children. The burgher, a good man of peace and local repute, once he had been properly molded by his anxiety, could be made to serve by accompanying a trained military agent into the camp of the enemy, where his appearance, reputation and character would mask the real spy's activities. Despite his forced labor of pretense, the burgher could be relied upon to behave amiably enough if often reminded that members of his family were the hostages held by those to whom the real spy, his companion, would report at the conclusion of their joint espionage venture.

Frederick's four classifications overlooked the modern patriot spy. The Prussian was a realist, a cynic—and an absolute monarch. Reigning sovereigns of his day were seldom in touch with genuine patriotism. The French Revolution had yet to fire Europe with nationalist enthusiasms. Threats and bribes, promises of promotion and gain, were the inducements that the spy-masters of Frederick's school understood how to use.

CHAPTER SIXTEEN

MR THURLOE AND MR PEPYS

THE GREAT PRESTIGE of Elizabeth's reign had been frittered away by the first pair of Stuarts; but it was to be magnificently regained, and even far exceeded, under the dominion of Oliver Cromwell. The republican years of England were few, which makes their achievements all the more illustrious. Cromwell's military organization was so superior to those of the Continent that many governments suppressed their abhorrence of regicide and sought to ally themselves with England. Protestants in the south of France were being hunted to death by the Duke of Savoy when Cromwell intervened. His great admiral, Robert Blake—who *founded* the tradition carried on by Nelson, Hawke and Jervis—enabled England to displace Holland as the ascendant naval power.[1] Algerine pirates no longer dared to raid shipping in the Channel or, as in the lax days of Charles I, take English slaves to Africa from the very coasts of Devon and Cornwall.

One of the chief ornaments of Cromwell's equally able diplomatic service was John Milton; while the "Blake" of his extraordinary secret service was John Thurloe. After Walsingham he was the most competent of England's directors of espionage and secret intelligence. Whether Elizabeth's or Cromwell's service was the more notably efficient is an academic question and as hard to decide from what evidence we have as are the relative merits of Walsingham and Thurloe. Considering the accomplishments of the former in spite of the queen's penurious appropriations for the safeguarding of her own life and regime, the palm would seem to go to Walsingham. John Thurloe, whose vigilance and manifold ingenuities protected the Lord Protector, was allowed generous sums which compare, in purchasing power, with the annual expenditure of the British Secret Service today—and which exceeded Walsingham's allowances in Elizabeth's most anxious year (1587) by the ratio of more than 23 to 1.

We only need turn the pages of Pepys, that matchless "secret intelligencer" of the Restoration, to learn from the complaints of the day how men recollected the brilliant performances of Thurloe. On February 14, 1668, Mr Pepys recorded:

> Secretary Morrice did this day in the House, when they talked of intelligence, say that he was allowed but £700 a-year for intelligence, whereas, in Cromwell's time, he [Cromwell] did allow £70,000 a-year for it; and was confirmed therein by Colonel Birch, who said that thereby Cromwell carried the secrets of all the princes of Europe at his girdle.[2]

Parliament returned to the topic of secret service only three days later; and the niggardly sum given Morrice for intelligence increases by fifty pounds according to Pepys's entry of February 17, 1668:

> They did here in the House talk boldly of the King's bad counsellors, and how they must be all turned out, and many of them, and better, brought in: and the proceedings of the Long-Parliament in the beginning of the war were called to memory: and the King's bad intelligence was mentioned, wherein they were bitter against my Lord Arlington, saying, among other things, that whatever Morrice's was, who declared he had but £750 a-year allowed him for intelligence, the King paid too dear for my Lord Arlington's, in giving him £10,000 and a barony for it.

Later that same year Pepys discussed espionage with a man who had been Cromwell's resident in Holland and had unquestionably directed an important segment of Thurloe's intelligence system, Holland at that time being recognized as England's chief maritime and naval competitor. And so the quaint Restoration gossip had this to preserve in his private diarist cipher as of December 27, 1668:

> 27th. (Lord's day.) Walked to White Hall and there saw the King at chapel; but staid not to hear anything, but went to walk in the Park, with W. Hewer, who was with me; and there, among others, met with Sir G. Downing, and walked with him an hour, talking of business, and how the late war was managed. . . . He told me that he had so good spies, that he hath had the keys taken out of De Witt's[3] pocket when he was a-bed, and his closet opened, and papers brought to him, and left in his hands for an [hour], and carried back and laid in the place again, and keys put into his pocket again. He says that he hath always had their most private debates, that have been but between two or three of the chief of them, brought to him in an hour after, and an hour after that, hath sent word thereof to the King, but nobody here regarded them. . . .

Downing, in the phrases of Samuel Pepys, sets forth the whole art of spying, which is essentially a threefold procedure: to locate the most reliable and valued information—and obtain it without being discovered—to transmit promptly to a superior whatever has been secured, and to leave the adversary in ignorance of his being deceived, so that what has been learned will not be nullified by his alarmed alteration of plan. If either the second or the third of these three is bungled, the original enterprise of the spy is completely eclipsed. Downing was able to confer upon King Charles and his ministers the same brilliant mechanism of espionage which he had developed at the instigation of Thurloe. However, there is a fourth—the final and least difficult—part of the espionage transaction, which anyone accustomed to serving Cromwell and Thurloe must have taken for granted. The heeding, or at least the mere reading, of the summary of intelligence! And so it was Downing's misfortune to have failure attend his best efforts as a veteran of secret service, when neither the king nor anyone else in London gave attention to what his agents in Holland garnered at the risk of their lives.

Secretary Thurloe's Protective Secret Service

John Thurloe was secretary of state both to Oliver and Richard Cromwell, but after the Restoration "the quiet Essex lawyer" sought to retire from politics and was never employed again, "though the King solicited his services." Charles II had good reason to respect Thurloe's abilities and endeavor to retain them, for no one man had done more to frustrate the innumerable plots of Charles' partisans, the exiled Royalists.

Blake's men-of-war had swept the narrow seas of Spanish ships, pirates and privateers; and so Cromwell's life and government were not seriously threatened until the Royalists turned from open warfare to political conspiracy. Plotters—far more numerous than the Jesuits and agents of Rome who had invaded Tudor England to strike at that other "usurper", Elizabeth—began swarming across the Channel in fishing smacks and every kind of trading craft. Cromwell's spies and military police formed the impregnable barrier against which they vainly hurled themselves. John Thurloe was "the linch-pin of the whole régime. As secretary of state he combined in his own hands nearly every portfolio of a modern cabinet, but he was also the chief of police and the head of the secret service."[4]

The annual grant of £70,000 for intelligence and counter-espionage seems to have been wisely invested to the very last farthing. It lined all sorts of pockets; Thurloe had agents everywhere, many of them high in the confidence of Charles Stuart. Plots continually incubating at Paris and Madrid, in the back streets of Brussels, Cologne and The Hague were reported to Secretary Thurloe with uncanny punctuality. The cabinets of France and Spain met behind carefully guarded doors; but Thurloe within a few days could read an accurate account of their "secret" deliberations. Oliver Cromwell is said to have been the only one who ever puzzled Mazarin. Cromwell was the cardinal's superior not only as a soldier but as a religious leader; he excelled him as an administrator and in everything else, save personal avarice; while Thurloe, Cromwell's lieutenant, could even have given the Italian a few lessons in subtlety, precision and the successful management of secret service. No wonder Mazarin was puzzled!

"There is no government on earth," Sagredo, the Venetian ambassador, wrote to the Council of Ten, "which divulges its affairs less than England, or is more punctually informed of those of the others." Scholarly intelligencers, penniless Royalists, simple-minded fanatics, exiled chieftains, fugitives from justice, young rakes and scoundrels who had broken the law—even "condemned men reprieved for the purpose"—found employment in Thurloe's time as operatives of the secret service. A good many of them "never knew that they were in his service. He intercepted letters with such regularity that the royalist postbag might as well have been delivered to his office. . . . Poor Hyde in France, with not a farthing to spend on anything" did not suspect that Thurloe "read him like a large-print book" and had reports on file of his "most secret plans almost before they were completed."[5]

Like Walsingham, a man of genius relying upon the curious special talent of Thomas Phelippes, Secretary Thurloe enlisted and depended upon the famous decipherer, Dr John Wallis of Oxford. Thurloe's ingenious interception of the royalist post would—without Wallis—have been censorship rather than espionage. And the Protector's enemies would have taken alarm and learned to communicate in some other fashion. Wallis, it appears, could "break" any code or cipher known to the intriguers of that age; and he dealt Charles' adherents such blows as the great British cryptographers—a Sir Alfred Ewing or Captain Hitchings—reserved for the Germans after 1914.

Thurloe, able as he was, and surrounded by expert assistants, had need of all his own and their capacity for vigilance, as Cromwell's life was threatened now from every corner. In 1654 the exiled, frustrated and poverty-stricken Charles—with scarcely one mistress he could call his own—had been inspired to issue a proclamation offering a knighthood and £500 a year to anyone bold enough to slay "a certain base mechanic fellow called Oliver Cromwell."[6] Thurloe's spies soon were revealing "a nest of murderous intrigues in many quarters"; and a new kind of police—a militia, not locally controlled, but under the command of army officers—came into being. England was divided into eleven districts, over each of which was a major-general,[7] commanding the militia in his area, supported by special troops of horse. The cost of this new and repressive organization was defrayed by an extra tax of 10 per cent on the incomes of the already impoverished Royalist nobility.

As a police measure taking all England into "protective custody" this innovation was a complete success, since Cromwell was not assassinated;[8] but as statesmanship it was deplorable. The new system of policing the realm had to be abolished in 1657, the very year which found Cromwell in gravest peril. A secret agent even advised Thurloe not to allow the Protector to read any more foreign letters, since one of them might be impregnated with a baffling poison.

Cromwell himself had been "worried by the Levellers with their clumsy, non-exploding fire-basket for 'their New Year's gift.'"[9] Secretary Thurloe's counter-spies detected Sir John Packington smuggling in munitions as wine and soap. Penruddock rose in Wiltshire; but the well-informed government exploded his rebellion, as it did all other Royalist risings, and scattered his band of followers. Army rebels—Overton, Harrison and Wildman—were as promptly suppressed. But the members of the "Sealed Knot", a secret society or club of Royalist conspirators, required widespread, constant surveillance and could not be rounded up. Thurloe's agents trailed an envoy of the "Sealed Knot" to Cologne and there discovered King Charles and Ormonde with one faithful body servant. Charles fled to Brussels, where Thurloe's spies were already waiting for him. Cromwell had declared war on Spain, "the great under-propper of Roman Babylon"; and one of his Brussels agents wrote Thurloe that the young king, impatient of the month-long siesta of the Spanish government, was wearied of "lurking behind the hangings with no part to act."

After the death of the Lord Protector, his successor, Richard Cromwell, retained John Thurloe as his secretary of state; and Thurloe struck at least one more blow at those who conspired against the Commonwealth by bribing Sir Richard Willis, a trusted and important member of the "Sealed Knot" fraternity. The greatest advantages expected from this stroke miscarried, however, when Cromwell's resident in Holland, George Downing—Mr Pepys' informant, already quoted—distinguished the symptoms of restoration at home and did himself the favor of warning King Charles that Willis had been bought. Thurloe could be lavish in his payments whenever the prize seemed alluring enough; but we come now to a celebrated spy of the Restoration who proved just how lavish Charles II could be in an affair of secret service, if the alluring prize was feminine.

Chapter Seventeen
ESPIONNE OF THE BEDCHAMBER

ACQUIRING THE FIRST MILLION is the hardest—in secret service as in every other form of remunerative labor; so hard, in fact, only two of the many accomplished spies of whom we have authentic record were able to collect that monument of wealth.[1] And one of them, Louise de Kéroualle, contrived her fruitful combination of favors, rewards and annuities by serving Louis XIV of France as a secret agent while developing an even more lucrative side line as mistress of the king of England. From the two royal treasuries in the year 1681 her allowances reached the incredible peak of nearly three million dollars, estimated in purchasing power today. Louise became Duchess of Portsmouth in England and of Aubigny in France and was evidently an all-around expert in the professions of spying and pleasing and the science of personal gain.

The ruling influences of Great Britain were then mainly exerted in the bedchamber of Charles II; and King Louis was too grand a monarch merely to hire a royal chambermaid. His own regal and catholic taste in women was never shown off to better advantage than when he came to appoint the agent who was to serve his interests by delighting Charles. And what caused the mission to seem infinitely more palatable to the potentate of Versailles, his conscience told him that by drawing the Merrie Monarch into the service of the Church of Rome his enticing French espionne would be helping to save King Charles' immortal soul.

Louise de Kéroualle made any form of conversion an epicurean experience. She seems, like Louis himself, to have been descended from the great Henri IV; but unlike Louis—who was the ancestor of increasingly incompetent Bourbons—she was destined to be the great-great-grandmother of Charles James Fox, that liberal and prematurely modern statesman whose feat it was to oppose Pitt and win immortality by keeping his great adversary in office for twenty years. Charles II must have had merely an academic interest in Henri of Navarre until he saw this sugarplum bestowed upon his court by the royal confectioners of France. A lovely, "innocent appearing girl with dark eyes, round, velvety cheeks and soft masses of dark hair", Louise came to England not so much to spy upon the British as to induce their sovereign to sell them out. There is every reason to believe that he would have shunned such a transaction if he had been able to pay any other price at the time, but he had little to offer save his honor and Louise represented a banker willing to discount Charles' honor at only a little below par.

The price of making Louise happy as Duchess of Portsmouth was, as we know, exorbitant. The "carrying charges" were to be endlessly burdensome, not to Charles, who was accustomed to being in debt, but to the English exchequer which he quickly infected with all his financial infirmities. And the downbinder upon the lady, merely getting her to settle in England—as her master, King Louis, intended—came to a terrific figure: Charles' consent to the odious Treaty of Dover. It was probably the most humiliating document ever offered a British sovereign for his signature, and, in some private concern for their historic repute, neither Charles nor Louis, its originator, ever did sign it. That possibly incendiary stroke each monarch left to one of his ministers.

Charles, in return for an annual subsidy of 3,000,000 francs and the "acquisition of Walcheren and the mouths of the Scheldt", bound himself to abandon the Triple Alliance and, at the bidding of Louis, declare war upon the Dutch. Everything hereafter was to be at the bidding of Louis, except, no doubt, Charles' getting in and out of beds, which he did with practiced and kingly grace. The French anticipated a Protestant insurrection would be provoked in Britain by publication of the terms of the treaty; and so they added to it a provision whereby the French monarch agreed to send military assistance to Charles in quelling any such outbreak. Obtaining such a treaty was doubtless worthy of the highest paid spy in history, for Charles quite candidly sold out to his French ally and put his throne and his people at the disposal of a Catholic overlord.

It is interesting to note that Charles' other favorite at this time was Nell Gwynne, "who did not cost the nation above £4,000 a year in revenue."[2] Nell shared the popular dislike of Louise, of course, and christened her "Squinta Bella", on account of the Frenchwoman's slight squint, and also the "Weeping Willow", because of her habit of "dissolving into tears when her royal lover refused any of her importunate demands." While to a woman who had been praising Nell's wit and beauty, Louise replied: " 'Yes, Madam, but anybody may know she has been an orange wench by her swearing.' "[3] And the story is told of an English mob one day hooting Nell's coach, mistaking it for the luxurious equipage of Louise de Kéroualle, whom the English called "Madame Carwell." And so Nell popped her pretty head out to cry shrilly: "'No! No! Good people! I'm the Protestant whore! The *English* one!'" Whereupon the people broke into cheers.[4]

Catholicism was a perilous faith to hold in the England of that day. There was the Popish Plot and many minor melodramas. Our friend Samuel Pepys was brought into the shadow of the gallows; and, though there is reason to believe that he was of the faith of his unpopular patron, James, Duke of York—soon to become James II for a brief turbulent reign—Pepys, a magnificent defensive fighter, contrived to clear himself of the menacing charges. He had also been accused of treasonable relations with France; but luckily for him his only accuser was a scoundrel and preposterous braggart, Colonel John Scott.

It was about this same time that John Churchill, the future military genius and Duke of Marlborough, was given his running start through the amorous intercessions of his sister Arabella, who was James's mistress, and of the aging duchess who was John's mistress. Presently James was deserted even by John in favor of William and Mary—that typical beginning for a dazzling career in the world of high politics and, in view of the improvement in the English monarchy, well worth the Jacobites' virulent condemnation. James was advised by a Jesuit, Father Petrie. His chief of secret service was the capable Sir Leoline Jenkins. A Mrs Elizabeth Gaunt was burned at the stake for the capital offense of having sheltered a rebel after Monmouth's ill-managed insurrection. In this case the rebel she had sheltered was allowed to bear witness against her and thus gain himself a royal pardon. British sense of fair play was outraged by that bargain and many another devised by the same biased minds. James had to go; at the Boyne even the Irish could not detain him.

In Russia a contemporary achievement was the initiation of political police under the personal supervision of the sovereign. In 1697 this predecessor of the notorious *Ochrana* was designated the "Special Office of the Tsar", and Peter the Great gave it much attention. Whoever wanted to accuse another of a crime against the state was required to appeal to the Office of the Transfiguration—the tsar's palace then being known as the Palace of the Transfiguration. Peter II abolished the political police bureau, now more simply entitled the "Secret Office"; but in the reign of Tsarina Elizabeth it was revived. The rack was humanely abolished as an implement of judicial inquiry;

but it was discovered that the knout was a simpler and equally effective means of achieving sworn confessions. We shall only hear of the "Secret Office" once more, after the December uprising in 1825, when Tsar Nicholas I had to surround his despotism with a sanctimoniously reorganized system of secret political police.

CHAPTER EIGHTEEN

DEFOE AND THE JACOBITES

THE CREATOR of the immortal adventurer *Robinson Crusoe* admitted that he had been employed by Queen Anne "in several honorable though secret services."[1] And that was putting it very modestly, for Daniel Defoe is one of the great professionals in all these centuries of secret service, a discreet giant among the legions of straining, posturing and boastfully "confiding" amateurs. Defoe, be it known, was in himself almost a complete secret service during the reign of the last Stuart sovereign of Britain; and he is our strongly endorsed candidate for everybody's "favorite secret agent" of these annals.

Defoe, the master of imaginative adventure and of uncanny realism, the journalist and novelist—witness his vivid *Journal of the Plague Year* or the account he developed from an obscure manuscript of the horrible sack of Magdeburg in *Memoirs of a Cavalier*—wrote millions of words in his fruitful and complex life but never a line about his own career as a secret agent of the crown. That reticence, deplorable to a posterity of admiring readers, is all the proof we need of Defoe's first rank among confidential emissaries. It emphatically distinguishes the veteran, the deft, trusted hand; for the best of them, operating and living discreetly for years, never get over an habitual cautiousness or lose their faith in the virtues of discretion.

In 1710 when Lord Godolphin was forced out of office by Queen Anne and yielded up the administration of British affairs to his successor, Harley, he personally recommended Defoe to the new ministry as a reliable and enterprising political agent. Defoe had done so well in the service of the Whig government—particularly in Scotland and the lairs of the Jacobites, whither he frequently journeyed in disguise —that the incoming Tories were well advised to make use of his established abilities. The author was forty-nine when *Crusoe* founded his lasting reputation. His earlier years had been packed with adventures; he had been twice imprisoned; he had suffered the indignities of the pillory in 1703; and acrid contemporaries even spread it around that his ears had been officially cropped. All of which was excluded from the "material" required by that superlative imagination. The gifted hand which could depict *Moll Flanders*, the pirate Avery, the highwaymen Sheppard and Jonathan Wild, took no chances with the secrets of the English government.

Having called this propagandist, spy and accomplished intriguer "in himself almost a complete secret service", it is possible to prove it, even though we are in want of his own testimony. Daniel Defoe attended Newington Academy—conducted by a Mr Morton—where one of his fellow pupils was that Samuel Wesley who married and begat Methodism. Three of Defoe's school friends were hanged for their participation in the uprising of the Duke of Monmouth.[2] And we may assume that those executions taught young Daniel a lesson, for ever afterward he avoided pretenders, attached himself to responsible ministers of state and was uniformly successful in making himself indispensable to the winning side.

It was a turbulent time of foreign wars, Jacobite conspiracy and impending threats of insurrections, and a man of Defoe's talents invaded political secret service at the risk of his life. Yet any student of the work of this extraordinary man will concede that, cramping as must have been his experience of the pillory, it was as nothing beside his prolonged self-exposure to writer's cramp. The gravest risk he ran all his adult years was that of working himself to death; and while no records of his actual accomplishments as a spy have survived, the confidence he manifestly earned, his continued employment by Whig and Tory governments, is a clear indication of his varied capabilities. As a propagandist there is evidence and to spare that Defoe was indefatigable, and as a journalist—before the machine age—all but unbelievable. The writing of his books was largely a pastime, light exercise for his leisure hours to keep his quill in trim.

He turned out pamphlets with effortless clarity and speed. He wrote three and sometimes four newspapers: a monthly publication —of nearly 100 pages—as well as a weekly and a triweekly. Part of the time he issued a daily. Gorki called *Robinson Crusoe* "the bible of the unconquerable"; but the castaway's celebrated labors in the vineyard of self-preservation must have seemed no more than moderate industry to his busy creator. Scotland was four hundred miles distant; yet when Defoe on one of his secret missions went into the north country he continued writing and publishing his reviews in London every other day. Even on the dire occasion of his being locked up in Newgate, he never stopped sending out manuscript to the printer.

Defoe was more than a single author, agent or masterly propagandist; he became a whole platoon of journalistic shock troops. Not only were his most famous characters fictional, but he himself was partly a figment of his own teeming imagination. He published some books anonymously, but signed his name to the introductions in which he recommended them to the consideration of the reading public. He encouraged himself in letters to his papers and reviled himself in letters to rival sheets. He corrected himself, he quoted himself, he plagiarized his own writings in works which he attributed to foreign commentators. He boldly reminded himself in print of his alliance with political gentry who were secretly employing him to oppose some policy of the government to which they belonged. Defoe, more than any man who has ever lived, permitted his aptitude for secret service to infect every other practice of his almost innumerable vocations.

Encircled in a Mist

A government spy for Lord Townshend, the secretary of state, during the critical insurrectionary year of "the '15", Defoe achieved this position as virtually an escape from prison. Enemies thought they had worked his undoing, but Lord Chief Justice Parker barred further proceedings against Defoe and personally represented to Townshend that the pamphleteer was a loyal adherent of King George I. Townshend therefore enlisted the services of the ostensible deserter, but it was agreed that the reconciliation between Defoe and the secretary of state should be so well masked that the journalist could remain in the "enemy" camp as a spy. The government nourished an acute grievance against the Jacobite press, whose seditious sniping was provoking a dangerous amount of popular ferment. If Defoe could continue to exploit an apparent antagonism to Townshend and the government, he might readily gain the confidence of the Jacobite editors. He was expected mainly to counter-act their treasonable broadsides by intercepting or taking the sting out of every article designed to embarrass the government.

Defoe seems to have been eager to join in this subterranean alliance. He became a "Tory" editor for Townshend in 1716 and continued in that role until 1720, helping to compose a Jacobite paper to "keep the Party amused", so that they would not start a far more violent one. In 1717 the government learned through various channels that the Jacobites were plotting another rebellion. Acting upon information obtained by secret agents—Defoe, perhaps, among them—the authorities descended upon the residence of the Swedish envoy, Count Gyllenborg, and uncovered a quantity of "incriminating" documents, chiefly correspondence between him and Baron Goertz, a distinguished Swedish diplomat serving as an ambassador on the Continent. King

Charles XII of Sweden straightway became the target of widespread English animosity; and Defoe conceived a project to harry and embarrass all the Swedes, including their king.

Nine years before, in 1708, the militaristic Charles XII with his eruptive Alexander-the-Great fixation had condemned a nobleman of Livonia, John Rhindholdt, Count Patkul, to be broken alive on the wheel. Defoe had never heard of Patkul until his execution, but it now struck the ace of English propagandists as an excellent time to revive discussion of King Charles' forgotten enormity. The resulting pamphlet, which appeared almost instantaneously, was a reputed translation of the original work by the Lutheran clergyman who had attended the luckless Patkul in his final hours. This "clergyman", however, has been detected by modern scholars as an unconscionable plagiarist, for in denouncing Charles and exposing to civilized contemporaries the condemned Patkul's anguish and innocence, he borrowed four whole pages from an earlier work concerning the *Wars of Charles XII* by Daniel Defoe.

Such an attack upon the Swedish monarch was not to be ignored, and Count Gyllenborg made strong representations to the British government, demanding severe punishment of the overcandid critic of foreign royalty. It was not yet an age when any commoner, let alone a mere "scribbler", could upbraid a living king with impunity. Defoe, however, had been given one more ministerial ax to grind; and so Count Gyllenborg was further embarrassed by getting nowhere with King George's ministers in pressing his counter-attack upon the pamphleteer.

In April of 1717, when Lord Sunderland succeeded Townshend, the ingenious Defoe obligated the government still more by contriving to attach himself—"in the disguise of a translator of foreign news"—to the Tory paper of Mr Nathaniel Mist. It was a pun of the time to say that Defoe "delighted to encircle himself in a mist"; and Sunderland for one was even more delighted, since Mist's *Journal* was the organ of the Stuart pretender. Defoe summarized his own secret purpose: "Upon the whole, however ... by this management, the *Weekly Journal* [Mist's] and *Dormer's Letter*, as also the *Mercurius Politicus*, which is in the same nature of management as the *Journal*, will be always kept (mistakes excepted) to pass as Tory papers, and yet be disabled and enervated so as to do no mischief or give any offence to the Government." He described Mist's correspondents and supporters as "Papists, Jacobites, and enraged High Tories, a generation whom, I profess, my very soul abhors."

His assignment was undoubtedly dangerous, but Defoe undertook it with relish. The advantages of employing a "government" editor who also happened to be a genius was soon apparent in the pages of Mist's *Journal*. Defoe was pulling one way and the Jacobites another, Mist meanwhile suffering spasms of anxiety, indecision and prosperity. The political articles savagely assailing the government were being displaced in favor of "diverting stories" and matter written in a bantering tone, which startled Mist's old readers but fetched in hundreds of new ones. Even so, Mist's *Journal* was still harshly criticized by the Whig organ, Read's *Journal;* and when, as was inevitable, Defoe's connection with Mist leaked out, the Whig press made merry, while the Tories were exasperated beyond measure.

As an immediate result, articles violently anti-government reappeared in Mist's paper. In October 1718 it published a letter signed by "Sir Andrew Politick" which so wounded sensitive ministers of the crown that Mist's printing shop was raided and searched for the original of the letter. On being examined, Mist swore that Defoe was the author of the offensive "Politick" letter. Lord Stanhope appears to have known all about it from Defoe himself, and no prosecution resulted. Soon afterward, thanks to Defoe's intercession, the imprisonment of Mist came to an end. And on two subsequent occasions the influence of Defoe arranged Mist's discharge from custody. While despising Mist's political opinions, Defoe seems to have dealt with him in a spirit of kindness and sympathy, like a missionary who struggles for the soul of the heathen who has already got him into hot water. Mist responded with nothing but partisan animosity, once Defoe's influence with the government had been revealed. Thus the two came to a parting, celebrated by Read's *Journal* on December 6, 1718, with a rhymed insinuation that they had quarreled over sharing the profits:

> "What strange adventures could untwist
> "Such true-born knaves as Foe and Mist?
> "They quarreled sure about the pelf,
> "For Dan's a needy, greedy elf."

Jacobite Conspiracy

From the day King James II fearfully abandoned his throne to an indeterminable date possibly associated with the coronation of George III or the declining years of Bonnie Prince Charlie, the British Isles were continuously athrob with Jacobite intrigues. After substantial research we may as well agree that the Jacobite partisans won and still hold an all-time record for miscellaneous conspiracy. This cost a great deal of time and money, and even a good many lives; but there is little evidence to show that it accomplished anything.³

The "Papists, Jacobites and enraged High Tories" were a fashionable set, and not to share their bigotries, fantasies and prejudices was almost as *démodé* as being in trade. The Jacobites were numerous and tenacious, obstinate and optimistic, fattening upon false hopes as the actual chances of Stuart restoration grew increasingly thin. Their creed transmitted easily from father to son, not only among the exiled Stuarts but even among the lowliest gillies of the Highland clans, so that layers of rebellion were held together by a rich icing of secret-service action, with two considerable insurrections—the '15 and the '45—occurring a whole generation apart. In between the Jacobite plotters had inflicted a "thirty years' war" of intrigue and agitation upon an era whose turbulence will be better understood by the American reader imagining what America would have been like had the surrenders at Fort Sumter and Appomatox come to pass in 1861 and 1891.

Even when there was no real conflict above the horizon there was little pacification and much low-voiced debate of civil war. It was not merely a game played by picturesque Scottish adventurers and the furtive envoys of Rome or St Germain; everybody seems to have taken a hand in it. John Wesley's mother was a Jacobite and his brother a Jacobite conspirator. The archives of the Jacobite "secret service" kept at Scots College, St Germain, are a library in themselves. With George III seated solidly upon the throne and Culloden a wounding memory, the traffic in clandestine travelers and intrigue did not abate. Even a mature Charles Edward Stuart is known to have paid London a secret "visit or two",⁴ with probably no more danger of detection than of being capsized with the responsibilties of an empire.

This prolonged cross-Channel traffic of the Jacobites will ferry us again from Britain to France as we pursue our investigation of secret service and political police. We find the police of both kingdoms dealt far more severely with domestic plotters than with foreign agents of military espionage. The military spies that France enlisted to work against Great Britain, however, were mostly Jacobites, who endangered themselves doubly by adding espionage to political conspiracy, and who, no matter how vital the mission or generous the compensation, never concealed their belief that the campaigns of the French were mere diversions intended to smooth the path of Stuart restoration. Maurice de Saxe, on being raised to the highest command, had taken immediate steps to organize a French Intelligence service; and his arrangements with the Jacobites in 1743 displayed a conception of the purposes and operative design of military intelligence far in advance of the ideas prevailing among the other victorious generals of his day. After the illness, retirement and death of Marshal Saxe the merits of the French Intelligence rapidly declined.

In 1755 one of its most influential directors was that M. de Bonnac, "an able and most active man," who was the French envoy to Holland. Two of the agents he had shipped off to England were Maubert and Robinson. The former wrote to Paris from London, advancing a scheme of financial sabotage. He would start a run on the Bank of England by circulating forged notes, which must be prepared for him by the best engravers in France. Louis XV was eager enough to frighten or embarrass any British government, but he could not bring himself to consent to any such lawless experiment. Maintaining his composure even in the face of Bourbon integrity, Maubert next reported having been able to "buy" a cabinet member. He hinted that his clandestine investment was Lord Holderness. But nothing extraordinary ever came of the alleged shady transaction. Robinson, Maubert's colleague, for his part spied upon the English so innocuously that, when they caught him at it and put him on trial, he was imprisoned in the Tower of London for only six months.[5]

It was a time of considerable slackness and inattention, a time when Viscount Dillon, eleventh of his line and hereditary colonel of the Dillon Regiment of the regular army of King Louis of France, could manage the affairs of that famous corps while residing in England. France and England went to war; but the Irish viscount, a soldier disdainful of hostilities, neither changed his residence nor resigned his command. De Bonnac had been recalled from The Hague and in his place was a new French minister, D'Affray, whose innocence led him straight into negotiation with Falconnet, a double spy much addicted to the golden guineas paid him by the British. M. d'Affray, after purchasing a fine cargo of bogus plans, saw through Falconnet and so turned gratefully to a more artful forger called Philippe, whose specialty was false information purporting to expose the British plans and operations in Canada.

Another double spy, Vautravers, a Swiss, found D'Affray so poor a match for his cunning that he went over the dupe's head and wrote directly to Louis XV. He was, he reported, incapable of learning the strength or objective of the new British expedition to the Low Countries. The English were extremely dangerous and clever if they could even fool him, Vautravers—he conceded—and the king of France would be well advised to sue for peace. Louis replied, suggesting that the Swiss give up diplomacy and resume his work as an espionage agent, for which he was being paid. At this period—1757—with Maubert and Robinson out of the way, a certain Dr Hensey was the only French resident spy in England. He was the brother of Abbé Hensey, a French diplomat, and believed himself importantly placed and secure in London. His intelligence reports appear to have done very little to enlighten the French government; but even so, the British detected Hensey and decided that he was dangerous. There would be no more gentleness, as in the case of Robinson.

Hensey's trial took place in June of 1758; and he received a shock that passed right through him and all over the European underworld of espionage when he heard himself sentenced to be hanged. Displaying an impressive indignation, tinged but slightly with malice, the abbé's brother addressed the court, demanding to know whether a spy dare be treated as a common felon.[6]

CHAPTER NINETEEN

BOURBON POLICE ESPIONAGE

AFTER the secret-service organizations of the two cardinals had helped to establish the Bourbon monarchy in the persons of the son and grandson of Henri IV, there had been no serious threat to the stability of the throne for more than a century and a quarter. We have seen Cardinal Richelieu laying the foundation stones of this immense security with the aid of an espionage service whose chief aim was the maintenance of his own security in control of the kingdom. Mazarin, likewise, was generally too preoccupied with the wars of the Fronde and other conspiracies of the aristocrats who despised him as an alien—a kind of "cardinal-carpetbagger"—to put his faith in government spies or police agents as compared with the clandestine and clerical operatives of his own private service.

Louis XIV, having passed his majority and begun to reign as the most accomplished young king of his time, very quickly changed all this. His police service was private still, but only because Louis looked upon France as his private property. The absolute monarch par excellence—L'état, c'est moi—his personal espionage naturally belonged to the police department of his personal realm. In the time of Le Grand Monarque we arrive, then, at the initiation of systematized political police, surveillance, postal censorship and peacetime military espionage.

Louis not only demanded system, efficient organization, but he provided the funds and authority which enormously enlarged the duties and powers of the French police. It was his admirable object to bring general security to the principal cities of France, wherein crime, license, disorder and dirt were indiscriminately commonplace. However, while thus conferring the blessing of stable government upon the French people, Louis operated at the substantial cost of crushing all remnants of freedom and independence out of them.

Louvois, after Colbert the most celebrated minister of state serving Louis XIV, kept spies in all the cities of France and with all bodies of troops. "M. Louvois was the only one to be well served by his spies," the Duchesse d'Orléans wrote with more obvious envy than accuracy. "In dealing with them he was liberal with money. Every Frenchman who went to Germany or Holland as an instructor in dancing, fencing, or riding, was in his pay and kept him informed of all that happened at those Courts." Another contemporary[1] reported: "There was not a military officer of any consequence in France, whose virtues and vices the Minister of War [Louvois] did not know to the last detail. . . . Not long ago, among the belongings of a maid who had died in the service of the largest hotel in Metz, were found several letters from this minister which make it quite clear that she was commissioned to inform him of all that passed in that hostelry. For her services he made her a regular allowance."

The directorial powers of the royal police were not, however, bestowed upon a minister of state or military commander but delegated to a lieutenant of police—called into existence in 1667—and presently advanced to the rank of lieutenant general. This functionary became all powerful, and he and his successors ruled Paris especially with a despotic hand until the outbreak of the great revolution. The head of the police had summary jurisdiction over beggars, vagabonds and lawbreakers of every class and kind. Crimes, great and small, were prevalent, particularly acts of fraud and embezzlement, Fouquet having just then been convicted of the peculation of public funds on a gigantic scale.

In the loftiest ranks of society there were tricksters and traitors. The Chevalier de Rohan was detected by clever spies while negotiating to sell several strong points on the Norman coast to a coalition of French enemies. This sensational plot, while important politically, hardly compared with the impact of the revelations concerning the Marquise de Brinvilliers, who made great strides in combining fatal doses of the new poison called "arsenic" with the diet of members of her family.[2] The streets of Paris resounded with tales of this elegant murderess; but they also resounded with the clash of rapiers and were made hideous by incessant public brawls. Every one went about armed; and the servants and retainers of influential noblemen were continually drawing their swords.

The lieutenant general of police faced a mountain-scaling task, but at least he faced it with an extraordinary complement of powers. His very word was absolute with respect to all offenses political or general. He could deal instantly with culprits caught in the act, arrest and "imprison any dangerous or suspected" person—a privilege no wider than the Atlantic Ocean—and in pursuit of suspects or alleged offenders he could enter and search private dwellings, or take any other step, no matter how arbitrary.

De la Reynie and the Imprisoned Books

The first lieutenant general of police was Gabriel Nicholas—who assumed the more patrician "De la Reynie" from his estate—a young lawyer who had been the protégé of the governor of Burgundy and subsequently earned the good will of the great Colbert. De la Reynie his contemporaries describe as grave, silent, self-reliant and possessing notable force of character. If his personal traits were those but seldom associated with the French courtier, he seems to have quickly won the confidence of his autocratic sovereign, and his conquest of rogues and conspirators thereafter became simply a command performance.

All the prisoners of state in the royal castles—Vincennes, the Bastille, Pignerolle and the other gloomy corners of oblivion—were given into his charge. He could interrogate them as he might see fit, and he could arrange to liberate or to forget them. There was a large armed force placed at his disposal, mounted men and infantry, nearly a thousand in all; and in addition he had taken over the original city watch, the *chevaliers de guet* or King's Archers, seventy-one in number.

De la Reynie marshaled his shock troops and proceeded to clear out the notorious Cour des Miracles,[2] a carbuncle among the boils and minor eruptions comprising the vast underworld of Paris. The police expelled and dispersed the garrison of this wicked citadel but, as is not unusual even to this day, merely gained a respite for Paris at the expense of the surrounding country. In the matter of disarming the nobles' servingmen, De la Reynie obtained a more lasting result. He published strict regulations, reviving the old edicts that forbade servants to come and go as they pleased, and denied employment to any whose papers were not in order. Then he apprehended a few recalcitrants, convicted and hanged them despite the wounded outcry of their influential masters. And when clubs, canes and huge sticks were substituted for the forbidden swords he invoked the law against those weapons also.

The lieutenant general's more intellectual exercises brought him fame as the first implacable censor of the press. Frenchmen, not yet completely cowed, published matter deemed libelous by a despotic government. There were subjects of King Louis foolhardy enough to circulate complaints against royal extravagance, military pillage, unjust judges and thieving financiers. But the police had complete authority over those infernal machines handled by printers and could deal out the law's swift vengeance to typesetter, author or publisher whose opinions neglected to conform. The most extravagant measures were employed to prevent the distribution of prohibited books; and philosophical works proved especially repugnant to the policeman's tastes.

It is curious to discover that books, when suspected, detected and taken into custody, were treated like criminals and consigned to the Bastille. Twenty copies were set aside for the governor, another twelve or fifteen were available to important officials, and the rest of the edition turned over to the papermakers to be torn up and sold as wastepaper, or else burned in the presence of the keeper of the archives.[4] Prohibited books were not imprisoned until they had been tried and condemned; and then sentence was written upon a ticket attached to the sack containing them. Condemned engravings were officially defaced in the presence of the keeper of the archives and the staff of the Bastille.[5]

Seizures of books were frequently accompanied by an order to destroy the printing press and distribute the bookseller's whole stock. But the police agents had a far more difficult problem to solve in their campaign against gambling and the prevalence of cheating. Following the extravagant and corrupt example of the court, everybody gambled, in or out of doors, anywhere, even in carriages when traveling a few miles or many leagues. Louis XIV, as he grew older and more youthful pleasures palled, played regularly and for high stakes. His courtiers took their cue from him; and the less elegant imitated them. The chance to win vast sums attracted any number of sharpers and *"grecs"* to the gaming tables; all kinds of tricks and cheating became the vogue.

The king repeatedly issued orders that the cheating must be checked; a functionary who had jurisdiction in the court, the grand provost, was even instructed to find some means of preventing it. De la Reynie at the same time was informing Colbert of the innumerable kinds of fraud his spies had found being practiced with cards, dice or *hoca,* a then popular game played with thirty points and thirty balls.[6] The lieutenant general of police made various suggestions: the cardmakers must be subjected to close surveillance; it was useless to seek to control the makers of dice, but they could be required to denounce everyone who ordered loaded dice; while as for *hoca,* it should be resolutely banned. The Italians, its originators, had soon despaired of the game's being played without cheating and so had prohibited it in their own country.

Gradually all games of chance, though still flourishing at court, were forbidden elsewhere. The king, growing more sedate under the religious influence of Mme de Maintenon, reproved the spendthrift nobles; but *hoca* and other games steadily grew in popularity. Louis promised De la Reynie to grant him power enough to abolish all gambling, but never hazarded the obvious expedient of launching his prohibition from court. Neither play—nor cheating—could be suppressed in the highest social circles of France, until the coming of the revolution made it a better gamble to try to cheat the guillotine.

Pompadour Reads the Mail

It is impossible to survey the procedures, follies and phobias of the whole succession of lieutenant generals from Gabriel Nicholas de la Reynie to Thiroux de Crosne, whose elaborate system of espionage caught the earliest tremors of, but could do nothing to prevent, the volcanic revolutionary disturbances that swept away the Bourbons and all their authorities. A few of these directors of the royal police were distinguished in some curious way, though hardly any were famous for great ability. D'Argenson, the elder, was universally detested and feared, but he cleared out the low haunts of thieves and criminals; and his merciless severities were as a rule in keeping with the brutality of the crimes which he punished. His son, the younger D'Argenson,[7] was the originator of "the law of passports which made it a capital offense to go abroad without one." Hérault, who excelled in every form of bigotry and intolerance, was noted for his persecutions of the Freemasons.

D'Ombréval was equally intolerant, but his distinction rests upon his implacable persecution of the half-mad fanatics known as the *Convulsionnaires*.[8] His agents were instructed to search everywhere for these culprits. He had them pursued "into the most private places, respecting neither age nor sex, and casting them wholesale into prison." However, the *Convulsionnaires* defied the royal police in publishing a periodical, *Nouvelles Ecclesiastiques,* which they printed and distributed in the very teeth of authority. And D'Ombréval's army of resourceful and unscrupulous spies could not find out who wrote it or where it was being printed. "Sometimes it appeared in the town, sometimes in the country. It was printed, now in the suburbs, now among the piles of wood in the Gros Caillou, now upon barges"[9] in the Seine or in private houses.

Many other ingenious devices have been credited to these audacious zealots. To get through the barriers they used a poodle dog that wore a false woolly skin over its shaven body; between the two the printed sheets were hidden and traveled undiscovered into Paris. On one occasion, it is said, the authors of this resolute propaganda grew so bold that, while D'Ombréval was having a house searched for their printing press, several copies of *Nouvelles Ecclesiastiques*, still wet from the press, were tossed into his waiting carriage.

The unprincipled Berryer owed his appointment as lieutenant general of police to the Marquise de Pompadour, whose creature he was; and with the ardor of the insufferable sycophant he diverted all the powers of his office to spying upon her rivals, learning exactly what was being said about her or against her, and avenging each attack with summary arrests. To oblige the reigning mistress of Louis XV, Berryer submitted each day an account of all the scandalous gossip which his agents found current in Paris. From that it was but a step to the felicities of the infamous Cabinet Noir—the government's bureau of postal espionage—by means of which every letter entrusted to the French post was read. A busy staff of confidential clerks, working directly under the supervision of Janelle, the postmaster general, took impressions of the seals with quicksilver, melted the wax over steam, extracted the letters from the envelopes, read them, and copied any parts deemed likely to concern or amuse the king and Pompadour.[10] The latter, most resolute captivator of the most indolent and easily bored of French monarchs, "always looked upon police *espionnage* as one of the most effective instruments of despotism.... The ministers-in-council were in the habit of meeting at her house and it was by her suggestion that spies had been despatched to all the European Courts."[11]

The Omniscient Vocation of M. de Sartines

If the foregoing police administrators seem ineffectual, narrow minded and vindictive, and almost willfully unsuited to their posts, we must recall that nearly everything they tried to accomplish had to clear a path for itself as a form of governmental innovation. In some fashion or other each lieutenant general was a pioneer, with the shortcomings of a pioneer, and with the disingenuous frailties of the typical French courtier of the seventeenth or eighteenth century. As they experimented with police spying and repressions, these conniving careerists were teaching the other monarchs of Europe what Asiatic rulers had already learned through centuries of despotic experience.

De Sartines, of all those who commanded the Bourbon police before the outbreak of the revolution, was the most indefatigable and talented. He gained his earliest reputation by means of a ruse which was characteristic of the man and his times;[12] but what fame his omniscient espionage system earned him after that was the result of exceptional police surveillance. A popular anecdote concerning his merit tells of a statesman writing to De Sartines from Vienna to urge that a notorious Austrian robber—"who has taken refuge in Paris"—be arrested and returned in chains to his native country. The head of the French police replied at once that the wanted man was not anywhere in France but hidden in Vienna. He gave the criminal's address and the exact hours at which he entered or left that place of concealment as well as the disguises he commonly assumed. All of which information proved correct; the robber was surprised and made prisoner.

The president of the High Court at Lyons ventured to criticize De Sartines' ingenuities of supervision, adding that anyone could contrive to elude the police if he only planned it carefully. He offered to wager that he himself could slip into Paris and remain there for a week without being discovered by the spies of the police. De Sartines accepted the challenge. About a month later the judge left Lyons, traveled secretly to Paris, and obtained lodgings in a remote quarter of the city. By noon of that same day he received a letter from De Sartines, which was delivered at his new address, and which invited him to dine—and pay the wager.

During De Sartines' term of office it became a whim of the fashionable to have in thieves and pickpockets to exhibit the artistries of their calling. To oblige his friends the head of the police would send a troupe of rogues to any great house, where they cut watch chains, slit pockets and filched snuffboxes, purses and jewelry to amuse a notable gathering. De Sartines, a Spaniard by birth and of "indifferent education", had come to Paris to improve his social position and increase his fortune. While doing both he improved the methods of the police and very greatly increased the number of his agents. He seems to have been the first minister of state in Europe to enlist "reformed" criminals and ex-convicts as professional detectives and spies. Reproached for initiating so questionable a practice, he countered: "Where should I find honest folk who would agree to do such work?" Yet we shall meet him again enrolling Caron de Beaumarchais as an agent to combat the menace of that strangest of all intriguers, D'Éon de Beaumont, who had got around to blackmailing the king.

Lenoir, successor to De Sartines, was a lieutenant general so addicted to espionage that he cared much less about protecting society than cataloguing its imperfections. His agents achieved something as close to absolute ubiquity as any secret-service network known to this record. Not until we come upon the volume of military espionage which Stieber, the peerless Prussian, spread over the invasion zones of France before 1870 shall we meet a similar horde of commonplace petty spies. Servants were only allowed to take employment on condition that they would keep Lenoir's police informed of all that went on in the houses where they served. Vendors in the streets were all in the lieutenant general's pay. He also bribed prominent members of the many existing thieves' associations; and they enjoyed his sufferance in return for betraying their confederates. The gambling houses were now openly "protected" by the police so long as they yielded up a percentage of their profits and reported the names of all clients and whatever occurred. People of social standing who had become entangled with the law were pardoned without trial or scandal if they agreed to spy upon their friends and guests and give information of everything Lenoir's tedious register of a brain thought worth the knowing. One of his best agents was a celebrated hostess of Paris, who gave costly parties and then came clandestinely, by a private staircase, to the headquarters of the police with her latest budget of intelligence.

Thiroux de Crosne, the last and not the least eccentric of these barometers of a declining royalism, had to tread gently about a city already mined beneath his feet. With the convulsions that would bring the ancien régime to an end quivering on the threshold of history, this official spent all his energies upon theatrical censorship, keeping his secret agents engaged in reporting how often this or that line or phrase of dialogue was applauded. De Crosne was ready to clap anybody into prison who dared affront a powerful aristocrat, and was far more eager to apprehend critics and pamphleteers than footpads, coiners, burglars or other nonpolitical malefactors.

The police, resolved to spare Louis XVI the contamination of reading the innumerable libels and manifestoes flashing into print, arranged to prevent all printed matter from reaching him. De Crosne's absurd abuses of the censorship were among the primary causes of the outbreak of the revolution; and this interdiction upon the sovereign's mind kept him from gauging the tendencies of his times or the sharply veering trend of public opinion. Growing weary of the vague and disquieting rumors that penetrated to the palace, the king ordered Blaizot, a bookseller, to send him everything that was being published. Soon he could surprise his ministers with the knowledge he had acquired; and that set them frantically to tracking down the "leak" in royal seclusion. Blaizot was easily discovered and whisked off to the Bastille. When the king, wondering why his freshet of pamphlets had dried up at the source, made inquiries, he learned that poor Blaizot was detained without trial by royal order for the sole offense of having obeyed a royal order.

Chapter Twenty

THE BEWITCHING CHEVALIER

THE THEORIES of despotic government exploited by the Pompadour and her creatures provoked so much political espionage that the level of ability in individual secret agents sank to the gutter—where, in any epoch of tyranny or terror, it is always best to begin looking for it. And yet into the middle of the eighteenth century, as a fitting herald of its many French celebrities of secret service waiting in the wings, there strolls a bewildering, adventurous figure who was soldier and spy, diplomatist and blackmailer, and probably the most gifted female impersonator who ever lived. That fascinating beauty who made the long hard journey to Russia in 1755 as a clandestine courier and emissary of Louis XV of France was Charles Geneviève Louis Auguste André Timothée d'Éon de Beaumont—the Chevalier d'Éon, who elected to visit St Petersburg as Mademoiselle Lia de Beaumont and who only thus succeeded in baffling the adversaries of France then surrounding Tsarina Elizabeth. The international situation was not unduly complicated, but in Russia an envoy of King Louis suffered an extraordinary handicap. Nothing could be accomplished at the Russian court without bribery; and agents of George II of England had been unscrupulous enough to get there first and corner the market.

King George suspected that France and Prussia had designs upon his precious native state of Hanover. And as this was an era when the English crown bought soldiers in any available foreign market, the British ambassador to the Russian court had offered a handsome subsidy of £500,000 if Chancellor Bestucheff would supply 60,000 rugged Russian peasants drilled and equipped for an heroic part in a quarrel they need not comprehend. Ambassador Dickens resigned and was replaced by Williams, who presently arranged a convention by which Russia agreed to march 30,000 men to the aid of King George or the allies of Hanover in return for an unspecified amount of English gold. The convention was not immediately binding but had to be ratified two months from the date of signing.

Having learned this much through anti-British intermediaries—who seem to have exhausted their capacity to serve him—Louis XV decided to reopen diplomatic negotiations with the tsarina, a stroke which would probably invalidate the English treaty. All his attempts to communicate directly with Elizabeth were frustrated, however, by pro-British Russians or agents in the pay of Britain; and when the Chevalier de Valcroissant made a resolute effort to tender his respects to the tsarina, he was taken into custody and imprisoned in a fortress, charged with espionage. Spies of the party headed by Bestucheff surrounded the tsarina. The chancellor, no doubt heavily bribed, did not mean to allow the bargain struck with the British king to be checkmated.

Now the young Chevalier d'Éon, who would one day be the object of many a famous wager, had disclosed much promise in his childhood, even though his mother—for some never clearly established reason—had dressed him in girl's clothes at the age of four,[1] and he had continued to wear those unnatural habiliments until he was seven. In adolescence he excelled both in the study of law and the exercise of fencing. He had taken his degree as doctor of civil and canonical law when his young companions were just beginning to master Latin, and had straightway been admitted to the bar in his native city of Tonnerre. A slight, delicate-appearing youth, who had excited only the ridicule of the reckless young men frequenting the city's best fencing school, D'Éon soon presented such skill with foils and rapier that he was elected grand prévôt of the salle d'armes.

An agile mind harmoniously conferred upon an equally agile, energetic body drew the chevalier away from quiet Tonnerre, celebrated for its wine rather than as a center of law or letters. He had composed a treatise upon the finances of France under Louis XIV, which brought him to the notice of that great monarch's successor. Louis XV had expected to employ D'Éon, lawyer and fencer, in his ministry of finance—where an agile step and subtle mind were welcome as the country sank steadily deeper into debt—but then the sudden need for a peculiarly gifted secret agent recommended this comely youth for the mission to Muscovy. Of all Frenchmen he seemed the best fitted to cross swords with Bestucheff.

The Lady Has a Book

D'Éon and his companion on the hazardous mission, a Chevalier Douglass, joined forces at Anhalt. Douglass was said to be "travelling for his health", an ironic label to put upon a French spy bent on thrusting his head into the icy jaws of Petersburg hospitality. Beauty of surroundings as well as travel seemed to have been prescribed for the health of Douglass, for he had brought along his "niece", the lovely "Lia de Beaumont." Having come to Germany by way of Sweden, Douglass further masked his Russian objective by going into Bohemia to look at some mining properties. His niece, presumably not much interested in mines, was an inveterate reader—slow but unrelenting. Young D'Éon, before ever setting out from Versailles, had been given a handsomely bound copy of Montesquieu's *L'Esprit des Lois,* which remained the constant solace of "Mademoiselle Lia", though she appeared to find it rather hard to digest. Or perhaps the serious-minded young lady was learning the whole work by heart?

There lay concealed between the boards of the volume's fine binding an autographed letter from Louis XV to the Tsarina Elizabeth, inviting her to enter upon a very secret correspondence with the ruler of France. The book also hid a special cipher which Louis wished the tsarina and her anti-British—potentially pro-French—vice-chancellor, Woronzoff, to use when writing him. D'Éon had to pose, then, not alone as a woman and dutiful niece, but as one so intellectually voracious yet optically indolent as never for a moment to let go of the precious printed hiding place of royal invitation and cipher.

Montesquieu's devoted reader was seen and described on this foreign journey, "her" world première in secret service, as "small and slight, with a pink and white complexion and pleasing, gentle expression." And the melodious voice of D'Éon went a long way toward completing his masterly disguise. He wisely chose to play the reserved and shy rather than haughty, coquettish, mysterious, or otherwise blessed damozel. It would have added a considerable handicap if she proved too attractive to men; and yet there is indisputable evidence that shows "Lia" did attract them. Court artists repeatedly solicited the honor of painting the portrait of "Mademoiselle de Beaumont." Several were so fascinated and eloquent about it, the commissions had to be granted. Paintings and miniatures survive to fortify D'Éon's renown as the first and greatest of impersonator-spies.

At Anhalt where the two impostors met to try out their uncle-and-niece masquerade, D'Éon and Douglass were accepted by fashionable society and urged to extend their visit. The excuse of health had to be trotted out in order to speed Louis' agents off along the rutted road to St Petersburg. Arriving at length in Elizabeth's capital, the travelers were welcomed to the home of M. Michael, a Frenchman profitably engaged in international banking.[2] Nobody questioned the fair "Lia"; but whenever pertinent queries beset Douglass he resorted to a painful fit of coughing and then added the obvious about his physicians' orders to spend some time in a cold climate.

Russia was cold enough, though not to "Mademoiselle Lia." Her confederate, however, made no progress; he was blocked by Bestucheff's agents on every avenue to the tsarina that a French gentleman in poor health, with an acknowledged interest in the fur trade and the manners of a courtier, could hope to travel. Douglass carried a handsome tortoise-shell snuffbox to which he clung as though it also was something by Montesquieu. Under the false bottom of that snuffbox were hidden the French agents' instructions and another cipher for their personal use. But Douglass had not yet employed the cipher as there was nothing to report—until his "niece" contrived to meet Woronzoff and found the vice-chancellor as well disposed toward France as King Louis' informants had predicted. It was Woronzoff who presented the lovely "Lia" to Tsarina Elizabeth.

The autocrat of all the Russias was an eccentric old woman who prolonged her life with a rich diet of flattery, youth and pleasure. And "Mademoiselle de Beaumont" proved a caterer's masterstroke. She represented *French* youth, foreign gaiety, a fragrant blossom strangely blown north from the garden of a monarch whose reign was already noted for adultery, having broken the record successively established by François I, Henri IV and Louis XIV. Elizabeth had heard of the scandalous *Parc aux Cerfs,* the first efficiently organized and systematically recruited harem ever conferred upon a Catholic king. And yet here was the lovely, innocent niece of Chevalier·Douglass more suitably adorning the court of St Petersburg.

Owing to his incomparable masquerade, D'Éon became a powerful favorite overnight and was presently appointed a "maid of honor" and then a reader to the aged empress. We may be sure that the first book "Lia" offered Elizabeth was her own treasured copy of *L'Esprit des Lois.*

To Lord Holderness in London the British ambassador, Williams, was soon confiding: "I regret to inform you that the Chancellor [Bestucheff] is finding it impossible to induce Her Majesty to sign the Treaty which we so earnestly desire."

Missions of Blackmail

The time came when young D'Éon, having brilliantly discharged several important diplomatic missions for King Louis, was officially recalled to Paris. It would seem that the tsarina was still devoted to him and that the feminine disguise had long since been abandoned, for Elizabeth is said to have urged the French agent to accept a post in her government and to have offered him a title and high rank in the imperial army. D'Éon, never more diplomatic, was able to decline without giving offense, and received a superb snuffbox encrusted with diamonds as a token of the old sovereign's admiration and esteem.

Louis XV appears to have been hardly less appreciative. D'Éon was publicly granted an annual revenue of 3,000 livres and regularly employed as a diplomatic representative. He was sent again into Russia and to other countries where some entanglement of statecraft called for his light, beguiling touch. At times D'Éon required heavier batteries of charm for his government mission, and so the fascinating "Lia de Beaumont" once again had to be powdered, perfumed, curled and adorned for the greater glory of French diplomacy. But when France went to war the young adventurer insisted upon taking his proper place in the army. He was made aide-de-camp to the Duc de Broglie, who as head of the royal secret service elected to employ his aid only in espionage and intrigue; however, D'Éon is reputed to have distinguished himself at a critical juncture of one engagement when he brought up an ammunition train while under heavy fire from enemy field pieces.

Being able to ornament the great world of court intrigue as an artless demoiselle, and discharging his duties on the battlefield as an officer and gentleman, D'Éon led a far more rounded life than it is given most professional secret agents to encompass. He was ultimately accredited to London as a diplomat and met with extraordinary success in his new field of duplicities. Acting as secretary to the Duc de Nivernais, then French ambassador, D'Éon busied himself behind the scenes while Louis XV and his minister, Choiseul, were endeavoring to negotiate a treaty with Britain which was meant to spare France from British attack until Louis felt prepared and ready to declare war. By what the *Cambridge Modern History* terms a "discreditable artifice", Nivernais' secretary had been able to forward to the gratified Choiseul accurate copies of highly confidential instructions to Bedford, with whom Choiseul was engaged in final negotiation of the treaty.

D'Éon's artifice—which was so effective it won him the uncommon distinction of being mentioned by name, as a spy, in a standard work of history—may seem discreditable, but hardly more so than the double-dealing of his royal master's foreign policy. It was clever enough, but deserves no fame as a master stroke of ingenuity. A congenial undersecretary of the British Foreign Office called upon Nivernais and D'Éon, it appears, while bearing a portfolio stuffed with official documents. The hospitality of the French embassy put him off guard, and some very excellent Chablis distracted him from D'Éon and the interesting portfolio. The chevalier excused himself for a moment; and as he left the room the portfolio went with him. Then, with a speed appropriate to the rare opportunity, he sifted through the contents of the portfolio and contrived to copy out all the secret instructions from Bute, intended to be seen by no one in France save the British negotiator, Bedford. The deceived undersecretary was still praising the Chablis and drinking more of it when D'Éon, with a word of apology for his absence, rejoined the ambassador and their English guest. The portfolio looked quite unruffled by its experience of French espionage.

The Duc de Choiseul gained immense advantage from this quick-witted and light-fingered enterprise. Bedford in all their final negotiations was repeatedly disconcerted "by the fact that the tenor of his instructions was perfectly known to Choiseul."[3] And because he learned nothing of D'Éon's exploit, Bedford persisted in the belief that he had been deliberately betrayed by his colleague, Bute, and so resigned the privy seal on returning to England. Subsequently, under the same misapprehension, he declined to accept the presidency of the council which had become vacant with the recent death of Granville. D'Éon thus curiously exerted a degree of pressure upon current British political alignments; not that it availed him anything, however, for his very successes in London were to signal the beginning of his own eclipse. He was indispensable to Nivernais, he was the trusted agent of Louis XV, whereat there fell upon his career the inevitable blight of the fading favorite, Pompadour, whose jealous suspicion of any confidant of King Louis was prompt and pathological.

D'Éon was now conducting a very private correspondence with the French king, while acting as an intermediary and transmitting to Louis the reports of an eminent military spy. After the crushing defeat at Rossbach of the Pompadour-picked incompetent, Soubise, the noted French engineer and military tactician, Marquis de la Rozière, had been taken prisoner by Frederick the Great. The French high command had immediately offered to exchange him for any one or any number of Prussians whom Frederick might name; and the king, in refusing, had observed: "As I have been lucky enough to take so distinguished an officer, I mean to keep him as long as possible." And so we come to the time when Rozière, having been exchanged, was risking a more uncomfortable form of detention by spying upon the English. He had been instructed to co-operate with D'Éon in London while making "a quiet but thorough study" of the Channel counties to decide "how a French army could best descend upon England."[4]

Now the energetic intriguer of the French embassy in London did more than receive and convey to Rozière the private admonitions and advice of their king; he kept a file of all original writings which passed through his hands. And the day was not far distant when he had need of just such a lance and buckler, for prodding and for countering foul and frequent blows. Louis XV had raised the chevalier to the

An old and authentic secret-service drawing: the "insect" with which a military spy masked his sketch of enemy fortifications.

diplomatic rank of minister plenipotentiary. The espionage mission along the English coast had been successfully concluded without detection, and the Bourbon "Bonaparte" was warmly cherishing his scheme of a surprise descent upon Albion. But suddenly the blow fell—upon D'Éon. A nobleman who as ambassador outranked him, a distant relative of his whom he had reason to account a personal enemy, was sent to London to supersede him. This was virtually a public demotion; he was a subordinate again. The jealousy of Pompadour and his clique of enemies had combined to pull him down.

The most persuasive complaint lodged against D'Éon concerned his extravagance, his insatiable love of luxuries. Louis had rewarded him with generous grants of money; but the chevalier persistently drowned himself in debt. He was not, however, defenseless against the barbs of calculated humiliation or without the equivalent of wealth. He had the letters of Pompadour's king—damning documents every one, exposing the plot against peace and against England, the Rozière and D'Éon spying, the insidious planning of invasion. Matters to inflame the English public, a cargo of high explosives if turned

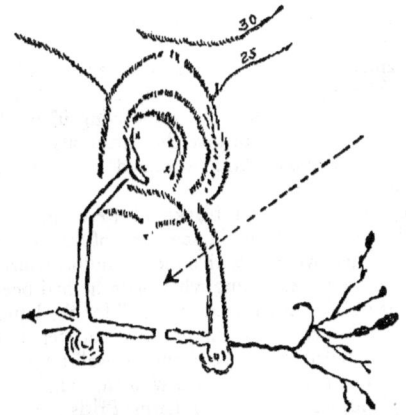

Design of fortifications concealed by the "insect."

over to the British parliamentary Opposition. D'Éon alone held these authentic grenades, which might readily provoke war between Britain and France, and only D'Éon knew where they were concealed.

From France came a peculiar outpouring of royal promises, threats, entreaties and commands. One missive reminded the chevalier how usefully he had served his king "in women's garments" and advised him to reassume feminine attire and at once "return to Paris." D'Éon went instead into a profound reverie. He knew all about that volatile commodity, the gratitude of princes. His enemies were triumphant; with Pompadour's ungrudging leverage they had overthrown and humbled him. But he seriously doubted whether his mere recall from London would appease their courtier appetites for vengeful demolition. D'Éon paid England the compliment of seeking sanctuary within the borders of a country whose state secrets he had formerly purloined. And he was not disappointed. English partisans and English justice did not retaliate by betraying him to the despised French autocrat.

John Wilkes, that unorthodox idol of the London masses, was D'Éon's friend and champion. But virtually all England seems to have enlisted in his cause. With a secret agent's instinct for self-effacement the chevalier tried at first to cover up his private warfare. But after he had been nearly poisoned—by his successor, the French ambassador, so he said—and there had been several attempts to kidnap him, he launched a campaign in the English press against his "alien" foes. D'Éon hired himself a bodyguard, men he had known in secret service, in the army, or French deserters living in England. He advertised his skill as a duelist to give the cutthroats on the other side something to worry about. And he rallied all his reserves of cunning and popular appeal.

Meanwhile, the fine arts of blackmail were quietly flaying the thick- and thin-skinned alike in the sanctums of the French monarchy. D'Éon addressed his sovereign with oblique candor, assuring him of his continued loyalty but mentioning what price he had been offered by his true friends of "the English Opposition" for the letters damnably exposing England's archenemy. Finding that counter-attacks of melodramatic violence failed them, the French Royalist agents resorted to the law. D'Éon lost his case in court, won the sympathy of half the people of England, and suffered no harm. British attempts to trace and arrest him were mere gestures of diplomacy. The man who dared to blackmail a king had simply disappeared into the custody of Wilkes and a resolute contingent of Bourbon-baiting partisans.

Another act of the melodramatic comic opera was played before an English audience, now as decisively divided for or against D'Éon as it was split, pro- or anti-Wilkes. French spies tried everything to trick, trap, discredit and ruin the beleaguered chevalier. Pamphlets of propaganda excoriated him. And his reply was a salvo right on the target: he published a few of King Louis' letters packed with indiscreet confidences. But he began only with the mildest, hinting bleakly of the hurricane to come.

This historic undercover struggle, fought in the dark with a liberal use of spotlights, became the fashionable fad of Londoners and might still be playing revivals if anybody had troubled to write a first-rate musical score. One day the chevalier heard weird cries and groans in the wall of his drawing room. Instead of reporting this incredible oddity, he took immediate action, begriming himself and some very elegant apparel to "clean" the chimney by thrusting up from the fireplace with his rapier. Whereupon he made prisoner a cringing chimney sweep who confessed that he had been hired by an agent of the French abassador to "haunt" the chimneys of D'Éon's dwelling. If D'Éon had reported hearing sounds the origin of which could not be discovered by outside investigators, that deranged imagining would have been used to support an insanity charge which his foes were now preparing to lodge against the diplomatist-spy.

Such maneuvering really alarmed D'Éon; and he hit back harder than ever, releasing more of the royal letters to be translated and published in England. He had heard tell of the girl inmate of the *Parc aux Cerfs* who, after Damiens' attempt upon the life of Louis XV —January 5, 1757—clung to her master on his return, crying: "Do not leave me, dear Sire. I thought I should have gone mad from grief when they tried to kill you!" And because "it would not have done for the mystery of the King's incognito to be solved,"[5] and the unfortunate girl had persisted in her fond identification, Louis had allowed her to be declared insane and confined thereafter in a lunatic asylum. D'Éon's blackmailing project thus became secondary to his dread of a more unscrupulous and powerful adversary. But the cards he had up his sleeve were all trumps.

What samples the British public had seen of the correspondence of Louis XV had provoked so much hostility, it became evident even to a Bourbon that D'Éon's campaign of revelations would, if he persisted, lead to war. Whereupon the chevalier practically dictated terms—in exchange for the letters, an annual grant of 12,000 livres and his renewed employment abroad in French secret service. D'Éon put no faith, however, in extorted concessions, and by way of continuing to safeguard himself held back several of the most incriminatory documents.

Negotiations for these were proceeding when Louis XV died. The new king and his ministers also appear to have respected D'Éon's invincible power to make trouble for France in England. But the price he was asking seemed altogether too high; and so a clever and practiced emissary was sent to London to bargain with the most celebrated adventurer of his day. This emissary was Caron de Beaumarchais, a considerable adventurer in his own right; and his coming to England at this time proved—quite apart from D'Éon's blackmail —of striking and historic consequence.

Chapter Twenty-one

CARON DE BEAUMARCHAIS, *ALIAS* NORAC

THE CREATOR of *The Marriage of Figaro* and *The Barber of Seville* was now forty-two and had crowded more than half his years with every form of excitement, speculation and public dispute, with duels, arrests, imprisonments and exiles, and with enough sentimental adventures even to provoke rumors that accused him of poisoning three wives, though he had never had but two and had poisoned neither of them. The son of a watchmaker, Augustin Caron, he had been apprenticed at the age of thirteen to his father's trade and, after various boyish escapades, had given his first proof of genius—a genius mainly for self-exploitation—by perfecting a design which made possible the manufacture of watches in very small sizes. Dainty Caron timepieces became the rage of fashionable Paris; and when a rival watchmaker borrowed the invention, its young originator scored a publicity coup by appealing not to the courts but to the august Academy of Sciences.

Presently he was *horloger du roi* and married to a widow some years his senior, whose wealth enabled him to purchase a patent of nobility. He soon abandoned watchmaking, for again his wife's affection and her widow's fortune intervened to secure him the desirable post of comptroller of the royal pantry. In appropriately rich attire he now supported the platter bearing the king's meat, and, since he had qualified with his title of nobility, he was even permitted to place it before the king. It is impossible here to survey the diverse foundations of the ensuing careers of Pierre Augustin Caron de Beaumarchais. He loved, it has been said,[1] "everything—renown, money, philosophy, pleasure, and, above all, noise." And we find him next a teacher of music, appointed to instruct those lonely ladies, the four neglected daughters of Louis XV.

It is curious to observe that this sedate and solacing enterprise marked his debut in a special kind of secret service. He was privately employed as an agent of the noted banker, Paris Duverney, one of the three Duverney brothers who had given a democratic demonstration in an absolute monarchy by starting life as potboys in their father's café. These Duverneys had boldly resisted John Law's paper-money and stock-jobbing craze, had trusted in gold and hoarded it, and even gone to prison for love of it. There was a Duverney employee named Poisson, and when this Poisson's daughter became the Marquise de Pompadour, the hard-money fortunes of Paris Duverney and his brothers had not only been "made" but made supreme in the kingdom of France. However, the statesmanship of Pitt and the generalship of Frederick the Great had terribly humbled French arms in the Seven Years' War; and Paris Duverney, adviser to Pompadour, had suffered a hard jolt from the recoil of Rossbach, Crefeld and Fellinghausen. Determined to re-establish himself in favor, Duverney decided to turn philanthropic and proposed, of all things, to found a young ladies' seminary at Saint-Cyr. This institution later became the famous French military academy; but all that was martial about its inception was the hope of making king, court and people forget a war that had cost France a million men, two and a half milliards of francs, and the catastrophic Treaty of Paris (1763) which amputated the Indies, Canada, several islands of the Antilles and Senegal. Those trophies passed to Britain; while France ceded Louisiana to Spain, an ally during the last years of the ruinous war. And to wipe away the stain of this stupendous misadventure the shrewd Duverney, who knew the trivial temper of the court and already had Pompadour's approval, engaged Beaumarchais, music tutor to Mesdames the king's daughters, to win for his philanthropy the measured enthusiasm of four obscure and maturing spinster princesses.

Beaumarchais traveled many roads thereafter, some of them simultaneously, but he was not regularly engaged in secret service until he had met with calamity and public disgrace. We cannot follow here the extended complexities of the Goezman case. Beaumarchais had been accused of forgery and of attempting to bribe a judge—through his wife—to render a verdict of acquittal. The French Parlement condemned him for that, required him to hear its verdict kneeling, and issued against him a decree of *blâme,* pronouncing him *infâme* and depriving him of French citizenship and all civil rights. There was, however, some compensation: "All Paris left their cards at my door the day following my conviction," Beaumarchais later on exulted; and a royal prince had entertained in his honor the very night after judgment was passed upon him. Beaumarchais had been unable to secure an advocate to defend him and so, in his own defense, had composed those *Memorials,* exposing the Parlement which was trying him with such fiercely abusive eloquence that he became the hero of restless, bankrupt, prerevolutionary France.

De Sartines, the minister of police, warned the convicted adventurer against his own popularity. "It is not enough," he said, "to be *blâme*"—to be disgraced—"one must remain modest as well." Our friend De Sartines was himself being exceptionally modest and adroit at the time, serving two masters, or political camps, with tact and the clearest conception of self-interest. Louis XV still lived and Du Barry was the favorite, with a host of enemies who must not be handled too roughly; for two of them stood waiting in the wings like posterity, a younger couple soon to ascend the throne as Louis XVI and Marie Antoinette. Sartines, having no presentiment of the mastery of Joseph Fouché, not unjustly considered himself the best-informed police minister France had ever had; and it was his patriotic resolve to stay in office until Louis XV died, and then live long in power with the new king.

The police minister, as the confidant of Du Barry and her enemies as well, had suffered a certain uneasiness when summoned in private by the king's mistress to hear her latest complaint. De Sartines of the many spies was actually humiliated not to know the cause of her present mental malaise before she knew it herself. It turned out to be that fellow Morande again—Théveneau de Morande, exiled author and publisher, whose best sellers were all limited editions because his real profession was blackmail. Morande generally used little pamphlets to sever the purse strings of his intended prey; often a title page was all that had to be printed and displayed. He had led a gay life in the French demimonde before police investigations spurred him to operate abroad; and Du Barry—whose progress toward the royal bedchamber had been largely a matter of installment selling—had once lived with Morande as his mistress. But now she wished that past of hers forgotten, aspiring as she did to a "Maintenon" or morganatic contract with the aging Bourbon monarch. Morande had lately touched off a little pamphlet which he proposed exporting from England to France. Entitling it *Mémoires secrètes d'une fille publique*, he had packed it with his warmest recollections of the light-o'-love, Du Barry; and all that lady asked of De Sartines was instantaneous buying off of the blackmailer and permanent suppression of his brochure.

Beaumarchais to London

The manifold accomplishments as well as the escapades of Caron de Beaumarchais were well known to De Sartines, and the police minister deemed him ideally available for the mission to Morande. Beaumarchais justified this confidence by conducting his negotiations with the blackmailer so deftly, he bought Morande's silence, his manuscript and every existing printed copy of the pamphlet. In that clean sweep of the exposé of Du Barry's promiscuous youth vanished utterly.[2] Morande had been astounded by the royal offer of 32,000 livres; and Beaumarchais had returned in triumph to claim his own reward—restoration of his civil rights—when the sudden death of the king upset his calculations.

There was only a brief delay, however, and then the secret agent went back to London as the representative of King Louis XVI. His prompt extraction of the shark's teeth of Morande persuaded the new regime that at last an instrument had been found to deal with D'Éon. Those secret and incendiary letters, even though the indiscretion of the previous reign, still threatened to provoke England and lead to hostilities. D'Éon, as a man of rank who had formerly made for himself a distinguished career in the French diplomatic service, presented a different and more complex problem from any with which Beaumarchais had thus far contended. He was a blackmailer, too, yet a favorite in England and a renowned eccentric, who demanded an exorbitant price to torment the French monarchy and frequently appeared in woman's garb to mystify the English public. Beaumarchais found him "smoking, drinking and swearing like a German trooper", and, despite the blackmail and the perplexing wardrobe, decidedly engaging and congenial. D'Éon belonged to the bohemian coterie of John Wilkes, to whom he introduced Beaumarchais; and it was thus that the Frenchman came to know Arthur Lee, then representing the American colonies in London. Beaumarchais was appearing under the transparent pseudonym of "M. Norac." Lee had suffered the continuous attentions of a cloud of spies ever since arriving abroad; but he was attracted to the French secret agent, whose extraordinary charm was radiating all over London now that it had warmed up D'Éon. Lee and Beaumarchais became great friends.

One experience of espionage that had afflicted Arthur Lee was novel enough to bear repeating. The American envoy was in Berlin, where the British minister at the court of Frederick the Great was Hugh Elliot, an ambitious diplomat but twenty-five years old. Through the agency of a German servant of his legation the Briton managed to bribe other servants at the Hotel Corzica, where Lee had taken lodgings. Whereupon Lee's private journal was stolen—"borrowed" —rushed to the British Legation and copied. Elliot was entertaining friends at dinner. Dropping everything but goose quills and espionage they all fell to and began writing down the American's thoughts and daily notations. It took them more than six hours; and then the missing journal was mysteriously restored to Lee shortly after he returned from dining outside of Berlin and detected his loss.

Even that master of secret-service technique, Frederick the Great, was revolted by the excessive "zeal" of Elliot. The Prussian king wrote his minister at London: "What a worthy pupil of Bute! What an incomparable man is your goddam Elliot! (*Figaro's* very language!) In truth Englishmen should blush with shame for sending such ministers to foreign courts."

The friendship that in London developed between Arthur Lee and the versatile secret emissary of France, M. Norac, led straight to the subtle undertaking of providing supplies for the insurgents of America. The colonial debt to Beaumarchais for his work in behalf of the "cover" firm he founded, Roderique Hortalez et Cie., is an old and familiar story. Possibly many readers have not considered that vital French munitioning of the American forces an episode of international secret service; and Beaumarchais himself, though he loved the conspiracy and his own star role, never treated it as a seriously clandestine affair. When the first ships were to sail "in secret" with arms and gunpowder for Washington's troops Beaumarchais moved a theatrical company to the port of Bordeaux, put on *Figaro* and made a kind of festival of the splendidly furtive affair.

Chapter Twenty-two

THE FURTIVE PRACTICE OF DOCTOR BANCROFT

THE CLANDESTINE NATURE of the preparations for helping the rebellious American colonies was purely a diplomatic artifice. It fooled nobody and was not expected to; for the English were completely and accurately informed by a brilliant Intelligence system, and the sovereigns of France and Spain needed only a very little salve upon their consciences. Great Britain had given them ample precedent for secretly assisting the insurgent subjects of a rival monarchy. When Spain was at war with Morocco, England had furnished arms of all kinds to the natives and had repeated the performance by arming the enemies of Spain in Algiers. Perfidious Albion—the Marquis Grimaldi, prime minister of Spain, wrote to the Comte de Vergennes—had even extended this traffic to the Orient, supplying arms to the Moors to attack "our people in the Philippines." And Vergennes knew from his own agents that it had been English ships which, during the recent insurrection in Corsica, had kept Paoli well provided with gunpowder and muskets.

What Vergennes seems not to have known was the caliber and range of the British secret-service operations on French soil, and especially in Paris, now that the governing classes of France were openly sympathetic to colonies which were in revolt against George III. Vergennes subsequently complained that everything the American representatives did was known to the English ambassador, Lord Stormont, "who was always plaguing him with the detail." And Arthur Lee, in his unprinted journal, continues: "No one will be surprised at this who knows that we have no time or place appropriate to our consultation, but that servants, strangers and everyone was at liberty to enter and did constantly enter the room while we were talking about public business and that the papers relating to it lay open in rooms of common and continual resort."[1] But the British had never been disposed to rely upon the Americans' probable want of precautions; the artlessness of American diplomats had yet to become a byword in Europe. The British were then, as in more recent wars, confining their blundering to the uniformed forces. They had, as John Adams said, sent troops to the colonies to quell a revolution that did not exist and managed to make a revolution. Lord Suffolk in London and his assistant, the Honorable William Eden,[2] in charge of secret service left no pocket empty of bribes and no confidential document unscrutinized in a masterly effort to regain what the British generals were losing.

For five critical years, from 1776 to 1781, the British Foreign Office and the British king—for the record shows that George III owned a Mogul emperor's relish for spy reports—were kept far better informed of America's international relations than either General Washington or the Continental Congress. This triumphant output of British intelligence was accomplished in various ways, of which espionage and the corruption of certain ostentatiously loyal "Americans" in France were the most fruitful. The embassy over which Benjamin Franklin presided at Passy was a far more productive bureau of the British Secret Service than anything later established near Paris—by making use of Bourbon partisans—during the revolution and Napoleonic Wars. Franklin's friend and confidential assistant, "the gentle and kindly" Edward Bancroft, M.D., F.R.S., was a British spy of such conspicuous—yet private—worth that he came to be granted a pension of £1,000 a year. Whatever Franklin knew, Bancroft was in a position to learn through some form of prying or inquiry easily misrepresented as devotion to his duties. And whatever Franklin knew that Bancroft learned was immediately transmitted to Lord Weymouth or Lord Suffolk. Franklin, whom the French approved and trusted, all unwittingly got secrets out of them which went straight to London; and often those same secrets never reached America, since Bancroft the obstructionist, the detainer of dispatches, was only second to Bancroft the spy and deceiver, the unsuspected thief of Franco-American confidences.

Benjamin Franklin has always seemed a unique and appealing diplomat, an ideal choice as colonial envoy to a powerful Old-World ally. He has appeared to most of us, his admirers, as typically homespun, shrewd and persuasive, and it is sad to reflect that the sagacious innovator, scientist and man of the world—a world visibly enlarged by his novel ideas—might be declared, with but few other contenders, the *most duped* representative of America ever sent to a foreign power in time of war. Walter Hines Page's famous Anglomania, 1914–1917, was a half-hearted trickle of encouragement by comparison with the help Franklin was duped into rendering the British during the War of Independence. And as if this were not the utmost of secret intelligence contrivances, Lord Suffolk made Bancroft a central gem in a jewel-encrusted setting of traitors and spies, one of whom was

Silas Deane of Connecticut, colleague of Franklin and Arthur Lee and an American commissioner.

The evidence of state papers and the correspondence of George III, some of it published as recently as 1932, is complete and incontrovertible. Arthur Lee, one of the first to suspect Deane, was subsequently joined by John Adams, Jefferson and many other eminent contemporaries. Franklin and John Jay reluctantly turned against the man when they learned that he had been consorting with Benedict Arnold. But by that time all the damage Deane could do had been done.

Bancroft and Wentworth

It further establishes the counter-espionage discernment of Arthur Lee that he was first also in denouncing Bancroft as "a spy in the pay of the British government." Lee presented this charge to Franklin himself and, what is more, submitted evidence. Bancroft had repeatedly visited London and whenever there "was closeted with the Privy Council." This information came to Arthur Lee from his brother William, whose extraordinary political career in England gave him many advantages for such impromptu counter-spying. William Lee was not only a successful tobacco trader but from 1773 to 1774 had served as one of the two sheriffs of London, being then elected alderman for Aldgate in succession to John Shakespeare. That a citizen of Virginia, one of King George's most rebellious colonies, should be chosen for this influential post a few weeks after the battle of Lexington strikingly exhibits England's "incongruous state of popular opinion at the time towards America. No American had ever before been an alderman of London,"[3] which was an office held for life. The alderman was a highly respected city official with the responsibilities of a magistrate and of a leader of the freemen, or voters, of his ward. If William Lee deemed Dr Bancroft's conduct worthy of suspicion, he was not one to be moved by idle or malicious gossip; and his warning deserved every colonial patriot's attention.

Franklin, however, would have none of it. His ordinarily temperate and gracious manner deserted him in the face of Arthur Lee's accusation. Edward Bancroft was his old friend and devoted disciple; and great men have a tender regard for disciples. It was Lee who was thereafter treated as a culprit and "marplot" and denounced for what now may be discerned as an historic perspicacity. Franklin's unsparing faith was all the cloak for his espionage that Bancroft needed; and Franklin's indignation seems to have largely disarmed the brothers Lee. With his spying to provide him a respectable income

Bancroft turned his agile mind to another vocation. He had the born conspirator's gambling instinct, faith in his star, and was always on the brink of enriching himself by some lucky speculation. Franklin seems neither to have noticed nor resented these palpable excursions from science, medicine or affairs of state, and it is curious to discover that it was Bancroft's *British* employer who pronounced his emphatic objections.

King George III felt as much abhorrence of stock gambling as any lamb who ever ran, bleating, fleeced and shivering, past the philanthropic façade of a stock exchange. Once the English sovereign heard about Bancroft's incurable tendency to forget the war and have his speculative fling, he began to accuse him of gambling with his honor also. "The man is a double-spy," George exclaimed.[4] If he came over to sell Franklin's American secrets in London, why wouldn't such a fellow return to France with a British cargo for sale?

Bancroft always did pretend to bring back to Passy a "budget of information", news of British troop movements, of the British fleet at sea and of ministerial plans—intelligence cooked up by his employers to sound important, but generally false or already so out of date as to be harmless. This was a form of protective coloration suggested by gentlemen in London, who respected Franklin's intellect and integrity and feared lest "the gentle and kindly" Bancroft might make one trip too many. Franklin's mistrust of him, once aroused, would put an end forever to the doctor's archdeception. France and England were not yet at war, but it would be no trouble at all for the French authorities to discover an excuse for expelling Bancroft from their country.

We observe then that George III, at least in affairs of secret service, was not quite the blind and cantankerous old despot that his colonial opponents professed to descry upon the throne. Bancroft *was* acting the double spy; and George's own ministers had sponsored the dodge. To fortify American faith in Bancroft's secret service the British ministry even had him arrested for espionage; whereat the Continental Congress was induced to pay the doctor a salary for his dangerous endeavors, and it is of record that he wrote a letter of sharp reproof when once his pay as an American spy was delayed in transmission.

It seems incredible that Bancroft's frequent visits to London did not stir Franklin's suspicions or, at any rate, remind the great man of the warmth and conviction of the charges entertained by the Lees. However, if Bancroft was posing as an American agent, of course he had to go to England to attend to his spying. Actually he went there for three purposes—to report to Downing Street, to keep an eye on his "personal speculation in the funds", and to confer with one who was generally his partner, both in espionage for Britain and in speculative schemes. This close friend and intriguing colleague was Paul Wentworth, who belonged to a distinguished family of New Hampshire, had lived long in London, and excelled Bancroft both in cultivation and social connections. Not that the doctor lacked for social graces or intellectual attainments; though a native of Westfield, Mass., and a pupil, according to John Adams, of Silas Deane—whose earlier exploits included teaching school—Bancroft had afterward been educated in England and as a physician, "a naturalist and chemist, a man of versatile talents, a friend [in due course] of Franklin and Priestly",[5] who made discoveries in dyeing and calico printing, he came to be well received. Intimacy with Wentworth was one of the proofs of his standing; for Wentworth was by way of becoming that imperishable landmark, an English gentleman. A distant relative of the Marquis of Rockingham, he was the owner of a plantation in Surinam, where, in fact, some of Bancroft's experiments with "Tyrian" dyes were made.

Caron de Beaumarchais, with his dramatist's eye for an engaging schemer, commended "Wintweth" as "one of the cleverest men in England." And yet Paul Wentworth—cultivated, speaking French "as well as you do, and better than I," Beaumarchais reported to the Comte de Vergennes, lacking neither property, influence nor opportunities—through some dubious caprice of his aspiring colonial's nature enlisted as a political secret agent. According to one who has of late most thoroughly investigated his character, intentions and extensive correspondence,[6] Wentworth loathed the term "spy", yet was an insinuating and ceaseless espion, who expected from the British as his rewards "financial compensation, a baronetcy and a seat in Parliament." Wentworth's price—which he never collected—was not excessive, for he seems to have possessed those qualities we find supporting the most effective campaign of espionage. He seldom ran any risks himself, to be sure, but was undoubtedly an invaluable, masterly recruiting agent. Even Edward Bancroft, that great innocent, lived to protest that all his involvement in the intrigues of Downing Street must be attributed to Wentworth's irresistible persuasions.

However true that may have been, once the good and scientific Edward found himself involved he made himself a professional of the game. Bancroft's spying upon his friend and patron, Franklin—contemptible though it may seem—might develop a trace of apology in the state of mind of many other persons born in America. The excuse for Arnold's treason was his alleged belief that the colonies would only win their "freedom" to fall into the despotic hands of the French Bourbon monarchy. Perhaps Bancroft also cultivated in his nicely balanced intellect the justification that, after all, King George's tyrannies had been demagogically exaggerated. But what about Bancroft the British spy and Bancroft the French spy—in Ireland? That mission of his was unadulterated secret service.

In Lecky's great *History of England* this agent reappears: "But, no documental evidence exists of a French agent having been in Dublin in 1784, it is certain that five years later, i.e. in 1789, one Bancroft, an American by birth, was sent on a secret mission from France to Ireland." Bancroft went as a *French* agent to Ireland, but his report—preserved in the Foreign Office at Paris, according to Dr Fitzpatrick—proves clearly that he was still playing his double game and primarily obliging the government in London. Bancroft's findings took on such a discouraging tone, all thoughts in France of assisting Irish rebellion on the same terms as the recent colonial revolution in America were straightway abandoned. This little-understood exploit of the spy may actually have been worth more to Britain than all his precious pilfering of Franklin's secrets.

CHAPTER TWENTY-THREE

CLANDESTINE SPIRIT OF '76

THE AMERICAN REVOLUTION was a small war which has grown increasingly larger because of the growth and power of the republic that it founded and the thoughts of men that it helped to set free. But the actual operations of secret service in that far-reaching colonial conflict have only very recently been weighed and measured. If we were still to depend on the standard works of history, it could be seen at a glance that, since Captain Hale and Major André were hanged, and Benedict Arnold fled to the refuge of the British camp, there was virtually no espionage or Intelligence worth mentioning in the struggle for American independence.

General Washington, however, was too skillful a soldier to underestimate the value of accurate military information. He had witnessed in his youth the defeat of Braddock who had firmly neglected to determine the strength of the defenders of Fort Duquesne. When Nathan Hale, a resolute but inexperienced and ingenuous patriot spy, failed in his important mission, the American commander in chief appeared both to deplore the sacrifice of a brave young life and to abandon the problem of secret service as a weapon or a measure of defense. Only a few years ago records were uncovered which contradicted this by proving that George Washington did a far more practical, necessary and characteristic thing. Hale, with only one life to give to his country, perished miserably without knowing that he was giving much more, a priceless example.[1] Warned by Hale's misfortune, Washington proceeded to enlist persons in a military espionage *organization* who would play the deadly game gaily and with spirit and would know how to keep their work really secret. And so well was the lesson of Nathan Hale's sacrifice learned by them that one hundred and fifty years had to elapse before anybody detected the chain of his successors.[2]

Messages of vital concern to the cause of the revolting colonies passed back and forth between General Washington and his supporters in the city of New York, not intermittently, not by lucky accident, but regularly and throughout the war of independence. Both espionage and counter-espionage were the result. If we take into account the poor equipment of the Continental forces, the inexperience of most of the officers, the primitive or pioneering aspect of the combat, of colonial fortifications, service of supply, naval co-operation and—including the British—plans of campaign, the impromptu development of efficient and thoroughly "modern" secret service is astonishing to find.

Washington was as cleverly and inventively served by his civilian intelligence corps as any European commander of his century. From Charles XII, Marlborough, Prince Eugene and Villars to Kellermann, Hoche, Moreau and Bonaparte, there was none who improvised a better service and none who had poorer means of financing that inevitably expensive arm. Amherst and Wolfe,[2] campaigning in North America, were practically without the assistance of espionage. Washington's spies, though less numerous, compare in caliber with the secret agents of Frederick the Great, the "father of Prussian spies", or with those of Maurice de Saxe, the father of most of the military secret-service innovations attributed to the genius of Frederick.

General Washington, as the leader of a cause, had the superior advantages which we shall presently find accruing to the British Intelligence in making use of French Royalists in its prolonged duel with Napoleon. Washington could rely upon the devotedness of partisans. Great risks and sacrifices might be asked of ardent young adherents to the colonial revolutionary cause; and sacrificial ardor is the very bloodstream of patriotic secret service. The first news of the first sacrifice—the hanging of Nathan Hale, which occurred some time in the month of September, 1776—was brought to the American forces by Captain John Montressor of the Royal Engineers, aide-de-camp to General Sir William Howe. He appeared on Harlem Plains, N. Y., and passed through the lines under a flag of truce, to be received by a group of American officers. Five months later the newspapers of the colonies began to publish garbled accounts of Hale's tragic misadventure in the service of his country.[4] He had admittedly blundered, had allowed himself to betray anxiety when questioned by the British, thus arousing their suspicion; and yet only through his failure was he able to exert a most salutary influence upon the Revolutionary cause.

On account of the event depriving Hale of his life and Washington of the valuable information that he was reputed to have had in his possession when arrested,[5] the American commander in chief became convinced of the need of improvising a secret service which, being more carefully planned and adroitly established, would prove far less liable to disappointing results. John Morin Scott was first delegated to organize a bureau of secret service, but before he could accomplish this—and for reasons never disclosed—he was required to resign. Whereupon Major Benjamin Tallmadge of the Second Regiment, Light Dragoons, was requested by Washington to undertake the task.

Tallmadge, Nathan Hale and his brother, Enoch, and Robert Townsend had all been members of the class of 1773 at Yale. It is possible, therefore, that some sentimental considerations influenced the selection of Tallmadge and the subsequent, and even more vital, enlistment of Townsend. Hale's classmates, whether or not they were also his comrades-in-arms, we may assume were the most aroused by his execution and most bitterly resentful of the harsh treatment which he was known to have suffered at the hands of the British provost, Cunningham.[6] Tallmadge may even have asked to be allowed to take charge of the new espionage system required in the vicinity of New York. That he had not had any more experience than Hale seems obvious; and the aptitude for military secret-service work discovered in him—the very instincts Hale had lacked—must have been mainly the result of one of those lucky accidents without which no war has ever been won.

The Code of the Black Petticoat

When an army major turns up in secret service there is always the likelihood he was transferred to it because of his undistinguished appearance on horseback or his inability to command a battalion of infantry; but when, in time of war, a civilian is found importantly connected with military espionage, it is more than likely that he has established his qualifications, consulted his conscience, and persistently applied for the post. Benjamin Tallmadge's great collaborator, Robert Townsend of Oyster Bay, N. Y., adds a name to the register of American colonial heroes that is little known and little honored in the United States today. Yet Townsend was the one dominating figure of the American secret service in the Revolution. Some records indicate that he was the personal choice of General Washington; it is indisputably evident that he earned and retained his commander in chief's confidence and gratitude. This young patriot of Long Island belongs in our "headquarters company" of instinctively gifted architects of secret-service organization; and the conflicts of North America will hereafter introduce only one other such self-made conspirator and civilian secret agent who, in a different war but in not dissimilar circumstances, proved Robert Townsend's peer—Miss Elizabeth van Lew.

When General Washington selected Townsend and Tallmadge to undertake the formation and management of a spy system in the city of New York, he was asking the former to wager his life against the vigilance of the British in and around their own general headquarters and the far more dangerous, vindictive counter-spying alertness of the Tories. And this was to continue for the duration of the war. Situated as it was, the port of New York provided an ideal base for the military forces of King George. With a strong fleet to blockade the coast and cover the line of communication and supply, with fresh convoys bringing guns, munitions and men, it must have been clear to Washington—and to any rebel observer like Townsend—that the island of Manhattan would be the last strong point in the thirteen colonies to cease being British.

Spying so near headquarters—all important as that was—combined with the never diminishing difficulties of getting reports through the lines, was the sort of mission that called for a veteran, some accomplished technician from the day and night schools of European intrigue. Washington, however, had no such operative to enlist; and happily, as it turned out, he did not need him. He had Robert Townsend, who had it in him to become one of the great amateurs of the patriot sport of spying; while Townsend had devotedly loyal and resourceful friends.

Abraham Woodhull, Austin Roe and Caleb Brewster—with Tallmadge always in charge of the Connecticut terminus—were the other links in this "chain", as Washington himself chose to call the men who so faithfully carried out his orders. At first these links of the well-forged chain that never weakened till American independence was won were masked by the nom de guerre, "Samuel Culper." But as the impromptu system of espionage discovered its own versatility and strength, the communicative tricks and concealments were improved. Woodhull thereafter signed himself "Samuel Culper, Sr," while Townsend became "Samuel Culper, Jr." To the end of the contest with the British, Major—presently Colonel—Tallmadge was referred to by all as "Mr John Bolton."

The master minds, Townsend and Woodhull, were endowed with youth, imagination, wealth and social position. They represented ideal "shock troops" to throw into an area overrun with Tories and turncoats. Townsend, though his home was at Oyster Bay, lived in New York and dipped into "trade", keeping a general store which was pretty obviously a blind as well as a first-rate magnet to British customers, who, when dropping in to buy, could be artfully pumped.

Young Woodhull stayed in his Setauket home, living there quietly and obscurely so as not to arouse anybody's suspicion. All the code messages that Townsend drew up were conveyed to Woodhull by Austin Roe, who was to communication what Townsend was to the espionage, but whose risks were the more acute on occasion as the chain system required that he spend the longest periods of time inside the British lines with incriminating papers upon him. Old documents —chiefly bills for fodder—have disclosed that he rode one of General Washington's horses. He kept it impudently stabled in New York City as a fitting neighbor to some of the elegant asses afflicting the English high command.

Roe's best disguise was his keen horsemanship. His name was frequently spoken in Revolutionary times; but like his colleagues he was not even remotely suspected of being an agent of Washington's secret service. He loved to ride in all kinds of weather; and riding from the heart of New York over the country roads of Long Island, he made frequent visits to the Townsend house at Oyster Bay, and often went beyond to Setauket, where he stopped at Abraham Woodhull's. And the object of these expeditions on horseback seemed outside the range of contemporary surmise.

As soon as Woodhull received one of the intelligence reports from New York, he hastened to the North Shore of Long Island to look for some wash on a clothesline. A black petticoat and a few handkerchiefs comprised the practical code of the spy chain at this point. It was the "fourth link", Caleb Brewster—an intrepid boatman, whose counter-spies were the winds and currents he surmounted while regularly plying his small craft from one side of Long Island Sound to the other—that hoisted the black petticoat to signal his arrival whenever he landed on the Long Island shore. The cove in which his boat lay was indicated by means of the arrangement of the handkerchiefs. Brewster, sometimes aided by Nathaniel Ruggles, also a patriot agent of the secret service, took the code messages—from Townsend to Roe to Woodhull—across to Connecticut where Tallmadge waited; and it was he who promptly transmitted them to General Washington.

As the espionage operations continued, Townsend sought to protect himself, Roe and the others by using invisible ink[7] and a complicated and arbitrary code. The first crude code of the secret agents was found to be inadequate, and a substitute was devised which was far more difficult to decipher because certain letters of the alphabet stood for other letters, and certain figures represented specific words, names of places or of individuals. Thus, a message from one of the "Culpers" reading—"Dqpeu Beyocpu agreeable to 28 met 723 not far from 727 & received a 356" translated to—"Jonas Hawkins agreeable to appointment met Robert Townsend not far from New York." The number 15 stood for advice; 286, ink; 592, ships; 711, General Washington; 712, General Clinton; 728, Long Island; 745, England. It was early in July 1779 that Tallmadge prepared a pocket dictionary in which this new and more baffling code was arranged. Undoubtedly copies were furnished the "Culpers" as well as American headquarters; but no exact copy of the code has survived,[8] and the only reference to it which has been found is in a letter from Washington, dated July 27, 1779.

The Counter-Spying Capture of Major André

General Washington gave strict orders that there should never be any delay in the forwarding of "Culper" messages. And only once did Benjamin Tallmadge venture to disobey, with results which may be said to have launched systematic military *counter-espionage* in North America.

British troops had occupied Oyster Bay, and British officers were quartered in the Townsend house. One night late in August 1780 the British Colonel Simcoe was entertaining a guest named André at the home of Washington's most effective spy. Sarah Townsend, Robert's young sister, supervised the serving of the dinner, and, as we shall see, gave thought to the kind of information her brother was always seeking for the American cause. Sarah saw a stranger enter and put a letter on the Townsend pantry shelf. It was addressed, she noted, to "John Anderson"; later she saw Simcoe's engaging guest open and read "Anderson's" letter and put it in his pocket. And still later she overheard André and Simcoe discussing the American's stronghold at West Point, where a great quantity of military stores—including much that Beaumarchais had shipped through his "cover" firm, Roderique Hortalez et Cie.—and magazines containing nearly the whole stock of powder of the Continental Army were known to be located.

Sarah Townsend, her suspicions increasing, now proposed and seconded herself as an agent of General Washington's secret service. Next morning she induced a susceptible British captain, Daniel Young, to send a messenger into New York to purchase supplies for Colonel Simcoe's entertainments. This messenger took with him a note from Sarah to her brother, Robert, informing him of André and "Anderson" and what she had heard discussed of the British objective, West Point. And no sooner did an English batman hand

Robert Townsend the message from Sarah than the links of the spy chain strained and grew taut under the pressure of one more emergency. Austin Roe was out of New York in no time and galloping over the scrublands of Long Island, Woodhull watched for the black petticoat, Brewster hoisted his sail, and so Sarah's warning came to Benjamin Tallmadge.

Now just before receiving the message from the "Oyster Bay branch" of the espionage service, Tallmadge had been handed a letter from General Benedict Arnold, in which the commandant at West Point mentioned that a friend, John Anderson, might pass Tallmadge's way. He requested that since Anderson was unfamiliar with the countryside, an escort of dragoons be granted to him. And right here we pause to pay further tribute to Washington and the unexceptionable secrecy of the Townsend secret service, inasmuch as Benedict Arnold, an officer of high rank and distinguished record, obviously knew nothing of Tallmadge's assignment as the fifth link in the invisible chain.

Major John André was well on his way to Arnold's headquarters when Tallmadge—disobeying orders—delayed Robert Townsend's latest communication by opening and reading it. What moved him to do so even the brilliant researches of Mr Morton Pennypacker have not as yet discovered. In the Townsend message Tallmadge found the same name, "John Anderson." He read what Sarah Townsend had heard André—or Anderson—discussing with Colonel Simcoe: how much the British Army stood to gain by seizing West Point. And Arnold's letter must suddenly have seemed ablaze in the palm of his hand.

Tallmadge continued to act with admirable initiative, changed his duties to counter-espionage and set out to trace and pursue the British major who now must be inside the American lines as a spy. However, as we know, André had already succeeded in making his way to West Point, where Arnold provided him with a plan of the fortifications and other documents, including an estimate of the attacking force required to take the stronghold. Ever since pretty Sarah Townsend had persuaded Captain Young to lend her the services of a British messenger, André's luck had been running out, and now it ebbed completely. The British sloop of war Vulture, in which he had ascended the Hudson, had been forced to drop downstream by the fire of an American shore battery. Meanwhile, André was conferring with the treacherous Arnold on the twenty-first and twenty-second of September. Upon discovering that he was cut off from the Vulture and must make his way overland to the British outposts, he accepted a pass from Arnold and "concealed" the incriminating papers, which were in Arnold's own handwriting, in his boot.

During the British occupation of Philadelphia the talented André had not only seemed to capture the affections of the Tory belle, Peggy Shippen—now Mrs Benedict Arnold—but also had played leading parts in those regimental theatricals which were among the chief diversions of the British garrison, together with the battles of Brandywine and Germantown. Perhaps assured that even a rebel army would not hang an amateur actor, Major André, before leaving Arnold, disregarded Sir Henry Clinton's explicit order,[9] disguised himself and thus became not a clandestine negotiator but a spy.

Three American militiamen, John Paulding, David Williams and Isaac van Wart, stopped André about 9 A.M. on the twenty-third at a point near Tarrytown, almost within sight of the British lines. His captors refused to abide by Arnold's example when the major promised them a generous sum in gold if they would escort him to the near-by English outpost. The bribe only consolidated their several suspicions; and they carried their prisoner straightway to Lieutenant Colonel John Jameson, commanding the Second Regiment of Light Dragoons. What words André used to persuade the cavalry commander to send him back to Benedict Arnold at West Point are forever lost to history; but André, the actor, must have read his lines with convincing distinction. And he would thus have escaped, as Arnold was to escape, if Tallmadge and the secret service had not turned up to prevent it.

Tallmadge returned to Jameson's camp that evening, heard about the prisoner, and that he called himself "John Anderson"—the very suspect Tallmadge, acting on the Townsends' information, had been seeking. Without revealing all that he knew, or how he came to know it, Tallmadge insisted that his superior officer order the prisoner intercepted on his way to West Point and brought back. Jameson reluctantly consented, but refused to recall a messenger who was carrying to Arnold news of "Anderson's" arrest.

Arnold was warned in time, owing to Jameson's blunder; André came to trial[10] and was condemned to die as ignominiously as Tallmadge's classmate, Hale, had died. André was liked by everyone; and the British put forth more exertion to save him from hanging than most of them devoted to the conduct of the war. Sir Henry Clinton may have regretted that the dictates of honor were so much more clearly defined than the principles of strategy. To one having his powers it must have been an aching temptation to exchange Arnold for André, thereby gratifying *both* armies. Sir Henry, since relieving

Howe, had violated nearly every known rule of good generalship; yet he could only be charged with indecision, poor judgment, leniency, or bad luck. If he had saved his accomplished young friend,[11] André, at Arnold's expense, however, he would have stood convicted of the unprincipled act of betraying a contemptible traitor.

Townsend in Dread of Reprisals

Agents of espionage who turn to counter-spying are more than likely to make trouble for themselves; and we find the Townsend chain was no exception. Having been instrumental in warning Tallmadge of the identity and probable mission of "Anderson", Robert Townsend seems to have feared some sort of betrayal, as a retaliation after the hanging of the popular Major André. He closed up his store in New York and kept it shut for three weeks. His accounts show that he spent about £500 at this time. General Washington's own carefully kept ledger reveals that, between 1775 and 1781, the American commander in chief spent but $17,617 on his espionage system, various payments being listed to "unnamed persons" in order to protect them from exposure.[12] The £500 expended by Townsend was a substantial sum in proportion to the whole secret-service outlay; and we may suspect that it came from his own pocket, that there were inferior persons with whom he dealt that might have denounced him —at least as an ardent colonial patriot—to the British, and that the sum he disbursed included "taking care of" the more doubtful with gifts or bribes.

One of the more personal of the "Culper." letters, dated eighteen days after André's execution, indicates that Robert Townsend left his post in New York City directly after the arrest of the English spy, without waiting for the more critical hours following his trial and condemnation.

       729   462   20th, 1780.

Sir, Yours of the 30th of Sept. & 6th of October are now before me. In answer to the first, W-s assurances are as much as I could expect. When I conclude to open another route you shall be informed of it. I do not choose that the person you mention, or any other of his character, should call on me.

I am happy to think that Arnold does not know my name. However, no person has been taken up on his information. I was not much surprised at his conduct, for it was no more than I expected of him. Genl. Clinton has introduced him to the General officers on parade as General Arnold in the British service, and he is much caressed by General Robinson. This will tend to gloss his character with the venal part of the enemy, but the independent part must hold him in contempt; and his name will stink to eternity with the generous of all parties.

I never felt more sensibly for the death of a person whom I knew only by sight, and had heard converse, than I did for Major Andre. He was a most amiable character. General Clinton was inconsolable for some days; and the army in general and inhabitants were much exasperated, and think that General Washington must have been destitute of feeling, or he would have saved him. I believe General Washington felt sincerely for him, and would have saved him if it could have been done with propriety.

The long time I have been out of town prevents my giving you any information of consequence. The army which embarked last week are generally supposed intended to make a diversion in Virginia or Cape Fear in North Carolina, to favour Lord Cornwallis—They take but few horses, but a number of saddles with an intention to mount a number of dismounted dragoons who are going with them. The Cork and English fleets are, I expect, arrived by this. I hope and expect that all my letters are destroyed after they are perused. I am yours &c.

SAMUEL CULPER Junior.[18]

With the exception of General Washington, all the men connected with the Townsend chain of secret service lived fifty years or more after the outbreak of the American Revolution. It is known that while he was President, Washington visited his former secret agents residing on Long Island. He appreciated the accurate intelligence they had forwarded throughout the war and was resolved that no harm should come to them. Documents relating to their espionage and to the work of other faithful spies[14] were sealed; and more than a century passed before the mysterious Culpers, senior and junior, were satisfactorily identified.

CHAPTER TWENTY-FOUR

LIBERTY, EQUALITY, FRATERNITY—INTRIGUE

CONSPIRACY, one may observe, is its own reward. Those induced to try it as an avocation are soon so enmeshed that all other considerations of the normal citizen lose significance. One dark night two men were sailing an angry sea in a frail, furtive craft that plunged and rolled and showed no lights. They were noted antagonists of Bonaparte, the Chouan leader, Georges Cadoudal, and a resolute Bourbon emissary, Baron Hyde de Neuville. As the latter describes it, in crossing the Channel they slept restlessly, and suddenly Cadoudal raised himself on one elbow and called with his powerful voice: "Do you know what we ought to advise the King to do? We ought to tell him that he ought to have both of us shot, for we shall never be anything but conspirators. We have taken the imprint."[1]

This occurred in the time of the Consulate, and the "king" was that prince called Louis XVIII, but as yet uncrowned, exiled, and in France all but forgotten. The anecdote reveals the typical optimism of your born conspirator, for Louis in the years of Consulate and Empire was politically so far removed from being Cadoudal's sovereign, he could only have had a Frenchman shot by committing suicide. However, the Chouan leader's observation is more typical of the France of 1789–1816 than any other to be mined from the mountain range of revolutionary memoirs.

The whole French nation took the imprint of conspiracy. It was in the air. It stands out as plainly as a trademark upon the age, upon most of the actors in the successive scenes of National Convention, Terror, Directory, Consulate, Empire and Bourbon Restoration. The bare record, naming and briefly identifying every known spy, counterspy, double spy, secret-service agent, every foreign emissary, petty plotter, or grand conspirator, every bribe-taker or bribe-giver, false witness, police informer, criminal impostor, or master of the intricate technique of political espionage, would overflow a small encyclopedia. For more than twenty-five years an ingenious, adaptable people lived under conditions which seem at once so furtive, frenzied and fantastic as to remain historically unique. England of the Puritans and Cromwell, the America of Washington, or even the Russia of Lenin and

Trotsky did not reproduce the same mingling of farce, tragedy, comedy and melodrama, the same glamor, horror and world impact. Never before or since has any land duplicated the devious superpolitics of this era in French history. Never again, perhaps, will the destiny of a continent hold the spotlight for that length of time in so artful and romantic a setting.

Pretensions of the rabble are nearly always comic; but the treacheries of desperate men in a time of social upheaval are the great revolution's leading donation to these annals of secret service. The whispered bargaining, betrayals, furtive informations and sinister conclaves of a typical day in 1793 or 1794 would crowd this volume. We can therefore give but little attention to other than the Olympian performers of the period, most of whom belong in the front rank, with few known peers and no superiors to be found among the Machiavellic brotherhood. France under the control of the jealous factions, the rival committees—of Public Safety and General Security—was aswarm with spies. A first-rate informer with a talent for wholesale, reckless denunciation was granted more privileges and deemed of greater value to the state than any soldier in the land. And it may be noted that there was no pervading sense of general security owing to the espionage of Public Safety, and no public safety anywhere because of the lurking agents of General Security.

A Spy-Persecutor's Persecution Mania

There was Héron of the High Police, a complex case, who accumulated dreadful power and a double income by getting himself employed by Public Safety to spy upon members of the Committee of General Security, who hired him to spy upon Public Safety. Héron's happiest occupation came, however, in denouncing his private enemies to one or the other of the committees which retained him. These quiet devastations of his personal acquaintance went a long way toward establishing his great repute for vigor, ability and faithfulness.

"When a person's name is slipped into a big list," said this instrument of justice and government, "events move by themselves. He is guillotined."[2] Yet such, we find, was not invariably the case; for, when Héron sought to divorce his wife, who had been unfaithful, by slipping her name into a "big list" of the condemned, one of his superiors refused to leave it there, thus preserving the lady for even more justifiable infidelities.

Since he was a police spy wholly without talent for genuine secret service, it is not surprising to learn that Robespierre and Fouquier-

Tinville were among those who defended him as "indispensable." Héron was a dangerous lunatic, but his lunacy did not endanger his admirers so long as it was kept within its disguise of patriotic vigilance. He—born in 1746—had served in the French navy; and just prior to the revolution a syndicate of bankers had paid his expenses to journey to Havana, where he seems to have failed to collect for them a large sum of money. But who knows? Possibly he did collect some of it, for ever afterward he hated bankers.

It was his rooted belief that they hounded him and spied upon him. Indeed, this spy felt surrounded by spies and was convinced that everybody was persecuting him. A number of people had declared him insane, and they were the poor fellow's tangible persecutors. During the attack upon the Tuileries in 1792 he had been wounded, and he had taken a hand in the massacre of the prisoners at Versailles; which sterling record commended him to the spymasters of the Committee of General Security. But soon, according to a more gifted operative of the High Police, Sénar—he who had declined to leave Mme Héron's name upon the list—General Security was mortally afraid of Héron, without daring to exclude him, "knowing the backing which he possessed from Robespierre."[3]

Sénar called him "Robespierre's *bouledogue*", and also "a veritable ogre ... the most crooked and perfidious of agents. He dominated, he influenced everywhere." Héron had somehow inherited the blood-drenched toga of the "brigand generalissimo" Malliard—Maillard of the September Massacre, whose gang of fifty ruffians one would rather have expected to soothe and poultice any persecution mania. But Héron still steadfastly believed himself persecuted. By his wife, the faithless trollop, and by her lover who had stolen thousands of francs from him, who can only have had thousands if he stole them from the bankers!

Yet this madman was encouraged, and he fed the guillotine robustly. Financiers got short shrift from him. Many were on his list, especially some who had complained about him; also his neighbors —for several of them had complained—his landlord, his least considered enemies, a few lukewarm friends, even a woman, a stranger —to him a hostile spy—whose sole offense was looking into his courtyard, all denounced at a time when an Everest of innocence could be toppled by the merest feather of suspicion. No wonder Héron's industry was admired and he "was considered indispensable for the direction of his gang, for big coups, for lively business. . . . He carried terror; he was smart at discoveries; the frightful system of devastation and cruelty caused him to be kept on."

When Héron walked abroad by day or night his garments sagged with weapons. He carried a huge hunting knife, two daggers, a belt bulging with loaded pistols, and usually there were two blunderbusses hidden beneath his cloak. Two of his gang, ambulant arsenals both, followed ever at his heels. He was desperately afraid, while inspiring the most widespread fear. Between him and Robespierre "everything was secret." Men from Héron's—formerly Maillard's—band of thugs were posted in the corridors of the Committee of Public Safety and "handed papers or letters to Robespierre, but always sealed and in secret . . . women and girls gave others to the infamous Chalabre woman"—the Incorruptible's crackpot feminine disciple. Still other documents were passed "to those on sentry duty" at Robespierre's lodging, the answers being generally "orders given to the Committee of Public Safety for a throat cutting or an arrest."[4]

"The names are called over, the heads fall, and pouf, pouf, the thing is done!" Héron exulted.

The more this crazed informer fell victim to his mania of persecution, the more the denunciations flooded in; and Robespierre—who was telling the Jacobins that they must "overthrow faction with a vigorous arm" because a "multitude of scoundrels and foreign agents are secretly forming a conspiracy to slander and persecute well meaning persons"—obviously cared little whether Héron's charges were the product of diligent counter-espionage or of dementia praecox. Robespierre was also served by reliable police agents and informers and was entirely correct in suspecting some form of foreign conspiracy. Except that it was not on foreign soil or managed by a foreigner; and only in minor degree financed with alien funds. The real conspiracy was as French as Robespierre. Its agents were Frenchmen and its objective was wholly devoted to the problems of France. This great Protean affair is still but imperfectly understood, and perhaps none will ever know just how deep it bored or how wide its tentacles of political torment were spread. But at least we know now the brain from which it sprang in serpentine resourcefulness, and we know the purse that very largely promoted it.

Robespierre's spies and the committees' spies never learned these facts about their most extraordinary foe, and so they called him a conspiracy. Behind the screen of their chronic mystification we may catch a hasty glimpse of the revolution's leading counter-terrorist, whose very name was meant to be whispered—Jean de Batz.

Chapter Twenty-Five

DE BATZ, THE GASCON WIZARD

THE ROYALISTS' HATRED of the revolutionary leaders of France was the natural loathing of a formerly privileged class for a plundering, upstart gang. Jean de Batz, baron of Gascony, was a Royalist die-hard who hated the revolution so long and virulently that he became its most prodigal terror. With infinite craft, with his own Gascon blend of vindictive relish and guile, he entangled himself in its plots, its rivalries and even its worst excesses. The revolutionary turbulence became his turbulence; for he encouraged every fanatic convulsion and sought to make the least political tremor an earthquake pulling upon the flimsy foundations of the state.

This anti-republican project was not one taking a few weeks or months, like an ordinary mission of secret service. The highly involved operations of the baron continued for years, until even he must have wondered—as the Convention's magnates, the schemers and agents of the committees, General Security and Public Safety, were all wondering—which was the natural ferment of revolutionary agitations and which the counter-turmoil called Jean de Batz.

The initial masterstroke of this incomparable conspirator seems to have been his discovery of nearly limitless resources. The lining of his pockets was always eminently negotiable; and while the government in Paris suffered a chronic emaciation of the purse, its archfoe's never stopped bulging with gold. And so with cynical extravagance he never stopped corrupting the starved wretches who were relief cases as well as republicans.

De Batz came, for example, at the summit of his powers to have absolute control over the transport department. He had even contrived to staff it with *ci-devant* royal servants—Murphi, huntsman of the late King Louis XVI, Bouchéri, Macherer, Blanchard, coachman of the king, Rouarre, the ex-bodyguard of Bourbon royalty, Hugué, a domestic of the palace, still devoted to the memory of "Citizen Capet." And through these and many other agents the Gascon could have "stopped the revictualling of Paris, or put an end to the famine that reigned there."[1]

A second stroke of sheer genius was the manner in which De

Batz protected himself. His bribes had reached so many spies and police agents that, even at the height of the Terror, it was the operatives of his principal foes who lived most in dread of his being arrested. Had the rash intriguer, through any oversight of theirs, come to stand before Fouquier-Tinville, scores would have been compromised and many a head less shrewd than the Gascon's would have tumbled before his into Sanson's basket.

Since the best detectives and informers enjoyed his bounty, it was imperative on two counts to keep Jean de Batz alive; and the only way to do that was to keep him at liberty *in Paris*. The baron's bribes were gold and never assignats, which he considered the perfect tender of trashy republicans; and there are garbled reports still to be seen in the French archives that reveal how determinedly although clumsily the spies of the committees protected their chief source of hard cash. In one of these stool-pigeonholed palimpsests he is discounted as a secondary danger to the republic, together with the banker Benoît, who is named "Benoîte", while the Gascon is mistily presented as "Baron de Beauce."

A Plotter's Apprenticeship

This adroitly managed obscurity of the master of Royalist opposition made him for years after the revolution a kind of fabulous figure adrift among catastrophes he was never suspected of influencing. Carlyle never heard of him; and even the great history by Madelin[2] fails to mention his name. It was as though the Baron de Batz, a nightmare to Robespierre and the actual motive force behind a dozen revolutionary climaxes, had never existed. He is thus our most perfect example of the historians' neglect of the secret sources of their material, as well as of the reluctance with which great concealments emerge from the deeps of their own design.

De Batz, who was no "German", as some have thought, came of a noble and ancient Gascon family. He was born in Goutz—now in the department of Landes—in 1761, and at the age of twelve was enrolled in the Queen's Dragoons. On December 8, 1776 he was commissioned ensign; but he was never seen at the headquarters of his regiment, a violation original enough even in those years of polite laxity to cause the Chevalier de Coigny, his colonel, to issue an order for his arrest. This was not, however, to take effect unless he put in an appearance, and Jean, it seems, was already submitting to his destiny in learning to disappear.

While obviously no soldier, he was dragooned by caste to pursue a military career; so in 1784 we find him on the road to Spain, where he tasted the more torpid routine of the Spanish army and neglected insignificant duties for another three years. It would be excellent practice to imagine at this moment that young De Batz stayed away from the Queen's Dragoons because he was already on secret-service assignment, in the modern European manner of listing officers as "retired" or even as deserters until they return from foreign espionage missions. That would explain the transfer to a Spanish regiment, perhaps; but would it explain his returning to France in 1787, being advanced to the rank of colonel and immediately retired on half pay?[3]

The years rolled by with an ever-quickening beat of political urgency; in 1789 the Gascon baron was a deputy to the States General, and in 1792 an émigré, soldiering again as an aide to the Prince of Nassau. De Batz, it is said, was so stirred by the rising of June 20, 1792 that he returned to Paris only ten days later at the risk of his life. On July 1 Louis XVI wrote in his diary that he owed the baron a very substantial sum of money. De Batz, we observe, was also a speculator. Like mild Dr Bancroft, he mingled it habitually with plots and intrigue; but the baron won, fortune after fortune, and he spent his own funds lavishly upon the Royalist cause. In that, if in nothing else, he stands forth as unique—a conspirator who could afford it, and who did not have to solicit a subsidy from any member of the English government.

Not many months later the king's debt to De Batz was on the point of becoming colossal, for the Gascon now plotted to rescue his condemned sovereign, and his plans held every chance of sensational success. He not only plotted to save Louis XVI but led the attempt in person. De Batz was that kind of plotter. One dark morning—January 21, 1793—a melancholy cortege slowly defiled through the gloom to the deep rolling of drums along the Boulevard Bonne Nouvelle. It came abruptly to a halt in front of the Porte St Denis. There was a strange and sudden commotion. "To my side, all who would save the king!" The signaling outcry of De Batz was accompanied by the flash of his drawn sword. He expected several hundred to join him in the attack, but there were only a few of his followers on hand. Republican counter-spying police had frustrated the bold attempt in advance by rounding up every suspected adherent. There was bloodshed, however, for those who rallied to the baron were not daunted by the odds. De Batz himself made a miraculous escape when it was seen that the heavy guard of soldiers doomed Louis XVI to proceed to the waiting guillotine.

Jean de Batz next prepared to save Marie Antoinette. This also was a plot of unparalleled audacity. He proposed on a certain day to have every member of the prison guard in league with him. The queen would be sent away under military escort and would thereupon simply vanish. His invariable necessity of engaging a large number of confederates was once again chiefly responsible for an heroic failure. Somebody conducted himself too confidently, rousing a ready police-spy suspicion. Marie Antoinette also—though the baron launched a second attempt—was not destined to be relieved of her martyrdom.

Saddened but undiscouraged by his failure to save either king or queen, De Batz reformed his program. It became nothing less than to destroy the revolution itself. He proposed enlisting his own growing corps of *canaille* and promoting such a series of political extremes and outrages, the decent majority of Frenchmen would become disgusted by republican institutions. His point of concentration was the legislature, the National Convention. He schemed to encourage the various sharply divided parties to mistrust and attack one another. He likewise had devout faith in the results to be obtained by corrupting officials. At the same time he displayed almost fantastic intrepidity, remaining in Paris all through the Terror, buying an estate for 530,000 livres at the very height of the Terror, being seen by Robespierre himself in the throng at the National Convention, yet slipping away or into some easy disguise before Robespierre's agents could gather to seize him.

"It is a remarkable fact that everyone who approached this audacious Gascon, everyone who, so to speak, entered his circle of attraction, instantly submitted to his influence," Lenotre has written. "He seems to have had some nameless moral force at his disposal, which enabled him to attract and keep the devotion of these people . . . they were faithful ever after—faithful to the death—to this man whom they had made their master."

Scores did, indeed, go to the guillotine when they might have saved themselves by denouncing De Batz—saved themselves, yes, and gained a large cash reward. Whenever he could arrange it, the baron rescued his detected partisans by paying out large bribes. Yet he refused to be blackmailed and complained to the president of the Committee of General Security when Burlandex, a Committee spy, attempted to extort 100,000 écus. De Batz was warned that his arrest had been planned as a fraud, devised with forged documents.

Eventually the baron was taken by a detective whom he could not purchase; but by a ruse De Batz got rid of incriminating papers he was carrying. From his cell he began to threaten the Convention, then nearly at the end of its course. The Terror had, indeed, killed off the revolution, which was precisely what the Gascon had aimed to do. He was not long under detention; there was too much that he might have *explained* if ever put on trial. Using his influence over the rabble, he raised the Sections one time more, only to stand aside at that fateful moment and witness the first historic "whiff of grapeshot." The *canaille* of Paris would no longer intimidate the politicians. A little Corsican artillerist had been found to defend the republican government; and so it is the Gascon baron's own fault if we leave him and turn to other scenes—he was in part responsible, it appears, for the dawn of Bonapartist destiny, which also ushers in Fouché, Montgalliard, Barnett, Savary and score of other extravagant adventurers.

Chapter Twenty-six
FOUCHÉ FACING FOUR WAYS

THE CUNNING OF JOSEPH FOUCHÉ repeatedly endangered him, but during the Terror it saved his life; and in spite of it he was able to squeeze through to the comparative repose of the Bourbon Restoration by compounding his duplicities and discounting his just deserts. Where Sieyès and other agile Frenchmen might boast that they survived the revolution, Fouché could whisper that he used it as a torpedo, a cloak and a ladder. It lifted him from the provinces to Paris, from humdrum obscurity to immense affluence and to what in an age of highly speculative standards passed for fame. He was a Jacobin, one of the regicides, the *"mitrailleur de Lyon"* who helped to extinguish masses of people with hideous whiffs of grapeshot. Yet all of this was glossed over, and the time came when his mere glance as minister of police upset more composure and caused more cringing than the explosions of cannon. In 1789 he was a dissatisfied churchman and teacher, impoverished and without faith; in 1815 he was the second richest man in France, and one of the most powerful in Europe, with unimpaired faith in himself. His was precisely the sort of fluid career everyone would try to imitate in a world without thick wits or moral integrity, with no principles or fastidious tastes of any kind.

Fouché was born in the seaport town of Nantes—May 31, 1758—of parents who were seafaring folks. Nearly all his ancestors had made their living on the sea; but young Joseph was slender, anemic and studious, boyish games exhausted him, and with many boats available he was soon made acquainted with the repeated taxations of *mal de mer*. However, he distinguished himself at school, and that display of intellect opened the only door in France with democratic hinges, the door of the Church. Since the expulsion of the Jesuits, the Oratorians had been in charge of Catholic education throughout the kingdom; and the generous, invisible realm of papal power welcomed clever youths, no matter how humble their origin. At twenty bright young Joseph was appointed a teacher of mathematics and physics, a school inspector and prefect.

It was a dignified rather than a promising post, and to the future master of spies and director of the imperial police it offered more opportunity to learn and gain in intellectual stature than to teach or to advance in clerical rank.¹ To be sure, had he elected to take priestly vows, a better path would have extended before him with inviting vistas of authority—priesthood, a bishopric, even a cardinal's princely estate. The Church of Rome, so much older and wiser than the decrepit but not venerable House of Bourbon, had long been giving the monarchs of France and all Europe this lesson of an applied merit system rivaling the claims of privilege and wealth; but for the most part the royal accidents of the Continent possessed neither merits themselves nor standards of merit, and chose to perpetuate the traditional system of their ancestors rather than hazard an experiment merely endorsed by the spokesmen of God.

Joseph Fouché was himself as conservative and cautious as any Capet of the line. He wore clerical garb, had a tonsure, and shared the monastic life of the Oratorians, but for ten years—and at a period of his life when not many young men are crafty, farsighted or adamant— he declined to be ordained and took no vows. Until he was thirty, as a kind of semipriest, cloistered, inconspicuous and seemingly void of ambition, he taught in convent schools. But by 1789 the political storm which was raging over France grew violent enough to leap from the Freemasons' clubs to the secluded cells of the Oratorians. Fouché had been stationed in Niort, Saumur, Vendôme and Paris; it is historically important that he happened to be in Arras when the first heat lightning of revolution began to illumine the long-overcast skies of plebeian opportunity. He was acquainted there with a captain of engineers, Lazare Carnot, and perhaps even more intimate with the nervous, thin-lipped, pallid and inordinately ambitious lawyer, Maximilien de Robespierre.² When Robespierre was sent from Artois to the States General at Versailles to join in drafting a new constitution for the kingdom, it was Fouché who could lend his impoverished friend enough money for the journey and the purchase of a presentable suit of clothes.³

Curiosity was drawing all young clerics' attention to the upheaval of society threatening France. The Oratorians brought politics into the refectories of Arras; and Fouché took his first revolutionary step. It was he who suggested sending a deputation to the States General to express ecclesiastic sympathy with the demands of the Third Estate. His superiors frowned upon such unscholarly enterprise and disciplined him by having him transferred to a Church school in his native town of Nantes. But one incontinent plunge into public affairs on that mighty eve of national metamorphosis dissolved the humdrum seminary teacher. His cassock was tossed aside; his hair was allowed to grow over the tonsure; and Joseph Fouché began addressing bourgeois political gatherings. A club was presently formed—they were now nearly as numerous as Frenchmen—and the ex-Oratorian turned orator got himself elected chairman of the *Amis de la Constitution* in Nantes.

The mercantile leaders of that community were ill disposed toward extremists. Fouché was a nicely balanced liberal. Most of the well-to-do citizens of Nantes had large investments in the colonies. And so Fouché had a "strongly worded memorial" sent to the new government of France, opposing suspension of the slave trade. This enraged the radicals but earned him the approval of the merchant class. And to strengthen his political hold upon those who would be the electors of tomorrow, he made haste to marry, winning a very unattractive "but handsomely dowered" girl, the daughter of a rich and influential bourgeois.

As soon as the writs were issued for the elections to the National Convention, Fouché declared himself a candidate. Campaigning in the best manner of modern democracy, he promised his potential constituents everything he could imagine they wanted; but, since Nantes was still far to the right of radical reform, he emphasized his anxiety "to protect commerce, defend property and respect the laws."[4] He skirted around the sins of the ancien régime by talking about the dangers of disorder. In 1792 he was elected and duly set forth on his journey to Paris, whither he had helped to speed his already notable friend, Robespierre, three momentous years before. Fouché the deputy was dogged every step of the way by Fouché the Jacobin, a grisly, imminent shadow. Fouché the victor over Robespierre, Fouché the minister of police, the millionaire and duke, the incomparable mender of private political fences, remained far off among the unimagined absentees.

The Making of a Minister of State

At the date of his election to the National Convention, Fouché was not quite thirty-three years old. Physically he was unattractive, and mentally, cautious, reticent and passionless. His face has been described as "extremely unpleasing"—narrow, angular and bony, with a sharp nose, thin lips almost always closed, and eyes, beneath their heavy lids, the greenish gray of bottle glass. One who met him somewhat later in his career remarked that the red of his "bloodshot eyes was the only touch of color in his sallow countenance." But even as a younger man, the practically unknown deputy from Nantes, he was like that: bloodless, and so lean that he "looked like a ghost." He seemed to lack vitality, sparkle was never detected in his eyes or vigor in his movements. Yet the tone of his voice was strong and emphatic, and though he might appear convalescent from some wasting disease, or a sufferer from chronic fatigue, he was actually enduring and wiry, with an unsurpassed capacity for long hours of hard work.

It is impossible to attempt in this space to weigh and balance, to appraise and delineate the shifting aspects of Fouché's career. He was one of the few men of his age who stood as solid as a rock upon visible foundations of quicksand. He survived not one "past", but half a dozen. He faced this way and that, like every successful politician; but he was conservative and radical, republican and Jacobin, Bonapartist and anti-Bonapartist, Imperial prop and Royalist retainer—all in such bewildering, nicely timed relation each to the other, one may only conclude he had no faith but Fouché, and no opinions he ever allowed to conflict with his stealthy pursuit of power.

There seem to have been two schools of French thought concerning this secretive and confounding Frenchman. In one we find Balzac, curiously alone. In the other are the critics who recall the massacres at Lyons with grape and canister, the Jacobin barely outwitting Robespierre, the master of intrigues and informers who, under the Directory, paid Josephine de Beauharnais well and regularly out of the police funds to spy in turn upon Barras and upon her husband. If Fouché—according to our early promise—is to be fairly judged in this record by the company of spies which he kept, then Josephine's acquisition was in itself convincing evidence of his genius. Balzac wrote of him as a "sombre, profound, and extraordinary man, whom few people really know." And again: "This remarkable genius which inspired in Napoleon something closely akin to terror, did not manifest itself all at once in Fouché. An obscure member of the National Convention, one of the most exceptional men of his day and one of the most misconstrued, he was moulded in the storms that were then raging."

Molded, yes; and in his pre-eminent role as commander in chief of the French police he did a very great deal to hold the worst storms within civilized bounds and steady a ship of state continuously rocked by soldierly ambitions. We shall soon again encounter Fouché, with his rivals, victims and skillful subordinates, while the European world waits for Waterloo. Let us stand aside then and allow the unparalleled molding process to proceed.

CHAPTER TWENTY-SEVEN

MONTGALLIARD THE UNMITIGATED

IN ALL THESE CENTURIES of unfolding intrigue and espionage there are few secret-service practitioners who disclose no redeeming trace of any kind. We have come, however, to the man who called himself "Comte Maurice de Montgalliard", whose schemes were too unsavory, whose bargains and betrayals too mercenary, even for an age incalculably corrupt, and whose least profitable activities proved historically the most malign. He was incapable of loyalty, no matter what cause enlisted his service or what leader rescued him from quicksands of debt. Those who helped him only earned his vindictive hostility; yet he was indifferent to affronts as to obligations when the moment came to change sides. Those who encountered Montgalliard and mentioned him in memoirs, writers who since then have had reason to dissect his varied depravities,[1] concede him eternal right to conduct the espionage school in hell as the most Satanic spy that ever lived.

A contemporary described him as of medium height, with pallid face and eyes which sparkled beneath heavy and almost jet-black eyebrows. His nose was long, his chin "like the toe of a boot", and he seemed to have a deformed shoulder, to be hunchbacked, with the general appearance of a "Portuguese Jew."[2] But research has detected that the jailer's book at the Temple does not mention any deformity of the prisoner, Maurice de Montgalliard, but that the description of his brother, Guillaume Honoré, depicts the latter as "hunchbacked on the right side."[3] If so villainous a character as Montgalliard had been a hunchback he would be utterly unbelievable. French imagination rather than Nature would seem to have turned out "this terrible Protean spy" in the complete make-up of melodrama.

His name, we learn, was Roques, which may have been near enough "rogue" to warrant the adoption of Montgalliard. He came of a noble but impoverished family of Languedoc, had been a student at the Royal Military College of Sorrèze, a cadet, a gentleman-at-arms in the regiment of Auxerrois, and then an officer of little courage or capacity who resigned his commission after two campaigns in

Martinique. He returned to France and soon contrived to force his way into the most exclusive circles of Parisian society. He was a member of "the little court surrounding Monseigneur Champion de Cicé, Archbishop of Bordeaux, who spent much of his time far removed from his flock, at the Abbey of Saint Germain-des-Prés." Montgalliard, ever pushing forward in his insinuating manner, developed an acquaintance with Jacques Necker, medicine man of anemic French finances; then he married one of his Eminence's goddaughters, a lovely girl just out of the convent and with a fortune of her own, who was further "overwhelmed with magnificent presents by his Eminence's *entourage*."

Two sons were born to this union;[4] but apart from his domestic felicity Montgalliard pursued his heady climb to the political and intellectual summits of the capital. With the outbreak of the revolution he tried his hand at stock speculation. Enrolled as a secret agent of the Bourbons, he played some part in preparing for the flight of the king. According to his own account—which is not necessarily holy writ—he lent Louis XVI a considerable sum of money; while the rest of his fortune was freely sacrificed in the interests of Queen Marie Antoinette, after her imprisonment in the Temple.

The dangerous and shadowy career of the man commences at about this time. He visited England; he crossed to Belgium and ventured to return to France. Though his name was listed among the émigrés, it was presently erased from that elegant company of the proscribed, an exceptional but not incomprehensible favor. It is plain that he now served both the Royalists and the revolution, that he had been cunning enough to engage a powerful protector. How else could he have remained in Paris during the Terror?—for there he was, and often close at hand to observe the manipulation of the guillotine "when the day's 'batch' was worth the trouble."

In May of 1794 he was charged with a mission to the Austrian headquarters and was there considered the personal envoy of Robespierre. Upon visiting the Duke of York, he also got himself presented to the Emperor Francis II. He had somehow "mysteriously" threaded his way between the outposts of two hostile armies, "dragging along with him the former priest of his native village, the Abbé Du Montet, whom he introduced as the tutor—*in partibus*—of his children." When the Duke of York sent him to London, he was welcomed as that social phenomenon, an aristocratic survivor of the Reign of Terror. He was the only available eyewitness of the tragic events which were already becoming legendary, a continual object of curiosity, introduced into the best clubs, and quoted in all the newspapers. Pitt received him; the Duke of Gloucester sent for him. Ministers, princes of the blood and fashionable noblemen vied in offering him entertainment.

At this time he published a pamphlet[5] which showed him curiously well informed not only as to current events but also the secret political motives of the day. At somebody's suggestion—it may even have been Pitt's—he returned to the Continent, and on his way to Switzerland, encountering an old acquaintance, a fellow cadet of the military college at Sorrèze, secured through him an introduction to Prince Louis-Joseph de Condé, exiled French commander of an exiled Royalist army.

The "Purchasing" of Pichegru

At this time—January 1795—the little army of émigrés strung out along the right bank of the Rhine was less than five thousand strong. It consisted wholly of French volunteers in the pay of Austria, which meant one loaf of "munition bread" and the equivalent of twelve cents a day for the men, nothing at all for the officers. So sketchy were the Austrian notions of pay that the Princess of Monaco, Condé's mistress, had to sell her jewels and plate to defray the most pressing obligations of the Royalist headquarters. To the Germans locally it was a perplexing alien spectacle,[6] this body of ex-magistrates, ex-landowners, ex-officers and "even bourgeois, carrying the knapsack of the infantryman or wielding the curry-comb of the cavalryman in a spirit of perfect equality. An equality of wretchedness. . . . At the mess of the headquarters staff they ate the ordinary soldiers' bread as cooked in camp. . . . The royal army was dying of starvation."[7]

Opposing it, encamped on the left bank of the river from Huningue to Mayence—and in a state of even more pitiable destitution—were the two Republican armies of the Rhine and the Moselle, soon to be united by order of the Committee of Public Safety under the command of Charles Pichegru, famous conqueror of Holland. Whereas the émigrés had their inadequate Austrian allowances, the patriot soldiers were paid in paper money that no beggar of the neighborhood would accept. The defenders of the Republic had neither clothing nor bread, could buy nothing with the assignats stuffing their pockets, and tore up the roots of the vines, or gathered clover, to be placed in their camp kettles as a substitute for vegetables. They wandered about in rags, without stockings or overcoats, and lived in the meanest mud hovels. Their officers were hardly better off, being forced to sell personal belongings and equipment as well as "horses and carriages to obtain a little hard cash."

Montgalliard, with the "perspicacity of the great adventurer . . . was quick to realise the peculiarities of the situation and the manner in which it favoured the exercise of his malevolent genius."[8] He offered to serve the Prince de Condé by helping to negotiate an English loan. On his own account he was relishing the prospect of a "magnificent coup." He had learned that England "in order to help all good Frenchmen to re-establish order and public tranquillity in their native country" had determined to subsidize the Royalist army.[9] And it was a simple matter to promise Condé to "persuade" the English to do for his cause what they had already decided should be done.

The prince moved his headquarters to Mülheim in Baden, and, lo, the golden lava of desperately needed succor actually began to flow from volcanic Britannia. In less than four months' time the impoverished Condé—who had been unable to allow his own daughter the sum of 500 livres—found himself possessing 500,000, in addition to the arrears of pay and the revictualing of his troops. With "amazement, but not without some anxiety, he saw a credit account of three millions and a half opened in his name for 'secret services.'"[10]

Condé might feel anxiety, but the Comte de Montgalliard stood all glib and ready to take a hand in this glorious clandestine disbursement. With his "boastful yet insinuating manner, and his skill in convincing his hearers of the truth of his statements he soon got the better of the weak and vacillating Prince and won him over to his infernal plot." Montgalliard was not alone in advocating the purchase of the Republican leaders; he was simply the most cynical and optimistic. The day would come when he would try to approach Bonaparte, "a little ragamuffin of a general" whom he considered ripe for a bribe.[11] But now, late in 1795, he began the gradual promotion of a scheme which was going to have the most profound influence upon France and all Europe, as well as on the fortunes of the "little ragamuffin" sprung from Corsica. Montgalliard proposed "buying Pichegru", most illustrious of the Republic's army commanders, and he even brazenly impressed Condé with his own itemized estimate of the price which must be paid. They need only offer Pichegru "the staff of a Marshal of France, the *cordon rouge*"—knighthood of the Order of St Louis—"and the *grand-croix*" of the same order, "the Château de Chambord for life, four pieces of artillery taken from the Austrians, one or two millions in hard cash, and a pension of a hundred and twenty thousand livres," and as a result the Republican forces would turn Royalist to a man, once again "the lilies of France would float over all the belfries of Alsace" and the fortress of Huningue would throw open its gates to the army of Condé.

And who was to be the man audacious enough to enter France, obtain an interview with the popular victor of Menin and conqueror of Holland, and invite him to betray his country? Pichegru was no fanatic Jacobin or lover of conflict. He had never troubled to hide his disgust for the negligence of the committees of the National Convention, blaming them for the wretched condition of his troops. However, it was known that at the general's headquarters three "representatives of the people, Rivaut, Rewbel and Merlin de Thionville" were installed and "scarcely left his side." This trio of watchdogs could not be included in the offer to Pichegru and would be perilous counterspies with whom to trifle or to bargain. Montgalliard feared that "the secret agent . . . wriggling into this revolutionary environment with the intention of corrupting the Commander-in-Chief" would probably be "treated as a common spy and shot without the formality of a trial."[12] Accordingly the prudent comte "decided to make a division of the fruits of his activity: he would keep the advantages for himself and reserve the dangers for his friend" and dupe, Louis Fauche, bookseller and publisher of Neuchâtel, who now stood second to none in the fervor of his Royalism and who called himself Fauche-Borel.

A Smooth Bore Loaded with Mischief

The cause of exiled princes is a magnet for all kinds of climbers, and the cause of the exiled Bourbons of France was as attractive to the Swiss bookseller who wanted fame, important friends and money as to Montgalliard who wanted money. The comte had discovered Louis Fauche during his recent travels which mingled the homelessness of the émigré with the observations of professional espionage, and his first shrewd glance had penetrated the bookseller's vanity and ambition. Montgalliard now overwhelmed the Swiss by summoning him to be presented to the Prince de Condé; and Condé—who "had learnt his lesson, and learnt it well"—nearly suffocated him by appointing him his personal emissary on the spot. Placing a hand upon the bookseller's breast, above his heart, he said hopefully: "You have a heart in your breast"—Fauche knew better; it was in his throat— "you will succeed!" And the reward promised was as princely as the gesture: "as soon as the Restoration was an accomplished fact, Fauche was to receive 'a million, the directorship of the Royal Press, the position of Inspector-General of the Libraries of France, and the Order of St Michael.' "[13]

Montgalliard, who describes this enticing promise, had no doubt suggested every word of it to Condé, whose verbal generosities were more inclined to royal vagueness. Louis Fauche was trebly seduced, by the prince, the princely gesture and the million; and he accepted the mission. From that moment he was intoxicated and blown up to unrecognizable proportions. If his negotiation with the Republican hero failed, a thousand louis were to reward him for his risk and trouble. But a million—the Swiss bookseller did not propose to fail! "If you see a citizen of Geneva throw himself from the window of a fifth storey," the Duc de Choiseul once observed, "you can follow him with perfect safety—there's fifty per cent. to be made out of it."

Fauche-Borel was allowed 7,200 francs for his initial expenses, but that was just a beginning. On the occasion of a later journey into Alsace the bookseller was stuffed like a Strasbourg goose—with cash; for Wickham, the English chargé d'affaires in Switzerland, had provided him with 112,000 livres to take into a country where the assignat for one hundred francs was worth exactly sixpence.

We cannot follow all the dodges, pretensions and maneuvers of Fauche, now at the start of his twenty years' service as a Royalist diehard and one of the most absurdly sanguine conspirators of the age. But in this affair of corrupting Pichegru he seems to have enjoyed not only the handsome British subsidies but some degree of beginner's luck. His speculation in statecraft and monarchist intrigue appeared to prosper; and he showered gifts upon the starved and miserably grateful Republican soldiers.[14] It is perhaps true that he bored and annoyed their commanding general and the chief object of his solicitations. Charles Nodier insisted that Pichegru, unable to endure more of Fauche's "firm guidance and encouragement" along the profitable road to Restoration, on accompanying the Swiss one day to the foot of the staircase, said to his aide-de-camp: "When this gentleman next calls you will oblige me by having him shot."[15] But the Directoire had begun threatening the same penalty for a quite different crime, on February 22, 1796, ordering Fauche's arrest as a spy "for the *émigrés* and the foreign enemies of France." This surely was a kind of fame; and yet how had members of the government in Paris learned so much about Condé's secret agent and Pichegru's plague? They had learned it from Montgalliard, as Fauche was, rather shrewdly for him, suspecting at the time. The shameless comte, a dangerous man to afflict with even a fancied grievance, had become not unreasonably embittered. He had settled down in Basle to attend to "the principal management of the negotiations"; and Fauche was instructed to correspond through him. But the buoyant bookseller was so soon convinced of his own political destiny and his unbounded influence in the Royalist camp that he had rapidly extricated himself from Montgalliard's toils. All funds, for example, passed directly from Wickham to Fauche-Borel; and Montgalliard—"sometimes reduced to asking my own agents, those whose fortunes I had made, for a sum of 20 louis"—could grind his teeth or tighten his belt, while estimating that this protracted revision of Pichegru's loyalties "must have resulted in nearly 280,000 livres passing through Fauche's hands."

With such pecuniary provocation there was only one thing that the honor of a man like Montgalliard required him to do—go over to the other side. Finding that the conspiracy he had instigated had brought him less profit than he hoped, he withdrew from it—ostentatiously pretending to have been cured of his love of intrigue—but not until he had sought to reap the aftermath by adroitly exposing the whole affair.

General Pichegru was relieved of his command and summoned to Paris, the first ominous symptom. Montgalliard had lately paid a visit to Italy, for "this devil of a fellow enjoyed the most singular immunities; his pockets were bulging with passports from many hands; he was able to travel through Europe in time of war as easily as we can walk the streets of Paris."[16] And in Venice he boldly presented himself to Lallement, a veteran diplomat, the minister plenipotentiary of the French Republic, chiefly to assure him that henceforward he stood ready to serve the nation with as much zeal as he had lavished upon the cause of the Bourbons—"not in the very least for reasons of interest and ambition, but because he wished to be associated with the glory of his native country."[17]

Inebriated with his own mendacity, Montgalliard hastened to call upon M. d'Antraigues, the principal representative in Venice of the legitimist pretender, Louis XVIII, anxiously placing at this agent's disposal his well-known devotion to the Bourbon monarchy. And in order to prove his resource and fidelity he proceeded to give D'Antraigues all the details of the Pichegru conspiracy, "the names of the agents entrusted with the negotiations . . . the date of their attempts, the results obtained, and those which were still anticipated—precious information of which D'Antraigues . . . who more than any had in his keeping the secrets of the *émigré* Court and nobility . . . hastened to draft a full statement at the dictation of his visitor."[18]

Montgalliard left Venice then, having done his worst, and abandoned, owing to his "diabolical intuition", a project of levying anew upon the British secret-service funds by launching an involved and voluptuous plot to rotate around the "purchasing" of Bonaparte, the same "'little ragamuffin' . . . of whom everybody was talking." The comte, upon being repulsed by Bonaparte's outposts, retired in the direction of the Tyrol, returned to Mülheim and proceeded to blackmail his alleged idol, the Prince de Condé. Saying he was about to abandon politics and purposed returning to France, he suggested that it would be dangerous for him to carry over the frontier all the secret correspondence sent him by Condé during the Pichegru affair. Whereat the prince, perhaps glad at last that this scoundrel's mask was off, agreed to pay him 12,000 francs for the compromising letters; and Montgalliard speeded away, taking a draft for 12,000 francs—but also the very documents he had sold.

The Ruin of the Ragamuffin's Rivals

At this juncture our trusty Louis Fauche-Borel happened not to be risking his life in France or in Pichegru's hearing and so was available to take up the pursuit. Montgalliard owed him seventy-five louis, whose recovery was a career in itself for any thrifty Swiss; but also the papers with which the fleeing comte's portfolio was crammed exposed Fauche's precious intrigues on almost every page. The chase proved a relatively simple one, for Fauche's capacities for secret service were considerable; it was only his vanity and nonstop flights of imagination that made him preposterous. In Neuchâtel—on his own ground—he found Montgalliard at the Hôtel du Faucon. There was "a quarrel, a violent scuffle, a bout of fisticuffs", and virtue seemed to triumph. Fauche-Borel swept from the battlefield, bearing with him, if not the incriminating letters, at least the address of "the widow Serini" at Basle where they were to be found. And there he recovered them and sent them proudly to Louis XVIII, without seeming to suspect that Montgalliard had copied or removed all of the really important papers.

Meanwhile the comte, though one of the proscribed aristocrats, had returned to France "without a shadow of difficulty" and was now waiting for his infernal maneuvers to yield him compensation and vengeance. He did not have long to wait. A few days later—May 16, 1797—Bonaparte's army captured Venice. The Royalist agent, D'Antraigues, was arrested on May 21 at Trieste and escorted to the Corsican general's headquarters. On him was found the detailed account, so impressively dictated by Montgalliard, of the secret service of Fauche-Borel and the treasonable negotiation with Pichegru. Bonaparte straightway dispatched this sensational narrative to the Directoire, and, if it hardly constituted positive evidence of treason, it "provided a terrible weapon to be used against Pichegru", who had just been elected president of the Council of Five Hundred.

At this time everyone was saying that the "Republic would end with a soldier." But among the victorious Republican generals Bonaparte was only a poor third, with Pichegru and Moreau—a very able commander, the future victor of Hohenlinden—the leading candidates. Pichegru, famous for his successes in Holland, enjoyed the widest personal popularity, and all parties were looking to him for some manifestation significant or decisive. A man of simple tastes, not at all ashamed of his humble origin, he lived modestly—he himself opened the door to persons visiting him in the Rue du Cherche-Midi—avoiding the pomp and circumstance of his celebrity and seeming actually to despise the advantages to be derived from it. Apart from his career in the army he had never been disposed to thrust himself upon public attention; yet even the directors, a majority of whom were hostile to him, treated him with caution and surfeited him with marks of respect. Pichegru was a victorious soldier and a man of the people, and his hour drew near.

The precise extent of this officer's intentional "treason" cannot be weighed and subjected to the X-ray at this late day or in this place. Montgalliard wrote of himself in 1810: "Above all, His Majesty [Napoleon] loves men of honor, and I am all honor." It is obvious that, having no conception whatever of honor, he therefore easily detected its abundance in himself. And since he believed the services of any man were a commodity—and had read or listened to the optimistic vauntings of Fauche-Borel—we may be assured he had grossly exaggerated to D'Antraigues that progress to date of the bookseller's temptation of the Republic's foremost general. Fauche, moreover, now boldly ventured into Paris, where other equally confident Royalists were strutting quite openly, certain of the coming of the pro-monarchist military dictator, and calling the baffled directors the "five shillings" because in English "five shillings can be changed for a crown."[10] And, combined with the treacheries of Montgalliard, the fatuity and indiscretion, "the childish love of fame or passion for gain" of Louis Fauche-Borel were bound to discredit and bring disaster upon the very cause which the bookseller plumed himself on serving with the utmost cleverness and resolution.

On September 4 came the coup d'état of Barras and the subsequent "shootings and deportations and imprisonments and pitiless reprisals of the weak yet triumphant Directoire."[20] Nothing of which overtook Fauche, the predestined contriver of other people's woes, for he was that kind of incorrigible plotter who disperses rather than suffers the consequences. He awakened to find himself placarded everywhere as "the chief agent of the King and the English Government"; and without stopping to admire this flagrant renown he made haste to disappear. It seems that he was concealed by a friend, a provincial lawyer, David Monnier, who had established himself as a printer, setting up his presses in some of the spacious deserted chambers of the Hôtel de Luynes; and because that "noble dwelling" retained the conveniences of a secret hiding place "contrived in the thickness of the wall" and a clandestine garden exit—having been "equipped in this fashion since the days of the Terror"—the Swiss bookseller was spared to promote further agonies of monarchism.

Charles Pichegru was arrested, tried and exiled to Cayenne. Escaping miraculously, he found refuge in London. He and Moreau —who had won a greater-than-Napoleonic victory at Hohenlinden[21]— were both still very popular with the army, and efforts were made to bring them together and effect a reconciliation between them, in order to oppose the dangerously thriving prestige of Bonaparte. The Comte de Montgalliard—who had sold himself to the Directory and the Consulate—and whom we shall meet again both as a Bonapartist police agent and a resurrected Royalist—hovered on the flanks of this strategy with other Consular spies. Then an obscure prisoner in the Temple, Bouvet de Lozier—alleged agent of Louis XVIII—attempted to hang himself, but the silken neckcloth he had used as a noose was severed in time; and from gratitude or breathlessness, he revealed all that he knew of a vast conspiracy, the object of which was the kidnapping or assassination of the First Consul.

The police acted swiftly. Moreau and Pichegru, Cadoudal—"the terrible Breton, a thickset Colossus, agile and impressive despite his obesity"—and more than a hundred others were arrested.[22] Pichegru, seeing his fame irreparably tarnished, committed suicide in the *oubliette* of the fearsome Tower of the Temple. Moreau remained under guard. And General Bonaparte's path to empire had been swept clear of martial obstacles.

Perhaps Napoleon was the Man of Destiny; possibly other fateful events—which did not have to occur—would have come along instead to glorify his genius for bloodshed and raise him up to the greatest heights. But to the student of secret service it is interesting to reflect that, if there had been no counter-revolutionary intrigues of the ardent

Royalist, Baron de Batz, none of Montgalliard's treacheries and avarice, and a good deal less of Fauche-Borel's vanity and zeal, a million young Frenchmen and multitudes of other Europeans might never have perished in the futile wars of the First Empire so soon to follow them all to the grave.

Chapter Twenty-eight
IMPERIAL SECRET POLICE

THE POLICE SYSTEM which Fouché created was both a network and patchwork—a wide-spreading network of sharp eyes and attentive ears, and a dubious patchwork of greed, shrewdness and bad character. The average police agent was either a needy, disreputable Royalist, like Montgalliard, or a scoundrel, like Veyrat or Bertrand, who had sprung from nowhere—or from prison—during the social convulsions of the Terror and its revolutionary subsidence. The rank and file of the all-powerful secret police were described as "a rabble of outcasts"; not the kind of instrument one would have expected to keep order throughout a complex and ever-expanding realm. Said Charles Nodier, who encountered them: "The precautions with which society has armed itself against crime are not a whit behind the expedients of crime itself in their violence and ferocity."[1]

It would be unjust to the genius of Fouché to assume, however, that he was deeply concerned about "order" as most of us conceive it today. If the age had been a tranquil one, the power of the police would have been limited and the role of Joseph Fouché made relatively insignificant. Small wonder then he seemed to dread tranquillity and was glad so seldom to be threatened with it while Bonaparte went on collecting kingdoms. From beginning to end of his career as head of the police Fouché's first objective was to maintain himself in that commanding position. He did not worry about disorders so long as his spies kept him warned in advance of the course that events were taking. His capacity to capitalize any sort of crisis, to remain cool, alert, impassive at the depths of a catastrophe, amounted to genius, even if his achievements mainly amounted to crime.

Fouché prospered and scored his triumphs as head of the detective and espionage services, despite the fact that all save a few of his lieutenants were men who suspected, despised and competed with him for the favor of the emperor. Veyrat, the inspector general, offers a perfect example. He had been a moneylender in Geneva before the outbreak of the revolution. Accused of issuing counterfeit notes, he had been imprisoned and afterwards banished, but he had turned up again in Geneva and had started his painful climb to wealth and authority by emerging as a pitiless Terrorist. Veyrat was an inconsequential shopkeeper of the Faubourg Saint-Denis, Paris, in 1795 and graduated into the police service two years later for the exclusive purpose of making money. Appointed by Minister Sotin, he was suspected and dismissed by Dondeau but discovered as a capable operative and reappointed by Duval.[2]

He was inspector general after the 18 Brumaire and very soon thereafter was notorious both for his greed and for the clever innovations by means of which he increased the revenue of his post. He resold to the Parisian booksellers the obscene books it was his mission to seize and introduced a sliding scale of petty corruption through which, for a fee ranging from 50 to 200 louis, he found it possible to avoid the suspects it was his duty to apprehend.[3] It was also his privilege to handle large sums of money without supervision. In the affair of the unfortunate Comte de Tryon, secret messenger of the émigrés, who was arrested and condemned to death in 1798, and of François, former tutor to the sons of the Comte d'Artois, who had become one of Fouché's "most intimate assistants", Veyrat seized and delivered to the treasury the sum of 239,000 francs. But his great sustaining strength, the main source of his powers of intimidation, came from his close friendship with Constant, Napoleon's valet. Veyrat was thus known to be in direct touch with the emperor as well as privately at the head of a special police who spied upon all the other police and kept Napoleon informed of all that was being planned at the Prefecture.

Comte Dubois, the prefect of police, was for years Fouché's subordinate, collaborator and jealous rival. Those who disapproved of him—his victims or his successors—have claimed that he cared for nothing "save retaining his post and increasing his fortune." To Fauriel he was a "tyrant . . . insolent, full of vanity."[4] To Pasquier the good manners of Dubois were almost microscopic; he had been corrupted by incessant association with criminals, police spies and informers, and had "lost all respect for himself and his influential post." Dubois had even granted himself a monthly pension of 5,000 francs, which he derived by farming out the "tax on gambling-hells." And he had awarded the comtesse, his wife—"daughter of an old serving-woman"—an annual gratuity levied upon the taxes on prostitution.[5]

Réal and Desmarest

MM. Réal and Desmarest were the chief lieutenants of Joseph Fouché, and it is a conspicuous tribute to them both that they retained their posts in the Ministry of Police while their discoverer, Fouché, came and went with the tides of his own oscillating fidelity. It seems to have been Réal and Desmarest who casually invented the modern system of spying upon spies, which honors its originators with its generally accepted French title of *contre-espionnage*. Differing from the bitterly condemned Dubois, Réal was to friends and victims alike a man of exceeding wit and shrewdness, who, according to Charles Nodier, possessed "regular features, although his expression charmed one, by the lucid transparent gaze of his blue eyes."[6] To Pasquier he "was not really so bad-hearted as one might be tempted to imagine, owing to a sort of joviality which never left him even in the execution of the most brutal measures."

Pasquier was evidently not given to applauding a colleague; but Réal is let off with the mere damnation of faint praise. However, a less prejudiced authority pronounced him "the complete policeman, from head to foot."[7] And it is significant that Réal was himself director of police under the authority of the chief justice during Fouché's first ministerial indisposition. It speaks eloquently of his caliber that, on Fouché's return, Réal resumed a subordinate position and remained efficiently at work in the department when virtually being supplanted as its master.

Desmarest in turn was subordinate to Réal, but his very able collaborator, chief of the Division of Public Safety and in command of the all-powerful Secret Police. He was an unfrocked priest and had formerly been a turbulent Jacobin. Madelin describes him as an excellent business man, rather out of his class, "intelligent, prudent, and able";[8] while no less a critic than Sainte-Beuve discerned in Desmarest "that gravity, that discretion, that are the mark of the honest man."[9] Both Réal and Desmarest excelled in the examination of prisoners, the latter especially having a deceptive, genial, almost hospitable manner which baffled the unfortunates interrogated by him. He made them believe they had found "an advocate and even a defender" and later left them astounded that the judge should have interpreted the evidence Desmarest offered so differently.

During the whole of the Empire these skilled officials were in charge of the secret service and political police. Either one, it appears, was the superior of Fouché—and of Savary, we may be sure—as an administrator of police. But they both lacked Fouché's blend of consummate double-dealing and concentrated self-interest and so remained inferior to him in rank in the Bonapartist hierarchy. The guillotine or firing squad was often the outcome of Réal's "humorous cross-examinations" and Desmarest's baffling inquiries. Yet both had been trained in Fouché's school, where knowledge and not blood was the foundation of power. For them the "all-important thing was to be 'instructed' "; they were not ready to dispose of a suspect who had merely incriminated himself, he must "lie in pickle" in a dungeon till he thought himself lost to the world and forgotten, and so, able to hold out no longer, came around to betraying his friends.

Réal and Desmarest showed the utmost versatility in recruiting spies and informers who could be made to serve the imperial police loyally and well, even though under compulsion. Their processes of compulsion were a dreadful enterprise, by which captured opponents of the regime were broken in spirit through every trick of confusion and threat, insinuations, tentative promises, physical degradation and moral torture. They systematically induced accused persons having political affiliations to spy for them and cooked Royalist suspects to a turn, with a rich brown gravy. When not in the imperial kitchen, they performed as a sinister pair of tailors whose styles were seen all over the Continent, and who manufactured turncoats for every conceivable occasion. They often made use of a disreputable device —called euphemistically a "test of Fidelity"—in that each victim and potential espion had to provide them with a permanent hold upon him by committing some "directed" crime at the outset. Evidence of this compulsory felony was then preserved with the other documents relating to the case and, if need be, found useful in discrediting him with any friends he had in a hostile camp, whose plotting he might be ordered to expose.

The Conscienceless Comte Again

The truly Napoleonic police service under Réal and Desmarest "stretched its tentacles all over Europe, and none of those who were 'wanted' by it, were they in Berlin, Rome, or Vienna, were able to escape its embrace."[10] Michelot Moulin, a Chouan who contrived to escape from an imperial prison, wrote in his memoirs: "All Switzerland, Germany, Prussia, and Denmark were under the influence of Bonaparte, to such a point that a word from his ambassador to any of these Powers was enough to send us back to France as prisoners." The Emperor Napoleon indeed supplied the threatful domination, while what Madelin called the "perfidious and motley" army of the secret police provided the eyesight and hearing.

That infernal marplot, the Comte de Montgalliard, had found it impossible to outwit them or make headway against their viligance and so had taken what seemed to him an obvious course and sold out the Royalist cause to become a Bonapartist. Hoping to win the favor of the authorities he "stooped to accomplish the vilest tasks for the police . . . accepted money from every party and every quarter, but was always overwhelmed with debts . . . always seeking to 're-establish himself' by speculating in this or the other commodity, or by betraying some victim" to the Consular police. His historian, Lenotre, even discovered the Montgalliard *dossier* in the *Archives nationales* and observes: "All but drowning in his own filth, he was rescued by Napoleon, who enlisted him among his secret informers, in which position, distrusted by all, he was closely supervised, so that he needed but to disregard a single summons and the watchers were on his trail, so great was the fear that he might accomplish some fresh betrayal."[11]

The long-forgotten entries of the *dossier* illuminate with burning clarity the infamous versatility of a master renegade. In Ventôse, year IV, from Hamburg we find Montgalliard—the Royalist recruiting agent—proclaiming the "purity" of his devotion to the Republic. In Nivôse, that same year, he denounced the "pretentious chatterbox" Fauche-Borel, whom he had himself induced to grow from bookseller to Bourbon emissary and secret agent. In Pluviôse he was reporting himself ready to expose to the world General Pichegru's treacherous negotiations, in which, as we know, he had taken a leading—and double-dealing—role. In Prairial, of the year XIII, he wrote Réal that he denied his own kin, having "blushed more than once in that I was born in a class to which all my enemies belong, because I have never been guilty of their vices." In 1810, now in prison for debt, he besought the rescuing intervention of the Ministry of Police and agreed to do anything asked of him if only he might be liberated and allowed a pension. Napoleon that same year took him on as a political spy; and Montgalliard at once was "only too happy to devote his life to that august service." By order of the emperor his debts were paid to the last centime: 78,417 francs and 45 centimes, the *dossier* reminds us. He was also granted a pension of 14,000 francs. And yet with the Bourbon Restoration he took up a new refrain, alleging that from 1801 to 1814, he had been "the captive of, or under the almost immediate supervision of, the man who had seated himself upon the throne of France."

The Ruse of the Secret Committee

If Réal and Desmarest could operate upon the foes of imperial France with such crooked instruments, they are, with their chief,

Fouché, entitled to recognition as inspired innovators of a repellently effective technique. Their defensive measures of counter-espionage were strikingly successful, and vital to a realm beset by multitudes of spies. The power of Bonaparte was always military power. Enemy agents tunneled his frontiers, thronged his cities and hovered around his armies, just as adventurous young officers sought to command them. The illegitimate aspects of his reign were concealed by nothing more substantial than cannon smoke; the very foundations of the Empire had been dug in the still-smoldering ruins of two other regimes. Revolutionists, in consequence, watched him and despised him as the latest monarchical oppressor of their country; and as the ruthless military usurper he was plotted against and spied upon by Royalists and émigrés, Bourbons, proscribed aristocrats and charlatans of vivid stripe.

It is such extensive, bold and persistent espionage that provokes great counter-espionage. In France after 1800 the opponents of the Corsican who were French became so numerous and varied, so vindictive and generally so impudent that alien secret agents never had to be employed by any foreign power seeking intelligence of Napoleon's government or armed forces. British, Austrian and Russian representatives, lurking on neutral ground, lavishly contributed the expenses of all kinds of spies and adventurers who riddled France with their "confidential" journeys and seem to have moved about in veritable procession, like a clandestine Roman triumph, with far greater display than discretion. The Royalist agents even dared for a time to wear a conspicuously cut V-shaped coat lapel as a symbol by which they might distinguish one another and proclaim their allegiance *in public*. But if most of the subterranean invaders were as harmless as their mannerisms now appear absurd, it was the brilliantly designed counter-espionage of Réal and Desmarest that diluted their venom and blunted their fangs.

In elaborating a project with which they originally hoped to entice certain Royalist emissaries, Réal and Desmarest themselves ventured rather close to a preposterous extreme, for they got around to expecting their deadfall to yield no less a quarry than the Bourbon Pretender. What it did produce was another masterstroke of counter-spying intrigue. Submerged at this time in that imperial insanitary service, the political police, was a forgotten man, Charles-Frédéric Perlet. After having established himself in Paris as a successful printer and publisher during the revolution, he had been ruined and banished because of incurable Bourbon yearnings and, upon returning from Cayenne and shipwreck, found his family in such pitiful destitution that he had to take any employment he could get, thus coming inevitably into the orbit of Desmarest as his tool. An authentic Royalist who had suffered dreadfully for his sympathies, Perlet had little difficulty in entering into secret correspondence with persons devoting themselves to the Bourbon cause in other countries. And this facility of contact inspired Desmarest and Réal—with the former as acknowledged originator—to create what the preaching-policeman, Pasquier, called a "demoralizing hoax": their famous "Secret Committee."

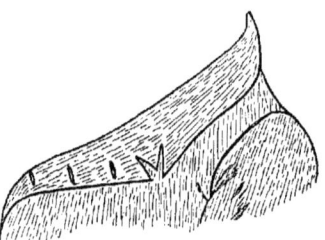

The V-shaped notch in the coat lapel, a sign by which French Royalist agents recognized one another, 1795–1804.

Perlet was instructed to tell his Berlin correspondent that he had come into touch with a number of influential men, ostensibly loyal to Napoleon but privately antagonized by his system and policies of government. These imperial magnates and army chiefs were represented as having formed a *committee,* and what a committee, involving grave personal risks but plotting to accomplish the overthrow of the emperor at the earliest favorable crisis. It was stated by the artfully inked pen of Perlet that the committee members preferred Bourbons to Bonaparte, that they were ready to join their strength to the faction desiring the return of that prince, yclept Louis XVIII, whose adaptability to exile, agility as a fugitive and submission to obscurity—as well as his less widely known exploits in consuming eighteen lamb chops at luncheon—seemed to make him the ideal post-imperial candidate. Since this committee of Desmarest's was wholly fictitious—reported as such to Fouché and mentioned satirically in the daily police bulletins read to Napoleon—its author was at liberty to extend his successful recruiting to any limits that he chose. Perlet conveyed the tidings abroad in his letters—which Desmarest dictated—and soon tired Royalist eyes began to glaze with emotion in reading hints of all the cabinet ministers, marshals, generals and other pillars of Corsican conquest who were changing without bribes or promises into subtle adherents of legitimacy.

There had, of course, been real committees of weight and thickness, especially thickness. One, organized by Hyde de Neuville, the Duc de Coigny, and the policeman Dupéron, [12] was incredibly entitled the "English Committee", perhaps because no Englishman paid any attention to it. The members had their own secret publication with another queer title, *L'Invisible,* as well as that Abbé Godard for their executive secretary who was so indifferent to caution he distributed *L'Invisible* and "pamphlets of Royalist propaganda in the public streets." Another committee had been more aptly named the "Royal Council", being created by Louis XVIII and composed of really eminent men who corresponded only with him.

Desmarest undoubtedly had these and similar Royalist agencies of the past in mind as life-size models for his fabulous Secret Committee. But also he could rely upon the monarchical aberration—"my people, my loyal subjects"—to make completely plausible this alleged sudden aversion to Napoleon on the part of his closest lieutenants. Had not ingenuous Bourbon envoys repeatedly approached Josephine, counting on her as a "Royalist" to plot against her present husband, the tyrant Bonaparte, because her first husband had been a vicomte? An even more ironic example of this school of thought concerned Marshal Berthier. Born at Versailles, his mother one of the chambermaids of the palace, he had been employed as a youth by Louis XVI in drawing maps of the country over which the king hunted; and none of the Bourbons "entertained any doubts as to the regrets which this brilliant past must reawaken in the heart"[13] of the man Napoleon had merely made his minister of war. The Royalist camp betrayed surprise when Berthier, approached by an aristocratic intermediary, politely declined to desert Bonaparte and go back to the map making.

Desmarest and Réal at first apparently had no greater object than the luring back to Paris of Fauche-Borel. That self-deluded harbinger of historic mishaps—who had been arrested and imprisoned—had engineered an ingenious escape but had been rearrested and returned to the Temple. On being transferred to the prison of La Force, a "sordid and infamous sewer", the bookseller's pride was deeply wounded. He had endured the humiliation of being lodged with low criminals for three days, had then talked his way out by assuring Desmarest he would become an invaluable operative of the secret service. Banished to Germany, but warned to keep in touch from there with the French police while starting the espionage he had voluntarily offered as the price of his liberation, Fauche-Borel did succeed in forwarding to Paris a document of considerable moment: an inflammable broadside from the Bourbon Pretender, as all good Bonapartists termed the future Louis XVIII, in which he assailed Napoleon and protested against his daring to occupy the throne of France. Fauche-Borel professed to have obtained his copy from the original; but, while thus genuinely serving Fouché's ministry in acquainting it promptly with a subversive Royalist declaration, the bookseller also had 10,000 copies of it printed for himself and began introducing them into France by every secret means at his disposal.

For this subterfuge Desmarest ordered him apprehended in Berlin as a traitor-spy. Prussian officials had promised to run down the impertinent scoundrel but actually warned Fauche-Borel and connived in his escaping to London. There, continuing his vast political correspondence, he deemed himself safe from the vengeance of even a Desmarest. But that imaginative policeman countered with the idea of the Secret Committee, troubling to create an entire provisional government which was to succeed Napoleon and deliver France to the Bourbons. Perlet, in whose letters the committee did all its lurking and plotting, was acquainted with Fauche-Borel and so "revealed" to him this promising growth of Royalism. And Fauche, characteristically inflamed with the belief that he alone could usher the cabal to its appointed place in French history, had begun deluging Perlet—whom he addressed as "Bourlac", employing a fearfully intricate code—with requests for further news, especially the names of all the prominent conspirators. These Perlet declined to entrust to paper, and he was instructed to hint that Fauche-Borel was the very man to slip over to Paris as a Bourbon envoy to treat with the committee in person. Desmarest expected the megalomaniac Royalist, ever eager to consort with the great, to rush right into this trap; whereupon it would be sprung, the committee disbanded, Fauche clapped into a noisome dungeon—and let him try to promise his way out of this one! We may, then, imagine the flattered amazement of Desmarest on learning—as he did from Fauche-Borel's torrent of letters to "Bourlac" —that his bold and seemingly authentic counter-spying concoction had taken in so conservative a man as Louis XVIII, his principal advisers, and even the British Cabinet.

Thereafter the hoax was enlarged and exploited by Perlet's extravagant "revelations", until Lord Howick, secretary of state in the British Foreign Office, acting in concert with the Royalist faction, agreed that a reliable negotiator must hasten over to meet and encourage the eminent patriots who were risking so much while privately undermining the French emperor. Fauche-Borel, gnawed by ambition on one flank but by his recollection of having tricked Desmarest on the other, found himself afraid to undertake the mission. Yet he argued that, as he was the close friend of "Bourlac", some member of his family should be chosen for the hazardous honor. He put forward his nephew, Charles Vitel, a gallant, artless young officer who had seen service in India with Sir Arthur Wellesley, the future Duke of Wellington. Vitel, soon afterward dispatched to Paris with an incriminating letter to Fouché hidden in his bamboo walking stick, was promptly arrested on Perlet's information, tried by court martial —he admitted his guilt—and shot as an English spy.

The Secret Committee, however, lived on, with Fauche-Borel, in spite of his nephew's tragedy, still its adoring prophet. Other agents were sent to get Perlet's list of members or to learn the date of the proposed uprising; but these well-paid individuals were reminded of Vitel and took such ready alarm, none of them accomplished anything. When it was seen by Desmarest that there was no longer hope of decoying to France a really dangerous spy or important Bourbon envoy, he informed Perlet that their complex imposture had flourished its last. But Perlet was unable to resist continuing to draw dividends from credulous Bourbon partisans; and when, in Savary's ministry, it was discovered by Desmarest that "Bourlac" still corresponded with the optimistic Fauche-Borel about the Secret Committee, he ordered Perlet dismissed from the service of the secret police, whose dupe he had largely been, and even had him detained for a time in the prison of Sainte-Pélagie.

We shall turn next to Ireland, where the patriot conspiracies and secret-service betrayals were marked at this time both by French revolutionary and Napoleonic influences. But first, what recoil ever developed from the Royalist faith in Desmarest's Secret Committee? In 1814 they were still looking for it; after Leipzig, the Allies' invasion of France, the banishment to Elba, Fauche-Borel and other puzzled Bourbon adherents searched widely in Paris for the underground structure of the committee that Perlet had described. All they found was the grave of Charles Vitel.

Chapter Twenty-nine
DUBLIN CASTLE'S CORPS OF DOUBLE-DEALERS

THE IRISH, in the pointed opinion of Samuel Johnson, were a truthful people because they always spoke ill of each other. It is possible that the Great Lexicographer had heard whispers about the Irishmen bought by Dublin Castle and employed in secret service. The leaders of the British government—having seen the American colonies lost not long since because rebel agitators and conspirators had been allowed to grow up suddenly into a party of independence, with military and naval establishments and diplomatic envoys sent to every European court jealous of England—were resolved to take no chances nearer home. There had always been an Irish Question; but the examples of the American and French revolutions trebled the urgency of Irish patriots desiring to govern their own land and the anxiety of Englishmen in duty bound to prevent it. As there was already a considerable armed force quartered upon Ireland, the only additional precautions which could be taken by Dublin Castle were more expansive activities of secret service.

The gentlemen who ruled in the king's name at the Castle were great believers in the fire insurance of secret service. The budget was sufficiently elastic and agents were plentiful, both espionage and counter-espionage proving congenial to the Irish political temperament. Unlike Robert Emmet and many another sincere patriot who suffered betrayal in this insurrectionary epoch, the gentlemen of the Castle had a clear and useful understanding of the "curious passion for theatrical double-dealing which was dearer to the average political plotter in Ireland than any theoretical liberty."[1] It was therefore the Castle's inveterate technique to stunt the growth of Irish liberties by retaining widely respected Irish "patriots" to betray automatically the plots or projects of their fellow patriots. And two hundred years of unfailing success were all the justification this corrupt practice of secret-service subsidies ever had to offer the superior authorities in London.

Gross stupidity and psychological blundering on the part of the English overlords was often glaring enough; and the grievances of the native Irish were a constant keening to high heaven. But how so many men with Irish names and good reputations could be found to sell their leaders to the Castle still remains incomprehensible; their perfidy had neither the excuse of intimidation nor partisan politics, and—since most of them had decent means of livelihood—it is hardly explained by greed, and not at all by bitter economic necessity. The time would come when the notorious Thomas Beach, who called himself—with a hireling spy's usual megalomania—Henri le Caron, would write a book[2] to prove his superior craftsmanship in betraying the Fenians and in imposing upon Egan, O'Donovan Rossa, Parnell and nearly all the other eminent Irishmen of his day. But that which may be included here in disclosure of Dublin Castle's most effective corps of double-dealers came to light only with the publication of the Castlereagh Papers and similar political documents, for whose canny dissection and interpretation the history of secret service is indebted to Dr Fitzpatrick.[3]

From the outbreak of the American Revolution to the ultimate exile of Napoleon the ferment in Ireland was unquestionably influenced by every adversary of England that chanced to take the field. Bonaparte was especially appealing—viewed from a distance—and many an Irish envoy visited the Continent to negotiate an alliance with the victorious First Consul and Emperor. London had to know about these threatening negotiations, and London always found a means of knowing. Progress, if any, was reported promptly, while the conditions of tangible French intervention were unvaryingly foretold. Sometimes the rebel envoys of Erin were mistaken by the Consular police or Fouché's watchdogs for British spies and seized as soon as they arrived in France.[4] In such a turbulent era of conflict and counter-revolution a general mistrust of strangers prevailed in all lands; but that mistrust, unluckily for a number of Irish patriots, was not extended to old familiar friends.

Through the years there were scores of such Irishmen, well placed, well connected and outwardly reputable, who faithfully served the Castle as its diligent spies. A few of them stand forth as betrayers of Olympian stature. There was Samuel Turner, whom nobody suspected, not even Newell "the informer",[5] then very much the confidant of Carhampton, commanding the English forces in Ireland. Turner—whose real value was such he came to rate a "pension" of £300 a year—was the spy that one day encountered Carhampton, his clandestine employer, while masked and adorned with a brilliant green stock; and when the British commander accosted him, deriding the color of the stock, an angry argument flared up. Whereupon Turner challenged Carhampton, and even threatened to post him as a coward when his challenge was ignored. It was indeed "a grand bluff" that worked to perfection, Turner—an overnight hero among United Irishmen—for a time even affecting to lie *perdu*. Not for months thereafter was he dangerously suspected by the patriot conspirators; though later he made for the haven of the Continent, and Pitt's noted secret agent, George Orr, declared Turner had fled in fear of assassination. However that may be, we find him next settled in Hamburg, the acknowledged agent of the United Irishmen and a friend and confidant of no less a patriot than Lady Edward Fitzgerald.

Turner, it seems, was known only as "Lord Downshire's friend" to those English authorities who cherished him for his perfidy. It was his lucrative privilege to inform upon Father O'Coigly, who was condemned and executed, though the chief witness against him— Turner—had to be spared appearing in open court. O'Coigly was one of those confirmed adventurers whose insouciance makes them seem typical of Erin, blotting out our recollection of the other camp aswarm with renegades; he proved bland, brave and ironic in the face of certain death. Lord Holland recalled that when O'Coigly's judge was "descanting on the mildness and clemency of the Administration" the accused quietly took a pinch of snuff and remarked "Ahem!" A different spy, Thomas Reynolds, was long reputed to have managed the undoing of Father O'Coigly, but years afterward it developed that Reynolds was himself unable to identify the real betrayer. That this notorious agent, a veteran "insider" of Pitt's Irish espionage corps, should be kept completely unaware of Turner's employment by the crown is all the proof we need ask of the genius of Pitt for the repressive manipulations of secret service.

MacNally

Samuel Turner was a barrister at law and an LL.D., and James McGucken, of Belfast, was the attorney who attended to much legal business for the United Irishmen. McGucken, like Turner, was in the pay of Dublin Castle, with many professional opportunities for earning a spy's rewards. However, it was Leonard MacNally who most outrageously combined the law and political espionage. With sinister enthusiasm he betrayed his own law partner, the fiancé of his partner's daughter, his clients, his friends and intimates, the cause he pretended to worship, the very people from whose good will he derived the income on which he ostensibly depended. It is surprising to find this plausible barrister-spy listed with Edward Gibbon, Horace Walpole, Cowper, Burke, Burns and other great names in a contemporary work entitled *500 Celebrated Authors of Great Britain now living*. However, the spy MacNally was also a playwright, one said to have been "popular with the pit and galleries", but yet, owing to the generous, inquisitive masters of the Castle, as little dependent upon long runs as upon the briefs from his other profession.

MacNally was a spy and had always been one. It paid him handsomely. Records which came to light years after his death show an enticing regularity of one-hundred-pound payments from the Castle to "L.M." The £1,000 reward for the betrayal of Robert Emmet, which MacNally also earned, was not recorded, being entered elsewhere to the dummy name of "Robert Jones." MacNally was the friend and partner of the distinguished John Philpot Curran, whose daughter, Sarah, was betrothed to Emmet. MacNally thus learned of the fugitive Emmet's hiding place at Harold's Cross and had even furtively visited him there to wish him well a few hours before Major Sirr and his police agents stole up and arrested the young patriot.

MacNally was fond of making speeches in which he denounced the English oppressor. And he always sent reports of the attendance at his meetings to the gentlemen of the Castle. When Jackson, a notable conspirator who had been betrayed by another Irish friend, left his private papers to his "dearest friend, Leonard MacNally", the spy straightway sold the papers to his English employers. On his daughter's account, Curran could not properly defend Emmet. MacNally volunteered to take his esteemed partner's place. That effectually doomed poor Emmet; yet when he was sentenced to death, it was MacNally who turned to him devotedly and leaned over and kissed him.

MacNally was described as "good natured, hospitable and talented", but he had a quick temper and was a resolute duelist. His willingness to fight accounted for a hip wound which made him limp. And his rapacious desire to increase his income can only explain his unspeakable espionage and serried betrayals. The spy-masters of the Castle noted a payment of one hundred pounds to their highly prized "L.M." on September 14, 1803. Robert Emmet came to trial on September 19. It was what a modern prosecutor would describe as "an open-and-shut case."

CHAPTER THIRTY

BRITAIN LEADS WITH A CUCKOLD

GENERAL BONAPARTE was now in Egypt, making "the rashest attempt history records",[1] wasting thousands of French lives and exposing a powerful fleet to destruction, yet soothing the insomnia of all the intriguers and politicians, who dreaded his ambition and had sent him as far away from Paris as a popular commander and his army were likely to consent to go. Though not quite as far away as Moscow; the directors' thoughts had not run off wildly in that direction. But doubtless they sighed with relief when Nelson at Aboukir destroyed the French fleet. What sacrifice could be too great to sweep such a competitor as the Corsican right out of the field?

Nevertheless, this young general's dangerous popularity did not abate—and for the ironic reason that the British naval blockade prevented the French public from learning the truth about their fantastic Egyptian expedition. After Aboukir Bay Bonaparte was "laid by the heels on the banks of the Nile", completely cut off from France by swift British cruisers, patrolling the Mediterranean like hungry hawks. But conversely the French republic was cut off from him and from all news of a war as inglorious and futile as any of modern times. The defeat before Acre where his own siege train—just captured at sea by the English—was turned against him, the army infected with plague, the shortage of provisions and the resulting horror of his prisoners massacred at Jaffa as a "military necessity"—all such deflationary tidings were suppressed by the vigilant enemy frigates, and the embryonic legend of Corsican invincibility suffered no miscarriage.

It was Nelson's practice to use his frigates to keep watch upon harbors which were the known bases of hostile fleets. Sometimes intelligence of fleet movements was conveyed by the scouting frigate. On other occasions—before Trafalgar being a famous example—the frigate transmitted its warning signals to vessels stationed to pass them on to the main battle fleet. English frigates throughout the long struggle with the French Republic and Empire played a lively part in operations of Naval Intelligence and even of secret service. We shall see how a noted British agent made use of the cruiser blockade to launch an extraordinary undercover attack upon General Bonaparte, with a candid hope that the young military genius would be slain.

John H. Barnett was the secret agent who devised this deadly speculation. A hard-hitting, unscrupulous Briton, he was Bonaparte's implacable foe. Deciding that the general must be susceptible to women, Barnett had sent a number of fetching sirens against the man whom England considered the gravest threat to world tranquillity. But with this preliminary campaign the British agent accomplished nothing. When a storm dispersed the blockading squadron, Bonaparte set sail from Toulon on his Egyptian expedition. Barnett aboard HMS Lion sailed after him.

The wife of a young Gascon officer named Fourès succeeded in getting to Egypt by going aboard one of the French transports in masculine disguise. General Bonaparte learned of her exploit and interviewed the lady. Officers' wives had been forbidden to accompany them on this adventure; but audacious Mme Fourès—"blonde and blue-eyed Bellitote Fourès" whom the French Republican army would soon nickname satirically *"notre souverain de l'Orient"*[2]—was one destined to prove that the commanding general would permit an exception.

This distraction of Napoleon from his conquest of the Mamelukes was first noticed by the sweltering Army of the Orient when he began driving about accompanied by the Gascon's wife. One smart aide-de-camp trotted beside the carriage, Eugene de Beauharnais, the general's own stepson. Eugene's mother had made rather a fool of her Corsican suitor when he was not so famous and infinitely more ardent, and she had ever been disposed to flaunt her own infidelities. At last, though France and Egypt were far apart, it was the general's turn. Tight as the British blockade might become, it could never keep this meteor of gossip from scorching the tongues of Paris.

Something soon had to be done about Fourès. Why not discover that "military necessity"—it would be an infallible excuse by the time they got to Jaffa—recalled him to France? A brave soldier, uxorious, yet not too submissive to deviate from a rigid code of personal honor, he could not be expected to remain more than temporarily dazed by the rapid social ascent of his pretty young wife since her first interview with General Bonaparte. When Berthier told Fourès that he had been chosen—as a special mark of his superiors' confidence—to bear important dispatches from the expeditionary headquarters to the government in Paris, the officer saluted proudly, then lapsed into anxious speculations about securing transport for two.

Berthier, in all campaigns nearly everything a chief of staff can be, reminded Fourès that his mission was perilous. The sloop of war carrying him to France must outsail British frigates, and there might be an engagement at sea. It would never do to expose Mme Fourès to such dangers; moreover, her husband would have problems enough in safeguarding his official dispatches and getting home with them alive.

Barnett Chooses a French Weapon

Fourès submitted; and the menace of his Gascon temper seemed to have been eliminated from the war zone of the East. But we turn now to John H. Barnett, cruising about aboard HMS Lion and pacing the deck like a caged king of beasts. Barnett was by no means confined aboard the speedy frigate. He merely made it his headquarters, operating clandestinely under the direct command of Sir William Sidney Smith. Often the English agent went ashore in a fast-sailing tiny craft which was kept at the disposal of Naval Intelligence. In a variety of modest disguises he managed to spy upon the French army of occupation.[3] He penetrated to Cairo, where he gathered reports from his many well-paid informers—domestic servants in a score of eminent households, or native runners, guides and clerks who drew less munificent wages in the employ of the French.

From this system of spies Barnett learned a great deal about the army's hero, the savior of French prestige, Napoleon Bonaparte, and from agents serving in the palace gained a perfect comprehension of the Corsican's bedside manner. Mme Fourès was the siren Barnett had failed to find and enlist; she was, however, devoted to her role as *"notre souverain de l'Orient"*, and no British bargain could be struck with her. That brought the secret agent around to weighing the possible utility of Lieutenant Fourès. But just then an ultra-obliging Berthier whisked madame's husband from the scene.

The fast French sloop Chasseur was assigned to rush Fourès and his dispatches past the squadron of patrolling frigates. Barnett heard of this, and his trim little fishing craft crowded on sail and swept him to the side of the Lion before the French ship put to sea. Thereafter began an unequal chase, with the Lion fast enough to overhaul the Chasseur and so heavily armed, the French craft could neither escape nor resist. Fourès was taken prisoner. He was not treated as a prisoner, however—he became the personal guest of the insidious Mr Barnett. It was diplomatically brought home to the husband of Bonaparte's mistress that his dispatches had hardly been worth the trouble which the chief of staff had seemed to lavish upon them. Through the clerks at French headquarters who were taking his gold,

Barnett had obtained copies of those dispatches. Fourès was confounded when he read them; and after a few more stinging innuendoes Barnett had found his weapon of destruction.

Fourès asked only to be allowed to give his parole, to be permitted to return to Egypt and avenge his honor. Barnett, closely in touch with the British commander, was able to promise both permission and means of transport. Fourès was taken to Cairo, after which stroke the extemporized conspiracy broke down.

The detailed truth of ensuing swift events has been obscured by the excellent opportunities for melodrama. Possibly the Gascon did brush past French and Arab sentries, to find his wife asleep in a palace room adjoining Bonaparte's. Perhaps he picked up a dog leash and was thrashing the naked, screaming adulteress when the Republican general from next door, wearing the eye of Marengo and Austerlitz, an imperial frown and a night-shirt, marched in to defend his love. But more prosaic accounts indicate that common sense stayed the officer's hand before he ever approached the sentries.

Fourès at least found that Barnett had not exaggerated. His wife was now living openly with his commander in chief. It is certain that he encountered them together; but Fourès was also aware of his duty as a French soldier and understood the army's plight, its need for its ablest leader upon this flamboyant adventure. He must likewise have reckoned Britain's stake in the matter and comprehended the motive in back of British considerateness. Barnett expected him to kill Bonaparte; and Fourès owned every impulse to kill him. And yet Fourès rebelled at being chosen the tool of combatant intrigue and a domestic dupe as well. Right there Barnett's scheme evaporated in the cooling reaction of Gascon temperament. Lieutenant Fourès resigned his commission and returned alone to France.

CHAPTER THIRTY-ONE

THE CONTINENTAL BLOCKADE

NAPOLEON SOON BECAME that man who—in the definition of Josh Billings—"tried to do too much and he done it"; and the threatful drive of such a personality made imperative the excellence of the secret service which, largely financed from London, continuously spied upon him, comforted his enemies and waited patiently to accomplish his ruin.

The French emperor on December 21, 1806, had hurled his challenge at the "nation of shopkeepers" in the famous proclamation of blockade, aggravated eleven months later[1] by the decree issued from Milan placing England "under the ban of the Continent." All communication was to be at an end, even correspondence between Europe and the British Isles was forbidden. Merchandise suspected of British origin was burned; travelers suspected of having come from England or stopped over in any British port were summarily imprisoned. A counter-espionage measure par excellence, yet much more of an offensive stroke than that, since Napoleon was not then seriously hampered by enemy spies or Royalist plotters.

Communication between England and the Continent, however, was by no means completely suppressed. What had never been regular and normal became altogether sub rosa, circuitous and abnormal. Smuggling had flourished for centuries, but now, with the attempted isolation of Albion, the veteran, the hereditary smugglers grew intensely active, an integral part of secret service and the paid confederates of government. Through them for a price secret passage to the Continent could be arranged by way of Heligoland, Denmark or Holland, or even directly across the Channel. Even so, to send a letter on its roundabout course from London to Paris required at least a fortnight, and the route and expense were continually varying.

When the blockade meant to ruin British commerce was promulgated in 1806 there already was in operation a secret system of transport and communication whose hazard, scope and intricacy surpassed anything elsewhere established in modern history. From the very outset of the French Revolution it had been exceedingly difficult to maintain communications with England; and, except for the fleeting

Peace of Amiens, this vigilant animosity was not to abate until Bonaparte went to Elba. Communication with England—enemy of the revolution, enemy of the Directoire, the Consulate, the Empire—was the crime which down to 1814 provided the courts martial with the largest number of victims. The French, adapting themselves to circumstances with their habitual ingenuity, practiced evading the Draconian port and frontier control laws of the revolution as a kind of apprenticeship looking to more profitable evasions in the time of the Continental Blockade.

It is of record that an adventurous citizen of Chambonas, in the department of Ardèche, having been entrusted with a letter for the brothers of Louis XVI, then at Coblenz, disguised himself as a shepherd with smock and crook, mobilized a flock of sheep, which he drove to Savoy, "grazing them on any chance pasturage, commons, and fallows," and no one troubled to search him or even demand his passport. At Chambéry he got rid of his sheep, discarded his smock and crook, and journeyed to Coblenz by the regular post without a hitch.[2]

During the Terror communication with foreign countries or with émigrés was a capital offense, and therefore it promoted a prosperous industry. At Saint-Claude peasants were ready to guide hunted aristocrats or alien secret agents through the mountains and across the Swiss frontier. It was the same in the Vosges. A woman living near Saint-Dié forwarded news, smuggled émigrés in and out of the country, reported to their kinsfolk remaining in France what was occurring along the Rhine, and transmitted jewels or money with scrupulous exactitude. Marie Barbe, a young girl of Bruyères, carried messages in all weathers from France to the Royalist army of Condé.

A twelve-year-old boy of the family of De Gonneville regularly traversed the whole of Normandy, carrying the most incriminating dispatches between the Royalist Frotté's headquarters and the coast; at night he customarily slept in the woods after hiding his messages some distance away under stones. For ten years the beautiful young chatelaine of Vauloue in La Manche, Mme d'Anjou, defied the shrewdest investigators of the revolutionary police. At length they abandoned their efforts to capture this intangible bearer of secret dispatches and hostess to Royalist or foreign emissaries.

The Iron Rock and Other Stratagems

No wonder, then, that upon the Continental Blockade being decreed it was immediately challenged by an experienced staff of operatives, "ready to snap their fingers at all prohibitions, and to enter into relations with the British cruisers maneuvering day and night in sight of the French coast."[3] The police prefect of La Manche had been told by an informer as early as 1805 that communication with Jersey was contrived by means of an iron box, painted and shaped to resemble the projecting boulders among which it was lodged on the Ile Chaussey. "Four persons have scoured the island from eleven o'clock in the morning to five o'clock in the afternoon," the prefect complained, "shifting all the boulders, probing all the recesses, without finding anything." It happened that "Chaussey" was a name applied to fifty-two small islets in that region, so that the work of the counterspies would involve "very long and difficult searches."[4] Which, be it known, never had any result.

Yet this useful "iron box" among the rocks or in the sand of the seashore, concealing messages and small parcels in transit, was repeatedly mentioned in contemporary British Intelligence reports. After nightfall a boat would put out from the British fleet and approach the shore. In order to spare the landing party the exposure of a prolonged hunt for the iron box or "rock", a Royalist agent posted on the cliff and smoking a pipe directed their search by drawing sparks from his tinderbox according to a prearranged telegraphic code.[5] Even the boats used in this traffic were especially built to withstand examination. They had secret hiding places both for letters and packages, so that it would have been necessary to rip them to pieces in order to discover anything. "Papers were sometimes placed even in the oars which were bored and prepared for this purpose."[6]

The contraband traffic between two countries officially closed to one another was effectually maintained and even *improved*, in spite of the Blockade. Consignments of money regularly passed between London and Paris, and drafts were drawn by English bankers on Parisian banking houses as though Napoleon were a myth and his strangling decrees a harebrained hoax. The English correspondence in time developed "express" messengers who managed somehow to cross the Strait of Dover by a direct though clandestine route, carrying the documents confided to them between the double soles of their heavy boots, or sewn into the collars of their coats—or simply in their pockets. They were resolute, shrewd and fearless men, generally unhampered by strong partisanship and yet absolutely trustworthy. What they did they did to earn a living; and a good living it seems to have been, since powerful interests were engaged, and government officials, rich noblemen and bankers paid handsomely for the speed that the "aces" of this curious company of postgraduate smugglers were able to promise them.

Hermely, the Breton, from the days of the Directory had been as regular as a ferry, plying back and forth between Paris and London. Police, informers, excise officers and coastguards meant nothing to him. And the Continental Blockade only succeeded in doubling his income. During one period the municipality of Boulogne was readily "persuaded" to issue false passports, a great boon to secret-service operations, but one soon terminated. M. Fouché got wind of the outlaw commerce and stationed in Boulogne the terrible agent, Mengaud, whom he called his "biggest bull-dog",[7] and that gap in the Blockade was at once marked Closed.

Hyde de Neuville, that Royalist agent of indestructible enterprise, landing in Normandy, congratulated himself on the "fairly easy" conditions of his journey, since he was able to make his way ashore with the water only up to his shoulders.[8] Often the agents and couriers, realizing that they were about to be taken into custody, had to get rid of compromising documents by eating them. And so the profession of express messenger had its bilious attacks as well as its bonuses. The "secret-service tissue" or extraordinarily thin tough paper used by correspondents of the period was a good deal more of a dose than merely eating one's words. Yet a certain Mme Chalamet is said to have managed to ingest a whole packet of letters when unexpectedly overtaken by Fouché's prowling policemen.

Ludicrous and uncomfortable predicaments were frequent; but every individual who set out to beat the Blockade assumed the risk of capital punishment. How many of the daring emissaries were detected and shot? One authority mentions fourteen names of comparatively well-known partisans. Scores and hundreds of others must have been slain while resisting capture or executed after an arrest and trial which left never a trace upon the records, not even a name in the meticulous archives of the French.

Audacious Abbé and Intrepid Nymph

A great number of priests were employed along the lines of communication between France and England. Two of them—for quite different reasons—became famous. The Abbé Ratel from the days of the Consulate had settled down in the château of a Mme de Combremont near Boulogne-sur-Mer. He was utterly brazen about it, making no effort to conceal himself and behaving like the master of the estate. He even persuaded his amiable hostess to receive Mlle Julienne Sper, known as Pauline and an ardent Royalist, "believed to be a kept woman," according to the files of the police ministry, who had passed some months under detention in the Temple. This young lady, whom the peasants of the neighborhood called *belle-peau*, was presumed to be Ratel's mistress. And from this excellent haven the abbé dispatched a stupendous correspondence. The English made it worth his while. He drew an annual salary of £600, of which £240 were for Mlle Sper, and collected £18,000 before any British official had the temerity to ask for an accounting. It was discovered that the secret-service correspondence supervised by Ratel had cost for a period of three years nearly 300,000 francs in excess of preceding expenditures. A considerable portion of this sum had stuck to the fingers of the abbé, and he was required to undergo the agony of making a substantial refund.

How differently expressed was the zealous Royalism of the Abbé Leclerc, alias "Boisvalon." Known, but not humorously, as the "man with the wall-eye", he was to a masterly biographer of the French revolutionary intrigants, "the perfect model of the conspirator, obstinate, active, adroit, enterprising, discreet, and—the most singular thing—disinterested."[9] He had not even tried to leave Paris during the Terror, and other Royalist agents serving the British had found him following the profession of a lawyer "the better to disguise himself" and also "so well-informed of all that was happening in France" it rather stirred their suspicions. From his hiding place in the Rue du Pot-de-Fer Leclerc had maintained a vast and unbroken correspondence, managing to collate "all the reports of all the Royalist agencies in France", and forwarding them to the exiled princes. As his reward, in 1803 he was summoned to Boulogne by Ratel, who revealed that Napoleon had lately conceived his tremendous scheme for invading and "conquering" England with a large army, that his camp was already being organized. The British authorities must be kept closely informed. Ratel himself was to be stationed in London, while to Leclerc would fall an eminently dangerous and difficult assignment —control of all the clandestine traffic of the French coast.

Gendarme patrols were now regularly scouring the countryside; while agents of the secret police, sent on from Paris, were developing a rigorous supervision over the hinterland between Dunkirk and Étaples. Spies, in short, were expected—and were to be discovered and shot!

Abbé Leclerc prepared to meet this Bonapartist challenge. He had neither château nor mistress, would accept no salary, and spent nothing upon his personal requirements. What refuge he needed was to be found in the homes of Royalist friends; and he seldom stayed more than a single night in any one place. He was always on the road in a little berline, driven by Pierre-Marie Pois, his faithful secretary, who also made constant use of several picturesque pseudonyms: Larose, Vieille-Femme, La Besace, Vieille-Perruque. With this slender equipment Leclerc—who was, on occasion, known by the names Bailly, Godefroid, Lepage, and his old favorite, Boisvalon—managed to send to London information as valuable as anything included in the *Bulletin de Police* which Fouché, throughout his ministry, daily dispatched to Napoleon.

Leclerc's espionage staff was small but select. An agent located in Brest, a highly placed official in the Ministry of War, served him well, as did another paid confederate—"still more highly placed"—whose post was in the administrative department of the imperial navy. In addition to the most absorbing details of military intelligence which he was thus enabled to transmit, Leclerc conducted a political correspondence of such interest and amplitude "as had never hitherto been known."[10] Maintaining uninterrupted communication with England, on a coast whose smallest coves and inlets were protected by army posts, and on which the whole strength of Napoleon's prodigious military machine was concentrated, Leclerc would set out in his little berline with his secretary, pass through Étaples, La Canche, L'Authie and the Somme, and then La Bresle, until he finally reached the district of Eu, which was not then occupied by the imperial troops. There he got in touch with needy fishermen, ordered a good meal and threw his money around, paying for everything in gold. Pois or "Larose", drinking cognac and repeatedly filling the glasses of the guests, would explain that he was a merchant who had to advise an émigré living in London of an unclaimed inheritance. Nothing political about this, just a matter of private interests! He would even read passages from the letter which he carried, no part of which could possibly seem compromising—unless it occurred to the listeners that there might be a secret message written in invisible ink between the widely spaced lines.

Some fisherman always was found ready to deliver this business letter to the English cruiser which the French boats often encountered in the Channel. For this casual service, while Leclerc remained in the background, the "merchant, Larose" offered twenty louis—nearly 500 francs, a small fortune. He was greatly assisted by Phillippe, a fisherman who also kept a grocer's shop at Tréport. This man recruited several friends, including the local schoolmaster, Duponchel,[11] and also his wife, a woman whose celebrated corpulence met the basic requirements of disguise without hindering her zeal or mobility. She made numerous journeys, carrying important packets for her husband, and received twelve francs for each journey. If ever questioned or arrested on the road, said Leclerc, she must insist that she "had just found the letters on the beach and was taking them to the police at Eu or Boulogne."

Leclerc, already past his forties and without physical attraction, seems to have exerted an inexplicable influence upon women. Since he was a priest it is not surprising that devout women, deeply attached to the Royalist cause, risked execution in offering him a refuge. But as his morals appear to have been irreproachable, we can only assume that his fanatical hatred of Bonaparte and the revolutionary cause proved irresistibly contagious in those aristocratic circles to which the "man with the wall-eye" had access. That alone—overlooking the "painful and annoying slander" of the time—accounts for the adventurous debut of his engaging accomplice, known as "the Nymph."

One of the Bourbon sympathizers with whom Leclerc now and again found a haven was a Mme de Roussel de Préville, widow of a captain in the Royal navy and a respected member of Boulogne society. Among other children, Mme de Préville had a daughter who, in 1804, was eighteen years old, a small and extremely pretty girl whose "hair and eyebrows"—according to a contemporary—"were chestnut, her eyes blue, her nose aquiline but well shaped, her mouth small, her chin round, and her face slightly flushed." She was called "the Nymph" because of her "beauty and graceful movements" and was "accustomed to adulation . . . full of gaiety, phenomenally frivolous, and inconstant and ingenuous to the point of folly. . . . Balls, receptions, and the adornment of her person, were her sole preoccupation."

Mlle de Préville was, it appears, the very opposite in age, appearance and character of that "perfect model of the conspirator" Leclerc. Yet so varied are the requirements of true secret service that the phenomenally frivolous young lady survives among the immortals of French political intrigue. Infected either with the exaltation of the Bourbon partisan or a yearning for masculine adventure, she became so enthusiastic about the counter-revolutionary work to which the resourceful abbé was devoting his life that she offered him her services. Leclerc accepted; he was ready to sacrifice everything to the success of his current undertaking; why not add this delectable ingénue to his little troupe of conspirators! And so, with sufficient guile to delude her mother and some thought still for the adornment of her person, Nymph Roussel de Préville—as she remains in the archives of the French police—disguised herself as a boy, borrowed the name of "Dubuisson", and set about traveling all the roads of the department as a Royalist courier and spy.

The girl was fascinated like many another by the mysteries of the "English correspondence",[12] and she seems to have been habitually rash, yet without impairing the safety of her comrades in their antipatriotic enterprise. She began by receiving letters conveyed by the elephantine but ardent "woman Phillippe", and passed them on to the abbé, her chief. Later she was authorized by him to pay some of the useful but minor operatives. She was often absent from Boulogne for several days at a time, "pushing as far afield as Dieppe or Amiens" alone, or in company with Pois. It happened also that one of her uncles, the Abbé de Laporte, was among the most active of Royalist agents on the lines of communication; and he is said to have frequently crossed the Channel to carry to England important dispatches brought to him by his hazard-hunting niece.

Progress of the English Correspondence

The French public had lately been told that "storms have caused us to lose some ships of the line after an imprudent fight", which propagandic great-grandsire of all the voluptuous understatements of the World War was merely breaking the news of the annihilation of Napoleon's navy at Trafalgar. That "imprudent fight"[13] of October 21, 1805, completed the ruin of the emperor's scheme of landing an army upon English soil; but he was already engrossed in other plans of conquest. Admiral Calder's victory in the Bay of Biscay three months before Trafalgar had caused Napoleon to snatch his troops from Boulogne and rush them across Europe in launching the campaign which would terminate brilliantly at Austerlitz. He was, however, "left with Britain in pitiless opposition, unattainable and unconquerable, able to strike here or there against him along all the coasts of Europe."[14] And the secret society of malcontents, romantic adventurers and hired accomplices, directed by Leclerc and, from a safer distance, Ratel, continued to operate and spread throughout the departments lying between Paris and the Channel.

Now the secret police under Fouché and Desmarest were never noted for accepting a good hard flouting with patient smiles. The alertness and perseverance of agents like Mengaud had closed one by one the gaps in the Blockade, and the gap at Tréport was bound in time to be detected and closed with a slam. A police informer managed to thread his way into the fringes of the Leclerc band—the usual counter-espionage technique—and Desmarest's men were soon hot upon the heels of the abbé, the Nymph and the faithful "Larose." Leclerc took refuge in Abbeville in the home of a Mme Denis, and there also Nymph de Préville was given shelter. Phillippe, the Tréport fisherman-grocer, upon being interrogated, confessed everything he knew, which was enough to send police agents and gendarmes galloping to Abbeville. Mme Denis' dwelling in the Petite Rue Notre-Dame seems to have been almost of Jesuit design, for neither Leclerc nor the "boy Dubuisson" could be discovered by the searchers. However, they so successfully intimidated Mme Denis herself that she led them to the hiding place of the documents which related to secret English correspondence.

Abbé Leclerc, it is said, made his escape late at night in the direction of Saint-Omer. The young girl separated from him and quietly returned to her home in Boulogne, telling her mother that she was outlawed, but innocent, and proposed to give herself up. Mme de Préville's stricken bewilderment can be imagined, for until this moment she had not had any suspicion of her daughter's reckless behavior. But she acted with admirable coolness and decision, sending the girl back to Abbeville to some relatives who lived there, and begging her to lie carefully hidden. But that was expecting too much of Leclerc's most extraordinary confederate. In "a town full of experienced police-officers, who had come down from Paris to find Leclerc's accomplices, she spent the day at her window, and twice went so far as to appear at a public ball. Then one day, perhaps in a passing fit of prudence, she disappeared."[15]

What became of her? With the abbé and Pois, his secretary, "*Nymph* Roussel de Préville, known as *Dubuisson*" was sentenced to death in default nearly a year later by the military commission sitting at Rouen. Phillippe and another fisherman, Dieppois, with the schoolmaster, Duponchel, were also sentenced to death—and they were not lucky enough to be in default. All three were executed. Nymph, unaccompanied, crossed the greater part of Europe in an effort to get to Russia but finally took ship for London where she ceased her wanderings. The British government bestowed on her, a minor condemned to death, an annual pension of 600 francs.[16]

Leclerc, having himself stayed awhile in England, then moved on to settle in Münster,[17] where he straightway began to gather together the broken strands of his secret-intelligence system. The imperial police had shut off his contraband postal service adjacent to Boulogne; but the lines of communication could be redirected to turn aside to Jersey and the Norman coast. And this the diligent abbé accomplished—with the help of his agents in Paris who had escaped detection and the never-failing sustenance of British gold.

Chapter Thirty-two
THE POWERFUL IMPACT OF POUNDS STERLING

THE CABINET MINISTERS of King George III were uniformly partial to intrigue and strategy. They spent money with lavish hands, a profound faith in the merits of secret service and a nice respect for the recurrent indigence of well-informed foreigners. Whereas their French opponents were always complaining of empty coffers and a chronic dearth of secret-service funds. The clandestine operations of Britain against Napoleon held an advantage, therefore, which we shall find repeated in the powerful combination of British Intelligence and blockade in the war with Germany a century later. Vital information could be bought from highly placed members of the Bonapartist regime and the support of neutrals gained by tactfully disbursed gratuities.

A large part of the program of espionage aimed at the Empire was conducted by British diplomatic representatives in Germany, the minister at Stuttgart, the plenipotentiary in Cassel, and especially Drake, the minister plenipotentiary accredited to the Bavarian court at Munich. Drake was so insinuating a dispenser of bribe money that he hired the director of the Bavarian post office, thereby assuring himself access to all the French correspondence. Even so, this English spy-master was gravely compromised when he was induced to employ one who happened to be an agent of French counter-espionage. Drake paid him well for misleading information, while he secured from the English diplomat important confidential documents which Napoleon hastened to make public.

Kunad, a Danish representative, and Forbes, the American consul in Hamburg, were able to support British secret-service operations by supplying false passports bearing Danish or American names. The American consul in Dunkirk was also alleged by the French to be so active in the interests of enemy espionage as to be virtually an agent of the British Intelligence.[1] In a letter which the emperor addressed to Rear Admiral Decrès, he warned: "English cruisers are making it a practice to board neutral ships about to enter our harbors, taking off a couple of members of the crew and substituting for them two spies, who are thus enabled to remain in French ports as long as the neutral ship remains." It was likewise discovered that subjects of neutral states, found on board prizes captured at sea, were often British agents who had been provided with foreign passports.

A motley army of hireling spies also served the British, and for certain missions of a routine nature were more effective than the numerous fanatic Royalists and Bourbon sympathizers who were posing as Bonapartists only for the purpose of saving their skins and covertly skinning the despised Corsican "usurper." Russians, Swedes, Spaniards and Jews, merchants, hawkers, peddlers, traveling mountebanks and women all listened to the siren song of golden guineas. And a torrential stream of intelligence poured into London from all corners of the Continent, most of which for the time being was inclosed in the sphere of imperial France by right of conquest.

The agents of Britain used many tricks and wiles in forwarding their reports, or were helped by such Royalist systems as that of the Abbé Leclerc in running them past the Continental Blockade.[2] But also much news was dispatched in the ordinary post.[3] Letters, ostensibly directed to a Danish, Dutch, Swedish, Spanish or American "cover", were written in codes as ingenious as any concocted in more recent times. The French intercepted and deciphered one letter in 1809 which was "written entirely in the staff-notation, and represented on the face of it a harmless musical composition." A message found in the wallet of a suspected person contained this diverting line: "Wash the linen I am sending you before you use it, in order to get rid of the stickiness." Which led to the detection of a report transcribed in chemical ink upon the hem of a petticoat. When a woman spy was discovered employing this very dodge in France during the World War, it impressed all beholders as original and unique.

A favorite—and nearly unbeatable—code trick of the enemies of Napoleon was the use of token words. There exists a confidential report submitted to the emperor by his Ministry of Police, which explains it has just been learned by French counter-spies that token words borrowed from music and botany are no longer to be employed by the British Secret Service—and that the vocabularies of watchmaking, catering and culinary arts are henceforth to be exploited in the fixed codes of the enemy.

In a later chapter the intelligence systems of banking houses are considered as phenomena of secret-service evolution; but this is the place to mention the operations in that line of the Rothschilds during the years of European turmoil dedicated to the sacred principle that a Corsican or any other upstart dictator is entitled to slaughter his millions, wear an ermine robe, and wed a young archduchess. The Rothschilds believed that Napoleon would lose in the race to ruin all of Europe before he ruined himself. They virtually gambled their financial existence and their lives upon this belief; and as the brothers spread out over a Continent turning rapidly French it became a problem of the first order to repudiate the destiny of Bonaparte and conserve the larger destiny of Rothschild. Not since the time of the Fuggers had Europe caught any glimpse of a private secret service working to such good purpose; and, apart from the British service at the core of Napoleonic antagonisms, it was probably the best in the encircling camp of the emperor's foes.

Napoleon had so often experienced the impact of pounds sterling that he placed every reliance himself upon the efficacy of cold cash. It did not always have to be cold or even legal. The police prefect, Pasquier, in his memoirs relates how his secret agents ferreted out a hidden printing plant where a number of skilled craftsmen were employed at high wages and only at night. The house wherein their mysterious work was done stood beyond the Barrier in the Plaine Montrouge; it was strongly guarded and heavily bolted and barred. The time—shortly before the expedition against Russia in 1812. Pasquier finally ordered a raid. His agents crashed in and stopped in amazement. The plant, as they had suspected, was counterfeiting bank notes; but not French or British. The notes they examined were Austrian and Russian. When the matter was referred to the Prefecture, an order came through commanding Pasquier to drop the affair. The chief printer was a M. Fain, brother of one of Napoleon's confidential secretaries, the one generally engaged in reading to him his favorite digests culled from private letters invaded at the bureau of postal censorship.

The counterfeiting, Pasquier was warned, enjoyed the emperor's personal patronage. The money being made was to be used in purchasing supplies during the forthcoming gigantic invasion of enemy lands. General Savary himself justified this unique practice to the correct Pasquier, saying that their imperial master only followed the example of the British. Savary we now find suddenly in command of all the Napoleonic police. Joseph Fouché, the genius, the adroit technician, having weathered sundry storms and dangerous calms at the ministry, having survived the suspicion and counter-espionage of Napoleon's brothers, had finally been discharged from office when caught having a fit of common sense.

Fouché could not approve the emperor's fruitless and desolating program of hostilities. Fouché saw no reason for avoiding peace with England, and, through an intermediary, a banker here and a banker there, especially a not too reputable M. Ouvrard, the minister of peace had ventured to open impromptu negotiations. Traveling by way of Holland, where a Bonaparte brother feebly flourished on the throne, Ouvrard and his negotiations had been found out. Napoleon considered this final insolence insupportable. Was Fouché now a British agent? Talleyrand had gone over—or been driven—into the Austrian camp, and was the alleged spy of Metternich. Fouché, too! The young empress and many another spoke urgently in his favor. Excuse him again, retain him in office! But Napoleon was in a mood. He had secretly ordered Savary to arrest Ouvrard, Fouché's friend and "shady" accomplice; Fouché had to be humbled and supplanted.

CHAPTER THIRTY-THREE

A CRACKPOT'S COUP

A WAR-MANIAC as aggressive and remorseless as the Emperor Napoleon can arbitrarily dismiss even a minister of police as resourceful, unscrupulous and thoroughly well informed as Joseph Fouché. He can turn him out like a groom, but he may expect to pass some wakeful nights putting out fires in the stables. It was characteristic of the Bonaparte of 1810 to replace a sharp and flexible instrument like Fouché with a blunt, pretentious tool like Savary; and it was characteristic of the Fouché of any year of his adult life to strike at the man who had humbled him by mining the path of his successor.

Savary had been given no choice in the matter. "You are Minister of Police. Take your oath and get to work,"[1] the emperor had barked at him. If the courtier and commandant of imperial gendarmerie would have preferred to dodge so ticklish a pilot's position, he was not allowed to admit it.

Fouché, the suddenly ousted creator of the most effective and far-reaching political police system of Europe—and, up to that time, of all history—was not departing discourteously. He was too adroit and well informed, too reserved and self-contained to undertake any futile open resistance. But he was possessed throughout his stirring, corkscrew career with a demonic humor, a puckish delight in making someone he had cause to dread or despise play the fool at his manipulating. Savary was now elected to the role, Napoleon having cast one ballot.

There was so much to be done, loose threads to be gathered together. Years of mounting authority, of accumulating despotic powers imposed upon Joseph Fouché a solemn obligation to his emperor and to France. He must welcome General Savary, Duc de Rovigo, make him at home in his new post, show him around. The incoming minister had every reason to hate Fouché and fear him, now more than ever; and yet he straightway allowed himself to be deceived by this consummate plotter whom he was humiliating, who received him in full-dress uniform with disarming cordiality.

Savary was incautious enough to grant his predecessor "a few days"

A CRACKPOT'S COUP   217

in which to set the ministry in order. Fouché could have attended to it in half the time. Aided by one trusted friend, he spent the next four days and four nights creating an impish hurricane of disorder. Every record of consequence was swept from the files, every document in that vast reservoir of espionage reports and political intelligence was removed to accommodate Fouché or embarrass his successor. Anything which compromised persons over whom it would still be desirable to have a hold was put aside to be taken to the retiring minister's estate at Ferrières. The rest went into the fire.

Precious names and addresses, names of those who had served Fouché as spies in the fashionable quarter of the Faubourg Saint-Germain, in the army or at court, were not to be inherited. Let Savary have the lower strata of shadows, sneaks and informers, of doorkeepers, waiters, servants and prostitutes—and let him try to run the police service with them. The general index was destroyed; lists of Royalist émigrés and the most confidential correspondence disappeared; some less sensational documents were given wrong identification numbers. The essential parts of the giant machine were thus scrambled with malicious zeal. Veteran agents and employees, on whom Savary would expect to lean, were bribed in advance to act simultaneously in the secret corps of the ousted incumbent, to report regularly to him who meant to remain their real master. In order to play this grandiose trick upon Savary, the wily Joseph had to destroy his own beloved lifework.

When finally he handed over his charge, he ironically produced just one significant document—already two years old—an abusive memorandum dealing with the exiled House of Bourbon. Savary, upon discovering how the ministerial archives had been plundered, hurried to protest to the emperor. Instead of proceeding on his embassy to Rome, Fouché had been resting comfortably at Ferrières, listening for the fanfarade of his dull rival's fury. But now the storm broke in earnest and lightning flickered around the jester's cap and bells.

Messages sped from Napoleon to Ferrières, demanding "the immediate surrender of all the ministerial documents."[2] Fouché was bold enough to intimate that he knew too much. Secrets concerning the Bonaparte family, those tiresome or troublesome brothers and sisters, had regularly come into his possession. But he had deemed it expedient to destroy them. If he had been too zealous . . .

The emperor was infuriated by this direct hint of blackmail. Various emissaries had already appealed to Fouché;[3] and to each he had returned the same blandly exasperating answer. He was very sorry— no doubt he had erred by an excess of caution, but all the papers had been burned. Whereupon Napoleon summoned Comte Dubois, chief of the private police and until recently Fouché's subordinate. For the first time in France a man, an official, was openly defying the dictator, and, striding up and down the room, Napoleon lashed at this rebel with furious and vulgar invectives.[4]

When Dubois visited Ferrières, the master of the house had to submit to having all his papers put under seal. This humbled rather than inconvenienced him, for he had been careful some days before to remove to another and more distant place everything that mattered. He had carried the little joke too far and, having yielded to the police emissary, at once began writing plausible apologies to the emperor.[5] But it was too late. Napoleon refused to receive him and sent him one of the most contemptuous dismissals ever addressed to a minister of state:

> Monsieur le duc d'Otrante, your services can no longer be congenial to me. You must leave for your senatorship within twenty-four hours.[6]

And the new minister of police was ordered to see to it that Joseph Fouché promptly obeyed the edict of banishment.

Savary Traces the Missing Spies

The Duke of Rovigo, having discharged that congenial duty, turned back to the task of commanding the imperial police in spite of Fouché. Though he tried promoting some of the low-class informers his predecessor had bequeathed him, he soon realized that he would need more reliable spies. He was, of course, entirely cut off from the skillful assistance of all those superior agents who had reported to Fouché personally, and on whom he had come to rely for his up-to-the-minute knowledge of the empire, its court and its capital.

A bit dull, very methodical, loyal and obstinate, Savary was no blockhead, and—possibly advised by Desmarest or Réal—he contrived to solve his problem of upper-crust espionage in a neat and expeditious fashion. He had found in his rifled offices a registry of addresses which Fouché and the friend had not thought worth mutilating. Intended for the messengers who delivered letters, this registry was kept by the confidential clerks; and Savary, believing most of them still loyal to the chief he had displaced, prevented their learning of his design by taking the registry into his private study one night and copying out the whole list himself. He found names which astonished him, names which he said[7] he would have sooner expected to find in China than in that catalogue. Many addresses, however, had no designation save a number or single initial; and these he suspected were the most valuable of all.

Savary, having acquired the addresses, began summoning each agent to his office by a letter written in the third person and transmitted by one of his messengers. He never proposed an hour for the interview but never sent for two of his prospects on the same day. Each secret agent came as requested, generally toward evening; and before he was shown in, Savary took the precaution to ask his chief usher whether this individual had often called upon M. Fouché. The usher had in nearly all instances seen the visitor before and could supply some information about him. By this means Savary prepared himself to take the right tone when greeting the newcomer—to be cordial or reserved, in keeping with the attitude of his predecessor.

He dealt in much the same way with those "specialists" who were identified by an initial or number. He wrote to them at their given addresses but dispatched the letters by confidential clerks who had done this service before—who, presumably, thought their new chief was acting upon the recommendations of Fouché—and who were known personally to the concierges of the houses where the agents lived. The Parisian concierge, champion of busybodies even in that time, was inquisitive about his, or her, lodgers' correspondence and knew exactly to whom should be delivered any letter with an initial or number in lieu of a name.

When one of these hitherto unidentified persons called, a little adroitness soon discovered his name. It sometimes happened that a formerly active agent made use of more than one initial. If his concierge had handed him two different letters, when he appeared at the ministry it was merely explained to him that the clerks had inadvertently written to him twice. In every case the summons contained a request that the letter should be brought along as a form of introduction.

Savary was so determined to surpass the efficiency of the service under Fouché that he tried out another method of gaining the acquaintance of the secret personnel. The cashier was ordered to inform him whenever an agent called to collect salary or expenses. At first, so suspicious were Fouché's people of the new management, very few persons presented themselves; but self-interest prevailed after a few lean weeks, and strangers began dropping in, "merely to inquire," as they explained. Invariably they met the new chief. Savary took each visit as a matter of course, masking his ignorance, discussing current events. Often after persuading a newcomer to boast of his services, he voluntarily raised the agent's rate of pay.

Plodding, methodical, persistent, he in time re-established all of the masterly Fouché's undercover connections. His next step was expansion and elaboration of the formidable system of espionage.

He wanted something even more searching and comprehensive than his predecessor had devised. In this he was encouraged by Napoleon, whose arrogance and megalomania had throttled Europe and were now weaving an invisible noose around his own neck. Presently this courtier and gendarme officer elevated to the control of the police had earned the sobriquet of *Séide Mouchard*—sheik of police-spies. He had, at last, whole tribes of surveillants and talebearers in his corps: factory workmen, cabmen and street porters, gossips and *gobe-mouches* of the clubs.

When fashionable Paris migrated for the summer and early autumn, Savary followed the most exalted personages right into their country homes. House servants, gardeners and letter carriers worked for him, and likewise many an unsuspected guest. Reversing the process, he actually obliged masters to spy upon their servants, each householder being required to transmit a report upon any change in his establishment and acquaint the police regularly with the conduct of persons employed there.

Such a suction pump of doubtfully incriminating trivia could expect only one reward. Savary became the best-hated man in the annals of the prefecture. Yet he appeared to relish any symptom of his remorseless efficacy.

He spared no one, bullied the clergy, increased the rigors of the wretched prisoners of war confined at Verdun and Bitche. Exercising with such great gusto his petty, vexatious surveillance over all Paris, over all classes throughout France—political, social and criminal—small wonder that he was universally despised.

Savary was avaricious—eaten up with vanity, able to run a high temperature of self-importance without spontaneous combustion. The perfect routine bureaucrat, lifted by chance to the pinnacle of all-time bureaucracy, he grew jealous of his rights and privileges and fanatic in vindicating himself on the instant he suspected his authority had been disparaged or curtailed.

Never perhaps a more inflated, unjustifiable pride—and never did it precede a more humiliating, justified downfall! Savary's pretensions as a director of imperial police were utterly exploded. Not by a rapier thrust from a Fouché or a Talleyrand; but by one half mad, who succeeded in shaking Napoleon's throne, who jarred the very foundations of parvenu empire and made its police minister sublimely ridiculous.

General Malet's Mania

Every conspirator deems it his privilege to overthrow at least one government, and no questions asked. And Malet—who had not done much soldiering, yet arrived at general's rank—was a born conspirator. A little off balance at times, to be sure, a crackpot but very resolute in all his larger lunacies, he earned a prominent place among the many devious, engaging schemers who embellish this record. Genius like theirs requires no special triumph or acclaim; its very extravagance and originality provide its own perpetual solace. Predestined intriguers of Malet's stamp can accommodate their lives to anything, even insanity, but never to tranquillity. They flourish chiefly in turbulent times and pay their way only in a coinage of added turbulence, spreading insomnia like a plague upon pompous official contemporaries.

Malet's army record was the kind that left almost everything to be desired. In June of 1804, when he was in command of the troops at Angoulême, the prefect requested that he should be cashiered. Napoleon, as first consul, was content merely to change his station and ordered him to Sables-d'Olonne. March 2, 1805 saw Malet's name suddenly lodged on the retired list owing to further brushes with the civil authorities in La Vendée. But he appealed again to Napoleon, now emperor, who indulgently reinstated him as an active officer on March 26. The following May 31 he was again retired because of certain financial irregularities, which decree, however, was never put into force, and Malet continued drawing the regular active-service pay. And what was his gratitude to the commander in chief whose lenity he had tested to the limit? In 1808 he was caught taking a hand in a conspiracy against the emperor and thereafter held as a political prisoner at Sainte-Pélagie; but he had some influence with Fouché, through which—before the police minister's downfall—he obtained transfer to the private asylum of a Dr Dubuisson in the Faubourg Saint-Antoine.

Seclusion there gave this general just the leisure his irrational perseverance required to work upon a new plot. And what resulted was an authentic masterpiece, owning an utterly reckless and brazen yet wonderfully simple design. Malet intended first of all to take advantage of the emperor's absence from Paris; and his own special talent for creating confusion, coupled with the delays and uncertainty of communication, would do the rest. He proposed to announce the death of Napoleon and declare a "Provisional Government", supported by bodies of troops of whom he meant boldly to assume command. All of which, when the hour struck, came about precisely as he had expected. This was Paris, the seat of Empire, the headquarters of a conqueror before whom German and Italian royalty trembled; and yet, save for one trifling mischance, the plot of the harebrained Malet would have been wholly successful.

Paris at the time was weakly governed. Cambacérès represented the emperor. Savary controlled all the police but, in spite of his organization of spies, knew nothing of Malet and next to nothing of the temper of the city below its glossy imperial surfacing. The prefect, Pasquier, was an honest, competent administrator, but not a man of action. The garrison of the capital was made up chiefly of raw levies, all the veteran divisions either facing Wellington in Spain or far away with Napoleon who led them to their—and his own—doom in Russia. General Hulin, the military commandant of Paris, was typical of his post and his calling, a sturdy, methodical and loyal soldier, unimaginative and naïve, a mere infant in arms.

At Dr Dubuisson's agreeable retreat, half asylum, half place of detention, the inmates were permitted to go about on parole, to associate freely with one another, and receive whatever visitors they pleased. General Malet was thus enabled to mature his plan, and, since the place sheltered other irreconcilables, he might readily have enlisted confederates. But there was only one other man at the *maison de santé* whom he cared to trust, the Abbé Lafone, whose audacity and resolution were quite the equal of Malet's, and whose long record of participation in hazardous Royalist plots against the Empire had stirred much irrational envy.

These two postgraduate conspirators kept their own counsel, for experience had introduced them to treachery and betrayal in many disguises. Malet knew that he could rely on the co-operation of two generals, Guidal and Laborie, with whom he had been on intimate terms in prison. But he proves himself to have been a real master craftsman, in that he prevented even this pair of anti-Bonapartist generals from learning the whole aim and extent of the conspiracy.

At the sanitarium Malet frequently had catered to his own whim by donning his full-dress uniform. The attendants were used to it and humored him; therefore it seemed strange to none that, when his "zero hour" came, at eight o'clock in the evening, October 23, 1812, Malet and his friend, the abbé, strode forth from the private asylum with the general in full martial array.

Presently he appeared at the gates of the neighboring barracks, spoke crisply to a sentinel and then to the corporal of the guard: "Conduct me to your commanding officer. I am General Lamothe."[3]

Malet borrowed this name to announce himself to the troops, not as a precaution, but only because Lamothe was a general officer whose reputation would be better known to the garrison of Paris. And Malet had other equipment than his monumental bluff. He had brought a sheaf of forged documents: the dispatch allegedly received by special courier, announcing Napoleon's death in Russia—the resolution of the Senate proclaiming a provisional government—and another investing him with supreme command of the garrison.

Duc de la Force

It is not strange that the asylums of the world have been densely populated with Napoleons in the six score years since Waterloo. The Napoleonic complex offers the best terminal facilities for delusions of grandeur. And Malet, on that night of the 23rd–24th, was in his element, quite unaware that he travestied every distinctive trait of the military monarch whom he envied.

Under his orders, officers were dispatched with strong detachments to occupy the key positions of the city, the barriers, quais and open squares. Another party was sent to the prison of La Force, where Guidal and Laborie were now incarcerated. And even their liberation was accomplished without violence, bloodshed or a hitch of any kind. Nobody ventured even to suspect the majestic fraud that the conspirators were perpetrating.

General Laborie, as soon as he had officially "reported" to his superior, Malet, was ordered away with troops to see to the arrest of M. Pasquier. Then, supported by Guidal—who seems to have been detained by the necessity of appearing in full-dress uniform—Laborie moved upon the Ministry of Police, where Savary, still unwarned, surrendered without a struggle. Malet himself prepared to lead another body of troops to the Place Vendôme. At the military headquarters of Paris he proposed to make General Hulin his prisoner.

The arrest of the heads of the police was managed without the slightest commotion or difficulty about 8 A.M. on the twenty-fourth, and they were conveyed under strong escort to the prison from which Guidal and Laborie had just emerged. Savary ever afterward was taunted with the nickname of "Duc de la Force", brief though his term of humiliating captivity proved to be.

Malet, meanwhile, had routed out Hulin and presented his credentials. They did not instantly overawe that matter-of-fact soldier. He made some excuse and turned to walk into an adjoining room to examine them. Malet could afford to take no chance and, drawing a pistol, he fired—the ball shattering Hulin's jaw. Having to shoot was the first mischance. Now came another.

Adjutant General Dorcet—only a secondary figure on the conspirators' list of those opponents who must be rounded up and imprisoned—happened to call upon General Hulin rather earlier than was his custom. Malet, once again flourishing the bogus credentials, brazenly received him; but an adjutant general is accustomed to papers, and one glance told Dorcet that these were forgeries. His keenness was very nearly his death warrant. Malet's deadly pistol was swinging up to take aim when Dorcet's aide walked into the room. Malet, who had emptied one barrel at Hulin, had not had time to reload. He had one ball left to fire—and *two* officers were now challenging him.

He might none the less have mastered the pair of them, who lacked his desperate incentive and unbalanced brain, but just then a squad of soldiers tramped into the room, and, obeying Dorcet and the aide, it was Malet whom they promptly overpowered. From that moment the extravagant venture collapsed. Savary and Pasquier were soon released from La Force; the confederates of Malet were arrested.

Napoleon returned from his immeasurably disastrous Russian campaign with an autocrat's appetite for scapegoats. What he had already learned from a distance of the Malet affair had nearly choked him with rage, but also it had filled him with foreboding.[9] The insecurity of his whole position in Europe, in France, in Paris, had been ludicrously exposed. He was furious with everyone, particularly loading the secret police with his familiar mixture of Corsican venom and guardroom abuse. And yet Savary, who must have expected a taste of Fouché's exile, was not removed from office.[10]

A prisoner—one whose conspirant obsession and irresponsible nature were well known—had been for more than six hours the actual, undisputed master of Paris. Malet's ruse, his dignity and confident demeanor had suborned or imposed upon superior officers. He had obtained the assistance of large bodies of troops, had thrown open prison doors, and shut them again upon ministers of state and influential functionaries. None had stood against him.

He and his accomplices had not made a single mistake. All the power vested in the most trusted adherents of the emperor had been nullified overnight by this crackpot's coup. Chance alone, a mere accident, had intervened. Even so, in thus holding up to ridicule the Bonapartist regime, Malet had succeeded beyond his liveliest anticipations. Inordinate as were his schemes, he can hardly have hoped to *rule* France; but if he meant to discredit the usurper, to engulf his minions in popular derision, that was precisely what he had done.[11] Like so many of the episodes of the dreadful invasion of Russia that same year, it counted as another onward step—toward Elba.

CHAPTER THIRTY-FOUR

AN EMPEROR OF ESPIONS

GENERAL SAVARY appears to much better advantage in his historic role as a recruiting officer, for it was he that discovered the talents of Karl Schulmeister, the Emperor Napoleon's invaluable agent of espionage, who is the Napoleon of military secret service. A century and a quarter have passed since the active career of Schulmeister came to an end; but unceasing intrigues of government and almost uninterrupted warfare have not produced a more effective or audacious espion. A people and a generation that endured more turbulence and conflict than any other of modern times, the French of 1789-1815 were bound to produce among so many extraordinary adventurers one pre-eminent military spy. Schulmeister was that man.

As recklessly unscrupulous as Bonaparte himself, he combined the resource and impudence—common to all great secret-service agents—with very special qualities of physical endurance and energy, courage, wit and histrionic gifts of the first order. Born on August 5, 1770 in Neu-Freistett, he was the son of an unattached Lutheran clergyman; but he grew up to nourish the agreeable conviction that he was of ancient and noble Hungarian lineage, and the momentous hour struck when he could certify his nobility by helping to forge the documents which proved it.

He was as extravagant in his private life as in military conspiracies. An eagerness for elegances—suitable to his exalted birth—led him, as soon as he could afford it, to employ the most noted dancing masters of the Continent. He aspired to fight bravely, to shine socially, and to wear the Legion of Honor; failing in the last of these ambitions, he made sure of the second by having himself taught to dance like a marquis.

He had, however, begun his life modestly enough, marrying a girl of his native Alsace named Unger and conducting jointly a provisions shop and ironmongery. His income was ample but chiefly derived from a very brisk trade as a smuggler. Like other Alsatians, he saw no reason for living so close to a frontier without allowing that circumstance to enrich him. Schulmeister was an accomplished and popular smuggler—or contrabandist, as he described himself—at the age of seventeen. He was never ashamed to admit it, declaring that it called for uncommon pluck and presence of mind in his locality. And even though he achieved note and great wealth in Napoleon's secret service, he continued to participate in smuggling enterprises.

In 1799 he became acquainted with Savary, then a colonel and a long way from his dukedom and Fouché's Ministry of Police. By 1804 the records show the smuggler definitely enlisted as a secret agent. Savary, now a general and one of Napoleon's favorite courtiers, charged Schulmeister with what still seems the most dubious and revolting secret-service exploit of the Empire: the luring into France of the Duc d'Enghien, that harmless young Bourbon prince then living in Baden upon funds supplied by the British and taking no perceptible interest in French politics.

Napoleon wished to intimidate Royalist partisans all over Europe and believed that the summary execution of an innocent relative of the proscribed Capets was just the right terrifying stroke. The Duc d'Enghien frequently visited a young woman of Strasbourg to whom he was deeply attached. Schulmeister found this out and straightway sent his assistants to remove her to Belfort, where she was detained in a country house near the frontier on the pretext that local authorities had listed her as a suspicious person.

Forging a letter in her name, Schulmeister sent it to D'Enghien, entreating him to effect her release from this unjustified internment. Her lover responded immediately. He believed that he could bribe her captors to allow him to convey her the short distance from Belfort to the territory of his protector, the Margrave of Baden. But Schulmeister was ready; and before the duke himself had actually set foot upon French soil, he was seized, hurried to Strasbourg and thence to Vincennes.

Only six days after his lawless arrest, as a Bourbon forbidden to return to France he was condemned by a preposterous court-martial. One of his last acts was to write to his mistress, explaining why he had failed to assist her. She, however, had served Schulmeister's purpose and been released, pathetically unaware of her part in the intrigue. That same night young D'Enghien was shot, his executioners compelling him to hold a lantern so that they might see to take aim. Savary is said to have paid Schulmeister a sum equal to thirty thousand dollars for arranging this matter. A costly Napoleonic whim! Talleyrand observed that the judicial murder of the Duc d'Enghien "was worse than a crime—it was a blunder." And mainly for this epigram has the savage episode been remembered. Whereas it exposed Bonaparte's barbarous conception of internecine politics and marked the debut of an adventurer who was to become the most formidable military spy in the history of France.

Schulmeister's combination of talents was made to order for conflict on a grand scale. Savary, who, with the execution of the young Bourbon, had moved nearer his goal of a ducal estate, presented the spy to Napoleon the following year, saying: "Here, Sire, is a man all brains and no heart." Napoleon—who would one day tell Metternich: "Such a man as I am does not care a straw for the lives of a million soldiers!"—chuckled with Savary, another warmhearted sentimentalist, over the unique cardiac omission in the case of the smuggler-spy.

Napoleon was fond of declaring: "The spy is a natural traitor." He often mentioned it to Schulmeister; yet there exists no record of Bonaparte himself ever having been betrayed by a military spy, whereas he disbursed large sums in order to corrupt more distinguished gentry on sale in the subterranean marts of treason.

Victories at Ulm and Austerlitz

Napoleon's campaign in 1805 against Austria and Russia was a perfectly timed and maneuvered military masterpiece; and that Schulmeister began his career in offensive espionage during this same campaign is significant. Napoleon had always endeavored to study the character of the generals his royal foes selected to defeat him. In 1805 Austrian hopes rested upon Marshal Mack, a soldier of no striking ability but great family influence, chiefly distinguished by an obsessing desire to atone for his previous defeats at the hands of the French. A confirmed monarchist, Mack would not let himself perceive that the Corsican usurper was really popular in France, that the nation generally supported him as a hero and military genius.

Karl Schulmeister made ready to prey upon this dull, simple-minded and easily misguided Austrian commander in terms of his own astigmatism. The spy first appeared in Vienna as a young man of noble Hungarian ancestry—the probable foundation of that ancient-lineage myth—lately exiled from France after many years residence because Napoleon suspected him of spying for Austria.

Mack interviewed the alleged exile, was impressed by all that he seemed to know about the civil and military conditions of France, and gladly availed himself of such fortuitous espionage. The spy became his protégé, was introduced by him into the exclusive army clubs of Vienna. Mack even obtained his vengeful "Hungarian" a commission

AN EMPEROR OF ESPIONS

and attached him to his personal staff. In the fateful autumn of 1805 they took the field together, Schulmeister, the spy, serving as the Austrian's chief of intelligence.

At this period of crisis Schulmeister's operations were fantastically complex. He contrived to keep Napoleon advised of every enemy plan and move. And besides communicating regularly—always a hazardous enterprise—he received large sums of money which he spent with a

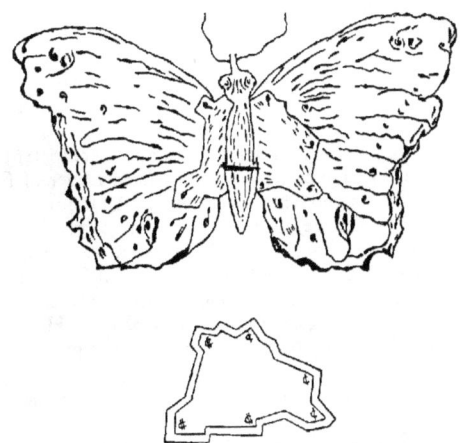

Entomologist sketch enclosing the design of an enemy fortress.

lavish hand and to very good effect. Like most educated Alsatians, he spoke German as fluently as French; and presumably he spoke Hungarian, else why would he have elected that nonessential nationality in preparing for his mission. But more than linguistic gifts were required to make him the favorite he had admittedly become in Viennese society. Even those with reason to fear or detest the spy conceded him a "clever rascal", with a pleasing personality and such manner and assurance he passed for an officer and a gentleman in Austrian court circles, disarming and captivating women and children and generals and nobles alike.

He had found two staff officers who would let themselves be bribed —a negotiation even more perilous than communicating from within the enemy's lines—and when he wanted to give Mack false information, it was confirmed by the apparently independent reports of these traitors, Wendt and Rulski. The optimistic marshal was made to understand that all his monarchist expectations of French disunion were steadily coming to pass. Schulmeister was receiving letters written to him by supposed malcontents in Napoleon's armies. They poured out gossip and eyewitness tales of military disaffection, civil turmoil and other national disturbances which would make any vigorous foreign campaign unthinkable. How gleefully Mack consulted these missives, likewise a newspaper that Napoleon had ordered to be printed especially for his spy's use. Copies of it were dispatched to Schulmeister with elaborate furtiveness; and in each copy were inserted a variety of items to support his mischievous intelligence and convince the Austrian general.

Now Mack was not a blundering, elegant incompetent unfit to command a guard of honor but an experienced leader of fifty-three, determined to succeed and hence overanxious. All too ready to believe what he wanted to believe, he proved a ready target for the sharpshooter from Alsace. France, said Schulmeister, was on the verge of insurrection—and Napoleon perforce must recall his best troops to the Rhine frontier. Whereupon Mack with thirty thousand men marched out of the strategically pivotal city of Ulm. He expected to pursue Marshal Ney and the retiring French vanguard. Instead he found Ney still at the head of an *advancing* army.

Ney was ready to give battle, which would have been surprise enough; but more puzzling still, Marmont and Lannes appeared on his flanks, then Soult and Dupont. Murat—to whom the spy now addressed his secret messages—closed the steel-tipped ring; and three days later, on October 20, the wondering Austrian "pursuer" surrendered.

Schulmeister, still the alleged Hungarian, carried himself and his desire for vengeance through the encircling lines of Frenchmen, effected a "miraculous escape" and boldly returned to Vienna. There, with more consummate guile and audacity than an army corps of average spies, he intruded upon the secret war councils over which the tsar and Austrian emperor joined in presiding. The spy professed to bring those disquieted allies encouraging news from a front that had ceased to exist. They had just lost one well-equipped army and had only two others to lose. Schulmeister persuaded them to listen to him, to consider seriously his suggestions of strategy which would discount the disaster at Ulm. Provided with forged documents seeming to prove his contentions, he cunningly led the allies astray while maintaining regular communication with Napoleon.

Arrest and Escape

Marshal Mack was believed to have been treacherous, and he subsequently was deprived of his rank, disgraced and imprisoned until the truth of his betrayal could be established by his friends.[1] Early in November 1805—a month before the majestic victory of Austerlitz—the first rumors discrediting Schulmeister flashed into circulation, and some officials who had all along mistrusted the engaging spy ordered him arrested. He was guilty enough, and he would surely have been tried, condemned and executed had not Murat moved his troops with such rapidity. The French occupied Vienna unopposed on the thirteenth of November, Kutusoff, who awaited strong Russian reinforcements under Buxhoeven, having had to retire and lose the Austrian capital or be attacked by a greatly superior force.

The speed of his rescuers saved Schulmeister for many another exploit. Austrian archives imply that Schulmeister and an accomplice named Ludwig Rippmann had been under arrest in the spring of 1805, accused of corresponding with the enemy. The disposition of these charges is not recorded; and since there is no mention of Schulmeister's escape, another transaction of bribery would seem to be indicated.

Being paid a small fortune by Napoleon, Schulmeister boastfully admitted collecting almost as much for his services to Austria.[2] It would, indeed, have been impossible for the spy in his loyal disguise to refuse payments from Mack or the Emperor Francis for the secret intelligence which he imposed upon them; yet his pride in these gainful double-dealings betrays a small, criminal mind. Napoleon, though generous to Schulmeister, appears never to have valued his work as, for example, Prince Bismarck in his time was to value the hardly more appreciable operations of Stieber, his "king of sleuthhounds." And such rewards as Schulmeister had from his commander in chief were not in proportion to the titles, privileges and estates Napoleon showered upon adventurers of no more consequence.

The masterly spy was always welcome to risk his life, not only in secret service—when he went as an observer into hostile countries, even undertaking a mission to England and Ireland—but also in battle where he proved a man of action and an intrepid soldier. With only thirteen huzzars he led a charge and captured the town of Wismar. At Landshut he commanded a troop, storming a bridge over the Isar and preventing the enemy from setting it on fire. Acting for Savary, whose confidence he always retained, he went back to Strasbourg to investigate civil disturbances. There during a sudden outbreak he confronted the ringleader of the uprising and shot him dead —a Napoleonic brevity in curbing public discontent with one pistol ball.

Upon Napoleon's second occupation of Vienna, Schulmeister was appointed censor of newspapers, the stage, publishing houses and religious establishments. Entrusted with this power, he displayed an altogether different and commendable sagacity, causing to be circulated broadcast among the races of Austria-Hungary the works of Voltaire, Montesquieu, Holbach, Diderot and Helvetius, all of which thus far in the Habsburgs' realm had enjoyed prominent reservations upon the Index, both papal and political.

The best personal description of Schulmeister was written about this time by Cadet de Gassicourt, Napoleon's apothecary:

> This morning I met the French commissary of police in Vienna, a man of rare intrepidity, of imperturbable presence of mind, and amazing penetration. I was curious to see this man, of whom I had heard a thousand marvellous tales. He inspires the Viennese with as much terror as an army corps. His physique is in keeping with his reputation. He has a bright eye, a piercing glance, his countenance is stern and resolute, his gestures are abrupt, and his voice is sonorous and strong. He is of middle height but very sturdy, and of a choleric, full-blooded temperament. He has a perfect knowledge of Austrian affairs, and his portraits of its leading personalities are masterly. On his brow there are deep scars, which prove that he has not run away from dangerous situations.[3] He is generous too: he is bringing up two orphans whom he has adopted. I talked to him about *The Recluses* (by Iffland), and thanked him for allowing us to enjoy this play.

This was in 1809, and Schulmeister, after leaving Vienna, was for a time commissary general of the imperial forces in the field. No matter what benefits he may have hoped to gain from the lucrative dispersal of army contracts and commercial favors, he was soon returned to duty in military secret service. But he was already a rich man, having purchased some years before the splendid Château le Meinau in his native Alsace and, in 1807, another large estate near Paris—the two having an estimated value of more than one million dollars today.

He had often directed a corps of spies, yet never entirely on his own, without being responsible to Savary, even when making his reports directly to the emperor. In short, though he now might style himself M. de Meinau[4] and live with the luxury of a lord, he was just an adroit and daring secret agent to the imperial military caste. He had begged his witty friend, Lasalle, that crack commander of light cavalry who perished at Wagram, to persuade Napoleon to confer upon him the Legion of Honor. Lasalle returned to say the emperor flatly refused, insisting that gold was the only suitable reward for a spy.[5]

Schulmeister's last chance came at the Congress of Erfurt, where through the representations of Savary he was chosen to direct the French secret service. And it is evident that he outdid himself in the depth, substance and variety of intelligence he submitted to Napoleon each day, for there were many notable persons to be spied upon, and the Corsican owned a villager's dread of missing any choice morsel of gossip. The Tsar Alexander was at Erfurt, amusing himself with Muscovite abandon; and Goethe—whom Napoleon had always professed to admire—was also there and in a mood for diplomacy, which caused his fellow genius some concern. Schulmeister wrote Savary that the emperor asked him every morning two primary questions: who has Goethe been seeing?—and, with whom did the tsar sleep last night? Inevitably some of Alexander's fair companions were agents employed by the French chief of secret service.

A less congenial task of Schulmeister's to which Napoleon regularly alluded was his keeping watch upon Queen Louise of Prussia. The Russian sovereign had shown himself disposed to admire and befriend this beautiful and greatly humiliated lady. Napoleon was bound to continue to humble the queen by blackening her character to the tsar if he could; and his chief spy—unimpeded by the Legion of Honor—was expected to dig up the smut.

In 1810 the career of Karl Schulmeister suffered an ironic twist of fate. In that year came the "Austrian marriage", imperceptibly signaling the downfall of Bonaparte and very plainly marking the decline of his ablest spy. Napoleon's domination over Vienna—which Schulmeister had certainly done much to assure—culminated in the wedding of the youthful Archduchess Marie Louise to her father's hateful conqueror. And an Austrian empress arriving in Paris brought with her such Austrian influences that the spy was driven into retirement. His intrigues before Ulm and Austerlitz had never been forgiven, though the individual gaining the most from them, who had been raised up to equality with the proud Habsburgs after Austerlitz, was now accepted as the consort of a Habsburg heiress.

An Austrian Never Forgets

Schulmeister, eschewing vain resentment, retired, but not into the camp of Napoleon's enemies as many another of his kind would have done, as Talleyrand and Fouché did do with no more to gain and less provocation. The spy, however, appears to have been genuinely grateful for his riches and estates. He was still the postgraduate smuggler and backer of smuggling projects, so he went to live comfortably at Le Meinau where his hospitality and charities won him the sincere homage of his fellow Alsatians.

Austrian animosity lasted until 1814. After the battle of Leipzig and the defeat of the French, Alsace was invaded by the Allies and a regiment of Austrian artillery was detached to bombard and demolish Schulmeister's home. During the Hundred Days he rallied to the emperor who had so casually dispensed with his services five years before. As a consequence, when Napoleon left Paris for Belgium and Waterloo, the former spy was one of the first to be arrested and only saved himself by paying an enormous ransom. That gravely crippled his finances; and when he sought to rehabilitate them it was not with smuggling, which he understood, but with stock and commodity speculation, which is too artful outlawry for a mere spy and smuggler.

He lost everything.

For five years he had known a steadily rising fortune; for ten he had enjoyed wealth and considerable authority. He might have kept something of both—as most of the really unscrupulous Bonapartists managed to do—but instead chance brought him down even as the meteoric splurge of Empire came to an end. Schulmeister retained besides his good nature the regard of his Alsatian neighbors; presumably he still danced like a marquis, though the estates to match that fashionable grace had been swept into other hands. Unlike a military autocrat's gratitude, his health and spirit endured. He was destined to live nearly four decades longer, until 1853, a poor but not unhappy citizen of France, granted by the government a tobacconist stall to tend in Strasbourg.[6]

One may remember Schulmeister with sympathy, not merely because of his final failures but also on account of the quality of the man. His successes now seem so personal; they had none of that bloodless, Juggernaut certainty which was to make the espionage feats of his Prussian counterpart, Stieber, a kind of road-roller demonstration. Schulmeister was treacherous when treachery was a patriotic expedient, but there is no record that he ever betrayed a personal friend. His guile was purely professional, his courage outstanding, and his social aims and patrician exertions were harmless and quite in character. Why should not a born smuggler or contrabandist try to smuggle himself into the contraband nobility of the First Empire?

CHAPTER THIRTY-FIVE

NAPOLEONIC ADVERSARIES

THE MEGALOMANIA OF A NAPOLEON is kind to the connoisseur of historical ironies. Schulmeister by his plausible treacheries helped hasten the conquest of Austria; and the resulting consideration—an eighteen-year-old Austrian archduchess conveyed to France as the bride of the conqueror—presently commenced paying off the Habsburgs' score against Schulmeister. Again, the mighty conqueror and expectant father—only a few months after Schulmeister had perforce abandoned his fruitful career of spying upon everybody, from Goethe to Queen Louise and the tsar—began dictating to the Duc de Bassano, his foreign minister, a complaining letter to Prince Kurakin, who was then serving as the tsar's ambassador to France. And that of which the momentarily peaceable and uxorious emperor complained were the secret-service activities of Colonel Tchernicheff, the Russian military attaché, a former aide-de-camp to the tsar. Tchernicheff, Napoleon fumed, was in Paris nothing more nor less than "an agent of bribery." He had been clumsy enough to be caught bribing a clerk of the Ministry of War, one Michel, who would now have to be shot. And Napoleon despised especially the sort of Russian espionage which caused him to waste a Frenchman and gunpowder away from the battlefield.

The emperor, as we know, could be a reckless spendthrift in secret service when it came to wasting Schulmeister and depriving himself of the services of the most accomplished military secret agent in the history of France. But he had excommunicated Fouché; he humiliated Savary and generally ignored the potent abilities of Desmarest. Who, after all, was Schulmeister and when would he ever again be needed? Where, in fact, was Borodino, or Elba—or Waterloo?

It is of interest, in relation to Schulmeister's ironic downfall, to discover that, of all those who served or studied Napoleon Bonaparte and described him at the time, or afterward, in memoirs, only the spy took notice of the quality of the emperor's voice. He reports it as being crisp and strident, rather high pitched, and adds that Napoleon's habit of speaking through his teeth gave a hissing effect to nearly everything he said.[1] Now that is not a courtier's description, and possibly the Alsatian's acuteness had denied to him that one most common deceit of flattery, so essential to the appreciated courtier.

Schulmeister, moreover, had come importantly upon the imperial scene too late. Engrossed in his own dynastic aspirations, Napoleon was beginning to be bored by the parvenu ambition of the victors and adventurers attached to his destiny. He would call the ex-smuggler "Karl", but he treated him like a lackey. And inasmuch as Schulmeister accepted this treatment and remained loyal in a mad charade of turncoats and selfish schemers, it may well have been that he was only a lackey with a genius for disguise and had disguised himself as a spy.

Colin Mackenzie and Colonel Figner

In the ever expanding or contracting—but always populous—camp of Napoleon's adversaries, who were the secret agents comparable to Karl Schulmeister? There was no identifiable secret agent enrolled on the side of Britain, Austria or their allies whose accomplishments seem to compare with his; nor were there many circumstances of Bonapartist frustration or defeat that suggest the interferences of some masterly unknown spy.

Blücher was acquainted with the French emperor's change of plan at a critical juncture of the campaign which resulted in the victory of the Allies at Leipzig, 1813, when his agents intercepted a note Napoleon had written to his young Habsburg empress. This loverlike and uncoded indiscretion did him considerable harm; after Leipzig he lost Paris, and losing Paris cost him Marie Louise. She had received the note, however, for Blücher, after making good use of its information, had it politely forwarded to her.

One of the Cossack guard on the raft in the Niemen at the signing of the Treaty of Tilsit was said to have been a noted British Intelligence operative, Colin Mackenzie. This is the kind of secret-service exploit which is both possible and probable. In our own time Paul Dukes has been knighted for successfully posing as a Russian in Bolshevist Russia and serving in the Red Army. And yet Mackenzie's espionage achievement might as readily belong among the legends, since nothing could or ever can substantiate it. Like the great operative he is alleged to have been, Colin Mackenzie wrote no memoirs. Presumably he wrote regularly instead to Pitt or Canning.

A signer of the Peace of Tilsit was the Russian vice-chancellor, Prince Alexander Borissovitch Kurakin, who soon moved on to Paris as the tsar's ambassador and to whom Napoleon wrote to complain of Colonel Tchernicheff. French agents visited the lodgings of the Russian military attaché in his absence and there found a letter of a highly compromising character. It was from Michel, a minor official occupying a trusted position in a special department of the French Ministry of War. Through the agency of the concierge of the Russian embassy he had opened communications with Tchernicheff, and he had sold him no less remarkable an espionage trophy than the complete plans drawn up for a projected invasion of the tsar's dominions by the Grand Army.

Michel wrote the attaché, demanding an increase of pay on the score of invaluable, timely and very confidential information which he had been able to supply in the past and would continue to supply. Napoleon heard of it from Savary and wrote Kurakin on March 3, 1812. But it was to turn out that Michel's treacherous commerce dated from 1804, from Fouché's time, when for two thousand francs he had conveyed to D'Oubril, a diplomatic agent of the tsar's government, military information of such striking character, it provoked Alexander I to join the Third Coalition.[2]

Thus Michel had brought Russia in against France on the side of Austria, Great Britain and Sweden. He was discovered to have operated as a spy with the aid of three accomplices, who were imprisoned. Michel was executed; which leaves unanswered the question of his value as an agent of secret service. Winter and the French themselves brought on the disaster of the Moscow campaign. Perhaps Michel merely encouraged the Russians to allow the conqueror to break his fangs upon their frozen citadel. From the Coulaincourt memoirs we learn that, despite all the French preparations for conquest, their gun carriages were improperly constructed to travel the Russian roads. And Coulaincourt had been Napoleon's ambassador in Moscow and had reported upon both the weather and the roads. If Michel through Tchernicheff informed Alexander of such systematic neglect of Coulaincourt's intelligence, he was indeed a valuable spy.

On the side of Russia, however, was one whose espionage exploits rank close to the Napoleonic master strokes of Schulmeister. The partisan Colonel Figner went brazenly into the French bivouacs around Moscow, disguised as a Russian vagrant or peddler, or at times as a French officer, since he had often visited France and owned a flawless command of the language. Information which he gained from these expeditions was practically all the secret service on which the tsar and his generals could rely during the French occupation of their country.

After the disastrous retreat from Moscow and the annihilation of most of Napoleon's army and all of his hopes of success against Russia, there were still strong points in the East to which the French held fast. One of these was Danzig, and in January of 1813 the Russians invested the city. Colonel Figner once more disguised himself as a French officer and contrived to penetrate the fortifications. The commandant of the fortress, General Rapp, received him; and the secret agent, conducting the masquerade with his customary skill, won Rapp's confidence and learned all that the besiegers wanted to know about the strength and morale of the garrison, their quantity of stores and munitions, equipment and caliber of guns. Rapp ultimately entrusted Figner with confidential dispatches to be carried to Napoleon, which, of course, were never read in Paris but gratefully received at Russian headquarters. No relieving force ever reached Danzig; and in spite of the French general's bold and capable defense, the fortress finally had to capitulate.

The Waterloo Campaign

A careful watch was supposed to have been set upon Napoleon and his little court exiled to Elba. Yet when the poverty and restlessness of the Bonapartist camp inspired their "escape" from the island, news of that startling event traveled no more rapidly than any other sensational tidings. There seems to have been no spy report which preceded the event and warned London, Vienna or Paris. Those expected to keep watch upon the exiled emperor were negligent or duped and lulled by the malarial somnolence of the locale.

During the Waterloo campaign the British Intelligence reasserted its superiority. Under the skillful direction of Colonel Hardinge, who made his headquarters with Wellington at Brussels, the secret service operated with invaluable speed and accuracy. An employee of the French Ministry of War and other lukewarm officials of the Bonapartist regime were in the British pay. While Fouché, as we know, operated shrewdly in behalf of *all* parties concerned—the Bonapartists, the Bourbons, the Allies and Fouché. Persons informed with curious exactitude about the impending operations of the French emperor wrote Hardinge daily; and there seems to have been no lack of both military and political intelligence in either Brussels or London. One question agitated everyone—would the troops given Wellington and Blücher be able to unite successfully against the powerful forces of Napoleon?

A secret-service message of the highest strategic importance reached

Hardinge in Brussels on June 6, 1815. It had come from France by way of Mons and reported:

> Officials familiar with the plan of the military operations state that the Emperor will go in person to Avesnes with the intention of carrying out a feigned attack from the Maubeuge side upon the Allies, while the main attack is to be made on the Flanders side between Lille and Tournay, in the direction of Mons.[8]

English agents sent Hardinge the most detailed accounts of Napoleon's army, its position, strength, armament and order of battle. And the strategy of the campaign which Wellington fought so successfully appears to have depended in large degree upon the findings of Intelligence. As early as the first week of May, a confidential document had been received, stating:

> Enthusiasm for the Emperor is strong in the Army, but not among the people. The National Guard will be induced to march only at the point of the bayonet. One lost battle will disperse the Emperor's forces, which cannot escape the influence of political factions.

This report, like the celebrated message which only reached Hardinge on the sixth of June, ten days before Ligny and Quatre-Bras and twelve before Waterloo, proved completely accurate. The most devoted of Napoleon's troops sacrificed themselves recklessly in the three momentous engagements, and then what had been a superb and confident army broke into defenseless fragments as the retreat from the Belgian battlefields changed rapidly to panic and rout.

CHAPTER THIRTY-SIX

HIGH PRIESTESS OF HOLY PEACE

NAPOLEON had now succeeded in "consummating the most difficult undertaking of his life—namely, losing his throne."[1] Immediately thereafter Europe witnessed another difficult undertaking, the rare example of a woman who was a spiritual zealot and past her first youth engaging in a contest with the leading diplomatic and secret-service intriguers of her time and winning an emperor to the cause she chose to espouse. The emperor was Alexander I, tsar of Russia, of whom one of his early associates had said: "He would gladly have every one free, provided that every one was prepared to do freely exactly what he wished." And the woman was the celebrated mystic, Baroness Barbara Juliana von Krüdener.

Europe, very weary after Leipzig and Elba, was practically exhausted after the Hundred Days. Everybody wanted peace, and deep-breathing exercises became the vogue, with Waterloo really one of the decisive battles of the world and St Helena a remote island, not a wishful mirage. Revenge was visited only on Napoleon and a few of his chief adherents. And the general liquidation of his conquests was arranged with more decency, attempted right thinking and want of cynicism than the future negotiators at Versailles (1919) would even pretend on the opening day of their deliberations.

France was restored almost intact to the commuting Bourbon dynasty. Everything on the Continent seemed to have been settled for a century to come, though three such influential personalities as Louis Napoleon, who was seven years old, Bismarck, born in 1815, or Victoria, four years his junior, could not be properly consulted. In defeating the Corsican it was believed that the French Revolution had also been beaten, as though Napoleon, save for purposes of propaganda or recruiting, was ever the embodiment of liberty, equality, fraternity. The peacemakers arranged their new world to make it as safe as possible for the divine right of kings. And there was an especial emphasis upon the "divine" because at the elbow of Alexander stood the spiritually exacting baroness.

This fascinating woman was an incurable romantic who had complicated a costly and agreeable existence by being simultaneously avid for youth, travel, love, the doing of good, the admiration of younger men, regal authority, and the discovery and beatification of her own immortal soul. She was born November 11, 1764, her father a wealthy Livonian, Otto von Vietinghoff, who became a senator, her mother the daughter of the famous Field Marshal von Munnich. At eighteen she had been married to Baron Burckhard von Krüdener, who was sixteen years her senior and presently the Russian ambassador to Berlin.[2] She was restless and enormously extravagant, and there was at least one "painful attachment" to a young officer, whose identity and accomplishments had to be confided to her husband. The baroness tried nearly everything, including the shawl dance hitherto confined to Naples and Emma Lady Hamilton; she tried literature, of course, and arrived finally at religion in an appropriate sequence. It was at Riga, after years of frivolous existence with and without shawls, that Baroness von Krüdener suffered conversion. Whereupon she set out for Karlsruhe to consult Heinrich Jung-Stilling, high priest of the occult pietists, whose doctrines had infected many royal courts, already dominated Baden, and were plucking at Stockholm and St Petersburg.

The turbulence and insecurity of the Napoleonic epoch had opened a wide avenue along which quacks of every stripe and complexion were busily carting home their harvest. New thought, faith, hope and piety, as well as pioneering experiments with diets and ventilation, easily surpassed the twenty-year vogue of cannon smoke. Baroness von Krüdener had a nice taste in palpable charlatans. She particularly attached to her a spiritual conjurer named Fontaine, whose wife came along in a complaisant minor role, willing to serve with those who only stand and wait so long as the baroness's fervor did not interrupt her conspicuous waste. Another who touched the Krüdener orbit was Marie Kummer, the noted medium. She had visited Tsar Alexander I but tossed away a likely prospect by immediately "reading" from her trance state what costly favors His Majesty was predestined to do for her. Alexander was attracted to religion and reform, but he was not that gullible.

Barbara Juliana von Krüdener had her first chance to appeal to him in 1815. She found the great man sitting alone, an open Bible in front of him, and it is said that when she began to speak he began to weep. Juliana kept him crying for three hours. He insisted, however, that she had enabled him to find peace; and so at his urging she and the Fontaines and other curious members of an entourage which was almost a sect proceeded to follow him—first to Heidelberg, and then, after Waterloo, to Paris. On this journey she must have been observed and investigated by any number of agents, reporting to Prince Metternich and other cynical gentlemen, who sought to answer the questions—what's her little game?—who does she work for?—and can anyone buy into the syndicate?

Peace and Prayer Meetings

At Alexander's suggestion, when the baroness arrived in Paris, despite the post-Waterloo congestion of that captured yet resigned city, she was provided lodgings at the Hôtel Montchenu, next door to the imperial headquarters in the Elysée Palace. A private stairway connected these buildings; and by means of this Alexander went each evening to take part in the prayer meetings conducted in her hotel suite by the baroness and the latest of her spiritual attachés, Empeytaz. The Fontaines were momentarily in eclipse, but they were still entrenched upon the pension rolls of the baroness, and so, it would appear, was Marie Kummer, the avaricious medium.

Colleagues of the tsar in reconstructing "a world of lasting peace" saw him dangerously surrounded by a coterie which, with the sincere exception of Baroness von Krüdener, was counterfeit and mercenary to the last degree. But there was nothing at the moment that anyone could do about it. Alexander's emotional response to the religious appeal of the baroness was genuine and profound. He had relieved the tedium of the Congress of Erfurt with that series of assignations so regularly observed by Karl Schulmeister, and now, perhaps for the first time in the annals of divine right and sovereign will, he was attending religious services clandestinely.

While the influence of the Baroness von Krüdener prevailed, all the negotiators and statesmen had to pay closest attention to this mingling of cultivated vagaries. The baroness was said to have first suggested the Holy Alliance, enough to assure any zealot of her place in history. Certain it is that she passed upon a draft of the treaty founding the Alliance, which Tsar Alexander carried to the Hôtel Montchenu for her study. Soon afterward vanity, which for all we know may be even the fault of angels, overcame her alleged mystical humility, and she began boasting about the influence which her beliefs, personality and prayers had attained in the shaping of current events.

Agents of the tsar and others hastened to report these indiscretions; and Alexander, who relished the contemporary glow of the spotlight as well as a golden throne in heaven, remonstrated with the baroness and advised her to return to her devotions. In spite of this threatening rift in *their* holy alliance, the Krüdener explanations had been so persuasive that the tsar, when preparing to return to St Petersburg, invited the baroness to accompany him. The spell which she had cast upon him seemed hardly to diminish, and it might possibly have maintained her power for years if her addiction to folk like the Fontaines and Marie Kummer had not gradually pried open the Russian autocrat's eyes.

After the baroness had journeyed elsewhere it was Metternich's turn; and the tsar passed completely under the sway of that courtly and vigilant reactionist. Six years later, when the insurrectionary outbreak of 1821 focused European attention upon Greece, the baroness undertook to reassert her influence over the ruler of Russia. She hastened to St Petersburg and implored Alexander to declare a "holy war" against the Moslems, very suddenly and belatedly noticed as the cruel oppressors of Christian Greeks. As the tsar had many millions of Christian subjects whom he and his predecessors had been systematically oppressing, he declined to lead the religious crusade and even set in motion diplomatic machinery which would gently expel the baroness from Russia if she persisted in resuscitating his conversion. However, a Crimean colonization scheme was soon enthralling her. She was still well to do and a veritable magnet for wealthy cranks and zealots. Her friends were many in all the pastures of faith, hope, reform and fermentation of the soul.

Soon afterward she died, having expressed the moderate deathbed conviction that she had done much good and so would be forgiven her follies.

The Rewards of Montgalliard and De Batz

The exploit—spiritual rather than amorous—of the Baroness von Krüdener in captivating for a season the most powerful autocrat of his age stands as something quite unique; yet it was truly in the spirit of those times. Europe was already suffering a grave relapse from revolutionary impulses of liberalism, and only the eccentricities of the individual made up for the stupidities of monarchs and the reaction of governments. Two of our liveliest acquaintances among the reckless and eccentric intriguers bred by the revolution and the Napoleonic Wars—the Comte de Montgalliard and Baron Jean de Batz—now take leave of secret service yet reappear in epilogues to their respective tragi-comedies.

Montgalliard, never abashed, a strictly lighter-than-air machine even when ballasted with all his decency and scruples, stood ready at any time to establish the truth observed in the statement—"The imagination of scoundrels is infinitely fertile, and they are endowed with powers of inventive penetration extremely rare in law-abiding men."[3] He had contrived to be the first to bring himself to the attention of Louis XVIII when the king, after twenty-three years of exile bordering upon oblivion, returned to ascend the throne of France. The Allies, having soundly thrashed Napoleon at last, desired the restoration of the Bourbon monarchy; and Montgalliard, after the years of martial rack and storm, broke out all over in rainbow stripes of Royalism. At Compiègne with his diabolic impudence he dared to remark in a casual tone to Louis whom he had endlessly slandered and derided with his pen: "Your Majesty has too much sense of humor not to have understood me! . . ." He commenced straightway to extol the virtues of the Bourbons, even as he had exaggerated his praises of Napoleon after the conqueror consented to discharge his debts; and he was given immediate employment, and petted and made use of, at a substantial stipend so long as Louis XVIII occupied the throne.

Being allowed to boast of his fidelity and noble sacrifices as a Royalist, he remained curiously exempt from any form of reprisals. In collaboration with the king he wrote a pamphlet,[4] "a manifesto, a model of petulant recantation,"[5] which affected to disclose his efforts in behalf of the exiled Bourbons. In it he referred affectionately to Moreau—who had died the year before—and to Pichegru, whose destruction he had accomplished almost singlehanded. "I have lived long enough to see the aims of these generals realized, to witness the recall of my sovereign . . . to the throne of Saint-Louis." He mentioned having "staked the honor of my name"—and then explained that the only way of getting rid of Bonaparte had been to "urge him towards the excessive", which thus explained why he himself had seemed to be "attached inseparably to the cause, the purpose, and the dynasty of the Usurper."

"I divined"—the pamphlet pursued—"the secret of his heart; he was dreaming of the crown, and I decided to place it on his head. . . . Fidelity to the King made this a duty." On such evidence, Clément de Lacroix justifiably wonders whether there was not between Louis XVIII and Montgalliard some "unconfessed complicity." This most Satanic of spies had learned so many secrets and had taken a hand in so many intrigues. "Perhaps his quiver still held some terrible shaft"; perhaps he had at some time been "the intermediary in some shady and dubious plan which it would be impolitic and scandalous to reveal." Since so great an historical detective as the late M. Louis Gosselin [G. Lenotre] was unable to discover either the origin of the "terrible shaft" or any trace of the "dubious plan", we may safely assume that M. de Lacroix's "perhaps" is permanent. It is possible, however, that Napoleon would have been less severe in measuring the rewards to Karl Schulmeister for really audacious military espionage if he had never encountered Montgalliard and his duplicities.

Unlike that infamous betrayer, Baron Jean de Batz had nothing whatever to conceal or explain when the Bourbon monarchy was restored. He had been a far more energetic Royalist than any of the Bourbons. He had fought the revolution as the paladin of reaction, he had undermined the Convention, suborned the committees and fanatically magnified the Terror. His retirement from conspiracy with the establishment of the Empire had been sensible; for the execution of D'Enghien in 1804 had vanquished the hardiest hopes of the Royalists, and—save as an English spy—there was little to be done against the solid administrative force of Bonaparte. His one stroke of assistance to that usurper, the inciting of the Sections for the event of the thirteenth of *Vendémiaire* which permitted the debut of the Corsican and his illustrious "whiff of grapeshot", had been incontestably accidental.

De Batz consequently presented himself at the court of the resuscitated dynasty with the air of a man who asks nothing because he deserves even more than can possibly be given him. On the seventeenth of September, 1814, however, he was made a Knight of Saint Louis. And the following March he was promoted by order of the king to the rank of field marshal, his commission to date from 1797. Louis had grave need of intrepid field marshals that month. Napoleon was already en route from Elba; and on March 17 the Bourbon ruler went again into exile. De Batz appears to have followed the king to Ghent and to have conducted himself in some consoling or resourceful manner, for on November 2, 1815—with St Helena now tenanted—his promotion to field marshal was confirmed. He at once requested active assignment, and on the ninth of the following March was given command of the department of the Cantal.

Though granted his urgent request, De Batz remained in Paris and on August 1 had not yet taken up his duties. He had married in the course of these recent events and also had contrived to antagonize the commandant of the Nineteenth Division, who wrote to the minister of war complaining of the baron's untrustworthy and vacillating character.⁶ The born conspirator was running true to type; but now when the minister of war ordered him rather curtly to proceed to his post or else resign his commission, he set out at once for Aurillac, arriving there August 4, 1816.

Paris seems to have called him as it has called so many; and in April of 1817 he returned to the capital on the pretext of an important lawsuit. There he tarried without permission until the thirteenth of November when, abruptly, the Bourbon ax fell upon one who had repeatedly avoided the revolutionary chopper. He was removed from his post and retired on half pay. Now it was a necessary formality to find him and acquaint him with this decision; and as a final touch of irony, the authorities had to call upon police detectives to trace the baron in order to tell him he was no longer a field marshal on the active list.

He was discovered at length, pleasantly residing at No. 34 Rue de la Chaussée d'Antin; and on December 30, 1818, his eccentric career as a soldier fizzled out with no more plots to redeem it. Two years later he begged to be restored to the active list, but in vain. Whereupon he retired in earnest—to that estate of Chadieu in Puy-de-Dôme, which he had managed to purchase under an assumed name at the very height of the Terror.

It is said that he was unpopular with the local peasantry. Such a confirmed Royalist could hardly appear democratic. And there were also rumors of trouble over an alleged forgery. The king could not save him but is reputed to have recommended an honor-refurbishing exit by means of suicide. Jean de Batz died on January 10, 1822; and the cause ascribed was apoplexy. But he seems to have been in serious difficulties, and, since he was buried by the roadside rather than in consecrated ground, there is some foundation for the belief still persisting at Authezat,[1] where the Château de Chadieu is situated, that the celebrated conspirator took his own life.

Chapter Thirty-seven
CARBONARI AND CAMORRA

CONSPIRATORS under oath abound in the history of every nation. It is probable that there has been a drop of blood pricked out to form a signature upon some clandestine parchment or manifesto for every drop shed in the greatest battle known to medieval or modern times. But apart from these makers of melodrama, who may even have the unique gift of being preposterous and dangerous at the same time —specimens of which type we shall presently meet in Baltimore, Md. —whenever a genuine secret society has turned to secular or political activities not far removed from government secret service, it has achieved significant results. It will never be forgotten that George Washington as grand master mobilized the Freemasons of the colonies at the outbreak of the American War of Independence. And their consolidated support, without becoming furtive or sinister, developed immeasurable influence in changing a rebel cause into a triumphant revolution.

The impression which resulted—of the Freemasons as potential insurgents—has survived to this day in certain states of Europe, notably Fascist Italy. But Italian politics has had too many examples of the power of the secret society grown arrogant and formidable to treat the matter lightly. The dread instilled by oaths of banded brotherhood derives from the insurrectionary endeavors of the Italian Carbonari and similar turbulent leagues. It is widely conceded that the Carbonari[1] branched off from the Masonic order. They cherished the most patriotic of motives, most of them were noble in conspiracy and disinterested as revolutionists; and while they accomplished much less than their minimum aspirations at the time, the pattern and influence of their movement spread afterward to many quarters of the globe, wherever tyranny swept down upon the barricades.

After Marshal Murat, Napoleon's famous cavalry leader, had reigned for a while in Naples as the imperial puppet, King Joachim I, he proved himself just another man on horseback. The Neapolitans, as much as any people of the Continent, were then entitled to complain that they had never known a just monarch or any perceptibly enlightened form of despotism. Imposition of Murat's authority, fenced about with sabers and bayonets, they interpreted as a kind of subregal last straw; and so the "best people" and others began conspiring with all the zeal which the Latin reserves for projects of stealth mingled with volcanic recklessness. Between 1808 and 1815 patriot "cells" or secret societies came into existence all over the country, the members being resolved and sworn to free it from foreign rule and win constitutional liberties. Either Murat or the Neapolitan Bourbons might have won the support of the Carbonari, provided either tyranny had shown the slightest disposition to fulfill some of the brotherhood's demands. But when the despots proved deaf as well as dumb, the patriot conspirators proceeded to foment insurrection with the useful watchwords of freedom and independence.

The Carbonari never weighted themselves seriously with a governing program. They never got around to agreeing upon what particular form of government they would set up when and if they succeeded in overthrowing the existing authority. One viewing them sympathetically from this time perspective cannot escape the suspicion that succeeding was not their paramount concern, that they cared for no program save their zestful plots and fermentations, and that belligerent opposition to the tyrant and the foreigner under circumstances of nerve-tingling melodrama was their sole, and thoroughly satisfying, reward.

Murat's minister of police was no Fouché but a rather engaging Genoese, Malghella, who gave much surreptitious aid to the earliest cells of the Carbonari and seems to have been mainly responsible for whatever was Italian and locally endurable in the puppet king's policy. Even Murat himself had granted the secret society some initial encouragement because he felt none too sure of the Italian "subjects" surrounding him and happened to be quarreling with his domineering brother-in-law, Napoleon. Later on, however, Lord William Bentinck, representing Britain from his base in Sicily, began negotiating with the Carbonari in the person of Vincenzo Federici—a leader popularly known as Capobianco—offering arms and subsidies and promising a constitution for Naples like that which had recently been given Sicily under British auspices. As a result, disorders inspired by the Carbonari soon broke out in Calabria; but Murat, a man of action if an incompetent king, sent a strong force under General Manhès to attack the insurrectionary element. Military repression put an end to Capobianco's rebellion; and he was captured, condemned and hanged in September 1813.[2] That effectually drove the Carbonarist movement underground. But the inexplicable Malghella used his powers as head of the Neapolitan police in continuing quietly to safeguard the Carbonari. He was even said to be a leading spirit in helping to organize them; wherefore, on the downfall of the Emperor Napoleon and all his brother kinglets, Ferdinand IV returned to southern Italy with the restoration of the Bourbons only to discover his kingdom aswarm with fervid plotters.

The secret society enrolled nobles, army officers, small landlords, government officials, peasants and even a few priests. Its organization was one of the curiosities of the age and so mysterious that in many respects it resembled an exciting game for boys. Its ritual was a fantastic composition of symbols borrowed from the Christian religion and from the trade of charcoal-burning, so extensively practiced in the mountains of Calabria and the Abruzzi. A Carbonarist lodge was termed a *vendita*—sale—and its members saluted one another as "good cousins", *buoni cugini*.[8] God was brought in as a sponsor of political intrigue, being elevated to the post of "Grand Master of the Universe", while with a trace of nepotism Jesus Christ was appointed "Honorary Grand Master." The Savior was likewise designated "the Lamb" by the active conspirators, and all were sworn to deliver the Lamb from the "wolf"—the wolf of tyranny, no longer Joachim I but Ferdinand IV.

Fire Bearers of the Bourbon Counterpoise

That monarch had settled down in comfort upon his throne with reaction around it like a Chinese wall. This happily restored Bourbon felt safe, and so he decided to have a civil war. The red, blue and black flag of the Carbonari was the acknowledged standard of revolt throughout Italy and remained so until the red, white and green displaced it in 1831. Ferdinand, who had been driven into exile, was antagonized by red and his royal person was only reminiscently black and blue, whereupon he placed an interdiction upon the Carbonarist flag and resolved to exterminate the Carbonari. The secretive and sympathetic Malghella had been superseded as minister of police by the Prince of Canossa; and unlike a famous barefoot emperor, Ferdinand went roughshod to Canossa, whose initial response in attacking the secret society took a typically reactionary and bureaucratic form. The police minister organized another society which he called the *Calderai del Contrappeso*—braziers of the counterpoise—and which he packed with members of the convict stripe, whom we have found throughout this history always overeager to oblige the profit-sharing agents of a despotism.

Mountain brigands and the dregs of the underworld of Naples—which was uniformly so vicious few people had suspected it could have dregs—were let loose upon the liberal and liberty-loving elements of this hallowed reactionist stronghold. As braziers of the counterpoise they committed "hideous excesses" upon the real and the supposed Carbonari, but never did more than drive the true conspirators underground.

It was no new thing to find a criminal element weighing heavily in Italian politics; and if in our own day one man with an aggressive jaw and an alpine ego has succeeded in pocketing politics, including the criminal influence, it is because—so say reliable foreign investigators—he initiated his drive to the Fascist summit by molding organized lawless elements into a secret police. The most complete criminal organizations known to Italian history were the Mafia and the Camorra. The former was a Sicilian order, presumed to trace its ancestry to a local cell—fiercely impregnated with evil—of the Camorra. For the purposes of these annals we need only take note of the parent body of rapacious underworld tyrants. The Camorra, an association at least four centuries old, had originated in the Neapolitan prisons where, upon the pretext of keeping a lamp alight before a prison shrine, a tax was levied upon all newcomers. The extortions of the Camorra were not long confined to inmates of jails. Those bold enough to resist the society's despotic power were injured or slain. Probationers, who had to attend to assassinations and pass other tests for a term of years, only shared in the society's loot as they proved they could both enforce and endure its discipline. From the *sala,* or small slice, one advanced to the *barattalo,* or half share. In time the full share, or *camorra,* was bestowed upon those sufficiently lawless, daring and vengeful. It was a little irony of the Camorra chiefs to divide their extortionist gains every Sunday, a day of rest for criminals who avoided honest labor every other day of the week.

So long as the masters of disunited Italy, in Philip Guedalla's phrase, "reduced patriotism to a conspiracy" there was bound to be a plethora of conspirators. One of the most picturesque of these was Garibaldi, an adventurer born to intrigue and espionage, who even fell in love with his future wife while gazing at her through a telescope. Prince Louis Napoleon—who mounted a throne as Napoleon III—was reputed to have leagued himself with agents of the Carbonari. When Austrian detectives came to arrest him in Italy, it was his mother, the vivacious Queen Hortense, who deceived them for eight days while her son recovered from a bout of fever. Another of the conspirator clan, virtually a whole conspiracy in himself, was Giuseppe Mazzini, who spent his adult years in a private underworld of patriotic frustration and furtive interviews. It was even his lot to die under an assumed name.

Mazzini did the same thing over and over in his twilight zone of not too practical intrigues. He might have been one of the greatest of secret agents or military spy-masters. Unlike De Batz, he suffered for want of a revolutionary background and was never able to foment the exact conditions of turbulence his talents really required. And we take leave of him here with a large allowance of credit for ultimate Italian triumphs from which fate cruelly excluded him. Moreover, by putting grains of sand or hairs between the folded pages of his letters he was able to prove that postal censorship was a secret vice of the British government, provoking an instant outcry and shocked interpellations in Parliament.

CHAPTER THIRTY-EIGHT

PROLOGUE TO SECESSION

WHEN we left North America to focus our attention once more upon the clandestine fermentations of Europe, the colonial rebels and agitators of violence had just cast off the shackles of polite paternalism and begun moving onto their historic pedestals as honored ancestors and respectable Founding Fathers. There were many American malcontents, dissatisfied with economic conditions or with their private gains from the war, as well as those whose suppressed Tory instincts made them deplore any form of republican government. But in all probability there was less secret service in the new and barely United States for a generation than we have discovered in contemporary France or Italy during a single turbulent fortnight.

In 1811, however—with Napoleon's empire already whispering ominously of a design for the conquest of Russia—we come suddenly upon one of those Americans who, having engaged in a notable campaign of secret service, earned almost immediate oblivion. George Matthews was sent down into Florida by President James Madison as a political emissary and secret agent. Matthews there took it upon himself to start a war with Spain; and he was personally occupied in besieging St Augustine when the recurrent integrity of political Washington caused him to be repudiated. He had been ordered to proceed "secretly" to Florida[1] but also to create a difficult double role by presenting himself to the Spanish authorities as the American commissioner authorized to take over the territory should the Spaniards desire to surrender it.

The Peninsular War was then cauterizing Spain, and the colonial office in Madrid had neither funds nor power. A new war between Britain and the United States was foreseen in 1811, and President Madison believed that the English would probably seize Florida as a base of operations. To prevent this, he appointed Matthews and Colonel John McKee, an Indian agent, to negotiate with the Spanish governor and secure if possible a cession of the provinces. They were to "fix a date for their return, if desired."[2] In case the commissioners were successful, a provisional government was to be established; but if unsuccessful, it was understood from the beginning that forcible possession was to be taken, should there be any reason to suppose a foreign Power was moving to capture the Floridas.

McKee seems to have abandoned this enterprise, leaving Matthews to carry on alone, which was very much to that gentleman's taste. He was a native of Ireland, had fought in the Revolutionary War, and had risen to the rank of general. No celebrated exploit of that struggle is connected with his name, but he was described as a man of "unsurpassed bravery and indomitable energy, strong-minded but almost illiterate."[3] Moving to Georgia in 1785, his indomitable energy won him election as governor the very next year. In 1794-95 he was again elected governor of the state, and some time thereafter, though entitled to be called both Honorable and General, he did not disdain to work for the War Department as a special agent on the Florida frontier.

Now the isolation of his colony, or its undoubted strategic importance to the British, did not sufficiently intimidate Governor Estrada, and he chose to resent it when Matthews began stirring up revolt among former Americans residing in the Spanish dominion.[4] Whereupon Secret Agent Matthews hurried home to Georgia, as ex-Governor Matthews raised a private army of sharpshooting frontiersmen and Indian fighters, and as General Matthews invaded the colony of Spain.

The Spanish minister at Washington protested vehemently. Matthews had captured several small towns on his way to take the capital, when from Madison and James Monroe—who had succeeded Robert Smith as secretary of state—there came the reluctant announcement that General Matthews had "misunderstood" the instructions of his government. Governor Mitchell of Georgia was appointed to replace him and directed to assist Estrada in enforcing order. Because of his unwanted versatility Matthews was dismissed; but his successor seems to have been given instructions no less opaque. Mitchell, it is said, was to obtain safety for the "revolutionists" in Florida, aid them as much as possible, and withdraw the American "troops as slowly as might seem feasible."[5] No better way of pursuing Matthews' imperial aim could have been contrived; and Mitchell made so much of his opportunities that the armed force Matthews had organized and commanded did not retire from Florida for fourteen months. Then—in May 1813—it moved to join the army of Andrew Jackson, who was himself presently ordered to renew the invasion and march upon Pensacola. Only a Congressional outcry checked this expeditionary thrust, and Old Hickory turned aside to the timely defense of New Orleans.

Sole Accomplishment of a British Spy

It was known at the time that George Matthews reported regularly to Washington. While discussing the necessity of occupying Florida to prevent the British from seizing it as a base, the American Congress sat in secret session, and many precautions were taken to keep the matter from becoming known. Matthews was in no sense, therefore, a filibuster or private plotter acting from selfish motives. Instead he typified the land-hungry American frontiersman of his age, who regarded himself as an agent—not a bit secret—of divine interposition and looked upon no boundary of the United States as final until it vanished into a sea, gulf or ocean. Matthews' conduct, as a government commissioner, was indefensible; and it is easy to understand why his project, carried on by his successor, has no forward place in the annals of the day. A blunt instrument adding one more note of apology to the sorry record of events surrounding the War of 1812, he has had to be ignored as he was formerly disowned.

Aggressive leadership was then mainly restricted to American naval commanders. Yet it is probable that Matthews would have continued in the confidential service of Madison and Monroe save for the outburst of national excitement that resulted from detection of a British spy. John Henry was the foreign agent who had been operating in New England and who was exposed by his own letters, which came into the hands of the President in 1812.[6] They revealed how he had been spending his time and English secret-service funds, subsidizing the press, undertaking to foment intersectional discord, and cultivating ponderously those pro-British sentiments already existing among New England Federalists.

When President Madison communicated Henry's correspondence to the Congress, unseasonable heat, horror and hysteria swept over the land of the free. An agent of British secret service active in Boston in times of peace! All of which helped prepare the country for three years of blockade, stagnation and largely inglorious war. But the first sufferer was George Matthews, who had to be curtly repudiated because of his resemblance to Henry and his deplorable improvement upon the heavy-handed intrigues of the Britisher. Whatever Matthews' crime in diplomacy, as a spy and secret agent he showed such enterprise and expansive industry as must here command him high rating in the slender biographical records of secret service in North America. The Irish ex-governor of Georgia was really too aggressive for conventional intelligence duty but might have become a military spy of outstanding excellence. Like Karl Schulmeister, whose contemporary he was, Matthews burst the seams of ordinary espionage and became the stroke of conquest he was only expected to prepare.

There was very little secret service of a professional mold in the three-year War of 1812 and not much effective work of the Intelligence on either side. This is surprising, for there were any number of living Americans who had been officers in the Revolutionary War, and some of them ought to have remembered General Washington's profitable dependence upon systematic espionage. And it is all the more surprising as a fault of the British, for Napoleon was beaten and exiled to Elba, and in 1814 the government in London could afford to train its heaviest guns upon the weaker American adversary. Thousands of Wellington's veterans from the Peninsular campaigns were put aboard ships and sent into the Gulf of Mexico. Where were the Intelligence officers, men of the caliber of Colonel Hardinge, who had been sharply trained by their prolonged contest with the secret service of the French emperor?

The politic repudiation of Matthews, dampening his ardor and his aggression on Florida, must have been generally regretted by the summer of 1814. In spite of Canadian and other bases available, the principal British operations on the continent of North America were organized to make use of Spanish hospitality. Pensacola was to become a veritable springboard whence the fierce old lion would pounce. And yet the War of 1812 was not to be that typical conflict in which Britain would "lose every battle save the last one." The last battle, Jackson's victory at New Orleans—fought more than a fortnight after the actual signing of the treaty of peace—was about the only land battle which British troops did *not* win. Jackson took up a strong position, he was anything but overconfident—leaving that to his veteran adversary—and, as we shall see, he contrived to be well informed.

Not until May 1814 had Jackson been appointed major general in the regular army and put in command in the deep South. In a letter addressed to Major John Reed, his aide-de-camp, and written at a moment of continuously mounting peril to the United States—written, in fact, only three days after the British invaders under Ross and Cockburn entered Washington, D.C.,[7] news of which American humiliation could not as yet have reached Mobile—General Jackson gives us ample proof of the timeliness of his intelligence and the value he set upon it:[8]

                                                                    Mobile, August 27th, 1814
                                                                           11 o'clock at night
Headquarters
   7th M. District
DEAR SIR

    At 5 o'clock this evening thro a confidential channel, I had information of the arrival and disembarkation of two or three hundred british troops at Pensacola with large quantities of arms, ammunition ordinance and ordinance stores, that the Orpheus, with 14 sail of the line, large transports and 10,000 men were to reach Pensacola this day, that 14 sail of the line, large transports and 25,000 of Lord Wellington's troops had reached Bermuda—and that the Emperor of Russia had offered England 50,000 troops to aid her and Spain to conquer and divide America—and in one month Mobile and all the country was to be in possession of the British—do not think this chimerical, bloody noses there will be before this happens—but without immediate aid the feeble force here must bend before such an overwhelming force—and there is no doubt but there are at least 35,000 British and Spanish troops on the coast and at Pensacola. I am anxious to hear from you, whether you are coming on or not—the business is too great for Captain Butler and myself and it will increase with the number of troops—I have ordered every Indian to be enrolled as soldiers and put under pay, this will alone deter them from joining the line of our enemy—and I have called into service the full quota authorized by the Secretary of War within 7th District.

    I hope the Tennesseans will do honor to themselves. I did intend to have forwarded, enclosed to Col. Butler, a short patriotic address. I have not time and must request you to have it done in my name. We must act with energy and effect or rest assured that there will be as sudden a decline of our liberties as there was of the Empire of Napoleon.

    My eyes are so sore and dim I cannot see. Requesting you will write me and inform whether you will accept or not—With compliments to Mrs. Reed, and all friends, respectfully

                                                          Yr Mo Obt Serv
                                                          ANDREW JACKSON
Major John Reed

    General Jackson's smashing success in the field came some months later, on January 8, 1815. Pakenham, his British antagonist, seems either not to have been well served by Intelligence or to have been incapable of comprehending the strength of the American defenses. No doubt he and his Peninsular War veterans were trained and disciplined to care nothing for raw "colonial" levies. But Pakenham himself and 2,000 of his men gave up their lives discovering the accuracy of backwoodsmen's rifle fire.

Before leaving the area of George Matthews' constructive espionage enterprise and of Jackson's military triumph, we must note two episodes informally representative of secret service at its best—or worst. In the conflict between the government of the United States and the Seminole Indians, the "slick Yankee" ingenuity and aggression of the former were bound to prevail; and Osceola, great chief of the Everglades tribal confederacy, was taken prisoner by deception *under a flag of truce*. Undying resentment growing out of such typical paleface perfidy—and not to be the last example of its kind in three centuries of persistent "pioneering"—embittered the aborigines of the watery fens of Florida for a hundred years. Only very recently, in 1935, through the personal intercession of Secretary of the Interior Ickes—who was "obliged to leap from log to log and stump to stump to reach their hide-out"[9]—was a treaty of peace officially signed, ending the state of war between the United States and the descendants of Osceola's braves.

In Andrew Jackson's time there was the piratical intelligence system of Jean Lafitte, a "picturesque villain . . . who instituted a reign of terror in the Gulf of Mexico" and established himself as "dictator in Galveston, with power to sell letters of marque to his fellow outlaws."[10] Lafitte and his men of Barataria were reputed to have come to the aid of Jackson, as combatants, scouts and spies, in defending New Orleans against the British. It was that same Lafitte, however, who was warned by his agents among the Creoles that the governor of Louisiana planned to offer a reward of $5,000 for the pirate's head and immediately made it an auction by bidding $50,000 for the governor's head. Romantic tales have been compounded wherein Jean Lafitte set forth for a dazzling fee to rescue Napoleon from St Helena. This secret mission, in the legend, actually brought him ashore on the prison isle and lurking outside of Longwood; but his backers had devised their plot too late. The dethroned emperor already lay dying.

Spain, even with British and American co-operation, could do little or nothing throughout the West Indies against such well-provided and completely informed marauders as those who followed Jean Lafitte and his equally ruthless contemporaries. During this period the Spanish government had all it could handle in trying to subdue and gradually losing control of its rebellious South American colonies, whence came "many of the pirate crews and the commissions under which the pirate vessels pretended to sail, although these commissions were more often than not forgeries or valueless papers bought from minor officials."[11]

Bolívar's Plague of Conspirators

Thus far we have had little to tell about the conquests and turbulence, the piracies and espionage of South America, not because that vast continent was spared the Old-World blight of perpetual intrigue, but because the men of classic ingenuity or low cunning have been so numerous and influentially active in other, more densely populated areas. The native Indians of Central and South America became impromptu intelligence agents instinctively protecting their own lands when the tribe of *conquistadores* descended upon them, and looked to them—with fair words and the ever-present threat of death or torture—for road maps and directions to the golden grail at the end of the New-World rainbow. And far out there at the end of a rainbow was just where the natives chose to send the greedy white men. In order to lure them on and away from their placid habitations, the Indians fed the *conquistadores* false and fantastic intelligence, not because they were unbaptized heathen bent on mischief, but because they profoundly distrusted baptized Spaniards.

We come now to the great Liberator, Simon Bolívar, whose habit and necessity it was to trust too many men who would play him false. Bolívar seems neither to have been materially helped nor impeded by systematic military or government espionage. But he and the cause to which he devoted his life were continually endangered by the Latin-American appetite for political conspiracy. Where George Washington had suffered a Thomas Hickey, a Conway, Gates, Charles Lee and Benedict Arnold, the "Washington" of Venezuela was destined to encounter a dozen of each and all the indescribable confusions of loyalty and purpose that afflict any people spiritually addicted to intrigue. Washington and Cromwell were fortunate "rebels" who could lead two of the great revolutions of modern times without ever having to behave like conspirators. Circumstances denied to Bolívar that equilibrium of unified and dispassionate command apparently reserved to the Anglo-Saxon revolutionist. Bolívar was himself a man of action rather than a plotter, but other republican plotters and agitators exercised an often momentous degree of influence upon his career and campaigns.

First among these influences was that exerted by Francisco de Miranda, one of the most picturesque adventurers known to the Americas or Europe in an age aswarm with them. Miranda, born in Carácas like Bolívar, but in 1756 and therefore more than twenty-seven years the other's senior, was a veteran soldier and hardened revolutionary conspirator with a price on his head when the future Liberator was an inexperienced fiery novice at the game of overthrowing Old-World "absentee" tyrannies. From his early youth Miranda had dedicated himself to the cause of Spanish American independence. He left Venezuela when still in his teens, gained his earliest military training in the army he had privately resolved to worst—that of Spain —and then served creditably in North America under the Comte de Rochambeau when French regiments led by that commander were sent to the aid of General Washington. Participating in the victorious American Revolution kindled anew Miranda's fanatic patriotism; and hastening home to Venezuela, he began plotting to effect the liberation of his native land. However, the young soldier of fortune was years ahead of his time. He encountered widespread apathy and suspicion, his schemes were betrayed to the Spanish overlords, and he barely escaped with his life.

Miranda visited England and the Continent, traveling more extensively than any other South American of his day. He even went as far afield as Russia, from which country he was later expelled at the instigation of the Spanish government, but not before his good looks and charming gallantry had promoted an amorous interlude. Catherine the Great looked upon her first Venezuelan and found him well worth her imperial while—or wiles—"an episode which to this day brings malicious satisfaction to Venezuelans."[12]

Having left behind the cold climate but warm welcome of Muscovy, Miranda visited Prussia, studied its formidable army, and reached France in time to enlist in the wars of the revolution. His rapid advancement followed. He was in command of the French force which besieged Maastricht and of the French left at the battle of Neerwinden. Being nearly involved by General Dumouriez in his treason, Miranda was tried and acquitted. That experience cooled his ardor for French liberty, equality and fraternity. But Venezuela was still in chains. He was subsequently rebuffed in England, and in America by both Jefferson and James Monroe. At length he found private sustenance for his plotting when Samuel Ogden, a merchant of New York, and others—in the winter of 1806—contributed money enough to equip what was the first of many filibustering expeditions designed in North America to explode politically somewhere on the southern continent.

Convoying two small transports, Miranda sailed in the brig Leander; but a warning of his purpose and the contraband he carried unluckily sailed ahead of him. The Spanish minister at Washington had a spy in New York who seems to have had no trouble in penetrating the conspiracy. Authorities at Carácas were promptly notified; and Miranda and his small force of revolutionaries—mostly *North* Americans—sailed straight for a coast that was armed and waiting for them. The swift little Leander escaped from the trap and got away to the neutral haven of Trinidad. Sixty of Miranda's followers were taken prisoner, however, and ten of them were hanged and their heads cut off and exposed on poles as a warning to various districts of Venezuela. This warning was curiously misdirected, as eight of the ten heads had belonged to citizens of the United States.

The Spanish minister's unforeseen triumph of counter-espionage proved typical of the breakdown of Latin-American insurrectionary movements for some years to come. It was equally typical of Francisco de Miranda's consistent disappointments as a liberator and of many subsequent North American enterprises of a helpfully rebellious nature down to the sorry affair of the Virginius and other disasters of Cuban intervention. But Miranda, like Bolívar himself, was a sturdy grappler with outrageous fortune. In Trinidad, with the virtual connivance of the British authorities, he got together quickly another expedition and was again discommoding his compatriot Venezuelans with a stroke of "liberation" in July of 1806. He managed to capture the town of Coro, only to find it hostile to all insurgents against the king of Spain. "The priests . . . instructed the inhabitants of this province that it had been invaded by a band of lawless hereticks and infidels, who came there only to rob them of their property and . . . deprive their souls of salvation by spreading damnable tenets and principles among the favorites of the Holy Virgin." Thus wrote one of Miranda's lieutenants at Coro. It might have come from stricken Spain in the summer or fall of 1936!

Miranda evacuated Coro and for the time being abandoned South America to its slothful, monarchist fate. He went to London and plotted there for four years, ultimately joining forces with the young firebrand, Simon Bolívar. Together they returned to Venezuela in December 1810. The politicians of Carácas were oscillating between loyalty to King Ferdinand VII and King Joseph Bonaparte, whom his imperial brother had enthroned at Madrid with historic instability. Spanish royalists were known to be counter-plotting all over the country; while Bolívar ardently advocated a declaration of Venezuelan independence. On July 4, 1811—the thirty-fifth anniversary of the North American colonies' Declaration of Independence —he persuaded an extremist club, the *Sociedad Patriótica,* to draw up a momentous resolution and submit it to the Venezuelan Congress. And as a direct result next day came Venezuela's hastily drafted Declaration of Independence, which Bolívar, who was no deputy, was not invited to sign. Miranda signed as deputy from the town of Pao.

The partisans of Spain sprang to arms, and hostilities commenced, with the veteran Miranda as republican commander in chief. He was one of those men whose personality easily cancels the most advantageous situation. It is said that he "surrounded himself with French officers, turned up his nose at native folks and ways and dishes . . . asked disdainfully: 'Where are the armies which a general of my position can command without compromising his dignity and reputation?'"[18] He and Bolívar were already showing the strain of their respective temperaments, the latter being deprived of important command; but he so distinguished himself when Miranda's force captured the pro-Spanish city of Valencia that he was allowed to regain his former rank of colonel.

Miranda failed to defeat the Spaniards under Domingo Monteverde, and when he abandoned his army and attempted to leave Venezuela, he was arrested by his own subordinates, Casas, Peña, Bolívar and others. Francisco de Miranda thereafter suffered the utmost degradation and died in 1816, "chained to the wall like a dog" in a Spanish prison at Cádiz. Bolívar survived the earliest insurrection and also the calumny that alleged he had helped to betray his chief, Miranda, to the Spaniards. Such episodes crowd one upon another in the remaining fourteen turbulent years of the Liberator's life. We cannot even enumerate here the number of assassins who all but succeeded in striking him down, the self-perpetuating cliques of turncoats and betrayers who sought to undo each conquest that gradually conferred independence on an immense area, today divided into six republics—Venezuela, Colombia, Panama, Ecuador, Peru and Bolivia.

By securing the password his enemies once nearly assassinated him at Calabozo. Spies betrayed Policarpa Salabarrieta, his courageous secret emissary in Bogotá, and that immortal heroine of Latin American insurgence was executed by a firing squad. Because their pay fell somewhat in arrears the garrison of Callao revolted and sold out to the representatives of the Spanish king. Similar mutinies interrupted the leader's great program of independence and unity. Mutinies raged and spread to the calamitous scope of armed rebellion. Revolution thus begat civil war; political ferment begat politicians; and intriguing civilians frustrated the soldier Bolívar with their ambuscades and sinister offensives.

At Bogotá one more plot was simmering; and the Liberator set his agents on the track of those who planned his assassination. Carujo, Galindo, Guerra, López, Silva, the French adventurer, Horment, the editor González! They had been holding secret meetings; officers and men of the garrison had been furtively approached. On the night of September 25, 1828, these murderers struck. Fergusson, Bolívar's Irish aide-de-camp, was slain; another favorite aide, Andrés Ybarra, was wounded. Only the resolution and audacity of Manuelita Sáenz, Bolívar's enchanting, daredevil mistress, saved his life. Manuelita forced him to jump out of a window when he would have tried to defend himself with a sword against men alert with carbines and pistols. Not long afterward "the upright and magnanimous" Sucre, Bolívar's ablest and most dependable lieutenant, was shot from ambush near the old royalist stronghold of Pasto. His wounds were mortal; the bullets of relentless assassins had cut down the hero of Ayacucho. Winning all the renegades but few of the battles, Spain in America thus slowly and painfully succumbed.

Abolition, Secession, Sedition

The space and attention to be given to the American Civil War, and to its leading secret-service operatives, are exacted both by the unusual character of many of those operatives and the novelty of their subterranean conflict, but also by the never-diminishing importance of the war itself. There was probably more espionage in one year in any medieval Italian city than in the four-year War of Secession. But the conspiracies, assassinations and intrigues of Florence or Venice, Milan or Rome had little significance apart from the dynastic or ecclesiastical politics of that day. Whereas the rather haphazard and often intermittent secret service of the American Civil War appreciably influenced the outcome of a struggle that altered world history. Confederate victory would have meant a Balkanized and embittered America, with Canada and the northeastern states the most compact and powerful, with the Far West disputed and perhaps divided, with further aggressions upon Mexican territory to extend the Confederate frontier and balance the North's new "northwest", with undoubted weakening or total abandonment of the Monroe Doctrine, dangerous—pre-1917—European alliances, and probable adventures in Latin America, multiplying the imperialist exploit of the Spanish-American War.

Compression has made it impossible for us to look too closely at the secret-service content of all the turbulent political phenomena—from the administration of Washington to that of Buchanan—which appear as a prologue to secession. In Jefferson's time France and Britain were renewing their death grapple, American seamen were impressed, and the embargo established; whereupon the merchants of New England began privately weighing and measuring their "right" to break away from a Union which was ruining their overseas trade. Federalists—Anglomaniacs, such as Timothy Pickering—actually ventured to conspire with the British against their own abominated government at Washington. Pickering hoped to counteract the bad effects of Saratoga and Yorktown.

Aaron Burr, who had deprived the Federal party, point-blank, of its last distinguished leader, cropped up anew with a conspiracy that would have led to his conviction in 1807 but for the great John Marshall's oblique conception of judicial integrity.[14] Burr's vanity and spleen, his renegade disloyalty to friends, partisans and patriotism, his ingrate's genius for saving himself by incriminating someone else—a generous Harman Blennerhassett, for example—confined him to the picayune destiny of a scheming malcontent, whose plotting to carve out a "Western empire" was doomed to failure and disgrace.

All this had its undertone of secret service, though there was then not any kind of federal police system, no military intelligence, no counter-espionage; and, characteristically, the plots and conspirators were more often exposed by accident or their own inherent folly. That was so when the notorious land pirate, John A. Murrel, undertook—in 1835—to organize an uprising of Negro slaves, river ruffians and criminals. Murrel was far more dangerous than a Burr or Pickering; and rumors of his plot first came to be circulated when a field hand could not resist bragging to a colored nursemaid about the impending massacre of the wealthy whites. But Murrel, the outlaws' "emperor"—the West was habitually too vast to germinate kings!—saw his thorough and formidable scheme exploded by the casual interference of an amateur detective of Tennessee, Virgil Stewart, who ought to be one of America's minor heroes but is not. So powerful was Murrel, the criminal and leader of *canaille,* and so well fortified his designs, that Stewart was put upon the defensive when exposing him and very nearly ruined himself with his now forgotten but then momentous espionage achievement.[16]

Other forms of secret service which flourished in America before the Confederate states seceded were mainly of a lawbreaking nature. Joaquin Murrieta of California—patriot insurgent to the Mexicans, bloodthirsty bandit to American settlers—was evidently served and in large degree protected by a very crafty intelligence system. In the Kansas-Nebraska prewar zone of violent contact the Border Ruffians and their militant foes revived the savageries of the French and Indian War, without any French and with very few Indians. That noxious rascal, William Clarke Quantrell, then calling himself "Charley Hart", began his career in this region of murder and rapine as a "detective" of invincible privacy. The worst homicidal guerilla in the red annals of American border warfare, Quantrell, with his band, in one August day of 1863 was to slaughter more than 150 defenseless citizens of Lawrence, Kan., and massacre seventeen unarmed boy cadets, besides looting and burning the town. But before those spacious years of rebellion he had to do his killing in more leisurely fashion, from ambush. As "Hart the detective" he operated alone, to the detriment and anguish of both sides of the slavery question; and in his own view it was a life of idyllic treachery. He first helped Abolitionists steal slaves as a matter of principle and then as a matter of personal profit stole them back again, either returning them for a price to their original owners or selling a batch of them farther South —at least once including a free Negress he had managed to delude and abduct.

John Brown's conspiracy emerged from the inflamed border country and was so feebly clandestine, it would have no place in this record, save that a real detective, Allan Pinkerton, alleged that Northerners of the Abolitionist faith employed him to try to rescue Brown after the failure of his forlorn hope at Harpers Ferry. When Pinkerton and his agents studied the Charlestown prison, they found it strong, guarded by soldiers, unassailable. Pinkerton had earned his difficult assignment through his partisan enlistment in the activities of the celebrated Underground Railway. That was improvised and lawbreaking "secret service" of a peculiarly native brand; and the Scotch investigator of Chicago, when not professionally hunting criminals, lent ardent support to the underground work of combating slavery. Righteous intriguers like Elijah Lovejoy, Philo Carpenter, Dr Dyer and L. C. Freer were operating an artful system that arranged the flight and total disappearance of fugitive Negroes. It is strange to discover, as we soon shall do, how little effective influence the Abolitionists' clandestine experience with their Underground Railway had upon the innovation of Northern—Federal—secret service when war presently broke out between North and South.

CHAPTER THIRTY-NINE

THE BALTIMORE CONSPIRATORS

THE SECESSION of the Southern States began like a plot conducted in public. It is now, perhaps, idle to estimate that an aggressively undertaken counter-plot, equally well publicized and embracing the activities of twenty thousand men—the losses at Shiloh or Gettysburg—would have disorganized the far from united Confederacy and limited the conflict to sixty days, largely in urban areas. The outcome would have been the same. The South, however, would have been repulsed rather than conquered; there would have been no stunting era of Reconstruction. But instead we have the record of feebly proposed Federal military intervention, giving the secessionists an immediate outward semblance of unity; while agitators and incipient assassins leaned against the bars at Guy's or Barnum's in Baltimore and bragged of their rebellious plans to Pinkerton detectives.

It was the president of one of the newly built railroads, Mr Samuel M. Felton of the Philadelphia, Wilmington and Baltimore, who had summoned Allan Pinkerton from Chicago with a party of his operatives to act as the company's private counter-spies.

"We have," said Felton, "good reason to suspect that secessionist plotters in Maryland intend destroying the property of the road, in order to cut off the Government at Washington from the Northern States. The ferryboats on the Susquehanna at Havre de Grace and our bridges below Wilmington seem especially to be threatened."[1]

The Federal authorities were neither prepared nor disposed to cope with the growing bitterness of the sectional controversy. They had no central organization resembling the military secret service or bureau of political espionage, then available to the more reactionary powers of Europe. There was in Washington no Army or Navy Intelligence, no investigative branches of the Treasury or Department of Justice; and if there had been any existent ancestor of these modern establishments, who would have taken the throttle and set them in motion? It was late in January of 1861. Abraham Lincoln had been elected to the presidency, but his inauguration would not occur until March.

At Mr Felton's suggestion, Allan Pinkerton moved first upon Baltimore, recognized as a hotbed of proslavery intrigue. The de tective proceeded to rent a house and, using the assumed name of "E. J. Allen", began circulating in those fashionable quarters of the city where violent enemies of the incoming Republicans were practicing agitation. One of the men under his command was Timothy Webster. Already an acknowledged star of investigative service, he was now being pointed—almost casually—toward his career as a secret agent of the North operating against the South, which he sustained with notable courage and aptitude for fifteen months and then relinquished tragically enough. Webster, a native of Princeton, N.J., was able to pass as a Southern sympathizer and soon contrived to enlist himself in a smart troop of cavalry then drilling and under arms at Perryman, its object the defense of the vital communication line of the Philadelphia, Wilmington and Baltimore Railroad from what was loosely termed "Yankee aggression."

Another Pinkerton ace on this strange assignment was young Harry Davies. After several years' residence in New Orleans and other Southern cities, he was familiar with, and capable of imitating or exploiting, the customs, chief characteristics and prejudices of the local gentry. He was personally acquainted with many of the leaders of Secession. Polished, good looking, of French descent, he had been educated for the Jesuit priesthood; but upon finding the discipline of that vocation distasteful to him he had, like a number of the European experts of these annals, turned to the congenial pursuits of secret service. He spoke three foreign languages and was widely traveled; but more than that, this perfect spy was endowed, in Mr Pinkerton's opinion, with all the persuasive powers that belong to the Jesuits.[2]

It cost him no effort save the spending of time and Mr Felton's money to impress the bloods of Barnum's Hotel and Guy's, who blended aristocratic bile with old Bourbon while keeping each other assured that "no damned Yankee upstart of a railsplitter ever shall sit in the presidential chair." But the one among them whom he chose to influence most was an obsessed youth named Hill. Of distinguished family, already an officer in the Palmetto Guards, a volunteer body such as that absorbing Webster, Hill seriously confessed to Davies: "Should I be chosen, I'll not fear to kill. Caesar was stabbed by Brutus —and Brutus was an honorable man. Lincoln need expect no mercy from me, though I do not hate him as much as some do. It is more love of country with me."

So an assassin was going to be chosen? An attempt made upon the life of Abraham Lincoln? The detective—now known as "Joe Howard of Louisiana"—used Hill to gain admission to the inner circle of plotters. That they were an actual menace could no longer be doubted.

Allan Pinkerton in his own orbit had found the police of Baltimore under the control of Marshal George P. Kane, an ardent Secessionist who had nourished the rank and file of his department upon radically rebellious notions. A keyman among the Southern partisans of Baltimore, Kane would not lift his hand in the event of their insurrection, except to fan the flame.[3]

Another leading spirit, wearing the very halo of a hothead—introduced to "Howard" by Hill, and by the detective to his chief, Mr E. J. Allen—was a man of Italian extraction called "Captain" Fernandina. By virtue of his Latin temperament, its wealth and warmth of utterance, as well as his professed resolve to yoke himself to the dangers of sedition, the "captain" was now welcome in all the exclusive public places, heard with respect, and treated familiarly even by those several cuts above him in Baltimore's well-defined social scale. Not only was he conceded military rank, though without a commission from any regular authority—an old and enduring Southern custom—but also he was the acknowledged organizer of one more of those companies of volunteers which were sprouting up from day to day with pious rebel enthusiasm.

Fernandina, however, had trained for his role of detonating agitator as the barber at Barnum's Hotel. He owned no slaves, had actually suffered in his business from the unfair economic competition of black body servants who did not have to be paid; yet shaving and trimming the hair of his wealthy slave-holding customers had somehow infected him with this overweening zeal in defense of slavery. And it seemed to the detectives a solid proof of the rashness and rebel ardor they had discovered that so many substantial citizens whom this man had formerly lathered and anointed now considered him their spokesman and a right gallant fellow.

Eight Red Ballots

Davies, the intimate of Hill and accepted with him as a disciple of the extremists' doctrine, at length was invited by Fernandina to attend a conspirators' meeting of the gravest importance.

He and Hill like the others—some thirty in number—were duly sworn, Davies perjuring himself with a mental reservation in order to defend his country. A kind of awe pervaded the assembly; though beholding his neighbors there, Davies was inclined to smile. He was surrounded by some of the least discreet and loudest tindertongues in Baltimore. How could *they* endure the secretive obligations all had just assumed?

Perfervid oratory is seldom the characteristic of the man of desperate action. In a box of white ballots to be passed to each member of the conclave there was supposed to lurk but a single red ballot. The conspirator drawing it was expected to say nothing but to regard himself as honorably fated when the appointed hour came.

Hill had learned, however, and confided it to Davies, that not one but *eight* red ballots were seasoning the awesome box. A necessary precaution against the eloquent but ineffectual, against cowardice, treachery or homicidal ineptitude!

Fernandina, the chairman, opened the meeting with a speech. His boiling point was uncommonly low at all times; a few ranting phrases and he was off, raking the champions of Negro freedom as one who vicariously felt the sting of the Abolitionist serpent. The lamps were dimmed still more, to conceal the designations of chance. The ballot box went around.

Davies drew a white ballot. And he could tell by Hill's poorly dissembled relief from nervous tension that he, too, had not dipped into the red. Eight men were leaving, each with the thought that on him and him alone rested the staggering responsibility of saving the South. Making some excuse to leave Hill, Davies hurried off to consult E. J. Allen; and after he had made careful notes of his crack operative's story, checking it with the warnings that had come from Timothy Webster, Pinkerton took the next train to report to Mr Felton in Philadelphia.

The slaying of the Republican President-elect as he was passing through Baltimore on his way to be inaugurated would be the "signal" of which Webster had been hearing a good deal—the signal for the burning of P. W. and B. wooden bridges, together with ferries and rolling stock throughout Maryland. Thus, at a stroke the nation would be made leaderless, the insurrection of the Slave States would be launched, and the capital of the land cut off from the despised Abolitionists of the North.

Conservative elements of the South had nothing whatever to do with the projects of Fernandina and his kind. Kane, the head of the Baltimore police, was surely in league with the plotters. Therefore, on arriving in the city Mr Lincoln would be left virtually unprotected. Only a few friends and party politicians were escorting him to Washington. And when—Davies had learned—cheering, hostile, or merely curious people began crowding around this small party at the Baltimore railroad station, a noisy "brawl" was to be started some distance off, giving the few policemen Kane would have on duty an excuse to go elsewhere. Then would the crowd close in around the little group of despised Yankees—a disorderly "rabble" pressing closest to Mr Lincoln. The eight holders of the red ballots would be there; and the fatal shot or knife-thrust must follow directly.

A swift steamer was to be stationed in Chesapeake Bay, with a boat waiting ashore ready to take the assassin on board. Without delay he would be carried to some as yet unspecified port of the deep South, where he surely would be honored as the heroic defender of States' Rights.

Corroborative Warnings

By an indirect route which the exigencies of politics seemed to necessitate, Abraham Lincoln was traveling toward Washington. He had left his quiet home in Springfield, Ill., on February 11, 1861, accompanied by John G. Nicolay, his private secretary, Judge David Davis, Colonel Sumner, Major Hunter and Captain Pope,[4] Ward H. Lamon and Norman B. Judd of Chicago. Allan Pinkerton was well acquainted with Judd and had already sent him two notes of warning, one delivered in Cincinnati and the second when the presidential party arrived in Buffalo.

Mr Lincoln reached Philadelphia on February 21, and through the intercession of Judd and Felton a private meeting had been arranged to enable the detective to present his evidence pertaining to the Baltimore conspiracy. Pinkerton submitted to a cross-examination as searching as any he ever experienced as a witness for the prosecution in a criminal case.

When he heard of Fernandina, Mr Lincoln said: "Then do I understand, sir, my life is chiefly threatened by this half-crazed foreigner?"[5]

"Mr President, he only talks like a maniac. One of my best men penetrated to the very core of the plot and learned how carefully every move has been planned. Fernandina's capacity to do you harm must not be minimized. Their conspiracy is a going concern."[6]

"But why—why do they want to kill me?"

The detective replied that it would be impossible for anyone of Mr Lincoln's mind and disposition—or, in fact, for any conservative Northerner—to comprehend the mad, hysterical feeling then prevailing against him in and around Baltimore. As the head of the government after March 4, he was expected to halt the disturbances in the Southern States, either by decisive tactics, as in President Jackson's remembered day, or by adroit measures of conciliation which would persuade the more tractable, the reluctantly belligerent majority, and cut the ground from under the incendiary elements.

In 1865 John Wilkes Booth, the half-demented ringleader of another shadowy plot of amateur assassins, killed Abraham Lincoln because again he was improperly protected, alien to counter-espionage, too confident of his fellow man, too approachable, democratic and kindly. In 1861 the Union was fortunate in having an obstinate Scot out of Glasgow on the scene in the capacity of impromptu counter-spy. Even a Lincoln could not make Detective Pinkerton concede[7] that there was little real harm to be feared from the "childish" raving and secrecies of Baltimore.

Samuel Felton, moreover, had gained corroborative evidence when a Southern friend of his, a Miss Dix, noted for her manifold philanthropies, came to him in Philadelphia with a private warning which she begged that he convey to the President-elect.

"This lady has proved her loyalty to the people of the South by innumerable acts of generosity," the railroad executive explained to Mr Lincoln, "but she cannot condone bloodshed and murder. She wishes me to tell you, sir, that there exists an extensive, well organized conspiracy embracing all the Slave States.

"They mean to seize upon the city of Washington with its records and archives. Then these plotters will proclaim themselves *de facto* the Government of the United States. They plan a *coup d'état* thus, very much in the European manner. At the same time they propose to interrupt all means of communication between the District of Columbia and the North, East, or West, checking any prompt transportation of troops to wrest the capital from their hands.

"Your inauguration would be prevented—or, Miss Dix said with tears in her eyes, your life would fall a sacrifice to the attempt at inauguration."

In the city of New York the able superintendent of police, John A. Kennedy,[8] had gathered some emphatic hints as to this same plotting from Democratic proslavery circles. Whereupon, venturing far outside his jurisdiction, he had ordered Police Captain George Washington Walling to send detectives to the seat of the brewing trouble in Baltimore and Washington.[9] These New Yorkers heard nothing but talk of insurrection.

The Counter-Plot

Abraham Lincoln had to yield. These must be many and serious dangers threatening him who personified Federal authority.

As a guest of Andrew Curtin, who would become famous as Pennsylvania's "War Governor", he was expected to speak that very evening in Harrisburg at a banquet arranged in his honor. But instead the President-elect was enabled to leave the banquet room early and drive to an obscure railroad siding where a one-car special train was held ready with steam up. Felton and Pinkerton were in charge of this historic journey, but with many a loyal assistant helping when and wherever required.[10]

It had been given out that Mr Lincoln, owing to a severe headache, had returned to the executive mansion with the governor. Even so, deplorable possibilities sprang from the undoubted presence in Harrisburg of Secessionist spies assigned to keep a close watch upon the movements of the Republican leaders. Samuel Felton owned enough authority to order the delay of all telegrams sent by way of Philadelphia; and to exercise this same censorship over the wires of the Northern Central Railroad, which led southward out of the capital of Pennsylvania, a trustworthy young lineman, Andrew Wynne, had been sent to cut them at an unfrequented spot. There would be no communication that night between a spy in Harrisburg and the simmering insurrectos on the Chesapeake.

Meanwhile, over an express track from which all traffic had been arbitrarily cleared by Felton, in a darkened coach attached to a fast locomotive, Mr Lincoln was being rushed to Philadelphia. There he changed to the regular night train of the P. W. and B., which had been delayed by Felton simply upon the excuse of an important package which must be taken to Washington that night. The package formally delivered to Conductor Litzenburg held only vintage newspapers of the year 1859, addressed to E. J. Allen, Willard's Hotel, Washington, D.C.

Arrived in Philadelphia, the President-elect kept his promise very amiably, submitting to all the precautions of the detective. He allowed himself to be represented as an invalid, with the celebrated Mrs Kate Warne of the Pinkerton staff posing as his attentive sister.[11] Having had reserved for them the last three sections of the last sleeping car of the train, the party—Lincoln, Ward Lamon, Mrs Warne, Pinkerton and his redoubtable general superintendent, George H. Bangs, the three operatives being armed—was able to go aboard without attracting the attention of other passengers.

Resolved to learn what had happened to Walling's investigators, Superintendent Kennedy of the New York Police Department was on that same train, quite unknown to the private detectives, who would have found him an intrepid reinforcement in case of an emergency.

Allan Pinkerton had made up his mind, however, not to meet with any emergencies. At his suggestion Mr Felton had sent out gangs of picked workmen to "whitewash" the railroad bridges. And while applying a white coating of a substance which, it was hoped, would do much to make the structures fireproof, they remained conveniently ready to be called upon in the event of an outbreak of violence.

In addition, there were heavily armed Pinkerton agents posted along the right of way of the P. W. and B., covering for that one night, at least, every bridge, siding and crossroad. Webster and Davies were at critical points, the former having moved up from Perryman to Perryville, where the train must wait to be slowly ferried across the Susquehanna. A final warning had come through from Webster, saying that the companies of railroad men were now drilling with the reputed purpose of safeguarding the property of the P. W. and B. But it was the investigator's acute opinion that they really meant to destroy rather than protect when the beacons of rebellion should blaze.

Every operative on watch had been provided with a dark lantern. Allan Pinkerton rode on the rear platform of the coach in which the President-elect was sleeping, studying the countryside through which they were passing and receiving signals from his men along the route. The welcome flash of Webster's light—"All's well! All's well!" —told him that the "enemy" had been caught napping.

The train rolled on, heading now into the stronghold of Lincoln's border foes. But from every bridge and vantage point the darting flashes kept up that running reassurance—"*All's well!*" At Baltimore there was not a sign of impending turbulence. The city was quiet, unsuspecting.

In the manner of the primitive and disjointed railroad facilities of that day, sleeping cars bound for the capital had to be drawn by horses through the streets of Baltimore to the station of the Washington line. One can imagine the tension of that small isolated group of guardians as their coach traversed the streets of a city which in spirit had already seceded. And then, having completed that passage uneventfully, they were compelled to wait two uncertain, perilous hours because a connecting train from the West had not pulled in according to schedule.

At length it arrived. Pinkerton and his associates completed the momentous preinaugural journey without having allowed Mr Lincoln to be seriously disturbed.

Next day, as word of this counter-spying exploit electrified the nation, fanatic partisans of the South broke into an uproar of derisive abuse. The wholly extemporized investigation was thought to reveal that a sinister web of government spies, a swarm of "damn Yankee" police agents, had spread subcutaneously over Maryland. There was, moreover, some partisan political contention in the North about the circumstances of the actual investigation; but no credit claimed for Allan Pinkerton could be denied him or his operatives when it developed that they had not only safeguarded Abraham Lincoln but assisted also in rescuing two of the New York detectives.[12] This pair had been exposing themselves to lynch law in a rabidly secessionist region, when that excellent "rebel" cavalryman, Timothy Webster, chanced along. And in the name of holy Slavery the Pinkerton agent promptly arrested them and marched his prisoners out of range of mob violence.

No raids or arrests for conspiracy in Baltimore had ever been contemplated; the times were much too critical. But Fernandina and the principal plotters were already gone from their favorite haunts. Guy's and Barnum's held no echo of them. Assassination, when not the act of the deranged, is generally the impulse of cowards who hope to exhibit a moment's audacity; and neither Davies nor his chief was surprised that those sworn to plunge a knife into the heart of the Abolitionist chose instead to thrust themselves into oblivion.

CHAPTER FORTY

AGENTS BLUE AND GRAY

THE HISTORIC EVENT of the Baltimore conspiracy is important not only because it protected Abraham Lincoln who was to save the American Union, but also because it showed better co-ordination of secret service and counter-espionage than would soon again be duplicated by either side in the spreading conflict of Secession. Mr Pinkerton and his detectives had returned to Chicago; but their combined operations in the critical weeks before March 4, 1861, so commended the Pinkerton Agency to the new Republican Administration that its chief and Timothy Webster were summoned again to Washington.

From dissension, agitation and the threat of armed uprisings the country had sped to the certainty of war. An organized rebellion was detonating nine Southern States; and the Federal authorities had only a scattered and distressed regular army. There were spies and Secessionist agitators swarming in every Northern center; and, since President James Buchanan had been intent on bequeathing his successor all the difficulties of his four years' neglect, there was not a trace of a Federal secret service to cope with them.

It was on Monday, the fifteenth of April, after the insurgent gunners of Charleston, S.C., had finished target practice upon Fort Sumter, that President Lincoln issued his first call for 75,000 volunteers. On the nineteenth the Sixth Massachusetts Infantry detrained in Baltimore to march across the city and proceed to Washington. And now all the worst—and most disparaged—predictions made by the detectives in February were confirmed by the actual violence eight weeks later. The agitations of Fernandina and his following, the undisguised hostility of local officials like Police Marshal Kane, found something at last to focus upon, something within reach; and the "Yankee" infantrymen, set upon by a great mob stirred to terrible ferocity, had to fight for their lives with bayonet and ball cartridges.

Following upon this sanguinary riot came a second demonstration which two months before had been anticipated in the Pinkerton espionage reports. At dawn on the morning of the twentieth the bridges at Melvale, Relay House and Cockeysville, on the Harrisburg road, and over the Bush and Gunpowder rivers and Harris Creek were destroyed by fire. This effectually interrupted railroad communications between the capital and the North. Telegraph lines were cut. And in Washington Mr Lincoln's government was shut up with a few battalions of soldiers and twice as many active if undisciplined partisans of disunion.

One of the first emissaries of the North to explore this no man's land of broken roads and arming factions was Timothy Webster. A dozen closely written messages from friends of the President had been stitched into the linings of his coat collar and waistcoat by Mrs Kate Warne before he set out from Chicago. And the Pinkerton agent had not only delivered these to Mr Lincoln's secretary[1] with creditable promptness but had also submitted verbal information leading to the arrest of a rebel plotter, who bore dispatches yielding up a wealth of evidence relating to secessionist intrigues.

The detection of the Confederate courier was an encouraging stroke; and Mr Lincoln sent for Webster to congratulate him. Another of the striking personalities of this record, Timothy Webster changed, it will be noted, in three months' time from private detective to professional secret agent and spy, to double spy, train watcher, government courier, and finally counter-spy—the principal roles of military secret service—without instruction and with uniform success. Some of this success was due, no doubt, to the disorganization on the Southern side.

One of Mr Lincoln's messages entrusted to the agent who carried a hollow cane was addressed to Webster's chief. The President invited Allan Pinkerton to come to the capital and discuss with him and members of his cabinet the formation of a "secret service department" in hopes of "ascertaining the social, political and patriotic relations of the numerous suspected persons" in and about the city of Washington. This was, in the light of the growing emergency, a dangerously restricted view, and, as worded, it was typical.[2]

The detective agreed. Southern agents swarmed in a cloud about the Federal preparations for war. They were just too numerous to be mistaken for spies; it seemed more like a convention or a "movement" of some kind. Nobody threatened them, kept them in order, or kept them from adding to the confusion. Their reports must have been confused, too; but they unquestionably worked great indirect harm. Had counter-spies existed to prevent their describing the preparations in the North, inadequate for war and too extravagant for a picnic, the South might have mobilized with less of eager jubilation.

Invention of United States Secret Service

At probably no other period of the rebellion was Federal police and espionage activity more imperative. For one of his many railroad-company clients Mr Pinkerton could have been hired to throw a cohort of his operatives into Washington and fumigate the community from the Alexandria Bridge to the Maryland line. The Scotch detective was a born counter-spy, wary, thorough and suspicious. He had given his opinion to the President and cabinet; they had seemed to approve; and Mr Lincoln had said he should hear promptly from the proper authorities. Doubtless, with but seven weeks' experience as head of the government, Mr Lincoln had believed that somebody could be prompt.

Three months later Allan Pinkerton became the first chief of an authorized and organized Federal Secret Service. He had not, meanwhile, been idle but had practiced the fine arts of military investigation as "Major Allen", a mysterious officer on the staff of General George B. McClellan.[3] Following a brief and masterly campaign in western Virginia, on July 27 McClellan had arrived in Washington, a popular new commander in chief for all the Union forces, whom Abraham Lincoln, just then at the dawn of all his painful gropings for a winning general, had hopefully appointed. The extent of the disaster at Manassas on the twenty-first had seemed to clear a path for this promotion; but also there were circumstances connected with it which issued a sudden call for the companion services of McClellan's little-known "Major Allen."

The accuracy of advance information forwarded to General Beauregard by Southern spies on duty in Washington had enabled the Confederate leader to prepare for the attack coming against him. McDowell, the Union's earliest victim of volunteer armies, had swept up to Beauregard with a number of those regiments which were to run away from their first battle not once but several times. Their advance lacked disciplined order even while the action favored a Union triumph. But then the weight of Johnston's reinforcements anchored the Confederate retreat; and not long afterward the rebel spies of Washington experienced their first dangers of the "front", being among those spectators nearly trampled to dust as a frantic blue stampede exploded upon the national capital.

Six days later General McClellan took command of a shamed and disorganized body of troops, which was still an army only because the survivors of Bull Run had all turned back in the same direction. There had been scandalous disorders in Washington after the humiliation of McDowell's force. Unruly stragglers, the remnants of companies, were much to blame; but the chief offenders were Southern partisans who celebrated with various acts of defiance. Martial law was thereupon belatedly proclaimed in the District of Columbia, with Colonel Andrew Porter of the Sixteenth Infantry appointed provost-marshal.

The Confederate victory at Bull Run was not only the first major success of the war, but also it was that action of the whole conflict most decisively influenced by accurate, promptly transmitted intelligence. Southern espionage scored more emphatically than it was ever to do again; and larger credit might here be awarded the Confederacy's secret agents in the District if their task had been really dangerous and of necessity clandestine, instead of resembling the blandest sort of press correspondence. Colonel Porter and Allan Pinkerton both were resolved to make it more dangerous. The regular police of Washington had shown themselves practically an advance unit of the Confederate army; and so in addition to other pressing duties, the provost and the military detective had to join with the municipal authorities in disciplining that force and adding to its ranks a few Northern men.

The newly established Federal Secret Service, with Pinkerton, or "E. J. Allen", in charge, acquired for its headquarters a dwelling on I Street. It had been plain ever since the rout at Manassas that the government's problem of suppressing Southern spies was a grave one. General McClellan, however, wished Allan Pinkerton to accompany him as a staff officer in the field and, it appears, bring his incipient Secret Service with him. The headquarters of McClellan were also probably a magnet for enemy spies. But Washington was the danger zone where they were harder to detect and could work the gravest harm; and either Pinkerton or his commander in chief should have recognized it. The organization of secret service thus began as an adornment of the army rather than a bulwark of the whole government.

"Mother Has Been Arrested!"

From beginning to end of the Civil War the ordinary hazards of professional espionage were doubled and trebled by the inexperience or downright incompetence of amateur staff officers assigned to impromptu Intelligence. Allan Pinkerton was merely the first of these, with past commitments to crime detection as a fair excuse for being a military novice. The important detail of transmitting information remained primitive and unsystematized so long as he was in charge; and only in rare instances did any of his colleagues or successors attempt to improvise either system or ingenuities of communication.

Allan Pinkerton, concentrating practically his entire investigative force upon the intricacies of Federal secret service, proceeded with so much groping, original sin and imitative error, he almost qualified for promotion to the command of the much misled Army of the Potomac. But he made no mistake when he built his earliest espionage corps around Timothy Webster. Pinkerton, to do him justice, seems to have discerned in Webster's willingness to volunteer that superlative aptitude for offensive secret service which he would demonstrate so convincingly through fourteen hazardous months to come. The whole training and career of Webster in the private detective agency had been equipping him for the larger perils and responsibilities of a secret agent in time of war. He had the requisite mental qualifications and extraordinary physical endurance—which, as we shall see, he was allowed to squander recklessly. Like that other Pinkerton operative, Davies—now thirsting for martial adventure and enrolled in a cavalry regiment—he was a priceless treasure to any government with a vast rebellion to suppress by force of arms.

Allan Pinkerton cannot be blamed for failing to enlist other geniuses. His fault lay in the natural blunder of requiring his only genius, Webster, to co-operate with a badly forged "chain" of less gifted agents, that indestructible stupidity of management which we shall find afflicting both sides in the mighty contest of the World War. Pinkerton never had at his disposal a large body of disciplined or specially trained operatives. Nowhere, either in the performance of his duties or in subsequent records dictated by him,[4] is there to be found any conception of the essentially military character of the work he sought to direct. Napoleon might proclaim with his habitually ethical view of combat: "The spy is a natural traitor." Mr Pinkerton seemed to believe that the spy is an inevitable civilian.

Before we turn again to the records holding the fate of the best male operative on the Northern side, let us see the new Federal Secret Service showing its teeth and really closing down upon a menacing agent of the Confederacy. It was Thomas A. Scott, then assistant secretary of war, who called upon Mr Pinkerton to submit a report upon the baneful activities of Mrs Rose Greenhow, living in the capital at Thirteenth and I streets. A widow, and reputed to be wealthy, she was an aggressive rebel agent and yet easily detected as a partisan of the South, for she refused to offend her conscience with pretenses of neutrality.

In one of his innumerable reports to General McClellan, Pinkerton refers to those suspects having "entrée to the gilded salon of the aristocratic traitors." That scornfully described privilege came to Mrs Greenhow by natural right and was maintained upon the strength of a widely quoted utterance of hers—that instead of "loving and worshipping the old flag of the Stars and Stripes" she saw in it only the symbol "of Abolition—of murder, plunder, oppression and shame." Yet nothing short of the most positive proofs would serve to justify her restraint as a Confederate spy. She had been a "leader of Washington society" in Buchanan's administration. Her niece—a granddaughter of the universally admired Dolly Madison—was married to Stephen A. Douglas. These insulations as well as her acknowledged wit and charm protected a not-unpopular form of guilt and would withstand a considerable siege.

Before Colonel Thomas Jordan, U. S. A., had resigned his commission and left Washington to become adjutant general of the Confederate Army at Manassas, he had discussed the importance of espionage and secret service with his sympathetic friend, Mrs Greenhow. She was eager to help the Cause; and so he hurriedly jotted down a cipher for her to use and recommended that she address him hereafter as "Thomas John Baycroft." When, later, she learned of the Federal plan of McDowell's advance upon Manassas by way of Fairfax Courthouse and Centerville, she enciphered a warning and found a Miss Duval who was willing to act as her messenger. Disguised as a "market girl", Miss Duval traveled with ease to Fairfax Courthouse, leaving the spy message at the home of a Federal officer, whose wife and daughter were dependable Southern sympathizers. Jordan thus obtained vital intelligence by a direct and deceptively ingenuous system of transmission.

The Federals, however, failed to keep their appointment; and Jordan and his superiors became alarmed lest Mrs Greenhow, as an amateur of espionage, had accepted and forwarded misleading information. Whereat General Beauregard dispatched a messenger of his own, one G. Donellan, a former clerk in the Interior Department, who bore a simple passport in Jordan's cipher—"Trust Bearer." Mrs Greenhow trusted him, and so he presently returned with a more comprehensive account of the Federal determination to attack Manassas. After the victory at that point and the Federal cross-country sprint known as Bull Run, both President Jefferson Davis and his victorious commanding general wrote generously of their "debt" to Mrs Greenhow.

She had launched her career as a military secret agent in April of

1861, and by November of that year the War Department and Allan Pinkerton were keenly suspicious of her continued residence in the capital. Considering the lean jaws of legislation that clamped down upon the most trivial of subversive actions or comment in America during the last year of the World War, it seems strange that Pinkerton agents had to prove the outspoken widow a rebel spy in order merely to retire her to uncommunicative seclusion. But in the Civil War partisans breathed more freely; and had condemning talk over teacups shaken the government, Washington would have been laid waste by that air raid months before Manassas. Assistant Secretary Scott was persistent about Rose Greenhow, described by him as a formidable spy who unwisely neglected to edit her conversation. And as soon as Allan Pinkerton and several of his men began watching the lady, they secured not only hints of her intrigue but evidence of the treason of a Federal officer whose attentions she was openly inviting.

Pinkerton found the windows of the Greenhow dwelling too high for observation from the ground, and it became his detective practice to take off his shoes and stand on the shoulders of his subordinates. Surveillance by that gymnastic-pyramid method clinched the case, and shortly afterward Mrs Greenhow was on her way to the Old Capitol prison. Adjutant General Jordan, on hearing of the spy's apprehension, felt called upon to apologize for his cipher—"Being my first attempt and hastily devised . . ." Allan Pinkerton was no less discomfited when he sought to use Mrs Greenhow's fashionable home as a trap for her confederates, or for Confederates in general. And only when Rose Greenhow's daughter had reached maturity was the simple cause of his discomfiture exposed.

Nobody bearing incriminating messages or otherwise involved in Southern intrigues called at the Greenhow home the day of her arrest, when agents of the Secret Service awaited them, because her little daughter—eight years old in '61—had climbed a tree adjoining the property and kept chanting to all passers-by whom she recognized: "Mother has been arrested! . . . Mother has been arrested!"

Mrs Greenhow Discommoded—Webster Hanged

Owing to the pressure exerted by her many influential friends, Rose Greenhow did not have to suffer court-martial proceedings or even long internment at the Old Capitol prison. Instead she was passed through the military zone and permitted to travel to Richmond on a flag-of-truce boat.[5] Timothy Webster, meanwhile, was matching Allan Pinkerton's counter-espionage triumph by insinuating himself ever more deeply into the ranks and councils of those partisans in Maryland who felt "cut off" from their fatherland of Secession. Impersonating the wiliest of rebels, Webster made each of his daring journeys into Virginia count as an exploit of his own private secret service in behalf of the South and its sympathizers. When a zealous Federal detective, the grim man-hunter, McPhail, caused his arrest in Baltimore, Pinkerton visited the "suspect" to interrogate him; and it was arranged that, on being ostentatiously escorted to Fort McHenry for internment as a rebel, Webster should be enabled to make a "bold break for liberty", escaping from trustworthy armed guards under orders to fire into the air. The spy returned to his Secessionist haunts in Baltimore at dead of night, was gleefully received, and lay in hiding there for three days before he slipped away again to report to Allan Pinkerton.[6]

Any public frustration of the Federal authorities quartered upon Baltimore was a cause of scarcely subdued rejoicing throughout the rebellious precincts of that city; and Webster, to maintain among his intimates the fiction of his escape, was thereafter obliged to behave more furtively inside Northern lines than when touring in his role as a Union inspector of Confederate armies. When he visited Richmond now he bore such credentials as opened all doors to him. He became the confidant of blockade runners—and reported their intentions to Washington and the Navy Department. He was importuned by enterprising gentlemen who hoped to arrange with a group of Baltimore's leading merchants to ship goods ostensibly to Europe, yet according to a plan whereby the unsuspected vessel—standing in close to the mouth of the York River—would transfer a valuable portion of its cargo to a smaller craft chartered to land the merchandise at Yorktown. The starved markets of the Confederacy made this and every other guileful project an enticing speculation, for already there had been a vast increase in the prices of innumerable commodities. Webster, without ever having heard the word *profiteer*, discovered himself so attractive to the breed, they crowded forward to consult him; and the spy took delight in exploding schemes intended to defy Union gunboats and batten upon the war necessity of the South.

At this prospering period of his secret-service campaign Webster began co-operating with three of Pinkerton's agents who, each in his special way, was a notable recruit. "Stuttering Dave" Graham had been dredged from the ranks of the Twenty-first New York Infantry to penetrate Virginia as a pack peddler. His vocal impediment was a histrionic masterpiece; and to help out the stuttering, his earliest specialty, he had been perfecting for years an epileptic seizure. As the South was still thick with combatants who were sure the war would be over in another three months, there were not many of them who cared to start in to question "Stuttering Dave." John Scobell was a Negro agent who devotedly served the cause which meant emancipation for his race. It would seem that Scobell was somewhat handicapped as a spy by that talent for hyperbole so characteristic of people of his color. Confederate batteries looked terribly formidable to the Negro agent and Confederate regiments sometimes spread out before him like the hosts of the ancient kings.

Yet this weakness of his was not unsuited to an agent working out of the headquarters of General McClellan, whose theory of effective military intelligence implied circling around an enemy sentinel and counting him from all four sides. In the vicinity of Richmond Scobell was useful, too, in operating with another spy, Mrs Carrie Lawton, as messenger and bodyguard while posing as her servant.

The second year of the Civil War began with Timothy Webster at the summit of his career as a devious but influential Confederate partisan. When a young Marylander named Camilear, noted as an advocate of Secession in the neighborhood of Leonardtown, ventured across the Potomac he was straightway arrested on suspicion of espionage. A word from Webster to the Virginian controlling Camilear's prison brought him forth and restored him to his home.

Webster's chef-d'oeuvre—with a safe conduct personally tendered him by Judah P. Benjamin, the Confederate secretary of war—was a tour he made in company with a government contractor who was buying leather for the use of the Southern armies. The spy thus visited Knoxville, Chattanooga and Nashville, returning to Washington by way of the Shenandoah and Manassas, and bringing such a carefully detailed account of all he had observed that his gratified commander in chief spoke to Pinkerton about granting him a month's furlough. Webster was no longer in robust health, having suffered severely from exposure. Rheumatism had afflicted him for a time; and he was still feeling twinges of it when he next escorted Mrs Lawton to Richmond.

McClellan's campaign in the peninsula was about to begin. The Secret Service was pouring all its efforts into observation of the garrison and defensive strength of Richmond. Webster suddenly turned silent—no word came through from him, though a report was long overdue. And now Allan Pinkerton, in spite of his Scobells, Grahams and other operatives who had returned safely from missions south of the Potomac, moved inexorably along the path that was to send Webster to his death. Two Federal agents, Price Lewis and John Scully, volunteered to go to Richmond and endeavor to repair whatever damage had been done to the feeble system of communication. Messrs Lewis and Scully—of British nationality—had much to recommend them as "neutral" visitors to the Confederate capital. But in Washington both men of late had been serving as *counter-spies*.

Webster was desperately ill in Richmond, stricken with inflammatory rheumatism, unable to escape, unable to move from his bed. Scully and Lewis found him at his hotel, tenderly nursed by Mrs Lawton and the object of much local solicitude. But, as Webster himself instantly foresaw, the two newcomers were suspected at once by General Winder's detectives. Presently both of Allan Pinkerton's investigators were in custody, accused of espionage, threatened with the gallows. Webster's illness, then, had utterly wrecked the Federal communicative system. Mrs Lawton, it appears, had had no means available to warn Pinkerton of his master spy's plight—which warning might at least have prevented this blundering "visit" of the two men, already recognized and denounced to the Confederate provost.

Intolerable pressure was brought to bear upon the two in prison; and when it was to be a choice between hanging or making a full confession, Scully broke down. Whereupon Lewis decided he might as well talk candidly to General Winder. If a few witnesses testifying that he and Scully had been Federal detectives in Washington had sufficed to get them convicted of espionage in Richmond, Lewis reasoned, Scully's disclosure of the object of their mission would be enough to convict Timothy Webster. And so it turned out, Scully and Lewis appearing as the star witnesses at their colleague's trial. As they swore Webster's life away, syllable by syllable they unwound the rope from around their own necks. Webster alone was condemned to hang.

Chapter Forty-one
LAFAYETTE BAKER AND BELLE BOYD

HIS mastery of espionage notwithstanding, Webster had never seemed close to the army but had remained, like his chief, a private detective investigating Southerners for a client who happened to be the government. General McClellan, however, was deeply concerned when word of the master spy's court-martial and the manner of his conviction reached headquarters; and at his suggestion Allan Pinkerton hurried to Washington to try to arrange some form of official intervention firm enough to impress Richmond and gain a stay of execution. President Lincoln agreed to call a meeting of the cabinet to determine what might be done in behalf of a man to whom the government was heavily indebted. Secretary of War Stanton said that he would use every resource at his command to save Webster, but that Scully and Lewis, who had betrayed him to gain a reprieve for themselves, deserved no official recognition.

Richmond had been a veritable sieve until a crack Union agent was in Winder's net; whereupon the Confederate capital seemed to move quite out of reach. Not even Mr Pinkerton was optimistic enough to suggest undertaking some form of rescue. There were vague discussions of reprisal. Ultimately it was decided to forward by telegraph and a flag-of-truce boat a communication to the leaders of the Confederacy, representing the lenient course adopted thus far by the Federal authorities in dealing with Southern spies—recalling how many of them, like Mrs Rose Greenhow, had been released after a brief term of detention, and that none so charged had been tried for his life or sentenced to death. This message was designed to intimate that if the rebels killed Webster, the Federal government would retaliate. Fortresses and other places of detention in the North were crammed at the time with candidates; and a more rigorous military regime contending with rebellion would simply have notified Jefferson Davis of the specific reprisals intended should Webster, Scully or Lewis hang. But Secretary Stanton's intimation was so diplomatically worded, the Confederate politicians chose to interpret it as permission to go right ahead—conforming to the tactics pursued by their generals, until rough campaigners like Grant and Sherman took the field against them.

McClellan, meanwhile, was creeping toward Richmond in the peninsula, was but four miles away when finally compelled to fall back to Harrison's Landing. He had been an American observer in the Crimea; and that war, which seemed to carry the waste and aimlessness of foreign adventures to the peak of imbecility, must have imparted to McClellan his more cautious conceptions of offensive strategy. Pinkerton's feeble ruse in authorizing the benighted errantry of Scully and Lewis had cost the North its hardest-hitting unit of offensive secret service. His abrupt resignation as chief of the Secret Service was in no degree related to Timothy Webster's undoing.[1] Following the Union victory of Antietam—which was to the South its victory at Sharpsburg—the command of the army was confided to Ambrose E. Burnside; and Pinkerton rather sharply reproved President Lincoln by declining to manage the spies or counter-spies for any commander supplanting his god, McClellan.

In the preceding months while Detective Pinkerton was rattling around in a position for which he seems to have had every qualification save experience and imagination, a new star was rapidly rising in the dim, uncrowded firmament of Federal military espionage. His name was Lafayette C. Baker; and he proved to be an artful officer, one of the few spies and managers of spies in America whose career and methods have engaged the studious appreciation of European experts. Though he attained to the rank of brigadier general during and directly after the Civil War, he began by spying for a Union commander without any enlistment or regularized army position whatever. Baker, like a true Yankee salesman, submitted a sample of his goods before naming his price or asking for a contract. Moreover, he approached his military career exactly according to the plan afterward much in vogue with the heroes of G. A. Henty and his imitators: he managed to present himself to the commander in chief and straightway attracted that soldier's favorable attention.

Spy as Itinerant Photographer

The gallant old veteran, Winfield Scott, sat in his tent wondering what Jeff Davis, Beauregard and the other Confederates had in mind. McDowell was in the field or on the edge of it with a Federal army of volunteers and militia whose fighting qualities had not been tried, like Scott's, in the Mexican War. Approaching the general, young Baker announced that he would like to go into Richmond as a Union spy. He believed he could successfully pose as a resident of Nashville and a Southern sympathizer. He would learn, he promised, all about the Confederate positions and resources in northern Virginia.

After questioning Baker, Scott decided to trust him. It was his curious notion to disguise himself as an itinerant photographer. We are accustomed to regard a camera as almost an insigne of espionage; during the World War any sort of photographic apparatus in civilian hands within cannon range of the front was deemed as threatening as an enemy air raid. The camera, however, was a novelty in 1861. Lafayette Baker's choice of impostures turned out to be perfect.

He had difficulty getting past nervous Federal pickets. He was fired at and challenged and chased, and twice he was taken up as a rebel spy. He managed to save himself by appealing to Winfield Scott; and the commanding general's intervention set him free to begin all over again. At length Baker gratefully found himself in the hands of Virginian cavalrymen; his inherent skill in the game of military secret service at once became manifest. The young photographer had with him about two hundred dollars in gold which Scott had given him. It should have aroused Confederate suspicions when he was searched, but it never did; he was mistaken for a poor man. He lugged along a camera which was broken and useless from the start; yet no inspiration of enemy counter-spies moved them to test his photography.

After a day or two of captivity and interrogation Baker was found so interesting a specimen that he was passed back from command to command, always meeting higher officers, always making progress as a spy, until he actually came to be interviewed in Richmond by Jefferson Davis, Alexander H. Stephens, the vice-president of the Confederate States, and by every important Southern general up to and including Pierre Beauregard. Baker seems to have toured all the regiments of Secession then training in Virginia. He brazenly promised fine results when "taking" a sort of panorama of a regimental mess at luncheon on some courthouse lawn. Ostensibly preceding Matthew Brady, he snapped his defunct camera in front of brigade headquarters and pretended to record the countenances of bewhiskered young generals and their younger and bewhiskered staffs— those group pictures, so dear to all organizations, and to newly uniformed warriors especially, which give one today the impression that the barbers on both sides of the Civil War were slaughtered to a man in the attack upon Sumter.

He was everywhere favored by that aristocratic attitude of the South which then looked upon a traveling photographer as no more than an odd type of peddler, perhaps a cut above a tinker or cobbler, but near kin to the strolling musician, actor, bookseller, itinerant farrier and such petty tavern clientele. Baker, even so, was technically under arrest almost all the while he spied and tarried south of the Potomac, was less often entertained in taverns than in jails and guardhouses. In Richmond the provost marshal was his guardian and kept him coolly under lock and key. He only escaped when President Davis ordered him taken to have an interview with General Beauregard, then commander in chief. Baker never hesitated to submit information he had supposedly picked up while passing through Washington; therefore, the Confederate leaders were as glad to detain and continue questioning him as he was pleased to be among them and observe what strength in war they were feverishly making ready.

By degrees he won the confidence of army men in Virginia and allowed himself more latitude in his espionage. Yet his failing ever to develop and deliver any of his pictures was remarked at last; that happened in Fredericksburg, where he was accused directly of being a Yankee spy. Lafayette Baker's crisis had come; he must go before a court eager to experiment with martial law—or else steal home to General Scott. He chose to spend the remainder of his gold in obtaining certain implements likely to aid his escape; and with bewildering ease, considering the gravity of the charge against him, he contrived his own enlargement. The jail that confined him was a rusty affair. He seems to have discarded it as readily as he did his photographer's outfit.

Traveling by night with every precaution, Baker drew near to the Union lines. There was a zealous young sentry who nearly shot him dead; but on giving himself up as a prisoner, the escaper at once demanded that he be taken before Winfield Scott. A commander in chief nowadays is seldom seen by spies save at victory parades. But again Baker's powers of persuasion brought him through; and Scott and his officers welcomed every detail of intelligence the ex-photographer was able to submit. He was commended for his daring; and his memory was prized as a vault of hidden treasures.

General Scott paid Baker according to his desire—got him a commission and placed him in the way of rapid promotion. He came to be provost marshal and presently was in control of his own corps of espionage or counter-espionage operatives. The compressions of this record exclude even a résumé of Baker's rise from grade to grade, until he wore the star of a brigadier general. We shall, however, meet him again.

The Longest Beard Ever Seen on a Spy

In the West General Grenville M. Dodge—who was to become far more celebrated subsequently as the builder of the Union Pacific Railroad—had been transferred to the command of the secret service and capably directed the activities of a hundred spies.[2] One of his operatives was a talented eccentric, "Colonel" Philip Henson, who in postwar years was to gain some renown and a meager livelihood by lecturing on espionage and the marked ingratitude of the Republic he had served, while adorned with a ten years' growth of beard six feet four inches in length. Henson, erect, measured six feet two; and when he allowed his superb beard to "hang untrammeled" it swept the lyceum platform, "fully six inches of it resting on the carpet." As a spy inside the rebel lines, Henson had displayed peculiar and equally virile traits. General Nathan Bedford Forrest, that superlative fighter, called Henson "the most dangerous Federal spy operating in the Confederacy", and regretted having overlooked an earlier opportunity to hang him.

On that occasion Henson had ventured into Alabama to visit his sister and had been arrested and then sent as a conscript to Virginia by order of Forrest. The spy could think of better ways of losing his life than facing the Yankees' new Enfield repeating rifles—"loaded on Sunday and fired all the rest of the week"—and so he waited until night and then jumped from a speeding Meridian and Selma Railroad train. Soon afterward he borrowed the papers of a retired Confederate soldier and made his way to Richmond on a spying expedition. When inflammatory rheumatism—poor Tim Webster's Nemesis—visited itself upon Henson he so far mastered that painful ailment as to escape with his life when a posse of suspicious Southerners approached the home of his relative, a Union sympathizer, where he had been stricken and where he lay concealed. Henson, without uttering a groan, let himself be lifted up and carried, safe if not sound, to a riverbank and to rescuers from a Federal gunboat.

"Colonel" Phil was that commonplace of European intrigue, a double spy—comparatively rare amid the strong partisanship of the War of Secession. General Dodge provided him with "samples" of authentic information concerning the Union forces, and with these Henson imposed upon Leonidas Polk. Henson was accepted by Polk as a valuable agent and regularly paid for a time in Confederate money, the perfect tender to a double spy. After the fall of Vicksburg General Dodge sent Henson to Atlanta; and it was during this eventful mission that he met General Longstreet and managed to impress him so favorably that he was even invited to travel upon the Confederate army commander's train. Longstreet at this period was moving to reinforce Braxton Bragg, and his advance seriously threatened the Union General Rosecrans. It is of record that Henson's espionage reports, forwarded by Dodge to Rosecrans, materially influenced the campaign in the West; and so Henson—who grew his fantastic beard to attract attention to his impoverished plight—was not unreasonable in complaining that his hazardous services merited a more grateful reward.

General Dodge was that kind of secret-service director who was bound to be loyally served, for he in turn risked charges of fraud in order to protect the anonymity of his agents. His superior, General Hurlburt, at Memphis insisted that he get receipts from those he paid to supply the Union command with information; but Dodge stubbornly appealed to Grant, who overruled the ridiculous order. It is amusing to learn with regard to this craze for secret-service "accounting" that three years after the Civil War it was discovered by some upholstered busybody of the Federal War Department that Dodge had disbursed a substantial amount of money to spies operating for Grant and Sherman, and so the department "peremptorily ordered him to make an accounting of the exact sum."[3] Dodge graciously referred the auditors of the War Department to the report of General Grant's provost marshal at Corinth, Miss. And only *nineteen years later* Dodge had this reply from the department: "Your secret service accounts for the years 1863 to 1865, amounting to $17,099.95 have been examined and adjusted, and are now closed on the books of this office." Probably the departmental files were being cleared out in anticipation of the red tape presently to be won in Cuba and the Philippines.

Both armies in the War of Secession preferred to call their military spies "scouts", the term "spy" being reserved to a limited class of civilian informants who remained behind the enemy's front and seldom carried their own reports through the lines. General Dodge was the first to employ his scouts to "run down rumors" of Confederate troop movements continually pouring in from partisan sources, and which otherwise called for a cavalry reconnaissance. As the Federal dragoons were notoriously ignorant and reckless in wearing out their mounts and overfond of raids and pillage disguised as reconnaissance, any mitigation of that wasteful pastime was a boon to Union commanders.[4] It was not difficult in a civil war for scouts to assume the manner, accent and uniform of the other side, which made both scouting and spying a widespread adventurous enterprise. But

Dodge seems also to have profited greatly from his shrewd selection of civilian agents; while his most successful espionage messengers were women. Some of his operatives were intrepid enough to remain inside the Confederate lines for months at a time. And to transmit their findings he developed an invisible chain of innocent-appearing feminine couriers. These Union partisans imposed upon Confederate provosts by "begging to go into the Federal lines to see relatives, who were refugees"—and in nearly all instances of urgent communication, a pass could be coaxed out of some gallant or sentimental Southerner.

Perhaps the most capable and aggressive foe with whom Dodge's men contended was a Confederate secret-service officer named Shaw, who elected to be known in the underground combat as "Captain Coleman". General Bragg was wont to rely upon his "scouts" and spies and displayed throughout the war great ability in organizing and directing them. Coleman was Bragg's ace of espionage. He had any number of daring exploits to his credit, until at length his luck changed—or so it seemed—and he was taken prisoner. James Hensal of the Seventh Kansas Regiment was an alert soldier in command of Dodge's scouts and counter-spies in the Tennessee Valley, and one day he and his men surprised and rounded up a party of civilians, all ostensibly engaged in the lawful pursuits of commerce but suspected by Hensal of dealing in cotton or other contraband. He did not recognize any of his prisoners, though one of them was Coleman and another Sam Davis, his intrepid messenger.

A Southern Hero and Heroine of Espionage

Davis alone was unfortunate enough to have incriminating papers found upon him when he was questioned and searched. "Where is your chief, Coleman?" he was asked a hundred times. But Davis persisted in answering that he did not know anybody named Coleman, that he had no chief and had not even spoken to a Confederate officer for weeks.

He was grimly reminded that as a spy he would be hanged or shot if he did not tell the truth. Neither threats nor promises provoked any confession exposing Coleman, who all the while sat among the nondescript, unidentified civilian prisoners, dreading that Davis would be tricked or bullied into some dangerous admission. Sam Davis, however, did not weaken as his superior feared and was executed as a spy without uttering the words he knew would save his life. Subsequently the undetected Coleman was exchanged as a harmless rebel sympathizer. And still later General Dodge heard from a

New York broker, Joshua Brown, how the much-wanted Coleman had slipped through his cordon owing to Davis' fortitude. Stirred by the Confederate agent's heroism, General Dodge later contributed to the fund collected in Nashville to erect the monument to Sam Davis, American hero and the Confederacy's "Nathan Hale" of the struggle in the valley of the Tennessee.

In 1864 a persuasive young man of patrician appearance came to be engaged by the Union side as a spy. He said he wanted only a horse and an order to carry him through the Federal lines, and in return he would bring back intelligence concerning the Army of Northern Virginia and the Confederate government at Richmond. Supplied with these and a little money, he vanished for a fortnight but then reappeared as he had agreed, bearing a letter from President Jefferson Davis to Clement C. Clay, the agent of the Confederacy in Canada, who was stationed at St Catherine's near Niagara Falls. The Union spy said that his envelope only contained a letter of recommendation; it was in Davis' own hand and allowed to pass unopened. Whereupon he became the regular courier between Richmond and Canada, and the dispatches he transmitted were all read and copied in Washington. To further this espionage it was necessary to duplicate both the paper and seals of the original wrappers, and this ultimately caused the Federal War Department to import from England the same paper Clay used in Canada.

One dispatch thus intercepted revealed a scheme of genuinely alarming sabotage.[5] Rebel agents were to set fire to New York and Chicago by placing clockwork machines in large hotels and places of amusement, such as Barnum's Museum, where they might be timed to ignite simultaneously, so that the fire departments in each city would suddenly have a great number of alarms to answer. General Dix, the commandant in New York, and John A. Kennedy, superintendent of police, were both incredulous when warned of this plot that Clay was manipulating from across the Canadian border; however, precautions were taken by police and military authorities. The St Nicholas Hotel in New York had a fire started by a clockwork device, and a few other fires broke out. But the infernal machines went astray in their timing; and none of them caused any considerable amount of damage or confusion.

During the first year of the war a report upon each meeting of President Lincoln's cabinet went southward within twenty-four hours, and nearly every Federal secret of any importance to the Confederacy was made known to Richmond with equal expedition. This efficient intelligence organization was largely composed of the postmasters of lower Maryland, all but three of whom in three counties were disloyal servants of the government that appointed them but loyal and active Secessionists.[6] As soon as operatives of the Federal Secret Service, now commanded by Lafayette Baker, had managed to overcome this internal handicap, offensive agents of a different caliber had to be combated. Southern spies like James R. and Charles W. Milburn, John H. Waring and Walter Bowie conspired and struggled against heavy odds which ultimately overcame them all. Bowie once contrived to escape from four Union detectives, who had him cornered at the Waring plantation on the Patuxent River, by making his exit disguised as a Negress with a washtub upon "her" head. The secret agent was stopped and questioned, and so far convinced the Federal operatives that he was a Negro servant of the Warings, they allowed him to pass. Later Bowie—whose other career in company with John S. Mosby's guerrillas was scarcely a shining beacon of heroism—was shot and killed after having pillaged a store at Sandy Hill. His sometime host, accomplice and rescuer, Waring, was taken into custody as a Confederate agent and all his property confiscated.

Abraham Lincoln had repeatedly interfered in saving convicted Southern spies and partisans from death; and in the case of such a celebrated rebel as Miss Belle Boyd it would seem that half the Union army was enlisted in furthering her espionage with acts of politeness and clemency. "A female spy is an engaging creature," the novelist, Joseph Hergesheimer, wrote in his study of Belle Boyd, "but in crinoline she has an especial, a romantic and absurd, charm."[7] Belle so skillfully enveloped herself in a cloud of crinoline that she succeeded both in exaggerating her merits as a "female spy" and in persuading her Northern enemies to condone her offenses like Southern gentlemen. She, an acknowledged Confederate sympathizer who had shot and killed a Union sergeant before she was eighteen, carried secret intelligence through the Union lines, not once or twice but a score of times—because of her "romantic charm", true—but mainly because no Federal officer cared to expose himself to unfavorable comparison with the uniformed chivalry of the South by being rude to a young lady whose design it was to have him and his men surprised and shot or made prisoner.

Belle Boyd, who was certainly, as Hergesheimer asserts, "the most famous woman concerned with official secret activities in the Civil War"—though not the most importantly effectual woman spy—has left a very clear impression that she was the kind of partisan who would have "stopped at nothing" to help the cause of the Confederacy. Yet, if we discount a few antique insinuations of Northern contemporaries, there is nothing to suggest she was ever more than mildly immodest in her espionage exploits. She fascinated men and could have played the traditional siren, enticing anything in boots and a uniform that had military information to disburse. But her opponents seem invariably to have been stupid or indiscreet without promises or compensation. Even when she was finally in custody, it appears she was neither seriously threatened nor searched. She had her trunks with her in jail and was able to conceal no less than $26,000 from the glance or grasp of her supposedly watchful warders.

Crinoline and Courage

The engaging Belle, daughter of a Federal official, was born in Martinsburg, then a community of Virginia. She was seventeen when the South commenced to mobilize; and only in July of that year of '61 she began to attract Northern attention. Invading soldiers attempted to raise a Federal flag over the Boyd dwelling, and when, as a loyal Virginian, Belle's mother objected, one of the more brutal of the detested Yankees spoke to her rather roughly and added injury to insult by slamming open a door which Mrs Boyd was injudiciously endeavoring to slam shut in his face. Belle, in her own words, "could stand it no longer." With "indignation . . . roused beyond control; my blood . . . boiling in my veins; I drew out my pistol and shot him. He was carried away mortally wounded and soon after expired."[8]

And that, in the modern phrase, was that—Civil War or no Civil War. Federal troops saw a good deal of the Boyds of Martinsburg for the next few months, but no more doors were thrust open by men in uniform when Belle's mother wished to slam them shut. Federal officers from the commands of General Patterson and General Cadwalader came and courteously investigated the casual killing; and martial law threw a protective arm of justifiable homicide over a Virginian belle not yet eighteen whose trigger finger had so convincingly reached the age of consent.

It was a justifiable homicide which further justified Miss Boyd's growing conviction that she was more than a match for Yankees. Soon afterward she won national recognition as a spy. We cannot enumerate all the risks she elected to run, the reports and dispatches she faithfully delivered, the thickening wits of Union adversaries that she appeared to solidify to the texture of solid skull. She was a born adventuress whose refined upbringing and caste inhibitions were largely though never completely dispersed in the burning maelstrom of civil war. With the correspondent for the New York *Herald* and various Federal officers quartered in her home, Belle was able to gain without effort a wide assortment of military information. On May 23, 1862, her news of enemy—of Union—strength became so imperative, she tried to induce any one of a dozen Southern sympathizers to carry a secret message to General "Stonewall" Jackson. But the local men were reluctant to rob Belle herself of simultaneous danger and glory; and so she set out, conspicuously clad in a dark-blue dress, white sunbonnet and "small frilled white apron." She had to run through crowds of Union infantry, and on, between the lines under heavy fire; and, though shot at by snipers, with an artillery duel screaming and crashing overhead, a hail of iron around her, a shell-burst seven yards distant drenching her with earth, she was able to wave her sunbonnet as the First Maryland regiment and Hay's Louisiana brigade acclaimed her grace and resolution with a welcoming cheer.

A friend, Major Henry Douglas, was the first to hear her intelligence. The combined forces of General Banks, General White and General Frémont were to be hurled upon Jackson's troops. Now Stonewall Jackson was one of those rare collectors' items, a master strategist who could make up his mind and a military commander accessible to the idea that patriot spies really risk their lives for the purpose of helping to defeat the enemy. He took action therefore as soon as Belle's report was conveyed to him, saved his inferior force and used it as an instrument of surgery upon the converging but as yet un-co-ordinated Union columns. After the victory he wrote with historic explicitness:

Miss Belle Boyd,
I thank you, for myself and for the army, for the immense service that you have rendered your country today.
                        Hastily, I am your friend,
                        T. J. Jackson, C. S. A.

Belle Boyd continued her generally impromptu secret services; and the newspapers of the North took full advantage of distance and sketchy communications to enlarge upon her beauty, army influence and audacity. The war seemed all but lost with this fair Virginian afield; but Belle made one grave mistake, entrusting a letter she had written Jackson to a Union secret agent who merely happened to be wearing Confederate gray. Secretary Stanton got the letter from General Sigel and straightway sent Cridge, a detective of the Federal Secret Service, to escort Miss Boyd to Washington. Cridge, to his young captive, was "low in stature, coarse in appearance, with a mean, vile expression . . . and a grizzly beard. All his features were repulsive in the extreme, denoting a mixture of cowardice, ferocity, and cunning." Cridge, in short, was not to be melted by even an "especial, a romantic and absurd, charm", and when *he* slammed a door, it had iron bars in it.

Belle was a difficult prisoner, eventually exchanged and personally escorted to Richmond by a Major Fitzhugh. The Richmond Blues presented arms, and at night she was serenaded by the city band. She was later at sea, she was in Britain, she met a Federal naval officer, Sam Wylde Hardinge, who succumbed at a glance and resigned his commission in order to make her Mrs Hardinge. There were vivid years of romance and celebrity ahead of her and of advantageous tours of lecturing when the war of sections was at an end. She was never ashamed to be known as "the Rebel Spy"; and it would have been an unhappy lyceum audience that mistook it for a term of opprobrium.

CHAPTER FORTY-TWO

CRAZY BET AND OTHER LADIES

THE MOST VALUABLE SPY opposing the Confederate States was also of Southern birth, Miss Elizabeth van Lew of Richmond, Va. This intrepid partisan has no peer in American history and few in all these annals. She is the only American woman ever to take part in military espionage in time of war, and within the enemy's country, who convincingly proved herself a master of secret service. It is odd, perhaps, that the sole candidate of the United States should be just this type of sheltered, cultivated gentlewoman; and it is a fact that, until we shall reach the behind-the-front activities of the World War, half a century after her day, there is no woman candidate of any land equaling her "masculine" range and caliber.

Elizabeth van Lew adapted herself to the more despicable necessities of espionage, betraying her friends, spying upon her neighbors, and intriguing against the armed forces of her hard-pressed native state. She not only risked her life but jeopardized her mother's and her brother's, exhausted the family resources, and persisted in her partisan conduct with invincible ardor despite repeated threats of mob violence. She overtaxed her frail physique, and likewise the capacity of Southern leaders to protect her or trust her, all because there was something she hated even more than her own deceitful practices. The thing she hated was slavery.

During the four years of war she paid an exorbitant price for the privilege of serving the Union clandestinely. A distinguished Confederate acquaintance surrounded her; and she was suspected in differing degrees by every resident of Richmond. Some believed her insane. And that she encouraged, sturdily masking her more subversive activities beneath the half-scornful, half-apologetic appellation, "Crazy Bet." It was, in short, impossible for true-blue Virginians to imagine a Virginia aristocrat opposing the Cause except on the impulses of a deranged mind.

They said that she was disloyal, that she wanted the North to win, that she had talked against Secession. And they were sure she was a rabid Abolitionist, for she had freed Negro slaves and never troubled to conceal her animus for the slave-holding institution. She was suspected, furthermore, of assisting "runaway niggers" and of hiding and helping Yankee prisoners of war to escape. And owing to her resolute effort, it was whispered in grim resentment, she had kept her brother out of a gray uniform.

Between 1860 and 1865 she was, in fact, suspected of everything that she did, or that she believed, or that she became—save the most desperate and threatful of civilian offenders. No one, whether grieving friend, hostile acquaintance, Confederate officer or counter-spy, ever suspected Elizabeth van Lew of being the vigilant, resourceful managing directress of the most consistently serviceable espionage system operating for either side.

General U. S. Grant spoke for the army and government of the North when he said to her: "You have sent me the most valuable information received from Richmond during the war."

Since Richmond was the capital of the Confederacy, the tribute of the Union commander in chief at once promotes Miss van Lew to the headquarters company of eminent espionage practitioners. Like Walsingham she spent her own money freely upon what she deemed the vital subterranean defenses of her country. Like De Batz, her every move or endeavor had to be impromptu and carried out against long odds in a city of all-encompassing foes. As final proof of her right to be numbered with the elite of the world's secret corps, she managed to accomplish nearly everything she set out to do and yet has come down to this day, from one of the most dissected and investigated wars of all time, as a modest little champion practically unknown.[1]

Upon the authority of General George H. Sharpe, chief of the Bureau of Military Information on the Federal side, the greater part of the intelligence received from the Richmond area by the Army of the Potomac—prior to as well as during General Grant's command—was either collected or transmitted by this incomparable woman operative.

She established five secret stations for the hazardous work of transmission, a chain of relay points whose terminus was General Sharpe's headquarters. The beginning of the chain was the old Van Lew mansion in Richmond, where she worked upon her cipher dispatches and received and sheltered the espionage agents who stole into the city on errands for the Federal high command.

There were times of dilated watchfulness and tension when no Union traveler put in an appearance, and rumors came to her of "damned Yankee spies" being arrested and shot. Whereupon she contrived to pass her own servants as messengers through the Confederate cordon, maintaining the vital supply of secret intelligence which reported conditions in Richmond. There is no record of her having attempted the perilous journey through the lines herself.

Complicating her military intrigues as no professional would venture to do, she brought escaped Union prisoners to her home and nourished and concealed them. They kept drifting away from Castle Thunder, from "the Libby" and Belle Isle; and the more this tireless woman heard from them of the life of the prisons whence they had fled, the more her scanty reserves were expended upon alleviating the condition of other Union captives shut up in Richmond. She carried them food, clothing and books—sometimes there had to be simple ciphers lodged in a worn old binding—and poured out her money, hundreds and ultimately thousands of dollars, until all the convertible property of the Van Lews had disappeared.

In witness of her generous expenditures, it was Van Lew money that even retained counsel to defend Union sympathizers prosecuted by the Confederacy. For many months, on the word of General Sharpe, her chief, this blend of conspirator and ministering angel was all that was left of the power of the United States government in the city of Richmond.

"A Woman of Delicate Physique"

Elizabeth van Lew was born in Virginia in 1818 but had been sent to school in Philadelphia, her mother's former home. The Pennsylvania city was never rabid about its antislavery agitation and contained hundreds of Southern sympathizers; yet Elizabeth returned to Richmond a convinced and disquieting Abolitionist. One of her first impulsive actions was to arrange for the freeing of nine of the Van Lew slaves. She also prosecuted a search for certain Negroes in bondage and bought them if she could, solely to reunite them with a husband or wife in the possession of the Van Lews.

There were like-minded Southern gentry,[2] of course, and so Betty van Lew's not too harmless eccentricity was overlooked or noticed with mild reproof by her neighbors and friends. Friendship in the case of the Van Lews was that famous Southern bond. The eminent Chief Justice John Marshall had been an intimate Van Lew friend. Jenny Lind had sung in the parlor of the Van Lews' Virginian mansion; where also the Swedish novelist, Fredrika Bremer, and any number of American notables had been entertained. A bit "advanced", the Van Lews, mother and daughter—but generous, hospitable and charming, no more than perceptibly handicapped as strong-minded women.

Elizabeth was forty-one when the marines commanded by Brevet Colonel Robert E. Lee stormed the enginehouse at Harper's Ferry and took John Brown prisoner. The hanging of the old man delivered her and her strong opposition to slavery into the camp of those "cranks and fanatics" sworn to abolish it. "From that time on" —she wrote in her diary[3]—"our people were in a palpable state of war."

The role she would play came to her without audition or rehearsal. She began at once to work for the Union, sending "letter after letter" to the Federal authorities, revealing conditions "down South."[4] She sent these letters through the mails; but if anyone in Washington gave heed to them it was some obscure and diligent clerk who counted for little in Buchanan's administration. Elizabeth's genius for espionage spared her, no doubt, from disillusionment when her efforts went unappreciated. She was observant, she kept on forwarding her reports and plotting against disunion. A supreme enthusiast, she was even intrepid enough to speak in the streets of Richmond as an Abolitionist.

Elizabeth was described at the time as a "woman of delicate physique", yet a small and commanding figure, a vivid personality, "magnetic, accomplished and resolute." The very captains of the Confederacy paid homage to her delicacy and charm; it took the groundlings to discover the mania of "Crazy Bet." Scorning an easy disguise of "loyal Southern womanhood" for her secret service, she declined to make shirts for Virginia's soldiers. Other ladies of Richmond sewed or knitted and, with the Yankee barbarians not too distant, engaged in pistol practice. But Mrs van Lew did not sew or knit, and Elizabeth slaved over genuine intelligence reports, improvising her own technique, relating as much as she could learn—which was often a great deal—about the Confederacy's mobilization.

Humanitarian instinct sent Elizabeth and her mother to the local military prisons to give aid to wounded men incarcerated after Bull Run and other early engagements. But it was presently noted at the War Department in Washington that the accuracy and importance of her intelligence was increasing through this daily contact with Union officers and men. One of the former was Colonel Paul Revere of the Twentieth Massachusetts Regiment, whom we shall meet again as her champion after the war and a devoted, lifelong friend.

The commandant at the repellent old Libby was a Lieutenant Todd, important on that account to Elizabeth van Lew, and not because he happened also to be Mrs Abraham Lincoln's half-brother. By taking him buttermilk and gingerbread she conveyed the impression that her kindness extended to South and North alike; and once she gained access to Libby Prison she found a mine of military information—at that time difficult for her to sift or even comprehend—in the whispered confidences of Northern prisoners.

This intelligence, obtained from the men most recently brought back under guard from the Confederate zone of combat, was passed to her in a score of ways. Questions and answers were hidden in baskets of food or wrapped up with bottles of medicine, not as yet made prohibitive in price by the Northern blockade. Or books which she had lent were returned to her with certain words faintly underscored. Sometimes, while other imprisoned Federals kept watch upon warders and sentries, she was enabled to interview a newcomer with much to tell her in a tense few moments of whispering, contrary to the strict regulations governing her prison visits.[5]

Few Confederate officers or men seriously exerted themselves to harass her with their suspicions. Her deep concern for the well-being of the Negro race was so well known, she seemed "queer" to the average Southerner; and with many casual eccentricities she nourished the conviction that her fanatic beliefs had turned her into a harmless lunatic. We must observe, of course, that her mother was never thought crazy and was probably the more endangered of the two. The lives of both women seem to have been repeatedly threatened by a seething community. Only the steady run of reverses which Southern troops inflicted on blundering Union generals throughout the first two years of the war spared the Van Lews from that mob violence which rises in all countries with the fermentations of defeat.

Newspaper articles openly condemned the "disgraceful" conduct of Miss van Lew and her parent. And yet, in spite of this campaign of denunciation, Confederate officers and government officials continued to call at the Van Lew mansion. Their after-dinner conversation generated a wide and valuable range of intelligence items; and she seems to have learned a headquarters trick of piecing them together or blending them with information gained from other spies or Federal prisoners of war. About the worst official rebuke that the cultivated, pitiable "Crazy Bet" ever sustained was the revocation of her permit to visit the military prisons. Wherever that occurred she put on her best frock and took up her parasol and went straight to General Winder, or to the office of Judah P. Benjamin, the Confederacy's secretary of war. A few minutes of frowning and polite reproof, a few more of moving appeal and feminine persuasion, and Crazy Bet was on her way home with a new prison permit, endorsed by Winder, the man whose counter-espionage service was entitled to sign her death warrant. On more furtive occasions, the crinoline and parasol were discarded impediments, and then "Crazy Bet" sallied forth in the guise of a common farmhand. The one-piece skirt and waist of cotton, seedy buckskin leggings and huge calico sunbonnet of this disguise were found among her effects a generation after Appomattox—the sole and significant mementoes of many a nocturnal expedition.

Jefferson Davis' Waitress-Spy

William Gilmore Beymer, to whom we are indebted for the investigations that led to the rediscovery of Elizabeth van Lew, rightly observes that her manner of reaching President Jefferson Davis "in his least guarded moments" gives proof of "her genius as a spy" and a director of espionage. She had owned a young Negress of exceptional intelligence and several years before the outbreak of war had arranged for the girl's manumission. She had even sent her North, paying the costs of her education; but when hostilities threatened, Miss van Lew wrote to the girl—Mary Elizabeth Bowser—and asked her to return to Virginia. This she did with the prompt obedience of gratitude and fidelity, whereat her former owner began coaching her for a difficult mission. With her training accomplished, Miss van Lew, through what artful recommendations we can only guess, had Mary Elizabeth installed as a waitress in the home—the White House —of the head of the Confederacy.

Here the record is torn away—for no spy-master that ever lived was more discreet in safeguarding subordinates—and a trail of mischievous deception grows dim. What did Mary Elizabeth Bowser overhear and report while waiting upon President Davis and his guests? How did she contrive, without ultimate detection, to transmit her findings to the Van Lew mansion? And were her reports as valuable as the nature of her employment suggests they could have been? No answers have been found for these questions. But it is evident that the spying of the Negress was never suspected, or she would have been severely punished as a warning to other members of her race.

Miss van Lew was not the "adventuress" type of spy as were, in varying circumstances, Emma Edmonds, Belle Boyd, Pauline Cushman and Mrs Rose Greenhow. She did not invade the enemy's lines and risk her life among keen-eyed strangers but remained among her own people in Richmond—her home which had happened to become the capital of the Confederacy—where she was known to everyone and where her social position unquestionably weighed as much in her favor as the masquerade of Crazy Bet. It was possible for her to transmit secret-service messages written in her private cipher by the hand of one or another of her own servants. Those faithful Negroes would never have thought of refusing to oblige "Miss 'Lizabeth"; and the uninterrupted success of her system of couriers must have resulted in large degree from their deceptively normal behavior.

	1	3	6	2	5	4
6	r	n	b	h	i	x
3	v	1	w	8	4	u
1	e	m	3	f	5	g
5	l	a	9	o	u	d
2	k	7	2	z	6	s
4	p	t	y	c	f	q

The private cipher of Miss Elizabeth van Lew discovered after her death, concealed in her watchcase.

Probably none of them ever fully realized the gravity of the work, which thus cloaked it in public with the unbeatable disguise of an ordinary errand.

Having procured military passes for her people to permit them to go from the town house to the Van Lew farm below Richmond, Elizabeth kept a steady procession of market-basket carriers on the road between the two espionage "stations." In every basket of eggs, for example, there was one egg that was merely a hollow shell with a tiny scroll of paper inserted and sealed over. A curiously restless young woman who was the Van Lew seamstress went back and forth through the Confederate defenses of Richmond carrying spy messages worked into or hidden among her patterns and dress goods.

Elizabeth van Lew, by way of exhibiting the efficiency of her communicative system, managed on occasion to "say it with flowers", a bouquet gathered in her garden of an afternoon reaching General Grant's breakfast table the following morning.

Second only to Miss van Lew's devotion to the Union was her anxiety regarding her brother John. Thus far he had been acting as a valuable "silent partner" in his sister's clandestine enterprises, running a hardware business which provided a good deal of the money that she spent in helping Federal prisoners. And now at last he was conscripted and ordered to report to Camp Lee, even though he had been declared unfit for military duty on account of his health. Rather than take up arms against the cause his family espoused, John van Lew deserted and was concealed by Union sympathizers on the outskirts of Richmond. He was still hiding there, awaiting a chance to make his way to the Federal lines, when word came that 109 officers had escaped from Libby prison through Colonel Rose's tunnel. This meant that Confederate vigilance would be redoubled and all suspected dwellings searched. John van Lew, as a deserter, had little or no chance of getting through the lines alive; while his very presence imperiled the poor family harboring him.

The Van Lews, mother and daughter, had been warned "there was to be an exit" from the Libby, had been "told to prepare." Whereat "one of our parlors—an off, or rather end room," according to Elizabeth's later account—was made ready. There were "dark blankets nailed up at the windows, and gas kept burning in it, very low, night and day for about three weeks;" and beds were even set up there for the comfort of the escapers. All of which suggests that the friendship of President Davis, General Winder and other leaders hindered official visitations so far as the Van Lews were concerned and proved a powerful deterrent upon effective counter-spying measures. Ladies of Belgium or the occupied departments of France, who in 1914-1918 had "dark blankets nailed up", would have been explaining their purpose to a German *Feldwebel* within forty-eight hours.

In Richmond were many who believed that Colonel Streight and a number of his escaping companions went directly from the tunnel to the mansion of the Van Lews. An entry of February 1864 in Elizabeth's long-hidden diary describes her actual encounter with Streight and other fugitives:

> 15th. I shall ever remember this day because of the great alarm I had for others. Col. Streight and three of the prisoners . . . were secreted near Howard's Grove. After passing through the tunnel they were lead

by a Mrs. G—— to a humble home on the outskirts of the city; there Mrs. R—— received them. By request of some of their number she came . . . for me, and I went with her to see them. . . . We had a little laughing and talking, and then I said good-by, with the most fervent God bless you in my heart toward all of them.

The Secret Guest Room

The Van Lews' "off, or rather end room" was not the most secret guest room in that Virginia residence; and her biographer, Beymer, believed that her reference to the "end room" with its curtaining blankets and extravagant waste of gas was so much "dust to throw in our eyes for some reason of her own." Not even in the carefully guarded diary did she allude to the really secret chamber that the house had afforded her or mention the spring door in the wall behind the antique chest of drawers. The Van Lew secret room extended like a long, low and narrow cell just in back of where the main roof sloped up from its juncture with the flat roof of the broad rear veranda. The garret of the house was squared, and between its west wall and the sloping roof was the concealed chamber regularly tenanted by some Union agent or fugitive throughout the years of civil war.

Existence of the hiding place was suspected all along, but Confederate searchers repeatedly failed to uncover it. A little girl, Elizabeth van Lew's niece, was unique in making the discovery that she did one night in stealing up to the garret to see where "Aunt Betty" was taking that heaping platter of food. Shading a candle with her hand, Miss van Lew stood before "a black hole in the wall", from which a haggard man wearing a worn blue uniform and with unkempt hair and beard stretched out his hand for the food. She saw him looking past Aunt Betty straight at her but hastily put a finger to her lips and then retreated on tiptoe. Later she ventured through the dark silent house, again stole up the attic stairs, and called softly to the hidden Federal soldier. He told her how to open the door, and when she had accomplished it, talked to her cheerfully. "What a spanking you would 've got," he said, chuckling, "if your aunt had turned around."

But for that recollection, disclosed by the niece of Elizabeth van Lew years after the event and after her death, the secret room would have remained undetected until the old dwelling came to be torn down. There was one other important recess hidden in the home of the valiant partisans, the "letter box" for espionage communications. In the library was an ornamented iron fireplace; on either side of the grate were pilasters, each capped by a small sculptured figure of a couchant lion. One of these was loosened, either by accident or intention, and could be raised like the cover of a box. It was in the small cavity underneath the lion that Elizabeth van Lew "posted" her military dispatches. Standing, perhaps, with her back to the mantel she would slip a message in cipher under the couchant lion; and after a while a servant would begin dusting the library furniture, approach the fireplace, take the small message from the cavity, and start within the hour for the Van Lew farm outside the city. She never gave furtive verbal instructions to her colored messengers, and, no matter how safe she felt from observation, her devious, theatrical manner of transferring to her accomplices the espionage reports meant for Federal commanders was not revised. Possibly that inflexible precaution saved her life.

Many attempts were made to procure her betrayal. Guests in her home were asked to spy upon her. She and her mother—in frail health, often ill from anxiety—were denounced, told they should be hanged, their home burned, and publicly "shunned as lepers." The military keeper of the prisoners was no longer Mrs Lincoln's kinsman, but a Captain Gibbs. Through some unidentified influence Elizabeth was enabled to bring this officer and his family into her home as boarders; and while they remained their presence proved "a great protection."

We may as well resign ourselves to a certain bewilderment about that residence of the Van Lews. Elizabeth and her mother were continuously afraid, but it hardly occurred to her to make matters easier by discarding a few of her clandestine chores. The house thus retained much of the congestion of a barrack, hotel, stable, secret-service headquarters and fine old ancestral seat. When the Confederate War Department began ransacking the whole South to round up more horses, Elizabeth hid the last Van Lew horse in a smokehouse. Soon, however, that obvious equine cache disturbed her; and so she moved the horse at night into her own dwelling—where Captain Gibbs and his family were sleeping—and stabled it in her study. The sound of the restless hoofs, we are told, she muffled by means of a thick layer of straw.

There were, then, Confederates in the Van Lew house, spies and spy-messengers in the house, Unionist fugitives, deserters and escaped war prisoners in the house, and a contraband thoroughbred trampling around in the master spy's study. And all records of the Civil War point to precisely that kind of intrigue and confusion mingled with instinctive hospitality, stirring partisanship and slack counterespionage on both sides of the battle front. It was not only "brother against brother", but a fervid contest of incalculable amateur enterprise.

Other ladies of secret-service persuasion behaved with the resolution of Rose Greenhow or the slightly exhibitionistic nonchalance of Belle Boyd. On the Union side were Emma Edmonds and Pauline Cushman, two famous female agents whose espionne ardor may be compared to Miss Boyd's or Miss van Lew's, even though their sectors of operation were less frequently brightened by the spotlight. Emma Edmonds was a Canadian woman, a nurse in New Brunswick but a spy for McClellan in the peninsula when Allan Pinkerton's inexpert organizing of *offensive* secret service was beginning to predict his resignation. Miss Edmonds ran second to none in the worship of excitement or devotion to the antislavery cause. At the battle of Hanover Courthouse she mounted a horse and served as General Kearny's orderly, galloping back and forth through the by no means delicate artillery barrage of that dawn of the breech-loading era. She is said to have made eleven journeys as a secret agent through the Confederate lines. And as the most curious undertaking of the whole war—Emma Edmonds elected in Virginia to disguise herself as a male Negro.[6]

The inevitable consequence was her being sent to live in the squalid Negro quarters of Yorktown. She could not disguise her distaste for that ordeal and paid five dollars to a substitute darky who had the easy task of being himself and suffering the only kind of food and shelter he ever had been provided. Still maintaining her pose by day Miss Edmonds was set to work upon the Yorktown fortifications. On another occasion she pretended to be a sentry, and on yet another she stole a Confederate rifle. The disabilities of the Negro race argued against her perpetuating the unusual masquerade, and on subsequent missions she appeared as an Irish applewoman. Just as in the case of Elizabeth van Lew and the other ladies, Emma was never afraid to complicate her secret service with the obligations of womanhood and the role of ministering angel. The Canadian nurse spent what leisure remained from her duties as one general's orderly and another's spy in looking after the sick and wounded. And when she found Allen Hall, a young Confederate soldier, neglected, desperately ill and dying, she remained with him to the end, though her position in hostile country was a dangerous one.

Pauline Cushman, in turn, was the "Belle Boyd" of the Army of the Cumberland and ranged widely over a combat area made extra hazardous by stragglers, renegades and undisciplined guerrillas. She was taken prisoner; and General Braxton Bragg, who used so many spies himself he was not too nice to dispose of the enemy's, ordered her to be shot. Her appeal for mercy was not transmitted to President Davis in Richmond. A different sort of appeal, however, came to the hairbreadth rescue of Miss Cushman. The Union General Rosecrans was advancing, hammering Bragg hard, and forcing his retirement. No Confederate riflemen cared about lingering to shoot Pauline; nor was there now time enough to arrange for her safe transport in custody. And so she—like Schulmeister in Austria—who had audaciously served the Army of the Cumberland, was saved by that force's rapid offensive.

The First Stars and Stripes in Richmond

Elizabeth van Lew was among those Unionists of Richmond whose urgings led to the hapless "Dahlgren raid." Acting upon reports received from her, the Philipses, father and son, and other spies, the Federal command sent Brigadier General Hugh Judson Kilpatrick—known as Kil and even Kil-Cavalry, owing to his reckless expenditures of horseflesh—together with the equally intrepid young Ulric Dahlgren upon the raid that came within five miles of Richmond and only failed when a treacherous Negro guide led the Yankee troopers astray.[7] Dahlgren, son of the distinguished Union admiral and himself a colonel when not yet twenty-two, was still on active service though his right leg had been shot off below the knee. He became detached from Kilpatrick's main force and, when riding at the head of about a hundred men, was shot and killed by an enemy patrol. The Richmond plotters took that tragic event to heart, blaming themselves and being resolved to rescue Dahlgren's body from among "the 10,000 grassless graves below Oakwood Cemetery." The intensity of local hatred and fear of Dahlgren convinced the spies that the Confederates meant to keep no record of his grave. But a Negro had reported the place of burial; and the expedition of nocturnal diggers had no trouble identifying the young colonel's body because of his amputated leg.

Having dug it up, they reburied it secretly in a metallic coffin which they sealed with a substitute for putty, of which there was no longer any to be had in Richmond. Contradicting the Union spies' belief, the leaders of the Confederacy generously sought to oblige Admiral Dahlgren and instituted a search for the body of his son, only to remain mystified to the end of the war when they could not locate it. Meanwhile, Elizabeth van Lew, who had taken a lock of the youth's hair, transmitted it to the admiral by means of her courier service.

In February of 1865, some six weeks before the peace, an Englishman named Pole was brought into Richmond by a Federal secret agent to assist him in getting information. The year before the North had gained much advantage from an espionage tour of the South made by a soldier of fortune who had been fighting on the side of the Union and had been wounded at Gettysburg. This was John Sobieski, exiled from Europe and the great-grandson of John III, king of Poland. Given an allowance of but $4,000, Sobieski—calling himself Count Kalieski, with his scars to show as a result of having engaged in a revolt against Russia—had gone to Havana and then Mobile, moved northward, seeing the camps and fortifications, having interviews with President Davis, Vice-President Stephens and other notables of the government, and even being escorted to the front to dine with General Lee. When he returned to Washington by way of a Gulf port and Havana, Sobieski had $332 left; and that superb investment was expected to be duplicated by this man named Pole, who hailed from England. However, he immediately denounced to the Confederate authorities his Federal guide, Babcock, a Northerner named White with whom he was to be quartered, and other Unionists who had aided him and Babcock on the way. When Miss van Lew heard tell of those arrests she experienced one more agony of apprehension. Pole, however, had been too eager to win Confederate applause and had thrown away his chance to incriminate her and many others.

When she saw that the fall of Richmond was only a matter of days, she had written to General Ben Butler, another of her correspondents, asking for a flag. And a great flag, nine by eighteen feet, was smuggled through the Southern pickets and added to the conglomeration of things hidden inside her home. As the local powder magazines blew up and the military evacuation was completed, a storming angry mob surged at last upon the mansion of Crazy Bet, carrying torches and preparing to make four years of threats a savage reality. But Elizabeth van Lew stepped out boldly and faced her embittered neighbors. "I know you, Tom—and you, Bill—and you——" she cried, calling off a dozen of the ringleaders' names. "General Grant will be here in an hour. And if you harm this house or any one in it, your own homes will be blazing before noon!"

That made sense even to a mob, and the last danger of violence dissipated. Presently the advance guard of men in dusty blue came swinging into the Confederate capital; but even before they appeared, the spy, who had hated most the war's compulsions of secret fidelity, raised the first Federal flag that proclaimed the surrender of Richmond.

Ensuing years were as grim and tragic for her as the tensions of wartime had been. President Grant appointed her postmistress of Richmond; she was tolerated in her office but socially ostracized to the end of her life. A just claim for $15,000—money expended by her to the priceless advantage of the Federal Intelligence system—was honored by Grant and every ranking general who knew of her work. But the politicians of Washington had other fish to fry in the boiling oil they called Reconstruction. Elizabeth van Lew never received a dollar of pay for her invaluable services nor had back one penny of her own funds lavished upon the cause of the *United* States. After Grant's administration she was promptly reduced to a minor clerkship in the Post Office Department, and even that grudging revenue was at length denied her. Passing her last years in abject poverty, she lived upon a pension from friends and relatives of Colonel Paul Revere—whom she once had sheltered and aided—and was still attended by loyal and aged Negro servants whose freedom she had been first in her community to declare.

Chapter Forty-three

REBELS OF THE NORTH

THOSE congenital civilians, the hotheads and die-hards who call for extermination of the enemy, for war *à outrance* until somebody else has shed the last drop of his blood, are a natural by-product of war, especially civil war; and both the adherents of North and South in the American War of Secession were edged about with an incendiary lunatic fringe. Some addicted to the Confederate "Cause"—the Lost Cause as it had already become—got in a final characteristic blow, the assassination of Abraham Lincoln. But other partisans of equivalent fury and a fanatic faith in the Union had the last word, for their counter-stroke was that assassination of the South itself, which its prophets called Reconstruction.

Allan Pinkerton, an excellent detective for railroads and other corporations, and, as we have seen, an accomplished counter-spy, had managed to protect President Lincoln when half the population of a rebellious state was plotting to prevent his inauguration. Mr Pinkerton's strong sense of faction, however, had taken him elsewhere; and now, after four years of fighting, the secret service had improved in espionage largely, it seems, at the expense of counter-espionage. The leadership and integrity of Abraham Lincoln were surely the greatest "valuable" in the possession of the government. And Lafayette Baker and his men failed, and failed miserably, in their prime duty of protecting it. The President, a true democrat, would no doubt have objected to pretentious safeguards. One can imagine him sincerely embarrassed even by such pomp and circumstance as an Old-World bishop or brigadier general would have mistaken for neglect. But Baker's was a *secret* service, and, though always tracking down applause, it might have learned through the long desperate struggle to protect its great leader unobtrusively and in spite of himself.

Baker, in ruthless methods, shady deals and unflagging self-interest, was unmistakably poured from the Stieber mold. But the Prussian spy-master never relapsed in vigilance or failed in loyalty to his chief, Prince Bismarck. The battle-ax of Crusader King Richard against a modern tank or armored plane would hardly seem more out of date than the precautions Baker's men were taking in 1865 against the loquacious malcontents and *known* irreconcilables of Washington. Suratt was a former Confederate spy, who had been set at liberty. All through the war—and Lincoln's generous nature had exercised a dangerous influence in this—aggressive Southern partisans were only detained at the pleasure of the authorities. And they generally pleased to forgive and forget in a few months' time, no matter what progress the rebellion was making or what the attitude or mental balance of the prisoner continued to be. John Wilkes Booth, far better known than Suratt as an advocate of Secession, was a ranting actor of the old school, a born rabble-rouser who, with the South now in the throes of defeat, had roused himself to a concert pitch of fanatic endeavor.

Operatives of the Secret Service did nothing to detect and explode the incipient conspiracy; and, when it had been carefully matured, they were in no position to prevent its desperate onset.[1] Instead of the oblivion to which his later involvements have consigned him, Lafayette Baker would survive as one of the most celebrated Union officers of the Civil War if he had done as much for Lincoln in 1865 as Pinkerton detectives contrived in '61. After the great President lay wounded and dying, Baker and his secret corps sprang into a frenzy of activity. They became so active, they all but overran the fugitive assassins. The usual controversy weighing responsibility for President Lincoln's death against the prompt apprehension of the conspirators at once began to rage. We shall neither explore nor revive it here; but in this writer's opinion no stroke of counter-espionage, no operation of defensive secret service, had anything to do with the identification and arrest of any of the Booth-Suratt accomplices. Military patrols managed the pursuit; cavalrymen with carbines rounded them up.[2] Those who had signally failed to safeguard the President were among the most frantic to avenge him. Lafayette Baker, shrewdly entrenched on the Washington political front, claimed for himself and his Secret Service so much unjustified credit that he avoided most of the justified blame.

The Secret Service and the "Whisky Ring"

Even so, the Secret Service, now that the war was over, suffered a marked degree of eclipse. Baker dodged about behind the scenes, making himself indispensable to the dominant clique of politicians while resolutely investigating everything that might be connected with their opponents. After the World War and the retirement from office of Woodrow Wilson's war-making administration, certain American political powers, encouraged by the "landslide" favoring the Republican party in the election of 1920, plunged straightway into the sordid transaction disposing of the Teapot Dome naval oil reserve as well as into other furtive bargainings and betrayals of public trust. By a quaint coincidence, the same Republican party was in control at the close of the Civil War when manipulations similarly corrupt were exposed to public approval. We find them differing from the scandals of the Harding Administration only in one particular: after the Civil War the Secret Service entangled itself in most of the corrupt practices it might properly have labored to expose.

When President Johnson was impeached by savage political headhunters, Baker at once set about impressing the nation with the extraordinary value of his abilities and services. He endeavored to prove that a certain Mrs Cobb had given bribes to members of Andrew Johnson's cabinet by way of procuring an easy pardon for ex-Confederates. Meanwhile, the very funds used in promoting the impeachment of Johnson were, it was said, contributed by distillers. None of Baker's investigators was clever enough to detect that; but a branch of the Secret Service connected with the Treasury Department was subsequently charged with having originated and organized the notorious "Whisky Ring", whose exclusive membership was restricted to distillery magnates and officials of the Republican administration.

Whisky taxes were divided with a furtive equity, half going to the corrupt intriguers and half to the United States Treasury. When the distillers' production slackened, the political "insiders" of the Ring urged them to increase it. Hundreds of persons were able to command some share of the loot; yet millions were involved, and even very minor politicians are said to have taken $500 a week as their slice. General O. E. Babcock of Grant's personal staff was widely believed to be a member of the Ring. When subsequently tried in St Louis he was acquitted, which did not blind the American public to his guilt. Only President Grant's personal influence, people maintained, had secured the acquittal. Babcock was definitely linked with the Secret Service and District Attorney Harrington in a scheme to have the latter's office robbed—whereupon they were ready to produce sworn "confessions" from the hired burglars, implicating in their "crime" a Mr Alexander, whose integrity and outspoken accusations were making the Ring nervous and resentful.[3]

Prompt exposure of this shabby plot, with many another example of misdirected espionage zeal, caused the Congress to abolish the Secret Service by a simple expedient of refusing to make appropriation for its agents' pay. Only a small force attached to the Treasury survived this exasperated massacre, and its activities were restricted to problems of currency and banking, the pursuit of counterfeiters or forgers of government documents and vouchers. Most of General Baker's operatives scattered over the land as a new and insinuating plague of private detectives.

The Molly Maguires and Ku Klux Klan

Many minor European turbulences—such as the Spanish insurrection of the Carlist *frondeurs*—have had to be passed over without discussion of their inevitable secret-service aspects. We cannot tell all the Old-World and New-World intrigues and clandestine exchanges that planted poor Maximilian on a Mexican throne and then abandoned him to the mercies of "the little Indian general" Juarez. Before that gallant pawn of Bonapartist imperialism faced the guns at Querétaro, June 19, 1867, he had come near to being taken in by a criminal who posed as a secret-service agent and had forged himself sundry "official" documents which convinced the emperor. This astounding rogue was Piper, the "invincible", a native of Paris, Ky., who was—with the all but fabulous Charlie Becker[4]—the most accomplished forger of the age. Piper, living comfortably upon the proceeds of his penmanship, was in league with the chiefs of police in a dozen large American cities. They guaranteed him protection from the laws which they sometimes felt inspired to enforce and were to receive in return a stipulated percentage of his gains. They also agreed to keep watch upon any money or bonds he might prefer to hide for a time and to act as his unofficial envoys in arranging settlements with citizens he had swindled. Furthermore, they agreed that, whenever too closely pressed, he should be arrested on some trivial charge and put in jail, whence his quiet departure from the center of disturbance might be much more conveniently routed. All of which was politico-underworld secret service of a dangerously effective pattern.

Piper's takings were large enough to maintain such a semiofficial system, and his armor of corrupt practices made him, in truth, invincible. According to Pinkerton Agency estimates, between 1857 and 1866 he obtained nearly a million dollars by raising checks and bank drafts and garnered fees amounting to almost half a million more by professionally altering court records, forging deeds and wills, or revising the numbers of stolen bonds so that they might be put upon the market. His tastes were international, and he was gathering no small harvest in Nova Scotia and other parts of Canada when he began to prepare the project by which the protégé of Napoleon III would be defrauded of four hundred thousand pounds of gold stored in the imperial treasury vaults at Mexico City. Piper went first to England, providing himself with a number of bills of exchange on French banks. He moved on to Paris, took obscure lodgings, and fashioned his masterpiece: the bills inflated to represent staggering sums, and letters which accredited him to Maximilian and Carlotta as a secret agent of the French government. In handwriting too familiar to be questioned, he advised the imperial pair to trust this envoy implicitly. They were to place themselves entirely in his hands should Mexican political conditions, upon his arrival, recommend their flight.

Piper enlisted three assistants to help him handle and transport the gold; but at Brownsville, Tex., these ill-chosen confederates lost their enthusiasm for a strange country where rebels like Juarez and Porfirio Diaz were now on the march. Pushing on alone, Piper presented his bogus credentials and gained an audience with the emperor. Maximilian, acknowledging the genuineness of the newcomer's authorization as well as the victorious onslaught of his Mexican foes, yet required five days to come to any decision. In the meantime he showed good faith, however, by ordering a count of the coin and bullion in the vaults. Piper at that moment stood within reach of the grandest coup in the annals of political fraud and impersonation; yet he was a thousand miles away from its accomplishment. On swept the Indian general, and the American would have needed a regiment of retainers to escort that golden treasure to the sea. He had several other consultations with Maximilian but likewise paused to consult himself. Those marvelously executed credentials from Paris would be a death warrant when the climax of Central American revolution overtook the emperor; and so reflecting, Piper made his escape not a day too soon. He was passing through Santa Fé when Maximilian fulfilled his tragic destiny.

Only two years later Piper was operating in Vermont, and there Pinkerton agents finally trapped him. It has already been observed that Lafayette Baker's men scattered over the United States as private investigators; and the rapid development of union agitation and labor unrest provided them a growing if highly competitive market. In North America, until well after the outbreak of the World War, there was never an official organization resembling the European model of political or secret police. But the work of secret police was performed nevertheless, minorities repressing other minority groups without legal sanction, taking the law into their own hands in lieu of respecting it.

The celebrated exploit of the Pinkerton operative, James McParland, alias James McKenna, in overcoming the powerful clan of "Molly Maguires" was virtually the debut in America if not in all the world of modern labor espionage. The wage scale and working conditions of the coal regions of eastern Pennsylvania gave the Irish Mollies great influence as champions of the downtrodden. They were directly descended from the Ancient Order of Hibernians, or "Ribbon Men", founded in Ireland about 1843 to intimidate landlords, or their agents and henchmen, and interfere with evictions. Like all kindred groups or secret societies banded together to redress wrongs, defeat the oppressor and enforce a private code of fair play, the Ribbon Men had soon become badly entangled in the coils of their own irregular authority. Criminals and bullies invaded the organization, diverted its aims and instigated tyranny of very sinister weight. Similarly, with the Molly Maguires in America, vicious elements invaded what had begun as a benevolent association.

Malign influences consolidate quickly. When the Pinkerton Agency was finally called in, the antilabor aspects of its proposed investigation were screened by the seemingly Molly-premeditated crime wave of violence and assassination encrimsoning the coal fields. McParland as the convivial "McKenna" managed to join the Mollies and become secretary to the "bodymaster" of the Shenandoah lodge. Thereafter his problems were three—how to drink so much bad liquor and not destroy his health, how to avoid exposure as a spy, and how to communicate with Allan Pinkerton. Often he had to use blueing as a writing fluid.[5] Both ink and lead pencils were an intellectual luxury among the Mollies—almost a snobbery—and liable to arouse suspicion. The Pinkerton spy there in the heart of Pennsylvania conducted himself precisely like an agent of military secret service, lodged behind the lines in an enemy country and subject to betrayal and execution. It was, however, the Molly Maguire leaders whom McParland ultimately betrayed, a famous feat of espionage which we may not pass over but which launched with deplorable vitality the modern craze for labor spying that employs in America today a veritable army—at least 150,000 strong—of sneaks, ex-convicts and corrupt informers.

The Molly Maguires went to the gallows or to prison largely because they attempted to originate the Prohibition-era technique of Chicago and other great American cities fifty years before politicians and business men were ready for an alliance. Contemporary with the combat of anarchy and espionage in the anthracite coal counties of Pennsylvania, the rise of the Ku Klux Klan marked another of America's extralegal and clandestine innovations which must have its minor place in the modern annals of secret service. "It was the night before Christmas" of 1865, and the place, Pulaski, Tenn., when six young men who had fought in the Civil War and now felt crushed by their poverty and poor prospects founded the Klan as a lark. Superstitious Negroes, reporting with awe the mounted "ghosts" they had seen, showed the earliest klansmen what a weapon they had found. And from its galloping start in Tennessee the Klan soon spread to all parts of the recently defeated South.

In 1867 the organization's first national conclave was held at the Maxwell House in Nashville without being suspected. The Confederate General Forrest was placed at its head, with the sanction of Robert E. Lee, who urged that the Klan be kept purely a "protective organization."[6] Responsible officers continued for a time in control, men like Generals Clanton, Morgan and James Z. George. But widespread growth was bound to invite an evil element. Violence and lawless abuses were inevitable, for the Ku Klux Klan dressed night riders in childish masquerade costumes to intimidate the ignorant, defenseless and rurally isolated—thus reasserting the superiority of the white landowning class.

Chapter Forty-four
BEFORE THE DELUGE

IN AMERICA the Union had been saved and Negro slavery abolished at a heavy cost; and even while Abolition had been dividing, enraging and arming the citizens of the United States there were other agitations on the subject of "human rights" and "slavery" disturbing the populations of enlightened countries in Western Europe. A new institution of police afflicted these lands, and a veritable panic of rumor, doubt and denunciation harassed the governments, excited the susceptible, and troubled farseeing, thoughtful men. The novel "reform" of an improved and uniformed police—in England, for example—was attacked as a secret scheme to enslave, an insidious determination to dragoon and tyrannize over a free people.

The Duke of Wellington was at the head of the British government in 1829 when Sir Robert Peel brought forward his measure designed to improve the policing of the kingdom and to extend and systematize its safeguards. And because the duke supported Peel's project, he incurred an extravagant odium. The immensely popular soldier, whom a grateful nation had rewarded so generously as to make him "the best paid fighter who ever lived", was now actually suspected of a deep design to "seize supreme power and usurp the throne."[1] Police spies armed with extraordinary authority were expected to dog the steps of respectable citizens, to invade their homes, make domiciliary visitations and exercise the right of search and interrogation on any small pretense or trumped-up story.

Wellington, of course, stood firm. He offered the object lesson of the horse patrol, which had done so much to clear the neighborhood of London of highwaymen and footpads. He reminded Englishmen of the early years of the century when scarcely a carriage could pass without being robbed and travelers had to be prepared at all hours to do battle with the armed thieves who attacked them. Yet he was still accused of some base ambition in raising this new "'standing army' of drilled and uniformed policemen", to be marshaled by the government and independent of local taxpayers' control. The appointment of Sir Charles Rowan, a military officer and veteran of Waterloo, as head of the police seemed to betray the Iron Duke's design of creating a "veritable gendarmerie", such as was just then fastening upon many absolute monarchies of the Continent. Popular aversion to the whole scheme of police, detection and crime investigation ultimately spent itself in abusive epithets applied to the new tyrants. They were "bobbies" and "peelers" because of Sir Robert Peel, and "raw lobsters" because of their blue coats, also "crushers", deriving from their anticipated heavy-footed interference with law-abiding enterprise, and "coppers" since they "copped" or captured His Majesty's lieges.

The admirable regulations framed by Sir Richard Mayne, who was presently appointed Rowan's collaborator, went a long way toward reassuring the general public. After a few years no subject of the British crown, save irredeemable knaves and rascals, would have thought of objecting to the new provisions for the maintenance of peace and good order, the protection of person and property. Such, however, was not the experience of Frenchmen. The oppression and espionage of the police was one of the chief survivors of the revolution; and restoration of the Bourbons had not restored the liberty which the governing classes of France—who remembered the *sans-culottes*—were still disposed to identify as license.

During these days of the revived monarchy crime was not too successfully suppressed, inasmuch as the efforts of all the police were concentrated upon a single blind objective: controlling opposition to the reigning power and prosecuting political independence. The detection of crime, it is true, was being undertaken for the first time as a distinct branch of police work, mainly upon the crude principle summarized in the phrase "it takes a thief to catch a thief." But we have not space here to illuminate the investigative genius of M. Eugène Vidocq, pioneer detective, who, until 1832 when he was forced to resign,[2] brilliantly exploited a troupe of police spies, ex-convicts and imperfectly reformed felons as audacious and disreputable as himself.

Prince Louis Napoleon, nephew of the emperor, had only climbed into the saddle as Bonapartist champion, presidential candidate and elected head of the Republic by way of adroit political intrigues. He, in short, had been a conspirator, and, like all of his tribe who scheme their way to eminence, he was passionately converted to the very measures of espionage and repression which had long repressed him. Upon becoming the founder of the Second Empire and proclaimed Napoleon III—an harmonic progression resulting from a rapid series of twists, turns and betrayals of public trust, disguised under that thrilling French euphemism, coup d'état—the usurping Bonaparte encouraged a horde of secret police to override every constitutional safeguard. The emperor employed an army of private spies, as well as the "police of the Château" commanded by Comte d'Hirvoix, whose duty it was to keep watch upon the regular police at an annual cost of some 14,000,000 francs.

The French people were at first rather delighted with the pageantry and drama of the new imperial regime. Napoleon in winning his way to the presidency had proved himself an accomplished politician, who rode in locomotive cabs, drank champagne with laboring men, and kissed infants held up to behold him; and even if, as a result of the coup, "arrested democrats overflowed from the gaols of Paris and the provinces into half the barracks in the country,"[3] a *plébiscite* which was genuine endorsed the change by a vote of seven millions and a half out of eight millions. Yet though there were comparatively few in opposition, Napoleon was too much the born intriguer not to suspect both those who cheered and those who held aloof. Before the Empire came to its vainglorious dissolution in the attempted "conquest" of Prussia there were six different secret police services with headquarters in Paris.

The emperor had his private troupe of spies, as we have noted, and M. Rouher, the premier, and M. Pietri, the prefect of police, were each similarly endowed. For some unaccountable reason the empress had a service of her own, perhaps occasionally useful in spying upon such of her rivals as Cavour's agent, the lovely Countess Castiglione. And two other private forces were under the respective supervision of MM. Nusse and Lafarge. All the agents thus employed were unknown to each other as government operatives; and so extensive was the interlocking and overlapping system of political espionage, half of Paris was kept busy reporting the generally harmless activities of the other half.

The Bombs of Orsini

Such extremities of mistrust—actually unduplicated anywhere in Western Europe, until the rise of Fascist dictatorships in very recent times—produced nothing of value, not even the right kind of precautions. It had to make a showing, however, and so it produced the celebrated, the sometimes infamous *dossiers*. These enduring little instruments of political blackmail were small portfolios or covers, one of which related to each individual in France, high or low, contented or insurgent, criminal or law-abiding, thought likely to require regular official observation. Many thousands of these *dossiers* were collected in the archives of the Préfecture, carefully catalogued and filed for convenient reference. They were made up of the generally calumniating reports submitted by agents—serious charges perhaps, but more often the most mendacious, unimportant specimens of gossip. The police informer without facts to represent his diligence had to fall back upon imagination; wherefore absolutely harmless folk were frequently accused of subversive practices.

But let us see how the political police of the Empire, so fecund in archives, dealt with really dangerous conspirators. On the night of January 14, 1858, the emperor, accompanied by the empress and General Roguet, drove in state to the Opéra in Paris. They were to attend a performance of *William Tell*, a "benefit" honoring a popular singer about to be pensioned. Outside the Opéra a crowd assembled to watch the arrival of Napoleon and Eugénie and their suite, who rode in three state carriages, escorted by a detachment of Lancers of the Guard.

The emperor's carriage was last and was a little delayed as it entered the archway while the two carriages preceding it put down the chamberlain and other members of the imperial suite. Just at that moment of hesitation there came a shocking blast of explosive, followed by a shower of bullets and blazing projectiles. Then a second vibrating crash and a third, and after that, darkness! The successive detonations had extinguished all the gas lamps. A quivering pause of silence was followed immediately by a hideous clamor—cries of the wounded and dying, the stamping and plunging of horses, shouts of frightened onlookers, the clatter of falling fragments and shattered glass.

Such havoc and carnage, panic and groping confusion produced a terrifying scene. Three bombs, thrown into the crowd surrounding the emperor's carriage, had killed a Lancer and killed or wounded numbers of spectators, 160 casualties in all. General Roguet was gravely injured; a bullet had grazed the temple of the empress, another had perforated the emperor's cocked hat. If the imperial carriage had not been lined with iron plates, all three of its occupants would have perished, for sixty-six bullets had scarred its exterior surface. Parisian streets literally ran with blood; the costume of Eugénie, the uniforms of attendants, were stained with it; great splashes marked the walls and the advertisements posted outside the Opéra. Yet with an admirable courage, to "allay the general consternation", Napoleon and his consort entered and took their seats in the imperial box as though nothing serious had occurred; and the whole house stood up to cheer them with thankful fervor.

Meanwhile, where were the police, the secret police, the police of the Château, and all the varieties of organized espions employed to keep watch upon each other? They were alarmed and they were raking Paris in search of assassins. One of the chief conspirators was, in fact, already in custody, but not "by a queer chance",[4] as some commentators would have us believe. Just before the first explosion gendarmes had arrested a foreigner named Pieri, or Piercey, who was recognized while sauntering about the neighborhood of the Opéra.

A new manifesto had lately appeared in Mazzini's organ, *Italia del Popolo* of Genoa; and wherever Italian irreconcilables gathered, the police were on the alert for symptoms of a reviving campaign of terrorism. Reports concerning bombs being manufactured in Birmingham had also come through to the Paris Préfecture. And those who meant to use them were beginning to move. London had sent a warning of the departure of one, Orsini, an addled and fiery conspirator, who traveled with three other disciples of Mazzini. The police of Brussels had warned of the dubious maneuvers of Pieri-Piercey.

Because this timely information from Britain and Belgium had not produced all possible safeguards, because the plotters quietly filtering into Paris had arrived unobserved and reached the Opéra unmolested, the minister of the interior, Baillant, and his subordinate, Prefect Pietri, were subsequently obliged to resign their posts. Yet even as reputations were exploding like the Italians' bombs, another was being made. M. Claude, a police official of much perspicacity, who had inspired the identification and arrest of Pieri, was one of the first to interrogate him; whereupon he visited the suspect's lodgings in the Rue Montmartre, to discover that he had been living at this cheap hotel under the name of "Andreas", and that Da Silva, an alleged Portuguese, shared his room.[5]

The latter, on being arrested and searched, was found carrying a passport issued by the Portuguese consulate in London but was easily identified as De Rudio, a political suspect who hailed from Rio de Janeiro. Suspicious articles were seized by the police in the "Piercey-Da Silva" hotel room: a revolver, ammunition, an ebony-handled dagger, and letters and papers which helped Claude in his swift process of identification. Both De Rudio and Piercey, or Pieri, were thus discovered to be acquainted with a certain ex-soldier, Gomez, alias Pierre Suriney, who had been denounced to the police by a waiter. Gomez unwisely sought to pose as an Englishman and had been acting as "servant" to the chief conspirator, Orsini. Shortly after the explosions the waiter had seen him looking out of the window of a restaurant across from the Opéra. He had appeared terribly agitated and added to the certainty of his detection by flourishing a revolver.

Orsini, a Latin enthusiast so imprudent and unreliable that Mazzini had nicknamed him the "Cracky", also had chosen to pose as a stolid commercial Englishman. He used the name "Allsop" and made that alias a bit more convincing by means of a code devised in terms of the manufacture and sale of beer.[6] Orsini, taken in his bed that very night, joined the other perpetrators of the bombing outrage in the police net into which two of them at least had rashly flung themselves. The secret police and the political police had accomplished virtually nothing. And even the achievement of the regular, the less secret and more energetic, police—as personified by M. Claude—was in the main a prompt seizure of lucky advantage rather than any procedure of coordinated defense and attack or one of those ingenious and involved investigative operations, typical of France in the popular mind, and certainly typical of a Vidocq, a Canler, Macé or Goron.[7]

The "White Blouses" and Other Provocations

Orsini and his confederates were tried within five weeks and condemned in two days. Orsini and Pieri went to the guillotine, De Rudio and Gomez to hard labor for life. The bombs of the plotters had mainly injured innocent bystanders, including the whole population of France. Flying missiles had left marks upon the emperor's carriage and on his mind; and deep, lasting scars were to be seen now upon French policy, both domestic and foreign. Tensions developed among the recent—Crimean War—allies; a strong protest went to Sardinia "against the export of Italian bomb-throwers"; and greater resentment was expressed because Orsini and the others had found asylum in Great Britain and there perfected their plans.

Parliamentary liberalism in France had been shattered like the gas lamps before the Opéra. Emergency powers were conferred upon the imperial authorities, enabling them now to detain or deport their opponents without trial, and a general, Espinasse, was appointed to administer "the soldierly illegality of this procedure." About four hundred arrests were made, all of persons having no connection whatever with Orsini or his bomb throwers. Espinasse devised the masterful expedient of requiring a fixed quota of arrests from each department of the Empire.

De Morny, the emperor's half-brother, had for a time dipped his deft, engaging hand into the tangled complexities of the secret police. A truly dazzling adventurer, dandy, connoisseur and speculator, De

Morny sketched in himself a perfect fictional portrait of the master of spies and intelligence technique. He had not been handicapped from birth by an obscure legitimacy, he proved skillful in applying official information to his private speculative deals, and in everything seemed more Napoleonic than the Third Napoleon, even without a drop of Bonaparte blood in his veins. Diversion of this brilliant amateur to other political pastures had left the imperial secret service virtually leaderless. It had to suffer the same mismanagement as any public branch of the government.

The most reprehensible result of this mismanagement was the special corps that became infamous as the "White Blouses", a network of provocative intriguers spread out over France. These furtive poseurs —incredible as it seems in an era of comparative tranquillity—were employed to incite the populace to riots and disorder, thus providing the uniformed police with pretexts for arresting and indefinitely detaining those leading spirits whose freedom threatened the "stability" of the regime. Such tactics inevitably hurried the decay of that pompous illusion; and when its final collapse occurred, many of the "White Blouses" were recognized as old *provocateurs* and "deservedly shot in the days of the Commune."

Sedan and the ensuing collapse, when it came, was as much the direct result of French preparations as a well-prepared scheme of the Prussians. We now approach the life and works of one of the very greatest of all our architects of both military and political secret-service organization, but on the way let us justly note the provocations inflicted upon Prussia by the government of Napoleon III. Operatives as malign as the "White Blouses" were covertly engaged in provoking even the least aggressive of the German states north of the Rhine frontier. It was the imperial espionage service that thus helped to incite war and made inevitable the coming of the Hohenzollern empire. But even Bismarck was hardly dreaming of that empire in 1856, when the "Techen affair" stirred the greatest excitement in Germany and held the attention of both the French and British press.

On July 24, 1855, there had appeared in the *Vossische Zeitung* an advertisement reading:

Yes, on the 24th of July, at 4 p.m. in Z.

Now this was a communication from M. Rothan, a secretary of the French Embassy at Berlin to Techen, former Prussian army lieutenant. Rothan was agreeing to meet him in Zehlendorf; but the French diplomatist did not keep the appointment, sending in his stead a certain Hassenkrug, who had been a Prussian police official but was at this time employed as an agent of the French Secret Service. Techen, a man seventy years of age, refused to negotiate through Hassenkrug; and so Rothan had to consent to a personal interview, which presently took place in the Tiergarten.

Techen delivered to the Frenchman copies of reports submitted by the Prussian military attaché at St Petersburg, Count von Münster-Meinhövel, containing much useful information about the Russian army and current conditions in Sebastopol, which was then being besieged by the Allies. Techen was also able to deliver extracts from the private journal of General von Gerlach, in which that influential officer made regular summaries of the political views prevailing in Prussian court circles.

Techen's information was of great and timely interest, and he received a substantial price for it, becoming a regular member of the system of espionage whose chief instigator was Moustier, the ambassador of Napoleon III. Many subsequent meetings with Rothan were arranged; but after a while Techen delivered his findings and received his pay more discreetly, a merchant, Hauptner, and his wife acting as intermediaries. Techen was now in touch both with servants of Privy Councilor Niebuhr and of General von Gerlach,[8] who were able to steal or copy letters and other documents whose contents Techen profitably purveyed to the French. Yet it appears that the employers as well as the employed in this unsavory business were either scornful of German vigilance or not bright enough to take the simplest precautions. On November 16, 1855, Bismarck was writing to Gerlach: "They are saying that Berlin postal officials are suspected of being in French pay. This is interesting to me, because on a certain occasion Moustier spoke to Manteuffel of a thing that happened here, and of which he can hardly have heard except through a letter of mine, that had reached Manteuffel only half an hour before. The words he used were almost the identical and somewhat unusual terms that I had myself employed. The incident has always been something of a mystery to me."

General von Gerlach wrote only twelve days later: "In the depositions they forgot to note that Manteuffel told me, that Moustier had questioned him about the contents of the letters in such terms as proved that he must have been already acquainted with them."

That was diplomacy of the kind which largely characterized the French foreign policy and foreign service under Napoleon III. And it was secret service of the same low and clumsy cunning which would mark the impending French contest with the invincible Wilhelm Stieber. Moustier's artless questioning of Manteuffel made Prussian authorities all the more certain of pinning the treasonable "leak" upon one or another of their post-office executives. On December 26 Von Gerlach confided to his journal: "This affair of the theft of letters in the post is taking a more and more sinister turn. The post office seems to have been opening letters and delaying the delivery of documents." But at length the suspicions of the Prussian investigators got around to old Techen, and in January 1856 he was arrested and interrogated. Having made an abject confession, he was duly convicted of treason; while Moustier and Rothan, exposed in the press of Europe, were so hopelessly compromised, they had to be recalled.

The German operations and intrigues of secret agents of the Second Empire did not abate but were merely turned over to new management. And yet a change, unanticipated by the French imperial regime and of incalculable consequence, was about to occur. For the first time since Scharnhorst and Stein outwitted Napoleon I, or, possibly, since Frederick the Great, Prussia was going to develop a secret-service department strong enough to take the offensive against the dominating Power of the Continent. The statesman who made this possible was Bismarck. The instrument of his undercover challenge was Stieber—the one unabridged cyclopedia of government intrigue in German history, a veritable pontiff of secret service, and the Iron Chancellor's most subtle accomplice among the charter members of that fervid guild, so dangerously active again today, which cultivates the Teutonic obsession that might makes *Reich.*

Chapter Forty-five

STIEBER THE SPY-MASTER

WILHELM STIEBER, the notorious Prussian spy-master, proved that a man may begin as a small sneak and by perseverance and devotion to his king and country lift himself to Olympian heights as a sneak and international scoundrel. The great intriguers and spy-masters of this history are many of them superior men, required by force of circumstances or the deep currents of national policy to condescend to cruel and base practices. Stieber from a petty, obscure and unpromising start developed himself into the most contemptibly talented patriot of his day. His underground work was shrewdly adjusted to Architect Bismarck's foundation plans of the new German Empire, a structure which did not collapse for forty-seven years.

With Napoleon banished to St Helena and his spies and armies scattered, we have seen high tides of triumphant reaction coursing over the Continent; and on the third of May, 1818, one who would come to be the craftiest defender of reaction was born. Stieber was the son of a minor official of Merseburg, a small town in Prussian Saxony; but there was nothing petty about his christening—the lavishness of Wilhelm Johann Carl Eduard suggests royalty—and perhaps someone suspected that this infant would live to hear the greatest Prussian of the century call him "my king of sleuth-hounds."[1]

In his boyhood the Stiebers removed to Berlin, and Wilhelm was soon being educated in the general direction of the Lutheran ministry. We have seen many a genius of espionage and secret service recruited from the clergy; but Stieber appears to have altered his own course and dodged into the legal profession. He turned at once to criminal cases and the inevitably congenial police work. In 1845 he was already a spy, for we know that he denounced to the Prussian civil authorities a man named Schloeffel whose offense was alleged to be liberal thought and labor agitation. Here was the first true "Stieber" touch, for Schloeffel had trusted him and confided in him, being the uncle of Stieber's own wife. After giving such proof of ethical atrophy his future in Prussia seemed to be assured.

The year 1848 found Europe in a peculiarly disturbed state. The pendulum of autocratic misgovernment had now swung so far to the right under Metternich's guidance that it seemed likely not to swing leftward at all but simply to fly off the handle and disappear into anarchy and chaos. Every political seismograph registered deep volcanic tremors; and the throne of many an absolute monarch became as shaky as a campstool. France was again republican. The recent advances of industrialism had fomented a new kind of agitation whose chief exponent was Karl Marx and whose doctrine was called Socialism.

Wilhelm Stieber needed just this tense situation to set him apart as a useful fellow, an intrepid monarchist and an informer dutiful enough to whisper into the very ear of the king. He was one of those fortunate malefactors who are enabled to serve the state without putting any tiresome curb upon their own criminal inspirations. He, who was to enrich the records of European treachery and intrigue for nearly five decades with the pride of a pioneer and the zest of a fallen archangel, displayed his singular ability from the first, in being able to enlist himself among the Prussian police before anything he had done could be charged against him.

Stool Pigeon and Radical Plotter

The evidence he had given against Schloeffel was not strong enough to convict him; but Stieber so managed his subtle part in the attempt as not to endanger his contact with the government or with the suspected radicals. He had to pose, of course, as an ardent liberal, pal of the workingman and partisan of Socialists. Whenever radical sympathizers were brought to trial he volunteered his professional aid. By "defending" them floridly and without charge he won his way into the very directorate of Prussian liberalism which his friends of the police were scheming to expose and suppress.

Frederick William of Prussia had inherited his kingdom but little else that was Hohenzollern. He was timid, futile and credulous. He lived in terror of mob violence; and Stieber soon contrived to turn that royal apprehension to his own account. As an *agent provocateur* it was necessary for him frequently to show off his partisan ardors and reassure the radical leaders and the turbulent rank and file. One day he put himself at the head of a particularly riotous crowd. In the guise of its spokesman he penetrated close to the quaking person of the king but at once revealed to Frederick William that he was Stieber the spy and whispered that all would go well, since His

Majesty was safely surrounded by him and his assistants. With those few words the young attorney welded himself to the secret service of Prussia's timorous sovereign.

While acting simultaneously as police agent and defender of the oppressed, as sublimated stool pigeon and radical plotter, he yet had time to build up a lucrative law practice. It is on record that in the five years of his young manhood, 1845 to 1850, Stieber had no less than three thousand clients for whom he appeared in court, and this among a conservative people to whom age and experience meant everything. Most of his cases had to do with crime, and he exerted himself almost always in the criminal's behalf. Since Prussia was never lawless to the degree of a modern American "crime wave", Stieber must have been legal adviser to virtually the whole underworld of Berlin. And then, when his success had excited much envy or admiring attention, its basic secret was rudely disclosed.

Stieber had still one other job—as editor of the police periodical. This excellent "inside" connection, a part of his reward from the grateful king, he was using to acquaint himself with whatever evidence the police had gathered to produce in court against one of his clients. It is hardly remarkable that he achieved his rapid fame as a criminal lawyer, the dazzling confounder of prosecutions, and one who, concocting impregnable pleas or alibis, was never to be overthrown by surprise testimony in the midst of a trial.

Exposure and Promotion

Revelations concerning the documentary sources of his magic caused a great scandal, but nothing came of it while the fainthearted Frederick William—who never forgot the riots—governed from Potsdam. Stiber in 1850 was even appointed commissioner of police, a job so much to his taste that, unable to foresee the future with its splendor of imperial conquests, he must have believed himself to have achieved, at thirty-two, the very pinnacle of his aspiration.

The following year he visited England, attended the World's Fair, and eagerly spied upon Marx and the radical groups of expatriated Germans then in London. But he complained in reports to his superiors that the British authorities would not join him in a scheme to harass these subversive elements of his own race. He decided he had been snubbed and crossed to Paris, where, however, he emerged as an "exile" and was generously befriended by Socialists and liberals. Obtaining from them a list of radical sympathizers still resident in Germany, he hurried home to supervise wholesale arrests. Soon he caused hundreds more to flee and seek refuge overseas; and we may reflect that Stieber directly influenced much of the best German immigration to America, in the decade before the Civil War, including such desirable types of citizen as Franz Siegel, Schurz and Jacobi.

Thus far the "king of sleuth-hounds" was only a kind of mongrel dog in the manger. The Prussian throne had become his altar, the favor of its occupant his household god; and if not yet a king himself, he was both a sly and rabid royalist who would use his spies and policemen to make every Hohenzollern subject a cringing copy of himself. Presumably the army of Prussia at this period meant to him no more than a force which might be used as gendarmerie should insurrection ever again threaten the government. He was delighted when Louis Napoleon's adherents contrived the coup d'état of 1852 establishing an empire in France, chiefly because it promised the wiping out of a radical haven, all those French headquarters of Communist agitation he had found so unpleasantly near.

Stieber's problems were international only when a Prussian whose liberty he hoped to impair eluded his agents and slipped across the frontier. He complained bitterly of both the liberals who stayed and the radicals who fled. Germans removed to North American particularly disgusted him. He could not resist intercepting their letters but, reading them, fumed over their glad cries of democratic discovery, their unanimous and unceasing outbursts in praise of the freedom their new refuge offered. Any such republican propaganda he deemed an affront to his own stinging patriotism. He grew righteously inflamed when German-Americans published opinions detrimental to autocrats and their secret police.[2]

It was now five years since the social tumult of '48. Having contradicted by cunning and force the slanderers of absolutism, Stieber and his kind could proclaim their gift to the German people. In collaboration with Wermuth, a police official of Hanover, he wrote a book depicting their battle with the dragon of Marxian revelation.[3] It was characteristic of him to include in it a list of dangerous radicals, Socialist or Communist partisans known to be at large. He wanted conservative authorities everywhere to know whom to be on guard against and to join him and his Teutonic colleagues in refusing asylum to persons whose liberal ideas were worse than cannon or pestilence.

Another five years, and the reward of autocracy's faithful servant came—in the form of dismissal. Stieber could prop up the king's throne, but not his wits. Frederick William was still a perfectly good autocrat, except that his agitations and lunacies were no longer intermittent; he was now insane all the time. And when the Prussian ruler was pronounced an imbecile he was relieved by an obstinate relative—afterward the Emperor William I—who thought that the feeble-mindedness of his predecessor had never been more abundantly exposed than in conferring upon such a man as Stieber the powers of the police.

Involuntary Vacation

No sooner was it understood that the regent considered the tireless *Polizeirath* a detestable and needless functionary than the latter's troubles began in earnest. For all his subtle endeavors, he had never been popular in any camp, not even when he was posing as a public defender and promising legal services free to the poor and oppressed. He had then come up for election to the Landtag—as a liberal, to be sure—and had been signally defeated. But now all the enemies he had accumulated in the thirteen years since he began as a spy gathered together their proofs and grievances and succeeded in having him brought to trial.

Stieber, badly cornered at last, saw no chance of retaining any position in the government or at the bar, and that counted terribly with him. Yet he had not defended three thousand persons of doubtful innocence without learning all the devious routes to acquittal. The record shows that he handled his own indictments with tactical genius. He contended that he had done his spying, inciting and betraying with royal authority, and by establishing that, however numerous or grave the offenses of which he was accused, he had never acted thus except by the king's command, Stieber maneuvered his foes entirely out of position. To convict him meant condemning publicly the ethical standards of a pitiable member of the reigning house, now confined in an exclusive sanitarium. It was impossible to prove that Stieber's conduct had ever been disloyal, privately vindictive or—within narrow monarchical standards—unpatriotic. He was subsequently removed from office, but in court he was acquitted.

Now in view of his leading role in the development of military espionage, counter-espionage and the technique of government secret service, it will be informing to see how he spent the years of his vacation between 1858 and 1863, when private life was curtly thrust upon him by the regent of Prussia. He was not idle but set about helping to reorganize the secret police service of the tsar. He had once been able officially to arrange the suppression of a scandal involving the wife of a Russian attaché in Berlin; and for his light touch in that affair he was remembered at a time when foreign employment was welcome to him.

He did not stay in St Petersburg, however, but was assigned to concentrate upon a device that would henceforth enable the tsar's agents to trace and apprehend suspected criminals even after they had escaped from Russia. He was given a sweeping commission—as well as generous pay and allowances—being expected to run to earth ordinary evildoers, forgers, counterfeiters, robbers, blackmailers and the like, and also political offenders, anarchist plotters and all manner of dangerous malcontents. So that Stieber really founded that system of external, and nearly world-wide, surveillance, the foreign branch of the *Ochrana,* which continued in operation until 1917. And in further proof of this man's unfaltering though rather curiously deformed patriotism, it is known that, even when disgraced as a police official at home, he never gave up spying for Prussia. He gathered valuable information about Russia and other countries all the while he was employed by the Russian crown.

Military items were still an unimportant matter to him. His most notable tricks of espionage had to do with the suppression of democratic tendencies; until there came that momentous day in 1863 when the course of his life was altered, the course of history wavered perceptibly, and the outcome of two European wars began to be determined in advance. He was introduced to Otto von Bismarck.

Statesman, Spy & Company

It was a newspaper proprietor, Brass, founder of the *Norddeutsche Allgemeine Zeitung,* who presented the ex-commissioner of police to the statesman, and who recommended him, too, in spite of Stieber's unpopularity with the regent who had become king. Two born conspirators thus brought together were never again to leave off a congenial dependence upon each other until the one had died and the other been thrust aside.

Bismarck was contemplating his first broad move on the Teutonic checkerboard. He had decided that overthrowing Austria would get him the right stage effects for an imperial production. The new Prussian army was fit and finished, certainly the superior of the Austrian; yet it seemed a commendable precaution to try to learn everything about the military readiness of Austria. He suggested that Stieber take charge of this preliminary incursion; and the spy eagerly accepted. He said he could do it alone.

In his own day a repellent, menacing personage, Stieber seems almost a humorous figure now, not because of inherent wit or irony, for he was intensely serious, but mainly because of his cynical realism in studying and appraising human nature. With a horse and wagon he proposed to drive about and investigate the Austrian military establishment while apparently attending to the most commonplace transactions. He wanted to go everywhere and be well received, so he loaded his wagon lightly—with cheap religious statuettes and obscene pictures!

He could be blandly commercial. He seemed to relish driving a bargain. Though he trusted nobody, he proved himself a "good mixer", readily winning the confidence of strangers. He was, in short, as gifted in military espionage, that dangerous game, as in the more accustomed practices of police spying. The Austrians never suspected him; and so he moved among them unobtrusively for months, gathering the data which was to astonish even a Von Moltke by its wealth of minutely accurate details.[4]

In 1866 came the Prussian conquest of Austria, one of the shortest and most decisive campaigns of modern times—but another confirmation of the saying that Austrian armies take the field to make the reputations of opposing generals. Owing to the intelligence supplied by Bismarck's chief spy, the army staff had been confident enough to draw up virtually a timetable of victorious advances. The soldiers of Prussia and its allies were better trained, better equipped and more expertly led than their adversaries, and they had little trouble in reaching the appointed objectives according to schedule. The one important battle at Sadowa terminated hostilities as well as the influence of Vienna in the politics of Germany.

In this happy spree of invasion Wilhelm Stieber played his first conspicuous part in eight years, directing a new squad of secret police designed by the chancellor for field service. Stieber seems to have pushed himself forward rather too suddenly at general headquarters. Aristocratic staff officers looked upon such a combination of spy and field gendarme as something lower than a lackey and refused to have him seated at their mess. Whereupon Stieber was invited by Bismarck to lunch with him privately. The chancellor doubled this rebuke by inducing Von Moltke to decorate the spy in recognition of the comprehensive excellence of his work in Bohemia.

The commander-in-chief yielded up the medal, but privately excused himself to his associates for having honored one whom they despised. Bismarck, not only an Iron Chancellor but a granite friend, countered by having Stieber appointed governor of Brunn, provincial capital of Moravia, during the Prussian occupation.

Social isolation appears to have disconcerted the spy as nothing else could, for he complicated his sinister career with every aspiration of the parvenu. His secret-service activities, however, smoothed the path of the uniformed nobility who shunned him. He and his agents had to guard the persons of the king and Bismarck, and of generals like Von Roon and Von Moltke, and also had to prevent enemy spies from getting hold of the secrets of headquarters. Thus Stieber—with Bismarck's consent and backing—initiated the first formal system of German counter-espionage. He added many a typical invention of his own to the original French model of the first Napoleon's counter-spies.

It was Stieber who devised the novelty of an exacting military censorship, covering examination of all dispatches, telegrams and letters from the front. This innovation mainly served to enlarge his own powers. Certainly it did nothing toward winning the war, for the victory was never for a moment in doubt. Austria's forces were kept on the defensive; and Stieber's own investigations had discovered that, compared to the fine new Prussian rifle, the enemy's weapons were obsolete. While reviewing this Austrian condition of helplessness and despair, he came upon his next martial improvement—organized military propaganda.

He convinced Bismarck that the spirit of the Prussian army, and of the civil population as well, would mount upon wings of his own manufacture if daily bulletins spread the choicest news of enemy losses and enemy panic, sickness, shortage of munitions, divided counsel and disaster. He really perfected a tonic cure without having met with the disease. Both civilian and army morale on the Prussian side was all that could be desired in a straightaway sprint to conquest lasting less than fifty days. But Stieber, a prodigious worker and greedy for power, persuaded the chancellor to let him establish a Central Information Bureau, and using what he called this "unobtrusive title" he began pouring forth Europe's pioneer samples of one-way war correspondence.[5]

In the public celebration following upon the triumph over Austria, the spy-master's merits were not neglected. He was restored to favor at Potsdam and appointed a privy councilor. King—soon to be Kaiser—William, who had formerly led the field in abhorring Stieber and distrusting all his works, now pronounced him a misunderstood and invaluable subject, and a secret agent deserving not only the usual cash rewards but honor and the public distinctions of the soldier.

Plots against the Second Empire

Between 1866 and 1868 Bismarck and Stieber pondered the oncoming war with France. Napoleon III was forcing it upon Prussia; and the chancellor grimly allowed the misinformed French emperor to stalk into the trap. Napoleon, with his customary credulity in external affairs, had digested a mass of haphazard intelligence and then *guessed* that Austria would defeat the new army of Von Moltke and Von Roon. As soon as Prussia had finished dictating terms of peace, the emperor of France wanted either to attack the victor or else extort an unearned share of the spoils.

Bismarck, remembering Sadowa, presented a bold front. Napoleon's army chiefs advised patience, reminding the shrewd politician and unwary diplomatist that his troops were in need of more up-to-date weapons. Union infantry in the last year of the American Civil War had been equipped with Enfield repeating rifles. Military attachés had reported upon these highly educated muskets; but in Europe the Prussian breech-loading needle guns were still the best available arms for infantry, and France possessed nothing so good. Correcting this omission straightway produced the *chassepot* and the *mitrailleuse,* believed to surpass every other type of rifle and machine gun then in use. Stieber, in 1868, visited the French to ascertain what deadly virtues lay in their new equipment.

But even before his most destructive tour of espionage began, something occurred which, if not illustrating any remarkable feat of espionage, will show how he endeared himself to an international conspirator of Bismarck's range. Through one of his still-existing Russian connections Stieber had obtained information respecting an attempt to be made on the life of Tsar Alexander II while he was visiting Paris. As the guest and potential ally of Napoleon III, the tsar was to attend a grand review in his honor at Longchamps, and there the Polish assassin would get in his blow. Stieber, after consulting his astute master, withheld a warning of this revolutionary plot until just the afternoon of the review.

French police officials, had they been notified well in advance, could have so completely checkmated the plot that it would have attracted slight attention. Stieber's calculated delay he made to seem like a last-minute discovery, and a frantic rush to aid the French in saving their royal guest. This forced the Parisian detectives to disturb the tsar and alarm his entourage, and then seize the plotters in a sensational fashion. But no crime had been committed; Stieber's mere warning was not legal evidence; and according to French law a severe penalty was impossible. Suspicion of an intent to assassinate Russia's sovereign was not a charge grave enough to get the alleged ringleader or his accomplices transported or sentenced to prison for long terms.

The tsar, as had been expected at Berlin, declined to see the judicial nicety in this. That Bonapartist upstart, he maintained ever after, had cared so little about a real emperor's life that he did not trouble to punish assassins who had all but succeeded. The result was estrangement between Alexander and Napoleon III, which was precisely what Bismarck needed if the French ruler and his marshals were presently to be lured to the slaughter.

Having done so much for the next war, Stieber now proceeded to do ten times more in making certain of Teutonic victory. He and his principal lieutenants, Zernicki and Kaltenbach, spent some eighteen months in France, spying, recording and measuring, while also placing whole brigades of resident agents to await the expected invasion.[6] During this fruitful tour the three sent a great number of code reports to Berlin, describing their progress; yet when at length they turned toward the fatherland they brought with them additional data filling three trunks. These Stieber checked through like ordinary luggage in an express car attached to their train.

CHAPTER FORTY-SIX

KING OF SLEUTHHOUNDS

IT WAS SAID by Schopenhauer that Germans are "remarkable for the absolute lack of that feeling which Latins call 'verecundia'—sense of shame." This may have grieved the philosopher and inconvenienced any number of his countrymen, but it has accounted for many striking developments of secret service. Wilhelm Stieber—as young attorney, *agent provocateur*, police official and military spy—we have seen to be one chronically afflicted with that "absolute lack." And his moral infirmity proved a continual boon to Bismarck and the House of Hohenzollern, as well as immensely improving to his own position in the state. He had never heard of inhibitions and did not know that he had none.

With the coming of the Franco-Prussian War in 1870 he was in his element. Subsequently he boasted that he had forty thousand spies lodged in the invasion zones of France when, on August 6, 1870, the defeat of MacMahon at Worth predicted the shattering of an eighteen-year-old imperial crown and the fabrication of another destined to "wear" more than twice that long.

Stieber, it is safe to presume, never had forty thousand spies. There may have been ten to fifteen thousand persons who had compromised themselves by accepting his gratuities for clandestine service. The biographer of Stieber, Dr Leopold Auerbach, conveys the impression that, if challenged, he could have supplied forty thousand names and even addresses. Yet a chain of five thousand spies suggests a vast department of state—disciplining, recruiting, checking their reports and compensating each agent according to his apparent deserts. It is a pity no one ever challenged the good doctor to produce his tally sheets; for the tale of that mastodonic service, that hippodrome of forty thousand spies, was still a living menace in European minds when Germany went to war in 1914.

Colonel Baron Stoffel, the French military attaché at Berlin from 1866 to 1870, appears to have been an alert observer. He heard nothing of the forty thousand, but he managed to detect many of the undercover preparations going forward from Stieber's notorious espionage bureau. He learned a good deal about Stieber, about Zernicki, Kaltenbach and their principal operatives. Proofs exist that Stoffel reported his suspicions to Paris;[1] but these uneasy admonitions merely earned him reputation as an alarmist.

France was still the most warlike nation of Europe. It was the customary thing for French troops to be brave and, on the Continent, generally victorious. The incapacities of Napoleon or his henchmen would scarcely account for the whole bewildering reversal. Worth on August 6—Sedan but twenty-five days later, and a great military Power had vanished from the contest! Stieber's boasts about *his* "army having the war half won" when it started must surely hold some measure of truth.

We know from Auerbach that the spy-master wrote proudly to his wife at this time, always upon the exalted topic of his growing intimacy with Bismarck.[2] Besides Zernicki and Kaltenbach, his crack lieutenants, he now had at his disposal 27 other officers and 157 agents and subordinates, a magnified force of field police, following the pattern determined by his smaller command during the campaign against Austria. And the chancellor, it seems, kept his chief spy within call, choosing him as a confidant on successive occasions, while each phase of the French debacle they had plotted together was making its record of unparalleled punctuality.

Spy as Census Taker

When he went into France to study the *chassepot* and the *mitrailleuse*, Stieber had understood his private responsibility. Should he pronounce the new French weapons vastly superior to the arms of Prussia, Bismarck would wait and adjust his shrewdly developing war provocation to whatever length of time it might take to deliver improved weapons to the German regiments. The spy's admiration for machine guns and rifles of the very latest model would, in short, embarrass his chief and obstruct his imperialist plans as German politics and foreign diplomacy had never been permitted to do. But again, if Stieber underestimated the *potentiel de guerre* and possible resistance of Napoleon's realm, the reaction in Germany would confer a kind of suicide upon the Prussian leaders.

Therefore, the spy-master had to declare for war entirely on the basis of his own observations and judgment or else impede the projects of the chancellor who was his very god. We shall see how often Teutonic agents or observers during the European war of 1914 blundered when trying to determine morale, resources and fighting power of an impending adversary. But in the critical year of

1869-70 Wilhelm Stieber did not blunder. He allowed for mistakes which he himself might make. Gauging all reports that he filed accordingly, he prepared to encounter much less advantageous odds than his near view of the sagging Bonaparte regime entitled him to estimate.

Overconfident and habitually slack, Napoleon's Ministry of War would have intoxicated a less coldly methodical espion. One of its spokesmen, Lebœuf, assured an anxious Chamber that the French army was ready "with not even so much as the button of a gaiter missing." Stieber, hearing of that, might justifiably have telegraphed the Prussian general staff to join him in Paris, or at least urged his superiors to attack before the incompetents could be found out and replaced by able men.[3] But doubtless possessing encyclopedic knowledge of gaiter buttons, Stieber merely consulted his notes and went diligently on.

He was the first "vacuum cleaner" in the annals of espionage, the first spy ever to work as a census enumerator. Roads, rivers and bridges, arsenals, reserve depots, fortified places and lines of communication were his foremost consideration. But he added an intensive interest in the population, in commerce and agriculture, in farms, houses, inns, and in local prosperity, politics and patriotism—in anything at all which struck him as likely to expedite an invasion or provide for the invaders.

When at length the Prussians came, bearing Stieber's data, civil requisitions and foraging were made easy. The village magnate with two hundred hens could expect to be called upon for so many dozen eggs. Were the hens not laying but going to market in person, Stieber's nearest resident spy would report the change when accounting for maximum local provisions. While if the villager objected to contributing eggs or fowls or whatever else he was known to have on hand, he would be marched before a provost who questioned the insubordinate with a hanging warrant in blank upon his table.

More than one thrifty burgher fainted when the cash assessment demanded of him showed an incredibly accurate calculation of his savings. Owing to Stieber and the horde of agents and subagents he had engaged to serve him, privacy in France was the first casualty of the war. This "omniscient" form of national intelligence has seemed admirable to many and, as a method of military preparedness, subtle, crafty and unique; yet even the Germans of the present day apologize for Stieber or omit mentioning his name, since his manner of gaining his ends was lawless in the extreme and often possessed of a cold ferocity.

Take as an example the Stieber report upon General de Gallifet, crack cavalry leader and the outstanding French hero of the disaster at Sedan, which was submitted approximately as follows:[4]

This officer is one who, under Napoleon the First, would have held the highest rank. A real Frenchman, with his heart in the war and a hater of all things Prussian. A fighter for the initiative, by every instinct a dangerous adversary and, for us, better dead. Should be watched; has no thought for anything in the present war but the success of the French arms.

Stieber's own operatives were encouraged to punish without mercy anyone seeming even remotely connected with French espionage. They disregarded the circumstance of the war being waged wholly in the enemy's country, with a dense population instinctively hostile or curious. Peasants and laborers were strung up and executed by slow torture when they had done no more than peer out at a German ammunition train or cavalry column. Bazaine and his best troops were blockaded in the fortress of Metz; Paris had been invested soon after Sedan witnessed the capitulation of Napoleon III and a large army. There was now nowhere for a French secret agent to carry his intelligence so that it might produce any serious recoil upon the Prussians. Yet even the most doubtful cases of spying were handled by Wilhelm Stieber with unbearable severity.

He had first tried his hand at wartime counter-espionage during the Sadowa campaign of 1866. It was not, however, until he plunged into the more imposing struggle with the Second Empire that he discovered his doctrine of merciless prudence in regard to counter-spying. In war, he maintained, a spy must have the "right" to kill an opposing spy, just as the uniformed combatant may fire upon a soldier of the enemy unless he promptly surrenders himself.

An enemy spy, he argued—generally addressing himself to Prince Bismarck, who seems to have had a strong stomach for that sort of thing—should be shot down as other antagonists are in battle. Yet if the spy was not slain but was wounded and made prisoner in the course of the espionage warfare, or, perhaps, captured unwounded, then his status as a spy must remain unaltered. And because of that he should be tried at once and executed.

Stieber evidently did not care how such harsh stipulations reacted upon his own agents. If their lives were forfeited, that was part of the hazard and the game. In counter-spying technique he particularly recommended the charge of "outrage", which appealed to him as the most plausible and convenient excuse for doing away with any suspected spy who might invoke the laws of war or humane precedent.[5] Let the suspect be shot because he had "attacked a convoy of German wounded", or because he had "fired upon an unescorted supply train" or upon a general riding harmlessly along escorted only by his equally harmless staff.

In Versailles the spy-master and his assistants occupied the mansion of the Duc de Persigny. Stieber had conducted himself with marked insolence ever since the invasion began, but here, in September of 1870, he began treating French and Germans alike to the nasty condescension of an upstart whose independent powers stem from obscure and lofty places. He always acted without consulting his military colleagues. Though the existence of martial law doubled his tyrant authority, he obeyed only Bismarck and the king of Prussia, and none of the generals dared to interfere with him or his agents. Deliberately snubbed and insulted by army leaders, he repulsed all their barbs with his rhinoceros hide and mounted rung by rung the mental ladder of his egotism.

His was now the arrogance of a rascal who has learned the joy of seeing better men afraid of him. For some trivial disorder he threatened to hang ten members of the municipal council of Versailles and wrote his wife with gleeful satisfaction, describing the terror he had inspired. It is said that he engaged five thousand poor citizens for a franc a day to gather in crowds and cheer the Prussian sovereign and other German princes whenever they appeared in the streets. And when at last the negotiations for the surrender of Paris began, he further accommodated Bismarck by posing as a valet.

Jules Favre came to Versailles early in 1871 to treat with the capital's besiegers. He was escorted to the house which had been Stieber's secret-service headquarters; and all during his stay within the enemy lines he was waited upon so expertly that he took polite occasion to compliment his German hosts upon the service accorded him.

In dealing with the Parisian envoy, Stieber elected the role of servant and discharged his menial duties with sinister relish. Favre was completely taken in. Every secret document and cipher he had brought with him, every letter or telegram he received, was exposed to the ransacking patriotism of the indispensable valet. Favre slept in Zernicki's bed, in a dwelling staffed exclusively with Prussian secret-service agents.[6]

Stieber and the Fair Sex

When Stieber had loosed his cataract of espionage upon France, he had included a great many women recruits, all of the baser sort—

as he stipulated to his assistants, "not bad looking but not too fastidious." He preferred a choice selection of subsidized barmaids, waitresses, servants in military canteens, and also domestic servants in the homes of French politicians and of the professional or official class. His men were mostly farmers or retired noncommissioned officers helped into jobs in various commercial lines; but he afterward conceded that their effectiveness as resident agents did not compare with the women.

In 1875 republican France had already begun to lift its head; the German Empire was still very new; and in both Paris and Berlin there was much thought of a war of revenge. The French General de Cissey was serving his second term as minister of war. This officer, while a prisoner of war in Hamburg, had known and become intimate with a charming young woman, the Baroness de Kaulla. Stieber, ever well informed about the "past" of eminent persons, learned of this affair, interviewed the baroness and, finding her also "not too fastidious", contrived to add her fascinations to his secret service. Giving her a large sum of money, he packed her off to Paris, where she was expected to reawaken in the minister of war those ardors which so often unlock official secrets.

The baroness did not have to exert herself, for she found the general disengaged at the moment and eager to renew the pleasant relationship which had ameliorated his capitivity. Such scandal as resulted was entirely due to De Cissey's verbal indiscretions. Paris, never more than fashionably interested in the mistress of a cabinet minister, could be profoundly stirred by anything threatening the young Republic's military reorganization. After an all-night secret session of the Chamber, the general would hasten to breakfast with his inamorata, whose Teutonic connections were more readily discovered than the Prussian chief had expected.[7] In the ensuing commotion De Cissey was ejected from office and the baroness from France, but not before he had prattled to her many confidences never meant to reach Berlin.

The new corps of resident spies—which Stieber began to distribute throughout France as soon as the terms of peace ending the Franco-Prussian War had been met—did not include any great number of Germans as had the cohorts imported before 1870. He comprehended the antagonism of the French after their humiliating defeat, and he therefore enlisted French-speaking Swiss, but also many other nationalities of the Continent. Almost any alien might be mistrusted as a Stieber hireling.

French counter-espionage was not for a decade to become sufficiently well organized or forceful enough to battle with this veteran on even terms. Stieber meanwhile found a new reservoir in the populations of Alsace and Lorraine, engaging those who were pro-German or individuals of a type easily controlled by the police as valuable recruits for his spy service. In 1880 he informed Emperor William I that, so thoroughly had he worked this vein, he now counted upon more than one thousand Alsace-Lorrainers as a sabotage corps. He had sent them into the employ of the French railroads, paying each 25 per cent of his regular wages as a kind of secret retainer. And should another war break out, at a word from him these agents would begin destroying or damaging locomotives, signals, switches and rolling stock. Stieber felt that he could paralyze French mobilization the very day the placards went up.

Spies that he controlled outside the public service were planted in factories, or as shopkeepers, or, in the case of most of his women operatives, as employees in hotels. The chief of German espionage had decided that if German capitalists erected luxurious hotels in foreign countries, he could insert scores of his secret-service creatures into their staffs and thus spy not only upon mysterious travelers but also upon the rich and distinguished persons who would frequent them. His hotel spies he expected to obtain information eventually applicable to subtle blackmailing schemes abroad; nor was he blind to the virtues of having them taught to steal or "borrow and photograph" important private documents from the luggage or dispatch cases of influential guests.

Knowing how to apply political pressure at home, Stieber had so formidably organized imperial espionage and counter-espionage that he could command a huge slice of all German military appropriations. Some of this money he poured into the international hotel industry; so that for years the best hotels everywhere were German owned and predominantly German in personnel; and not all attentions they rendered a guest were itemized upon his bill.

Stieber next tried to extend his sway by means of subsidies to banking and other international businesses, always with the idea of expanding an already overgrown system of intelligence. In some instances he undoubtedly succeeded, or established those concerns which were no more than masked bureaus of secret service.[8] But the German was a trader from the days of the Hanseatic League; and it would be idle to represent—as many did during the World War—that all Teutonic commercial enterprises overseas from the time of Stieber until 1914 had the primary purpose of government conspiracy and espionage.

Stieber, keenly aware of the growing power of the press, and having already helped to sponsor the semiofficial Wolff telegraphic news agency, organized a special branch of his intricate department to study foreign opinion and keep track of foreign publications. He made it a practice to learn what motive—or subsidy—lay in back of any strongly anti-German article or editorial. If certain publishers or writers seemed to him to hate Germany, he sought to know their grievance; and if any kind of cash transaction would correct this enmity he was disposed to buy liberally in the right markets. He is reputed to have purchased newspapers in nearly every neighboring country to popularize simultaneously antimilitarism, the ideals of pacifism, and pro-German sentiment.

Even without his natural enthusiasm for any new form of political deceit or domination, Stieber would have been compelled to instigate imperial propaganda. Both before and after proclamation of the empire, the Prussian yoke had rested painfully upon the smaller German states. Hanover especially caused much uneasiness in certain quarters; and Stieber kept a corps of operatives continuously assigned to look out for and counteract dangerous internal resurgences.[9]

The spy-master's razor-edged capacities as a plotter did not rust, no matter how peaceable the late Victorian world of his declining years became. He had sent his crack secret agent, Ludwig Windell, into France; and there he was serving as the coachman of General Mercier, the new minister of war. Mercier was fond of inspecting fortifications. And Windell, the spy, drove the French general right into any restricted zone or fortified area that his ministerial position required and permitted Mercier to visit. Thus Stieber kept up the old game, while continually inventing new tasks for himself; and, if he could not recover the raptures of invasion in 1866 and '70, he retained Bismarck's unsparing support and was the right-hand man of the most powerful German in the world.

The "Green House"

As minister of police Stieber could delve into any crime or conspiracy. After the imperial machine began running smoothly, he started in to save William I and the great chancellor from sundry assassins and divers other subterranean perils—many of which are now known to have been promoted by his own operatives. On the surface it was a great day of German unity and patriotism, of stirring acclaim for the war-born empire and fatherland. And Stieber even grafted his espionage ideals upon *"Deutschland über Alles."*

He made it seem every good citizen's privilege to undertake some secret mission which to the private individual acting for himself would have meant contemptible deceit and well-deserved ostracism. He knew how to manage the zealous rank and file with appeals about patriotic duty. Yet he had learned that the rich and influential, the minor royalties and nobles, owned always a much more worthwhile access to imposing secrets than would any spy he might train or hire. This led him to the final innovation of his long and artful experience in mingling underworld practices with the powers of government.

In Berlin he opened the notorious "Green House", a resort for people of consequence, where every form of excess or vicious indulgence was sumptuously encouraged, all under the happy pretext of offering notable libertines an almost providential privacy. Since they came to the "Green House" to forget themselves, Stieber arranged to remember for them. While there was never even a suggested limit upon any of his clients' behavior, if they were prominent persons the memory of it would be made to last forever.

Each event at this rendezvous was, in short, well known to the police because police agents managed, staffed and protected it. Sinister little histories of a debauched and abominable society were hidden away by Stieber in his private file. And at need he used that file to extort co-operation—even from royalty—so that the imperial secret service when operating in the highest altitudes might never move ineffectually.

Social ambitions induced Stieber to try to promote himself and his family through the same kind of sublimated blackmail. He was wealthy now and inflated by his years of bureaucratic despotism; and if the mere threat of scandal and exposure served Prussia, why should not the same lever elevate the head of the police? Dread opened a few doors to him; but, apart from the business of state, his intimate acquaintance was as parvenu as himself. Such pressure as he was able to exert opened him a path, like some mushroom growth, up the backstairs of fashionable Berlin.

Yet if he received only inferior invitations, he had been decorated twenty-seven times. He had the diplomas and medals to prove it; so that when he lay fatally stricken with arthritis in 1892 he must have deemed himself great, his career a useful and honorable one. Useful it had surely been. But whatever prize he had sought in his life had been won by stealth, and now it was the end. No hereafter would hazard its future by undertaking to reward or to punish him.

Bearing witness to his unsparing devotion to Germany, to Prussia and to Hohenzollerns, personal representatives of the emperor and of the other rulers of states paid him their last respects. His funeral, in fact, was well attended; but there seems to have been an embarrassing levity among the mourners. Many perhaps were there to reassure themselves that the autocratic old sleuthhound was really dead.

CHAPTER FORTY-SEVEN

LESSONS FROM A SCHOOL OF HARD KNOCKS

THE GERMAN CONQUEST of Napoleon III and the French set in motion a train of events which, despite several flag stops, found their inevitable terminus in 1914; but that was not foreseen even by Bismarck at the time of his adroit founding of the German Empire and isolation of republican France. The government of successive Hohenzollerns was distinguished by a nearly continuous assertion of its own political importance and military readiness; and it was flattering still to allow the sinister reputation of the secret service, established and directed by Stieber, to extend its cloak of past triumphs over all ensuing undercover activities of Berlin, even the diplomatic. This concealed a generous indulgence in post-Bismarck blundering and ineptitude and allowed the *surviving* German Intelligence and espionage system to fall into decay, without any German noticing it or any potential opponent ceasing to fear it.

Stieber has been treated at considerable length in this record because nearly everything he started, or for which he seems even remotely responsible, has proved a hardy and malignant growth. It was Stieber who gave modern secret service its impress of consistent, premeditated ruthlessness, in peace as well as in time of war. Governing ruthlessness and police terror were no inventions of his; yet there had been little studied ruthlessness before his debut, but generally the fluctuating, desperate expedience of incompetent monarchs, ministers of state or military commanders. Stieber borrowed the trampling brutalities of armed invasion and exploited them in secret service as a preferred pattern of official conduct.

If he was incapable of making the desired lasting impression upon the caste-mentality of Prussian officers, his influence upon the Austrians and French—when the character of his assault upon their countries became fully understood—was enormous. The real "Stieber influence" thus mounted for decades in those and all other countries so near to new Germany they could hear the constant saber rattling; while the gospel of the Stieber police echoed harshly in the palaces of St Petersburg. He had set the Russians a particularly potent example, since neither the tsarist military espionage nor the operations of the *Ochrana,* or secret political police,[1] had known much effective organization before Europe began imitating Prince Bismarck's masterly subordinate.

It was Stieber also who infected his contemporaries with the secret-service cult of the cashiered "officer and gentleman." This recruiting dodge was founded upon the theory that a man of good breeding who has ruined himself socially and has had to resign his commission may "redeem" his patriotism, and perhaps some of his debts, by inflicting his bad character upon the neighbors. Prince Otto Hochberg, scion of a noble house but himself an unconscionable gambler and cardsharp, became one of wily Wilhelm's most useful operatives. Such a man is likely to cheat even his own rehabilitation, though a secret service of the Stieber mold had its special resources for enforcing discipline. Hochberg brought to espionage and international intrigue the same crooked zeal with which he had won his brother officers' money; and there were a number of his unsavory sort employed to attend to the more precarious chores of government after 1871.

The Code of Revanche

It must not be inferred that the influence of Stieber, either at home or abroad, was of calculable weight and dimensions. Germans and French alike at that time were careful to minimize his contributions to the victory and resulting dissolution of the Second Empire. His compatriots discounted the work of the German spy-master because of his sinister methods and unpalatable notoriety, and also because it was repugnant to all good Teutonic minds to allow anything to dilute the fame of the army. The French on their part—except in official archives—largely ignored Stieber until a generation had passed and the researches of Paul and Suzanne Lanoir admitted him to the company of *Les grands espions.*

The Franco-Prussian War is perhaps too easily struck off as a medal, with the emperor surrendering at Sedan on one side and Paris being surrendered on the other. But if we analyze the exact nature of the postwar Stieber influences, we find that the spy-master dealt with considerable French opposition, especially after Sedan, when the strong nationalistic impulses of the French replaced enfeebled and delinquent imperial impulses. The code of *Revanche,* still vital at the time of the Armistice in 1918, was already invoking French sacrifices—from secret agents as well as soldiers—before either Metz or Paris surrendered. The imperial armies of MacMahon and Bazaine did not fight so well in 1870 as the improvised hosts of

Gambetta in '71; and the latter, though confronted with invasion, a beleaguered Paris, Bonapartist defeatism, and the treacherous maneuvering and bargaining of the oligarchs of the Bank of France,[2] even found time to improvise an extensive and powerful counter-espionage.

The secret-service organization of Napoleon III, a numerous and heavily financed corps, ought to have opposed Stieber effectively before war ever came. But the imperial detective bureaus had little chance to learn counter-spying so long as they were nagged by internal quakes and recoils, with the attendant necessity of spying upon foes of the Bonapartist regime. We have noted in the chapter preceding how Baron Stoffel's reports from Berlin were avoided by the discriminating. Napoleon III never got over allowing courtiers to sift his foreign intelligence. The misguided estimate of Prussian "defeat" in 1866 was somehow accounted for; and Stieber's continuing activities were viewed from the same obtuse angle that minimized the preparations of a Von Moltke, Bismarck or Von Roon.

Now Gambetta's secret service, while virtually an improvisation of the battlefield, showed vast improvement over the imperial agencies for which it had to be hastily substituted. The German generals were nonplussed by the unexpected resistance of a beaten nation; and so was Wilhelm Stieber. Prince Bismarck had hoped to make peace with Napoleon after Sedan. The submission of an emperor and his army seemed a better political risk to the victorious invaders than trying to negotiate with rhetorical republicans, already beginning to stir up the country with talk about "the honor of France" and *Revanche*. Napoleon, a disconsolate prisoner of war at Cassel, was enabled to send M. Régnier, under German auspices, to Metz to ascertain how Bazaine's army felt about re-establishment of the French Empire. And from Metz on a somewhat similar errand General Bourbaki—"in a remarkably roomy suit of civilian clothes" belonging to Bazaine—was allowed to run the blockade, visit England and consult Eugénie.

Gambetta's secret agents, who ran the same blockade in the opposite direction, entered Metz in vain, however; there was no prolonging the siege. It was true that Chanzy, whose *moblots* were to cover themselves with glory and blood in the snow outside Le Mans, ought to have captained Gambetta's scrub team, the Army of the Loire, instead of the capable but timid D'Aurelle de Paladines. Even so, strategists concede that, had Bazaine not surrendered Metz when he did, thus releasing the army of the Prussian crown prince, the Loire army stood a first-rate chance of raising the siege of Paris. Garibaldi had his *francs-tireurs* in Burgundy; and "admirals on horseback" led bravely blended detachments of *gendarmes* and *Spahis*. Gambetta was seeking to mold a kind of sketchy, twilight republic—"*la République sans les républicains*"—into an invulnerable defensive machine. He was not, as Thiers branded him, a "raving lunatic", but a bold and formidable patriot with a talent for tactics as well as for talk. Were they not his orders to D'Aurelle de Paladines which defeated the Bavarians at Coulmiers,[3] the only French victory in the war?

Gambetta was preaching war to the bitter end, death rather than dishonor; and many a French agent was finding death an obscure as well as bitter end. While Stieber's field police obviously discovered in the regenerated French government at Tours an opponent whose high resolve inspired a counter-offensive and whose resource made it threatening even to well-entrenched invaders.

The Second Empire Lost; the Second Bureau Found

On October 9, 1870, we have Von Moltke writing to Major-General von Stiehle: "In the bottom of a snuff-box found on the person of an emissary of the French government, there was discovered the original of an edict signed by Favre and Gambetta, deferring the elections once more."

Five days earlier Von Moltke had issued this order from his headquarters at Ferrières: "We have proof that communication is still being maintained between Paris and Tours by runners. We know here that one of them reached the capital on the 4th inst. To men whose alertness leads to the capture of couriers carrying government dispatches, a reward of one hundred thalers is to be paid for each separate case."

With this incentive couriers were brought in who proved to have important French dispatches sewn into waistcoat linings or concealed in sticks and twigs. Other messages were found in boot soles, cap peaks, in an artificial tooth, even in a ten-centime piece which had been cut through, hollowed out, and fitted together again, "the joint being rendered invisible by the use of vinegar." Some of the most vital communications which the Germans detected were hidden "in rubber-coated pellets . . . swallowed when danger threatened. There were emissaries who had had to swallow the same pellet several times. The Germans would search French prisoners suspected of carrying messages, strip them, give them a strong purge, and keep them under constant observation. If no suspicious signs had been

350 THE STORY OF SECRET SERVICE

observed in the course of a week"—and Stieber seems the very Prussian whom the Almighty would assign to invent colonic and excrementary counter-espionage!—"the patient was generally released

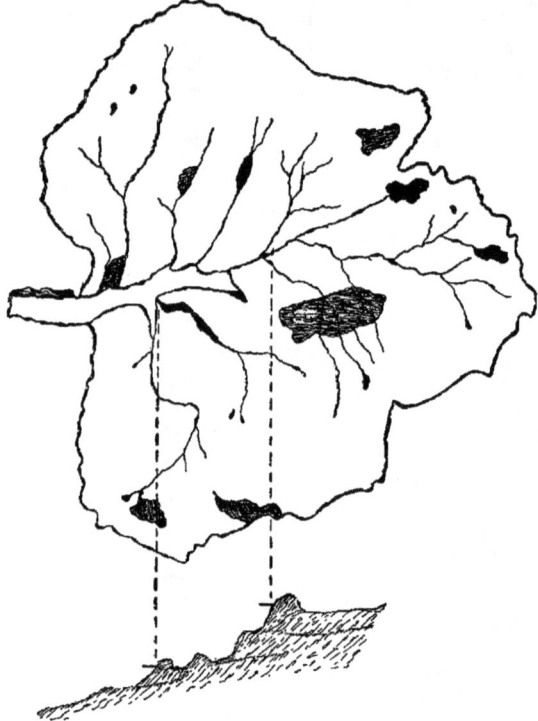

An authentic diagram of modern military espionage as interpreted by the secret service after successful transmission.

with a warning not to be caught again in similar circumstances. The guilty were shot off-hand."[4]

The shootings, however numerous, were never able to out-number the intrepid volunteers, once the French nation was really stirred, not to perpetuate the shabby imperial regime, but to resist foreign invaders.⁵ The agents and couriers who so gallantly maintained the secret-intelligence service were most of them countrymen, merchants, carters, foresters, and customs or excise officers, whose work had made them very familiar with the invaded areas of France. Gendarmes, soldiers and sailors also were diverted to the hazards of espionage. Many of these agents pretended to be Belgian subjects; and Stieber's men were kept busy scrutinizing fraudulent passports. Throughout the campaign the French spy-masters made the serious mistake of underpaying those who volunteered for perilous missions, either promising more than they were able to pay or else promising too little. The customary reward for taking dispatches through the German lines ranged from fifty to two hundred francs; often no more than ten or twenty francs were paid, peasant couriers especially being victimized in that fashion.

There were many devoted patriots who risked their lives boring through the Stieber network without thought of gain. One incredible fellow offered to disguise himself as a Prussian *Uhlan,* and, since he spoke no German, to have his tongue cut out so that he could not speak at all. Another, a peddler named Macherez, who had sworn to avenge the burning of the village of Jussy by the Prussians, carried a vital communication from field headquarters to the commandant at Verdun and then went on to Metz, yet refused a payment of 1,000 francs, declaring himself rewarded enough by having had the privilege of outwitting the enemy. Some agents would have taken the risks less rapturously if they had understood the character of their missions. There was, for example, a message smuggled out of beleaguered Metz at capital risk, dated October 26—three days before the surrender—and received by Gambetta in Tours, where no copy of the code used by the Army of the Rhine was to be found. Gambetta had to send Bazaine's dispatch on a second perilous adventure into Paris; and after a third desperate journey it was brought back to Tours, decoded at last, on the seventeenth of December.

Patriotism and national honor, the campaign of home defense which Gambetta inspired, greatly improved the caliber of the individual secret-service operative in the dreadful autumn of 1870 and the winter of 1871; but now, long afterward, we cannot determine how much Wilhelm Stieber, by threat or example, contributed to that improvement. His influence, whatever its impact in war, chiefly provoked the rival French services to combine and expand soon after peace was restored. The Second Empire might be lost forever; but the *Deuxième Bureau* of the French General Staff was found; and some of the worst practices of the secret police remained.

Stieber had put his own brand upon the German, Russian, and other departments of political police. Labor espionage, too, and that sleepless vigilance which allows no respite to malcontents, visionaries or any known partisan of the politically defrauded and socially underprivileged, owed some details of undercover organization and merciless technique to Wilhelm's infectious form of Prussianism. The *dossiers* were not, however, of his origination. And the secret-service foundations of France as a free Republic after the German triumph and the Hohenzollern Peace of Frankfort suggest to us much less learned from Stieber, the victorious foe, than inherited from Fouché, or even from De Sartines, the forgotten Royalist.

A vast cargo of *dossiers* was destroyed in the incendiary fires of the Commune. And the criminal populace rejoiced in this destruction, but not for long, as one of the first acts of the re-established conservative government was to order the precious *dossiers* reconstituted. This was an immense labor, calling for reference to all the archives of prisons and tribunals, newspaper files and public documents in general. Yet within two years *five million* new records were ready, interred in eight thousand boxes. That monument—composed, in the words of a noted police prefect, M. Andrieux, of "all the gross calumnies and truculent denunciations that form the basis of such documents"—was surely a republican work in the pure tradition of the clever De Sartines. And so were the seventeen assorted "shadows" covering Walsin Esterhazy, who will turn up presently in the affair of Captain Dreyfus. Whereas the dead hand of Joseph Fouché seems to have directed the French Secret Service when it set to work upon General Georges Boulanger. The general-politician's valet, one Georget, was a police spy, and so was the valet's sweetheart, efficaciously employed as lady's maid to Boulanger's mistress, Mme de Bonnemain. When the general had to flee to Brussels, both valet and maid trooped along. Boulanger never stopped dreading en route the secret police and their detection of his flight. His arrest would have been possible at one of twenty stops before the train crossed the frontier; but the police agents were only instructed to escort the unlamented "man on horseback" as he furtively rolled into oblivion.

The French Republic, in spite of the indemnity exacted by the Prussians, was able to provide funds for police espionage that touchingly respected all the least democratic Bourbon and Bonapartist traditions. Major Arthur Griffiths, the British police authority, was distressed to find in Paris spies "among all classes of society . . . even today; in drawing-rooms and in the servants' hall, at one's elbow in the theatre, among journalists, in the army, and in the best professions"—as well as in the oldest. Having observed the continuity of political secret service in France and prepared for the strong revival of the military secret service after the terrific defeat inflicted by Stieber and his clandestine corps, we must give passing attention to the intelligence and espionage practices of international bankers and other dominant individuals. Tsarist Russia then takes its place in these annals of the past century with its own peculiar extravagances of political police, espionage and provocation. Whereupon we shall arrive inevitably in France once again and come to a pitiable bystander named Alfred Dreyfus, whose destiny it was to bring such penetrating obloquy upon the Military Intelligence service of the French Republic that it rose, as from a deathbed, killed its doctors, and attacked its own chronic infections.

CHAPTER FORTY-EIGHT

PRIVATE PATRONS OF INTELLIGENCE

IT IS ONE OF THE CURIOSITIES of this record that the only individuals who have ever had private espionage or intelligence systems equal in effectiveness to those of governments, or of political plotters ambitious to govern, are churchmen, bankers and criminals. The church spies were largely a natural phenomenon of the past when the temporal power of cardinals, bishops and enriched monastic orders was often superior to that of any other compact propertied class. Down to modern times, however, well-organized criminal bands and far more securely established banking houses have made use of certain forms of secret service—generally for the same reasons, protection and profit. But with this difference, that where the criminal has sought to gain intelligence so that, when he breaks the law, his chances of being caught are reduced, the banker more virtuously employs it in order to prove, if he gets caught, that he did not break the law.

A practice of being professionally well informed was so long ago cemented into the cornerstone of international moneylending that the exploits of master criminals or politicians or clergy in this same line, and even of many princes and elective governments, seem like debts repaid in the flattering coinage of imitation. Secret intelligence of a variety which would nowadays be news, on the screen, "on the air," and a torrent flooding from high-speed presses, was once upon a time a precious commodity. The price was high because of inferior distribution, for consumers were plentiful and the production of events tremendous.

Princes, clergy and lay politicians did the scheming and whispering; criminals attended to the eavesdropping or stealing. While the banking and merchant classes paid as dearly for this information as for the rich fabrics and spices, or frankincense and myrrh, brought by caravans from the East. It was like buying life, accident and fire insurance, a weathervane, and acquaintance with the intimacies of court circles, all for the upkeep of a few lean and slippery spies. It was the price of liberty and the cost of living—in turbulent regions, the cost of keeping alive. Changes in government might be frequent;

PRIVATE PATRONS OF INTELLIGENCE 355

tax levies, imprisonment and death would be constant. The present was always painful and the future uncertain; and even the richest bankers could not muster the wages of a reliable seer.

When the great De' Bardi and Peruzzi banking families of Florence were induced to lend Edward III of England large sums of money with which to fight the battle of Crécy, they had their agents in the war zone. These spies hovered around Edward and reported upon conditions in France, upon the English military strength, the king's skill as an army commander, and his excellent chances of winning. The total amount advanced—in loans whose collection could obviously never be enforced—was 1,365,000 gold florins, equivalent today to more than £7,000,000 sterling.[1]

Edward and the English were completely victorious at Crécy, attesting to the accurate perceptions of Florentine intelligencers. But since their champion never repaid his war loans, Crécy was the ruin of its Italian promoters. Simply because they had to depend upon spies, when they needed a soothsayer to warn them that centuries later it would be convenient for the English and all their allies to borrow even more heavily upon the security of success, and win, and repudiate the loans.

The Fuggers of Augsburg were a greater house of bankers and business men, who learned at frequent intervals about the very diet of European monarchs and every item of interest concerning them or their noticeable subjects, whether en route to the cradle or finally enshrouded for the grave.[2] The Fugger *News Letters* were virtually an associated press; they transcend secret service, for the German Fuggers were to money what the Hohenzollerns became to Prussian infantry. Papal elections were prayerfully financed from the vast coffers of Augsburg; while they habitually bribed the electors of the Holy Roman Empire in favor of the candidate who had passed the Fugger Intelligence tests. Even the illustrious Emperor Charles V was but one more heavily backed Fugger favorite—well connected, safe and sane, though the son of pitiful Mad Juana—a Habsburg elevated to a vast dominion of absolute power by depending upon his creditors.

It was the Fuggers who restored to the considerations of European statecraft the manipulation of money and credit in the grand manner, known to Imperial Rome, and which we know as international finance. They were actually so skillful in controlling credit and investing their money that they anointed more bankers than kings or emperors, permanently establishing the financier on his still-unshaken throne as partner of the heads of governments. However, from the time when Sir Francis Walsingham engaged the Lombards to delay the victualing of the Spanish Armada, we have seen the secret service conniving with bankers. In order to avoid being used in matters contrary to their private interests, the great banking families, from medieval down to modern times, prospered according to the speed and accuracy of their systems of espionage and intelligence.

The Medici, the Fuggers, the brothers Rothschild, all recognized the need to excel in secret service. If their spies were as well organized and managed as some private department of state, they resembled in their business activity the exchequer of an imperial state. Transactions involving millions in gold, in human lives, unseating dynasties and obliterating frontiers! Even overcoming distances in an age of indistinguishable roads and imaginative maps, their couriers had to be as swift and daring as their spies were alert and conscienceless.

Of the twists and turns of nineteenth-century speculative expansion we have here no space to tell. Spies were employed upon it; numbers of them traveled continually back and forth, crossing oceans and continents, meeting, watching, dodging, or denouncing other agents and private emissaries.[3] Ministers were said to have fallen when they had merely been found out. Mergers, monopolies, concessions, bankruptcies followed the flags of empire. Wars were fought over markets or sources of basic supply, only to have them captured from the sidelines by some disengaged neutral. And through all the intrigues and moral oscillations of politics and the "profit motive", credit has religiously stiffened or relaxed, like a corpse demonstrating the influences of rigor mortis. Substitutes for the Medici and Fugger banks have been found; but no substitutes for the spies or for the power of money.

Outlaw Masters of Counter-Police

Criminals with a marked talent for espionage seldom have met with notorious success in crime. It is not even true that criminals spy more cleverly than policemen. In most lawless regions it has been *easier* to keep watch upon the police than to keep an eye on the furtive practices of the criminally inclined; and it is on this account that our record may not fairly pass over the private intelligence or "counter-police" systems which have been developed in all quarters of the world to assist the depredations of the most dangerous outlaws.

Among these there seems to have been only one, Belle Starr, who personally served a kind of criminal apprenticeship in the role of spy. Belle, as a child of the border country, spied with enthusiasm for Quantrell and his guerrillas when her brother enlisted in that unspeakable battalion during the American Civil War. However, the criminal exploits of Belle Starr—which endeared her to Signor Lombroso as the "petticoated terror of the plains"—came some years later, were notorious for their recklessness, and showed little trace of early experiences in an outlaw branch of Confederate secret service.

Looking backward, but only to the formidable adventures of Dominique Cartouche, we discover secret service devoted to criminal pursuits and criminals organized into an army—a veritable bandit brigade, having every military distinction including discipline, and every weapon except artillery. Cartouche "the unconquerable" possessed such great qualities of leadership, it was the misfortune of France that it had no means of transferring him from the command of the underworld to the command of its armies. His name, however, is synonymous only with successful crime exploited on a grand scale.

In October of 1693 a saddler named François Louis Cartouche, residing in the Rue Pont aux Choux in Paris, registered the birth of a son, Louis Dominique. After the execution of this son the saddler confessed that a nobleman and dignitary of the Church had brought him the outlaw chieftain as a babe and had paid him large sums of money to rear the child and keep him unaware of his true parentage. Since Dominique grew up to be wholly unlike his insignificant "father" and brothers, there is much that seems to endorse the saddler's confession; for the outlaw evinced nearly all those qualities of reckless courage, wit, arrogant leadership and rapacity then peculiar to the patrician classes of France.

Dominique at the age of fourteen was sent to a famous Jesuit school, where, it is said, young François Marie Arouet—as yet unrecognized as the immortal Voltaire—was also enrolled. The saddler's son was treated with brutal disdain by most of the other pupils; and his wandering life of adventure, which changed to an all but revolutionary campaign of lawlessness, is but one thing more we may attribute to the high-spirited French aristocracy and the "discipline" of the Jesuit fathers.⁴ Resenting the inequalities and suspicion he encountered at the school, Cartouche ran away to the conventional refuge of a troupe of strolling acrobats. He was a short, hardy and muscular youth, with a bright face of such exceeding innocence that his earliest followers dubbed him "The Child." Like other great captains of the bandit peerage he was both an athlete and a born actor. The facility with which he learned to change his appearance soon came to be the marvel of the underworld. Cartouche might emerge any day as a gay young noble of the regent's dissolute entourage; but the next he would be a soldier or abbé, and the day after a gambler, a broker elbowing the throng at the Bourse, or one of the wits idling at the recently "arrived" Café Procope.

This sort of impudent display was good advertising; for it was the plan of Cartouche to double and redouble—not his shares in John Law's bank or the "Mississippi bubble"—but his own audacious following, to make new and useful recruits continually. He wanted to have his agents spread out everywhere, so that they might gather information as spies or render aid as accomplices. It was his fertile idea, quite unique at the time, to "retain" honest men as informers and confederates without impairing their good repute or positions in the community, which made them of value to his organization. A number of the police thus came into his employ. The official at the door of the Royal Bank in Paris was an agent of the master criminal; while several of the clerks in that and other financial institutions were clandestine "Cartouchiens." At its greatest strength the band of Cartouche exceeded two thousand, a small army of specialists.[5] All were sworn to obey the chief's orders. He in turn never squandered his forces upon profitless or ill-considered, spectacular undertakings, and showed them repeatedly that he identified their interests with his own.

The numbers and devotedness of his comrades, his shrewd tactics and eagerness to be first in facing dangers, coupled with the outlaw's curiously "modern" appreciation of the value of accurate intelligence, explain the formidable power he accumulated. It was an extravagant age of the great god Financier—and made to order for any well-disciplined corporative kingdom of thieves. John Law's topless towers of company promotion in North America, in Senegal and far Cathay had excited the cupidity of the whole nation. Nobles and parvenus alike were spending their paper millions with the ostentatious ease of men who make money without earning it.

The fabulous furnishings, golden adornments and precious gems with which they celebrated Mr Law's democratically apportioned delusions of grandeur, became the abundant spoils of Cartouche and his band. Royal Archers, prison warders, high court officials could be heavily bribed and added to the outlaw's espionage and insurance system, just as millionaire cooks and lackeys were buying equipages more sumptuous than the regent's coach and four. Even noted surgeons, whose patients by day included the socially elect of Paris, were engaged to accompany Cartouche on his nocturnal raids, so that any wounded among his partisans might be attended with instant skill.

Such audacity and depredations threw the police into an ostrich posture from which they pretended there was no criminal at large named Cartouche, that the word was a label chosen by an evil association of robbers and thieves to intimidate honest folk. In reply Cartouche began making public appearances and deriding the authorities with imprudent regularity. He and one of his lieutenants, Poil de Feu, or Sanglade, with a few companions, would intrude upon some merry gathering. "I am Cartouche," he would explain, drawing a weapon, and either put the whole company to flight or detained them for a bout of systematic robbery. Again, he had twenty of his followers, dressed and made up to resemble him, appear in as many different quarters of Paris at the same hour.

The police seemed powerless to round up the real Cartouche and equally unable to cope with his robber army, now operating in units of fifty or more. Cartouche and his men had stolen plate from the palace, the jeweled sword hilt of the Prince Regent, and later made off with his great silver candlesticks, which exploit disturbed one of his many assignations.[6] Growing disgusted with the futility of the police, Gaston d'Orléans, the regent, called in the military authorities, gave them limitless powers, and posted a dazzling reward for the apprehension of the chief outlaw, dead or alive. Every garden wall and window in Paris was now protected with spikes and iron bars. A regiment of the royal guards was kept constantly under arms. While Cartouche was protected, however, by his own mobility and excellent spy system, the precautions of the government were of no avail.

If he had neglected counter-espionage, he was hardly different from his contemporaries in never having heard of it. His band had grown so numerous, it could not deny membership to every treacherous nature. And what military mobilization, agents in disguise, all the energies of the police and government had been incapable of contriving, a heavy bag of gold pieces at last accomplished. One of the Cartouchiens, a certain Duchatelet, was found to have his price; and the king of Parisian lawbreakers landed quite unexpectedly in the toils.[7] "You'll not hold me," he promised his captors; and many people, convinced of his magic, believed this boast. He had his spies in every prison, and he expected to be delivered from the foul dungeon where he was kept chained to the wall and unceasingly watched by four warders when not being examined or put to the torture.

Cartouche endured all the awesome judicial agonies, including a great agony of mind as it became clear to him that his formerly obedient followers were now leaving him to his fate. He once nearly effected his own escape and was removed forthwith to the practically impregnable Conciergerie. At length, after the executioners had exhausted their maiming arts, Cartouche was brought to the Place de la Grêve, where an immense crowd assembled to see him broken upon the wheel. It is said that he still anticipated rescue; but when he saw no movement in the throng, he abandoned his resolute silence and confessed, naked and wrapped in a cloak, there beside the engine of execution, dictating an account of his crimes and accomplices that "filled thirty-six sheets of paper closely written."[8]

Before he perished horribly, details of soldiers and police were swarming over Paris to rake in the rogues he had implicated. Nearly four hundred arrests were made; and soon both the scaffold and gallows had long waiting lists. The confession of Cartouche, vindictively incriminating those he despised for deserting him, as well as other admissions dragged from his principal accessories, disclosed the secret of the outlaw's comprehensive spy system. More than half the tradesmen of Paris had been receiving stolen goods; some of them, to be sure, unwillingly, for Cartouche had luxurious tastes and generally had insisted on settling his debts by payment in kind. Most of the city's tavern keepers were likewise exposed as agents or informers affiliated with the secret-intelligence service that Cartouche had made peculiarly his own.

Other Secret Services of Organized Crime

We must travel far, both in miles and in years, to get from Paris of the Regency and the minority of Louis XV to New South Wales and the "Kelly country" about 1870, for the notorious Ned Kelly and his gang were protected by an improvised system of spies, scouts and informers which seems to have been only second to the "secret service" of Cartouche in helping to resist the forces of the law.

The Kellys, who were so confident of their individual prowess that they never sought the thousands of active followers the French outlaw dictator had prized, gained absolute supremacy over an area of 11,000 square miles. Ned Kelly and his brother, Dan, with their chief lieutenants, Steve Hart and Joe Byrne, used scores of friends and sympathizers in that huge tract to keep them regularly acquainted with the movements of the police as well as to give them timely notice of gold shipments, heavy bank deposits, or other portable treasures. And those inhabitants who did not covertly assist the bushrangers were afraid to give information against them, because the Kellys could count upon more supporters than could the officers of the crown. Large rewards were posted, inviting betrayal of the outlaws. There had formerly been no more than fifty constables on duty in the whole area of the Kelly country; but after the Wombat encounter, when the bushrangers shot and killed Sergeant Kennedy and two of his three men, strong reinforcements were mobilized by the colonial authorities.

The celebrated Australian black trackers were added to the secret agents of the police who sought to undermine the stronghold of these desperadoes in that northeastern triangle of New South Wales. A number of the Kellys' friends were arrested; but there was little to be learned from them and no evidence against them, and so they were released. When the total amount of the rewards offered climbed to £4,000 a former Kelly confederate, Aaron Sherritt, was moved to reveal that Ned Kelly and his comrades planned a raid upon the bank at Jerilderie on the Billabong, between Wagga Wagga and Deniliquin. The bushrangers, however, completed this crime and rode off with their spoils before the authorities could assemble forces strong enough to prevent them from crossing the Murray. It appears that the Kelly brothers with Hart and Joe Byrne, advised by their superior intelligence service, were accounted the equal of at least a hundred policemen.

Old Mrs Byrne, mother of the reckless Joe, was also one of the most persistent of the outlaws' spies. She discovered constables hiding in Sherritt's hut and hastened to warn the bushrangers of their former ally's treachery. Whereupon Dan Kelly and Byrne had an accomplice draw Sherritt from his hut at night by a ruse and shot and killed him, with the four constables assigned to safeguard the betrayer only a few yards distant. Excitement in the colony was intensified by this outrage and by many another—such as the bushrangers' capture of Euroa, a town less than a hundred miles from Melbourne, where they cleaned out the local bank adjoining a police station.[9]

It remains to be noted that the very excellence of Kelly espionage led finally to Kelly extermination, inasmuch as the reports of their spies provoked the bushrangers to one of the most extravagantly evil and rash attempts in the annals of crime and killing. The Kellys learned that all the available strength of the police was to be sent up against them, that a special train would be dispatched to Beechworth, near which place—as the authorities had learned from *their* spies—the bushrangers were now secretly established. The train was to be rushed up on Sunday, when there was no ordinary traffic; and the outlaws prepared to wreck it by tearing up the rails at a point near Glenrowan where there was a cutting with a long downward slope over which the train must go. Constables, detectives and black trackers would thus "be swept away wholesale at one fell stroke." If any of them escaped, they were to be shot down as they crawled from the debris of the train. The Kellys then proposed to pillage Benalla and other neighboring townships before a new contingent of police could be raised, gather up all the plunder they could manage, and leave the country.

The outlaws expected by striking such a foul blow to terrify all Australia. The scheme—as something conceived and to be carried out by only four criminals—was Napoleonic; but luck no longer favored them, and their last homicidal designs produced a murderous recoil. Bold in executing their well-plotted campaigns and uniquely served by their spies, the Kellys were quite without parallel among underworld champions in that they had fashioned for themselves "veritable armor that was bullet-proof, made of old ploughshares, iron pots and scrap iron." The self-appointed destroyers of Australian peace and police fell upon the community of Glenrowan on Saturday evening, captured the local hotel near the railroad line, and used it as a prison structure, into which they swept all the inhabitants of the district.

One of these prisoners was a grave and ingenious man, the local schoolmaster, Curnow, with ideas of his own about secret service. He ingratiated himself with the bushrangers, who spent hours "in jollification, joining their prisoners, with whom they were on excellent terms, in sports and games, drinking and playing cards to while away the time till midnight"[10] when the police train was expected to reach Glenrowan and be wrecked. Curnow persuaded one of the Kellys to release him just at midnight and then hastened to find a lantern and a red cloak. The train was two hours late; and Curnow succeeded in planting his danger signal some distance ahead of the long stretch of broken track—which the bushrangers that morning had forced two railway laborers to demolish under threat of instant death.

The police special, and a second train bearing more reinforcements, were stopped just in time. In the ensuing "battle of Glenrowan" the armored bushrangers, despite the odds against them, stood siege for hours. Little skill or judgment was displayed by the commanders of the constabulary, and in the first volley their chief, Superintendent Hare, was badly wounded. Several of the outlaws' prisoners locked in the hotel were hurt by the "wild and indiscriminate" rifle fire of the police. Hare's lieutenants telegraphed to Melbourne for artillery; but such an engagement could only have one outcome, and it ended before the train bringing a field gun, with gunners and munitions, arrived. Byrne had been slain early in the combat. Dan Kelly and Hart gave up only by committing suicide. The noncombatant prisoners finally escaped from the hotel; and Ned Kelly, though painfully wounded, nearly got away on horseback. Being overtaken, he saw his reign was over; and later he went to the gallows "with undeniable courage and seeming repentance."

Other bandit barons have given lessons to governments in their own improvisations of espionage and intelligence corps. Corsican outlaws—Romanetti, Spada and their many predecessors as monarchs of the *maquis*—had almost the entire island populace to spy for them upon the gendarmes and the well to do. We find that espionage, in the best Oriental tradition of far-reaching stealth, favored the evil fortunes of Raga, the Malay "Prince of Pirates", who for seventeen years dominated the Straits of Macassa, between Borneo and the Celebes. This maritime public enemy, "remarkable for his cunning, intelligence and barbarity, the extent and daring of his enterprises, and his disregard for human life . . . had his spies everywhere,"[11] and lived up to his oath to take no European prisoners. He relished striking off the heads of captured ships' captains with his own sword; but after some of his pirates had surprised and massacred most of the crew of the Salem schooner Friendship, the United States government sent Commodore Downes in the frigate Potomac to carry on the tradition of Preble and Decatur; and Prince Raga and his thieving lieges were obliterated by a savage attack in which the Americans took the Malayan forts by storm.

It is probable that nearly all piratical organizations founded their solvency upon a masterly use of information bought from spies. Lilius, the journalist, who investigated at considerable hazard the hereditary pirate powers of the China seas and Bias Bay, even found secret agents of the pirate queen, Lai Choi San—*The Mountain of Wealth*—inside of the Victoria Jail, Hongkong.[12] But from that contemporary ingenuity we had best turn back once more to the most significant events of the latter half of the nineteenth century. A famous European journalist—who brilliantly represents his profession in these annals of secret service—stands waiting in the wings, ready to re-enact his public-spirited duplicities.

CHAPTER FORTY-NINE

DE BLOWITZ AT BERLIN

THE CONGRESS OF BERLIN in 1878 was an austere affair which accomplished even more than its sponsors set out to do, canceling for Russia the results of the victorious war upon Turkey but also managing to scramble the political situation in southeastern Europe so as to threaten chronically the peace of the whole Continent. While the *tuchans* of statecraft conferred and intrigued, Stieber and his spies and informers circled about the gathering. And all the other great Powers were represented more or less secretly by agents of their Intelligence departments. It remained, however, for a comparative outsider to score the secret-service coup of the Congress, and, in fact, one of the finest practical demonstrations of secret-intelligence technique of the nineteenth century.

Wilhelm Johann Carl Eduard Stieber in behalf of Prince Bismarck had proved his mastery over France, Austria and other adversaries. But Henri Georges Stephan Adolphe Opper de Blowitz was to prove his mastery over them all, including Stieber and his Iron Chancellor. Representative of the *Times* of London, Henri de Blowitz was already nominated by many as the greatest newspaper correspondent of the age.[1] And it was the heroic age of newspaper correspondence, with government propaganda still being served as hors d'oeuvres, not a ten-course dinner. De Blowitz, therefore, attended the Congress with the polite resolve to turn it inside out and show it to his readers.

The Congress of Berlin, primarily designed to checkmate Russia, was meant to be a most mysterious affair. The weight of practice in high politics always inclines toward the arriving at judgments and conclusions *in camera*. Bismarck proposed to alter the map of Europe, affecting the lives of millions of its people, privately; and to that end he ordered Stieber to stand by and then proceeded to swear those in attendance at the Congress to complete secrecy at its opening session.

There was to be no impeding of the acts and decisions of the assembled statesmen by ill-timed criticism or suggestions from mere bystanders whose fate had yet to be determined. And there was to be no interference with the fermentations of diplomatic intrigue by public debate of methods and aims before those methods had resulted in, and the aims had been realized in, the treaty product of the Congress.

All of which hermetical planning omitted a single calculation—De Blowitz. In one of the most influential exploits of journalistic history the correspondent of "The Thunderer" proceeded to send his paper authentic accounts of the day by day deliberations of the Congress. And then, to cap his remarkable series of newspaper "beats", he enabled the *Times* to publish the text of the Treaty of Berlin at the very hour it was being signed in Berlin.

This not only outmaneuvered Prince Bismarck, but—as nobody appears to have observed at the time—it completely unstiebered Stieber. And yet, though it is fitting and proper to include this master coup of the always masterly Mr de Blowitz in the annals of secret service, it must be added in fairness to him that his secrecy was secondary or even tertiary, that he was denied many of the subtleties and protective colorations of the professional spy. Any correspondent of so famous and respected a paper as Mr Delane's was a marked man; and De Blowitz arrived in Berlin to report the cloistered sessions of the Congress with a reputation of the highest order. Yet his being such a celebrity, and precursor of the X-ray, availed him nothing at the start, when he began his usual procedure for breaking through the "whisper proof" reserve of the assembled negotiators. There was that agreement and pledge to keep the proceedings veiled with Mohammedan caution. Delegates either would not talk because they mistrusted Henri de Blowitz, or they wanted to favor him but were even more intimidated by the German chancellor.

The correspondent, however, had the cards stacked against furtive diplomacy from the beginning, having managed to get a friend and confederate connected with the Congress as an attaché. By means of this friend he was able to obtain the articles adopted and other concise information after each daily session; and armed with such leading facts the correspondent managed his ensuing interviews so as to bring out fairly complete accounts of the progress of the deliberations.

The Hat Trick

In order to throw a disgruntled Bismarck and his agents off the scent, De Blowitz made use of a simple stratagem. He and his accomplice never exchanged documents, never met, never appeared to be acquainted; nor were papers meant for De Blowitz ever delivered to any chosen point or waiting intermediary. The two merely happened to dine each day at the same restaurant. Both wore hats of the same pattern and approximate size, and on leaving they exchanged hats. Reports of the session of the day were concealed in the friend's hatband.

The capable reporting or professional wizardry of Henri de Blowitz was displayed in giving to the public against all odds the details of their business as transacted by their diplomatists, destined to serve more than idle curiosity or legitimate interest. He helped in one memorable instance to make a success of the Congress itself and to prevent great speculative losses.

On the morning of June 22, 1878, the *Times* was able to publish the agreement effected the previous night between Great Britain and Russia regarding the Bulgarian question. That question had raised such majestic difficulties that the sittings of the Congress had been suspended, and Mr Disraeli, either from adroitness or in all sincerity, had engaged a special train for Monday, the twenty-fourth, to leave Berlin.

It would have been a disastrous rupture; the whole Continent anxiously waited for news; and the strategist of the *Times* did not fail his vast public. The agreement was reached at midnight on Friday, the twenty-first, and became known in London at six o'clock the next morning, and in the rest of Europe at eight or nine. If De Blowitz had not been able to telegraph his editor as he did, Saturday's stock exchange maneuvers would have brought on a virtual panic. Many people would have been ruined. But the speed with which he dredged up the deepest secrets of Berlin and flashed them to London made stock exchange manipulations impracticable.

The famous journalist is said to have gained many enemies among those gentry who were gambling upon an Anglo-Russian break. All of which was but a prelude to the crowning triumph of his career, a career that seems to have been mainly devoted to beating diplomatists at their own game.

The Congress was soon to adjourn, and De Blowitz, who had never meant to do less, secured and published the Treaty of Berlin hours before that document was to have been benevolently exposed to public view.

"If I were asked to choose between all the orders and decorations in the world and the treaty I should select the latter," he told a delegate.[2]

"And how are you going to get it?"

"I have just had an assurance that Prince Bismarck is highly satisfied with what I wrote on our last conversation. He thinks I have rendered a service to peace. I am going to ask him to reward me by communicating the treaty to me."

The friendly delegate reflected on this probability for a moment, then he said: "No—do not ask him until you have seen me again. Walk out tomorrow between one and two in the Wilhelmstrasse, and I will see you."

Next day this delegate came up to De Blowitz and said hurriedly: "Come for the treaty the day before the end of the congress. I promise that you shall have it."

He kept his word. With consummate craft De Blowitz had seemed to persist in appealing to Bismarck for an early copy of the treaty; and, on the grounds that such a favor would enrage the press of Germany, he had been refused. He thus was able to assure himself that the treaty would not be given out in advance to anyone else.

With everything except the preamble of the treaty in his possession the evening before the end of the Congress, De Blowitz induced another of his friends among the delegates to read him the preamble which had just been drafted. This he memorized in the course of the one reading.

He had already announced that he was going to leave Berlin without waiting for the assemblage of statesmen to adjourn, professing great resentment because the German chancellor had denied him an advance copy of the treaty. To disarm the suspicions of his fellow correspondents, he showed them the prince's letter of refusal; and so his abrupt and unseemly departure was ascribed to pique.

The complete text of the still "secret" treaty was flowing from the presses of the *Times* in London, as De Blowitz triumphantly crossed the German frontier. Prince Bismarck might growl and storm[3] and Stieber's agents whisper their multiple suspicions of the delegate-betrayer—who, however, was never identified. Henri de Blowitz had completed his brilliant task of secret-service reporting by turning this last dramatic coup.

CHAPTER FIFTY

THE *OCHRANA*

OF RUSSIAN Intelligence and espionage there has been little to tell. The tsars' military secret services in war or in peace were fabulously expensive, and in most wars an equally fabulous failure. The average Russian in order to do himself justice had to be paid to spy upon other Russians.[1]

This is easier to prove than to explain; but if there is any non-psychological reason for it, perhaps the antique "practice makes perfect" offers a solution. The practice of internal espionage never reached perfection in tsarist Russia but did attain its maximum recorded growth. From the nightmare reign of Tsar Ivan the Terrible and his *Opritchina,* the people of Russia endured some concentrate or other of political police, its surveillance, provocations and despotic travesties of legal procedure. No one, living or dead, may be quoted to tell us what Russia was like without such espionage, for it was endemic in Muscovy, and the only sovereign who tried getting along without it—Tsar Alexander II—sought immediate refuge in declaring the greater part of his realm in an abnormal state, which amounted to martial law.

Other mitigations were attempted but always in some typically Russian form, experimental and transitory. Liberalism of the nineteenth century was coming down the decades a painful step at a time, and elsewhere the secret-police services were limiting themselves to keeping suspects under observation. But the Russian system, also bent on progress, moved in a diametrically opposite direction, taking over the punishment of accused persons by administrative process. Thus the tsarist government preserved in judicial proceedings that secrecy which all other reactionary rulers had long ago restricted to the service of surveillance.

With Oscar Wilde, who wondered of London whether the fogs caused the people or the people caused the fogs, one may ask if there was something so rebellious and sinister in the Russian nature that it required all that special police supervision, or something so secretive and domineering, it best expressed itself in the espionage and repressions of political police? Agents, informers and spies numbering into the thousands were a conventional segment of the population. Perhaps they were avaricious, cruel or corrupt, but they were not sterile. And after centuries there must have been, by 1900, a substantial percentage of all the tsar's subjects above the peasant-artisan class who either belonged to the police service, or had formerly done so, or who were related to or descended from officials, gendarmes, agents and spies. A kind of hereditary clan of vicarious autocracy!

Two Russian witnesses of great distinction may be called to give testimony.

"To whatever party Russians may belong, in their cruelty they are all alike." And Maxim Gorky adds to that trenchant opinion his further belief that cruelty is as obviously "the most prominent feature of the Russian national character" as humor is of the English character.

Cruel, domineering, oppressive—and secret!

Hear as second witness the historian, Michael Pokrovsky:

> The proceedings of the court were strictly secret. Not only did they take place behind closed doors, but in the hall of justice there was neither defending counsel nor accused present. Only documentary evidence was placed before the judges, and on the strength of that the sentence was pronounced. Not judicial proceedings only were secret; the whole organization of the state was secret. All sittings of the higher authorities were held *in camera;* the most important ones were especially secret. Almost every official paper was marked "secret"; in the Foreign Office there were no documents at all that were not secret. If they wanted to indicate that something was really to be kept secret, it was marked "very secret," because the word "secret" by itself had lost all meaning.[2]

Under such conditions, with this ideal and ritual of privacy in government, to have had any powerful division of the police which was not *secret* police would have been unbearable.

Oh, Dry Those Tears

The Tsar Alexander I had been, according to the standards of his time and certainly by intention, a civilized, humane citizen of the world and enlightened despot. He was followed, as so often happened in the alternating current of the Romanoff-Oldenburg dynasty, by the tyrant, Nicholas I, whose mind was medieval and whose hand held the throttle perpetually in reverse. Nicholas looked upon tyranny as a religion rather than a sport and seems to have preferred it to warmaking, horse racing, or the explorations of the boudoir.[3]

This monarch of all and much more than one man could have surveyed in a long lifetime never would delegate authority if he could help it. Yet he had inherited absolute authority over an empire too vast to be controlled by an individual who fell perceptibly short of omnipotence. Nicholas therefore achieved "the most truly Russian creation by endowing cruelty with definite form,"[4] in founding the Special Corps of Gendarmerie, a merciless mechanism to govern by intimidation the whole of tsardom.

Count Benckendorff was appointed the first commander of this force, and with due ceremonial he came to bow before Nicholas and beg a few words of explicit instruction disguised as advice. The tsar made no formal reply but pulled out a white handkerchief, handed it to Benckendorff, and, with a flair for the majestic and the banishment of reality as well as revolutionaries, commanded:

"Dry the tears of the oppressed. May your conscience and the conscience of your subordinates ever remain as stainless as this linen!"

Whereupon the count began making sure of a regular output of oppressed together with the stipulated freshet of tears. And as a special touch of his own he brought on some of the worst trembling attacks of the nineteenth century. Everybody feared the attentions of the gendarmerie; and not only private citizens but every other official of the Russian government stood in dread of Benckendorff.

Benckendorff would probably have been satisfied to do no more than inspire the dread and trembling. It was Nicholas who wanted the more reluctant tremblers *hurt*, who wanted to *hear* knees knocking together and catch the timid whisperings from closets or under beds. Thus came about the formation of the bureau of private police espionage, the terrible "Third Section" of the tsar's Court Chancery.

Its chiefs were empowered to decide at their own discretion the fate of every Russian subject. Thenceforth any resident of Russia might have a police agent drop in on him and intimate that, for the good of the state and the preservation of his health, he must leave "within three hours" for Archangel or Akatuisk. Such a decree, if once issued by the "Third Section", admitted of no protest, legal defense or process of appeal.

"The Liberator"

At the very outset of the reign of Nicholas I there had occurred the insurrection of the aristocratic military conspirators known as the *Dekabristi*. Being imbued with ideas fathered by the French and American revolutions, and, to a great degree, imported into Russia by Tsar Alexander I, they sought to force concessions from the new sovereign. But there were to be no concessions for thirty-one years, or until a second Alexander ascended the throne. The rebellion was swiftly and harshly suppressed in December, 1825; the ringleaders were hanged, and over a hundred of their followers, officers and young men of good family, exiled to Siberia.

The reign of Alexander II began far more agreeably; yet never was the dubious prophetic adage about a good beginning's promise of a bad ending to be so clearly established in fact. The new tsar would not believe that severity alone paid dividends of obedience and a long life to the rulers of Russia. He restored many privileges and emptied many prisons. The story goes that when, on his thirty-ninth birthday —in April 1857—he looked about for more victims of his predecessor's "Third Section", to order them released, there was nobody confined in the dreaded Troubyetskoi Bastion of the Fortress of St Peter and Paul.[5]

Famous as "the Liberator" of the serfs, Alexander also sincerely endeavored to be the liquidator of the tsarist political police. He favored a lenient police system; and as the pendulum of autocracy swung gradually leftward from the extreme right where Nicholas I kept it shackled, official heads went rolling off in a thoroughly Muscovite manner. General Dubbelt, the pet of Nicholas and most despised of his espionage tools, was obliged to abandon a career which made an art of sinister repression and yet had done no little to enable Nicholas to die a natural death.

A diligent informer handed in a report of an insolent comment he had heard at the St Petersburg Chess Club when some player's king was in jeopardy; whereupon Alexander threw the paper in the wastebasket and tossed the spy twenty-five roubles, adding: "You are dismissed the service."

He was ever disposed to profit from the example of his predecessor, who, in the opinion of many, had been submerged by his own creations of secret police and gendarmerie. Benckendorff, whom Nicholas had made chief of one and commanding officer of the other, had come gradually to wield in these twin capacities the more widespread and absolute governing power. Alexander, on his part, disapproved of subterranean compulsions and made serious attempts to introduce into the empire modern forms of Western judicial procedure. His zeal caused an edict to be published requiring all legal proceedings to be held in public. He substituted the oral method of conducting a case for the old bureaucratic paradise of working with documents only; and for grave criminal offenses he even initiated trial by jury, as novel to a land of Asiatic cast as it was characteristic of Britain or America.

Political offenders were, however, excluded from the jury courts, and public attendance at trials of revolutionaries remained within the discretion of the judge and prosecutor. Alexander's unaffected instinct for liberalism came into violent collision with the strongest elements of the tsardom, but especially with the solid front of the Russian official classes, which, for a generation, had been the instruments of Nicholas' pitiless tyranny. It was, however, the insurgent patriots of Poland, who preferred any sort of Polish government to the best Russian brand imaginable, that did the most in convincing the liberal tsar of his permanent need for spies and strong bodies of police. With fanatic venom the revolutionaries hunted the tsar, planning trap after trap, and in the end they were successful and killed him with a second bomb as he left his carriage courageously to see to the injuries of members of his Cossack escort who had been wounded by the first explosion. The new tsar had no taste for bombs, and the first measures he instituted for his own protection related to the imperial police organizations. Thus the notorious *Ochrana* or secret police came into being, perhaps the most typically Russian, the most costly and ponderously inefficient political secret service that ever stirred up hatred and promoted dread.

Having experienced its rigors and made sport of its clumsiness, the Bolshevist rulers of Russia, after climbing into the saddle, whimsically exposed many archives of the *Ochrana* to public ridicule and review. Any prolonged investigation of the *Ochrana* will largely confirm an early impression that it was something imagined first by Lewis Carroll. The Russian secret police could be savage and formidable enough; but the general tone of the organization was destructive rather than deceptive, and since it ended by destroying itself and all it was designed to preserve, the total effect is ludicrous.

Despite heroic labors of expenditure, expansion and repression, the *Ochrana* never learned to apply more than two methods of protecting the tsar, members of the Romanoff family, or officials of the government—those perpetual clay pigeons of the revolutionary assassin fraternities. Agents of the *Ochrana* followed and recorded the hourly movements of every Russian, regardless of class, who had any degree of intelligence or mobility. And by a very rigid enforcement of passport regulations they kept track of travelers as perfectly as of those who remained at home. The second method was founded upon a childlike faith in the dependability of the average *agent provocateur;*

and it is the abject betrayal of that faith—or bureaucratic delusion—which we shall discover in the chapter following.

It is well before exploring the depths of police provocation to see how the "shadowing" methods of the *Ochrana* were made to count. The great Leo Tolstoy visited St Petersburg in 1897 and was dogged by spies of the *Ochrana* from the moment he left his train. In published reports we observe that only one condescended to describe him as the "well-known writer"; to another of his shadows he was "Retired Lieutenant Leo Nikolaievitch Tolstoy." One of the greatest of then living artists and a ponderable spiritual force in Russia and the rest of Europe, to the political secret service he was only a "lieutenant" whose file card at the war ministry had been marked "retired." Tolstoy at this time was also the best-known man in the empire, but the welcoming report—that which begins with his leaving the railroad carriage—minutely described his costume, even his hat, and took note of the color of his hair. No disguises the great man might elect were going to fool the *Ochrana!*

As a final eccentricity of those trained to safeguard the foundation stones of Russian imperialism, the police reports record the hour and minute Tolstoy entered a shop, purchased tobacco, remark how much he paid, and when he resumed his stroll—follow him to a restaurant, take account of his menu for luncheon, how long he remained at table, and what his meal cost him. And yet that sort of apprehensive tedium was not strictly Russian, but universally *political police*. Archives of the secret service in Vienna, not long ago made available to scholars, show that matter concerning Louis Kossuth, the celebrated Hungarian patriot of the nineteenth century, was regularly filed under the heading: "Criminals."

However, to know the administrative marvels of the tsarist *Ochrana* we must not be diffident about meeting *provocateur* spies. Nothing exposes the soul of that vast surveillant and repressive police organism more thoroughly than the intrigues and exposure of its most incredible prize. His name was Azeff, and he has also been called "the Russian Judas"; but, perhaps, as we trace his career in revolutionary circles as an *Ochrana* agent we may decide even Judas can be libeled.

CHAPTER FIFTY-ONE

AGENT PROVOCATEUR

THE *OCHRANA* might have had additional thousands of spies and informers on its payroll, it might have suspected everyone rather than almost everyone and had them all shadowed, with the shadows of shadows and *their* shadows streaming off like a chain gang to the farthest horizon of secret-police punctilio. Even so, there would have been no marked significance attached to the tsarist organization, and its notice here would be merely for stolid, methodical inquisitiveness and ludicrous excess. The *Ochrana* chiefs, however, were courtiers and bureaucrats before they were guardian detectives. They were ambitious men whose duties brought them close to the throne and whose careers depended less upon the order and tranquillity of the empire than upon the good will or whim of an absolute monarch. Their principal opponents, liberals, revolutionaries and Nihilists, were violent and aggressive, but at best sporadically active. If the times were quiet, the police service was presumably in full control—but promotions were few, the careers languished. Terrorist conspiracies and radical disturbances were what the vast espionage works needed to keep that single majority stockholder aware of his faithful foremen and glad to reward their labors. Therefore the fomenting of turbulence and the meanest practices of detection were harnessed in tandem by subsidizing that most odious of sneaking scavengers, the *agent provocateur*.

Azeff was the provocative spy to whom the enduring reputation of the *Ochrana* owes its deeper shades of infamy. There were many *agents provocateurs;* their employment was—and is—standard political police and labor espionage technique; but Azeff was provocative with a difference.[1] His revolutionary plotting had satanic gifts of leadership about it. Plots which he devised and directed came off. His spying and secret denunciations scarcely congested Russia's prisons, but the bombs of his terrorist confederates began rocking the Romanoffs.

At first the Russian police supported him, and he preyed upon his fellow revolutionaries. But, proving himself a man of action in the company of debaters and dreamers, he was soon thought so necessary to the "Battle Organization" of the social revolutionary cause that its substantial funds were given into his keeping. He still took the pay of the *Ochrana* and submitted regular reports as an agent. The people he now denounced, however, were of little consequence, while the assassinations he managed were able to extinguish—among others—the tsar's most influential uncle. That, one may hazard, will never be surpassed by any *provocateur* in practice or unborn, Olympian or Plutonian.

Azeff was born in 1869 in the district town of Lyskovo, in the Grodnensky province, the son of a poverty-stricken tailor, Fischel Azeff. He was the second child of a large family—three boys and four girls—and he seems to have known in his childhood and youth that grinding poverty of the slums which in all lands produces misers and criminals, drudges, derelicts and an occasional multimillionaire. And any number of stool pigeons and police informers also, but few even approaching the caliber of Azeff. Those who could, endeavored to escape from the "confines" imposed upon the Jews by the Russian government at that time; and when young Azeff was five years old his father did, indeed, break away in an earnest effort to improve the family fortunes.

The Azeffs settled down in Rostov-on-the-Don, then rapidly developing as a center of industry and commerce in southeastern Russia. Rich in wheat and coal, the region was experiencing that commonplace American necessity, a boom; and the more enterprising flocked to a place where capital was easily found by anyone sufficiently resourceful or unscrupulous. Fischel Azeff seems to have had scarcely a particle of the character which bitter need rather than heredity must have transmitted to his son. He went in for trade and opened a drapery shop but in a flourishing speculative atmosphere was able to do no more than survive.[2]

Stringent domestic sacrifices gave all the Azeff children the opportunity of an education. The sons were sent to a gymnasium, where the future police spy finished his course about 1890; but beyond that schooling the parental resources could not extend. Azeff now had to turn his hand to many kinds of employment: he gave lessons, he was a reporter on an obscure local paper,[3] and held a clerical position in an office, before branching out in the more opulent capacity of commercial traveler.

He appears to have still been very dissatisfied with the meager life permitted by his income. Acquaintances he had made among the revolutionary-minded youth at the gymnasium, coupled with his genuine thirst for knowledge, convinced him that Rostov, though a thriving, flashy town, was not a big enough world for him. The local gospel of quick and easy profits had, however, profoundly influenced his character; since greed and unscrupulousness became the very foundation stones of what may be euphemistically described as his life ambition.

At the beginning of 1892 suspicion fell upon him as one involved in distributing a treasonable manifesto. A number of his school friends were already in custody; and Azeff seems to have guessed—and guessed rightly, the archives of the police confirm it—that his own arrest was being considered. That was the finish for him at Rostov. He anxiously resolved to go abroad, was wholly without funds for the enterprise, but by an easy snapping of moral fiber took care of that basic deficiency. As a salesman he had received a consignment of butter from a merchant. This he sold for eight hundred roubles, and at once was on his way. May of 1892 found the young absconder in Karlsruhe, Germany, enrolled at the Polytechnic.

A number of Russian students were attending this school, among them many of Azeff's Rostov acquaintances. He eagerly joined the Social Democratic circle while taking up the study of electrostatics. But very soon his old bugaboo of financial distress was hampering his work and vanquishing all other interests. The eight hundred roubles, however husbanded, had gradually melted away. He gave those he met the impression that he was suffering painfully from hunger and cold.

A Fifty-Rouble Informer

On April 4, 1893, he sat down and wrote his first letter to the *Ochrana*, offering to sell his comrades' secrets and spy upon their revolutionary activities.[4] This step which was certainly not unavoidable, since other poor students found honest ways to subsist, must have seemed a peremptory necessity at the time. It was going to put him in possession of more money than the best technical education would ever permit him to earn, and it was going to make him so notorious that, as long as there are studies of abnormal behavior, government intrigue, police espionage or plain perfidy, his name will live.

Not until May 16 was a reply sent, and that a very typical one, hesitant, evasive and disingenuous.

"We know of the Karlsruhe group"—though actually the *Ochrana* scarcely knew anything about it and had only made some inquiries after receiving Azeff's offer—"and we are not very interested in it;

therefore you are not of a such great value to us; nevertheless, we are prepared to pay you—on condition, however, that you reveal your name, for we have strict principles and will have no dealings with certain people."³

Azeff replied at once, the wage he demanded being "delightfully low" at fifty roubles a month. Yet he still felt reluctant to give his right name, lest revolutionary agents should somehow intercept his letters and expose his attempt before it profited him anything. Even so, the *Ochrana* was at least clever enough not to be baffled by a novice. Simultaneously with the student's offer to the political police he had addressed a letter in almost identical terms to the Rostov gendarmerie. And by means of this he was identified before his second message reached the police department. Comparatively few Rostov people were living in Karlsruhe, and their names were known. It was a simple matter to trace the author of the letter by the handwriting.

Shifty as it made him out to be, the report upon Azeff forwarded from Rostov said nothing to affect the "strict principles" of the *Ochrana*. Indeed, the student's personal character seemed precisely what the secret police required in a higher-educational informer:

Ievno Azeff is intelligent and a clever intriguer; he is in close touch with the young Jewish students living abroad, and he could thus be of real use as an agent. It can also be assumed that his covetousness and his present state of need will make him zealous in his duty.

Rostov's hearty endorsement made the *Ochrana* eager to engage such a specialist. A few days after the receipt of Azeff's second letter, a special memorandum was prepared in which it was pointed out that he could be very "useful" to the state and that the price he asked was "moderate"; and on the tenth of June, 1893, no less a functionary than the assistant to the Russian minister of the interior set the seal of his approval on this memorandum. The most iniquitous and incalculable *agent provocateur* of secret-service history had been retained for the protection of the tsardom.

Azeff received his first salary in June of '93; but though his material condition had been recklessly remedied, he was too smart to begin spending his pieces of silver imprudently. His comrades had reason to know how hard it was to earn an honest mark locally, and they were aware of the financial straits of the Azeff family. Therefore, he had to remain ostensibly poverty stricken, but he began working on a solution he had already evolved, writing letters of eloquent appeal to every kind of charitable society or institution, particularly those designed for Jewish relief. And on the pretext of wishing his friends to correct his indifferent German, he showed them these letters. When his ceasing to starve came to be remarked, there would be gossip explaining his new source of income.

Police employment effected a much more apparent change in his revolutionary ideology. Arriving at Karlsruhe, he had been as "moderate" in his attitude as in his subsequent demands upon the *Ochrana*. He opposed extreme measures and tended to support the Marxists. But once in possession of his fifty-rouble stipend, he swung to the left and the very tip of extremism. By 1894 he had earned the respect of the dominant radicals by his logical advocacy of terrorist methods.

It was Azeff's shrewdest stroke to pose as a "man of action" in company overweighted with wishes, dreams and theories. He professed dislike of speeches but volunteered to undertake a variety of organizational errands. This cleverly enlarged his acquaintance; and as he gradually permitted himself to "have money", he managed a series of journeys into Switzerland, or to neighboring German towns, attending all the more important revolutionary gatherings and lectures.

The novice spy was in Zurich as soon after his police initiation as August, 1893, where he invaded not only the public meetings of the International Socialist Congress but also the private conferences of Russian representatives and émigrés. A safe investment, that truly moderate wage of the *Ochrana!* And in 1894 he arrived in Berne and made the acquaintance of the couple Zhitlovsky, founders of the incipient *Union of Russian Social Revolutionaries Abroad*. Since their organization was just starting to grow, the Zhitlovskys naturally welcomed recruits; and Azeff joined the *Union,* suspecting he might turn it to some account. It was to enable him to become one of the founders of the Social Revolutionary party!

At Berne he also met a young woman who was to influence his life profoundly, his future wife, then a student at the university. A sincere and convinced revolutionary, making her way alone with splendid ardor and self-denial, she saw in Azeff one who shared her aims and ideals. That he talked revolt and terrorism mainly to cover his connection with the tsarist secret police never occurred to her. It had, however, begun to occur to a number of sharp observers of the spy's meteoric radicalism. In Rostov he bore the reputation of being capable of anything which would result in his private gain. And his appearance in itself was neither fanatic nor reassuring. Heavily built, with a puffy, yellow, unprepossessing countenance, thick lips, a low forehead narrowing toward the top and a general aspect which repelled the sensitive, he was easy to suspect of any deceit or chicane. Yet when a student named Korobotchkin, having accumulated all the vague mistrust of Azeff to nourish his own physical distaste, publicly called him a spy, the general sympathy was lavished upon a zealous comrade "unjustly accused." Azeff's position was not even threatened; while Korobotchkin, having nothing with which to support his denunciation, was condemned and expelled from the student circle as a malicious slanderer.

This, the first of many such annihilations of the truth, could happen even though some comrades in Karlsruhe were discussing Azeff suspiciously soon after his first reports to the *Ochrana,* in June of 1893. News had then come from Rostov that the recent arrests there were thought to be the result of information sent to the gendarmerie from abroad. Azeff had seemed the most likely informer. Yet no one had troubled seriously to investigate him or the unformulated accusations; and the matter, subsiding into talk, had diminished steadily as the various students completed their courses and scattered. Truly the "man of action" at fifty roubles a month was a lion safe in devouring at his leisure the lambs of rhetoric, radical philosophy and honest idealism.

The Hundred-Rouble Terrorist

It is not surprising that Azeff, by the end of his university course, was solidly established in Russian student circles and accorded general respect. He now possessed a considerable library of unlawful publications, from which his comrades were permitted to borrow, on payment of a small subscription fee. He was acknowledged a hard worker, a subtle organizer, an upholder of the terror and a conspirator of mark. Generally the spy was elected chairman of student gatherings. He still persisted in refusing to address public meetings; but that uncommon elocutionary continence only lent great and sensational weight to his thoughts when he consented to unbosom a few of them.

The keen revolutionary publicist, Vladimir Burtzeff, who alone would eventually be able to expose the *agent provocateur,* recalls that when he published the first number of his *Narodovoletz* (The Freeman) advocating the assassination of the tsar, a letter from Azeff was the only sympathetic response which came from his readers. Contemporary accounts reveal the impression which Azeff produced on the youth of that period: "a leading personality"—"one outstanding in devotion to the Revolution and its ideals!"

He must have talked to them—when he talked—in the same spirit in which he now constantly wrote to his wife. His letters to her, according to one who has read them, were full of "the deep sorrow of a 'popular bard', and at the same time of the ardor of a fighter burning with the fire of idealism."[6]

And his reports to the *Ochrana* were equally successful.

The perfidious student of damnation and electrodynamics had long received a bonus every New Year's. But so regular and valuable were his reports covering revolutionary activities abroad, and their relation to sympathizers in Russia, that in 1899, as a reward for information supplied, his salary was doubled. Moreover, the strict principles of the secret police gave his sinister vocation a slightly religious touch by granting him, in addition to the hundred roubles a month, a bonus at Easter as well as at New Year's.

This promotion was nicely timed, for in 1899 he also received his diploma of electrical engineer at Darmstadt, whither he had gone from Karlsruhe to specialize in the subject. He seems to have expected to continue his espionage abroad and even secured himself an engineering post in the firm of Schukert of Nuremberg. The *Ochrana*, however, prepared to outbid that commonplace future. Revolutionary agitation was growing even faster than the repressive energy expended upon it, and there was a manifest demand for an agent of Azeff's character in Moscow.

He was promised the necessary influence to obtain a good position as an electrical engineer, likewise another increase of undercover income from the police. And so in the fall of that year he set out for Russia, bearing extraordinary introductions in duplicate. The Zhitlovskys warmly recommended the spy to all their friends and sympathizers; while the secret police were almost lyrical in presenting the terrorist to Zubatoff, celebrated chief of the Moscow *Ochrana*.

Zubatoff of the Secret Police

In Zubatoff the tsarist government had found a deadly opponent of the revolution; and Azeff found in him a director and collaborator with whom the ambitious, the appropriately covetous, agent could go far. Zubatoff himself had mixed in radical circles in his youth but soon had suffered reform. Getting in touch with the *Ochrana*, he had —in his own phrase—begun to "undermine the revolutionary conspiracies with counter-plots", a fascinating pastime which might have lasted as long as Azeff's had not his denunciations led to raids and arrests which stupid police officials allowed to recoil upon him.

Once his double-dealing was exposed, Zubatoff had openly entered the service of the *Ochrana*. He therefore understood perfectly the delicacy and hazards of the never-crowded profession which Azeff now was ornamenting. Even at the sacrifice of many minor plotters whose Siberian quarantine Azeff might steadily have instigated, Zubatoff meant to protect him in artful ways determined by his own student experience.

Azeff was a skilled informer, a spy—why not, then, an *agent provocateur*? In other countries provocation had been used intermittently, at specific periods of political tension or tyranny; as a consequence, it had never become traditional. But the revolutionary ferment in Russia throughout the nineteenth century had caused provocation to be established as a system, to the development of which the best brains of the bureaucracy were devoted. Zubatoff's brain was the best at this time in the whole police organization. And Zubatoff's brain was quick with schemes for making use of Azeff.

The secret-police projects of Azeff's new chief went considerably further than the detection and arrest of isolated malcontents. As a firm believer in autocracy, he recognized that its principal danger lay in the revolutionaries winning the confidence and support of the laboring masses. If the republican movement of the intelligentsia became a mass affair, Zubatoff realized, it would never be possible to control it by merely repressive measures. The strategic problem, then, as he saw it, was how to split the opposing forces—how, in short, to sow dissension between the revolutionary intelligentsia, whose aims were political, and the working classes, who favored the revolutionaries only because they sympathized with the workers in their effort to improve material conditions.

Zubatoff was notoriously self confident, vain and domineering. His manner of dealing with the problem was bold and intricate, though "distinguished by its complete lack of understanding of social processes." With the utmost relish he pursued a dual policy. He supported labor legislation, often taking the part of the employed in important disputes with employers after making sure that the controversy was wholly economic in character; and he even obtained permission for the workers to organize lawful societies *under the control of the police* for the defense of their economic rights. On the other hand, he deliberately encouraged the spread of revolutionary extremism among the discontented professional and intellectual classes.

He is said to have declared in a moment of rash candor: "We shall provoke you to acts of terror, and then crush you."[7]

To this end he paid great attention to the "secret agency" with which he infected revolutionary organizations. After his retirement he was moved to admit: "My connection with the 'secret agency' is my most precious remembrance." He deemed himself a master of secret-police provocation and knew how to recruit and control turncoats, double spies and renegades, an aromatic crew. It is certain that he was expert in keeping "their tracks covered", and that he owned some special magic in teaching them how to gain admission to the innermost conclaves of revolutionary authority.

Addressing a group of *Ochrana* officials as to their confidential relations with undercover agents, Zubatoff once advised: "Gentlemen, you must look upon your collaborators as you would upon a woman whom you love and with whom you are conducting a secret intrigue. Watch over her as the apple of your eye. One rash step, and you have dishonored her in the eyes of the world."

In a letter written after the public exposure of Azeff as a spy, Zubatoff summarized his character thus: "Azeff's was a purely mercenary nature . . . looking at everything from the point of view of profit, working for the Revolution for the sake of personal gain, and for the government out of no conviction but also for the sake of personal profit." Yet at the outset of their collaboration Zubatoff took his own romantic advice and was as tender with Azeff as if he combined the best qualities of a beloved one with the solid merits of a shipment of crown jewels. It was undoubtedly through him that Azeff obtained his good position as an engineer in the Moscow office of the General Electric Company. The spy also became affiliated with the Intellectual Aid Society, whose membership included the elite of Moscow's intelligentsia; he contributed to the paper published by this society, persistently widened his acquaintance, and attended all the meetings and banquets to which an "advanced thinker" and graduate of a foreign university might be invited.

Zubatoff saw to it that Azeff was a model of discreet reserve in his dealing with the revolutionary leaders. Declaring himself a sympathizer was enough; the potential *provocateur* must not force his attentions upon them, ask questions, or display curiosity about their acquaintance, their meetings or program. Thus, by subtle degrees, Zubatoff groomed Azeff for his incomparable role as a double spy, as an initiate and presently a leader of the most secret fraternity of Russian terrorism.

The Battle Organization

Azeff confined his police espionage to no single cult, bloc, coterie or revolutionary "cell" but kept Zubatoff minutely acquainted with everything that he learned while ceaselessly revolving in circles of radical energy. From him the chief of the Moscow *Ochrana* heard for the first time about the directors of the local "Committee of Social Democrats", about various illegal printing presses, and the "Social Democrat Library." Zubatoff found especial delight in Azeff's relations with the *Union of Social Revolutionaries,* the most promising contact which the spy had derived from the introductions pressed upon him by the ardent Zhitlovskys.

This *Union* was now rapidly extending its sphere of agitation and was publishing a paper—"Revolutionary Russia"—which was on its way to becoming the central organ of the whole Social Revolutionary movement. Azeff let it be known that his own "experience" abroad made him doubt the feasibility of establishing either large organizations or revolutionary publications inside the Russian frontier. He favored publishing abroad, since the forces of police investigation, provocation and repression were too powerful to wrestle with—save in one way, and only one, the waging of ceaseless subterranean warfare by means of the Terror.

"Terror is the only way," Azeff repeatedly declared. And naturally this conviction of his gradually commended him to the partisans of assassination.

When Karpovitch[8] shot and killed Bogolepoff, the minister of education, Azeff went about privately exulting. "Well, it seems the terror has begun!" In this he was conforming to the zealot-characterization that he had draped upon himself while living abroad; but now it was also stimulated by the hovering, paternal Zubatoff, who worked upon the role of "Azeff the decisive revolutionary—Azeff the calculating terrorist—Azeff the born leader" like a playwright whose every performance is a critically studied première.

Even though Azeff set a low value upon the purely intellectual agitations, or nonterrorist impulses of the revolutionaries, he was always ready to lend them a useful hand. Argunoff, leader of the *Union,* required a "solid but not too unwieldy roller" for the secret printing press. Azeff volunteered to procure it, alleging that a trustworthy friend of his, an engineer, had factory facilities permitting him to make it without police interference. The roller was, however, made with the assistance of the *Ochrana,* so that it might later serve as one of the principal clues leading to the detection of the *Union's* clandestine press.

Azeff was enabled to denounce various leaders of the *Union* without seeming to be implicated; and when, almost by accident, Gershuni, leader of the "Battle Organization" was arrested at Kieff,

Azeff was ready and groomed for the vacant post of command. He impressed all his revolutionary comrades—and Zubatoff—as the ideal man of action who should now become general manager of terrorism. One of the most incredible chapters in Russian history, in *all* history, thus began to be written very stealthily yet with frequent discharges of dynamite.

Azeff proved he could *act* terror as brilliantly as for years past he talked terror. His secret cohort of idealistic killers gave him the devoted obedience that is rarely accorded to inferior captains. Azeff was a great plotter, a thoroughly menacing social avenger—but all the while he was in league with the secret police. When the Grand Duke Sergius was bombed, his horrible end won the chief of bomb throwers a garland of undercover acclaim. Another plot, another loud report, and Plehve, the justly hated minister of the interior, had gone to his unmentionable reward. Plehve was an arrogant fool; and it is ironic to learn how he failed to take precautions—though he knew he had earned the hatred of more than terrorists—simply because he was sure the *Ochrana* had in Azeff himself an "inside" informer who would warn of any serious plot before it culminated.

The active prosperity of the "Battle Organization" under Azeff's despotic control might have attained the pinnacle of slaying the tsar. Azeff insisted that he had no dearer objective. However, the remorseless suspicion and clever detective work of the revolutionary editor, Burtzeff, and the curious indiscretion of the police official, A. A. Lopuhin, resulted in Azeff's exposure, or—shall we say—the exposure of the *Ochrana,* for the recoil upon the secret police was catastrophic. A police spy had actually devised the assassination of the tsar's uncle! And of Plehve, the ministerial head of all the police! Who would ever be secure hereafter with the very government subsidizing its own destroyers?

We may not proceed farther along the path of police provocation either as an art or a neglected commercial career, for we only come up against the enigma of Azeff's divergent loyalties. Was the fellow a monster of deceit? Was he a terrorist using the police—or a secret agent whose very success overpowered him? Once so deeply involved as he became with terrorism, it meant his life to try to moderate the program he had sworn to execute. Rather than risk his own life, he preferred to sacrifice more eminent Russians.

Plehve at least was a target of his natural selection. Azeff, lavishly though he was paid by the police, was never paid enough to stop hating Plehve. The minister of the interior encouraged pogroms to distract the tsar's subjects from their growing radical impulses. There had been a dreadful pogrom at Kishenev, alleged to have been fomented by Plehve himself. Hundreds had been wounded or killed; and there had been a particularly brutal massacre of children and infants, "whose heads had been dashed against walls." Azeff is said to have shown himself as overjoyed as any fanatic in his organization when the bombing of Plehve was reported.

"That's for Kishenev," he exulted. And in 1912, meeting Burtseff in Frankfort on the Main, he said reproachfully: "If you had not exposed me then, I would have killed the Tsar."

Chapter Fifty-two

THE DEGRADATION OF ALFRED DREYFUS

THE affair of Captain Dreyfus was a pogrom conducted by members of the French General Staff. They were brazen and overbearing rather than acute conspirators and only sustained their treacherous artifice by an impregnable *esprit de corps*.

At nine o'clock in the morning, October 15, 1894, a fateful Monday morning which a generation of Frenchmen would have cause to regret, Dreyfus reported at General Staff headquarters in Paris at No. 10-14 Rue St Dominique. He was in mufti, according to orders, and believed that he had been summoned to a general inspection of staff probationers. To his surprise none of his fellow probationers appeared, however; and Major Georges Picquart of the Intelligence, with a few words of casual explanation, escorted him to the office of the chief of the general staff.

Neither the chief, De Boisdeffre, nor the deputy chief, General Gonse, was there; but Dreyfus, growing still more puzzled, found waiting a solemn group of officials which included M. Cochefert, director of the Sûreté, and a certain major of the General Staff, the Marquis du Paty de Clam.[1] This insipid soldier but authentic nobleman adorned the staff without elevating it, displaying the strangest zeal for all sorts of maneuvers except those of the battlefield. A precious aesthete who had written novels, an amateur of occultism and the friend of Jesuits, he was happy even in his transient glory as first accuser of the luckless captain.

On that morning of the fifteenth Du Paty de Clam said to Dreyfus: "General de Boisdeffre will be here in a moment. In the meantime, you might do something for me. I have a letter to write, but I have a bad finger. Would you mind writing it for me?"

There were half-a-dozen army clerks in the adjoining room, but Dreyfus, correct and attentive, took up the pen. After dictating from memory two sentences relating to the treasonable crime which was to be attributed to the captain, Du Paty de Clam exclaimed: "Why, what is the matter with you? You're trembling!"[2]

Much was eventually to be made of this. Du Paty de Clam as a court-martial witness submitted that Dreyfus at first had trembled but that next he showed no uneasiness. Both these symptoms were deemed important by the military judges. If the accused had trembled, it was his guilty conscience—while not trembling continuously thereafter meant he had already been warned, and that only a hardened traitor could so completely dissemble his emotions.

At the time Dreyfus saw nothing but hostility in the marquis major's ejaculation, and he was accustomed to hostility from certain individuals. He thought Du Paty de Clam had reference to his bad handwriting. It was a chill autumn day with a north wind blowing; he had only been indoors a few minutes and explained that his fingers were cold. When he resumed, his hand was steady and the writing clear.

Du Paty de Clam had advocated this test, wishing to create "psychological evidence" against the suspect. And now he stood up, savoring the one great moment of a mediocre career. "Captain Dreyfus," he intoned, "I arrest you in the name of the law. You are charged with high treason."

Dreyfus stared at his accuser without uttering a word. He offered no resistance when Cochefert and an assistant stepped forward to search him. Dumbfounded, he spoke with an effort, stammering, protesting his innocence. Then he cried out: "Take my keys. Go to my home and open everything. I am innocent."[3]

Du Paty de Clam had kept a revolver in readiness under a file. He now let it be seen; and Dreyfus shouted wildly: "Put a bullet through my head." The marquis turned away with a significant gesture, saying: "It is not for us to kill you." Dreyfus gazed at the weapon for a moment, seeming to arrive at a dreadful conclusion. His hand crept toward the revolver butt; then he jerked it back suddenly, as though it had been scorched. When he spoke again it was with renewed composure. "No. I will live to prove my innocence!"

All through this tense drama a Major Henry of the Intelligence—whose army career and personal repute were to be as inflexibly bound up in this case as the destiny of Alfred Dreyfus—had been standing in back of a curtain. Now he accepted the captain's rejection of suicide as his cue and stepped forth, taking him in charge. Dreyfus was removed to the military prison in the Rue du Cherche-Midi.

Flimsy Proofs and Strong Prejudice

The arrest and incarceration of the artillery officer followed in accordance with the plans of anti-Semitic members of the General Staff and was based on the unsupported conjecture of Alphonse

Bertillon—already famous as the inventor of anthropometric identification[4]—that a certain document of 700 words, unsigned and unaddressed, was in the handwriting of Dreyfus. This document, thereafter to become world famous as the "bordereau", was a kind of Judas' invoice, enumerating five plans or papers of military importance which the writer was in a position to secure and deliver for a price.

Dreyfus was kept "in solitary" at the prison from the day of his arrest until the fifth of December, when he was at last permitted to engage counsel and write to his wife. She and other members of his family had been warned by General Staff officers that they would best serve his interests by doing nothing and maintaining a discreet silence. Though not even permitted to know the nature of the charges against him, they had followed this advice with anxious exactitude.

The accused man had been interrogated again and again. His home had been thoroughly searched. But no particle of new evidence could be found to add to the flimsy proofs of his alleged treason. He was still so bewildered and appalled, so inutterably alien to any sense of guilt, that he could offer little or no defense. He could only deny his guilt, assert and reassert that he never had plotted to betray French army secrets, point out that he had no motive, that he did not need the money. Dreyfus' emphatic solvency may have inspired some envy among those of his colleagues who had to struggle along on their army pay; it surely inflicted weird flights of fancy upon his more virulent traducers. Why should he sell out for a comparative pittance a career he had worked so ardently to win?

The youngest of three brothers and three sisters, he had been born October 9, 1859, at Mülhausen, in Upper Alsace, where his father was a well-to-do manufacturer of textiles. In 1872 Bismarck's brand-new German Empire was, in accordance with the terms of the Treaty of Frankfort, allowed to compel the inhabitants of Alsace-Lorraine to declare their nationality; and the Dreyfus family, with one necessary exception, elected to remain French and had moved to France. The exception was the eldest brother, Jacques, long past military age and willing to become a subject of the Kaiser in order to stay at Mülhausen to conduct the family business. The two younger brothers, Mathieu and Alfred, took up residence in Paris.

When he was nineteen years old, Alfred began his military education at the *École Polytechnique*. Two years later, in 1880, with the rank of cadet second lieutenant of artillery, he was attending the *École d'Application* at Fontainebleau. On October 1, 1882, he received his lieutenant's commission and was ordered to the Thirty-first Regiment of Artillery at Le Mans, a year later being transferred to the mounted artillery attached to the First Independent Cavalry at Paris.

Pursuing his military career with the sort of diligence that often antagonizes more indolent inheritors of family tradition, Dreyfus was promoted to captain in the Twenty-first Artillery on September 12, 1889, and then detached for special study in ballistics at the *École Centrale de Pyrotechnie Militaire* at Bourges. That winter he was betrothed to Lucie Hadamard, the daughter of a Parisian lapidary, and also passed the examinations for the *École Supérieure de Guerre*—the French Staff College—which he entered on the twentieth of April, 1890. The following day he was married.

His high rank in the class, upon graduating two years later, made it impossible for even prejudiced army bureaucrats to ignore his ability, and he was brevetted to the General Staff—the first Jewish officer to be so honored. He entered that powerful administrative organization on Janury 1, 1893, as *stagiaire* or probationer. He was at the time a captain detached from the Fourteenth Artillery; if all went well his probation would naturally end on the thirty-first day of December, 1894; and as early as May of that year he was ordered to pass the last three months of it on active service with the Thirty-ninth Infantry of the Paris garrison. He would not, therefore, be required to attend the autumn maneuvers of the army.

This was an important point, for the writer of the treasonable "bordereau" had closed with the sentence "I am just off to the maneuvers"—which was contrary to Dreyfus' orders received the preceding May. Experts had decided that the writer must be an artillerist because he mentioned a new and secret gun-recoil brake, and that he was probably a General Staff probationer. This narrowed the suspects down to four or five officers; and notorious anti-Semites saw to it that only Dreyfus was seriously investigated.

Points in favor of the accused captain were carefully ignored; which was all the more imperative since no evidence worthy of consideration by an honest court ever turned up to incriminate him. According to the German record of this celebrated judicial farce, the manner in which the "bordereau" came into the hands of the French was explained in two different ways during the course of subsequent diplomatic exchanges. On one occasion it was stated that the document was obtained *par la voie ordinaire* [through the usual channels] which meant, from the wastepaper basket of the German military attaché, Colonel Max von Schwartzkoppen.[5] This explanation was false. Though the charwoman was bribed to deliver the contents of that basket regularly to a French secret agent, she could not have thus acquired the "bordereau" because Von Schwartzkoppen had never had it in his hands. Obviously the second explanation was the true one: that the document was stolen before it reached the attaché.

In accordance with the prevailing French fashions of counterespionage "control", the German attaché was being shadowed, an Alsatian agent named Brucker having been assigned to that duty. He applied himself to it so diligently that he even contrived to establish intimate relations with the wife of Colonel von Schwartzkoppen's concierge. Thanks to this agreeable blend of surveillance and infidelity, the colonel's private correspondence was very closely watched.

Brucker upon going through it one day came across the fateful "bordereau" and saw at a glance what a prize he had uncovered. Hastening with it to Major Henry, he demanded a substantial bonus for having made so important a discovery. Such cash rewards were also in vogue as a measure of Intelligence technique. Henry would probably have liked to get rid of the highly explosive document; but Brucker would feel cheated if he did. He dare not destroy the "bordereau" then, because Brucker knew of its contents. And this was but the first of the strange compulsions which were to snare with incredible malignity an innocent man.

Esterhazy

The real, but punctiliously undetected, author of the "bordereau" was a member of the General Staff, Major Ferdinand Walsin Esterhazy. A racial mongrel and military adventurer of a type that any shrewd country banker would have mistrusted on sight, he had been accepted by responsible French officers without misgiving and assigned to confidential duties. In 1881, for example, this man had been sent abroad on foreign service. His mission, like nearly everything else about him, remained obscure; but he had been suspected of espionage. Even so, in 1894, thirteen years later, he was an ornament of the French Intelligence.

It was known that he had served with the Roman Legion in 1869. And prior to that there was some vague hint of his having resigned from the German or the Hungarian army. He had come into the French Foreign Legion, and the shortage of officers in the Franco-Prussian War had accounted for his transfer to the regular army.

The major often let it be known that he was a cadet of the noted Hungarian family of Esterhazy, but he never got around to proving it. His parentage and his past were left to polite conjecture, even as his future was foredoomed to shame and want. But at the time of Dreyfus' automatic immolation he was doing rather well for himself, since Colonel von Schwartzkoppen had him on his private payroll at 12,000 marks a month. Before Yves Guyot denounced him in his paper, *Le Siècle,* Esterhazy had copied and transmitted 162 important documents to his German employer. Years were to elapse, however, before the French military authorities permitted the treason of this enterprising scoundrel to be brought to their notice.

The "bordereau" discovered by Brucker was written upon very distinctive paper. It was particularly thin and light and could not be bought in any Parisian shop. Only one officer used it as notepaper, and that was Esterhazy. And only one officer knew of this, Major Henry, his colleague of the Intelligence. Henry kept silent about it.

Whether the "bordereau" was written as a serious offer or wholly for purposes of provocation, with Henry scheming to embarrass the German embassy, and Esterhazy—an already subsidized betrayer—holding the pen, no amount of journalistic and political inquiry has ever been able to determine. It is interesting to note that the Germans cheerfully bribed Esterhazy but also believed that Henry had meant to us him against them as an *agent provocateur.*

However contemptible Esterhazy appears as a treacherous adventurer, however abominable the anti-Semitism of a military clique that would convict, disgrace and even reconvict an absolutely innocent brother officer, it is Henry who deserved—and ultimately earned—the gravest condemnation for his zeal in arranging Dreyfus' ruin. In the summer of 1894 a member of the French counter-espionage service had been arrested at the frontier. General Auguste Mercier, the minister of war,[6] had promptly ordered his release without revealing his name, thereby drawing upon himself a hot fire from the radical press. When the investigation of Dreyfus' alleged guilt was disclosed to him in all its pitiful emptiness, Mercier thought of dropping the whole proceedings. But Henry caused the *Libre Parole* to move in the matter and inspired a renewal of the press campaign which exasperated Mercier and compelled him to make a court case out of the feeble counter-spying allegations.

The Secret Court-Martial

Gobert, handwriting expert for the General Staff and the Bank of France, had examined the "bordereau" and compared it with many specimens of Dreyfus' handwriting.

"They are not the same," he affirmed.

When Bertillon contradicted him, the General Staff abandoned its own expert in favor of his rival of the Sûreté.

"What did you find when you searched Dreyfus' flat?" the chief of the General Staff inquired.

"He had made away with everything," lamented the Marquis du Paty de Clam.

"And when you first accused him?"

"The Jew turned pale."

"Does he confess?"

"He still denies everything—but, sir, his words do not ring true."

The General Staff clique, having chosen its victim, would not have accepted any substitute, not even an actual traitor.

General de Boisdeffre troubled to consult M. Forzinetti, director of the military prison in the Rue du Cherche-Midi, who had been in closest contact with Captain Dreyfus from the day of his arrest. "'Since you have asked me, Sir, I must answer you,' said the prison director. 'I think you are on the wrong track. Dreyfus is as innocent as I am.'"[7]

And Forzinetti believed that the chief of the General Staff was virtually confessing his own belief in Dreyfus' innocence when he remarked: "The Minister of War has given me *carte blanche*, but he had better settle his Dreyfus affair for himself."

Millions of others would have recognized the artillery captain's guiltless and tragic position if everything had not been kept profoundly secret. The nature of the accusation, the evidence alleged to exist, the procedure against him—all very secret for reasons of state!

The radical press was still clamoring, as only the French press can clamor, but without really knowing anything, or even suspecting what was afoot. Furthermore, the German Embassy was denounced as a "hive of spies" and there were demonstrations before it, causing the ambassador, Count Münster, to demand from the French foreign minister, Hanotaux, both reparation and satisfaction.

At this time Münster was endeavoring to inform various French statesmen as he had already reassured Berlin: "About Captain Dreyfus, no one at the Embassy, not even Colonel von Schwartzkoppen, has ever known or heard anything."

That, of course, was also kept secret.

An indictment had been drawn up containing anonymous police reports, intended to show that the accused officer was both a libertine and gambler. Something had to be done to account for the treasonable inclinations of a brilliant and ambitious man whose combined income of army pay, revenue from the Mülhausen factory and from his wife's ample dowry was more than 50,000 francs a year.

The court-martial began on December 19, lasted four days and was wholly secret. The procedure consisted of attempts to turn the suspicions, insinuations and conjectures of the interrogation and indictment into legal evidence.[6] One episode will illustrate how crudely this was accomplished. A witness was permitted to testify that an "honorable person", whose name he was not required to divulge, had informed him that Alfred Dreyfus was a traitor.[9] This was solemnly introduced and made a deep impression upon the seven military judges, none of whom was, like the defendant, an artillery officer.

Major Henry as a counter-espionage specialist was allowed to make a statement in the absence of the accused and the defending counsel, so that neither Dreyfus nor Maître Demange could know what incriminating new "evidence" had been offered against the prisoner.

And after the judges had retired to consider a verdict, General Mercier caused to be laid before them eight documents with a covering letter. Now only one of these documents had any reference to Dreyfus, but, by the phrasing of the covering letter, all were made to incriminate him. The one document which referred to him was an intercepted code telegram, presumably from Von Schwartzkoppen to his chief in Berlin. And had the French decoding been correct it would have completely established the innocence of Dreyfus. By not permitting the defense to examine this "evidence" the judges violated Article 101 of the Code of Military Procedure. Since they were intent upon convicting him, it was well that the violation occurred.

The court proceeded to find the captain guilty of having "delivered to a foreign power or its agents a certain number of secret or confidential documents concerning the national defense." His sentence of life imprisonment in a fortified place was not deemed severe enough. He must first be degraded in the presence of the garrison of Paris.

This ceremony was carried out on the morning of January 5, 1895, on the parade ground of the *École Militaire* with the troops drawn up in a hollow square and, as a foreign observer put it, "the usual French theatrical show." His officer's insignia was ripped from Dreyfus' uniform, his sword broken and cast upon the ground. This was followed by the "rogue's march" around the square, Dreyfus at almost every step crying out "I am innocent!"—only to be answered by yells of hatred and derision from the crowd gathered without.

The most dramatic account of the affair was published in *L'Autorité*, a paper bitterly hostile to Dreyfus. By a curious irony it was that very report, abusive and prejudiced, which first aroused sympathy for him abroad and even raised disturbing doubts as to his guilt.

Prejudice in France continued riding high, so high, in fact, that an *ex post facto* law was passed to designate the penal colony of Cayenne, French Guiana—the *guillotine à sec*—as the "fortified place" of his perpetual imprisonment. And, contrary to French usage, his wife was not to be permitted to join him there.

Dreyfus arrived in the colony on March 15, and for a month he was held in the convict prison until huts could be erected for him and his guards on one of the small islands in the bay.[10] This was the never-to-be-forgotten Devil's Island, which, since Dreyfus' ordeal there, has fastened its name upon the entire penal colony. In the vestibule of his hut a sentry was stationed day and night. The prisoner was forced to do his own cooking, washing and cleaning, and only received matches in exchange for an empty box.

He has written how insects devoured his food and his books, particularly mentioning his encounters with the "spider crab, whose bite is poisonous."[11] Dreyfus was permitted to take exercise over about half an acre—a treeless triangle formed by his hut, the landing wharf, and a little gully which once had sheltered a leper camp—until, in September, 1896, a rumor reached the Colonial Office that he had tried to escape. As a consequence of this he was put in double irons for several weeks and the island fortified.

At its origin and up to the moment of Dreyfus' proclaimed conviction by the court-martial, his case had remained relatively unimportant, interesting only army circles. But with the deportation of the "traitor", the affair was projected into the turbulent arena of French party politics. Gradually it assumed international proportions. The Dreyfusards became a powerful camp. The army plotters would not yield. France was threatened with a conflagration.

Chapter Fifty-three
PICQUART AND ZOLA: THE COUNTER-DETECTION

ON THE FIRST OF JULY, 1895, Georges Picquart, now a lieutenant colonel, became head of the Intelligence. He was a brilliant staff officer, the youngest man of his rank in the French Army. His future promotions up to chief of staff, perhaps minister of war, could be discerned without consulting a sibyl.

In due course and "through the usual channels" he came into possession of the renowned "petit bleu"—an express letter, so called because of its color. This striking bit of evidence was not easily deciphered. More than fifty jagged pieces had been found and put together, and the threading network of tears somewhat confused the sense of the message.

It appeared to have been written to a spy by Colonel von Schwartzkoppen, who, for some undiscoverable reason, had torn it up instead of posting it. Brucker or another agent in his stead had obtained the wastebasket's conglomerate treasure.

Picquart scanned the lines:

DEAR SIR:
Regarding the matter in question, I would first like to have fuller details. Will you please let me have them in writing? I will then decide whether I can continue my relations with the firm of R. or not.

Bearing the signature of a capital "C", which was already known as a code sign used by Von Schwartzkoppen, it had been addressed to:[1]

Commandant Esterhazy,
27, rue de la Bienfaisance,
Paris.

"Another Dreyfus!" was Picquart's startled thought.[2]

He was shocked and astounded. But worse shocks were in store for him; and his astonishment grew as his superiors repeatedly warned him against further investigation of this evidence, since it tended to exculpate Alfred Dreyfus.

Picquart was not only a staff officer but a soldier, a crusader, honest, obstinate and careless of his own security. He returned to the charges and was finally forbidden to speak of them. To make sure that, if he disobeyed, his voice would be muffled by distance and desert, he was removed from the staff, November 16, 1896, and ordered to Africa. His new commanding general was advised to assign him to a post of danger.

This was implacable undercover warfare. To venture to defend "that Jew" was to become monstrous, a traitor, a blasphemer, a knave —and no gentleman. Yet two events took place in 1896 which were profoundly to influence the vindication of the lonely man on Devil's

THE HANDWRITING OF ALFRED DREYFUS

Island and his exiled champion in Tunisia. First, an article appeared in the Paris *Éclair* of September 14, discovering the long-sought "new fact" necessary to gain a review of his case: that Dreyfus had been convicted in violation of Article 101 of the Code of Military Justice. Second, on November 10 *Le Matin* published a facsimile of the "bordereau," with the inspired editorial comment that all who had specimens of Dreyfus' handwriting must now be convinced that only he could have written it. This disclosure was to have precisely the opposite result.

Mathieu Dreyfus, brother of the condemned captain, circulated leaflets and posters displaying a photograph of the "bordereau," and Paris stirred to the second dramatic chapter of the celebrated case— the counter-detection of Majors Esterhazy and Henry.

The latter fought the suspicions which were gaining ground. In Basel he had a conference with an emissary of the German General Staff who had sought the meeting in order to declare that Dreyfus was absolutely innocent. The German representative gave such particulars that the French authorities would readily have been able to recognize Esterhazy as the guilty person had not Henry alertly cut the German short whenever he started to allude to the real culprit.[3]

THE HANDWRITING OF FERDINAND WALSIN ESTERHAZY

However, the fitful breezes that whirled Mathieu Dreyfus' handbills over Paris were blowing up a gale. A banker, M. Castro, who had handled speculative accounts for Esterhazy, saw the facsimile of the "bordereau" and recognized his client's handwriting. Picquart, too, had managed to communicate to a Dreyfusard his reasons for suspecting the alien major.

The Intervention of Scheurer-Kestner

This evidence was privately brought to the attention of the vice-president of the French Senate, M. Scheurer-Kestner. An elderly and respected man of science, who had never seen Alfred Dreyfus or any member of his family, he had become disturbed lest a foul judicial error had been committed, and he had been working away quietly upon the case for months.

Now, on October 30, 1897, the senator called upon General Billot, who had succeeded Mercier as minister of war in April of the previous year, laying before him the proofs which exposed Major Esterhazy's treasonable transactions. At once the French government was propelled into the fray. The Church took sides against the "Jewish

THE EVIDENCE OF THE "BORDEREAU" WHICH SENT CAPTAIN DREYFUS TO DEVIL'S ISLAND

The illustrious Alphonse Bertillon, having perpetrated an "identification" that any one-eyed illiterate could discredit from these writing specimens alone, went on with unimpaired assurance to develop his world renown as a master of the new methodical crime investigation and criminal identification.

traitor" with all the bathos, bias and bigotry in which clerical partisans excel.

One must study the newspapers of that day to appreciate the vicious extravagance of these allies' attack, the unreasoning fury of army, Church, politicians and the press they controlled, against any one who merely asked that Dreyfus' conviction be examined. General Billot impatiently repudiated Scheurer-Kestner's proofs. Whereupon Mathieu Dreyfus addressed an open letter to the minister of war on November 15, denouncing Esterhazy as the author of the "bordereau" and, hence, the traitor. On the eighteenth *Le Figaro* gave its circulation a bomblike boost by publishing certain treasonable letters which Esterhazy had written to a Mme Boulancy.

The accused major, with the swaggering insolence characteristic of his type, now demanded an investigation and then a court-martial. The army tried him on January 10–11, 1898, and dismissed all charges, the president of the court stating that the case of Alfred Dreyfus was finally disposed of, and it had merely been a question of deciding whether Esterhazy was, or was not, guilty of treason. Being triumphantly acquitted, he resumed his pampered role as the darling of Church and State.[4]

It was Picquart and not Esterhazy who was the General Staff's chosen villain; and Picquart, in this perspective, seems to have been the real hero of the Dreyfus case. He had been ordered back to Paris in November; but he firmly refused to testify in Esterhazy's behalf, since it was contrary to his own avowed convictions. And so, on January 13 he was tried and found guilty of having communicated official documents. His sentence was sixty days' close arrest.

On that dark day, however, another Dreyfus champion strode into the arena, for on the thirteenth the celebrated novelist, Émile Zola, published his *J'accuse*. It was a great moment for French justice and the salvation of the soul of France; an ominous one for the intrigants and manipulators of secret service at the Ministry of War.

A truculent editor—who had formerly taught in a young ladies' school in America and had married one of his pupils—Georges Clemenceau, sharpened his claws as the "Tiger" of France by printing in his paper, *L'Aurore*, the novelist's slashing counter-attack. Zola denounced the criminals of the military hierarchy from Mercier down, the judges of the Dreyfus and Esterhazy courts-martial, and the handwriting "experts", inviting prosecution on charges of criminal libel.

The Third Condemnation

Zola was duly prosecuted, only to meet with the same disaster in court that had overtaken Picquart and Dreyfus. He was fined and condemned to a year's imprisonment. On appeal his conviction was reversed by the highest court of the Republic. Despite pressure from the government, the judges realized that a defender of abstract justice was defending that for which they themselves stood. Whereupon the government and clerical press denounced them in language of unspeakable fanaticism. They were termed "servile, cowardly, rotten, corrupt"; and a new trial was decreed.

The Dreyfus affair had entered its most virulent phase. At Zola's second and third trials he was spat upon, howled at and struck by well-dressed men and women of the privileged class who monopolized all tickets for the spectators' seats. Such few editors who stood by the principles of justice and equality before the law were actually risking their lives. Clemenceau, for one, wrote almost daily in *L'Aurore* during 1898-99 upon a theme which would have seemed platitudinous under any other circumstances: every Frenchman's right to justice![5]

The cause of Alfred Dreyfus had become the cause of the plain everyday citizen, subject to the despotism of invisible powers, lacking influence, distinction or fortune. Dreyfus had not been poor—though the factory in Mülhausen had to be sold in 1897 to defray the heavy expenses incurred by his family in continuing to try to establish his innocence—but he was a little-known member of an unpopular race. And he was imprisoned illegally and kept in prison by the whole weight of government, caste, army, Church and press.

Enlisted to aid him were just the handful of disinterested men, ready to make any sacrifice so it seemed, in order to win him the justice which was his due. The lives of these pioneer Dreyfusards were continually threatened; and Leblois, his heroic counsel, was fired upon and wounded. But instead of stimulating the populace en masse to a demand for fair play, the campaign of prejudice excelled in gaining recruits. Public cowardice was never more palpable, most of the deputies when presenting themselves for re-election trailing at the heels of the government in a timid pack.

Indiscriminate denunciation of Jews was then even more scathing, unjust and outrageous than its obvious parallel in Nazi Germania of 1935, because the French excel their Teutonic neighbors in volatile spirit and eloquence. But does not this extract from a candidate's speech—assailing an opponent in 1898—convey an up-to-date overtone of Hitler *über Alles?*

He has dared to say: "I do not know if Dreyfus is guilty or not"—which is at once stupid and infamous; *stupid because all Jews are traitors;* infamous because he thus endeavors to shake the structure of the army by throwing a doubt on the *competence and loyalty of its chiefs.*

The speaker was not a Göring or Streicher, but one named Teysonniere, and he snarled and shrieked his way into the Chamber of Deputies.

At the last as at the first of the Zola trials nothing was allowed to be asserted which would reveal the truth about the condemnation of Dreyfus. Only one sentence of the famous letter *J'accuse* was used as the basis of the libel charge: that Esterhazy had been acquitted on orders. Henry, who had been promoted to Picquart's place as head of the Intelligence, was a key witness for the prosecution. Zola found himself a victim of the same juridicial Juggernaut he had ventured to arraign; and, after two appeals, believing that he had vainly sacrificed himself, he fled to England and was convicted by default.

As events soon turned about, his sacrifice was anything but in vain. The sensational nature of his trials, his self-imposed exile, and Picquart's still emphatic declaration—"I can prove the guilt of Esterhazy and the innocence of Dreyfus"—drove Henry to an egregious blunder that ultimately answered every good Dreyfusard's prayer.

The "faux Panizzardi"

As chief of Intelligence, Henry decided that it was his duty to strengthen the "guilt" of Dreyfus beyond all doubt. As if anything more were wanted by his enemies, or anything else would weaken the fidelity of his friends! And so Henry caused to be forged a document which he placed in the Dreyfus *dossier*—one which was to become notorious as the "faux Panizzardi."

Colonel Panizzardi was the Italian military attaché; and from letters of his—harmless old missives, filtered through those ubiquitous "channels"—a document was put together implicating Dreyfus. The Italian officer appeared to have written his German colleague, explaining that he, Panizzardi, intended saying nothing in Rome, and that Von Schwartzkoppen should say nothing in Berlin, about their mutual relations with the condemned artillery captain.

This menacing fake was also available to use against Georges Picquart, who had not yet been sufficiently punished for daring to accuse Esterhazy. Picquart had been dismissed from the French army on February 26, 1898, his powerful foes reluctantly denying themselves another sadists' circus of shorn-off buttons, mutilated braid and broken sword. On July 13 he was rearrested, charged with forgery, and kept in solitary confinement.

Zola had definitely turned the tide, and Picquart's defense could only be his stoutly reiterated accusations. The minister of war, now Cavaignac, entrusted Captain Cuignet—who was certainly no friend of Dreyfus—with the reclassification of all the documents in the case. They were known only from photographs that Henry had prepared which reproduced them persuasively in torn or crumpled condition. The originals had hardly been touched.[6]

Working by lamp light Cuignet came to the pièce de résistance, which, not yet known as a "faux", was dramatically entitled the *document Vercingetorix*. He held it up to the lamp and was as startled as Picquart had long ago been startled by the "petit bleu." One can almost imagine this staff captain wondering what to do, so rare was a straightforward or impartial act in the circles to which he had been elevated. Would honesty be too impulsive?

This *document Vercingetorix* was an absurd forgery, composed of two different kinds of paper. The top and bottom, bearing a genuine "Dear Friend" and Panizzardi's signature, were paper of a faint bluish tint; whereas the lamp light shone reddish through the middle, the incriminating portion of the missive.

Cuignet, to do him justice, hurried to Cavaignac; and to do *him* justice, the minister of war never hesitated to expose a shocking scandal, bound to provoke a ministerial crisis and his own retirement from office. Under the impulsion of a national event he conducted himself as a man of honor.

Picquart, of course, was still under arrest. Henry was recalled from leave. Yves Guyot's *Le Siècle* had already printed staggering evidence of Esterhazy's relations with Von Schwartzkoppen, and then a sworn statement quoting both the German attaché and Colonel Panizzardi in proof of Esterhazy's authorship of the "bordereau."

Henry had used all his cunning—which was never great—and all his influence and authority—which were dangerously far reaching—to hold back the avalanche of decency and fair play. On August 30, 1898, the game was up. He was confronted with his guilt by the minister of war.

Henry sought to deny everything, to blame that desperate betrayer of his caste, Georges Picquart. But presently he broke down, confessed to having instigated the forgery of the Panizzardi evidence. Three years, ten months and fifteen days before he had lurked behind a curtain while Du Paty de Clam intoned his arrest of Dreyfus. Now another curtain was descending upon the last act of his tragedy of miscalculated counter-espionage; agents of the Sûreté were waiting to lead him away.

On the following morning this hopelessly mired malefactor drew a razor across his throat and was dead when they found him in his cell.[7]

The Struggle for Vindication

Esterhazy fled to England. But the proceedings against Picquart were not dropped; he was indicted for forgery on September 21. And that gallant rebel nourished no illusions about the caliber of his adversaries.

In court he declared: "This is probably the last time that I will be able to speak in public. I would have the world know that if there be found in my cell the rope of Lemercier-Picard,[8] or the razor of Henry, I shall have been assassinated!"

Nine days previous Du Paty de Clam had voluntarily retired on half pay. The opposition was beginning to sink into oblivion, but at a glacial speed. Picquart was not released until the twelfth of June, 1899.

Dreyfus by then had been brought back from Guiana—and what efforts of will power even that modest achievement had cost! As soon as Henry's guilt was acknowledged, and Esterhazy's advertised by flight, an immediate review of the Dreyfus conviction had been demanded, and, incredible though it may seem, as defiantly resisted by a very articulate Old Guard—or rear guard, for retreat had really begun —of powerful prejudices. Revisionist proceedings initiated in the *Chambre Criminelle* broke down; but the *Chambre Réunie* ordered the prisoner brought back to France. There on June 3, 1899, the *Cour de Cassation,* supreme tribunal of revision and appeal, quashed the conviction of 1894 and gave its opinion that the "bordereau" had been written by Esterhazy. Dreyfus was sent before the *Ille-et-Vilaine* court-martial sitting at Rennes, so that the military hierarchy might "rectify its mistake."

The anti-revisionists had one more poison dart to blow, however— another forgery, the absurd "bordereau annoté de Guillaume", a document with alleged marginal notes by the German emperor. On its account the second court-martial found Dreyfus guilty "with extenuating circumstances" and sentenced him to prison for ten years.[9] Ten days later, on September 19, 1899, he was pardoned by President Loubet.[10] The Waldeck-Rousseau ministry of "Republican Defence" feared a revolution if Dreyfus were reconvicted; and he agreed to accept the pardon on condition that he should still be free to establish his innocence.[11]

In 1903 he petitioned for a revision of his case; and at length, in January 1906, eleven years after the original condemnation, the *Cour de Cassation* quashed the conviction of '99 and completely exonerated Dreyfus. He was restored to the army with the rank of major and decorated with the Cross of the Legion of Honor. In its final judgment the supreme French tribunal thriftily made note of the fact that he had "declared his intention to refrain from claiming the financial compensation to which, according to Article 446 of the Code d'Instruction, he had a right."

Meanwhile, an act of amnesty prevented the state from proceeding against the criminal witnesses and judges; but those who had been prosecuted for attempting to establish Dreyfus' innocence were formally exculpated and rehabilitated. Picquart, who had suffered even more than Zola for having inflicted moral integrity upon the schemes of a General Staff cabal, was reinstated with the rank of general. When Clemenceau was forming his first cabinet, he satisfied his own and the high gods' appetite for irony salted with justice by making that substantial soldier his minister of war.

And the end was not yet. Émile Zola having died in 1902, a French Chamber made him belated amends by voting a sum equivalent to seven thousand dollars for the transfer of his remains to the Panthéon. This ceremony took place on the fourth of June, 1908; and while the minister of education, M. Doumergue, was delivering his address, an excitable onlooker drew a revolver and fired pointblank at Major Dreyfus.[12] That officer's bad luck, however, had not come home with him from Devil's Island, and, though wounded twice, both wounds were superficial.

The would-be assassin, Grigori, upon being interrogated, proclaimed that he had wished to strike not at Dreyfus but at "the system." What system? Dreyfus—who voluntarily retired from the army in 1909, three years after having been reinstated—represented no one and made no effort whatever to capitalize either his world-renowned martyrdom or his absolute vindication. Perhaps he was a symbol of those disorganized but uncompromising partisans of his, who would fight even to the death for the legal rights of an average man.

It is rather Grigori, the inexpert marksman, who seems to have stood for some kind of system of inextinguishable bias, since, when he came to trial, French justice relapsd to another of its giddy spells, and he was promptly acquitted.

In a case of such grave significance, liberating its foaming niagaras of emotion, no fair return could ever be made to all of those who deserved reparation. During the years of Dreyfus' disgrace, members of his family had endured virtual ostracism. How now to do away with every social and financial impediment devised by the enemies of the "Jewish traitor"?

Prejudice, of course, had borne hardest upon the young. In 1894 his brother Jacques' two elder sons, who were being prepared in Paris for the military schools of the Polytechnic and Saint-Cyr, had been compelled to abandon their careers. The next two sons had been literally hounded out of the *Lycée* at Belfort.

And yet two years later, when almost everyone in France unfortunate enough to bear the surname Dreyfus was having it legally changed, this resolute man summoned to him his two remaining sons, now of military age, and said:[13] "You will leave your father's house and return to it no more. You will go to France where your name is scorned and despised, but you will preserve it. It is your duty. Go!"

The German Reaction

Alfred Dreyfus, when war broke out in 1914, presented himself at once for active service, was brevetted brigadier general and put in command of one of the forts of Paris at St Denis. At the end of the war he was made a lieutenant colonel and commander of the Legion of Honor.[14]

A German victim of the war was Major General Max von Schwartzkoppen, who died in the Elizabeth Hospital, Berlin, in January 1917. As Esterhazy's chief customer of 1894, a sworn statement by him at the right moment would have saved Dreyfus those five terrible years of imprisonment and six more of frustration and uncertainty; but it is now known that the German military attaché was officially forbidden to speak. When he lay dying, however, his wife[15] heard him cry in his delirium:

"Frenchmen, listen to me! Dreyfus is innocent! He was never guilty! Everything was intrigue and falsification! Dreyfus I tell you is innocent!"[16]

Military tribunals have never been noted for their impartial procedure. French politics, chronically turbulent today, were hardly tranquil when the Republic was only entering its twenty-fourth year. Yet that Dreyfus—a Jew whose talents were so distinguished that, even though personally unpopular, he could not be denied staff appointment—should twice be convicted of treason without a particle of evidence against him, while Esterhazy the *ex curia* traitor was acquitted, undoubtedly caused a grave impairment of French prestige.

In Germany it seemed all too apparent that the government and army leaders of France and its military secret service had lost nothing of their vulnerability discovered in Stieber's heyday. The Dreyfus affair unquestionably renewed in France the post-Sedan tensions and humiliations and revived the spy mania and suspicion generated by Stieber's horde of espions. Caste brigandage had despoiled the artillery captain's best years in the army, depriving the Republic of a brilliant staff officer; but the crime of his antagonists is most significant because of its profound effect upon the "next war" psychology of Berlin, of Paris, and of a hundred million potential foes. It influenced the formation of the Entente and hastened the outbreak of hostilities.

This appears to have been foreseen at the Wilhelmstrasse, where the earliest—1894—fulminations of the French press were closely observed and speedily resented. The German ambassador, Count Münster, complained to Foreign Minister Hanotaux, and Kaiser Wilhelm wrote on the margin of a state paper: "Approved. Münster should demand urgently the fullest official satisfaction. Otherwise I will proceed vigorously."

Münster proceeded so vigorously that the French premier, Dupuy, practically assured him Germany was in no degree involved in the guilt of Dreyfus. As Dreyfus was not guilty, this was more than a diplomatic truth. Dupuy himself was the innocent dupe of Henry, D'Aboville, Fabre, Du Paty de Clam and the other staff conspirators. But when Münster submitted his report to Berlin, the Kaiser wished to have issued a public statement of the admission Dupuy had made. To that end Chancellor von Hohenlohe wrote the ambassador on January 4, 1895, requesting him to procure from the French president confirmation of Dupuy's statement, concluding pointedly:

If this be the case, his Majesty the Emperor expects from the loyal friendship of the President of the Republic that he will publicly and officially set this fact to right, whose longer beclouding is calculated to embarrass the stay in Paris of a representative of the Ever Highest Person.

No demand could have seemed more awkward to President Casimir-Périer. How could any member of the government affirm that the traitor had not had any relations with the embassy of the Ever Highest Person when Dreyfus had been convicted on contrary evidence?

When in 1897 Senator Scheurer-Kestner, Picquart and Mathieu Dreyfus launched the counter-offensive which, ultimately, destroyed the conspiracy and liberated Dreyfus, diplomatic reports again began streaming toward Berlin. Count Münster wrote the chancellor, "I have never myself doubted that Dreyfus's conviction was an injustice." On the margin of this Kaiser Wilhelm wrote, "Neither have I." A second report affirmed the illegality of the verdict of the French court-martial; and again the Ever Highest Person observed, "Such view I entertained formerly, and am still of that conviction."

The Waldeck-Rousseau government of "Republican Defense" was anxious about the insurrectionary outbreak which threatened as Dreyfus' second trial approached. The premier in his extremity besought Wilhelmstrasse to release even one of the Esterhazy documents it had received after the arrest of Dreyfus. M. Delcassé, then foreign minister, asked that Von Schwartzkoppen—who, of course, had been replaced in Paris—be allowed to make a deposition in Germany. Both the Marquis de Gallifet, minister of war, and Maître Labori, junior counsel for Dreyfus, wrote personally to the Kaiser, the former endorsing Delcassé's request, and the latter urging that the military attaché be granted permission to appear in person at Rennes.

But Wilhelm was now not only ever highest but adamant.

On the margin of Labori's entreaty he wrote: "Imprudent—of course, out of the question." And on De Gallifet's: "How does all this concern me? I am not Emperor of the French; moreover, the court martial does not want it."

The fear expressed by the French war minister that if Dreyfus were reconvicted there would be a revolution, and that the very existence of France as a nation was in danger, extended the Hohenzollern vocabulary hardly at all.

"Richtig!" he wrote, and also, "Ja!"

Chapter Fifty-four

THE FRENCH REACTION

COLONEL DREYFUS is said to have been especially proud of his four years' service in the World War. He would have been justified in laying claim, if he chose, to even larger credit. His disgrace, his widely deplored and prolonged sufferings had led to many radical revisions of the military establishment of France, revisions which counted heavily in the war, in its hours of strain, its days of defeatism, its months of mutinous tension.

This was particularly true of prewar reforms effected in the General Staff and Intelligence. However, while the camp opposing Dreyfus survived there was nothing precipitate about these reformations. Virulent prejudices are not to be curbed by judicial fiat; and, though growing older seems to moderate and mellow the radical, only death will cure a reactionary.

Picquart had been punished for being right, which, as a later chapter will show, was so ineradicable a trait of the French higher command that they even communicated the infection to some of their British allies[1] during the conflict with Germany. Moreover, as the espionage bureau and *État-Major* absorbed the successive shocks of possible collusion, Picquart's dismissal, the suicide of Henry and Esterhazy's fugitive admission of guilt, there was being contrived on a lesser scale, with no anti-Semitic bias or umbrage of caste, a parallel proof that the typically French *management* of spy and counter-spy, even more than spying itself, was peculiarly crooked and callous.

The case of the secret agent, Lajoux, never gained the attention it merited. This was principally on account of the contemporary agitations of the Dreyfus affair; but also because Lajoux, unlike the artillery specialist, was not just an utterly innocent bystander, dragged in by feeble chicane to hide other crimes behind Jew-baiting ceremonies, but rather a clever secret intriguer of the Henry-Esterhazy stamp. He had willingly and even proudly involved himself in a series of hazardous and slippery transactions, all under the head of clandestine service to *la patrie*. In consequence, anything that happened to him was no more than the "worst" which the professional spy must expect. And yet it was not in the code for ranking French officers, much indebted to this man,² to rack themselves and lie awake, devising his treacherous ruin.

Lajoux had served in the French army for ten years, taken part in the comfortless Tunis campaign and risen to the rank of noncommissioned officer. About 1890 he was living in Brussels, honorably discharged, but out of work, penniless. Richard Cuers was then chief of Germany's secret-service "expedition" located in the Belgian capital; and having struck up the usual café acquaintance with Lajoux, he worked around to the delicate point of suggesting that the former French N.C.O. become a German spy. Lajoux admitted his great need, hinted he might accept. Cuers made him a handsome offer; and the Frenchman professed his willingness to agree. Yet poor as he was, on that same day he wrote to the French minister of war, describing what had been said to him by Cuers, and concluding: "If you approve, Sir, I shall keep in touch with this person and hear all that he has to tell or ask, and perhaps you can make use of me."

This, of course, meant becoming a "double spy", and that meant double pay. Lajoux was out of the woods if all went well. He had, however, impressed Richard Cuers—who was the best imitation of Wilhelm Stieber the German service was to find in a generation— and his shrewdness afterward seemed manifest to officers of the French Intelligence with whom he collaborated. And any man of sense must have realized that he would gain longer and better remunerated employment if he worked fairly and exclusively for the Germans. Thus it appears that the poverty-stricken ex-soldier was inspired by the truest motives of patriotism from the first hour of his dealing with Cuers. French Intelligence officers never got around to understanding that in Lajoux; but if he was pained and surprised, we need not be, for those same officers were soon to become the flagrant champions of race and caste who all but dismembered France with their home-brewed "guilt" affecting Alfred Dreyfus.

When the chief of the General Staff gave his consent,³ Lajoux was enrolled in the *section de statisque,* becoming within the same week an accredited French and German espionage operative. Cuers paid well but expected his money's worth; and one questionnaire after another was now fired at the French "traitor", conveying a dangerously penetrating assortment of inquiries. French fortifications, mobilization plans, equipment tested but not yet issued to the army, and many other matters were touched upon repeatedly. And Lajoux had to respond plausibly or forfeit the German spy-master's confidence.

The answers he delivered to Brussels were drawn up by a member of the French Intelligence staff and invariably submitted to the chief of the General Staff and his deputy for approval. Since a great deal of accurate information had thus to be sold Cuers, who would have instantly detected clumsily fabricated nonsense, the little game the French officers were playing *was,* in a literal sense, treason. A strict interpretation of French law covering the delivery "to a foreign power or its agents" of "secret or confidential documents concerning the national defense"—that accusation waiting for Dreyfus—might have sent any one of these players to Cayenne. Permission given by the chief of the almighty General Staff, with his deputy as witness, protected Intelligence from the ever-shifting quicksands of French parliamentary interpolation.

For three years Lajoux sustained an unruffled masquerade. Almost every week a list of questions was received by him and promptly answered. The German Intelligence was thus encouraged to congratulate itself upon obtaining up-to-the-minute information; while French counter-espionage operatives chuckled over their certainty of learning what the other side did not know, and that which, in Germany, seemed most to warrant interrogation.

How to Suppress a Spy

"When at length the questions became more and more precise in form, it was, of course, increasingly difficult to supply such answers as would continue the deception and prevent suspicion from being aroused," the Second Bureau of the French General Staff later vouchsafed.[4] "Lajoux, as an accredited agent of the foreign power, had acquired a mass of valuable details concerning military matters and the spy-system of that state [Germany], which he had communicated to us. When the other side observed that the answers were becoming vaguer and that, about the same time, several of their agents in France were being arrested, they ceased to trust Lajoux or to show their hand."

Easy as it is to prove dead intriguers stupid, we may assume that the arrests in France compromising Lajoux had to be made if the culprits were to be taken at all. A kind of inevitability generates in the career of a spy as accomplished and well placed as Lajoux. The more useful he becomes, the more certain it is that his duplicities are going to be found out. If his collaborators in Paris had thought only of conserving his imposture, they would have dared to make use of very little that he communicated to them. As a consequence his imposition upon the Germans would have diminished in value to a degree which made conserving it no longer worth while.

On the other hand, making use of what he reported induced the same depreciation by warning his German employer against him. Lajoux, as they said, was *brûlé*. To the modern American underworld a confederate is "hot" when he draws upon himself the concentrated attention of the police and newspapers, and, if he is notably combustible, the Department of Justice. Lajoux, to the French Intelligence technicians, was not merely hot but burning. In acute cases of that nature there could be only one treatment they felt safe to prescribe—the incinerator. Where Lajoux might be left to burn himself up and become, patriotically, harmless.

Secret agents are not dismissed so much for cause as because—and Lajoux, in spite of nearly six years' devotion and a fine record, had to go because he knew too much. There was, in addition, the ever-handy inference that he might be a double spy who had elected to redouble and actually work in an honest fashion for the adroit and generous Cuers. Again, there was the evidence of a meeting between the German spy-master and Lajoux in Luxembourg, whereat the French, keeping them both under surveillance, had arrived at the conclusion that Lajoux was gravely compromising the Second Bureau by letting it become generally known that he was one of its men. The mere fact that such alleged misconduct cancelled the other "proof"—as to his having often dealt fairly with Cuers—made no difference; *both* suspicions were counted against him.

Lajoux was therefore advised to prepare himself for a second honorable discharge from the French army. He might count on three months' pay but thereafter must shift for himself, aided only by his former superiors' fervent wish that he tell nothing, write nothing, and drop off the face of the earth. It was made cruelly clear to him that further employment in secret service would be out of the question. No one thought to suggest a clerical position or the decent retirement with pension he would seem to have earned.[5]

Picquart and his chronic symptoms of integrity[6] had just been packed off to Tunis—November 16, 1896—and Major Henry was now in command of the Second Bureau. He felt worried about certain matters known to Lajoux which might discommode himself and other superior officers of the Intelligence, and, as we know, when Henry was worried he was capable of the most reckless and malign activity. The department he directed, which owed such a great deal to Lajoux, now condescended to the worst abuses of slander and blackmail. To all who would have stood by him Lajoux was represented as a liar, drunkard and grasping extortionist. While he was absent from his home in Brussels, a French agent broke in, damaged his furniture and stole his private papers. That took care of the authentication of any memoirs which the spy might undertake to write, either vindictively or because of future need. And even this stroke—which would seem wholly justifiable to espionage officers, whether Lajoux was threatening or docile—failed to satisfy Henry, whose emissaries next sought to induce Mme Lajoux to leave her husband and start suit for divorce, in consideration of a generous bribe. She was expected to brand him publicly in the Parisian press as a traitor.

After his wife resisted this conspiracy, Lajoux himself was taken into virtual custody by a ruse. Two police agents, assuring him that they had come to escort him to a meeting with General de Boisdeffre, with whom he had just been in touch by telephone, persuaded the spy to go with them to an institution which proved to be the asylum of Sainte-Anne. Lajoux was detained there for a week but then released when a medical board certified him as perfectly sane. The French espionage service had no room for him on the payroll but agents to spare in hounding the poor wretch. After his lucky escape from the asylum, he fled to Genoa; but by "warning" the Italian authorities that their visitor was a dangerous lunatic, the French made his new refuge unbearable.

At length, through a negotiation in which threats and fear weighed heavily, Lajoux was convinced that he had best accept a one-way third-class passage to South America. Major Henry, with nothing on his conscience save the ruin of Dreyfus, the undoing of Picquart, and the use of forgeries for the protection of the treasonable Esterhazy, could discover no excuse to have Lajoux transported to Cayenne. But when, late in 1897, the former spy was put aboard a vessel at Antwerp, bound for São Paulo, Brazil, the French Intelligence chief and his minions were aiming close to the mark.

Chapter Fifty-five

THE ACCREDITED SPIES

LIKE SOME CRIMINALS, the influences guilty of provoking the great war of 1914–1918 were of bad ancestry and noticeably bad character from birth. It has been seen how the imperial aspirations of the surviving Bonapartes and the Bismarck-Hohenzollern camp stalked each other down the middle decades of the nineteenth century, with one or the other bound to prevail, one or the other certain to be afflicted with sore and bitter impulses of revenge. When the Prussians and their allies, more than a little indebted to Stieber and *his* allies, won in overweening fashion, the French licked their wounds, unbelted the indemnity, and settled down to simmer with resentment and suspicion. And since we now must behold a defeated Germany fermenting in the French manner, it becomes obvious that another war had to follow the Franco-Prussian War. From the seventeenth-century victories of Turenne and Marshal Luxembourg to Blenheim to Fontenoy to Rossbach to Jena to Waterloo to Solferino to Sedan, French arms had been alternately victorious. Bismarck tried to isolate the Third Republic after crushing the Second Empire; and the counter-development of the Franco-Russian Entente set about forging its iron ring around Germany. But events were really following a pattern, and these diplomatic frays and forays, like the battles and the spying, were not so much causes of the World War as an integral part of the pattern of intermittent truce.

Extraordinary political changes were manifested between 1890 and 1910 which would ultimately bring British, Russian, Serbian, Italian, Roumanian and, finally, American armies into the European field as allies of France, a coalition without precedent in modern military history. The whole Continent, however, had been surfeited with the legend of the imperial German juggernaut. Awe or dread of the Kaiser's invincible war machine was actually or potentially world wide; and none had done more to cultivate this, or recruit future adversaries, than the Germans themselves. It was not a stroke of Entente secret service to invent *"Der Tag."* Even the post-Stieber secret service of Germany was maintained as a universal bugaboo, quite on a par with the regular saber-rattling calisthenics.

Meanwhile, the spies of France, Russia and England were comfortably underrated. The expenditures of Paris, the enormous outlay of St Petersburg, deserved better than a defensive reputation. And yet how could the stealthy step of innumerable anti-German espionage agents drown out the swashbuckling fanfaronade of Potsdam?

There is not any clearly defined date, or even year, when the imitators of Stieber began to excel his Germanic successors. The German decline was already marked at the time of sly old Wilhelm's death; while the French, after suffering disasters in battle and a change of government, had set out at once to enlarge and improve upon the espionage organizations of Napoleon III, which had always been too large, but perpetually aimed in all the wrong directions—a defense of the Bonapartists rather than of France. It may have been in this period that military attachés earned their title of "the accredited spies." We have witnessed the transactions involving Schwartzkoppen and Esterhazy, so tragically harmful to Dreyfus. But for all the Hohenzollern display of arms and Potsdam saber rattling, it can not be said that Teutonic attachés were ever the chief offenders. Possibly the terrific recoil of the affair of Dreyfus moderated the German officers' zeal for official espionage.

Russian attachés, however, were notoriously suspect. It was never a great problem to detect them; the difficulty lay in getting them to leave. Colonel Zantiewitsch, a Russian military attaché accredited to Vienna, was a popular officer and favorite in society, yet detected in a case of bribery and espionage. He could not be arrested without a serious diplomatic affront to the tsarist government; but at a state ball one night the Austrian emperor, Franz Josef, "cut" the colonel with pointed discourtesy. Zantiewitsch knew his signals—he had been found out!—and so within a week he engineered his own recall.

Colonel Bazaroff, the tsar's military envoy to Berlin in 1911, corrupted so many officials in the Cartographical Department of the German War Office that he was warned to leave the country within six hours or face arrest. Bazaroff was brazen enough to resist expulsion, complaining that it was an insult to him and his august position to bring up against him the mere evidence of a sergeant major. However, the German authorities swept him over the frontier. Colonel Michelsen, his predecessor, had departed the same way and for precisely the same reason. No wonder there was tension and talk of an "inevitable" war.

Italian military attachés were also "accredited" spies. In 1906 Major Delmastro gravely compromised himself and had to leave Vienna. During a tour of duty with the Turkish army Lord Kitchener—then a major—secretly drew "magnificent maps" of Syria and Palestine which would one day prove of immense usefulness in the campaign of General Allenby. British officers seem to have acquired a Stieber-itch for espionage. Three of them—Trench, Brandon and Bertram Stewart —were caught and convicted in Germany, and were imprisoned there until Wilhelm II ordered their release as a complimentary gesture at the time of his daughter's wedding. Sir H. M. Hozier and Captain Hall, R. N.—father of the British Chief of Naval Intelligence during the World War—had respectively labored with infinite patience to establish intelligence branches of the army and navy of Great Britain.

The undoing of three men of the caliber of Trench, Brandon and Stewart was a ponderable blow to British Intelligence prestige and enormously helpful to Teutonic propagandists of *"Der Tag"*; yet the pioneer work of Hozier and Hall was not to be wasted, not an ounce of it, and the devotion and ingenuity of their successors at "I" were the gains and defenses they had sought in anxious expectation that the general and "inevitable" war would keep all its appointments.

CHAPTER FIFTY-SIX

MESSENGERS TO GARCIA AND AGUINALDO

THE Spanish-American War of 1898 had insurrection both as a cause and an effect. After the mysterious blowing up of the second-class battleship Maine in Havana harbor and other equally questionable provocations, the people of the United States were ready for war. Public resentment had long been fevered by the oppressive regulations of Weyler, the aged Spanish governor general—"Bloody" Weyler to newspaper readers and the people of Cuba, who would have to wait thirty years for a Cuban, Machado, to make Weyler seem merely tentative and Christian in his cruelties. But humanitarian influences, however resentful, never meant to promote an armed conflict; while the Spaniards were almost humbly desirous of sparing themselves from American attack. The war simply began because no powerful interests at Washington were opposed to it. And beginning as a crusade to abate the evils provoking insurrection next door, it ended ironically with American volunteers shooting insurrectos a hemisphere away.

There was a minimum of diplomatic intrigue preceding the declaration of hostilities. Influential agents of intelligence were the newspaper correspondents who roused both the world and the government at Madrid with their shocking exposure of conditions in the Cuban concentration camps. Spanish conscripts in Cuba were likewise enjoying no healthful holiday; and other Spaniards aboard obsolete warships were going to sink or suffer. The monarchists ruling Spain did not need espionage to warn them of the prospects of their overseas forces; and yet war came, in support of the headlines, after Madrid had conceded every American demand.

When, only sixteen years later, the Austro-Hungarian Empire found this an agreeable precedent for thrusting chastisement upon war-weary little Serbia, the American public was revolted by the spectacle. Probably the same public would have rejected the political maneuver in '98 if it had been allowed to measure the potations of pride Spain was offering to swallow. But the Spanish-American War was not the kind that grows up to become a horrible example. If munitions manufacturers ever have to pass around samples they should choose it as a model, together with some of those even milder punitive expeditions against virtually weaponless tribesmen. Death when it occurred was just as final; wounds were as painful; the embalmed beef as unpalatable as profiteers could pack it. Fever that did not wait upon the invasion of tropic jungles, but raged in Tampa and other Gulf cities, did as much execution every week as all the rifles and cannon discharged by receding *conquistadores*. This price in casualties, however, seemed so trifling after thirty-three years of peace and Indian fighting that even sentimental ballads of the day had to exaggerate it or hark back to the slaughter of the "Blue and the Gray" at Shiloh and Fredericksburg. The fever camps were obscured by the victories and the ample parades—it made '98 *the* year for parades—and so also was the cost in money, actually so insignificant that it could be removed from the national debt by transitory nuisance taxes.

The war with Spain, to Americans who wanted it and who won it, was a standardized affair of perfect decorum, one hundred days' duration, a quartette of serious battles, two on land, two at sea. And the operations of Intelligence or military secret service were in perfect accord with the rest of the martial production. The American government saw that there would have to be armed conflict, no matter how often Madrid apologized for the mystifying tragedy of the Maine. Colonel Arthur Wagner—not President McKinley—sent for a subordinate, a first lieutenant in the Ninth Infantry and a West Point graduate, Andrew Summers Rowan, and told him that the War Department wanted to get in touch with General Garcia—Calixto Garcia y Iniguez—leader of the Cuban insurgents. Rowan had written a book, *The Island of Cuba,* so skillfully drawn from authentic sources it failed to expose that he had not yet visited Cuba. And so a peculiarly difficult assignment was thrust upon him. His instructions were oral—he carried no messages. He was to find Garcia, learn the strength of the insurrectionist forces, what supplies they needed, Garcia's plan of campaign, the morale of his followers, and whether he would coöperate with an American army of invasion. This meeting occurred on April 13, 1898, or twelve days before the actual declaration of war.

Rowan's mission was exceptionally hazardous,[1] for, in addition to penetrating tropic jungle, it was suggested that he find out all he could about the Spanish forces also. In civilian clothes he sailed first to Kingston, Jamaica, where he established invaluable and secret contacts with certain exiled Cuban patriots. From Jamaica it took thirty-six hours to reach Cuba in a fishing craft owned by Cervacio Sabio. A

Spanish patrol boat stopped Sabio, but he had Rowan hidden and cleverly pretended to be a lone fisherman whose luck thus far had been bad. However, it was good; and on the twenty-fifth of April—the very day that the United States declared war—Rowan opened the invasion by landing in secret at a point on Oriente Bay. Cuban guides were waiting for him in a remarkable demonstration of insurgent teamwork. The ensuing trip through the jungle consumed six days—the putrid water, the intense heat, the insects, and numerous Spanish patrols combined to promote the utmost hardship. But Lieutenant Rowan, who carried no "message to Garcia" save his superior officer's instructions, gained the camp of General Rio, was given a horse and a cavalry escort, and was sent on to meet Garcia who was besieging the town of Bayamo.

When the American officer convinced the insurgent leader of his identity, Garcia said he needed artillery, munitions and up-to-date rifles. He needed them so badly that within six hours he had the exhausted American on the road again, traveling with three of his staff and heading this time for the northern coast of Cuba. The second jungle penetration took five days and was no improvement; Spanish patrols were everywhere, and the men had to travel mostly at night. Finally they came to the coast and located a hidden boat, which was so small one of the Cubans had to turn back. It had only gunny sacks for sails, yet in it the three voyagers managed to avoid patrol ships and keep afloat during a severe storm. They made Nassau, were quarantined two days owing to a threat of yellow fever and then, thanks to the intervention of the American consul, were transported more comfortably to Key West.

For this extraordinarily well-executed mission of secret service Rowan was promoted to the rank of captain. He subsequently had a distinguished army career in the Philippines and was decorated for gallantry in the attack on Sudlón Mountain, attaining the rank of lieutenant colonel of volunteers. From Key West he had hastened back to Washington where his exploit was acknowledged with a degree of public acclaim.[2] But since he was a regular who continued to serve against Spain in a contest mainly productive of naval heroes, the merits of his performance as a secret agent were somehow disregarded by political appointees at the War Department.

Only twenty-four years late, in 1922, his grateful country awarded this officer the Distinguished Service Cross—the citation acknowledging the unique value of his mission, together with its special bearing upon the American victory over the Spanish forces in Cuba.

The Spies of Ramon Carranza

When Fitzhugh Lee, American consul general at Havana,[3] and Captain Charles D. Sigsbee of the USS Maine testified before a Congressional commission, each said that he believed Spanish officials were responsible for the blowing up of the American battleship. Whereupon the naval attaché of the Spanish Legation, Lieutenant Ramon Carranza, sent challenges to both. The proposed duels were not permitted. But the lieutenant reached a high-C of belligerence which the Spanish navy afloat was not equipped to maintain. When the Spanish minister[4] was handed his passports, he set out for Madrid by way of Canada but left Carranza behind, with headquarters in Toronto and Montreal, which he required ostensibly to wind up the business of the legation. Carranza's real assignment, however, was espionage.

This seems to have occurred to the American government almost immediately; and agents of the Secret Service of the Treasury Department were diverted from their ceaseless pursuit of counterfeiters to take up the practices of counter-espionage.[5] The house in Tupper Street, Montreal, rented by Carranza was their first objective. Not a day passed without some one of them—a succession of gas inspectors, bill collectors, salesmen, insurance agents, job-seekers—contriving to enter the dwelling and have a word with the Spanish lieutenant.

A naturalized American citizen of English birth, one George Downing, alias Henry Rawlings, was first to succumb to the blandishments of Carranza's cash bonus. An American operative secured the hotel room adjoining that occupied by the Spaniard in Toronto and actually overheard the conversation in which he recruited Downing, a former yeoman aboard the United States armored cruiser Brooklyn. This spy was shadowed from the Canadian city to Washington. Secret Service men struck up acquaintance with him on trains; specimens of his handwriting were secured. Downing, though he now called himself "Alexander Cree", visited the Navy Department soon after arriving in the American capital, stayed for a short time, then returned to his lodginghouse and remained for about an hour. When he came out he posted a letter, which was read by the counter-spies as soon as Post Office inspectors could be added to the case. Dated May 7, 1898, and addressed to Frederick W. Dickson, Esq., 1248 Dorchester Street, Montreal, Canada, it used no cipher but reported that "a cipher message" had just been sent from the Navy Department to San Francisco, ordering the cruiser Charleston[6] to proceed to Manila with

500 men and certain machinery for making repairs to the squadron of Commodore George Dewey. It stated further that a message had been received from Dewey at 3:30 P.M. and was being deciphered.

A warrant was issued upon this incontrovertible proof of espionage; and Downing's arrest followed.[7] With such a precedent of leniency toward Confederate spies in the Civil War, it is unlikely that a death penalty, or even a long term of imprisonment, would have been prescribed in the Englishman's case, although, as a naturalized citizen of the United States, his offense was treason as well as spying. But the former yeoman took his predicament with all the gravity it deserved. Lodged in a military prison, he refused to discuss his arrest and brooded deeply for three days, then chose a favorably unguarded moment and hanged himself in his cell.

The energetic naval attaché of Spain had thus far gained little intelligence of real import; but he was still rolling in resources and willing to deal generously with "neutral" assistants. It was his scheme to induce Canadians or Englishmen of military experience to enter the States in the guise of ardent adventurers, enlist in the American army, and thereafter conduct a simple sideline of messages to "Dickson" or some other "cover" address. Their daily observation of the strength, equipment, training and morale of the American forces was well worth the bonus he promised. Upon arriving with combat units in Cuba or the Philippines, his agents were instructed to desert. An unostentatious gold or silver ring, bearing on the inside the inscription *Confienza Augustina,* was supplied each potential deserter, who was assured he need only send it to the local Spanish commander to earn a substantial welcome.

When his secret-service recruiting failed to prosper, Carranza, who hated America, had recourse to the typically American expedient of engaging a private detective agency. Among the first prospects discovered by this candid breach of Canadian neutrality were two young Englishmen, known to the records as "York" and Elmhurst. Each was out of work and low in purse, each plied with food and drink— especially drink—by a representative of the detective agency, then proudly presented to the Spaniard. And each, when he sobered up, found that he had agreed to serve as a spy. "York" hastened at once to explain his plight to a former commanding officer; he did not want to spy upon Americans nor on anybody else. Carranza's detectives, realizing his defection, shadowed him and even took the curious precaution of giving him a severe beating. Whereupon he left Canada by the first cattle-boat, but not before he had given his railroad ticket to a friend to be redeemed, likewise the code-marked ring.

And the friend confided all this to the American consul, who promptly notified Washington.

Counter-spying operatives were thus advised to be on the lookout for British recruits with plain new rings. It was also arranged to have a record kept of all telegrams sent to or received from Montreal and Toronto at telegraph offices located near a military base or training camp. In Tampa a man who gave the name "Miller" presently tried to enlist. His application was delayed when the Secret Service learned that he had telegraphed to Montreal. The reply which came for him was intercepted. It read:

> Cannot telegraph money today. Move from where you are and telegraph from some other place. Write fully regarding stocks at once. Will wire money and instructions on receipt.

It was signed "Siddall."[8]

American agents in the North soon located a Canadian bartender, Siddall, who admitted that he had lent his name, for a consideration, to the private detectives working for Carranza. "Miller" was now taken into custody, documents found in his possession proving his name was Mellor. At about this same time young Elmhurst turned up in Tampa and managed to enlist in an American regiment. But "York", who had been induced to return from England, compromised him by giving testimony about their experiences together in Canada. This identification of Elmhurst removed that impending espion from the fever-ravaged training camp at Tampa to the safer, if closer, confines of Fort McPherson. And there he stayed until released and deported at the end of the war. While Mellor, who had never really functioned as a spy, paid with his life for having ventured into Florida, dying in prison of typhoid fever.

A letter written him by Carranza was secured by Agent Ralph Redfern—afterward a noted chief operative of the Secret Service, in charge of its bureau in Boston—and this document, besides helping to convict Mellor, added much weight to the growing evidence of the Spaniard's violations of Canadian neutrality. Carranza had fought obstinately, trying to promote a kind of one-man campaign on the North American continent. Undoubtedly some of his hirelings dabbled in espionage, but many a sharper preyed upon his patriotic ardor; and little or no intelligence of a damaging nature got through to him in time to be transmitted via Madrid to the Spanish commanders. Meanwhile, this blatant intriguing wearied the Dominion authorities; and when at length the señor departed for Europe, it was at the request of the Canadian government.

Americans on the Offensive

There were few spies in the United States and relatively few spy scares, though some six hundred persons were denounced to the authorities during the Spanish-American War and duly investigated. What really monopolized the nightmares of the more excitable people of the eastern seaboard was an imaginary "Armada" expected to sail from Spain with better speed and guns than the Elizabethan naval menace and better aim than Christopher Columbus. Cities and seaside resorts of the Atlantic coast in the summer of '98 were seriously alarmed; and the government, which knew better, could neither impart nor explain its perfect feeling of security.

Any truthful explanation would have exposed to certain detection an admirable secret agent. Having Spaniards for foes provided America one considerable advantage, owing to its long frontier shared with a Spanish-speaking nation, and its many loyal citizens of Latin-American descent. It was possible to find a reliable operative who might pass as a native of Central or South America; and many more could have been enlisted if the war had been prolonged. The lone agent ordered to try his luck in Spain was a Texan of Spanish ancestry and a graduate of West Point.[9] He arrived in Madrid in May, using the name "Fernandez del Campo" and posing as a wealthy Mexican of pronounced Spanish sympathies.

Stopping at the capital's best hotel, he made no advances and presented no letters of introduction but let his dislike of the "Yankees" be understood and gave it out that his visit to Madrid must be brief. Members of fashionable clubs, military officers and officials of the government met him, accepted his casual invitations, were sumptuously entertained and also enriched by one who lost money at cards with the insouciance of inherited manners and income.

Cádiz interested him, he said; but he declined letters of introduction to the governor of that port and to Admiral Camara. It was, however, Camara's slowly preparing fleet that represented the goal of his mission. The tactics of cordial reserve which had seduced Madrid were equally appreciated by the elite of Cádiz. Presently he met the governor; and it was but a step—a single dinner invitation—from him to Camara. In order to dine with the admiral it was necessary to go aboard a fast steamer which the Spanish government had very recently purchased from the North German Lloyd. The American spy heard officers aboard this vessel complaining about its condition. The German company had disposed of a ship that ought to be re-christened the Caveat Emptor.

"And when do you sail to give the damned Yankees a thrashing?" queried the partisan from Mexico.

"It will not, alas, be possible to sail for six weeks. There is still so much to be done."

The secret agent allowed his emotion to be misinterpreted. And so it became imperative to prove to him just why the deplorable delay was unavoidable. He was shown all over the former German vessel and by degrees put together an accounting of the whole fleet's armament, munitions and stores. Subsequently he managed to investigate the dockyards and arsenal of Cádiz, and even learned that, though Camara was to sail under sealed orders, his objective was known— the Philippines and the destruction of Dewey's cruiser squadron.

This was the vital intelligence he had come to Spain to secure. American communities, from Boston to Savannah, were still living in dread of a Spanish raid and bombardment. But such fears were without foundation. Cuba was blockaded by a much stronger American fleet, with Cervera's cruisers penned up in Santiago harbor; and now Camara was destined to steam thousands of miles away from the North Atlantic.

The secret agent is said to have been invited aboard a launch of the Spanish Admiralty[10] to witness the departure of the "Armada." A friendly naval officer pointed out to him the torpedo tubes and other offensive and defensive improvements hidden on the renovated vessels. Shortly after this event, the American appears to have dropped his guard prematurely or grown a bit careless, drawing police suspicion upon himself. He had sent off daily reports to Washington— cabled, presumably, via Paris or London—and there was much danger of detection in this necessary procedure. His keenness, however, did not desert him. Even as he discovered police agents watching his hotel, he was packing his luggage off to the Tangier boat, and he contrived to reach that craft unmolested after paying his bill and making an elusive exit by a service door.

The American Navy Department, thanks to the enterprise of this one operative, had complete information about the only Spanish fleet unaccounted for, even to the quantity of coal in the bunkers of each of Camara's vessels. The spy, returning safely to Washington, was privately honored for his wholly successful mission. But since a "Spanish" secret-service agent of his caliber was peculiarly valuable to the great northern neighbor of Latin America, his identity for years was closely guarded and his achievement never publicly honored.

When the United States presently came to terms with the government of Spain, all 7,083 of the Philippine Islands were ceded to the victor as a kind of imperialist debutante's bouquet. A matter of twenty million dollars was paid to Madrid for three centuries' lethargic improvement of the archipelago; but the new management got a stubborn Filipino insurrection thrown in for nothing. Many a young patriot, therefore, after enlisting to liberate the starved and exploited Cuban, found the war removed to a far-distant tropic island, where every shot of his Krag-Jorgenson would be answered from ambush by furtive little brown men who took him for a tyrant.

This grievous epilogue to a war of humane intervention might have lasted as long as the insurgents were skillfully and heroically led. General Emilio Aguinaldo was the directing brain and firebrand of the insurrection and a talented exponent of guerilla tactics. Nothing less than a master stroke of military secret service would serve to round him up and draw the teeth of the revolt; and it was a young officer belonging to a regiment of Kansas volunteers who produced that unexpected master stroke.

Frederick Funston had missed the technical training derived at West Point, but he had some things that no amount of education anywhere in the world could provide: a resourceful mind, a love of adventure, the spirit of leadership, and red hair. In spite of the hair—which was the very opposite of Filipino—this soldier, who was fortunately not too tall, disguised himself as a native and with a few companions, also disguised, found his way through the trackless jungles of Luzon. Funston's object was to make a surprise raid upon the remote inland headquarters of Aguinaldo and take him prisoner. And in this daring enterprise he was completely successful.

Then began the return journey, which was infinitely perilous. Dodging pursuers who knew every yard of their line of retreat, fording or swimming jungle streams, escaping bullets and poisoned arrows, avoiding even more poisonous serpents and insects, they brought their prisoner safely through to American army headquarters. As Funston had hoped, when setting out against such great odds, the capture of Emilio Aguinaldo virtually broke the back of the insurrection and thus accomplished what ten generals and forty regiments could hardly have done in another year of costly guerilla warfare. Such an adventure of secret service transcends the mere exploits of spying and communicating spy reports. In Funston's case, too, it was not quickly forgotten. He rose rapidly through all the grades of his profession and was a senior major general of the regular army in 1916 when, after the "bandit" raid on Columbus, N. M., President Wilson placed him in command of the forces mobilized along the Mexican border.[11]

It was while the dangerous drudgery of pacifying the Filipinos still engaged American troops that the Boxer uprising startled the world and inundated China. Regiments hastily transported from Manila joined the large contingents of Japanese and Russians, together with British, Germans, French and others, in the famous march of the Allies to Peking. The very conditions of this unique campaign discouraged noteworthy feats of espionage and secret service. Ample information concerning the Chinese upheaval, the strength of the Boxers and the desperate nature of their assault upon the "foreign devils", was obtained from Occidental refugees[12] and native converts, the distracted "rice Christians" of the mission schools. As for Intelligence and counter-espionage, the invasion zone from Tientsin to Peking was familiar ground to most of the forces concentrated around Taku on the Chihli coast, and, being vastly superior in discipline and equipment, the Allies simply mistrusted all Chinese and drove forward, behind a screen of skirmishers, to the relief of the beleaguered legations.

CHAPTER FIFTY-SEVEN

THE SOUTH AFRICAN WAR

THERE WAS NOTHING that resembles the modern organizations of British Intelligence and secret service in operation at the time of the conquest of the Boer republics in South Africa. The disorganized uncertainties of the Crimea seemed to prevail, rather than the earlier traditions and excellences of the struggle with Bonaparte. Nevertheless, British Intelligence owes much to the South African campaign, and even more to imperial experiences in India and other quarters of the East.

The outbreak of hostilities, though foreseen by Boer and Britisher alike, found the imperial government and its armed forces quite unprepared, with regard to Intelligence as with every other necessity of hard campaigning. Espionage activities gradually increased. In August of 1900 an English lieutenant of artillery was captured by Boer scouts, tried and convicted as a spy, and shot. Other arrests were equally accidental. The reminiscences of Winston S. Churchill and the late Richard Harding Davis, who attended this conflict as war correspondents, suggest that neither the nature of the country nor the temperament of the Boer was conducive to widespread or systematized counter-espionage.

African natives rendered both sides the most valuable service in scouting and spying. The British hired Kaffirs and Zulus, especially some of those accomplished cattle thieves of the border country, who were trained both by instinct and practice to travel through the Boer lines without detection. The reports conveyed by native runners were frequently written in a novel cipher, which was Hindustani spelled out in Roman script. Messages were inscribed on small bits of paper, rolled up into a tiny ball and pressed into a hole bored in a stick, the opening then being stopped with clay. Other African spies, prospering in British employ, learned to smoke incessantly and carried an extra pipe with their message hidden beneath tobacco in the bowl. If threatened with capture, they were ready to light the second pipe and burn message and tobacco quickly with seeming vigorous enjoyment.

Natives of German Southwest Africa, recruited as secret-service runners, adopted a different device. Pressing the sheet of paper into a tiny pellet, they inclosed this in the kind of tinfoil that is used in

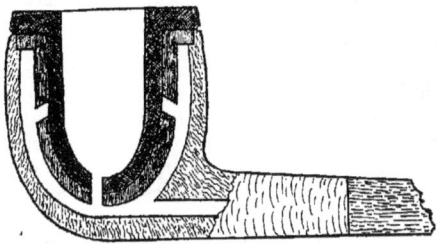

FOR SMOKING AND CONCEALING:
The more up-to-date pipe of a military secret agent, arranged by a unique internal device to permit smoking and the simultaneous concealment of cipher notes and messages.

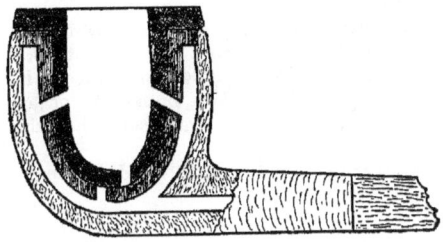

IN TIME OF DANGER:
By a slight turn the inner bowl of the spy's pipe is altered to allow burning tobacco to consume incriminating written matter concealed inside the pipe.

wrapping tea. Half a dozen of these homemade shiny beads might be worn on a string around the neck. In the event of trouble threatening the runner, he need only drop the string on the ground, where it would lie inconspicuously among the stones. Having been careful to remember the precise spot, he could return and recover it as soon as danger passed.

By means of fire and smoke signals—with which the North American Indian was also formerly adept—African natives kept the British informed of the strength and movements of the Boer forces. Sir Robert Baden-Powell, defender of Mafeking, has paid tribute to the secret-service abilities of a native assistant, a Zulu known as Jan Grootboom. A famous guide and hunter, he had come regularly into contact with Europeans, wore European dress and spoke English fluently. He was altogether trustworthy and possessed those traits of courage and cunning which frequently have distinguished the Zulu tribesmen. His British chief found him immensely resourceful in operations of the most perilous or complex character.

Lord Kitchener, as chief of staff, initiated several projects designed to improve the Intelligence strength of the army. But one such scheme was the not too-original convocation of a "Peace Committee", including, of course, the necessary ingredient of disloyal Boers. This committee was never meant really to agitate for peace, except as it might facilitate espionage at a critical time when the Boer commandoes were breaking off a hopeless campaign and scattering, to resort to guerilla tactics until the British should exhaust themselves in trying to round them up.

The superannuated "committee" dodge did not bewilder the rough vigilantes of the veldt; for witness a dispatch published on January 13, 1901: "The agents sent by the Peace Committee of Boer prisoners in Pretoria were captured by De Wet, on the 10th of January. One of the emissaries, a British subject, was shot. The other two were flogged."

That one word *captured* probably dissolved the committee.

Dr Leyds

An organized system of secret service had been unknown to the Transvaal, as elsewhere in South Africa, until the energetic Dr Leyds became secretary of state. The service which developed under his patronage was a curious imitation of many European services and, within a few years, one of the most elaborate and costly in the world. It also appears to have been the worst managed. Agents engaged for the work had no experience beyond that of police informer; and there was neither professional efficiency nor amateur enthusiasm in the ranks.

Dr Leyds did not take charge himself, nor yet delegate some competent executive to run the service for him. At the height of this ambitious confusion there were no less than *eleven* separate organizations in the Boer Republic, each nominally its principal bureau of espionage, intelligence and propaganda. Each was controlled by a different chief. Nor was secrecy a prime characteristic of these interlocking, over-lapping secret services, for it has been said that the only members who did not know all about one another were the heads of the eleven departments.[1] Waste and corruption were inevitable. As the result of a mere practical joke—inspired by interdepartmental jealousy and petty vindictiveness—the tidy sum of £5,000 was wasted upon an investigation, or one third of the total amount which Germany appropriated that year—1896—for its celebrated military secret service.

The objectives of the secret service established by Leyds were quite above reproach. Never sinister or aggressive, they took the legitimate form of defending the Boer government, and a law-abiding people, from the prejudicial attacks and criticisms regularly appearing in the press of the British Empire. Since Continental papers took their tone from them, and even North American opinion was influenced, the distortions gained the widest possible circulation.

Before 1899 Leyds had learned a great deal by trial and error. The waste of funds was still incredible; but results were no longer microscopic. His mastery of the propagandist's art as an "undertone" of secret intelligence turned much of the Continent, as well as many Americans, against the British and in favor of the Boers. When war came Leyds's propaganda suffered an amusing setback, however, for "the weak, defenseless farmers" managed to win all the early engagements. Sympathizers fond of an underdog cause were as much taken aback as the British army; but those temporarily alienated were replaced by the multitudes, chiefly German and Irish, who thought that the hard Dutch skull thrust into the lion's mouth was going to break off all his teeth.

Leyds paid some court to the Irish and Irish-Americans but mainly devoted his prewar attentions to the Continent, especially Germany. As the Transvaal and Orange Free State were making heavy purchases of German arms and munitions, it was not impossible to enlist Teutonic champions, right up to Kaiser Wilhelm and the austere General Staff. Leyds brought many Germans into the service of his country, and secured them easy, high-salaried positions, to the disgust of many native Boers. That several of these favored ones were also agents of the German government seems probable; but even if it were certain, it would not prove—as some have professed to believe —that Dr Leyds was himself a paid German partisan.

He was as ready to employ Englishmen if any were available. The first agent he sent to London was Reginald F. Statham, an Englishman long resident in the Transvaal and Natal. This man's highly remunerative post was merely "watching" the British press. He would have been identified in America as a "lobbyist" whose client was a government rather than a private company or organization; and when he allowed himself to be identified in England as a subsidized Boer champion, his usefulness was at an end.

Neither British nor Germans served Leyds as expertly as their liberal salaries entitled him to expect. It was the *Netherlands Zuid Afrikaansche Spoorweg Maatschappij* which proved most serviceable as the medium and agent of Leyds's secret service, with its general manager and secretary, a Hollander named De Wilt, linking the interests of the railway company to all the undercover projects of the Boer statesman. A great weapon discovered by Leyds and De Wilt was advertising; and editorial opinion all over South Africa was "modified" by extensive and generally superfluous buying of space. If no copy "writing up the country" was ready for insertion, De Wilt astonished the public by lavishly announcing minor alterations in train schedules in the columns reserved for his advertisement.

Leyds, managing to enlist more subtle operatives than Statham, ultimately had a private correspondent in every great city of Europe. All salaries were paid through a European banking house, such communications as Leyds sent from the Transvaal being worded so innocuously as to stand any inspection. He learned adroitness in dealing with his collectors of intelligence and, by treating each agent as if he were indispensable, eventually created a loyal, effective secret service.

Yet even this was to be of no avail in preventing the collision that cost the Boers their independence. Dr Leyds had little to do with military espionage of the Transvaal; while in Europe his service seems to have broken down as the crisis at home grew overwhelming. Sir Edward Marshall Hall, famous English barrister, believed that H. J. Bennett, whom he vainly defended in 1901, had been acting as a Boer spy; but Bennett lost his case and was condemned for murder without having his political affiliations investigated.[2] If he was a spy, he was certainly not one of Leyds's men; and his chances, both for espionage and long distance communication, were slim indeed.

In the decades since the South African conquest, a remarkably well-ordered secret-service department has exercised strict, if subterranean, control over the traffic of the celebrated diamond fields and, to lesser extent, of the gold-mining industry of the Witwatersrand and adjacent districts. Defending the great diamond monopoly, this service has been long devoting its acknowledged talents to relentless warfare—the enemy being that indistinct horde of spies, agents, smugglers and all-around adventurers of the I.D.B. fraternity. Independent diamond buyers sound like prosperous, resolute citizens; but in South Africa they are committing a crime. And so the secret-service agents of the monopolists do police duty and criminal investigation and are only included here by way of illustrating a curious problem in economic motives and patriotism.

Since Africa is the dark continent, in race if no longer geographically, it is appropriate to find that the very best spies and intelligence agents were—and, in some regions, still are—the native witch doctors. These cunning black wizards were freely employed by Boers and British, wherever obtainable. The success of the witch doctor's prognostications was wholly dependent upon his talents for observing, inquiring and the unsuspected extracting of information. In a venerated role, combining most of the obligations, and all of the prerogatives, of doctor, lawyer and priest, the African witch doctor was bound to gather together a huge stock of gossip, rumor, confessions and miscellaneous facts. And his fame rested largely upon his capacity to remember all of it and make use of it at the right moment. What could have been more expertly designed to train any one, white or black, for military secret service?

CHAPTER FIFTY-EIGHT

SPIES OF THE RISING SUN

THE GOVERNMENT and people of Japan have been giving a Western varnish to the lacquer of their Asiatic civilization with unparalleled zest and rapidity; and in nothing have they shown more zest or talent for rapid imitation than in organizing and operating up-to-date systems of political police and military secret service. Intelligence departments of the army and navy came long before the secret police, since the mikado's minister experienced no trouble for a generation, or until very recently, with Japanese inspired to imitate the radical elements of other lands. However, the ultimate importing of popular aspirations—suffrage, liberty of the press, higher wages, better living and working conditions—produced its inevitable increment of civilian spies and police informers to keep the long-buried bombs from being fused.

The Japanese appear to have become so imitative, not through servility or want of capacity, but because of a passion for speed. Improvising abruptly a complete modern civilization—and keeping it "modern"—left no time for experimental branching out along distinctive racial or geographic lines. The systematic use of government or army spies was as extreme a transformation as discarding the lance or musket in favor of the magazine rifle. Japan, unlike the great empire of the Mongols or Hindustan, does not seem to have shared the Asian tradition of authority sustained by comprehensive espionage. And as a method it was not congenial to the ruling caste of knightly autocrats, who governed almost to the present century by direct action, not furtive intimidations.

An old *samurai* with a new sword was not required by law or custom to wait for the next war. He simply strode to the nearest crossroads and tested his blade by carving off the head of the first commoner who happened along. The decapitated man had neither the arms nor the skill to defend himself; and, if by odd chance his feelings had been consulted, he would have only been expected to profess a peasant eagerness to accommodate the honorable weapon by hastening to his honorable ancestors.

That dutiful, submissive spirit readily translated itself into the most exacting obligations of patriotism. And when the nationally stirred and consolidated Japanese recognized the need for Intelligence and espionage in war and international relations, an instinctive self-sacrifice more than offset their lack of experience.[1] In September of 1904 two Japanese clerks employed in commercial emterprises at St Petersburg were arrested by the *Ochrana*. They had lived in Russia for a number of years; and both were discovered to be naval officers. They had long and carefully established themselves in the life of the Russian community and developed many social and mercantile relations connecting them with the affairs or personnel of the Russian navy. One of these patriot spies, in order to strengthen his position and make possible his marriage to a Russian woman, had already joined the Orthodox Church and was faithfully observing its ritual.[2]

The Russo-Japanese War

The war with Russia, 1904–1905, witnessed the world première of the Japanese Secret Service as a powerful offensive instrument. In the historical notes he contributed to the German Field Service Manual (1908) as reserved a military commentator as Colonel Immanuel pointed out how completely the espionage organization of Japan had mastered its European foe. And this in spite of the Russian government's large expenditures and invariable reliance upon spies. Other authorities have gone so far as to ascribe the victory of the mikado's forces to the remarkable industry of the Japanese secret agents.

Only a few weeks before the outbreak of hostilities an *Ochrana* operative, possessed of no little skill as well as the resounding name of Manasevitch-Manoiloff,[3] had contrived to secure a copy of the codebook used by the Japanese Embassy at The Hague. Now the codes of Japan are peculiarly involved and difficult owing to the complexity of the language, which, to most Occidentals, is a rare and defiant code in itself. With the aid of this codebook copy, however, the Russians were enabled to read all diplomatic correspondence of the rival government at a period of swiftly developing tension.

Possibly such advantages only hastened the conflict, for the attitude of the Japanese was uncompromising, whether coded or in clear. And the gaining of all that "inside" information seems to have been turned to little account by the Russians. There was always at home the turgid leviathan of bureaucracy, capable of frittering away any excess profit; and as soon as Japanese representatives were allowed to discover that something was wrong, they changed to a new and more baffling code.

General Harting, an experienced officer detached from the foreign division of the Russian political police, was ordered to Manchuria to develop a system of counter-espionage in the theater of war. He was provided with ample funds. But though a few daring spies of Nippon were caught, the superiority of the Japanese espionage in the Far East, once asserted, was never to abate until the end of the conflict. In spying Russia also seems to have run a poor second. Agents of the *Ochrana* circled around every Japanese diplomat or official in Europe; but in the war zone, from Port Arthur to the Siberian border, a far more vital area was dominated completely by Japanese counter-spies.

In the fall of 1904 a Russian soldier, disguised as a Chinese, was detected near a Japanese encampment through some minor mishap and brought to trial upon charges of espionage. He had no defense to offer. The court martial convicted and condemned him to death. But his bravery, fine bearing and evident ideal of devotion to his country all profoundly impressed the officers with whom he came in contact. After the sentence had been carried out, a full report of the proceedings was forwarded by the Japanese Intelligence to the headquarters of the Russian commander in chief, Kuropatkin. This statement eloquently praised the courage and patriotism of the unfortunate spy. And months later the tsarist government made public a striking and chivalrous commendation, at that time unique in Western warmaking;[4] yet such was the Russians' addiction to secrecy, even when the Manchurian conflict had ended, the real name of their "Nathan Hale" was never disclosed.

The army and navy officers of Japan were not inferior to those of any other modern Power in breeding, education or ingrained class consciousness. However, they recognized the "coolie" aspect of Asia to Occidental eyes and, while privately resenting this arrogance, never hesitated in line of duty to take advantage of it by submerging themselves and their secret-service missions in the coolie mass. Any sort of inconspicuous or menial employment—as steward aboard ship, barber, waiter, cook, valet or porter at an hotel, laborer or domestic servant—was not only accepted but solicited as an effective "cover" for purposes of espionage.

Long before the outbreak of war Port Arthur abounded in Japanese spies, who had disguised themselves as Chinese or Manchus and were concealed by the swarming native populace of workmen, peasants, traders, servants and bandits on vacation. Chinese secret-service estimates[5]—rather like those of an umpire—held that every tenth or twelfth coolie was a Japanese. All the Celestial servants of certain regiments forming part of the garrison, the First Tomsk, the Twenty-fifth and Twenty-sixth Siberian Rifles, were agents of Japan. So were half the porters on the Liao Tiah Shan Railway. While the most favored post of all, even though the most arduous, was that of a laborer employed in the construction of the Russian fortifications. Japanese officers, said to have been of field rank in some instances, rendered invaluable service to their emperor in thus slaving away with coolie gangs upon parapets, gun emplacements and trenches which other soldiers of Japan were going to storm.

The location of the electric power station and main transmission lines, the "hidden" position of the searchlights among the fortified hills, and the distribution of mine fields designed by the Russians to make the harbor impregnable—all were made known to the mikado's admirals and generals by agents of the Intelligence. And with what result? Japanese spies were not only honored at home but may be credited here because of the indisputable nature of *their* military achievements. To cite two examples: the great searchlights, expected to dazzle Japanese attackers, whether by sea or land, were straightway put out of action by the accurate gunfire of Admiral Togo's fleet; and, in the course of five attacks upon Port Arthur, only one of the admiral's ships was destroyed by a mine—later admitted to be a mine which had broken adrift.[6]

China's Reservoir of Spies

In spite of the evident willingness of Japan's officers to sacrifice themselves, Intelligence proved decently disinclined to waste their gifts or throw their lives away. Sabotage attempts were in the beginning reserved to particularly audacious agents or officers. But in the early part of 1904 Russian patrols stumbled upon two men in Mongolian attire who proved to be Japanese officers. They had made their way into Manchuria, slipping around the Russian flank, and were now near a main railway line, prepared to destroy telegraph lines—soon to be so necessary to the tsar's commanders in contradicting each other's orders[7]—damage the railroad itself and do what harm they could to the railroad repair works near at hand.

When brought before a court martial at Harbin, neither enemy made any effort to lie to the Russians. *Sabotageurs* of their rank had never been met before; and it must have taken all the heroic candor of which the accused were capable to convince their judges that they were not brilliantly disguised student bomb throwers from Warsaw or Kieff. Ultimately the military court condemned them to lose their soldier status and to die by hanging, all on account of the "crime" of sabotage creeping into secret service. The sentence, however, was modified to death before a firing squad, by order of General Kuropatkin, in consideration of their rank and courage.

Thereafter the espionage chiefs of Japan employed Chinese along the danger-strewn front-behind-the-front, which proved economical in many ways. For a few roubles each the secret-service operatives of Japan found they could hire competent Chinamen to work against the Russians. Being ordinary inhabitants of the country, they aroused comparatively little suspicion, even at a time when the Russian chiefs were themselves employing Manchurian residents to spy upon the oncoming Japs. The available Chinese were, apart from the useless peasant-coolie class, mainly those who had served the Russians heretofore as interpreters, couriers or clerks. They knew that they were justly subject to Japanese suspicions, yet they had not fled because they owned a bit of property or had settled their families in the now disputed province.

It was a simple matter—and the very essence of Occidental espionage technique—for Japanese Intelligence officers to warn these suddenly stranded Chinese that, if they cared to avoid arrest, they must prove their affection for the new conquerors by enlisting as spies. Additional recruits were found in those thrown out of work and stripped of all their worldly goods by the usual devastations which war inflicts upon noncombatant populations. Japanese spymasters gladly took advantage of the misery which Japanese invasion was causing and paid not more than the equivalent of twenty-five dollars a month to their Chinese confederates, while the war-rocketed cost of living continued to rise.

The organization of this military espionage was as systematic as Japanese ability to imitate system could arrange it. Along the army front bureaus were set up, under the command of Intelligence officers whose duty it was to control the whole service in their sector, make payments, receive and sift information, and pass on to headquarters a summary of whatever they obtained. Corresponding to these stations were others on the Russian side, managed, of course, by Chinese, who were responsible for the actual espionage—in towns behind the lines, along the railroads and at all concentration points of Kuropatkin's army.

Each Chinese spy, in turn, worked with two or three other persons whose job it was to carry the information he had collected to the Chinese bureau head. Whence it was conveyed by the boldest of the carriers through the Russian outposts to the Japanese advance front. Unwieldy as this may appear, it was one of the most swiftly operative espionage organizations ever instituted in an enemy zone of combat. The Russian front never exceeded a depth of sixty versts.[8] Therefore, a spy, using three runners, could receive and answer urgent inquiries sent by Japanese Intelligence in three to four days' time, maintaining almost an uninterrupted flow of information.

The Chinese carriers of this dangerous tide of news were peddlers or coolies from the poorest class of town populations. Poverty, so unescapable as to be virtually hereditary, was their best disguise, since they were hardly to be distinguished from the pitiful throng of beggars roving about Manchuria. For carrying one message across the most perilous zone they were paid five roubles and were so enchanted with that stipend, they are said never to have been conscious of the capital risk they were running.

Circumstances led the Japanese to form another type of espionage mission, embracing several groups of three or four spies who operated from a central base—generally well behind the Russian front—and were each assigned some very exactly defined problem to solve, such as reconnoitering a specified defensive position, or army corps, or observing a particular troop movement on a limited frontline of offensive. That Mislichenko's Cavalry Corps was expected to make a surprise attack on Inkou and the Japanese railroad communications was known at the headquarters of Field-Marshal Oyama two weeks in advance, or some days before the plan was revealed to the units assigned to participate. Reports from a group of independently operating spies had furnished minutely accurate details of the proposed enterprise. And the resulting counter-measures of the Japanese command caused the Russian raid to break down in complete failure.

These spy groups were provided with ample means, since it was desired that each group should have funds enough to establish its own center. This was generally a small shop, such as a baker's shop, which would be visited by people of all classes, including officers and soldiers, from whose conversation a good deal might be learned, and to whom casual questions might be put without exciting suspicion. Espionage in this adroit manner was only undertaken by the senior agent of the group, while the other Chinese busied themselves as clerks, waiters or attendants, or, away from the shop, as beggars or peddlers.

Stratagems of Old Asia

General Harting's counter-espionage organization, which was by now spending a small fortune monthly, began to achieve some results. Spying was still practicable; but the transmission of findings became increasingly hazardous. New dodges and devices had to be tried, one of the most ingenious of these being the working or braiding of the code message into a Chinese runner's pigtail. That engaging Venezuelan example of the modern soldier of fortune, Rafael de Nogales, was for a time an agent of the Japanese Intelligence and conspired in Port Arthur with an old Chinaman he called Wow-Ling. It was this spy's individual virtue to have several hollow gold teeth——

> Every night, after tracing and retracing, sometimes for hours, on the dirty mud floor of our room and by the light of a candle, the outlines of the various entrenchments which we had come across that day, Ling would write down and draw with the help of a magnifying glass our mental notes and pictures on a diminutive piece of very thin, parchmented tissue paper, about one-third the size of a cigaret paper. After I had examined it and declared it O.K. Ling would roll it into a ball, the size of a pin-head, and "file it away." He would pull one of his three or four hollow gold teeth out of his mouth, place the paper ball into it, shut the empty tooth with a piece of wax and push it back into its original place.[9]

The "portable files" of this crafty Chinese spy were eventually crammed full—only to be discovered and confiscated. His captors were native police agents of Yuan Shi Kai, who became president of the Chinese republic in 1912, but who at this time was declaring himself in on the heavy disbursement of Russian bribes. Wow-Ling, having unluckily been taken in a general roundup of Port Arthur's suspects—which the Venezuelan had the good fortune to avoid—was tortured to death after the fashion of Celestial inquisitors. The intelligence treasures of his hollow gold teeth were discovered when the teeth were removed as legitimate booty of the torture chamber.

Lessons of this nature taught the Japanese espionage service not to allow information of great importance to be put in written form. The spy was ordered to commit it to memory and communicate it orally to none but the Japanese officer in charge of the bureau employing him. In the guise of a coolie or peddler, the spy who carried no communications in writing, who was cunning enough to eschew furtive actions, who submerged his individuality in the Chinese multitude ever moving from place to place, would only be detected by rare accident. And even in the most suspicious cases it was impossible for counter-spies to convict these agents of Japan by discovering upon them any material evidence of espionage.

This was made possible by a favorite stratagem of the peddler's pack. The disguised spy would carry in his basket goods of various colors, which might, if black, brown, red, gray or white, correspond to certain military formations. By the same dodge, each separate class of goods represented a different kind of weapon. Thus, pipe tobacco might stand for heavy batteries, cigarettes for field guns. To add complexity the spy-peddler might also have for sale pipes or cigarette holders. Notes in Chinese characters would be inconspicuously written upon these articles. Separated, the notes meant nothing whatever; but when arranged in a special order, they transmitted comprehensive reports. With the mingled ingenuities of two Asiatic races at the disposal of Japanese Intelligence in Manchuria, it is not surprising that it won most of the skirmishes along the "underground" front of military secret service.

According to General de Nogales, it was "an acting secretary of state of the Empire of Korea", an adventurer named Evans, who enlisted him on behalf of the Japanese and sent him to Port Arthur to pose as a peddler of watches—Swiss watches at bargain prices offered by a Swiss peddler, because Stoessel, the commander of the Russian fortress, was a Swiss. Evans was "a shrewd business man" to the young Venezuelan, and one resolved to make himself a millionaire: whereas to Yuan Shi Kai he was "that abominable man ... who is trying to sell Korea to the Japanese."[10] Evidently this Korean "adviser" was both the responsible head of, and cover for, Nipponese espionage in Korea, Port Arthur, and the Liaotung Peninsula prior to the outbreak of actual hostilities.

While the British were rather openly backing Japan, the government of China—mainly in the person of Yuan Shi Kai, favorite of the Dowager Empress Tzu-Hsi and viceroy of Chihli, whose spies were everywhere—did all in its power to hinder Japanese ascendancy. Owing to Japan's proximity to China, it seemed even then a more malignant threat to Chinese territorial integrity than the sprawling imperial designs of the tsar.

In 1904–05 it was easy to regard "little Japan" as the weaker belligerent and underdog, and to applaud the exploits of the Japanese army and its secret service. Japan, moreover, was obviously determined to make its debut as a World Power under the most pleasing auspices and therefore fought a generous, thoroughly old-fashioned "professional soldiers'" war. When revolutionary elements in European Russia aspired to take a hand in the struggle, looking to Russian disaster as a gain for their cause, the Nipponese high command refused to co-operate. The Polish agitator, Pilsudski,[11] traveled secretly to

Tokyo to beg military support in fomenting a Polish insurrection; but the mikado's representatives would have none of him. They sought to win the war by fair means and *in the Orient*, to gain prestige as well as their first foothold in Manchuria while accomplishing the eviction of the Russians. Helping to overthrow another imperial dynasty would have violated their own rooted belief in monarchy, absolutism and divine right.

The leading result of the Russo-Japanese War, so far as it pertains to this record, was its radical influence in altering the foreign policy of St Petersburg. Great-Serbia, Pan-Slavism and the rather recklessly nurtured antagonism between Austria-Hungary and the Balkan Slavs became the diversion of the Russian Foreign Office. Thus the defeats in Manchuria reversed the Romanoff imperialism, so that a head-on collision with the Habsburg imperialism was inevitable. But before we focus our attention on the development of that fateful explosion in the Balkans, we must observe one other theater of secret-service operations—South America—virtually isolated from the governing technique of modern Europe, yet a harbinger of the political police systems that fortify European dictatorships today.

CHAPTER FIFTY-NINE

WATCHDOGS OF DICTATORDOM

THE POLITICAL "BOSS" in Latin America has generally disdained to stoop to the electioneering chicaneries practiced by politicians of the United States. It has perhaps been a matter of local pride to differ in that—and other—degrees from the envied, suspected Colossus of the North; and apparently it has been found cheaper, not to promise the voter what he will gain if he votes for you, but to convince him that he will be shot if he votes against you. The greedy and garroting grip of the dictator has left its mark upon the windpipe of nearly every one of the South and Central American republics. A few have been prodigal and existed continuously under some thinly veiled form of tyrannic misrule. Some others have prospered, though never excessively, or with even a considerable general improvement of living standards, simply because the natural resources of the land were so rich they overflowed the pockets of the plunderers.

Such dictatorship has meant administratively a special blend of spurious progress, repression and neglect. It has also meant a curb upon free speech and free assembly, a gagged or subsidized "opposition", and a corrupt press. And it has always meant spies and hired informers, petty tyrants and petty grafters, together with dungeons, flogging, torture, martial law, exile, executions, and habeas corpus only as an undertaker's privilege. It has called, in short, for every extremity of ruthlessness in the operations of political police.

Whereas the detective of North America has been habitually cartooned as a "gumshoe", walking softly upon rubber heels, the typical government agent of Latin American dictatordom wears the iron heel and aims for the citizen's neck. Any suspect who may prove hard to convict, but whose nuisance value is subject to inflation, will be shot while trying to escape. Long ago that became basic police technique in Latin America, whose second and third oldest professions are despot and revolutionist. The yoke of Madrid was joyously thrown off, yet after generations of liberty and popular suffrage there were many Latin-American republics at the turn of the century to which the monarchies of Spain or Russia could have been removed as a program of liberal reform.

Among so many political generals who seized despotic power there were bound to be monsters. In little Paraguay was one who had all the sadistic viciousness of Ivan the Terrible, without any of that evil tsar's sixteenth-century excuses of ignorance or widespread want of compassion. Paraguay had formerly experienced a benevolent absolutism under the Jesuit missionaries who ruled the land firmly and virtuously for over a hundred years. The native Guaranis were governed as children—disinterestedly so far as men, churchmen or saints, in a position of absolute authority, can be disinterested, but enjoying a perfect communism in their secular life. General Francia changed all that. He was an anticlerical fanatic who became dictator, who found his pleasure in watching the execution of his victims and kept them waiting upon a bench in view of his palace windows until he chose to give the signal to have them shot.

The police terror which he founded enabled his nephew, Carlos Antonio López, to take over the dictatorship when Francia died. Carlos' specialty was extortion rather than sadism; while the people bowed down and the graft rolled in, he was content—and Paraguay had to be. On his death his eldest son, Francisco Solano López, was the natural candidate for the post of *El Supremo*. Francisco had been living in Europe and he imported a narrow-gauge Napoleonic complex and a mistress, Eliza Lynch, a typical cocotte of the Second Empire. Patterning his political ambitions after the fashion of Napoleon III, this monstrous López brought ruin and death to Paraguay, reducing the male population by hundreds of thousands. It is practically impossible to report upon the Irish-born Eliza Lynch in a work that must be admitted to the mails. López was about equally dominated by her and by his virulent mania. He had his own mother publicly flogged for opposing his abuses of power; and the torture and execution of women became a conventional policy of the despotism. López' spies were everywhere; none, high or low, evaded the net of this unspeakable tyrant. Pursuing an aggressive and arrogant course in foreign affairs, López provoked an alliance of his neighbors to form against him. The common soldiers had to be driven to the war under the lash; and then this "Napoleon", descended from a half-caste Brazilian mule-driver, drove his army on to defeat and almost to extinction.

He ruled for eight years, the "Black Plague" of Paraguayan history. And every Latin-American dictator since then has owned or acquired some of the López traits. Their stories—the plots, the espionage and intrigues, the wenchings, the killings and the sordid pillage—read like the swashbuckling inventions of melodramatic fiction. They were natural Fascists a generation or more before the famous march on Rome; and it is deplorable to note that, however democratic its government at home, the usual North American technique of intervention in Latin-American affairs has fomented and openly defended the worst manifestations of Fascist dictatorship. One of the most disreputable dictators enthroned in Central America today obtained his start in the Caribbean world by serving as a spy and informer of the United States marines.

General Juan Vicente Gomez of Venezuela, seizing power during an uprising in 1908—when Cipriano Castro was abroad—held on to it thereafter by every known contrivance of repression to the day of his death, a reign of twenty-seven years, and a record for uninterrupted control of a South American state by a single individual. To maintain his authority Gomez "organized what was probably one of the most efficient systems of secret police in the world. For every uniformed policeman in Caracas there were a dozen plain-clothes detectives and spies who haunted theaters, hotel lobbies, restaurants, saloons and street corners, always on the alert for snatches of revolutionary conversation. Strict censorship kept unfavorable foreign opinion from the people of Venezuela."[1]

The general was called "El Benemerito" by act of Congress; and to some commercially-minded observers he regained for his country "the century of progress ... lost through a perpetual reign of revolutionary terror." Gomez' terror was stable and not revolutionary. His own son, trained to succeed him, a vice-president of Venezuela and a general in its army, he sent into exile when his name was linked to an abortive revolt. No doubt many of the stories told against the dictator were the fabrications of his well-flattened enemies. "Take your choice, señorita," he was reputed to have said to the daughter of a prominent family who, claiming the right of a spirited aristocracy, resisted him. Opening a desk drawer Gomez handed her two papers, the deed to a fine mansion in Maracay—the little town in which he lived in preference to Caracas—and a warrant for her father's arrest. "She loves him now," it was presently whispered in the cafés; but the whisperers may all have been Gomez' professionals.

Another charge described his having certain enemies suspended from the meathooks in a butcher's shop. It was a fact that agents of his fired from a motorcar into a mass meeting of women in a public square. And the imprisonment and torture of agitating university students gave his foes their greatest propagandic weapon. American business men spoke of Venezuelan oil concessions and Venezuelan motor roads. When "El Benemerito" died, his prison of La Rotunda yielded up quantities of leg irons, racks, thumbscrews and fire-blackened instruments of the medieval torture chamber.

Chapter Sixty

TRAPPING AN ARCHTRAITOR

ALFRED REDL was a spy-master and a spendthrift, licentious, homosexual, and an unconscionable traitor, who made such a brilliant impression upon his fellow officers that they expected him some day to become chief of the Austro-Hungarian General Staff. Redl came of a comparatively poor and socially obscure family, yet earned a staff appointment and rose rapidly in one of the most exclusive, caste-controlled military establishments of modern Europe. To scale without influence the heights that had confronted him required keen intellect, immense industry and indestructible aplomb. Redl possessed all those qualifications, and more. He was a clever linguist, with shrewd personal knowledge of the principal countries of Europe. Military history and Intelligence technique were his hobbies.

In 1900 when General Baron von Giesl was the head of the secret service he appointed Redl chief of the department of espionage and counter-espionage, the *Kundschafts Stelle* or information service, or, for short, the "K.S." Until 1905 Redl was the Austro-Hungarian director of Intelligence, and he won the admiration of the army leaders by the efficiency of his department. He caught some of the smartest spies on the Continent; he contrived to obtain many of the best-guarded secrets of neighboring Powers; it was said that he could not fail. Yet for more than half that time Redl was really devoting himself to the interests of Russia.

He made the "K.S." in Vienna a secret museum of counter-spying. If any one of its military staff was at all interested in a visitor, his photograph—full face and profile—could be taken, also his fingerprints, and every word he spoke recorded on a gramophone disc, and this quite without his knowledge. No matter where the visitor chose to sit, two cameras could be focused upon him with favorable lighting. Shortly after he had been ushered into an office, a telephone there would ring. The officer on duty had rung up himself by pressing his foot on an electric button underneath the table. In the midst of the ensuing dummy conversation the officer would motion toward a closed cigarette case on the table, inviting his caller to take a cigarette.

The metal exterior of the case was treated with minium and would retain the fingerprints of anyone handling it.

If his vis-à-vis did not smoke, the officer would allow the phone conversation to "summon" him from the room, apologizing, and snatching up as he departed a portfolio to carry with him. Thus was exposed a second portfolio, marked *Secret*. And few who invaded the central bureau of the "K.S." were of a type to deny themselves a passing glance at anything which seemed confidential. The surface of the second portfolio was also treated with minium; and if the visitor resisted its temptation, then a different ruse would be tried, and so on and on until one at last was successful. While all this time a hidden instrument had been transmitting every oral sound to a gramophone record in the next room.

When Von Giesl was transferred in 1905 to the command at Prague —one of the most vital posts of the empire—he insisted that Redl come with him as his chief of staff. So great had been the efficiency of the "K.S." under Major Redl that his promotion to colonel was promptly authorized. He took up his duties as second to Von Giesl in Prague, leaving behind him the record of his clever and prodigious industry as an incentive to his successor, Captain Maximilian Ronge, and the whole Intelligence staff. And it is ironic to note that the legacy of effective counter-espionage which Alfred Redl left behind him was, in eight years' time, to cause his own catastrophic exposure.

In 1908 came the annexation of Bosnia and Herzegovina, which provoked the animosity of the Serbs and led directly to the tragic collision with Russia. Ronge was kept on the alert by his new chief, General August Urbanski von Ostromiecz, who had succeeded Von Giesl as head of the imperial secret service. Moreover, Ronge was always aspiring to out-Redl Redl. A new form of viligance devised by Ronge was a secret postal censorship. Only three men—Ronge, his chief, and the officer they placed in charge of this Viennese *Cabinet Noir*—knew the real motive behind the innovation. The rest of the staff, though sworn to secrecy, was told that it was meant for the detection of customs swindlers. On account of that mild prevarication examiners at the bureau of censorship paid particular attention to letters coming from points on the frontier.[1]

Kronen from Eydtkuhnen

On the second of March, 1913, two envelopes were opened in the Black Cabinet. Both had been addressed: *Opera Ball, 13, Poste Restante, General Post Office, Vienna*. And they came, according to their postmarks, from Eydtkuhnen in East Prussia, on the Russo-German frontier. One inclosed bank notes to the sum of six thousand Austrian kronen and the other yielded eight thousand, or a combined equivalent of more than twenty-seven hundred dollars. As neither contained any covering letter, it was natural for the censors to suspect them. Eydtkuhnen, moreover, was a little frontier station well known to spies of every nationality. The "K.S." returned both letters to Poste Restante and resolved to have a look at the individual who would call for them.

On one side of Vienna's general post office, in the Fleischmarkt, there was a small police station. Ronge ordered a wire installed between it and the Poste Restante counter. The clerk on duty there would only have to press a button to set a bell ringing in one of the rooms of the police station, and he was to do this the moment the letters were asked for and be as slow as possible in handing them over. At the police station two detectives were to be ready day and night to hurry out when the bell sounded and detain for questioning the person receiving the letters.[2]

A week went by, everything was ready, but the bell did not ring. March and April, and still no one had called for the letters; fourteen thousand kronen lay unclaimed. But on the eighty-third day of waiting, Saturday afternoon, May 24, the police alarm began to clamor for attention. One detective was out of the room; the other was just then washing his hands. Yet in two minutes' time they had overcome their surprise and were sprinting across the Postgasse.

The postal clerk complained of their delay and said the man had just gone out "to the left." They reached the street only to see a taxi rolling away, and the only taxi in sight. The two men stood right there for twenty minutes, as reluctant as tardy schoolboys to report their failure and hear their superiors' comment. Hence another choice bit of irony enters the Redl case, for the detectives' blighted effort and aimless lingering in front of the post office provided a major clue. Presently a taxi came by, which one of them recognized as the cab whose recent passenger had certainly been the receiver of the letters. Hailing it they asked the driver where he had driven "their friend" —the man he had picked up in this very street about twenty minutes before.

"To the Café Kaiserhof."

"We'll drive there too," said the detective. And on the way he and his partner thoroughly searched the interior of the taxicab. They found the cover of a pocketknife, a little sheath of gray suède, and nothing more. At that time of day the Café Kaiserhof was almost empty; no doubt he had doubled on his tracks in another cab. There was a taxi stand not far distant, and here the detectives learned that a gentleman had taken a cab, about half an hour ago, to be driven to the Hotel Klomser.

Going to that hotel, they asked the portier if anyone had arrived in a taxi during the past half hour. Yes, several had; the guests in Number 4 and Number 11, and also 21 and 1—Number 1 was Colonel Redl.

One of the investigators showed the portier the pocketknife sheath. "Take it, and ask your guests, as you get the chance, if any one of them has lost it."

The portier, true to his profession, was glad to oblige the police. One of the detectives stepped aside and began to read a newspaper. Presently a well-groomed man in smartly cut civilian clothes came down the stairs and gave up his key. It was Number 1.

"Pardon me," said the portier, "but has the colonel by any chance lost the sheath of his pocket knife?" And he held out the grey suède cover.

"Why, yes," said Redl, "of course that is mine. Thank you." Then he hesitated. Where had he last used his pocketknife? In the first taxicab—removing the money from the letters! He glanced at the portier, who was hanging up the key. Another man stood near, apparently engrossed in his newspaper. Redl pocketed the sheath and walked to the door.

The detective who had been reading sprang for a telephone booth and called "123408"—the secret number of the headquarters of the political police in Vienna. And the chief officers of the "K.S." were now hearing what had happened in the past exciting hour. The "Opera Ball, 13" letters had been called for; their recipient had used two taxicabs in trying to throw off possible shadows but had carelessly mislaid the sheath of his pocketknife—which sheath, on his own admission before a witness, had been established as the property of Alfred Redl—the well-known Colonel Redl, chief of staff of the Eighth Army Corps, stationed at Prague.

One can imagine the stricken bewilderment of those officers of Austrian Intelligence. Their former leader, their painstaking teacher, and still their model and inspiration! Captain Ronge hurried to the post office to make inquiries. At the Poste Restante counter in Vienna all persons asking for letters had to fill in a brief form:

> Nature of packet—
> Address on packet—
> State (if possible) where from—

He was able to take away the form which had been filled in by the man receiving the "Opera Ball, 13" letters. From a concealed shelf in his office he took down a slim, neatly bound volume. It was in manuscript, a forty-page document written by Redl and considered by him too confidential to be sent to a printer.[3] It represented his advice to his successor at the "K.S." and was the last thing he had done there before being promoted to Prague.

Among numerous subtleties of espionage and secret service, it summed up his five years' experience as a detector of spies and now it was going to detect a master spy.

Proofs of Treason

Ronge placed the little post-office form upon a manuscript page. There could be no question about it—the handwriting was Redl's. He had received suspicious postal packets containing large sums of money. That did not prove him a traitor; he might merely be acting for somebody else in a private matter. But coming from Eydtkuhnen, that border "funnel" of secret-service conspiracies!

The reverie of the Intelligence captain was interrupted by one of the two detectives who had been shadowing Redl. Did he bring fresh proofs? "In fragments," he answered grimly. He was taking a number of raggedly torn scraps of paper from his pocketbook. With the anxious Ronge he bent over these pieces, fitting them together.

In half an hour the small puzzles were conquered. Ronge and the detective studied the proofs they had gained. Beyond all doubt Redl was a spy and a traitor.

The bits of paper had been obtained in a curious way. The two detectives had shadowed Redl as he walked away from the Hotel Klomser. Looking back and recognizing the man who had stood in the hall of the hotel reading a newspaper, Redl quickened his pace. This was a game he had often helped to play, but never before as the one pursued. Only seventy yards from the hotel, at the corner of the Strauchgasse, he managed to give his shadows the slip.

A few yards down the street, on the right, the detectives had a view of Wallnerstrasse. No Redl! Taking thought, the detectives agreed he must have entered the old Exchange Building. It had three exits, two into the Café Central, and the other through a passage into a large open square called the Freiung. They gambled on the passage to the Freiung—and there, sure enough, caught sight of their quarry. As Redl reached the square, he looked back, saw the two detectives, and once more quickened his pace.

He was heading down the long Tiefengraben, and as he could not seem to outdistance his shadows, he tried strategy. Drawing some papers from his pocket, he tore them up and threw them down without looking to see what they were. The staff colonel appeared to realize that his being trailed so persistently could only mean his treason had at last been exposed. It was too late to worry about "evidence"; the one thing to do now was to give these men the slip—be alone for a while—try to think of a way out.

Redl hoped the shadows would stop to pick up his papers, but neither of them did. On they came until, at the Konkordia Platz, they reached a rank of taxicabs. Redl did not take a cab, as his pursuers could easily do the same. He walked on. But one of the detectives jumped into a cab and was driven hurriedly away. Redl continued his strained, urgent patrol about Vienna, along the Heinrichsgasse to the Franz Josef Quai—down the Schottenring's mile length—into the Schottengasse and back to his hotel.

Where had the other detective gone? He had driven to the spot where Redl's torn-up papers dotted the pavement, collected all he could find, and hastened with them to Captain Ronge. At the "K.S." it was thus learned that Redl had been carrying in his pocket a receipt for the dispatch of money to an officer of Uhlans, Lieutenant Hovora. And three receipts for registered letters to Brussels, Warsaw and Lausanne. Ronge smiled bitterly as he read the last three addresses. A "black list" of known Intelligence bureaus of foreign Powers which Redl had prepared was in his file; and it included these three addresses.[4] Ronge now reported his findings to the chief of the Austro-Hungarian secret service, General August Urbanski von Ostromiecz, who was so shocked by the news that he hurried to convey it to his superior, General Conrad von Hötzendorf.

At his hotel Redl had found Dr Victor Pollack waiting. "Alfred, we dine at the Riedhof," he reminded him, and the colonel agreed, excusing himself to change into evening clothes. Pollack was one of the most distinguished legal authorities of Austria and had often been Redl's collaborator in court proceedings connected with espionage cases. The detective had overheard what was said, telephoned his superior, and then went to the Riedhof to interview the manager.

When Pollack and Redl sat down to dinner in a private room, their waiter was an agent of the secret police. But he heard little, as Redl could not match his friend's gaiety and hardly spoke except when they were alone. Pollack that same evening had occasion to repeat Redl's private conversation when he went to a telephone and, to the astonishment of the waiter-detective, rang up Gayer, the Viennese chief of police.

"My friend, you are working late," said Pollack.

"I'm awaiting some developments in a rather important case," said Gayer, and listened while Pollack described Redl's difficulty. The colonel had seemed moody all evening, had apparently suffered a psychological disturbance—had confessed to his friend of moral lapses, magnified anxieties, various delinquencies and misdemeanors. But, of course, nothing about espionage or treason.

"Overwork, probably," Pollack explained. "He asks me to see to it that he goes back to Prague immediately and that the journey be made as comfortable as possible. Could you provide him with a companion?"

Gayer said it would be impossible to arrange anything that night, adding: "But calm the colonel, and tell him to come straight to me in the morning. I'll do all I can for him."

Pollack returned to the private dining room. "Let us go," he said to Redl in the "waiter's" hearing. "I am sure we shall be able to arrange matters for you."[5]

Pollack left the waiter-detective perplexed and worried. He had heard the lawyer telephone to the chief of police, and then tell a spy and traitor that somthing would be *arranged* for him. Was the affair to be hushed up? Had powerful General Staff influences cut in to prevent the legal processes of retribution? The treason of Alfred Redl was, if possible, to be hushed up. But not in a way that would spare the traitor. The detective's worry and perplexity were as nothing compared to the reaction of such responsible commanders as Von Ostromiecz and Conrad von Hötzendorf. The latter, interrupted while entertaining friends at the Grand Hotel, was privately advised of the treason—Redl—the Eighth Corps. "Just the point where treason may be most deadly! If Plan Three is gone . . ."

The commander in chief is said to have perceptibly aged in a few moments, for Plan Three was the ultimate expression of the technical and tactical skill of himself and his staff.

"We must hear from his own lips the extent of his treason. Then," said Conrad, "he must die. . . . No one must know the reason for his death. Call together four officers—you, Ronge, Höfer and Wenzel Vorlicek.[6] Everything must take place tonight."

At 11:30 Redl took leave of Pollack and returned to his hotel. At midnight the four officers, in full uniform, called upon him. He had been sitting at a table, writing, and now he rose and bowed. "I know why you have come," he said. "I have spoiled my life. I am writing letters of farewell."[7]

"It is necessary to ask the extent and duration of your—activities."

"All that you wish to know will be found in my house in Prague," said Redl. He then asked if he might borrow a revolver.

None of the officers was armed; but fifteen minutes later one of them returned with a Browning revolver and handed it to the colonel. And now, left alone, and at the end of the somber spiral of his treacheries, he wrote on a half-sheet of notepaper, in his firm legible hand:

Levity and passion have destroyed me. Pray for me. I pay with my life for my sins. *Alfred*

1:15 A.M. I will die now. Please do not permit a post-mortem examination. Pray for me.

He left two sealed letters, one addressed to his brother, the other to General Baron von Giesl, who had trusted him and recommended his promotion to Prague. Fate had sardonically used that trust and that promotion to work Redl's undoing. If his abilities had not won him the complete approbation of his superior, he would probably have stayed on in Vienna; and while retaining his place at the "K.S." through manifest aptitude for secret-service work, Redl might have continued for years to cover up his treachery by means of subterfuges impossible to the chief of staff of an army corps at Prague.

Chapter Sixty-one

THE COSTLY TREASON OF ALFRED REDL

THE OFFICERS assigned by the chief of the Austrian General Staff to interrogate Redl and make sure of his immediate "execution" had established themselves in the Café Central, ordered coffee, and, tense and silent, prepared to wait out the night. One of their number had been left to keep watch upon the door of the Hotel Klomser; and every half-hour this man was relieved.[1] Not until five o'clock in the morning did they take any further action. Then, summoning to the café one of the detectives who had shadowed Redl, they gave him an envelope addressed to the traitor and told him to deliver it personally. The detective was warned what he might find and instructed to return without raising any alarm if the colonel was dead.

Arriving at the Klomser, the detective explained his errand to a drowsy portier, then went up and knocked at the door of Room No. 1. When he received no answer, he tried the door. It was unlocked. He stepped into the brightly lighted room, to find Alfred Redl lying in such a position that it was evident he had stood in front of a mirror with a strong light shining upon him when he fired the shot into his brain. The agent of police came away at once, closing the door and going out past the sleepy portier on tiptoe.

A few minutes later the telephone rang, arousing the portier. It was a request for Colonel Redl to be called to the phone. Whereupon the night portier went and discovered the body, just thirteen hours after the two "Opera Ball, 13" letters had been picked up at the general post office.

The hotel management immediately notified the city police; and Gayer, the chief, and a physician hurried to the Klomser. No further intrusion of the military authorities was to occur.[2] But Redl's devoted valet, Josef Sladek, a Czech, tried to interest Gayer in a clue he had discovered. The Browning revolver was not his master's. Four officers had paid him a midnight visit. It might be murder! Gayer took the servant aside, however, and spoke to him earnestly, thereby sealing his lips so that newspaper men on the following day could not get Sladek to utter a word.

As soon as Conrad von Hötzendorf had been informed that Redl had shot himself he appointed a commission consisting of a colonel and a major to go to Prague by special train. Their search of the dead officer's house was conducted in the presence of General Baron von Giesl; and the results of this investigation were sensational. Redl's home was luxuriously furnished—documents showed that in 1910 he had bought a costly estate—in Vienna he owned a large house—during the past five years he had "bought no fewer than four of the most expensive motor cars."[3]

He had been thought by his brother officers to possess private means; but actually he had lived like a multi-millionaire. In his wine cellar were found one hundred and sixty dozen of champagnes of the finest vintages. It was then discovered that in nine months he had received from Russia about sixty thousand kronen. That was ten times his colonel's pay; yet the extravagances of his mode of life hint that the accounts uncovered failed to reveal the full amount. The tsarist secret service was always notably liberal; and Redl probably was worth five or six times the sum indicated, or the equivalent of at least sixty thousand dollars.

Perhaps the most curious touch of all to this extraordinary affair was given in Prague, after his death and owing to the investigation of his dwelling. The greatest possible precautions had been taken to keep the treason secret. In all Austria but ten people knew the facts—the commander in chief, the highest officers of the secret service and of the War Office, and chief officials of the Vienna police —and each of the ten took a special oath not to breathe a word of it. Even Franz Josef himself and his heir, the Archduke Franz Ferdinand, were to be kept in the dark. And yet these measures of secrecy failed because the best locksmith of Prague was also a crack football player.

The locksmith, Wagner, could not play with his team, Storm I. on Sunday May 25, 1913, and, as the *Prager Tagblatt* reported next morning, his team had been beaten, score 7–5, largely on that account. The captain of Storm I. was a subeditor of the *Tagblatt,* and when he visited Wagner on Monday to inquire about his absence, he learned how the locksmith had superseded the fullback at the imperative command of ranking army officers.

Wagner, in short, had been employed to force his way into Alfred Redl's house and then to pick or break the locks on all its drawers, cabinets, wardrobes, chests, desks and cupboards. These had yielded up great quantities of papers, photographs, a good deal of cash, and maps and plans. Some of the papers, he had heard, were Russian. And the officers seemed utterly confounded and kept exclaiming: "How is it possible?"—"Who would have imagined it?"

Instantly the football captain was superseded by the journalist. As a subeditor he had handled in that day's issue the message coming from the official Vienna Correspondence Bureau. It told "with regret" of the suicide of Colonel Alfred Redl, chief of staff of the Eighth Corps—"a very gifted officer who would have risen to the highest rank." The colonel, having gone to Vienna "on a professional mission, in a moment of depression, brought about by weeks of insomnia, had shot himself." But Russian documents—photographs and plans—a commission of officers sent to search Redl's house a few hours after his suicide! That meant espionage—it meant treason!

The captain of Storm I. had unearthed a sensational secret; yet now that he had his story, he dare not print it. So stringent was the censorship in Bohemia, even in 1913, that the most guarded editorial exposition of "the Redl case" would have only meant a police descent upon the newspaper office, suspension of the paper, and jail sentences for as many as the staff as could be incriminated.[4] But the Czech and German public of Bohemia had taught themselves to read between the lines and even to peer "behind the paragraph." To let their readers know, then, that Redl was a spy and betrayer of his country, the captain of Storm I. and his editor concocted this "denial" for the *Prager Tagblatt* of Tuesday, May 27:

> We are asked by a high authority to contradict rumours which have been spread, particularly in army circles, about the Chief of the Staff of the Prague Army Corps, Colonel A. Redl, who, as already reported, committed suicide in Vienna on Sunday morning. The rumours are to the effect that the colonel had been guilty of betraying military secrets to a foreign Power, believed to be Russia. As a matter of fact, the commission of high officers who came to Prague to carry out a search in the dead colonel's house were investigating quite another matter.

Moreover, the football captain was the Prague correspondent of a Berlin paper; and by the twenty-eighth all Europe was reading his exposé of Redl's perfidy and suicide. Austrian officers, when questioned, were at pains to belittle the importance of Redl the spy. Only since the World War has it been possible to determine the full impact, the incredible scope and frightful cost of the staff colonel's decade of treason.

Masterstrokes of Treachery

He had begun to spy in 1902 and for ten years had been Russia's leading foreign spy. He had made a specialty of aiding Russian counter-spies, had denounced scores of persons acting as spies in Russia. Some of these were his personal friends and devoted subordinates at the "K.S." And he had sacrificed them to make more secure his own position as an agent of the Russian service. In order to earn the good will of the tsar's Intelligence directors, he had ravaged the empire's archives as well as its secret service. Not only had he denounced his own men on foreign service, but he had contrived to assist Russian spies sent into Austria-Hungary. He had been invaluable when it came to trapping and betraying to the Russians any "Redl" of their own forces who notified Vienna he had secrets for sale.

What—apart from the rifled files of the "K.S."—had he sold of Austro-Hungarian military secrets? The preliminary and hurried examination at his house in Prague developed a tale of unparalleled treachery. From the great mass of copied documents, codes, ciphers, letters, maps, charts, photographs, police records, confidential army orders, mobilization plans, reports on the condition of railways and roads, it became all too painfully clear that there was little he had not betrayed.

Plan Three was assuredly a victim of his rapacious trafficking. The complete scheme for military action against Serbia should war come with that bantam of the Balkans,[5] it had been sold to Russia, which meant that the Pan-Slavic partisans at Belgrade now knew all about it. Plan Three was the avowed masterpiece of the Austro-Hungarian General Staff and the pride of Conrad von Hötzendorf. Years of thought and strategical study had gone into it; they might modify it here and there, but its main features hardly could be changed. Examining Plan Three would have given the Serbian General Staff an X-ray photograph of the best minds of the Austro-Hungarian army. Marshal Putnik, a brilliant officer, was at the head of the Serbian staff. It is said that he concentrated upon the copy of the plan which the Russians sent him until he knew it by heart.

With what result? When the war came in 1914 all the world was astonished by Putnik's generalship. He and his heroic little army inflicted terrible losses upon the Austro-Hungarian invaders—who thus were still paying for Redl's champagnes and motors.[6] Thrice the Austrian high command tried variants of Plan Three—now known as Plan B (Balkans) as distinguished from Plan R (Russia)—and thrice the Serbian Voivode checkmated it. It took overwhelming odds and a shortage of all materials to expel him and his gallant troops from Serbia,[7] for to the last he had his mind attuned to enemy conceptions of tactics and strategy.[8]

Examination of Redl's papers shed light upon many a revolting transaction, as, for example, his crafty undoing of a brother officer and a Russian colonel. The Archduke Franz Ferdinand, visiting St Petersburg, had been so well received by the tsar and his court that on his return journey he asked the Austro-Hungarian military attaché to reduce espionage in Russia to such a degree that it would no longer disquiet the Russians. The attaché left the royal train at Warsaw, stopping there two days, in which time a Russian colonel visited him, offering to sell a complete plan of a Russian offensive upon Germany and Austria-Hungary. Despite the archduke's recent instructions, this seemed too rare a "bargain" to miss; and so the attaché came to terms with the Russian.

Redl heard of the deal and immediately went into action: a tsarist agent who, at need, would put the whole Austro-Hungarian service to work—for Russia. As head of the military secret service he was first to lay hands upon the Russian plans. He prepared and substituted a palpably fraudulent set of plans, to make it appear that the St Petersburg attaché had not alone disobeyed the Archduke's order but had been ridiculously duped. The attaché was reprimanded and recalled. Redl then returned to Russia the genuine plans, safe in the knowledge that only he and the discredited attaché had seen them, and that the latter had not had time to study them.

Lastly, Redl informed the tsar's Intelligence of the guilt of the colonel who had proposed the sale—which officer committed suicide on learning he had been betrayed. Redl's accounts noted proudly that by this odious exploit he had earned one hundred thousand kronen.

No exception can be taken to his suggesting that he "earned" what was then equivalent to twenty thousand dollars. To the Russians he demonstrated his value beyond the peradventure of a doubt; for he not only saved their secret plans and all the toil which staff officers put upon such speculative—and highly negotiable—paper, but he prevented both the Austro-Hungarian and German general staffs from learning of the formation of a considerable number of new Russian army corps. As a consequence it has been argued that the traitor directly influenced the ruin of three empires.

"If," said the late Count Albert Apponyi, "we had known of the existence of those army corps, our General Staff—and the German staff also—would have recognized the hazard of a quarrel with Russia, and would have been able to prevent our 'statesmen' from driving us into war in the summer of 1914. Hence our absurd war fever and our crushing defeat.... That villain, Redl, denounced every Austro-Hungarian spy in Russia, suppressed reports that leaked through in spite of him, and delivered our own secrets to the Russians."

The Hekailo-Acht-Wienckowski Affair

Documents found hidden in the house in Prague also showed how close to betraying himself Redl had steered in the first months of his infamous double dealing. Only the skill with which he played his triple role of spy, counter-spy and spy-prosecutor disengaged him from a dangerous complication. In 1903, shortly after Redl began pocketing bribes from Russia, a young man named Hekailo, a clerk in the army depot at Lemberg, was arrested on a charge of misappropriating funds. An inquiry resulted in his being released; but he immediately fled the country. Two months later, Redl called upon Dr Haberditz, a noted lawyer of Vienna often engaged for military cases. Haberditz had conducted the investigation of Hekailo and was surprised to hear Redl allege that the clerk had been guilty of espionage on behalf of Russia, that he had betrayed the plans for the co-operation of Austria-Hungary and Germany in attacking Russia by way of the Thorn region. Redl explained that he had discovered Hekailo's present whereabouts from an intercepted letter, the fugitive having written a Lemberg friend that he was now "Karl Weber" of Curityba, Brazil. Since spies could not be extradited, Redl urged Haberditz to demand Hekailo's extradition on the ground that he had committed extensive thefts; and this was done.

Hekailo at length was put on trial in Vienna; and Redl produced most damaging proofs against him. While his superior officers admired his dazzling performance, Redl brought forth as if by magic a succession of photographs, letters, sketches and various documents sent to the address of a governess in the family of one of the ranking officers of the Russian General Staff in Warsaw. Redl told his superiors that it had cost him thirty thousand kronen to obtain these proofs.

Redl and Haberditz took turns trying to make Hekailo confess, but without result. At one point Hekailo answered a question put to him by Redl: "Sir, how could *I* get at such plans? Only somebody at General Staff Headquarters here in Vienna could secure them to sell to the Russians." And that, though the accused clerk could not know it, was a proper solution of the case. Under severe pressure Hekailo was persuaded to name as one of his confederates, Major Ritter von Wienckowski, stationed at Stanislau. Next day Redl and Haberditz visited that place and had the major arrested. Half a ton of documents was seized and a third person implicated—the keyman, Captain Acht, personal adjutant to the general commanding at Lemberg. Soon all three defendants stood in the dock, and the trial was now a European sensation.[9] But as suddenly Redl's whole attitude suffered a curious change; where Wienckowski and Acht were concerned, he became more their defender than an expert witness appearing against them.

Haberditz objected, and his relations with Redl became so strained that he approached Redl's immediate superior, bluntly expressed his suspicion that Redl had been bribed, and demanded another officer of the Intelligence be detailed to assist him. But the accusation was brushed aside—Redl, the clever, the inexorable pursuer of Austro-Hungarian adversaries, a traitor—what nonsense! And a fortnight later Redl shamelessly reversed himself, once again becoming the unrelenting prosecutor; whereupon the trial ended with Acht and Wienckowski drawing sentences of twelve years' imprisonment, while Hekailo was tucked away for eight years.

Why had Redl performed his barometric evolutions in full view of a general court martial? Among his papers at Prague was the grim revelation. In the first place, it was he who had sold to the Russians the plans of the Austro-German offensive via Thorn. But in addition to his fee, he had insisted that his foreign employers strengthen his position by enabling him to capture the attention of Vienna with a startling spy exposé. As Hekailo had fled to the wilds of southern Brazil, he was no longer of value to the tsar's Intelligence, so the Russians sacrificed him to oblige Redl, told where the fugitive might be found, how to extradite him, and turned over the peculiarly complete "court case" against him.

Redl had said he spent thirty thousand kronen, but those admirable proofs really cost him nothing, and the money vanished into his private exchequer. However, it was not all to work out as smoothly as that. The Russian chiefs were profoundly disturbed when Hekailo implicated Wienckowski, whose arrest brought Acht into Redl's toils. Those two officers were accounted the best spies in league with Russian Intelligence in all the border country. The military attaché of the tsar found occasion to call at Redl's office and ordered him to contrive the acquittal of the pair, or else . . .

We may assume that Herr Redl's gramophonic recording device at the "K.S." was cut off that morning while the attaché spoke his piece. Redl knew that he need expect no mercy to be shown him by the Russians. They paid their spies with an open hand and punished them with a heavy one. And so he had to risk the progressive antagonism of Haberditz by trying to influence the court in favor of Acht and Wienckowski.

Caught at last between the suspicions of his civilian colleague and the brutal candor of his employers, Redl could only strike a bargain. And what he developed was characteristically cold blooded. The Russians agreed to forgive the condemnation of the two officers—for a price. In court, when the trial was nearly concluded, Redl referred to a certain incriminating document which, he said, had been obtained at great cost. A Russian major attached to the General Staff at Warsaw had "borrowed" it and forwarded it to him.

Redl confided to the court that this major was a man who had given Austria-Hungary, where his true allegiance lay, the benefit of his best services. The theft, however, had been traced to him; and he had been tried, convicted and recently hanged. Even mentioning the tragedy seemed to affect Redl profoundly, so indebted was he to the Russian on account of his aid. But the truth was this. Conniving to save himself when he could not save Acht and Wienckowski, Redl had undertaken to betray one of the best spies serving the "K.S." to the Warsaw counter-espionage authorities and supply them the evidences of his guilt. The Russian major was the secret agent whom Redl delivered to the hangman as his part of this unspeakable bargain.[10]

"Levity and passion have destroyed me," he wrote before squeezing the trigger of the borrowed Browning. He might have written—"destroyed me as I, coldly and without conscience, have destroyed many others—as, even from a suicide's grave, I shall yet destroy my thousands and ten thousands."

Austro-Hungarian losses in the four Serbian campaigns have been estimated as high as half a million casualties. Redl, it appears, was directly or indirectly the author of between 20 and 30 per cent of these. How many soldiers of the Dual Monarchy were killed or wounded on the Russian front in actions or disasters related to his espionage and treachery there is no way of attempting to compute. By hiding from the Austro-Hungarian General Staff, and, hence, from their German allies, the existence of strong new Russian formations, the hireling traitor nourished the fire-eaters of Vienna. By camouflaging the hazards of a contest with the tsar's empire, now largely recovered from its Manchurian misadventures, Redl played into the hands of every vainglorious "war party" in the capitals of the Continent. To that degree he helped work the ruin of Austria that trusted him and of Russia that enriched him.

Without minimizing the influence of this corrupt colonel as the undoubted master spy of prewar Europe, however, we must proceed to other and to primary influences which contributed more extensively to the coming of the great war. And they also belong to the annals of secret service. Sweep a dozen Redls from the scene, and what remains? Incendiary plots and rivalries all over Central Europe; the endemic conspiracies and antagonisms of the Balkans; the Pan-Slavic upsurge and its ingrained enmity toward Austria-Hungary, which the magnates of Vienna and Budapest wholeheartedly reciprocated. We shall find that agitators, bombmakers, spies, terrorists, assassins, all those desperate "patriots" of nationalism were as guilty as the cunning "patriots" of imperialism, the diplomats, generals and politicians, in fomenting the struggle which began in the Balkans. Alfred Redl, alive, contributed to these channels of turbulence and intrigue more misunderstanding, deeper suspicion, darker treachery. His post-mortem contribution was an extra round of slaughter.

CHAPTER SIXTY-TWO
SECRET COMMITTEES OF MACEDONIA

TO SPEND AN AFTERNOON in the Bosnian capital of Serajevo—June 28, 1914—not a quiet afternoon but one of stern event, sinister and measureless, we must look backward many years to the revival of Balkan nationalism. And we must look again at the Treaty of Berlin. Henri de Blowitz of the London *Times* could cannily expose the secret exercises of balance, bargaining and barter which produced the treaty. But once that negotiated paper went into effect, it was beyond all the chancelleries, all the newspapers, diplomats, agents and spies of Europe to cope with its irreparable consequences.

The Greeks, Roumanians and Serbs had won their freedom from the rule of the sultan before the middle of the nineteenth century. The Bulgars, without any vestige of independence for over five hundred years, had to wait another whole generation. They had actually lost their instinct of pride and prestige as a nation, every vivid remembrance of ancestral glories, until a monk from the celebrated retreat at Mount Athos, whose name was Paissi and who had been born somewhere in Macedonia, wrote his own rugged narrative of a rugged race of men, *History of the Bulgarian People, Their Kings and Their Saints*. No concoction of a board of master propagandists ever produced a more immediate, spreading effect than that simple text in the crude and ancient Bulgar tongue. The peasants so long enslaved by the Turk learned of battles and conquests when, under Simeon the Great, the Bulgarian realm was virtually the Balkan peninsula, learned of the Macedonian chieftain, Samuel, who for a brief time restored Simeon's empire,[1] or of the fierce Khan Kroum who laid siege to Constantinople and whose drinking goblet was the skull of the Emperor Nicephorus, encased in gold.

The Balkans being what they are, this sort of thing had a very invigorating influence upon the Bulgar peasantry. In 1835 the first Bulgarian school was established at Gabrovo; and by 1870 the Bulgarian Church, hitherto under the authority of the Greek patriarch of Constantinople, was recognized as an independent institution. Political agitation developed inevitably. The people whom Father Paissi had inspired began forming revolutionary committees, whose first able leader was Vassil Levsky. Disguising himself as a monk he journeyed from village to village; and because he preached a strange new religion called *Liberty* he was known as the "Apostle."

Vassil Levsky was extraordinary in his own time, but typical of his class and country ever since. He was successful in spreading a network of revolutionist conspiracy from the Adriatic to the Bosporus and presently threatened the corrupt old Turkish empire with the fire and sword of revolution. Like many a pioneer plotter of insurgence he was destined to guide his people chiefly in martyrdom; for Ottoman agents managed to arrest him; and he was hanged at Sofia while the Bulgar villages seethed. Shortly after Vassil Levsky's execution, as though his death were the signal he had promised them, the revolutionists struck. In April 1876 a band of young rebels led by the twenty-eight-year-old poet, Christo Boteff, boarded an Austrian vessel, the Radetsky, carrying large bundles which, they said, contained carpenter's tools. But as soon as the boat pulled away from the Roumanian shore, this band—two hundred strong—unpacked what proved to be uniforms and weapons. The former were authentic Viennese operetta, adorned with bronze lions rampant as a symbol of revolt; but the latter met most of the requirements of a simple program for slaughtering Turks. Like pirates they seized the vessel, but only long enough to transfer themselves to a point on the Bulgarian bank of the Danube where Boteff meant to begin his campaign.

This uprising spread swiftly and hotly across the parched prairie of Bulgar resentment. Boteff, however, was picked off by a Circassian sharpshooter and the revolt itself crushed with similar precision and dispatch. When the Turkish troops warmed up to their historic trade of massacring Christian women and children, they turned in a record at Batak, with five thousand defenseless folk tortured and slain. Thus the insurrection which Vassil Levsky had fomented and Boteff planned to lead brought on the Russo-Turkish War that resulted in the freeing of Bulgaria.

The Turks were careless enough to do a good deal of their slaughtering within range of enterprising newspaper correspondents. And these genuine horror stories had the same influence upon public opinion as similar columns written about Weyler's savage counter-revolutionary procedure as the "strong man" sent to pacify Cuba. Gladstone denounced the "despicable Turk"; and his pamphlets arraigning the atrocities were widely circulated. Gradually Western Europe convinced the tsar that he was protector of all the Slavs. Russian armies marched into the Balkans, beat Osman Pasha at Plevna,[2] and drove the Turks before them to the gates of Constantinople. With backs insecurely pressed against the Bosporus, the sultan's emissaries were willing to sign the Treaty of San Stefano, a document lamented to this day in the Balkans because it stipulated that all Balkan lands inhabited by Bulgarians should form one independent Bulgar state. Bismarck and Disraeli, however, stepped medicinally upon the scene. If Turkey was the "sick man of Europe", treatments which had failed him for fifty years must still be faithfully prescribed from Berlin.

At the ensuing congress, where we have only observed the intelligence prestidigitation of M. de Blowitz of *The Times,* ink was spilled that spread out in staining rivers of blood. San Stefano's bargain with the Moslem bankrupt had been dictated in cannon smoke. There was a rough army surgery about it; and the wounds would probably have healed. Using cigar smoke, the horse traders now concealed everything but their relentless guile in dictating to the victor on behalf of the vanquished; and once more from its Asian interment the corpse of Turkish sovereignty tottered back into Europe.

Comitadjis *of the Imro*

As a substitute blessing the ostentatious Treaty of Berlin outraged everybody. Macedonia was restored to Turkey for further alternative bouts of insurrection, massacre, uprising, subjugation. Eastern Rumelia, with Philippopolis as its capital, was set up as an autonomous province with a governor who must be a Christian appointed by the sultan. And what was left of the Balkan lands ceded at San Stefano was allowed to solidify as a nominally independent Bulgar principality.

No sooner were these inflictions made known to regions of the recent Turkish overthrow than fierce-looking mountaineers began laying in ammunition. "Macedonia for the Macedonians," Mr Gladstone had exclaimed; and Macedon took this for its slogan. Agitation for an independent Macedonian state has persisted with hardly any interruption down to the present moment. We are now tracing its secretly infectious influences upon the breaking out of the last great war; but it would be only a matter of a few notes and references to continue uncovering those incendiary powers of provocation which will endure to the outbreak of the next.

The Imro—or *International Macedonian Revolutionary Organization*—came into being for the sole and direct purpose of making Macedonia an independent state.[3] The founder of Imro was Damian Grueff, native of Smilevo, a village of carpenters near Bitolia. He had studied at the State University in Sofia; but his revolutionary impulses had to be obeyed, and in 1893 he discovered the kind of outlet that he and his compatriots required to save them from separate and fruitless attacks of spontaneous combustion.

Dr Christo Tatartcheff, Grueff's collaborator, became the first president of the central committee of Imro, wisely located in the nearest great seaport, Salonika. Local chapters were readily formed in every city and town of Macedonia. Many of the organizers were schoolteachers; and other leading spirits obtained teaching appointments to conceal from the Turkish police their real object in locating where the organization needed them. Grueff contrived to get himself appointed inspector general of Macedonian schools which was a perfect "cover" for his peregrinations as a revolutionary evangelist.

At first a society exclusive and secret, Imro expanded with the rapidity of a business catering to some basic popular need. The whole countryside, even to the most isolated small villages, was traced over with revolutionary cells. Teachers, priests and peasants, tradesmen, students, artisans, shepherds, and many housewives took oath upon an open Bible with dagger and pistol symbolically crossed upon it. These hundreds swore to fight, at the cost of their lives, for the ultimate liberation of Macedonia. As the organization spread, a system of control developed through local, subcounty, county and district committees, each linked to its neighbor, and all submitting to the supreme authority of the central committee at Salonika. It is said these novice revolutionists patterned their society after that of the Italian Carbonari;[4] and if that is so, they greatly improved on the pattern, despite—or, possibly, because of—far more intensive and savage opposition.

Imro was not long able to confine itself to underground civilian propaganda. A congenial transition from evangelical plotting to action began with the earliest attempts to supply the masses of Macedonia with arms. The first rifles and cartridges were smuggled over the frontiers from Bulgaria and Greece; but many more were bought on the spot from Turks who cared less for politics than developing a profitable traffic with the mountaineers. Agents of Imro were even sent to Belgium and Hungary to study the chemistry of explosives and the art of making bombs. It was a great day for the revolutionary movement when several small bomb foundries were secretly established right under the noses of Ottoman police spies on Macedonian soil.

For two years the finely spun network of conspiracy continued to strengthen and prosper; and none of the sultan's many spies and informers caught a murmur of its fermentation. Couriers went back and forth with important dispatches, munitions were brought in and stored at strategic points, bombs were distributed to neophyte assassins. The first intimation of the existence of this concerted plot came by accident; and subsequently a similar mishap led to the uncovering of the well-armed organization itself. Members of Imro at Monastir wanted to see what the new bombs of Macedonian make looked like; and a peasant, Andon Stoyanoff, was allowed to transport several of the iron balls, unloaded, so that they might be examined and admired. He hid them in sacks of rice packed on his mule, but on the way fell in with Turkish revenue men whose chief concern was the tax upon tobacco. When they thrust their iron spears through the rice sacks, hunting for contraband tobacco, the spearheads rang strangely upon the bombs. And when the rice was poured out, the peasant's relation to an amazing Balkan plot was exposed.

Andon Stoyanoff, being subjected to the usual Turkish "third degree", endured all the agonies that police curiosity can prescribe, said not a word about Imro, and became famous among Macedonians for his fortitude. But the secret organization had too many adherents, covering too much territory, to remain undetected indefinitely. Two years after the episode of Andon and the sample bombs, in November 1897, a robbery and murder occurred in the village of Vinitza, which had a mixed population of Turks and Bulgars. Since a wealthy Moslem had been robbed and slain, the Turkish police followed their customary procedure and tortured his Bulgarian neighbors. The robbers were a notorious band who had come over the frontier from Bulgaria and returned before any pursuit could be organized. Seeking the band's alleged accomplices in the Macedonian village gave the police both an alibi and a week end of their favorite indoor sport.

They made a thorough job of torturing the Christian "suspects" of Vinitza. Yet all bore it heroically until a woman broke under the strain and confessed, not about the robber band, but that there were rifles and ammunition hidden in her home. The Turks at once made a house to house search, discovering some fifty rifles, a dozen cases of bombs and cartridges, and a quantity of gunpowder. Thus by mischance was Imro's preparedness bared to the cold scrutiny of police investigation.

Sultan Abdul Hamid and his councilors had lately conferred on the Armenians their biennial massacres. A Cretan insurrection was coming to a boil. And now this echo of volcanic rumbling in supposedly subdued Macedonia!

Were the Turkish resources of tyranny near to exhaustion? A celebrated destroyer of Bulgarians, a *valie* from Skopye, Hafuz Pasha, happened to be at liberty, likewise the notorious police sadist, Dervish Effendi. These two were given carte blanche to deal with the Macedonian Bulgars, which meant that they would deal themselves *carte rouge*. The utmost of cruelty and bestiality were let loose upon the people,[6] and continued for two months until British correspondents and special investigators of the British Embassy at Constantinople extorted a countermanding order from Yildiz. Thousands meanwhile had been tortured, imprisoned or slain.

Nothing less than extermination will stop the spread of national revolutionary impulses. Centuries of repressive maladministration have proved that, which accounts for the police mentality of so many despots, dictators and ministers of state who seriously entertain schemes of salutary annihilation. The "Vinitza affair" brought Imro into the open, at first invisible but no longer secret, and then no longer invisible. The days of the subterranean civilian conspirator were at an end. The organization now was typified—and defended—by bands of armed men, called *comitadjis*,[7] who dared to dispute with the Sultan's police and military detachments their power over life and death in Macedonia.

The *comitadjis* were both a revolutionary secret service and an informal gendarmerie, and because they effectively combined these two capacities they must be noted in this record as unique. The need for such armed and disciplined patrols developed soon after the exposure of Imro by the Turkish authorities. As the merciless "investigators" of Hafuz Pasha and Dervish Effendi combed over the land, hundreds of Imro partisans fled into the mountains. Instead of leaving them a burden and a problem of scattered fugitives, they were made strong and useful, which brilliant stroke is credited to Gotsé Deltcheff,[8] who composed with Damian Grueff and Pierre Tosheff the general staff of the revolutionary organization.

Groups of armed men had always been used as convoys for ammunition trains, and the first patrols of *comitadjis* continued that duty, while gradually gaining experience as punitive and policing contingents. In villages where there were no Turkish army posts or police stations, and only Macedonian inhabitants, the *comitadjis* openly conducted themselves as a force of gendarmes. Elsewhere their expeditions were nocturnal; their presence felt rather than perceived.

Imro, having taken possession of the forests, lodged armed reserves in mountain strongholds and planted secret agents in every village and town, was transformed from a furtive popular intrigue to a cooperative military machine. And the Ottoman government was its unwilling partner in ruling Macedonia. Exploits of the *comitadji* bands inspired the lethargic peasantry, while rifles, bombs and knives of *comitadjis* curbed the zeal of despotic Turkish officials. Living in terror of Imro raids, great landowning overlords allowed the hard lot of the long-enslaved Christian population perceptibly to improve. Many a petty tyrant who felt immune to intimidations was more or less painfully liquidated. Thus, by means of a guerilla campaign of intervention, this well-armed and combatant "secret service" virtually liberated expansive rural areas.

Secret Preparations for Revolt

By a secret evolutionary, even more than violent revolutionary, process, Imro was on its way to capturing administrative control of Macedon. But the *comitadjis* were lineal descendants of those mountain Robin Hoods, the *haiduks*,[9] whose traditional insubordination to the power of the Turk inspired all the earliest endeavors of the Balkan peoples to escape the thrall of Constantinople. And so, together with the struggle for freedom, there was an ingrained Macedonian zest for reprisals. After many centuries of Turkish oppression, freedom itself—if suddenly granted by divine intervention—could not have seemed more sweet than viewing over the sights of a fine new Mannlicher a uniformed Turkish target.

One of the memorable, and yet typical, exploits of the *comitadjis* at the turn of the century was the raid upon the town of Melnik.[10] The designer and director of this engaging lunacy was Boris Saraffoff of Nevrokop, who had resigned his commission in the Bulgarian army to plunge into the conspirant revival and guerilla offensive of his native Macedonia. At the head of a band of rebels in 1897 he captured Melnik from its Turkish garrison and held the town for twenty-four hours. This was purely a revolutionary demonstration, without strategic importance, but it electrified the countryside as it was meant to do, and made Saraffoff an international celebrity. Many of his followers were brigands by instinct and inheritance. Only a leader of masterful purpose could have prevented their looting the city treasury and the homes of wealthy inhabitants. But Saraffoff held in check their preference for pillage, thus insuring the political significance of the achievement. Henceforth, until his assassination in 1907,[11] he was to be one of the most influential exponents of Macedonian liberation.

He became the permanent European agent for Imro. Of distinguished appearance and romantic personality, he was welcomed to the most fashionable drawing rooms of the Continent, where he put forward every conceivable scheme for replenishing the revolutionary war chest. By making love to the daughters of British and Belgian capitalists, he obtained many large contributions. In Geneva, London, St Petersburg, Vienna, "the handsome figure of the Macedonian could be seen in the company of gorgeously attired ladies, usually mature and ugly, since the young and beautiful ones understood little about national movements and the funds that were needed to keep them moving."[12]

Saraffoff's projects frequently skirted the borders of absurdity. When he heard that the Macedonian monks in the famous monasteries at Mount Athos had fabulous amounts of gold concealed in moneybelts or the monastic cellars, he rushed to levy upon this patriot hoard, only to be rebuffed. During the Spanish-American War he called upon the United States consul in St Petersburg to offer an invincible Macedonian legion to the cause of "Cuba libre" if, in exchange, the American government would supply Imro with guns and munitions for its combat with the Turks. The consul explained that America's man power was more than adequate. Imro's itinerant lover fared better in Switzerland, where an eccentric Englishman with an unmarried daughter old enough to be the mother of the dashing *comitadji* was interested in Macedonia to the tune of 50,000 gold francs. Saraffoff, who lived in Geneva at the Bellevue Hotel under the name of "Nicholas", made similar attempts upon American moneybags. Having no title to match his operatic manner, he was wined and dined but never subsidized with dollars.

Two *voyvodas* of Imro, Zandansky and Christo Tcherno-Payeff, had a different idea of capitalizing American concern for oppressed peoples. The pair kidnaped Miss Helen Stone, a missionary from Boston, Mass., and held her captive in the mountains until a ransom of 14,000 Turkish pounds had been paid.[13] During her captivity, a period of about two months ending on January 18, 1902, Miss Stone became a convert to the cause of Imro and afterward lectured in America on its behalf. Yet the kidnaping did Imro harm beyond price; and nothing said by Miss Stone entirely counteracted the widespread conviction that, like the bandits of China, the Macedonian insurgents were a mere underworld of thieves and assassins who would even prey upon foreign missionaries.

Imro needed many times seventy thousand dollars—though hardly at such a cost in sympathy and prestige—for Imro through the past decade had been preparing for war. The revolutionary high command —in 1903—set the date for the uprising late in the summer so that crops might be given a chance to ripen. Quantities of food as well as medical supplies and ammunition were secretly stored in mountain holds; and the Turkish spies and military forces were none the wiser. Often the peasantry staged eventless festivals, brideless weddings and corpseless funerals to cover up their insurrectionist activities. Thus arms were withdrawn from villages to be removed to some more strongly defended depot; or a leading *comitadji* might be enabled to escape in the guise of a bride, a priest, or as the temporary occupant of a coffin, from a district watched by police spies and blockaded by Ottoman guards. Recruiting proceeded without interruption, the agents of Imro moving about unmolested in their habitual disguises of peddlers, monks, muleteers and beggars. All of this, mind you, was a gigantic conspiracy, a form of revolutionary secret service; and even conscription was practiced in Macedonia; the new conscripts were drilled and clandestine maneuvers held in the mountains.

The small local bands were formed into companies numbering from seventy to a hundred. At length a disciplined force of 15,000 marksmen awaited the signal of revolt. Damian Grueff, and his "general staff" colleagues, Saraffoff and Alexander Lozantcheff, gave that signal on August 3; and as night descended upon Macedonia a flaring chain of great bonfires carried the war cry of rebellion far across mountain and plain.

This remarkably devised but hopelessly overmatched insurrection lasted two months and twenty days. For more than a fortnight the *comitadjis* swept everything before them; then an amazed and angry sultan changed his field commanders, replacing the tentative Omer Ruzhdi Pasha with Nazar Pasha. The latter at once concentrated an army of 264 infantry battalions and began borrowing some of the tactics which had recently served the British in mopping up Boer detachments in the final, guerilla chapters of the South African War. He used strong cordons to isolate each mountain, his infantry moving upward and narrowing in as they combed over the terrain by cautious advances. When *comitadji* bands slipped through the cordon, to reappear on mountainsides which had been fumigated, Nazar Pasha resorted to the last extremity of ruthlessness. He ordered his troops to burn and ravage the Macedonian villages and massacre their inhabitants, who were already sustaining the greatest hardship. By this efficacious infamy the revolt of Imro was brought to an end.

Terrorist Pawns on the Balkan Chessboard

The field army of *comitadjis* had been outnumbered about twenty to one, had fought 239 engagements and, in having 994 men killed in action, had inflicted—according to admittedly partisan estimates—nearly twenty times that number of major casualties upon its foes.[14] Macedonia was neither freed nor utterly vanquished; and Imro dissolved into its scattered cells of secrecy, but only to continue for another decade the struggle against degradation and bondage. Many influences led to the First Balkan War in 1912. The Macedonian agitation for freedom was certainly important among them. The ceaseless sniping of the never quite extinguished *comitadjis* had as certainly weakened the Turk in a region with exposed Grecian, Serbian and Bulgarian boundaries where he needed to be strong. And when the conflict came, it found Imro mobilizing, the *comitadjis* taking the field to fight heroically beside Bulgar, Serb and Greek in overwhelming the armies of the sultan.

Now the Balkan allies, each advised by one of the great Powers, were not altruistically pouring out their blood to set up a rival Balkan state in free Macedonia. When the Turkish armies were speedily defeated, the Bulgars, who had operated mainly in Thrace, discovered that the Serbian and Greek troops were not going to retire from Macedonian territories assigned in the allies' prewar secret treaties to Bulgaria. That infuriated the *comitadjis* as much as their being denied autonomy, for of the three allies they were least antagonistic to the government at Sofia.

The territorial delusions of grandeur affecting Athens and Belgrade brought on the interallied or Second Balkan War. This sharp contest might have been called the Typically Balkan War, since it was a free-for-all with no fouls counted and no holds barred. Roumania discovered its profit motive and joined with Greece and Serbia in jumping upon Bulgaria. The Young Turks at last displayed the agility of youth by likewise rushing in to beat the Bulgars—sneaking back into Adrianople, from which place they had been expelled after a siege. Only the *comitadjis* of Macedonia failed to react to that automatic magnetism of the winning side.

Standing up loyally to fight beside the Bulgarians, they took care of scouting, guerilla attacks and secret service, but saw the Bulgar armies, which had done the best marching and fighting in the First Balkan War, defeated by a confederation of all their neighbors. In May 1913 the Balkan states signed the Treaty of Bucharest—subsequently ratified at Paris—by which Bulgaria lost heavily, and which conferred, among other ill-gotten gains, the greater part of Macedonia upon Serbia and Greece. For such spiritually crucifying results had Imro struggled through the years of conspiracy, insurrection and warfare. The victory of the "liberators" was in many respects now more repugnant to Macedonians than their former existence—as a geographical unit, with the people enjoying certain national rights—under the corrupt and frequently discomfited sultanate.

Imro at once began plotting to challenge this diplomatic outrage. Todor Alexandroff, who would come to be known as the "greatest of the *comitadjis*", was in command; and the archweapons of secrecy and terror—first sharpened upon the Turk—were ground to a fine razor edge for use against new tyrannies, most of which survive and are resisted in Macedonia to this day. The structure, operations and disappointments of Imro are important to this record chiefly because the European situation for many years has made that secret-service society of Macedonian teachers, peasants, ex-brigands and *comitadjis* a kind of parent organization of terrorists. It is an ironic fact that Imro—incapable of contriving its own promised liberation of the small area of Macedon—has indirectly helped to bestow new forms of government upon vast regions and upon millions of people.

Chapter Sixty-three

BLACK HAND IN THE BALKANS

IT WAS a long open season for conspiracy. To appreciate that fully we must visualize a Europe divided by a broad belt of popular discontent, extending from the Balkans to the Baltic. Once it had been buried forever, the Europe of 1906–1914 was lamented in retrospect as something tranquil, expansive and precious; yet more than half of it during that "golden age" of Edward VII and Wilhelm and Nicholas the Last was resentful and simmering with revolt. Contiguous provinces excited by sullen, scheming minorities lay across the most civilized of the continents like a saddle, and in that saddle rode a knight errant of nationalism, spurring and whipping his restive steed.

The Poles held one of the key positions in the broad dark stripe of discontented peoples. Led by indomitable conspirators, Pilsudski, Moscicki, Daszynski and their insurrectionist partisans, the subjects of three empires were resolved to bring about a national amalgamation of the broken Polish state. The Czechs and Slovaks of Austria-Hungary sent the more accurate inkwell hurlers and liveliest of parliamentary disturbers to Vienna, but the Czechs as a government problem hardly excelled the Habsburgs' Croat, Roumanian or Italian Irredentists. The resultant "secret service" of all these minority agitations was a cataract of plans, outbreaks, frustrations and not too-theatrical stealth and martyrdom.

The Italian subjects of old Franz Josef not only contributed "Irredentism" to the arguments of other racial camps but also represented a peculiarly insidious threat to the Dual Monarchy, inasmuch as the blood brothers with whom they sought to become "reunited" lived in Italy, an Austro-Hungarian ally in the Triple Alliance. It was especially the Dante Alighieri Association which set the other minorities a pattern for the propagation of Irredentism. Publicly the sole object of this association was to cultivate the Italian language; but its agents were lodged in Trieste, Pola, Trent, Gorizia, Rovereto and many smaller towns, all of them working in close accord with the Italian General Staff and Intelligence Service. The association was proscribed in Austria, yet great numbers of Italianate Austrians belonged to it. And since it was expected to deliver to Italy valuable secret information relating to the army and frontier defenses of Austria-Hungary, it had to enlist the services of Austrian officers of Irredentist sympathies.[1] These became known as *amici*—friends—because they did not work for money but to promote the dissolution of the Habsburg empire.

While the Austro-Hungarians and their subject peoples had tyranny, autonomy and nationalism to wrangle over, desperate economic inequalities and grievances were largely obscured from them. One might expect that intelligent, farsighted monarchists—surely informed by their political police of the seething base of antagonisms on which the thrones were resting—would have banded together to restrain each other's minorities. But instead, for purposes of espionage, propaganda and infectious agitations of separatism, it was the common secret-service technique to use those minorities as if each imperial government had no intractable elements of its own.

Russia was accustomed to finding Poles and other anti-tsarist revolutionaries granted asylum in Austria-Hungary. This occasioned a few protests, neither loud nor long sustained, however, for Russian secret-service activity within the Habsburg empire had become almost a revolution in itself. From the late 'eighties, when war with the Dual Monarchy began to seem inevitable, Russian military espionage recruited its helpers among the subject nationalities of Franz Josef's polyglot realm. Large groups of spies were engaged and generously paid, not alone with money but with promises of ultimate independence. This from the tsar's government, then employing ten thousand agents and informers to police its own malcontents!

Often as many as twenty agents formed an Intelligence group, the vast espionage net being cast over the entire monarchy, from the Carpathians to the Tyrol and the plateau of Bosnia. During a whole generation, as we have seen, nearly every Russian military attaché sent to Vienna was compromised by his plots and spying and had to be sent home again. In addition, consuls of the tsar were active in espionage, and so were Russian priests and members of the embassy staff. In eastern Galicia the Ruthenians, racially akin to the Russians, rendered them enthusiastic service. Deputies, judges, lawyers and priests took part in subterranean activities.[2] The Ruthenian schools and associations became centers of Pan-Slavic and Great-Serbian propaganda and gave shelter to its agents.

Enviable Industry of the Serbian Regicides

The conflicting nationalities of Austria-Hungary might already have been recognized as utterly unmanageable, yet Count Aehrenthal's statecraft proceeded in 1908 to attach two more inevitably turbulent provinces to the quaking patchwork of empire. The revolution of the Young Turks permitted, among other Balkan upheavals, that Austrian feat of brigandage known as the annexation of Bosnia and Herzegovina. With Italian, Czecho-Slovak, Polish, Ruthenian and Roumanian "Irredenta" forming a cordon which all but enclosed the Habsburg frontiers, genius at the Ballplatz had to express itself in thus acquiring an even more combustible Slavic or Serbian "Irredenta." Aehrenthal's stroke astonished Germany and Italy, who, though allies in the Triple Alliance, had not been consulted. Elsewhere in Europe the government reaction ranged from the cynical or pained surprise of France and England to the indignation of Russia and Turkey. Little Serbia was in a frenzy.

Aehrenthal had discussed the annexation with the Russian foreign minister, Isvolski, and the latter had expressed willingness to agree to it in return for Austro-Hungarian support in revising not only Article 25 of the Treaty of Berlin, which dealt with Bosnia, but also Article 29, which prevented the passage of Russian warships through the Dardanelles.[3] But before Isvolski could sound Great Britain or France, Aehrenthal told old Franz Josef that Russia had consented, and proclaimed the annexation to the world. Sir Edward Grey, the British foreign secretary—supported by France and Russia—proposed a conference of all the signatory Powers to review the Treaty of Berlin. Germany and Austria-Hungary at first agreed; but then word came from Vienna that the annexation, being settled beyond recall, was not subject to discussion.

As the weeks passed, the Balkan strain increased. Turks effected an injurious boycott of Austro-Hungarian exports. And the frenzy of the Serbians did not abate. Their national "future", they exclaimed, had been blighted by the Austrian violation of the treaty, which, if it ever should be revised, ought to reunite them with their racial brothers of Bosnia. The "war of pigs" was waged between Austria and Serbia, doubling the price of bacon in the Dual Monarchy. Conditions along the Danube were close to the breaking point, with three Austro-Hungarian army corps opposite Belgrade and now virtually raised to war strength. Russian agents reported an apparent concentration of forces in Galicia which could only signify Vienna's expectation of war.

Russia, however, was ill prepared for war; and certainly for this war, which Germany would surely enter on the side of the Austrians. The Russian army was still recuperating from its disasters in Manchuria. Revolutionary outbreaks which had followed the Far Eastern misadventure were just subsiding. On March 22, 1909, the German Ambassador, Pourtalés, called upon Isvolski to reveal such diplomatic finesse as a steam roller might have envied. Unless Russia immediately recognized the annexation of Bosnia, and induced Serbia to do likewise, there would be war. "Immediately" meant as soon as the Russian Council of State could be summoned.

The council deliberated for four hours and in the evening submitted unconditionally. Serbia, shorn of its powerful ally, had to back down in the same humiliating fashion; and it was only through the intervention of Sir Edward Grey that Aehrenthal permitted the Serbian "consent" to include this sardonic euphemism: ". . . sure of the peaceful intentions of Austria-Hungary, Serbia will bring her army back to the condition of the spring of 1908."

Both St Petersburg and Belgrade had submitted under duress. If war in the field against the Dual Monarchy and its formidable German accomplice was a poor risk, Russia already had its secret-service campaign against the Dual Monarchy geared to just such a period of armed, resentful "truce." Serbia, bitterly hostile, now joined in this subterranean fray. Both the mechanism for violent conspiracy and a hearty enthusiasm for terrorist acts were among the Serbian national assets.

The Great-Serbia agitation, even before 1908, had extended into Croatia, Slavonia, the southern part of Hungary, Bosnia, Herzegovina and Dalmatia. It was managed by a secret organization, the *Narodna Odbrana,* at the head of which was General Bozo Jankovic, and whose ultimate objectives were insurrection and, in case of war, the rendering of assistance through espionage and sabotage to the Serbian army. Imro, its Macedonian neighbor, had influenced it strongly. Schools known as "comitadji schools" had been established at Cuprija and Prokupplie to train squad leaders, recruited from ex-service men, schoolteachers, and priests of the Greek Orthodox Church. There was, it appears, much overlapping of membership, Imro agents mingling with the plotters of the Serbian society; for at this time, even though Imro's ties were stronger in Bulgaria, Serbs, Greeks and Russians were all regarded as potential liberators of Macedonia.

Officers of the Serbian Intelligence belonged to the *Narodna Odbrana,* which ostensibly provided a "higher culture" for the Serbian or Slavic subjects of the Dual Monarchy. But the Austrian counter-espionage service was not to be deceived by the harmless "educational" program with which the Serbs—in this borrowing not from Imro but from the Dante Alighieri Association of Italian Irredentism —masked their insurrectionist designs. The society might form alliances in Austria-Hungary with sports clubs, student corps, antialcohol leagues and cultural federations. Its origin, however, was as bloodstained as any association of meat packers; and the blood had been royal blood.

The *Narodna Odbrana* was also the society known as "The Black Hand", founded for purposes of mutual protection by those Serbian regicides who, in 1903, had broken into the palace and hacked King Alexander and Queen Draga to death.[4] There was little enough secrecy about that monstrous flourishing of cavalry sabers. Colonel Mashin, one of the chief conspirators, was Draga's own brother-in-law. In one night's massacre about fifty other persons lost their lives, the Obrenovitch dynasty came to an end, and Prince Peter Karageorgevitch was set upon the throne. The new King Peter accepted Mashin as his first minister of public works, thereby assuring the officers of the secret "Black Hand" all the *mutual* protection at home that they desired.

Once banded together, this deadly society nourished the dream of Great Serbia with savage patriotism, combining the discipline of Imro, or of the early Jesuits, with the terrorist procedure of Russian Nihilism. A powerful influence in domestic governing circles, the association is said to have initiated Crown Prince Alexander, Pashitch, the prime minister, and Putnik, the army commander in chief. However true that may be, our chief interest lies in the acknowledged fact that the leader of *Narodna Odbrana* in May and June of 1914 was Colonel Dimitriyevitch, chief of the Serbian Intelligence. Thanks to the industry of the organized regicides, and by an ironic blend of fanatic conspiracy and government secret service, the Black Hand of the Balkans raised its homicide quota from fifty to millions in eleven years' time, by provoking the World War.

Assassins Provocateur at Serajevo

Amid all the obscurities and counter-charges as to "war guilt" there is now little doubt that the chief of Serbian Intelligence, acting *in that capacity* as well as in his even more secretive role as head of *Narodna Odbrana*, devised and organized the plot to murder the Habsburg heir during his visit to Bosnia. Since 1908–09 the incitements had steadily multiplied. The Serbs could forget neither the annexation nor the humiliating and clumsy "diplomacy" which had made them yield and assent to it. Bellicose speeches and publications, espionage, rumors, frontier incidents, nationalist propaganda, all heaped up the fuel supply. And then came Austria's deliberate restraint upon Serbia at the victorious conclusion of the First Balkan War.

The weakness of Turkey, the example of the Italian conquest of Tripoli, encouraged the Balkan allies to oblige Imro by claiming autonomy for Macedonia. As we know, the Greek, Serb and Bulgar combination won handily; and Serbia prepared to take over its share of the spoils, by agreement—Northern Albania. That meant a Slav state on the Adriatic; and Austria-Hungary, flatly rejecting the idea, began to mobilize. Russia, as great sponsor of the small countries' ejecting the Turk from Europe, answered—five years after the Aehrenthal-Isvolski exchange—with mobilization. But this time Germany was not in a belligerent mood and joined with France and Britain to forestall the European peril. Creating an independent Albanian state sent Serbia into Macedon to carve out some promised compensation; and as a result of the ensuing dogfight of the Second Balkan War, Serbia came out the chief territorial gainer, mainly at the expense of Bulgaria.

Vienna restlessly observed this new and unanticipated forward step of the Great-Serbian movement. In the summer of 1913 the Austro-Hungarian General Staff urged an immediate attack upon the war-exhausted Serbs. Germany still favored a more temperate attitude, yet bestowed upon Russia a fresh affront by extending German control over the reanimated military forces of the sultan. Russian statecraft countered with a bid to Roumania, which obvious gesture toward the creation of a new Balkan alliance gave Vienna another attack of imperial jitters.

Police and military espionage backed by force was the only remedy that occurred to the rulers of Austria-Hungary in mastering the discontent of their subject minorities. And a strangling dose of the same remedy was what their acute minds prescribed for an external state, Serbia, whose crime was its magnetic influence upon the empire's diverse and straining internal parts.

In the summer of 1914 Austrian army maneuvers were to be held in Bosnia. The Archduke Franz Ferdinand, as heir to the throne, planned to attend them and then, accompanied by his wife, pay an official visit to Serajevo. It was announced that he would enter the Bosnian capital on June 28—which was the anniversary of the total

Serbian defeat in 1389 at Kossovo Polye, "the Field of Blackbirds."' In Serbia this was not mistaken for coincidence.

It has been noted as an Olympian irony that the perfervid Slav nationalists, in seeking to demonstrate against Austro-Hungarian oppression, singled out and murdered the only man of influence in Austria who was their friend. Franz Ferdinand had given much thought to a rehabilitated imperial structure in which the several minorities should be bound together, not by spies and fear and force, but in liberal federation. To Bosnia's Slavs, however, he symbolized the tyranny of Vienna; and to the extremists of the "Black Hand" he was the more menacing because his dream of racial reconciliations within the empire might extinguish their dream of Yugoslavic union, the indispensable prelude to Great Serbia.

Colonel Dimitriyevitch would not gain an exalted place in the history of Military Intelligence, but as a director of assassins he rates a limited, repulsive fame. Enlisting a dozen youths, most of them under twenty, he incited them to a fanatic pitch of homicidal martyrdom. Under his authority they were given bombs and Browning revolvers and trained in their use. Money for travel and maintenance was provided them—also cyanide of potassium for suicide, as a last resort.

The government of Prime Minister Pashitch was already at war with Imro over the administration of the newly occupied Macedonian territory and on the same score had earned the hostility of the *comitadjis* of the Serbian Black Hand. Postwar revelations leave no doubt but that Pashitch and several of his colleagues had learned something of the terrorist conspiracy. And orders are alleged to have been passed to all frontier posts to prevent the secret agents crossing into Bosnia. However, the frontier guards were members of *Narodna Odbrana*, and they were with Dimitriyevitch to a man. They ignored the civil government—and every one of the novice assassins got through to Serajevo.

The Serbian minister at Vienna, Yovanovitch, went to the Ballplatz, where he saw one of Count Berchtold's assistants, and murmured something vague about the archduke's special danger in Bosnia. This was filed, if at all, as a very fine specimen of calculated Slavic impudence.

Franz Ferdinand understood the dangers of his visit. He had endeavored to dissuade his wife from coming with him, but as an officer and the heir to the throne he felt bound to fulfil his engagements. In such circumstances the Austrian police and military authorities would ordinarily have taken elaborate precautions. But instead only cynical indifference to the safeguarding of the highly unpopular "liberal" heir was on display in the Bosnian capital.

General Potiorek, the provincial military governor, did almost as much as Colonel Dimitriyevitch to facilitate the program of Serb assassination. Various explanations have been found for this soldier's negligence. His congenital incompetence—supported by many defeats he sustained as an army commander in the World War—is among the more charitable.[5] Police were conspicuously few. No soldiers lined the streets; and not even a reserve of gendarmerie had been provided. Every arrangement invited confusion and disaster. In Belgrade the invitation had already been accepted.

Differing in all things from the Austro-Hungarians, the Serbians' plan had been carefully made. At least seven agents of the Black Hand took their stations at the most favorable points. Each of the old city's three bridges was covered by one or more of the assassins.

Death to the Archduke!

The first Serbian attempt was made on the way to the town hall; but the back of the archduke's automobile deflected the bomb, and only two officers of his suite were wounded. After some delay, the royal party proceeded to the town hall, where the pardonably indignant Franz Ferdinand had to listen to the usual addresses of welcome. Upon being told that the bomb thrower had been arrested, he uttered his bitterly prophetic observation on an aged and rotting monarchy which was only to survive him fifty-two months: "Hang him as quickly as possible or Vienna will give him a decoration."

Police precautions seemed not to improve, and Count Harrach, owner of the automobile, who sat beside the driver, said to General Potiorek: "Has not Your Excellency arranged for a military guard to protect his Imperial Highness?"

The governor of Bosnia drew himself up to read an historic line of comic relief where none whatever was needed: "Do you think Serajevo is full of assassins, Count Harrach?"

The archduke proposed a change of route in leaving the town hall, so that he might visit the hospital to which the two wounded officers had been hurried. Count Harrach said he would stand on the left running board to shield the archduke; but Franz Ferdinand motioned him to his seat, saying: "Don't make a fool of yourself."

In their original order but at an increased speed the four motorcars rolled out into the dense throng. The entrance to Franz Josef Street was blocked by the unpoliced crowd, which made a lane, and the cars in error turned back to the former route. Potiorek, who sat facing the royal pair, gave an order to the chauffeur, and their car slowed down and came close to the right-hand pavement. Whereat a young Serbian student named Princip—not the most promising of Dimitriyevitch's patriot killers[6]—fired two shots at three meters' range, both with fatal effect.

The archduke continued to sit upright, his wife sinking upon his breast. A few murmured words passed between them. No one realized at first that they had been struck by the assassin's bullets. In Viennese court circles the heir to the throne was reputed to protect his body on occasion by wearing an exquisitely wrought shirt of chain mail. Princip's first shot had severed the artery in his neck, the second piercing the Duchess of Hohenberg through the abdomen.[7]

News of the crime outraged all of Europe—except Austria and Serbia. The Serbian press took few pains to hide its jubilation, and the Serbian public took none at all. As for the Serbian government, exhausted after the two Balkan wars, it had every incentive for peace and a chance to consolidate its recent gains. Yet it neither undertook nor offered to investigate the complicity of its subjects, scarcely troubling to conceal the participation of many of its own officials in the plotting of *Narodna Odbrana*.[8]

The Austrian police investigation was a little masterpiece of perfunctory bureaucratic dabbling in obvious facts. After a fortnight Wiesner, who had been sent to conduct it, made the report that, while societies and officials of Serbia were implicated, there were "no proofs of the complicity of the Serbian Government. . . . On the contrary there are grounds for believing it quite out of the question."

Whatever the dynastic indifference of the court at Vienna,[9] the crime of the double assassination had whipped up the fury of the mob. There were violent demonstrations against Serbia in many cities of the Habsburg empire and attacks upon Serbian representatives and establishments. The British consul general at Budapest reported conditions in Hungary as a "wave of blind hatred of Serbia and everything Serbian . . . sweeping over the country."

Thus Franz Ferdinand and the woman he loved and had wed in defiance of etiquette and emperor virtually died in each other's arms, the victims of a people with whose aspirations the archduke sympathized, the symbols of a blow struck at Austria's governing classes who were suspicious of, and bitterly antagonistic to, them both. And those two vain and profitless killings at Serajevo were the first of a four-year inferno of similar sacrifices.

CHAPTER SIXTY-FOUR

THE COMING OF WORLD CATASTROPHE

THE MAGNATES of the Austro-Hungarian General Staff and Foreign Ministry now had their Pan-Slavic provocation. In one of the many pigeonholes of the Ballplatz there lay a document three years old. This was the notorious ultimatum, drawn up to be used against Serbia when occasion should arise. And here was the perfect occasion.

The assassination of the heir to the throne, cause of so little public grief and so much private rejoicing, could not have been more correctly timed and appointed if the Austrian "K.S." rather than the Serbian Intelligence had procured the crime. It was already late in June; and Europe had its tradition of decisive battles—Waterloo, Solferino, Custozza,[1] Sadowa, Sedan—fought in the summer. That allowed the Central Powers a month in which to prepare. If Berlin would consent to repeat the bullying tactics of 1909 against Russia, the ultimatum could be dusted off and gravediggers beckoned toward Belgrade.

So consistent had been Vienna's Great-Serbian grievance that a few minor changes in the phrasing of the ultimatum would bring it up to date, fit it to the circumstances of the hour. And Berlin did consent. On the morning of July 7, Count Hoyos returned to the Ballplatz with an answer that in resolute, provocative encouragement[2] exceeded the most lurid hopes of the war party at Vienna. All that they had felt against their small Slavic neighbor but had not dared to express they now would be allowed to proclaim in a bellicose roar.

The Austrian chief of staff, Conrad von Hötzendorf, could dip his pen in what he thought was ink and set down the exulting and prophetic "Germany would stand on our side unconditionally, even if our advance against Serbia let loose the great war. Germany advises us to set matters in motion."[3] At once a veritable melodrama of "secret service" was enacted with all the agents and performers gentlemen of imposing eminence.

Said Count Berchtold, the foreign minister: "We will not hand in the ultimatum until after the harvest and after the close of the Serajevo Inquiry."

"Rather today than tomorrow," Conrad replied, "so long as the situation is what it is. So soon as our opponents get wind of it, they will get ready."

"Care will be taken that the secret is kept most carefully and that no one knows anything of it," the foreign minister reassured him.

"When is the ultimatum to go out?"

"In fourteen days—on the 22nd July," said Berchtold, adding: "It would be a good thing if you and the War Minister would go on leave for a time, in order to preserve the appearance that nothing is happening."[4]

The two archconspirators then spoke about the attitude of Roumania and the possible intervention of Russia.

"As to whether we are to go to war with Russia we must be perfectly clear at once," Conrad has reported himself declaring. "If Russia orders a general mobilization, then the moment has come for us to declare ourselves against Russia."

Berchtold asked: "If we enter Serbia and have occupied sufficient territory—what then?"

"With the occupation of territory nothing has been attained. We must proceed until we have struck down the Serbian Army." A self-inflicted trial of chastisement that—due in no small degree to the late Alfred Redl—would cost 500,000 Austro-Hungarian casualties!

But suppose, the foreign minister wondered, the Serbian army should retire?

"Then," said Conrad, "we demand demobilization and disarmament. Once things have got that far, the rest follows."

Whereupon the fascinated Berchtold begged him to take no steps now "which could *give us away*—nothing must be done which would attract attention."

In that sibilant atmosphere of back-stairs intrigue the measureless calamity of the great war was generated.

Berchtold Erases the First Serbian Attack

The illustrious Count Berchtold ordered the ultimatum to be presented in Belgrade at six o'clock in the evening of Thursday, July 23. Originally he had fixed the hour at five o'clock; but in the true spirit of Machiavellian diplomacy he conceded the hour's delay to disconcert the Russians and French. President Poincaré and Premier Viviani had been visiting St Petersburg. Sixty minutes' difference would make certain that they had left the Russian capital on their homeward journey.

Even the German chancellor and foreign minister were not exempted from Berchtold's passionate secrecy. They only read the text of the ultimatum on the afternoon of the twenty-second; but though they found the terms startling and excessive, they made no move save the easy one of sitting down to await the inevitable. Nothing was done to recall or amend the circular note already sent out to instruct German ambassadors in Paris, London and St Petersburg—a note in which, while still unaware of the Austrian demands, Wilhelmstrasse pronounced them "moderate and proper."

The ultimatum required Serbia's submission within forty-eight hours. And promptly at 6 P.M. on Saturday, the twenty-fifth, the Serbian reply was handed to Baron Giesl, the Austrian minister. Well aware of the Austrian resolve to attack, the authorities at Belgrade accepted the demands with scarcely a whisper of protest. It was the German Kaiser's jubilant opinion—expressed in a note to his foreign minister, Von Jagow—that: "The few reservations that Serbia makes in regard to individual points can in my opinion well be cleared up by negotiation. But it [the reply] contains . . . a capitulation of the most humiliating kind, and with it every reason for war is removed."

Count Berchtold had the same Serbian reply but a wholly different set of conclusions. And he no longer felt constrained to keep them secret. His power to darken the future of Europe and arrest the material progress of mankind was at that hour satanic. An ocean liner bearing a cargo of virulent *bacilli* could not have represented greater peril. This was, in fact, Berchtold's only greatness.

Diminutive and devious, fashionable, foppish and a follower of the turf, the Austrian foreign minister was immensely rich, the scion of a noble house, and of about the caliber of a light target rifle whose single shot could provoke the cannonade of twenty thousand heavy guns. He was, in the mordant phrase of Mr Winston Churchill, "the epitome of this age when the affairs of Brobdingnag are managed by the Lilliputians."[5] And yet, though history may expose him and a thousand ironies flay his fame, Berchtold's terrible invocation of slaughter can never be revenged with words.

Almost at the moment Kaiser Wilhelm was congratulating himself that the danger of war was past and "a great moral victory" won without need of firing a shot, Berchtold was telegraphing Belgrade that "the Royal Serbian Government not having answered in a satisfactory manner the note of July 23, 1914 . . . Austria-Hungary consequently considered herself henceforward in a state of war with Serbia." The Belgrade authorities, kept well informed by sundry agents of *Narodna Odbrana* scattered through the provinces of the Dual Monarchy, had commenced to mobilize even as they submitted.

No compliance, they suspected, could be submissive enough for the Austrian war party and General Staff, whose mouthpiece was the little dandy enthroned at the Ballplatz.

To be sure, economic and colonial rivalries and many other influences had long been propelling Europe toward the abyss of war. But Count Berchtold, almost singlehanded, propelled two empires into *this* war. It was expected that the old Emperor Franz Josef would prove reluctant to put his signature to the declaration of war against Serbia. When the document was presented to Count Paar, the septuagenarian aide-de-camp observed:[8] "This may be all right, but all I can say is that men of eighty-four years of age don't sign war proclamations."

Berchtold, however, had armed himself against the wisdom, conservatism or obstinacy of a venerable monarch. Together with the unsigned proclamation he took the liberty of laying before His Majesty a report that the Serbians had fired upon Austrian troop transports on the Danube—that the conflict had, indeed, already begun. The declaration offered to Franz Josef concluded with the challenge, "the more so as Serbian troops have already attacked a detachment of Imperial and Royal troops at Temes-Kubin." Such was Berchtold's commonplace yet fatally potent invention. No Serbian attack had occurred. Hostilities might still have been avoided, for not a shot as yet had echoed over the Danube.

After the emperor was moved to sign the document which was to have every consequence save the one intended, extirpation of Great Serbia, Berchtold punctiliously erased the sentence that exploited the fictitious engagement at Temes-Kubin. Next day he explained that the report was unconfirmed. But war had now been declared, its very declaration producing the necessary frontier clashes. It was therefore too late for Franz Josef to reconsider a decision extorted by the first of many thousands of fallacious communiqués.

CHAPTER SIXTY-FIVE

THE SHEEP'S CLOTHING OF WILHELM STIEBER

THE military secret services of Europe had all believed themselves to be competent and prepared, ready for anything. Most of them straightway proved that they were ready for anything except what they all had been helping to prepare—a general war. Because of the assumption that a first-rate service is never demobilized, the abruptly belligerent Powers found themselves shorthanded. Too many aggressive and talented officers had been rewarded for espionage missions or other Intelligence work with release from such duties and promotion to regular branches. There were few reserves to be called up for mobilization, since every one available, trained and trustworthy, was already on duty according to the service's full *peacetime* strength.

Here was an insidious defect that even the great Teutonic reputation for formidable military readiness could not long conceal, though it carries something of the impact of a news release today—twenty-two years after—to pronounce the German Secret Service of August 1914 the least adequate of them all. We are accustomed to think of the German preparations for the great European conflict as about the most perfect example of military thoroughness and foresight made known in modern times. How curious, then, to uncover the confession of Colonel Walther Nicolai, the General Staff officer who commanded the German secret service throughout the war, in which he admits: "The War was looked upon as wholly a military affair, and therefore remained in the Military Intelligence Department. But it only dawned gradually on the General Staff how defective the Intelligence Service of the Government actually was. In Charleville one morning I had to deliver a message from General von Falkenhayn, then Chief of the General Staff, to Von Bethmann, the Imperial Chancellor. He asked me to sit down for a minute: 'Do tell me how things are with the enemy. I hear nothing at all about that.' A different picture from that which, I believe, was presented by the Intelligence Service under Bismarck!"[1]

A different picture, true, a veritable panorama the ironic implications of which seem wholly to escape the captious staff colonel. That immensely effective "Intelligence Service under Bismarck" was personally created and despotically managed by Wilhelm Stieber. Had Bismarck, as imperial chancellor, ever been required to say—*do tell me how things are with the enemy*—he would not, like the luckless Von Bethmann, have been asking Walther Nicolai, admiring disciple of Erich Ludendorff, "with his sergeant's face,"[2] who suspected and despised all civilians. He would have been applying to a civilian who merely happened to be his own masterly disciple and the greatest director of secret service in German history.

It was not good form in the German army, however, to remember the crafty work of Stieber, nor even to mention him by name. Yet great victories had been won and an empire established with the aid of his powerful secret service. To deny its achievements and neglect the conveniences of such espionage as his was an odd and inexplicable way of serving the Pan-Germanic dream.

Colonel Nicolai attempts to explain it:

> From time immemorial Staff-Corps officers had preferred practical service on regimental staffs to life in Berlin and the more theoretical work there. So when war broke out, the best of them were found filling General Staff posts at the front. . . .
>
> These circumstances reacted on the secret service. Its central organization, too, was transferred to the front. Of the few officers trained in this service the best were rewarded by being released for work on the regimental staffs, and the remainder were shared among the army commands as Intelligence Service officers. There was a general idea that secret service, espionage, would find its field of action primarily in the theatres of war. But on account of the rapid progress . . . in the West, where a military decision was first sought, strong skepticism prevailed in the army commands regarding the possibility and the usefulness of espionage. This went so far that one army command, on the advance through Belgium, left the intelligence officer behind in Liége as needless ballast.[3]

And this was the allegedly formidable prewar German Secret Service, from which officers after expert training were "rewarded" by being "released" to the routine of a regimental staff!

Nicolai continues:

> It was also not without significance in an army in which the feeling of subordination was very strongly developed that the chief of the Intelligence Service was, in years of service, by far the youngest departmental chief of the High Command and considerably younger than the chiefs of the General Staff at the front and the departmental heads at the War Office. The civil authorities, too, were accustomed to a more powerful representative on the General Staff than a major.[4] I must emphasize these personal considerations because they help to make credible the difficulties

which our Intelligence Service met with in its work, and why it remained such a long way behind what the enemy had achieved by long pre-war training and by being supported by statesmen determined to fight and win.

Conscious of the lack of preparedness in the secret service, the authorities had, before the War, certainly tried to find out, by means of great strategical war-games, what demands would be made on this service if war occurred. But these theoretical studies were kept within tactical and strategical, or at least within military, bounds. They were concerned neither with the investigation of economic and political conditions in enemy States nor with propaganda there. A world-wide intelligence service had never been the subject even of theoretical consideration. Reality, therefore, put every past conception in the shade.

Every past conception except the Bismarck-Stieber conception, which had been exclusively Teutonic and had flourished but a generation before!

German "Enemies" of the Prussian Army

It is that old army platform of the failure of the civil government on which Nicolai takes his stand. "The tasks set to the military Intelligence Service in peace had been completed on the outbreak of war," he complacently avers. In fact, he prevaricates, as we shall see, but allow him to continue: "In peace this service had been the sole means of getting information about the military position of the enemy states." Nicolai has so consistently proclaimed the weakness and cowardice of the civil authorities during the years since they died and ceased to defend themselves that it has lately brought him his reward. To digress—in a Berlin office adjoining one in which those free and liberal Nazi scholars are composing their anti-Semitic history of the Jews, Walther Nicolai is composing a Nazi indictment of the civilian conduct of the war of 1914-18, the only war of modern times that Germany expects to lose.

However he may have qualified for his present role of martial propagandist, many of his admissions and complaints relating to the German Secret Service in the World War are blessed with the candor of the defeated side which can afford to tell the truth. Nicolai describes with feeling those police officials who arrived by appointment at his field headquarters, wearing "knee-breeches and long stockings and felt hats with a sprig of chamois hair, and believed that in such equipment they would achieve success in the 'secret' army police."

Germany was not alone in that plight, the amateur secret agent

THE SHEEP'S CLOTHING OF WILHELM STIEBER 489

of all lands being generally either comic in person and mental equipment or grotesquely misinformed upon the subject of espionage and counter-espionage—or both. Not only was personnel inadequate, but funds were, with the exception of two of the combatant services, everywhere insufficient. Great Britain had enough; Russia, too much to learn to spend it effectively. But there is a low moaning note in Nicolai's lament that in 1912 the Russians were enabled to expend "about 12,000,000 roubles"; whereas the ever niggardly *Reichstag* had been induced to vote the German Intelligence a 50 per cent increase, from 300,000 to 450,000 marks, only that session. A step up to indigence from absolute penury!

It is likely that reports of spies disclosing the tsarist extravagance were confided to startled German legislators. Moreover, the "Army Estimates for 1912 were drawn up under the personal influence of Colonel Ludendorff"—one destined never to be at a loss when competing with Russians.

Out of the increased subsidy, to Nicolai "this small sum"—which did demand a certain elastic knack in stretching it over the "costs of both espionage and counter-espionage"—the presentable fraction of 50,000 marks was "saved in 1913 for use in the event of extraordinary political tension." Such a Spartan example of thrift, only the year after spurring *Reichstag* members to recognize the Ludendorff "influence", was characteristic of the kind of hard schooling and self-discipline which turned out that high-powered engine of warfare, the German General Staff officer. It is also significant that presiding experts of the select corps known as the *Nachrichtendienst*,[3] Major von Lauenstein and Nicolai—who had never been allowed half the funds they wanted—should be inspired to pinch and skimp and put aside a nest egg the year before Armageddon.

It will occur to the reader that "extraordinary political tension" must have been perceptible to *intelligence* chiefs in 1913. And even as small a sum as one ninth of the total German subsidy might have been disbursed to ease the Austro-Balkan aggravations and thus have prevented the outbreak of war. Modern Intelligence and secret-service departments, however, are never paid to protect a country from itself or its ruling classes. Nor are they expected to govern historic events while studying them in process of gestation. Intelligence, in theory, neither foments nor prevents hostilities, but assembles information about those openly, secretly or potentially hostile, while impeding the pursuits of their agents, intriguers and spies. No new indictment may, therefore, be drawn from this record, placing any branch of the German Secret Service in the dock beside those firebrands, fools and fossils who tricked Europe and the world into the homicidal-suicidal experiment of 1914.

A general admittedly can never be quite sure he *is* a general until he commands troops in battle. A statesman, too, must inspire and aggrandize his state, or he dies without knowing whether he is even a footnote of history. But the chief of secret service has his year-around job in spite of the longest lapses of peace. No master of spies need urge them to help start a war, just to see how they work; for if he is a master, he already knows how they work. He knows how little even the best of his agents can achieve which may be publicly credited to them—or to him.

The German Intelligence defect, then, was not actual connivance with the Berchtolds and Conrads, the war party of Vienna or the saber rattlers of Potsdam, but something rare in Prussian history—want of vigilance, vision and preparedness. Since there was no Bismarck in all Germany, the hope of discovering another Stieber was never bright. That masterly wolf in varied woolen disguises left no garments which could be cut down into uniforms for staff officers or draped upon a graduate of Charlottenburg, Lörrach, Antwerp or any other "spy school." German espionage, "in the theatres of war" or elsewhere, was unable to overcome having been left at the post, very much as Nicolai excuses it. On the other hand, German counter-espionage was equally handicapped at the start and always understaffed, yet it learned its job and grew strong, to continue to the end of the struggle a feared and respected adversary.

German Readiness in England

The people of Germany, including many courtiers, officers, editors and politicians, seem to have been entirely unprepared for the counter-balancing blow of the British joining the *entente* of France, Russia, Serbia and Belgium. English officers like Captain Trench and Captain Brandon, and Bertram Stewart, had been arrested and convicted of espionage and confined in German prisons. Every symptom showed England in league with the so-called "ring" of Teutonic foes; yet the surprise of the British declaration of war was the loudest of many August detonations.

The resulting hatred, the imprecations spurring *Gott* to strike England, suggests that the German nation had a more frightening comprehension of that invincible factor called Sea Power than the Kaiser's army or admiralty staffs permitted themselves to obtain. The kind of first-rate Intelligence service that Stieber exemplified in reporting the truth about the superiorities of the *chassepot* and *mitrailleuse* would have spared Potsdam and Wilhelmstrasse their malaria of myths. Britain was not afraid to fight, was not fatally riven by Irish civil war, was not incapable of mobilizing its radical labor elements. The British navy could guarantee not less than a draw in any conflict permitting a Continental blockade. God was, indeed, the only reserve to call upon in striking at England, for Germany, even blessed with Zeppelins and U-boats, was not in a position to capsize that obstinate isle.

Nothing, however, seems to have been derived from German espionage in Britain which abated fundamental Intelligence and diplomatic blunders.[6] A good deal of attention and money, and not a little stealth, had been expended upon the development of a spy system covering England. Its agents, largely under the control of Gustav Steinhauer, were distributed to allow for every contingency, except the two most important: (1) the detection of one of their number, and (2) the outbreak of war between Great Britain and Germany. The caliber of the spying was nicely gauged by the quantity and quality of the spies employed—plodding and methodical, rather than adroit or enterprising. And the day had to come when the German Admiralty and General Staff would deplore this thoroughly Teutonic infirmity, a day when Entente counter-espionage learned all about that "spy chain", for the British quietly rolled it up like a flag of truce and put it away in a cool, dry place.[7]

Several years before the war Kaiser Wilhelm had been visiting in London, and British operatives made responsible for his safety chanced to observe the curious conduct of one of the members of his suite. This officer was known to them as the acting chief of German Admiralty Intelligence. With the culpable imprudence that so often distinguished his Hohenzollern master's public utterances, this naval captain called at the modest establishment of a barber, Karl Gustav Ernst, located in the Caledonian Road. Thereafter the British counter-spies devoted a good deal of attention to this obscure Londoner. Ernst, having been born in England, was technically a British subject. For sixteen years he had occupied the same modest shop, and for an unknown period of time he had also earned an extra pound a month by acting as a secret-service "letter box."

His pay was small, but the trouble and risk were inconsiderable. Letters of instruction to spies came to him in batches from German Intelligence headquarters. As they already bore English postage stamps, Ernst merely consigned the lot to the nearest post office. Replies which came back to him he straightway forwarded to his employers at Charlottenburg, or, on occasion, directed them to some "cover" address in a neutral country. Except for names and addresses —which rarely changed—he was allowed to know very little about the centrifugal force that he kept in smooth operation. He was neither a technically trained agent nor an individual likely to be endowed with a Prussian officer's esprit de corps. It was left for his superior, owning all those eminent qualifications, to give the whole show away.[8]

British counter-spies, given that slight, destructive clue, had proceeded to open and read the mail addressed to Ernst, whether from the spies in England or their masters abroad. For many months, prior to the outbreak of hostilities, the German espionage service in Britain all unwittingly enjoyed the closest British supervision.

Steinhauer, Not Stieber

Gustav Steinhauer was not the indiscreet "superior" cited; however, his own account of his contact with German espionage in Great Britain proves how much he also was to blame for its complete and damaging breakdown. A former private detective, who had gained some experience in America with the Pinkerton Agency, Steinhauer discloses an actor's flair for disguise and a commercial traveler's flair for the expense account. He also seems to have suffered from the same infirmity Allan Pinkerton brought to the Federal Secret Service in the American War of Secession in that he could make nothing of military or naval espionage save crime investigation.

He has described himself without diffidence as "the Kaiser's Master Spy", which not only casts a spotlight upon his mediocre achievements but rather illuminates the prewar standards of German secret service. Compared to ingenious operatives of the war years— Henrichsen, Max Wild, Silber, Schtaub, or Bartels,[9] who accepted the capital risk of serving Germany in enemy lands—the "master", Steinhauer, was scarcely a spy at all. What time he did not spend, when on duty abroad, complaining of his employers' parsimony he devoted to a reverent regard for his own safekeeping. No first-rate German Military Intelligence authority thinks enough of his services to mention him by name; yet as an agent of the political police, under Muhl and Von Tausch,[10] he seems to have made a creditable detective reputation. In spite of his vanity and passion for disguise, he was a born counter-spy, persistent, alert and unscrupulous. England and the Allies were greatly obligated to whatever German chief diverted him from that to espionage.

Ten days before the outbreak of hostilities, in the last week of

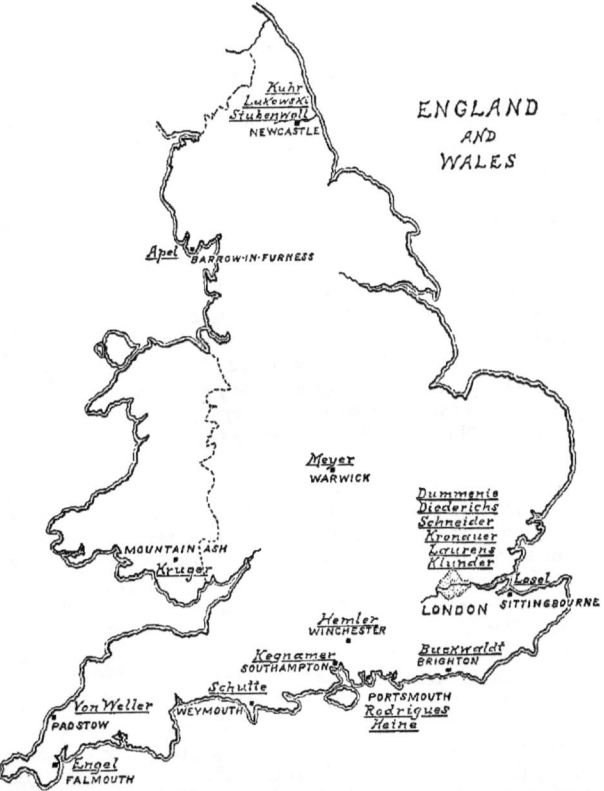

GERMAN AGENTS ARRESTED IN ENGLAND: AUGUST 4, 1914

This map, disclosing for the first time the exact location of the various spies distributed over the kingdom, further points out the dangerous concentration of British war industries and depots, a defect in this era of air bombs and professional sabotage which the British government is now endeavoring to correct.

July 1914, there were twenty-six agents of German Intelligence in England. Steinhauer was among them, the spy-master, the directing brain. He had come from Belgium, from Ostend, in fact, for his conception of secret service beckoned him to the most agreeable resorts of the Continent in season; and he now traveled about, meeting and arguing with his spies, who would not take seriously his warning of the imminence of war. They had lived too long in England to suspect the martial capacities of the British people. They were, in short, totally incompetent to act as military secret agents in the event of war. And the British had no intention of allowing them to improve with practice.

Steinhauer went down to Walthamstow to call upon Kronauer, a barber, who had been stimulating the growth of German espionage in England for many years. But, behold, the British were "covering" Kronauer. This police surveillance was easily detected by Steinhauer, always expert in counter-espionage. He alleges[11] with curious naïveté that it had been "known in Berlin for some time past" that Kronauer was "having his correspondence opened."[12] Steinhauer believed the operatives watching the barber's shop were mainly engaged in laying a "crude trap" for himself. He avoided it, turning his "double overcoat" and otherwise observing his ritual of emergency disappearances. But as he hastened elsewhere, the spy-master eased his conscience by sending Kronauer—and his other correspondents, barbers, bakers, headwaiters and small tradesmen—a warning in code to be ready for hostilities. This took the form of an innocuously worded message scribbled on post cards which he put into those same mails "known in Berlin" to be inspected by British counter-spies.

War was now dangerously near; but Steinhauer still had to go north to study the potential naval bases of the Grand Fleet. This vital—and curiously belated—errand was made the more hazardous for him by the well-remembered "mission" of another German agent, Dr Armgaard Karl Graves. It is clear that Steinhauer had no use for the doctor even before this journey to Scotland reminded him of Graves' portentous blundering in that corner of the United Kingdom. He describes Graves both as "a smooth-tongued impostor" and "a double-dyed rascal", who was "never a spy of mine." Graves was one of those artful "adventurers" who were then "continually giving the world the impression that Europe was overrun with spies and agents of the German Secret Service."[13]

Graves had certainly helped give the Scots that impression in 1912 by getting arrested in Glasgow, brought to trial in Edinburgh and, on being convicted, sent to Barlinney Prison for a term of years. He served only eighteen months, however, and subsequently compensated himself for that by going to America and publishing an autobiographical book, *The Secrets of the German War Office*. It appeared by chance in such happy relation to the sudden outbreak of war in Europe[14] that it had a large and profitable sale and, while producing neither serious nor very startling revelations, resulted in an inevitable sequel.

It was Graves—according to Steinhauer—who scraped an acquaintance with one of the staff at a Scottish hotel and "was introduced into a club by that gentleman as 'my friend, the German spy.'" On which account, late in July of 1914, Steinhauer felt that he must practice the utmost circumspection. Posing as a fisherman and imposing upon a friendly Scots angler, he made his way to Scapa Flow. By fishing there with a knotted line he took soundings and thus answered the German Admiralty question—can the great battleships of the British navy anchor in Scapa Flow?—with an affirmative.

What seems puzzling even to this day about Steinhauer's mission is the long delay of German Admiralty Intelligence in getting around to wonder about Scapa Flow. Commencing about 1909, the German and British navies had prepared for a duel to the death. Every armor belt put upon a new German warship, every cannon put aboard, was done in expectation of fighting the British. *"Der Tag"* meant more to the German navy than to any other offensive service. Yet German Intelligence waited until The Day was at hand—until war in the North Sea was all but an accomplished fact—before ordering Steinhauer to investigate a natural, and nearly impregnable, base for the Grand Fleet which even then was mobilizing to match the threat of German land and sea preparations.

CHAPTER SIXTY-SIX

THE DRAMA BEGINS: DOWN WITH THE CURTAIN

THE TIME HAD NOW COME to stop oiling and polishing the vast and beautiful machinery of European militarism and start drenching it in blood. Highways of the Continent trembled to the thud of iron-shod marching men. No more parades, no more autumn maneuvers—Serbia was arming to resist annihilation; Austria-Hungary was mobilizing; Russia was mobilizing.

On the morning of the thirty-first of July 1914 General von Moltke, chief of the German General Staff, signed the order that a state of *drohende Kriegsgefahr*—threatening danger of war—should be decreed at midday. That was really Mars's last hurdle, and he kicked it aside with a grunt of satisfaction. Germany at once began to mobilize, then France, then Belgium, which was small but had its own special ultimatum, and finally, the British Empire. All the great civilized Powers, not excepting the most distant and neutral—a whole civilization changed forever in the course of seven days.

A British staff officer is said to have remarked that his country would probably repeat the experience of the Napoleonic Wars: begin the war with the worst Intelligence Service in Europe and end with the best. Surveying the immediate achievements of the other Continental services leaves the impression that Britain's "worst" did rather well. Certainly it began as the luckiest in counter-espionage, largely owing to the blunders of its enemies.

The personnel of the counter-spying branch consisted of only four officers, three investigators and seven clerks. However, a special detective division of New Scotland Yard and the whole police force of the British Isles could be enlisted in the pursuit of enemy spies.

Gustav Steinhauer had paused in his flight to warn his Edinburgh agent, a music-hall pianist, George Kiener. It was this spy's novel conviction that the oncoming war would not affect him, as the great Powers about to be embroiled were—England and Russia. Otto Weigels, the German agent in Hull, had laughed at Steinhauer's warning; and yet now, as the British closed in upon the "Ernst chain", Weigels was one of the few who managed to avoid the net. Steinhauer merely had written to Schappman, his Exeter agent, and had told him to pass the alarm on to Ernst in London. Schappman escaped; and Steinhauer, of course, got away to Hamburg with plenty of time to spare. Ernst and twenty-one other German agents were arrested on the fifth of August, the morning after the declaration of war.

Those in London were rounded up by detectives, while telegrams to chief constables caused the simultaneous apprehension of the rest. And thus a curtain, more baffling than any London fog, enfolded Great Britain, blinding German Intelligence. The Prussian General von Kluck has acknowledged his surprise when the First Army struck at Lanrezac's left flank and encountered British regulars.

The Defense of the Realm Act—"Dora," with the justly celebrated "teeth"—was not yet in force when Ernst and his "chain" were taken into custody. Many of his secret-service correspondents were subjects of the Kaiser and could only be interned for the duration of the war, no light sentence. The barber earning a pound a month,[1] whom Steinhauer, the master spy, had sought to rescue with a post card, eventually suffered seven years' penal servitude.

The Mission of a German Nathan Hale

This fortunate extinction of the German espionage system in England—which marked the beginning of the British luck—yielded prompt and ponderable dividends. The British Expeditionary Force crossed the Channel without hindrance or hostile observation. And had that body of regulars been twice as large, its impact of surprise, felt only by Von Kluck, would have extended to the invading armies of Von Bülow and Hausen and might have changed the course of the war on the Western Front. Even without weight of numbers, the surprise contributed materially to the maneuvers of retreat and strain known as the "battle" of the Marne—in that it had earlier helped to save Sir John French's army and the French Fifth Army of Lanrezac from a smashing disaster.

Those two forces, comprising thirteen French and four British divisions, by the twenty-third of August had—under Joffre's orders—nearly thrust their heads into the steel jaws of a German trap. The First and Second armies of Von Kluck and Bülow were closing on them from the north, and Hausen's Third Army from the east. Military critics give three reasons for their timely escape: Lanrezac's caution in hesitating to advance across the Sambre, the premature attack of the German Second Army, and the arrival of the British on the left flank unknown to German Intelligence.[2]

"Am I surrounded by dolts? Why have I never been told that we have no spies in England?" the Kaiser is said to have stormed when he learned of the promptness with which Sir John French's army had reached the battle line.⁶

Solemn General Staff experts agreed with the All Highest that every German plan would now have to be revised.

"A first-class spy must be sent to England at once," Wilhelm commanded, "and above all a German whose patriotism can be relied upon."

German Naval Intelligence was the more concerned about this espionage defect, the British army still being regarded as too small and "contemptible" to worry Military Intelligence. Apparently having no "first-class spy" on hand, Naval Intelligence hurried the hapless Reserve Lieutenant Carl Hans Lody off to Scotland. Since he volunteered to act as an emergency replacement, his handicap of total inexperience was not counted against him.

Lody knew Britain well, having been a tourist guide for the Hamburg-American line. He spoke English fluently "with an American accent", a detail largely overlooked by other German spies in the war who sought to pose as Americans. In September 1914 he turned up in Edinburgh bearing the passport of an American tourist, Charles A. Inglis, with his own photograph substituted upon it. Mr Inglis had lately visited Berlin, had applied for a visa, and had waited while Wilhelmstrasse unaccountably "mislaid" the document that introduced Lody to the British port authorities. On the demand of the American Embassy, Inglis was supplied with another passport and the customary apologies. Lody meanwhile had sent a telegram to Stockholm, had removed inconspicuously from an hotel to private lodgings, and, hiring a bicycle, had begun to explore the vicinity.

As a novice secret agent, he suffered from an excess of zeal and a disproportionate ability in covering his tracks. He asked too many questions, showing a dangerous keenness about the harbor at Rosyth, and displayed anything but a casual tourist's attitude toward British naval affairs. Lody fell under suspicion with the filing of his very first telegram. It was addressed to Adolf Burchard of Stockholm—not yet a charter member of the vast Suspect List of British Naval Intelligence—and in it Lody unwisely sought to exhibit himself as one rejoicing in sentiments hostile to Germany. But even that early in the war the censors were not so gullible; a person writing *at* them too obviously deserved in return a good deal of extra attention. Spies after Lody were to try this transparent stratagem by post, and their letters were invariably delayed to be tested for secret-ink writing.

In Lody's case it seemed neither neutral nor American to spend a cable rate in exulting to another neutral about German reverses.

He wrote Burchard five times. Only one of these letters was allowed to reach Sweden, and that one because it helped to confirm the rumor, fantastically typical of the first months of the war, about a Russian army landing in Scotland and being transported thence to France, for action on the Aisne. His picking up and communicating this false report does not reflect on Lody's intelligence, for at the time leading military critics and correspondents were devoted to that welcome host of Russians.[4] As brave and promising a young man as Carl Lody, given any respectable amount of secret-service training, might have become a dangerously effective espion. Instead his life was gratuitously squandered. To comfort the Kaiser and "replace" the lightly expended Ernst "chain", Lody was hustled off to an enemy land without the simplest protective initiation into subtleties of codes, ciphers or even invisible inks.

Thus the luck of British counter-espionage continued. This first substitute for Steinhauer's resident spies was shadowed from Edinburgh to London, back to Edinburgh, from there to Liverpool, to Holyhead, to Dublin and Killarney. He was heading for the naval base at Queenstown; but his last letter to Burchard, intercepted like the others, seemed to be proof enough, and he was arrested by the Royal Irish Constabulary at the request of Scotland Yard.

Lody Goes to the Tower

After his downfall became known in Germany—and this did not come to pass for many weeks—secret-service and military notabilities there mentioned Lody only to blame him. They said that he had blundered—a wartime epidemic to which they alone were thought to be immune—and that by arousing British vigilance against mobile agents, he had been instrumental in causing the detection and death of many other spies.[5] But nothing that Lody did showed any want of initiative or assurance, while almost everything he did exposed the hurried incapacity of the German Secret Service, which had neither trained him as a spy nor wisely directed his espionage mission.

On the thirtieth of October 1914 he was brought to trial in London before a court martial that extended itself to do honor to British justice and accord an enemy fair play. Major General Lord Cheylesmore presided; and to a distinguished member of the English bar, Mr George Elliott, was assigned the hopeless task of defending the German agent. Lody was specifically charged with having posted on the twenty-seventh and thirtieth of September two letters which were addressed to Karl I. Stammer of Berlin,[6] and which conveyed information about recent British military preparations and defensive measures. It developed that there had been found in Lody's luggage, besides the forged passport, a notebook containing naval data and various addresses in Hamburg, Berlin and Stockholm. He had saved copies of a telegram and of four letters sent to Burchard. Had he been encouraged to pack and carry along his uniform as a senior lieutenant of the imperial naval reserve it would not have proved more incriminating.

His reports were described to the nine officers of the court as the best that had thus far fallen into the hands of British counter-spies; their "accurate observation and clear expression"[7] were especially emphasized. Lody offered no defense, save as a man who had done what he conceived to be his patriotic duty and stood not in fear of the consequences. It was stated by his counsel that his grandfather had been "a great soldier who successfully defended a fortress attacked by Napoleon," and that the accused had hoped to emulate that military resolution. Happening to be in Berlin at the outbreak of the war, he had immediately placed himself at the disposal of the Admiralty, and on being found physically unfit to be certified for active service, he had accepted assignment to the secret intelligence branch.[8]

"I am not here to beg for mercy for him," said Mr Elliott. "My client is not ashamed of what he has done. Many would gladly do for England what he has done for Germany, and may actually be doing it at this moment. Whatever his fate may be, he will meet it as a brave man."

Lody more than fulfilled that prediction. His fine bearing and undeniably sincere devotion to his native land recommended him to the mercy of the court or of higher British authorities. Yet at that critical hour a commutation for any flagrant case of German espionage was deemed a harmful and unjustified advertisement of weakness. The enemy would be anxious to replace the defunct "Ernst chain" in the British Isles, and this replacement could only be discouraged by executing the engaging naval agent as a deterrent example.

Lody's quiet acceptance of the capital penalty, his composure and resignation up to the moment, early in the morning of November 6, when he faced a firing squad in the Tower of London commanded the utmost respect.[9] Sir Robert Baden-Powell has written: "In the Lower House they spoke of him as of a patriot who had died on the battlefield for his country."

At the last minute, when the time had come, the condemned agent said to Lord Athlumney, the provost marshal: "You would not, I suppose, care to shake hands with a spy?"

"No, I don't think so," the British officer replied. "But I shall be proud to shake hands with a brave man."

CHAPTER SIXTY-SEVEN

INTELLIGENCE AND SECRET SERVICE

TO ENEMY and neutral observers this immediate, this unanticipated and almost unbelievable breakdown of German espionage was a disconcerting shock. The peoples and governments of Europe for a generation had been dreading another monstrous onslaught of Teutonic spies. But where were they? The usual fantastic spy scares filled some of the vacuum, and yet not all of it. If the Germans from the very outset were not doing their best, it must be a trick.

It is perfectly apparent today how the German Secret Service at the beginning of the World War came to fail as it did, and also why, in various isolated instances of the undercover combat, the Germans later managed to score some degree of success. The Kaiser's armies were able to tip their bullets and bayonets with terror. Frightfulness—*Schrecklichkeit*—was their premeditated strategy from the opening day of the conflict.[1] And in attempting to counter the Allies' blockade, the German navy with its sinister application of unrestricted submarine warfare developed a form of sea-going frightfulness not inferior to the deeds of the Barbary corsairs, or Caribbean pirates, whose unwanted captives—as a source of innocent merriment—walked the plank. But neither the original organization of the *Nachrichtendienst* nor the training of its earlier operatives warranted reliance upon this character of combat. Later on, in sabotage, counter-espionage, and an occasional mission of offensive secret service, German agents managed successfully to borrow their military or submarine comrades' philosophy of frightfulness and terror. Without frightfulness even the clandestine Teutonic combatant was off form, hampered and unhappy.

It took time for the Intelligence experts of the Entente allies to discover this; and their initial perplexity had a good deal of influence upon the waging of secret-service warfare. If the Germans were not making historic blunders, what desperate new ingenuity were they endeavoring to screen? Or were they really accomplishing a lot which had not been detected? These were troubling queries; though not so confusing as the truth—since confirmed by Nicolai—that the German command was so arrogantly confident of winning a quick decision on land, it felt little interest in spying upon the Allies' futile attempts to escape the consequences of their own rash belligerency.

Alleged thinking on *both* sides at length got around to the facts by stumbling over them. And to the Entente it now became wonderfully and painfully apparent that the enemy was doing his best in secret service with such pitiful results they would have to be concealed.

It would have been too hazardous, for example, to permit the British public to suspect that there was not one dangerous enemy agent at large in the United Kingdom. Fortunately, even at this time, the war propagandists were ready for the most complex requirements of their calling—namely, to make the enemy seem: (1) utterly savage and demonic, (2) ever more powerful and threatening, and yet (3) never more than temporarily victorious. To belittle a foe's achievements while continually exaggerating him as a threat was necessary from these early months of the war until the last dud had furrowed the mud of Flanders, because both the morale of the "home front" and the zeal of the raw recruits must be simultaneously stimulated. And there was no better way of accomplishing this neat blend of quake and bravado than by magnifying the influences gathering behind all the German efforts.

By rumors and direct distortions it was regularly hammered home that, though the Kaiser was losing every engagement, he still might win—and recruiting (conscription) must not for a moment abate— by encouraging his captains to resort to some terrible new stratagem of cold ferocity and monstrous cunning. Beyond the enemy's battered, wavering armies lurked one or more giant intellects, pursuing the unspeakable ideal of a sudden, annihilating stroke.

Throughout the war the German Secret Service was so misrepresented. The Germans were winning most of the time on land and making themselves increasingly troublesome at sea. What if their offensive espionage were often at fault, misguided, clumsily ill informed, and at times, both in the West and East, downright ridiculous? The secret-intelligence corps of the Kaiser's forces could be all the more comfortably recognized as a constant stalking terror and issued regularly in nightmare form to civilians and combatants, like war-loan propaganda, or ammunition, rations and medals.

Revanche *without Readiness*

The vast confusion attending the outbreak of a general European war seems to have been anticipated by hardly any of the stupendous intellects which had wrestled so long with the provocation of the conflict. Mishaps, blunders and oversights of major consequence battered every front as the war's first creeping barrage. Waste, stupidity and carelessness were already in the ranks, the kind of conscripts who cannot be rejected, who clutter the battlefields and never get killed. Some of the outstanding errors of Intelligence seem to have been prepared months and years in advance, and some of the more perverse—the very antithesis of intelligence—had a calculable effect upon history.

The French had spent forty years contemplating *revanche,* the recovery of Alsace-Lorraine and atonement for Sedan and the surrender of Paris. Yet what first-rate military Power ever prepared so long for one "inevitable" conflict and succeeded in overlooking so many of its inescapable requirements? With the single exception of the light field gun—the immortal .75—France was not ready and might almost appear the victim of a sudden surprise attack. The French Intelligence—whose voracious concentration upon the Teutonic menace had sent Dreyfus down to ruin, Picquart to imprisonment, Lajoux into exile, and, at vast expense, absorbed, wrecked or cruelly distorted a thousand more clandestine careers—began the World War with its heaviest contribution to victory, *German* victory. Two German soldiers took the field in August 1914 for every one that the French General Staff had been led to expect. Its Intelligence advisers "during the crucial days when the rival armies were concentrating and moving forward . . . counted only the active divisions" when estimating the German strength, though formerly French Intelligence had accepted "the possibility that the Germans might employ their reserve formations at the outset;" thus we learn that the "fundamental flaw in the French plan was that the Germans had deployed twice as many troops as the French Intelligence estimated, and for a vaster enveloping movement."[2]

Since 1906, when the celebrated Graf Schlieffen was succeeded by the younger Von Moltke as chief of the German General Staff,[3] nine new German divisions had become available. But even though allowed an eight-year interval in which to correct past errors and make allowances for the new formations, French Intelligence experts perpetuated their dangerous fallacy and passed it on to General Joffre. His imposing "Plan XVII", of the school of *offensive à outrance,* was based upon this wrong estimate; which was one of several reasons why "Plan XVII" broke down and had to be replaced, virtually upon the battlefield.

In this theater of operations—and long before the hostilities that everyone anticipated had actually commenced—a vital espionage achievement had been allowed to go disastrously astray. It was a case of the inconvenient impact of certain spy reports obtained by the Belgian Intelligence. Little had been spent by Belgium upon military espionage until 1912; but then, as the tensions of the Continent failed to abate, it became unpleasantly apparent to the authorities at Brussels just how events were shaping themselves. Treaty guarantees of neutrality would never survive any swinging into action of the Germans' "Schlieffen Plan."[4] A few secret agents were thereupon employed, mainly because the rumored weight of new German siege artillery had begun pricking the composure of the Belgian army chiefs.

Fortifications at Antwerp, Liége and Namur were optimistically reputed to be "strong" and even "impregnable." Yet they had only been constructed to withstand the fire of the German 21-cm. or the French 22-cm. guns; and the Japanese had already used 28-cm. ordnance in battering at 202 Meter Hill and other main defenses of Port Arthur. And so Belgium's spies visited Austria and Germany, learned all they could about the latest models of Krupp rifles and Skoda howitzers, and came home with a pregnant warning. The Austro-German allies were equipping themselves with cannon half again as large as Japan's 11-inch siege-howitzers!

One espion is even said to have brought back a detailed, accurate description of the huge 42-cm. Skoda guns. But for this neither he nor the Skoda works received any recognition. It was considered "too late" as well as "too costly" to reconstruct the Belgian fortresses so that they might withstand the incomparable pounding which the new siege guns would be able to inflict upon them. Moreover, the Belgian General Staff felt that giving official credence to such bad news would only disturb the commander in chief, who was also their popular king.

Ludendorff Unlocks Liége

Leaving those fortresses to their fate proved a blunder of the first magnitude. Liége, for example, defended the "bottle-neck" through which the two great German armies of General von Kluck and General von Bülow must be poured before they could deploy fanwise and strike southward at the French and British. Liége guarded no less than four lines of railroad that were the only means by which the German invaders could be supplied once they swept into action. In order to clear this vital Meuse gateway into the Belgian plain north of the Ardennes, the German General Staff had prepared a force of six infantry brigades with a mass of artillery, cyclists and motor cars—and held year after year near the Belgian border on a *peace footing* of constant readiness to strike. The spies had also told gentlemen in Brussels all about that destructive spearhead, but even so, nothing more could be done to mitigate the unpreparedness of Liége.

That German van of invasion in 1914 was commanded by General von Emmich. The mobilization even of the superbly organized German armies would require weeks; but to Von Emmich's force Liége was a matter of days measured in hours. Nearly three weeks before the main shock of the enormous rival armies could begin, Von Emmich's six brigades must fall upon Belgium's key fortress. All of which happened in accordance with Schlieffen's strategic program and Von Moltke's faithful modification of that masterpiece. But it only occurred because of the emergence and intervention of a new German staff genius; and even he would have been deprived of his laurels and his eventful stroke if Liége had been made a little more up to date. And the Belgian war budget had been elastic enough for what little was desperately required.

According to plan, the German command sent Von Emmich and his six brigades over the Belgian frontier on the night of August 6, 1914, violating a neutral state and defying Britain in order to carry a vital defensive position by a *coup de main*. However, their surprise attack failed; even the long-drilled German storm troops blundered. The ring of Liége forts did not surrender, and in the darkness and confusion those columns feeling their way between the forts "lost their direction and hung on the verge of disaster." Whereupon from the wings stepped a Prussian officer whose name would soon be known around the world and whose reputation for superlative abilities—whether he always had them or not—would fortify both military and civilian morale in Germany through the darkest hours. His name was Erich von Ludendorff; and his superiors already knew him for a brilliant member of the General Staff, though "a man whose opinions had been so strongly expressed that it had been thought expedient a year before to remove him from Berlin to a brigade."[5]

That brigade was now in disorder and on the brink of a severe reverse, the more damaging in itself and to the whole German assault because of its significance at the very outset of the war. Ludendorff "suddenly appeared from the gloom," took charge of a column that had mislaid its general, and added to it all other disorganized units within his reach. Then he found the right road and, leading his troops forward, entered the city. Connecting the Belgian forts were no intermediate works of any kind to impede his advance; and at dawn, singlehanded, Ludendorff was calling upon the citadel of Liége to capitulate. He bluffed its commander into assuming that a great surprise attack had mopped up the outer ring of forts—which were not at the moment firing their guns to expose this fraud, since they were not being attacked—and so procured the citadel's surrender with its entire garrison. Holding the city enabled the Germans to besiege the forts from every side, but they resisted stubbornly and were only reduced one by one when the great Skoda howitzers were brought up to register direct hits with their terrific shells.

A noted military critic[9] has written that the "destructive power" of those howitzers "was the first tactical surprise of the World War." And certainly the blasting impact of the 42-cm. shells gained another world-wide advertisement for German might and military brains. Yet there is every reason to believe that Germany's foes were not surprised; they knew that howitzers of such caliber and field mobility were being made, even as later in the war they had ample foreknowledge of the manufacture of the long-range Krupp guns which shelled Paris. The Germans' "tactical surprise" at Liége was generated in the main by Entente Intelligence and General Staff officers whose complacence and lethargy were not to be disturbed by the febrile alarums of secret service.

The Russians Afield with a Code of Candor

In the epilogue to his recently concluded history of Europe, H. A. L. Fisher ruefully observes that: "The tragedy of the Great War was that it was fought between the most civilized peoples of Europe on an issue which a few level-headed men could easily have composed, and with respect to which 99 per cent. of the population were wholly indifferent." But the truly "level-headed men" were not those with supreme authority in the so-called citadels of civilization. The civilizing process had polished up the leisure of a continent but sharpened no wits keen enough either to prevent the war or win it with humane rapidity.

Witness the Russian staff's childlike faith in the durability of Colonel Redl's treason. That great villain and "greatest spy of prewar Europe" had been dead about fifteen months when, late in August 1914, Russian armies came sweeping into the Austrian province of Galicia, employing a formation allied to the purchased secrets of Vienna. No Russian strategists had sought, like Serbia's skillful Putnik, to "think all around" the disclosure of enemy plans. And what Redl had sold, by a desperate endeavor, had been revised by the

Austrians since his suicide. Yet the Russians allowed for no variants and pressed majestically on. Redl had revealed that his country's main force would assemble in the region of Lemberg. But now the Russian vanguard discovered the principal enemy concentration behind the line of the San River, to the west of Lemberg—which unsportsmanlike move disconcerted some of the most gorgeously decorated general officers on the Eastern Front. Superior numbers—and lavish subsidies to spies and traitors—entitled the Russians to an overwhelming triumph; but their relying upon intelligence months out of date led them perilously near to a good sound thrashing. Alfred Redl's depravity had caught up with him, however, and it was too late to ask for their money back.

When other great armies assembled for the invasion of East Prussia, the German staff sergeant, Wolkerling, was serving a fifteen-year prison sentence for having sold to the tsar's attaché, Bazaroff—among a variety of German military secrets—the plans of the small, but strategically important, frontier fortress of Lötzen. General Rennenkampf, commanding the Russian First Army, expected to capture Lötzen with ease; and it was imperative that he do so if his advance were to continue in accord with the invasion schedule prearranged by his superior, the northern army-group commander, Jilinski. However, the Prussian commandant of Lötzen sturdily resisted, answering a summons to surrender by firing upon, wounding and making prisoner the Russian officer and trumpeter sent with old-fashioned magniloquence to invite his submission. Now even though the Russian Stavka had acquired by purchase the Germans' own plans[7] of the permanent defenses of Lötzen, Rennenkampf marched up to this obstruction without bothering to bring along "a few heavy howitzers", and therefore was incapable of reducing it. Failure to overwhelm the fortress had an almost immediately fatal influence upon the actions and maneuvers known as the first Battle of the Masurian Lakes, September 9-14, 1914. Rennenkampf, barely avoiding such envelopment and ruin as had overtaken Samsonoff's Second Army at Tannenberg, escaped with a loss of 45,000 prisoners, some 200 guns and nearly 100,000 casualties.

In the next chapter we shall discover a luckless officer of the tsar's gendarmerie, Colonel Sergei Miasoyedoff, standing trial and being summarily executed for various military offenses including espionage which, it was alleged, betrayed to the enemy the strength of Russian positions in East Prussia and contributed heavily to the German triumph at Tannenberg. There is not the slightest doubt that Hindenburg, Ludendorff and their brilliant staff officer, Hoffmann, were kept minutely well informed of the Russian armies' operations; but no spy that ever lived could have done for his German employers what Russian generals did for them with unassuming negligence. The Russians were equipped with a powerful wireless apparatus, and when the history of the Eastern Front is ultimately distilled it will be that apparatus which ranks first as the most decisive German accessory of the war. After Marconi signals had saved passengers and crew of the Republic and called rescue ships to the timely aid of lifeboats launched from the sinking Titanic, no sane man would have deplored the invention of wireless. And yet, had there been no such communicative device available in 1914, the course of the war would have been inestimably altered. One and possibly two Russian armies would have been spared initial decimation; the Austrian defeat at Rava Russka could have been turned into a catastrophe. Austria-Hungary, never again to be so strong or aggressive after losing the professional core of its finest army in the series of battles that made up the Battle of Lemberg,[8] would have lost in addition General Auffenberg's Fourth Army had there been no Russian radio.

What would such a knockout scored in the sixth week of the war have done to Austro-German plans? Threatened Germany with invasion by a great force of victorious Russians, dislocated the whole German recovery in France after the setback of the first Marne. Would there ever have been a drive upon the Channel ports or upon Verdun? The millions of casualties saved from those futile unfought battles might have been recklessly consumed in other actions unforeseen; but it is still not absurd to suggest that the Russians' misuse of their field wireless prolonged the war for months and years and thereby tragically confused its outcome. The Russian code or field cipher was not, as alleged, sold to German agents by Miasoyedoff. And if it had been, that might only have bewildered the German high command, since the Russians habitually exchanged vital wireless communications without using any code whatever.

A German wireless station in the fortress of Königsberg picked up messages in clear, disclosing the strength and intentions of both Samsonoff and Rennenkampf. This colossal blunder revealed that Rennenkampf's army could not come up in time to fight beside the Second Army if Samsonoff were attacked. "In addition to this," Hoffmann observes,[9] "the order confirmed the information we already had as to the strength of the Russian forces, and . . . we were very glad to know the exact objectives of the individual enemy corps."

Small wonder that this, coupled with Rennenkampf's excessive inertia, his subsequent relations with the German adventuress-spy, Maria Sorrel, and his remembered quarrel with Samsonoff in the Russo-Japanese War,[10] gave rise to charges of treason and espionage. But why need Germany corrupt the treacherous or hire spies? The doom of Tannenberg was already on the air five days before Von François' First Corps and Mackensen's Seventeenth completed the bequest of the national renown of Hindenburg-Ludendorff to a Germany then badly in need of major heroes.

Only eleven days after Tannenberg the tsar's oracular field wireless turned from promoting Russian disaster to prompting the escape of an all but encircled adversary. General Ruzski's Russian Third Army was pressing hard upon Auffenberg's Fourth Army. Plehve, in command of the Russian Fifth Army, who had extricated himself from a similarly dire envelopment on August 31, now turned and swept around Auffenberg's left flank, preceded by Dragomiroff's cavalry corps. Neither Auffenberg nor his superior, Conrad von Hötzendorf, was aware of the great strength of the Russian forces traversing the rear of the Austrian Fourth Army. In such critical circumstances reports from spies and Intelligence summaries are out of date in an hour, granting they are ever received. But the Russian Stavka had means of correcting every enemy lapse; and on the morning of September 11 the radio—which could still be intercepted and translated without any hindrance from cipher or code—spoke up once more, commanding two corps of Plehve's advancing host to reach the hamlets of Brusno and Cieszanow that same day. At once Auffenberg realized his extremity and began a rapid retreat to the southeast. Guided thereafter by an electrifying series of Russian orders—sent by wireless, in clear, to other Russians—the Austrian general was enabled in the nick of time to drag his worn and battle-strained battalions from the steel jaws closing upon them.

In East Prussia another opponent of the Russians mystified and hampered them by the very acts which led to his being dismissed from command. When General von Prittwitz broke off the Battle of Gumbinnen on August 20, 1914, his decision—so uncharacteristic of German obstinacy in the face of superior numbers—baffled the Russian "victors" and left them groping and cautious, mistaking his timidity for a ruse. Prittwitz, however, encoded his communications, so that most of the harm he did was done to himself. After he assured Von Moltke that he might not even be able to hold the line of the Vistula he was removed in favor of an older and all but forgotten veteran, Hindenburg. Thus, looking behind the scenes long after the event, we discover each of the mighty Powers slipping and stumbling into the death grapple. The complexities of the World War being what they are, this record can only serve as a spotlight hereafter, picking out certain of the more dramatic and outstanding personalities, encounters and episodes to be found in the secret-service theater of combat.

CHAPTER SIXTY-EIGHT

THE QUICKSANDS OF TSARDOM

THE HOLY MAN RASPUTIN may have been all kinds of a sinner, but there is no evidence to be found which supports the charge that he betrayed his imperial benefactors. Rasputin was assassinated by the aristocratic conspirators who gathered at the palace of Prince Felix Youssoupoff on the night of December 16, 1916; and ever since then persons endeavoring to misinterpret or dissemble the obvious reasons for the breakdown of tsarist Russia have sought to suggest that the monk was a German spy. It has never been proved, however, that he was subsidized by, or even in touch with, the many Teutonic agents of pro-German Russians who spent the war in Petrograd. Austrian and German Intelligence or Secret-Service officers have not been reluctant to describe certain plots involving bribery of Russians which they advanced on the Eastern Front;[1] but none has ever mentioned so much as hearing about a transaction enlisting as valuable an ally as Rasputin would have been to the "K.S." or *Nachrichtendienst*.

The monk was, moreover, unvaryingly spied upon; every step that he took set a battalion of police agents and shadows in motion. He was so powerful at court that the most arrogant official of the secret police did not dare to mention his name and referred to him in reports only as "The Dark One." But let us see what kind of surveillance the *Ochrana* chiefs conferred upon the favorite mystic of the empress. On April 1915 Rasputin decided that he ought to take a few days off, to recuperate from the wearisome round of playing healer, prophet and parlor god before his admiring audience of Romanoffs. He therefore traveled to Moscow, staying at the home of friends and throwing the police of that city into a panic of attentive apprehension. Agents of the *Ochrana* appear to have penetrated the house from hour to hour. Rasputin's excessive drinking was noted, likewise an excess of jollification. There were complaints lodged in the neighborhood because of the noise he made; and while drunk the charlatan kissed all the servant girls who came within his reach. Even those kisses echoed numerically in the police reports—made public with many others found in the *Ochrana* files by the Soviet authorities after the revolution.

In being taken for a drive in a cab, so that the bracing air might sober him up, Rasputin was still closely observed by the unblinking eyes of the *Ochrana*. The cost of the ride was even noted; and since the peasant-monk's capacity for carousal was only dilated by his oxygen treatment, the next page of the police report escorts him to a variety of cafés where he spent the whole night enjoying himself with friends, his conduct gradually "assuming a sexual-psychopathic character." Rasputin, after a very little sleep, was abroad again, this time accompanied by the prettiest of his hosts' housemaids. Three such days left the *Ochrana* spies limp and gasping, and then—no doubt with thankful sighs—they saw "The Dark One" to his train.

A comprehensive police report of all that had occurred in Moscow was now forwarded to the chief of the *Ochrana* in Petrograd, passing from him through the prescribed ceremonial channel to General Junkovsky, then undersecretary for home affairs. The general was tactless enough to suppose that Nicholas II wished to be accurately informed as to the character of the man on whom the palace was currently doting, and so he handed the *Ochrana* report to the tsar. Soon afterward "the Minister of the Interior, Prince Shtsherbatshov, received a communication from the Tsar suggesting that he might find another more suitable post for his Assistant. General Junkovsky naturally drew the proper deduction from this Imperial reprimand and went into retirement."[2] A year and eight months would elapse, with the monk assuming an ever more "provocative and overbearing manner", before police divers had to go down into the frozen Neva to move Rasputin's body from that retirement to a more decorous one.

The Alleged Treason of Soukhomlinoff

In 1916, with imperial Russia drained and tottering, the tsarist government was careful to sabotage whatever remained of public confidence by causing the exposure and condemnation of its minister of war. Much convincing "proof" of the guilt of General Soukhomlinoff has been published in the twenty years since his treason trial ended in conviction. He himself survived both his disgrace and the revolution, escaping into Germany where he "vindicates himself in able memoirs."[3] As shrewdly informed an observer of World War and Continental intrigues as Winston Churchill has called him "certainly the scapegoat of disaster."

Soukhomlinoff, serving a sentence of life imprisonment, was released by Lenin in the general amnesty of tsarist prisoners. It is, therefore, imperial rather than Soviet partisans who have kept alive a legend of the heinous crimes of the war minister and his accomplices; and it would be easier to accept the court-martial verdict in this celebrated treason case if we knew nothing about the bureaucratic conspiracies and undercover practices of tsarist Russia. The old general's trial was held *in camera,* with too many "secret witnesses." Moreover, Soukhomlinoff happened to be married to a young and very fascinating woman—admired by some of his brother officers—who was also a social liability since she was a Jewess from the then severely anti-Semitic city of Kieff.

The army career of General Soukhomlinoff had been a long and distinguished one when he became minister of war in 1909. He had fought at Plevna in 1877 and had risen thereafter through all the grades, both in commands and in the Russian General Staff. Kuropatkin had asked him to serve in Manchuria as his chief of staff, and Soukhomlinoff declined, saying that he did not know the theater of operations well enough, but would gladly accept a subordinate command. Which hardly suggests the scheming traitor and bribetaker! Three years of fumbling attempts to reform the tsar's army and revive its morale followed the disastrous war with Japan. Then, in 1908, Nicholas II dispensed with the committee of grand dukes and other hereditary tacticians and asked Soukhomlinoff to become chief of the Russian General Staff. The best military minds of Europe conceded this an uncommonly sagacious move; and the next year, at the age of sixty-one, Soukhomlinoff was appointed minister of war.

We might follow this general in his aggressive endeavors to reorganize the Russian army and bring it up to date as a powerful, responsive instrument of modern warfare, on a par with its Austro-German rivals. But to understand the inner workings of the tragedy that overtook Soukhomlinoff we had better pause to spy upon the significant reorganization of his own household. While commandant in the Kieff district the general had acquired an incurably romantic determination to possess another man's wife. His charmer was a schoolteacher, and the wife of a schoolteacher who had discovered her fascinations and lifted her up from an obscurity even greater than his own. General Soukhomlinoff found her not only willing but ambitious, and, as his passion was both mature and consuming, he chose to marry the lady. It had thereupon been arranged to grant the husband a leave of absence so that he might travel abroad; and when he unguardedly set forth into this sabbatical snare, the necessary divorce was manipulated. Even in an orthodox country few Russian administrators were then equal to the job of impeding the pleasures of a general.

Madame Soukhomlinoff—for they were married with equal expedition—was no longer obscure, but now the adored and petted wife of the commandant at Kieff. Yet she was still a Jewess in a city which had been the scene of the notorious Beiliss "ritual murder" trial and other episodes almost as rabidly anti-Semitic. She had, however, made an impressive match and was presumably accustomed to the prejudices of the Ukranian city, where she had long resided before a general noticed her. She was Soukhomlinoff's second wife; and he was so delighted with her that he discounted social frictions. He sought to indulge her in everything, and very frequently she traveled abroad. At Wirballen on the main railroad line into Germany there was stationed a Colonel Sergei Miasoyedoff, commanding the frontier guard. He was immensely courteous to all important travelers, on which account he was said to have once been invited by the German Kaiser to hunt upon his demesne at Rominten. This officer of gendarmerie was glad to win the approval of a distinguished superior by favoring his young wife. Mme Soukhomlinoff, encouraged in every extravagance, when abroad, even more than at home, spent her time buying things; and the day came when it was whispered that Colonel Miasoyedoff had helped and even guided her in smuggling in Parisian luxuries.

We need not deal at length with the political animus of Goutchkoff and his followers in the Russian Duma which prompted them to strike at Soukhomlinoff, the minister of war, through his wife and her friend, the colonel. As an indispensable friend Miasoyedoff had followed the Soukhomlinoffs to St Petersburg, and there he entrenched himself. The minister of war, ever eager to oblige his wife, rather recklessly declined to heed all the antagonistic gossip accusing the colonel. That Hohenzollern invitation to Rominten kept cropping up, together with other insinuations, some of them stated so openly they amounted to categorical charges. But Soukhomlinoff appointed the colonel his confidential aide. Goutchkoff charged Miasoyedoff with specific acts of treason and espionage. A duel resulted in which the Octobrist leader, a noted pistol shot, fired into the air, while the colonel fired but missed. To friends who protested Goutchkoff's failing to take aim he said with prophetic animosity: "I did not wish to save the rascal from the gallows!"

The zealous Russian commander in chief, Grand Duke Nicholas, complained that, whenever Russia went to war, spies and traitors created a housing problem in the tsar's capital. And since this was palpably true, General Soukhomlinoff seems to have been reckless and defiant in maintaining intimate relations with an accused "German spy" at the Ministry of War. Had Miasoyedoff been tactful enough to suggest a transfer, in some nonpolitical post he could have lived down his deplorable notoriety. Instead, war with Germany swept upon the empire, exposing all the quicksands of tsardom. Winston Churchill and many other eminent authorities bear witness to the excellence of General Soukhomlinoff's work at the War Ministry. The huge army was equipped and ready; railroads and transport facilities had been improved according to the schedule of a five-year plan, not yet completed. Mobilization of the "armed strength of Russia and its assembly in the battle zone" suffered no breakdown. Soukhomlinoff's program of army reorganization was put to the test and the whole colossal enterprise punctually accomplished.

However, in May of 1915 the minister of war was removed from his post and arrested on charges of neglecting war preparations, of treacherous communication with Austrians and Germans since the outbreak of hostilities, and of accepting bribes. The examining magistrate, Kotshubinsky, showed the chief of the imperial police a letter which he characterized as "convincing proof." The letter was from the Austrian merchant and suspected spy, Altschiller, addressed to Mme Soukhomlinoff and posted from Carlsbad. It mentioned that it had been raining, the roads were in poor condition near Carlsbad and "long walks . . . out of the question." When the pertinence of such mild pedestrian gossip was questioned, the excited magistrate exclaimed that the simple phrases concealed an intricate "Austrian code." And when M. Vassilyev persisted in his skepticism, the examining magistrate waved him away with, "The devil knows what the man meant!"

Throughout the trial the public prosecutor failed utterly to prove that General Soukhomlinoff had received any large amount of money from abroad, or that his wife, extravagant though he admitted she had been, had aided him in either receiving, concealing or expending sums large enough to be accounted a bribe to a minister of state. Yet against such feebly concocted accusations Soukhomlinoff's admitted, and extraordinarily valuable, services in reforming the Russian army from 1908 to 1914 were allowed to weigh not at all. The old general was convicted and monstrously condemned, barely escaping with his life.

Colonel Miasoyedoff had an underling's luck and was hanged. Brought to trial at Warsaw as early as February of 1915, the three charges against him alleged, first, that he had engaged in espionage for Germany on the East Prussian front, and, second, that he had stolen two terra-cotta statuettes from an abandoned dwelling in

East Prussia. This was lugged in as "plundering under arms." The third charge seemed an extension of the first and has been described as "incomprehensible." The court martial was made up of two General Staff officers and one regimental officer, while no representative for the defense was admitted. The chief witness, an officer whose testimony was discredited after the revolution, dealt only with the allegation of espionage, Miasoyedoff's betraying of the strength of the positions of Russian forces in East Prussia having, it was insisted, materially helped the Germans to win their annihilating victory at Tannenberg.

Miasoyedoff was described as an officer of the Intelligence Service, yet his once having come to the Dembowa-Buda section of the front and asked a number of questions was introduced against him. The

Interior design of the incendiary "crayon" pencil, one of the most novel and destructive sabotage instruments perfected during the World War.

verdict of the court martial was guilty, and its sentence—degradation and death by hanging. Vassilyev has stated that Miasoyedoff was acquitted by one court martial, but that "at the express command of the Grand Duke Nicholai Nicholayevitsh a second trial was held", ending with the desired sentence of death. Soukhomlinoff, be it noted, was still minister of war, but allowed to do nothing to reprieve or exculpate his friend and former subordinate. It was brought out at the trial that Colonel Miasoyedoff when arrested had "made a bad impression by his distracted answers to questions." He denied his guilt and reasonably accounted for the distracted answers, saying that a charge of betraying his country was so amazing and preposterous he did not know how to answer it.

After conviction he asked for permission to telegraph the tsar and to take leave of his mother. Both requests were denied. He then attempted to cut his throat with a piece of glass broken from his pince-nez. Military Russia so languid or relaxed behind the lines on other occasions was terribly brisk about disposing of the man who represented the first step of "intrigue and faction" in its overwhelming of Soukhomlinoff. Colonel Miasoyedoff, contrary to every code of procedure or tenet of decency, was hanged within two hours[4] of the rising of the court that had condemned him.

CHAPTER SIXTY-NINE

SABOTAGE

AS EARLY AS 1915 the great war settled down to the most horrible form of combat—a grinding contest of attrition, whose first casualties were maneuver and strategy, and whose ultimate cost was an extra million lives. The Entente, with numerical superiority in the West, proceeded upon the happy conviction that at least three Germans must fall for every four French or British effectives, and that, in consequence, at some indeterminable date there would only be a vast No Living Man's Land called Germany into which enfeebled little groups of Entente survivors would pick their way as conquerors. Yet in the midst of this program of calculated destruction of the enemy's human resources, very little new thought was brought to bear upon sabotage or the calculated destruction of the enemy's vital material resources.

Sabotage, as the word implies, had hitherto been the assumed concerted action of common and lawless folk, the reeking farm laborer or grimy factory worker theoretically provoked to trample the property of the privileged classes into the mire with wooden sabots. The World War, however, taught us that the worst anarchists of all are stupid generals or a hidebound staff, and that no greater malefactors can be met than officials of government claiming the right to kill or ruin, requisition or demolish in the purest spirit of defensive patriotism. And the war taught us further that, wherever effective sabotage did occur, it was the contrivance of men of scientific education and even cultivated tastes. The most accomplished chief of *sabotageurs* active during the conflict must have had several pairs of patent-leather "sabots", for he resided at a plutocratic yacht club, went regularly to his "office" in New York City like any attorney or merchant, conferred there with his agents as though they were clients or salesmen instead of spies and bombmakers, and frequently accepted invitations to dine in public at the Ritz-Carlton.

Of similar technicians of sabotage in Europe, and particularly in its zones of combat, there is little to tell. Where countless shells were bursting, air bombs exploding and fires igniting, who could detect an occasional "accident" devised by a furtive amateur hand or by a professional agent of sabotage? Moreover, acts of demolition or incendiarism—even when obviously accidental or but faintly suspected "hits" of sabotage—invited furious reprisals in noncombatant areas. And so the British and French were as a rule rather reluctant to encourage or order such behind-the-front attempts, as their chances of seriously impeding the enemy were slight compared with the inevitable excuse thus given the Germans for new local penalties and exactions upon the invaded regions of Belgium or France.

The French authority, General B. E. Palat, records[1] his conviction that two major strokes of luck really saved Verdun in the terrible months of 1916: the fortunate destruction of all the German 42-cm. howitzers by the accurate fire of the French long-range guns, and the blowing up of the great artillery park near Spincourt, where the Germans had accumulated 450,000 heavy shell, which they *kept fused*. Such carefree vulnerability was in itself a form of "sabotage" endemic throughout the war zones—the negligence of a subordinate or the tradition-saddled mulishness of a superior officer. Yet, regardless of the condition of those thousands of German shell, what was it that detonated the first of them? The Spincourt disaster has never been publicly claimed as a master stroke of Entente secret service, either in locating the park for the benefit of aerial bombers or in exploding it directly as a feat of sabotage; and General Palat is almost alone in acknowledging its vital influence upon the preservation of French morale and the maintenance of a key position on the Western Front.

The Allies appear to have felt uneasy about the ethics of sabotage and to have left most of the achievements in that line to be claimed for Germany; though Compton Mackenzie in an unsuppressed volume of his war memoirs[2] has told about a colleague of his in the British Intelligence who devised a plan for blowing up a certain bridge near Constantinople. This officer was uncommonly thorough. He obtained samples of various kinds of coal used in that part of Turkey in order to select a few large pieces and forward them to England, where they would serve as models for the casings of the bombs which he had promised to supply his hired Levantine *sabotageur*.

Sabotage, though it remained an isolated method of attack, seems to have produced the inevitable agent of counter-sabotage. The German military attaché at Bern made the acquaintance in 1915 of a Russian exile who appeared eager for any sort of anti-tsarist commission. And as he seemed familiar with all parts of Russia, an ideal mingling of interests began to simmer. What about the trans-Siberian railroad? This potential spy and agent of sabotage said he knew every verst of the trans-Siberian. He even agreed, when the mission was broached to him, to return secretly to Russia and cross Siberia to the Yenisei River where he would blow up the railroad bridge. A first-rate job of demolition would interrupt or hinder for months the vital flow of Japanese munitions to the Russian front. The Russian, whose name was Dolin, received complete instructions, traveling expenses and a generous fee—with a double reward promised him if he escaped and the Yenisei bridge did not. Whereupon Dolin journeyed boldly into Russia and reported himself to the chiefs of the *Ochrana* and General Batioushin. A cheat and trickster who lost his nerve? Not at all; a trickster, but only along the broad patriotic lines of secret service; for Dolin had tricked the German from the start. He was a responsible agent of the *Ochrana* and had been sent to live in Switzerland to keep watch upon its community of Social Revolutionaries.[3]

Rintelen and Company; and the Rudder Bombs

The one organized *campaign* of sabotage during the World War, unique of its kind and unduplicated in modern times, was conducted in North America rather than in any zone of the vast European conflict. It began many months before the United States declared a state of war against Germany, and it diminished in degree as the national government at Washington grew unmistakably belligerent. This justly celebrated sabotage attack was Germany's single achievement in secret service which lived up to the exaggerated prewar reputation of Teutonic intrigue and military espionage. Though ostensibly but a side show of the European embroilment, it was veritable warfare striking at American citizens who had believed themselves at liberty to sell as they pleased to Britons, Frenchmen or Russians. It was primarily an attack upon the traffic in arms and munitions, upon vessels of any nationality whose cargoes were more or less directly bound for the battlefield. All of which we know, not from adroit counter-espionage, but from the notably candid account of his work written by the chief of the German sabotage mission, Naval Captain Franz Rintelen von Kleist.[4]

The Allies complained of American munitions on the score of inferior quality—premature explosions that killed their own gunners or infantry, or duds that would not try to kill anybody. The Germans complained more vehemently of the same munitions because, while the Entente blockade closed the North Sea, they could not get deliveries of contraband from America. And although the blockade was a lawful instrument of war, and wholly British, the Germans seemed to heap more of the blame upon Americans, whose fault was that they consented to sell to customers they could reach and not side with customers who could not reach them.

In her volume of reminiscences, *Footnote to Folly*, Mary Heaton Vorse describes the public reaction she encountered in Germany after the Lusitania had been torpedoed with great loss of life. "It serves them right," they said of the drowned Americans. "Travelling on a munitions ship! Why should they travel on a munitions ship? People who travel on munitions ships must expect to be blown up."[5]

The Germans grew rapidly more sensitive about the munitions ships from America, especially those not so fast and famous as the Lusitania, which somehow escaped the attentions of roving U-boat commanders. And thus they came—by a process of trial and error with all the best types of torpedoes—to undertaking their program of sabotage to be directed from the American side of the Atlantic. Captain Rintelen was a happy choice for the high command of this subterranean mission. His energy and leadership, as well as his correct and deceptively engaging manners, almost counteracted the pro-German provocations of such attachés in the United States as Von Papen and Boy-Ed, such diplomats as the ineffable Dumba, and all their *Kolossal* brood of imitators. Rintelen made a little war in America and yet antagonized fewer Americans than the German diplomatic Thors and Wotans, who thought they were trying to make peace.

Sabotage—after the Rintelen model—was really an agreeable game; and, make no mistake about it, future wars are going to rely upon regiments of rintelens, and detonate, ignite and demolish opponents with vivid effect and quiet contentment. The German naval captain, upon arriving in America, readily recruited a corps of enthusiastic, fiercely patriotic and formidable Teutons. Rintelen implemented these *sabotageurs* with such accessible commodities as lengths of lead pipe, sulphuric acid, chlorate of potash and sugar. An infernal machine as simple as the "cigar" illustrated would start a bunker fire in a munitions ship after it had put to sea. It was no trouble at all in the beginning to introduce short lengths of pipe, with the ends plugged, into the bunkers or holds of munitions carriers loading for the war zone.

Bunker fires soon were erupting on the Atlantic ship lanes like chicken pox in a kindergarten. And bunker fires required the masters of endangered ships—whose explosive, inflammable cargoes were not designed for overheated holds—to flood them, checking the flames and brining the munitions. Waterlogged cargoes of shells and cartridges were theoretically valueless; but "salvage" is a word with as much emergency latitude as sabotage, and munitions cargoes which had been landed, dried out and somehow refreshed after being baked and bathed were undoubtedly delivered in many instances to the battle front. No wonder American-made shells gained their bad reputation for a high percentage of duds! The German *sabotageurs* thus earned an extra dividend by adding fuel not only to the cargo boats but also to the antagonism already well developed between

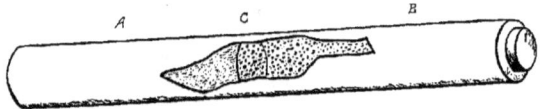

THE SABOTAGE "CIGAR"

A. Compartment of the length of pipe containing sulphuric acid; B. compartment containing sugar and chlorate of potash; C. the copper partition gradually penetrated by the acid which thus operates within this simple incendiary bomb as a timing device.

American "profiteers" and their urgent yet suspicious Entente customers.

Besides those innocuous-looking lengths of pipe—incendiary bombs of a nicely timed and dependably simple structure—Rintelen and his agents used other infernal machines fashioned to be mistaken for tinned foods, childrens' toys, or ordinary lumps of bituminous coal. It remained, however, for one of Rintelen's chief accomplices, Lieutenant Fay, to invent the war's most unique time-bomb, so contrived that it could be attached to the rudder of an anchored vessel, and the rudder would attend to timing its own devastation.

Fay, financed by Rintelen, worked out his invention in an isolated place. He built himself the stern of a ship and attached to it a genuine rudder. To this rudder he fixed a detonator, the tip of which carried an iron pin that was needle shaped at the lower end. The pin was connected with the rudder shaft itself; when the shaft turned, the pin turned with it, gradually boring its way into the detonator, until eventually it pierced the fulminate and caused an explosion that at least blew off the rudder.

Fay's One-Man Marine Attack

The German *sabotageur* injured himself in testing his device, yet persisted until he could always make his models work, and then started manufacturing the bomb in a handy form. Soon thereafter in a hired motorboat he went out into New York harbor one evening, pretended to have engine trouble, drew up alongside the rudder of one of the larger munitions transports and made fast. He was able to attach his explosive machine and push off, undetected. Presently, with the same sputtering motorboat, he succeeded in repeating his operation. Two big ships now carried his curious bombs. The results —in terms of destructive secret service—were immediate and gratifying. The ships put to sea, and each met with a startling, mysterious accident, suffering great damage to the stern as well as losing its rudder. One of them had to be abandoned by its crew and left drifting as a derelict off the Atlantic coast; while the other signaled for help and was towed into the nearest harbor.

These triumphs over cargoes meant for the slaughter of his fellow Germans caused Lieutenant Fay much additional trouble. He no longer dared to flounder about an American harbor in a seemingly defective motorboat. Should he drift toward any anchored vessel's rudder, he would at once be suspected of sabotage and put under arrest. But the German agent was young, reckless and resolute, as, indeed, he needed to be, for his next resource in attacking the munitions carriers called for an exhibition of iron nerve. He made a small platform of cork and mounted his detonating machine upon it. Under cover of darkness he swam out into New York harbor—no mean feat in itself —and pushed his dangerously burdened raft ahead of him. Upon coming to the vessel whose position he had carefully noted, he managed to transfer his bombing device from the raft to its rudder. And for weeks thereafter Fay pursued his daring nocturnal campaign not only in New York but also in Baltimore and other North Atlantic ports—one man against all the shipping chartered by a voracious Entente to bring them war supplies.

The munitions transports, however, multiplied so rapidly that American harbors soon were swarming with them; and not only improved police protection, but quite unofficial British and French counter-spying reached out strong arms to shield them from enemy agents of sabotage.[6] Captain Rintelen's whole outfit of conspirators was not powerful enough to interrupt the regularity of so many loadings and well-disguised sailings. Even Fay's exhausting labors had to come to an end. The German mission, which had accomplished the difficult and hazardous task of violating a great nation's neutrality to make war upon more formidable and popular foes, now struck on a broader front—a final desperate effort—by financing Irish agitators against England, and by fomenting and subsidizing strikes in munitions factories and among the dock workers of leading Atlantic ports.

Rintelen's activities came to an inglorious end through the constitutional or calculated stupidity of Captain von Papen,[7] the German military attaché at Count von Bernstorff's embassy in Washington. Clumsy messages, easily intercepted and deciphered by the British, reported Rintelen's return to the fatherland in a "neutral" disguise. The master *sabotageur* was, of course, identified and taken off the Holland-American liner, Noordam, carrying him home; and, after a courteous encounter with Sir Reginald Hall and his assistant, Lord Herschell, at British Naval Intelligence headquarters, the captain was appropriately interned at Donington. When the United States entered the war, the extradition of Rintelen was demanded, not as a prisoner of war who had fought against Americans, but as a criminal guilty under existing admiralty and civil law. Extradition was duly granted, and the German naval *Kapitänleutnant*, being tried in a federal court, was sentenced to Atlanta penitentiary for a term of four years. Rintelen and many of his champions have complained against such crude American treatment of a "Von", a naval officer and a gentleman. He may, however, reflect today that in most Continental countries impassioned by the losses and rigors of the war he would have been condemned as a spy and shot.[8]

Not all the secret undertakings of the *sabotageurs* had come to light at the time of Rintelen's conviction or were even known before the termination of the war. Some ships were incredibly lucky. A sturdy old German liner bearing the appropriate name of De Kalb made trip after trip to France as an American army transport, and only when that tour of "captive" duty came to an end was the vessel's crankshaft found to have been cut *four fifths through* by the German agents of sabotage. Similarly, the Norwegian freighter Gyldempris, after loading at New York in January 1917, carried and discharged various cargoes until late July, the last of these at Naples, where the steamer's afterpeak was cleared out. Two powerful dynamite bombs, fitted with detonators, were thus discovered belatedly under the ship's effects in the afterpeak.

Europeans inclined to discount their countries' war debts by a comparison of casualty lists hold to the belief that nothing really happened to Americans in the war and that their losses were trivial. None among the belligerents, however, suffered more damage or disorder from the sabotage conspiracies of one or the other European combatants; and none had a case to match the mystifying disappearance of the USS Cyclops. This big naval collier was last reported at a West Indies island on March 4, 1918, while transporting a cargo of manganese from Brazil. The Cyclops was equipped with the most up-to-date wireless installation; and yet this great seaworthy craft never was heard from again.

The American consul general at Rio de Janiero, A. L. M. Gottschalk,[9] who was one of the naval vessel's fifteen passengers, is said to have received rather a dubious "warning" about the dangers of going home aboard the Cyclops, which he promptly communicated to her captain, Lieutenant Commander G. W. Worley, U.S.N.R., so that the utmost vigilance ought to have been exercised by officers and crew. And yet no radio flash, no SOS came from the collier. Nor was a tropical hurricane or rare volcanic upheaval reported on her course. It would seem probable that German *sabotageurs* lurking among the populous Teutonic centers of Brazil or the Argentine contrived some swift, unimaginably sudden death stroke. How else could a collier—a great, slow, well-founded ship go down when nearing the gulf coast of America without even being able to spread one urgent blur of dots and dashes on the air?

CHAPTER SEVENTY

SPECIAL MISSIONS

AMERICA HAS SEEMED, largely from want of provocation, to lag behind Europe in developing the subtle contrivances of military secret service. In the American Civil War, however, we have noted the invention of telegraphic wire tapping and other novel deceptions. And it is an American whose skill and exploits are imperishably attached to the outstanding innovation of espionage in the World War. Indeed, that innovation—employment of the airplane in putting spies over an enemy's lines at night—has no pressing rival as the best single improvement of method in the annals of secret service. It was first attempted during the Balkan Wars of 1912–13; and, after that curtain raiser, the same young American adventurer turned up on the Western Front where the use of "air-spies" and the practice of "special missions" came on side by side with the new technique of army aviation.

Lieutenant Bert Hall began as an army flier in 1912 with the Turkish forces opposing Bulgaria. Born in Kentucky, he had spent his childhood in the Ozark Mountains and grown up to become an automobile racing driver and later a pioneer aviator.[1] In the Balkans he was flying a French monoplane, the Turks having hired him to take care of their air scouting for the not excessive fee of one hundred dollars a day in gold. But the sultan's armies—with Serb and Greek as well as Bulgar opponents—were compelled to fight entirely on the defensive. They met with successive defeats at Kirk-Kilisseh and Lule-Burgas, October 24 and 29, 1912; and their ancient stronghold of Adrianople was besieged by a Serbo-Bulgarian force. When it dawned upon them that they were losing the war, their chief interest in flight centered upon retreating safely toward Asia Minor.

Hall had done good and faithful scouting, and nothing but scouting, having ignored Turkish hints that he might be able to drop explosives upon their victorious foes. And now when his pay stopped, he stopped —taking himself, his monoplane and his energetic French mechanician over to the side of the Bulgarians, who hopefully engaged him to fly for them at the same daily wage. He had become well acquainted with the new defensive positions before Constantinople while in the service of the sultan; and it was suggested to him now that he try landing behind the lines at Tchataldja to do a bit of spying. The American pointed out the differences between scouting, which he had enlisted to do, and any form of espionage. But for a bonus he agreed to assume the special risks of trying to land a Bulgarian secret agent inside the Turkish lines; and this, even with the crude flying equipment of that dawn of aviation, he managed to do.

When the Bulgars repeated his Turkish experience, however, defaulting in their payments at the end of thirty days, the pioneer war pilot decided that his changing sides had been a mistake; and he was packing up to leave when put under arrest as an enemy spy. This typically Balkan method of distracting a creditor grounded the American flier in a rather bleak locale. As a soldier of fortune he was deprived of his citizen's right to appeal to a representative of the United States; and as he had never denied having formerly worked for Ottoman generals, it was going to be impossible to *prove* that he had ever stopped working for them.

Being tried by court martial, he alluded to the sums his captors owed him, and in return they sentenced him to be shot. Luckily his French mechanician, André Pierce, had never put much faith in Bulgarian integrity, and now, avoiding arrest, he carried his share of their profits in gold to some higher authority. A few hours before the appointed dawn of the "spy's" execution, the Frenchman emptied his pockets and the American went free.

August 1914 saw Hall begin repaying his debt to French presence of mind. He enlisted in the Foreign Legion on the second day of the war. After three months of fighting, his skill with a plane was discovered, to gain him transfer to the flying corps. He presently became a member of the Lafayette Escadrille—at the close of the great war being one of the few survivors of that famous company of "airdevils."[2] Even prior to the formation of the escadrille, Hall as a French army pilot was picked for the assignment which aviators came to know—and dread—as *special missions*. Getting in and out of the German battle zone with spies! This duty required, first, flying in the worst light, for just at break of day was the only hour then deemed safe for the spy, and, second, bringing the plane down on an unfamiliar and unprepared landing field. The return journey was hardly less hazardous; and in a few days, a week, or a fortnight the whole exploit had to be repeated, as soon as a carrier pigeon winged in with its tiny message reporting the agent ready to return to the French side of the line.

Hall, in working upon this innovation of offensive espionage, had to improvise his methods as he went along. Owing mainly to his coolness and piloting skill, he delivered several spies with their baskets of pigeons and brought each of them home again, without a single mishap. On one occasion, however, he appeared to suffer betrayal. The spy's request for transport came in; and Hall flew over before dawn to pick up his man at a field near Rocroi.[3] German counter-espionage agents were informed of the exact hour and place of his landing. Machine guns and riflemen awaited him; but it was Hall's luck and salvation to have the trap sprung a second too soon. Their long vigil and nervous tension had made his enemies impatient, and their opening burst of machine-gun fire was the American's signal, literally, to "fly" for his life. He zoomed up out of range. By his instinctive, bold maneuvering, the plane got off and away with its wings badly riddled, Hall suffering a slight thigh wound. Not long afterward, on account of his demonstrated excellence as a pilot of special missions, and for other flying services, he was decorated with the *Médaille Militaire*.

The air transport of spies, from this tentative beginning, came to be a regular duty in the flying corps of all the belligerent Powers. And numerous improvements in the routine of the stratagem were devised to help pilot, passenger or both. The landing of the plane was presently made, if possible, somewhere near the dwelling of a resident agent, who could shine a strong light up his chimney—visible only to one circling directly overhead—if, after careful scouting, it seemed safe to try to land. Signaling thus also came to the aid of the flier when he returned to pick up his spy. If for any reason an agent of espionage could not be ready at the appointed hour, the resident spy's signals spared the aviator a perilous, futile landing.

Judicial Dangers

Legal questions arose in regard to the pilot's position before a court martial should he chance to be taken prisoner in company with a spy or directly after having landed such an operative in the midst of the enemy. There was no existing rule of warfare in the Hague conventions which applied to an aviator caught while taking part in any form of espionage; moreover, in some quarters the laws of war were receiving a good deal of concentrated inattention.

A test case soon developed from the curious misadventure of two airmen, Bach, an American in the French flying corps, and Sergeant Mangot. Each of these pilots succeeded in landing his spy; but both came to grief when taking off in turn from the impromptu landing field.[4] They tried to work their way overland to a neutral frontier but had no means of disguising themselves and were quickly traced from the broken planes and made prisoner. Conducted to Laon and there brought to trial on grave charges of espionage, the luckless pair were cast for the unenviable distinction of helping to establish an international precedent. But Jimmy Bach was a genial young adventurer and well to do; he was able to afford the luxury of a distinguished civil attorney coming on from Berlin to defend him and his French companion. At the first trial, October 20, 1915, no decision was reached; a second, on the thirtieth, resulted in the charge of espionage against both aviators being dismissed. Bach and Mangot as prisoners of war spent the next three dreary years imprisoned at Nuremberg.

On all special missions thereafter it was arranged to put the secret agent in uniform, with civilian clothes underneath. Once he had been landed, he hid the uniform and set about his spying in civil disguise. But when the night arrived on which the pilot was expected to reappear and carry him off on their return flight, the air-spy again donned the uniform that would save them both from court martial.

The Allies gained greater advantage in sending spies over by plane and, therefore, developed the practice in spite of aviators' candid distaste for such missions. Belgium and the thirteen conquered departments of France were open to French or British secret service, with scores of more or less obscure landing places available, and hundreds of patriotic men and women willing to lend a hand. Paying as little as seven hundred francs—then about the equivalent of one hundred and thirty dollars—the spy-masters engaged former residents of Belgium who could be put down near their homes or in neighborhoods where, actually, they knew every foot of the ground.

To obtain that same familiarity behind the Allies' combat zones, German officers of espionage had to bribe a French or Belgian renegade—at best some rascal they had liberated from a jail of the occupied territories. And while such an agent might know his way about well enough, he was handicapped by his own record and his likelihood of being recognized by local authorities. Convinced after many experiments that this duel of the air-spies would always go against them, the Germans could only expand their defensive vigilance. Microphones were installed to pick up the vibration of an airplane engine in those ideally remote sections where an agent might be landed.

The Allies countered by reducing their pilots' special-mission landings from two to one. Hereafter the spy came down by parachute, which was appropriately noiseless, making his descent as a rule in a district covered by a resident agent. Espionage thus produced its most fantastic wonder of the four years' contest, with secret agents floating down out of the darkened sky upon a foe who anticipated their coming and yet would have had to disengage every soldier from every battle, trench line or reserve area on two fronts to stand watch over all the partisan French or Flanders fields spread out to welcome and conceal them.

A Campaign with Balloons

Most of the air-spies were men too old for duty at the front. Being trained in the handling of carrier pigeons, they would take as many as six with them, to send back at intervals bearing speedy reports of their findings. Each started off with complete instructions and an ample supply of French and German money, and, upon landing, sought the nearest line of communication and then threaded his way up to the front. Germans, too, were eventually enlisted in this work on the side of the Allies, chiefly Alsatians and Lorrainers, who had lived in France since the declaration of war—avoiding military service —or soldiers who had deserted or been taken prisoner.

The progress of hostilities made planes and pilots ever more precious;[5] and the French on their part grew increasingly "careless" about sending over for agents at the end of their espionage tour, many being left to shift for themselves when the last of their pigeons had come winging home. Air-spies thus deserted either fell into the hands of the Germans or made their way to Holland by a devious route. French consuls there were instructed to look out for them and return them to France. Many of the spies were advised, if a rescue by airplane failed them, to turn their furtive journey overland to account by destroying railroad lines, bridges and rolling stock in the rear of the enemy forces.

As a further economy of pilots and planes, a new secret-service venture was launched, the air-spies now being transported by balloon. This completely eliminated the betraying noise of the airplane motor but owned few other advantages. The average spy-balloon had a diameter of 8.5 meters and held 310 cubic meters of gas. It could only carry one person and had a range of travel between twenty-four and thirty-six miles. Balloon-spies were trained in England for a period generally lasting four weeks, during which at least six trial flights were made, two of them by night. The inevitable baskets of carrier pigeons accompanied the air-spies adrift in balloons.

It takes all kinds of courage to make a war; there were many brave enough to volunteer for espionage duty who yet had no wish to fly, to pass over anti-aircraft batteries, or to land in the dark by balloon or parachute after leaping from a military plane. To provide for the nervous ones who would agree to undertake the journey but balk when the crisis came, a new style of plane was constructed. Under the fuselage, between the wheels, there was built an aluminum compartment to hold the spy and his parachute. Only the aviator controlled the door of this compartment, and when he decided to open it, the spy fell out with his parachute attached.

Special missions produced real Intelligence results. As a consequence their scope was steadily magnified in order to harass the enemy. Rather than the temporary activity of a single spy, the aim now became organization—the founding of a regular branch of the espionage service to be carried on by local agents who would be secretly recruited and trained. Bright minds in 1917 actually began wrestling with the problem of a kind of correspondence school which would be conducted for those Belgian or French civilians who might be induced to assume a share of the perils of espionage.

From planes large numbers of carrier pigeons, propaganda bulletins and secret-service pamphlets were dropped in an effort to instruct the inhabitants of the occupied area in gathering and transmitting information. Small baskets were used, holding two pigeons; with silk parachutes attached, they floated gently to earth. In each basket, besides food for the carriers, were directions for handling them, questionnaires to be filled out, specimens of vital intelligence, some French money, and always a ringing printed appeal,[6] expected to kindle the patriotic ardor of poor folk who had gone hungry and humiliated about their meager daily tasks through three years of hostile invasion.

German counter-spies discovered a great many baskets of dead pigeons in lonely districts behind the lines.[7] But these, it was clear, represented only a small fraction of the quantity of pigeon baskets which the Allies now distributed. Carriers in flight were constantly being observed; and, though it needed superb marksmanship to shoot them down with an army rifle, in about a dozen instances that was done. Each time, according to the German record, the pigeons were bearing amateur reports of genuine military value—an astonishing average.

That passion for chips and scraps of information with which Intelligence usually dominates military secret service caused the Allies to continue expanding this system until the day of the Armistice. Pigeons were dropped not only by plane—often too conspicuously—but also by means of small balloons, some five meters in diameter, to which an ingenious mechanism was attached for letting the pigeon cages free. This type of small balloon carried a wooden cross, to each of the four ends of which a pigeon basket was fastened. In the middle of the cross was a box holding a simple, alarm-clock device; after the flight had lasted a given length of time, it automatically released the baskets with small parachutes attached, and eventually allowed the gas to escape from the balloon. With rather naïve intent not to arouse suspicion, each carried the legend: "This is a German balloon; it may be destroyed." Still later a slow-burning fuse was employed in place of the clockwork, setting the balloon on fire soon after the pigeon baskets had been released.

Carrier pigeons are very sensitive and were exposed to death by this ordeal if not found at once. Secret service therefore added to its many routine chores the distribution of news balloons. These, with a diameter of only 60 centimeters, were made of a light-blue tissue paper and difficult to see in the air. Any ordinary gas jet would inflate them. Packets dropped generally contained three of these balloons, folded, with minute instructions as to how they should be used. Sometimes chemicals were included, allowing the isolated finder to manufacture gas at need. But since the paper balloons when filled could only be dispatched with a favoring wind, they never compared to carrier pigeons as message bearers.

Harassed villagers behind the German combat zone continued to be the target of Intelligence; and the bulletins showered upon the potential spies grew ever more intense.[8] By the winter of 1918 there were special-mission aviators of the Allies scattering pigeon cages and news balloons even over the remote districts of Alsace and German Lorraine.[9] Their final achievement was the aerial distribution of wireless sending sets, excellent of their kind, the latest Marconi model, with four accumulators, 400-volt dry batteries, and 30-meter antennae. By means of them messages could be sent about 30 miles. Packets with these contrivances which were dropped by parachute carried, in addition to the usual directions and advice, brief instructions in ciphering. And the peasants and lonely dwellers of those war-stricken regions persevered not only in hazardous spying but also attempted to transmit spy reports in cipher by wireless telegraphy.

CHAPTER SEVENTY-ONE

GENIUS IN THE NEAR EAST

NO LIST of great amateurs of espionage may be compounded hereafter that does not include the name of Colonel T. E. Lawrence—Lawrence of Arabia. This young Englishman of acknowledged genius, odd seclusive traits and earnest scholarship was an effective agent of Intelligence and espionage before proving himself one of the most formidable captains of irregular troops in modern history. As a guerilla leader, Lawrence organized a campaign of desert warfare that raised his strange camel corps of tribesmen to a peak of strategic importance quite out of proportion to its strength, equipment or field of combat. Penetrating the Turco-German lines at will, he—sometimes with only a few native followers—blew up bridges and troop trains, and committed other acts of legitimate military sabotage. His disguises appear to have been masterly; he not only managed to look like an Arab chief, he thought like one, making the Arabs' tribal aspirations his very own and patterning his conduct upon the standards of Arabia.

Lawrence was both an efficient spy and a self-taught spy-master, never without adequate intelligence of the enemy forces coming against his variable command; and the findings of his espionage system, together with the impact of his guerilla thrusts, proved of inestimable value to General Allenby in his Palestine campaign. Colonel Lawrence, however, has written so vividly of his own exploits, in secret service and other military pursuits, the reader may well be referred to that extraordinary narrative. All of his adventures have been brilliantly described; his fame is as secure as it is well deserved.

In Asia Minor and the Near East the British contended with several agents of German Intelligence who seem to have shared, each in some astonishing degree, the special abilities of Lawrence. General Allenby's Intelligence officers called two of their most enterprising antagonists Preusser and Francks; but they might as well have been ticketed Missing Persons A and B for all the advantage derived from knowing them by name. Preusser, the more elusive and mysterious of the pair, had Lawrence's exceptional knowledge of the Near East and Lawrence's mastery of disguise. To his Turkish allies this German operative was "the Bedouin",[1] and it is said that on at least three critical occasions he visited Egypt and successfully penetrated the British headquarters at Cairo. Between Suez and Constantinople, in a politically disturbed region difficult for travelers and singularly unsafe for secret service, Preusser seems to have gone about pretty much as he pleased, either spying himself, or collecting information from lesser agents, native residents and local scouts in Turkish or German pay.

Wolfgang Francks had spent years in various colonies of the British Empire, seeking his fortune—as a sheep rancher in Australia, a merchant in Bombay, a journalist in Capetown—and only finding the eventual necessity of trying his luck at something else. He never ceased being German, no matter how much he grew to resemble a British colonial. The war came; and Francks hurried home to volunteer. He had a routine post in the heavy artillery until he volunteered a second time—for duty as a secret-intelligence officer and for transfer to the Jaffa-Jerusalem front. Francks convinced his superiors that he knew the country well, that he could swear like an Australian sheep raiser, that he could even pass for a British staff officer. And by one of those rare accidents he was actually given the assignment that he was best qualified to undertake.

Francks reached Palestine just as the Turks began to feel the full weight of Allenby's offensive pressure. Having his "perfect command not only of English but also of several of its dialects",[2] and an extensive military wardrobe, he began turning up here or there as a British or colonial officer; and such was the variety of his equipment and the versatility of his personations, he never presented himself as the same man twice. It was relatively simple to get into the British camps. Unlike the tense and vigilant situation in France, the British and Turkish lines lay parallel to each other in a limited zone and then trailed off into a semineglected, flanking no man's land, which replaced the mud and shell holes of Picardy with a waterless waste of desert sand. If Francks rode out far enough he could slip around the end of the line and into the opposing camp. On other, more pressing occasions he was put over at night by plane and landed by means of a parachute.

He was always in British uniform. Of fine figure, easy manners, possessed of technical knowledge in nearly all military branches, he conspicuously paraded the uniform of the staff, red tabs, "pips," numbers, every detail complete; and no one challenged him. His divisional insigne was chosen with care and belonged to troops stationed at some distant point in the Jaffa-Jerusalem line. Another time he affected the blue tabs and special insignia of the ordnance staff, which attire permitted him brazenly to "inspect" a regiment of artillery. He acquired on one occasion an exact explanation of an impending barrage. He was adept at cutting and splicing telephone lines, attaching his own small telephonic apparatus and listening in on official conversations; and such was his talent for imitating British voices that more than once he managed to issue contradictory orders.

The British never grudged him credit; in fact, all that is known of this German genius comes from former enemies who have paid tribute to his histrionic daring. When the war ended Francks vanished utterly, like so many of the more gifted members of his profession, and to date no reminiscences have come from his hand. But until the close of the Palestine campaign he vanished only to reappear in some other sector of the front, concealed by a new and equally plausible guise. Repeatedly he compelled hurried and awkward changes of plan, besides inflicting progressive annoyances upon every British officer that in any way resembled him. Scores of suspects were stopped though upon some urgent errand, had their orders subjected to exasperating disbelief, and were detained for an hour awaiting counter-spies' identification as the menacing Major Francks.

A Brother and Sister of Jaffa

The British might be plagued with "Major Francks" scares; yet on their side was many an officer of Intelligence grounded in the ways of the East and all its devices of warfare, adapting or improving upon the stratagems of the Old Testament. Sir George Aston, himself connected with a branch of the vast British Intelligence, has told[3] how neatly certain of his colleagues contrived to liquidate one of the best of the Turkish spies. Secret agents on duty with Allenby's Egyptian Expeditionary Forces got on the track of a dangerous spy whose zeal and ingenuities seemed to threaten the success of Britain's plans and the lives of many British soldiers. He had to be stopped; and the expedient chosen cost no more than £30. Approximately that amount in English bank notes was inclosed in a letter addressed to the spy, ostensibly rewarding him for secret services he had rendered the British. This letter was intercepted, just as its originators intended; but with, perhaps, greater finality than they expected, the flimsy evidence of that cash enclosure was accounted strong enough to condemn him. Without adequate investigation the Turko-German authorities shot their very effective agent, fearing him as a "double spy" whose treacheries might endanger them as much as he had actually endangered the British.

In that same theater of the war, during the Palestine campaign, a lad of nineteen belonging to a well-to-do Jewish family of Jaffa made a hazardous contribution to the British offensive, which, he hoped, meant the liberation of his own people. Young Aronson's patriotic ardor and bitter hatred of the Turk were shared by his sister; and the pair found they could turn themselves into spies with little effort, since an influential German staff officer had been quartered in their parents' home.[4] Each day offered some opportunity to go through his papers or ask him naïve and flattering questions. Moreover, both brother and sister had friends with no less promising opportunities for espionage.

They soon accumulated a budget of urgent information; and now a method of communicating with British headquarters had to be devised. Owning a boat, Aronson solved the problem by rowing out in it and along the coast until he came abreast of the Turko-German right flank, which rested on the shore. A good deal of caution and some more pulling on his oars brought him past the British left flank; then he landed and gave himself up for questioning by Intelligence officers. They commended the youth's pluck and initiative and were grateful for the information he delivered. After a few special missions by rowboat, Aronson was recognized as their best spy in that district. His base was now with the British. He had seemed to vanish from his home, but he still used the boat, rowing out and around behind the Turkish trench system; while his young sister served as collector for all their comrades and ranging amateur spies and met Aronson at night to transmit whatever had been learned.

Jaffa fell to the British and their allies on November 17, 1917. Jerusalem surrendered twenty-two days later. But before this, their final expulsion from Palestine, the Turko-German authorities and police became viciously alert. It was the cruel misfortune of Aronson's young sister to be arrested by military police at the end of October. Because the German staff officer had lived in her home, she feared to involve her brother, their spying friends, and innocent members of all their families. The Turks tortured her, but she would not talk; and so they finally killed her as Jaffa was being evacuated. The brother learned of her fate and is said to have borrowed a machine gun from his British army acquaintances. One time more the small boat carried him out and around the lines; he landed at Jaffa in the midst of terrific commotion and straightway added to the turmoil, for he located a few of his friends and they went Turk hunting.

Aronson was destined to become a trusted, useful attaché of the British Syrian administration. But there was an Old Testament flavor to the vengeance he sought for the sister who had helped to win what she could not live to enjoy. Turkish inquisitors at police headquarters had flung her into a loathsome cell, had whipped and burned her flesh, and pulled her finger nails one by one when she refused to incriminate her accomplices. And Aronson and his hastily recruited squad of irregulars shot Turks till their ammunition had been exhausted, stragglers and prisoners, sick and wounded—the Ottoman uniform was all the target they looked for. Moslem gendarmes, it was known, had beaten the young Jewess with a rattan cane until she could not feel their finishing stroke. The retribution her brother visited upon gendarmes and soldiers was as terrible as that; but rather it is the impromptu and masterly espionage contrived by these youngsters which arrests our attention and earns them patriot renown.

Wassmuss of Persia

Twice monthly British Intelligence at the War Office printed and circulated a comprehensive map purporting to show the distribution of enemy forces throughout the Eastern theaters of war. And for nearly four years this map displayed a vast segment of Persia on which there was a word of eight letters, printed in red and inclosed by an ellipse: *Wassmuss*. The area covered by that solitary word was somewhat larger than England and France combined. All southern Persia, in fact, lay under the influence of a lone German consul, young and resourceful—he was in his middle thirties at the outbreak of war—who came to be almost as legendary a figure east of Suez as T. E. Lawrence himself. Observers on the British side have even called him the "German Lawrence."[5]

To the General Staff of the British army the name on the map stood for an individual adversary accounted the equal of two army corps. Before the war Wassmuss had represented Germany at Bushire, his consulate there being the most impressive of all similar edifices. Kaiser Wilhelm II, at the time he visited the Holy Land and dazzled the populace with a spectacle of himself prancing about on a milk-white steed, had heard of the enterprising young consul in Persia; and thereafter Wassmuss received a generous extra allowance for entertainment, propaganda and ostentatious imperial display. The Persian situation in August 1914 was curiously confused, with a kind of local war already in progress, one of those affairs that no one could officially recognize. The prize in sight was the oil fields, which the Germans coveted no less than the British. Under an international agreement a neutral gendarmerie had been installed to maintain order; but this force was Swedish, and the guns on the Marne had only started firing when Entente agents in Persia discovered that Wassmuss had the "neutral" police in his pocket.

Those candid and overbearing impulses of self-interest, which have solved so many ethical problems of British conquest in the Orient, came to the aid of officers arriving in Bushire with troops and war vessels to enforce their opinions. Since the neutrality of Persia had been grossly violated, said they, it now had simply ceased to exist. Very well, said Wassmuss—addressing a mere handful of subordinates —though, my friends, we are far from the main war, we will not be exiled from this country, for even here much may be done.

German diplomatic and consular representatives were accepting their passports and heading for Berlin wherever the British spheres of influence spread out before British guns and bayonets. But Wassmuss, inspired by the crisis of conflict, elected to stay and put up a fight. First, however, he had to break through the British cordon. This he succeeded in doing by a commonplace yet adequate ruse;[6] and when he escaped one night he went on horseback, astride his favorite pony and carrying off that one among his officially seized and sealed bags which he knew he was going to need. It contained nearly 140,000 marks in gold, which had been part of the war indemnity paid by France to Germany after the disasters of 1870–71 and reserved in vaults at Berlin for over forty years until sent out to Bushire soon after the outbreak of the European war.

Wassmuss galloped away and reached the hill country, where he instantly ceased to behave like a fugitive. He had powerful native friends of long standing, deferential, warlike and well subsidized. He at once set about capitalizing his devotedly acquired knowledge of native dialects and familiarity with the traits and inclinations of the Persian tribesmen. Wassmuss sought to act as a chief agent of German secret service, a director of military and political espionage all along the Persian Gulf; but also he elected to hold southern Persia as completely as possible under German influence, hamper the British oil transactions, and endeavor to keep the hill tribes in such a state of ferment that every move by British armed forces in that quarter of the world would provoke their active hostility.

Once he had mapped out his campaign of obstructive tactics and spying, the German consul let nothing divert him from his plans. He felt he must give an overpowering demonstration of Teutonic friendship for Persia. And what was his amazing, characteristic stroke? He married the daughter of one of the most influential Persian chiefs. Religious differences were adjusted and the alliance of "two great races" negotiated with all the excesses of formality that could be generated by old Oriental custom competing with European diplomatic punctilio.

These annals abound in the adroit dodges of master intriguers; and we have had to omit hundreds of clever routine stratagems owing to the crowded scene of many centuries and the limitations of space. There is no single act in the vast vaudeville of secret service which quite compares with Wassmuss' wedding. Contrary to custom, the happy bridegroom insisted on defraying all expenses; and the father of the bride, having already enjoyed a substantial German subsidy, was told to invite all the local elite with whom he was not privately at war. Wassmuss for his own part asked about everybody else in that corner of Persia. He had the backing and encouragement of the Berlin Foreign Office; and it is understood that the costs of his grandiose entertainments were deducted from secret-service funds. Besides the horde of relatives and friends of the bride's family, an enormous retinue of peasants and commoners gathered to help celebrate the nuptials, symbolizing the unity of Kaiser and Shah, or Wilhelmstrasse and the oil fields.

In this inelegant secondary assemblage were craftsmen, farmers and fishermen, shepherds, porters, dock laborers and seamen, whose surprise at being bidden to the feast was hardly greater than their admiration for a foreigner rash enough to issue such a blanket invitation. But Wassmuss' hospitality yielded curious dividends. Brugmann, his industrious German assistant, circulated among the guests with an ample supply of cash and an interpreter. Spies were recruited on the spot. British Intelligence subsequently estimated that more than half the natives who gorged all day at Wassmuss' wedding breakfast were enlisted in the masterly espionage network he developed between India and Suez and the banks of the Tigris and Euphrates.

It proved a good deal more advantageous to have a Persian core for his far-flung scheme than the generally imagined remoteness of Iran might indicate. From Bombay and other Indian ports a vital traffic had to flow continuously toward the Red Sea and Mediterranean or into the Persian Gulf. Wassmuss contrived to have a great many small craft on innocent-seeming errands cross and recross the ship lanes leading from India. Already begun or impending were the campaigns in Mesopotamia and at the Dardanelles, in Palestine and German East Africa; while in Armenia a Russian army moved upon Erzerum and Trebizond. Spies dispatched by Wassmuss from his hill retreat were able to approach the communication lines of every one of these expeditionary forces of the Allies.

The amount of intelligence that came pouring in upon him would have suffocated a man of less efficiency and determination. Besides the capable Brugmann, he had only one other German and a Swiss clerk to help him. Practically all of his field agents were native Persians, ranging from the highest to the lowest caste. At the outset one of his most resourceful operatives was a Swede, Dr Lindberg, whom British counter-spies deemed themselves lucky to take prisoner in 1915.[7] Not only was Wassmuss' "headquarters staff" swamped with information, but he found an even harder problem to master in devising a system of communication. The studiously checked and summarized reports of his corps of native spies had to be forwarded promptly to General Liman von Sanders, the commander in chief in the Near East, or to some other German authority. The fighting ranged from Gallipoli to Ctesiphon; and the Germans were always being shifted to some point of emergency. Even so, the intricate messenger service devised by Wassmuss never failed to keep in contact; and a flow of valuable reports covering British or other transports, reinforcements, casualties and supplies proceeded steadily to Von Sanders and his aides.

Two Lakhs of Rupees—Dead or Alive

It is conceded that Wassmuss' acute observation of the British advance in Mesopotamia did much to prolong that doleful and costly campaign. And a good while before this was even suspected, merely for his nuisance value on Persian soil, the British paid him the compliment of offering £3,000 for his capture, dead or alive. Steadily their valuation of the menace of the man expanded until the last bid—in 1917—was almost five times greater. Two lakhs of rupees, or nearly £14,000, for an obscure German consul; and spreading across the map still, printed in red: *Wassmuss*.

Some of his projects recoiled upon him. When he tried to foment a native uprising in Afghanistan he squandered his diminishing cash reserves and kicked up only a momentary cloud of dust. Nevertheless his "marine division" maintained its pace. Large sailing vessels went as far as Singapore to gain him a truly imperial perspective; while the small boats of his "fishermen" slipped back with news of every military transport from India, Australia or New Zealand which touched at Aden or steamed through the Strait of Ormuz. By 1916 he was not only immobilizing thousands of British troops but had impudently started to arm and equip the more pro-German tribesmen; so that four warships had to be sent into the Persian Gulf for special patrol and blockade, and there they remained—Wassmuss' fleet—trying to intercept the dhows that now brought him munitions of war as well as naval intelligence.

At the summit of his successes in Arabia, Colonel Lawrence hardly disturbed his foes more proficiently. Indeed, to many unprejudiced observers of all the Eastern conflict, Wassmuss, in a far more isolated position and with little backing, seemed to surpass the young English adventurer in the scope of his malign achievements, the concrete results obtained as much by diligence as by stealth or surprise. And to his credit it may be noted that Wassmuss—in heroic vein—rose to his greatest heights of singlehanded prowess as the German chances of winning the war manifestly faded. If he had no victories to brag about, he switched his native audience to a diet of lies. And what lies! When General Haig massed his new armies for the "blood bath" on the Somme, Persian opinion veered sharply away from its former conviction that peace would be dictated from Berlin. Whereupon the German conspirator countered with a stupefying conquest of his own. The Kaiser's armies had invaded England; and as a gesture of contempt, King George himself had been publicly executed! "Special correspondence" of that muzzle velocity naturally carried far.

Similar brazen concoctions enabled Wassmuss to hold his own for another twelve months. The indispensable Brugmann had been secretly dispatched to India, there to bestow a wreath of rash promises on every native ruler presumed to be dissatisfied with British domination. But vigilant agents of counter-espionage trailed the very craft on which Wassmuss' spy embarked and so were able to limit his exercises in Hindustani to less than a week. Having arrested Brugmann, the British respected a daring and persistent opponent[8] and refrained from shooting him, as they were legally entitled to do. They were satisfied to imprison him "for the duration", knowing that now the energetic Wassmuss was left virtually alone among tribesmen turning hostile. Russia had collapsed; but Americans were being fetched thousands of miles in defense of their homes and had turned the numerical tide. Presently Foch began his great counter-offensive of July 1918; and news of the successive German defeats spread even to the hill country of Iran. The Persian chiefs, aware that giants were fighting to the death, felt a strong personal inclination to pick the winning side. And they grew furious as it became evident how Wassmuss had deceived them.

What offended them most—the funds of the plausible intriguer were now exhausted; no more gold could be drained from the fast-emptying coffers of Berlin. He poured out paper promises. As his position grew more desperate, natives talked openly of bringing him to "justice"—which meant the German should pay with his life for the bribes he no longer was able to pay. And yet none seems to have suggested delivering him bodily to the British in order to collect that majestic reward. Postwar inquiries have explained this lack of intelligent avarice among his followers. The British had simply bid too high for a lone German. Hard-bargaining Persians were positive that no individual could be *worth* two lakhs of rupees.

A howling mob of his native creditors finally surrounded Wassmuss' dwelling and demanded payment and a measure of vengeance. And here this isolated adventurer, who had so cunningly exploited them, rose to the critical occasion and duped them one time more. It was all a matter of showmanship. He commanded silence. He ignored the rabble crowding him close as he stalked to the center of an open space carrying a long black pole with a length of wire and other makeshift devices attached to it. This was his wireless telephone. He drove the pole into the ground, and boldly "rang up" the caliph. He had turned Mohammedan and taken to wearing native robes with the first serious ebb of Austro-German fortunes in the field; and now as a follower of the Prophet he complained to an attentive caliph, complained loudly of the kind of hospitality he was finding in Persia. To be absolutely frank about it, Caliph, these once-friendly Persians have turned rather nasty, brandishing knives and spears, and threatening to shoot with ammunition made in Germany which he had himself distributed among them.

Then the caliph replied, being heard indistinctly, yet using the same local dialect. And he also was brutally candid, assuring the entirely surrounded German of his friendship and powerful protection. Let Wassmuss be harmed, however little, by Persian violence and half the countryside would suffer for that single indiscretion.

"I thank thee, Caliph," said the German convert.

He pulled the pole out of the ground, still ignoring the throng whose rage had subsided. A respectful path was opened to him as he turned to retrace his steps. He was safe for the time being. But only a few weeks later, when word came of the Armistice, his father-in-law at Ahram agreed it would be wiser for him to slip away without relying further upon even divine intervention; and so the German agent vanished from the hill country where he had defied the British Empire and ruled as an uncrowned king.

Chapter Seventy-two

ADVENTURERS IN ESPIONAGE

THE WORLD WAR enlisted thousands of adventurers in espionage, killed a good many of them, enriched or ruined others, and conferred an astonishing amount of "free" publicity and enduring celebrity upon a few of them. From earlier conflicts we have seen a Belle Boyd, a Stieber or Schulmeister emerge upon the lecture platform, in his grateful country's honors list, or in print, to claim a measure of temporary renown; but out of the great struggle of 1914–1918 have been mined real nuggets of secret-service fame. This may be credited in part, at least, to the grinding of the propaganda machines which fought for both sides in the World War. Some of it, too, has been mere notoriety; generally where nothing more than notoriety was deserved. It is curious to reflect that Mata Hari is still a household word in communities whose best-informed citizens would fumble for the name of the general who conquered Jerusalem or Bagdad. And, putting the "Javanese" dancer aside on account of the special exploitation of her "past", it is no less curious to discover that nearly a dozen secret-service reputations have come out of the war period with at least as much chance of prolonged survival as any but the top rank of military heroes and statesmen.

In *The Crater of Mars*, Ferdinand Tuohy's reminiscences of all fronts, there is an entertaining chapter he calls "A Company of Legend" that gives an experienced war correspondent's impression of the ultimate hardihood of World War reputations. Among a group of twelve outstanding personalities that provides Mr Tuohy his most "picturesque list" are to be found Nurse Edith Cavell, Mata Hari and "'C' of the Admiralty"—Captain Mansfield Cumming—each of them representing the secret-service contingent in unadulterated form. But this list also includes "Campbell of the 'Q' ships", Lawrence, Rasputin and Feisal, whose widely divergent roles seem more nearly allied to Intelligence excursions than to the maneuvers of fleets or the shock of mighty armies. Seven, therefore, or 58.33 per cent, of the author's enduringly picturesque dozen were more or less closely connected either with the adventures of spy or counter-spy or with some other branch of secret service. The list has a candidly British flavor, including as it does Lieutenant Warneford and "Swinton of the Tanks." Were it to maintain its standards of choice but extend its national lines and double its number, who will deny that the names of "Alice Dubois" and Gabrielle Petit, Wassmuss of Persia, Roger Casement, Captain von Rintelen, the German sabotage chief, Sir Reginald Hall, and the German spy-master called *Fräulein Doktor* should be added? We may then—without affront to combatant services—assume that the percentage is maintained, and that more than half of all picturesque or especially dramatic or romantic participants in the great war belong in large degree to these annals of secret service.

In chapters immediately following we have some report of the strikingly individual specialists mentioned. It will not, however, be possible to do justice to all the luminaries of the espionage conflict whose ultimate fates have been more obscure. The French had a great spy in Marthe Richer, and the Germans employed a remarkable adventuress in Maria Sorrel. The latter became the mistress of the Russian general, Rennenkampf, and perished miserably on a crudely improvised gallows when that incompetent's enemies caught up with her. Rennenkampf's blunders in the World War are today a commonplace of the disastrous Russian campaigning in East Prussia. And not this history or any other will ever be able to determine how much of the blundering should be charged against the general and how much credited to the artful spy, Maria.

Marthe Richer, a pioneer prewar aviatrix known to masculine rivals as *l'Alouette*—The Lark—volunteered to go to Spain in June 1916 as a French secret agent. She was the widow of a slain French officer, and it was her avowed intent to fascinate Von Kron, a German espionage chief. Fascinate him she did, extorting not only conversational indiscretions but documents and codes also, and the key to his private safe. She obtained as well a substantial sum in cash which she did not keep but faithfully transmitted to Captain Ladoux, her chief of the neglected and impoverished Fifth Bureau of counterespionage. Only very recently was this exceptional woman spy awarded—in spite of the outcry of a shrill camp of moralists—a long-recommended Legion of Honor.

Before we proceed to a review of the career and martyrdom of one of the war's most famous heroines of Belgium, there is one more audacious and defiant young lady whose unique impudence ought not to be excluded from a record of authentic secret-service novelties. She was already of note in the demimonde of Brussels, and she did not greet the German invaders of August 1914 with much perceptible

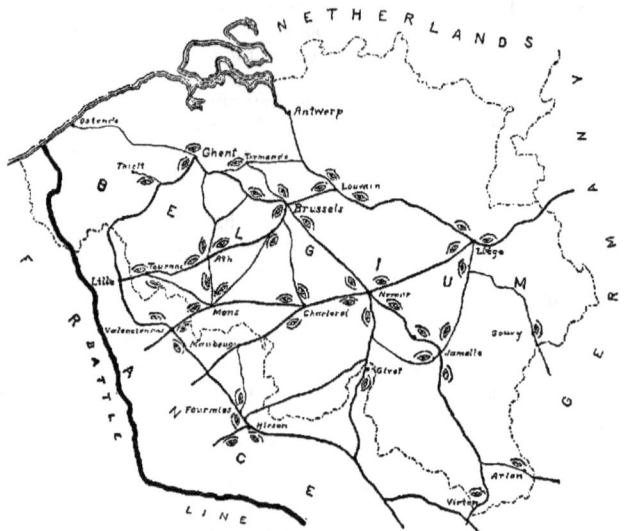

ESPIONAGE SYSTEM OF THE BRITISH SECRET SERVICE
SPREAD OUT BEHIND THE GERMAN ARMY ON
THE BRITISH FRONT IN FRANCE; EVERY
EYE IS A SPY OR A GROUP OF SPIES

March 1918 saw this network, designed to gather and transmit military information, at its highest state of efficiency. And yet, while served by perhaps the most elaborate espionage and train-watching system ever operated within a zone of combat, the British army suffered its most shattering reverse of modern times in the Battle of St Quentin, March 21-29, 1918. A general staff and high command, however promptly and accurately informed, contrives to win or lose its modern engagements quite apart from considerations of efficient secret service.

repugnance. Presently her notoriety was on the increase, for she was observed devoting herself to Von Bissing, the German military governor, whose unpopularity lasted as long as he lived and is still epidemic in certain sectors of Belgium. But Von Bissing, before the war ended, had died. His local mistress, surviving him, was still a flourishing young demimondaine in 1919 when her arrest was decided upon by Belgians then specializing in reprisals. The charge against her was a grave one: she had publicly shown herself in sympathy with the invader.

Mlle Angèle—to give her a name—was ready enough to confront her accusers. By the capriciousness of the life she had led him, she declared, senile decay had advanced more rapidly in Von Bissing's case. In short, she had hastened the day of his death, which an oppressed populace had applauded as openly as they dared. For their joy Belgium owed her a debt, said this minx. Moreover, she professed to have given much aid to the Belgian secret service—and this could not be contradicted. And lastly, if brought to trial it would be necessary, she reminded her accusers, to tell the names of all those prominent persons, both men and women, who during four years' oppression had applied to her and privately received through her influence with the German military government, a succession of small favors, permits, special exemptions, and the like. Strange to say, the arraignment of Angèle was not abandoned, yet it appears to have been postponed forever.

Chapter Seventy-three

THE MARTYRDOM OF EDITH CAVELL

EVERY DAY, almost every hour, of the 1,564 days that the great war lasted saw German soldiers conducting themselves with exemplary discipline and valor. And about every third day of the dreary, all-consuming struggle other Germans, secure in administrative posts not too near the front-line trenches, contrived some stroke of firmness and heroics which would make the soldiers' conquest more remote and the defeat of Germany more vindictive. The punishment of Nurse Edith Cavell was one such feat—a nearly perfect display of clinical technique in amputating the laurels of victory.

The squad of uneasy reservists routed out before dawn on the morning of October 12, 1915, given rifles and ordered to shoot a defenseless woman was, all unawares, overweighing the best that a Hindenburg or Ludendorff, a Hoffmann or Falkenhayn, and armies of resolute infantry could accomplish on the battlefield. The German proconsuls of Belgium had felt that they needed "to make an example." And so, with the aid of their counter-espionage service, they chose a gray-haired English hospital supervisor of unblemished record and keen, benignant face and indecently hurried her to a barbaric martyrdom. Thus presenting themselves with the finest example of enemy recruiting poster[1] since medieval churchmen of the Anglo-Burgundian faith burned the Maid at Rouen in 1431!

Miss Cavell was not even remotely connected with espionage. And she was not charged with spying but with "conducting soldiers to the enemy" under Article 58 of the German Military Code. In 1914 the German army, after a succession of rapid conquests from Liége to the surrender of Antwerp, had settled down to inflict unrelenting durance upon seven million Belgians. Young men of military age were soon escaping, however, in large numbers from the occupied kingdom, intending to join the remnant of King Albert's army which had evaded the German cordon at Antwerp and moved along the coast to take up its position on the extreme left flank of the Allies' line. There were also hidden about this superficially subdued country a great many British and French soldiers, wounded and stragglers, left behind in August when their commands were hurled back into

France by the superior forces of Von Kluck and Von Bülow. They would not surrender; and so, with the noteworthy advice and assistance of Lieutenant Colonel Gibbs of the West Riding Regiment, who had been wounded at the battle of Mons, a civilian organization was formed to pass them safely out of the country. It was for the crime of devoting herself to this patriotic endeavor that Nurse Cavell suffered the death penalty.

Though in time the work became a craftily managed and closely knit conspiracy, at the start the "conspirators'" motives were only humanitarian. They had no thought of making war upon Germany in behalf of the Allies. The small British expeditionary force, stubbornly retreating from Mons, had to abandon many wounded. Local ambulances organized by Belgian doctors gathered them up, and thereafter they were cared for and sheltered in civilian hospitals, infirmaries and private homes in La Bouverie, Wasmes, Frameries, Wiheries, Pâturages, Quiévrain and other places in the vicinity of Mons.

Few of these British casualties were discovered by the Germans. They had posted proclamations ordering the inhabitants to report all such cases; but that only roused the combative instinct of loyal Belgian civilians. Who would turn crippled and weakened men over to a hated enemy to be herded off behind barbed-wire fences as prisoners of war? At the clinic of a Dr van Hassel in Pâturages a number of wounded soldiers were entirely overlooked by the much-occupied invaders. This greatly stimulated many different schemes for smuggling British, French and Belgian convalescents out of the combat zone.

Lieutenant Colonel Gibbs recovered from his wound at Wasmes, and, even before the first battle of the Marne had checked the field-gray avalanche, he was moving groups of service men overland to Ostend. They were given money, rations and Belgian identity cards, easily obtained at that confused period; while local patriots gladly volunteered to act as their nocturnal guides. As late as October 8, 1914, General Rawlinson was in the vicinity of Ghent with a mixed force of British regulars, French territorials and a brigade of *Fusiliers Marins*.[2] But the fall of Antwerp compelled virtually the total evacuation of Belgium. Under British impulsion the Belgians opened the sluices and the sea poured over the flat country, stopping the German right wing. Ostend no longer was available as an outlet for Gibbs' operations, and new channels of passage had to be developed along the Dutch frontier.

The electrified frontier barriers which came later in the war were then no part of the problem. But a major difficulty was the want of places of concealment midway to the border, where the fugitives might wait until the moon was favorable and a large enough group had assembled to be passed into Holland. The *passeurs*—most of them veteran smugglers—took as many as a dozen or a score at one time.

Dr van Hassel came to Brussels, hoping to gain assistance. He knew Miss Cavell professionally as the supervisor of a nurses' school in the Rue de la Culture and carried his appeal to her. As she had been nursing wounded since the outbreak of hostilities, it appears that she willingly accepted this further patriotic opportunity. The first British soldier to be sent to her was Sergeant Meachin of the Cheshire Regiment. Others followed in increasing numbers; and she had to enlist the aid of her friends, many of whom agreed to conceal one or more of the furtive wayfarers in their homes. This was the launching of the so-called Cavell organization, which the Germans were subsequently to find so menacing and subversive. Nurse Cavell merely besought trustworthy friends in Brussels to harbor an overflow of escaping convalescents.

Patriotism Not Enough

War propagandists were to make much of Edith Cavell's "last words", spoken at the moment of facing the German firing squad: "As I stand here in the presence of Eternity, I find that patriotism is not enough." The probability of this having been invented by an emotional journalist after her execution is, of course, very great. But it is now seen that the moving phrase attributed to her might well have saved Miss Cavell and her colleagues from disaster had they heeded it.

The members of the Cavell organization, while firmly linked together by common ideals of patriotic duty, were scarcely "organized" at all. There was never a captain, a responsible skipper at the helm or a skillful hand upon the throttle, no fair division of the work and the risks, and oftentimes some pretty sketchy teamwork. Loosely allied groups were only united by their attempt to outwit continuously the best counter-espionage operatives at the disposal of the German government. As more than one postwar investigator of the "organization" has observed, the wonder is that it held together for nearly a year in spite of an encircling cloud of renegade informers.

Dr Tollemache Bull, a member of the British colony in Brussels—and himself arrested in 1916 after much activity in aiding war prisoners and young Belgians of military age to escape into Holland[3]—has told of Edith Cavell's difficulties: of her faithful endeavor to guard the interests of the school for nurses which she directed, and her conflicting desire never to refuse any patriotic task that offered. Because of this spirit of self-sacrifice, less courageous persons imposed upon her. To Dr Bull she complained that as many as thirty-four soldiers had been brought to her at one time from the Borinage, or Mons district. He believes that she clearly foresaw the fate which must overtake her.

Owing to her martyrdom, every contribution she made to the group operations was exaggerated at the time for propagandic purposes and has continued out of focus ever since. She had many intrepid and competent associates. Though her name will ever be attached to their efforts, she was not their directing head and would have been incapable of serving for a day as she did without their presence in outlying areas.

Around Mons the vital work of collecting the men and dispatching them toward Brussels was supervised by M. Capiau, who from the first had performed heroic labors in picking up and caring for the Allies' wounded, and who continued to manage his part of the system with unobtrusive efficiency. He was fortunate in enlisting the active co-operation of Prince Reginald de Croy, and his sister, Princess Marie, and these scions of an ancient mediatized house undertook to lodge some of the fugitives in their château at Bellignies. A courageous Frenchwoman, Mlle Louise Thuliez, sought out men hidden in the forest of Mormal and even ventured as far as Cambrai. Besides procuring the necessary Belgian identity cards, Capiau enlisted trustworthy men to guide the fugitives to Brussels. The Comtesse Jeanne de Belleville offered her château at Montignies-sur-Roc as a refuge for recovered British wounded.

Enlarging this activity to transport the scores of Belgians and Frenchmen desiring to enlist in their respective armies was a process of haphazard evolution rather than semiofficial design. Other civilian committees were now applying themselves exclusively to this form of clandestine recruiting, and, since the men they passed along were able-bodied young natives who spoke the language, were easily guided or disguised, and had few of the disabilities affecting British stragglers or wounded, it is not surprising that some of them appear to have done so much without being detected. So bold and untiring were these amateurs that one committee put 3,000 men across the frontier in four months; while another moved 800 in the same period over a longer and more dangerous route.

As the impromptu plotters understood the risks they incurred, it was not difficult to attract some of them to espionage or other forms of secret service. While no principal member of the Cavell group was ever seriously charged with spying, it is evident that some had taken part in the publication and distribution of propaganda. Philippe Baucq, one of Nurse Cavell's most talented and energetic colleagues, was intimately connected with the publishing of *La Libre Belgique*, that eczema of printer's ink which ceaselessly irritated even the rhinoceros hide of Moritz von Bissing, the German governor general. And it now appears that counter-spies directed by Pinkhoff and Bergan were trailing Baucq to locate the latest hiding place of the propaganda newspaper's printing press when he unwittingly led them to the very core of the Cavell organization.

Various renegade agents—Gaston Quien, Louis Bril[4] and Maurice Neils—have been credited with the betrayal of the English nurse and her comrades. While the odious Armand Jeannes boasted to a Mme Werres of Liége that he had been instrumental in the condemnation of 126 Belgians, French and British, including Edith Cavell. But it would seem that German surveillants, at the heels of Baucq on account of *La Libre Belgique*, luckily stumbled upon the Cavell-Croy-Thuliez-Capiau-De Belleville chain—to their own intense satisfaction. Shadowing Baucq had acquainted them with his habit of taking a pet terrier out every evening before he retired; and so they arrested him in the street on the night of August 11, 1915, allowing him no chance to warn his own household. Surrounding his home at once, the enemy agents from the Rue Berlaimont forced an entry. Baucq had kept nothing hidden in his house to be discovered in the event of a police search. Even so, the Germans chanced upon the weakest link of the Cavell chain, which, though they did no more than breathe upon it, ruinously snapped.

A Chain as Strong as Its Weakest Link

It happened that Louise Thuliez had a few hours earlier arrived from Mons. When questioned at the Baucq dwelling, she gave the name of "Lejeune"; but she had allowed herself the paramount indiscretion of carrying on her person a notebook containing the names and addresses of many of her collaborators. And her false identity card, counter-signed by Commissaire Toussaint of Pâturages, offered the Germans their first clue to the locality of the intrigue outside of Brussels.

Four days later, on the fifteenth, secret-service men were knocking at the door of the nurses' school, and Edith Cavell was arrested.

Capiau was arrested. Thirty-one more followed them into isolation cells, a lucky exception being Prince Reginald de Croy, who contrived to escape. With no great degree of cunning, the Germans informed each member of the captive band that all the others had confessed in order to avoid the maximum penalty—and he, or she, would best do likewise. A number were duped by this antique but deadly artifice, so that Stöber, the German military prosecutor, marched into court with a plethora of proofs.

Appearing for the numerous defendants were two German and three Belgian attorneys, MM. Braun, Braffort and Sadi Kirschen. They divided up the defense of the thirty-five prisoners, Miss Cavell being in the Kirschen group.[5] Stöber set to work; and the rest was little more than a heel-clicking, solemn formality. Bergan and Pinkhoff of the invaders' counter-espionage service were the witnesses for the prosecution. A certain amount of justice crept in, since eight of the accused—all of whom had in some degree violated the German Military Code—were acquitted and discharged. Twenty-two others received prison sentences ranging from three to ten years' hard labor. Mlle Thuliez, Louis Séverin, the Comtesse de Belleville, Baucq and Nurse Cavell were condemned to death. But two of these were deemed a sufficiently imposing example; and so the first three had their penalties commuted to life imprisonment.

The American minister, Brand Whitlock, representing the British government in Belgium at that time, had been asked to intervene. Informed of this, the Germans passed sentence at 5 P.M. and set the execution for dawn of the very next day. Mr Whitlock, however, was somehow warned of their cruel and incredible haste, and, though seriously ill and confined to his bed, he addressed urgent pleas for mercy to the German authorities, while instructing Hugh Gibson, first secretary of legation, to wait upon them in person. Gibson acted in concert with the Spanish ambassador, Marquis de Villalobar; and after some difficulty they broke down the evasions of the executive head of the German political department in Brussels, Baron von der Lancken. This veteran of the European or highly glazed school of diplomacy assured his visitors that he sympathized with them and would do all he could; but further imparted that he knew he could do nothing. Reprieves, pardons and all major portions of mercy emanated only from Von Bissing, vicegerent of the All Highest, whom Teutonic propagandists at that date were naming "the Vicegerent of God." The Spanish envoy and Gibson hastened to appeal to the governor general. But Von Bissing was not feeling merciful that evening,[6] and at dawn Edith Cavell and Philippe Baucq[7] were shot.

The Prohibitive Price of Rescue

Miss Cavell at her trial had admitted helping some two hundred British, French and Belgian wounded soldiers to escape from the occupied region. With impartial kindliness she had also nursed many wounded German soldiers. Discipline, however, denied them a chance to appear as her character witnesses. Both she and Baucq confessed that they had realized the seriousness of what they were doing, and also that they had been in "communication with the enemy", having heard from fugitives after their safe arrival in Holland. As many Belgian soldiers in civilian disguise were being sent into the country as spies and *sabotageurs,* the German high command and military secret service had every reason to adopt strong measures in trying to suppress this traffic. Whatever the question of outrage, then, of obscene haste or martial severity in executing a woman of the character of Nurse Cavell, in terms of counter-espionage the sweeping roundup of the Cavell group was a redoubtable stroke for Germany.

On the side of the Allies there were keen minds enlisted in secret service that began revolving some plan or other for an effective counter-stroke. The French espionage mission established in Rotterdam by Joseph Crozier had been uncommonly successful in getting its confederates released from Belgian jails. Nurse Cavell and her associates were lodged in the prison of Saint-Gilles in Brussels, and Crozier's people had even met with success in liberating one of their number from that frowning institution. We have it on the authority of Crozier[8] that a certain "Abbé de L."—a holy man who had co-operated with him and with Miss Cavell—came to him in Holland with word of the nurse's arrest and the anxious proposal that Crozier engineer her rescue from the prison before she could be brought to trial. Crozier agreed to make the attempt. But he warned the good abbé that any notoriety attaching to her case would be fatal to a scheme of liberation. Judicious bribery and the white-hot glare of the Allies' propaganda could not work together.

Everything went well and quietly for a day or so; but then the secret services of Great Britain "abruptly refused to follow in that path." Crozier, being tacitly warned away from the plot by his chief, Colonel Wallner, concluded that "the interested services already had at hand, in the people used for their regular work, the elements necessary to the success of their plans, and that any new help would be superfluous to them."

Crozier had believed he would have to spend not less than one thousand pounds. This price was pronounced excessive by the British

Secret Service, though it had nearly unlimited funds at its disposal and was willing to pay as much as two thousand pounds for a single trip into Germany by a certain "neutral" business man. Crozier, being a realist in secret-service technique, the only spy-master of his time to acknowledge candidly having had to "execute" informers and menacing adversaries, infers without smugness or affected horror that the British cared little about the heavy cost of bribery in Saint-Gilles prison but accounted the real cost of the Cavell rescue—sacrifice of one of the greatest potential pro-Ally arguments of the war—prohibitive. This may explain why so many British officers since then have kept on assuring us that the nurse was executed strictly in accordance with martial law.

It seems that the last letter written by Nurse Cavell was addressed to the Abbé de L. And he, desperate to save his friend, hastened with it to the highest British authority in the Netherlands. The abbé was asked to part with his cherished letter "for a few days"; and it was never returned to him. What inexpedient admissions or complaints can that letter have contained? Crozier had it quoted to him by the abbé, and he respects his friend's confidence, merely hinting his own private opinion that the British, so far as threatening or decisive endeavors in her behalf were possible, really abandoned Miss Cavell to her executioners. The representations of Minister Whitlock and the Spanish ambassador, though ardent, sincere and encouraged from London, were never more than diplomatic formalities. Neutrals' protests had little influence at that period of the war in reversing the decisions of the German war lords.

In justice to the governor general, Von Bissing, who dispensed justice strictly according to European army standards, Prussian, French or any other, we must observe that he was not alone in denying Miss Cavell her escape from martyrdom. And if the British became the chief beneficiaries of that martyrdom, it must count as a master stroke of propaganda rather than diplomatic negligence. Prior to President Wilson's decision in favor of a declaration of war the British endeavored to ship at least one seaman of American nationality aboard every vessel in danger of torpedo attack in the submarine zone. Propaganda was as clean a weapon as poison gas; and with the best blood of Britain being martyred at Gallipoli, Loos and on the Somme, the life of a nurse or a neutral deck hand was simply an additional weapon to be employed whenever made available.

So artfully and continuously were these weapons employed that Von Bissing, who was no Bourbon, forgot nothing and was disposed to learn a very great deal. The nearly world-wide reaction against

Germany on account of the legally permissible executions of Captain Fryatt, Gabrielle Petit, Baucq and Edith Cavell taught him his lesson. And in many succeeding instances of far more flagrant violation of the martial law—the espionage convictions, for example, of "Alice Dubois" and her lieutenant, "Charlotte", whom we shall presently meet—Von Bissing was just and almost ostentatiously lenient.

Whereas the French, while even surpassing the British in exploiting every harsh military necessity of the "Hun", were themselves implacable to the end of the struggle in the execution of women offenders. Mata Hari was shot after a farcical trial, Maria Sorrell hanged by the Russians without any trial whatsoever; and many German and Austrian women whose motives were purely patriotic suffered the death penalty. As the news of their service and self-sacrifice filtered through the heavy-duty propaganda machine of the Entente, even German women in espionage were cleverly mated to the Huns.

CHAPTER SEVENTY-FOUR

THE REAL FRÄULEIN DOKTOR

THE most extraordinary woman on the German side was the secret-service operative whom her French and Belgian foes called "Mademoiselle le Docteur." Since, unlike Mata Hari, she was never caught, interrogated, photographed and shot, there has been no limit to the malign ingenuities which have been ascribed to her.[1] Now the career of this curious intellectual adventuress, while far from prosaic, was actually so "normal" in time of war that it may be believed. She even turns out to possess a few striking resemblances to Joan of Arc: she was humbly, zealously, completely patriotic; and, though she replaced peasant simplicities and spiritual fervor with sophistication and attainments of the mind, she was destined like the Maid to become a legend even while still an active participant in the war.

At the University of Freiburg, early in August 1914, this studious young woman put aside her work of research and began writing letters, all of which were sent to the same address: *Oberste Heeres-Leitung*—German G.H.Q. She started her bombardment before the 42-centimeter Skoda howitzers commenced to demolish the ring of forts at Liége; and she was still writing—but had received no answer—when the German invasion swept into Brussels.

This persistent applicant was *Fräulein Doktor* Elsbeth Schragmüller. She came of a family established in Westphalia for several centuries and as a girl had frequently traveled to foreign health resorts with her grandmother. Enjoying many cultural advantages, she acquired a fluent command of English, French and Italian. She had taken her degree of Doctor of Philosophy at Freiburg only the year before, and her dissertation, *Die Bruderschaft der Borer und Balierer von Freiburg und Waldkirch*—a study of ancient Teutonic guilds—had recently come from a Karlsruhe printer.[2] Members of the university faculty had found Fräulein Elsbeth's brain considerably above the average. She was twenty-six; inexperienced and acquainted with warfare only in books, but persevering, resourceful and resolute. Applying herself to a new objective, she had contrived to learn the names of officers most influentially connected with the General Staff bureau of information, espionage and secret service—the *Nachrichtendienst*.

She wrote to Major Karl von Lauenstein, but he was too deeply concerned with his own web of intrigues in the East; and when he did not reply, she next besought Lieutenant Colonel Walter Nicolai to enroll her as one ready to serve in any useful capacity *at the front*.

It did not occur to her to inquire about hospital training or any form of strictly feminine war work. She wanted to help *fight* the war. At length when her answer came, bearing the General Staff seal, it enclosed credentials admitting her to the military zone, together with orders directing her to proceed at once to Brussels. There she found a thorough Teutonic administration had assumed control of the invaded kingdom, and that her own destination was a routine post in the civil censorship bureau. This was monotonous yet vital work in the midst of war and invasion; it proved an apprenticeship which detained her little over a fortnight. She passed upon more mail than any of her fellow censors, and from these hundreds of banal communications she managed to extract many items of solid military interest, some of them timely enough to be forwarded directly to General von Beseler, commanding the army corps then besieging the city of Antwerp.

One day, late in September, Von Beseler sent for Captain Refer, an intelligence officer attached to his staff.

"What about this Lieutenant Schragmüller?" he asked. "I have been getting his reports, and practically every bit of information he has submitted has turned out to be reliable. Who is he?"

The captain had to confess that he did not know.[3] "Probably some subaltern who lived in Belgium until war was declared. Many a bright young fellow has been waiting for just this opportunity."

"Find him and send him here to me!"

The "lieutenant" was never found; but the next day Fräulein Schragmüller came from Brussels to report at Von Beseler's headquarters. She was slender and blonde, with rather a wistful face and keen eyes. Her whole bearing suggested a quick, comprehensive intelligence.

The general and his aide, having recovered from their respective jolts of surprise, were particularly impressed by the visitor's intense blue eyes. She seemed unembarrassed and answered questions candidly; in attending to her duties as a censor, she explained, she had tried to be as helpful as possible.

"Your reports, Fräulein," said Von Beseler, "have shown an extraordinary grasp of military strategy and tactics." He advised her to continue the vigilant reading of "enemy" mail, then startled her with a promise of promotion: "As soon as we have taken the city and cleared the Belgian Army out of Belgium, I shall recommend you for appointment to our Special Intelligence Corps. You will be sent to 'school' for a time, Fräulein, and will be allowed many opportunities to learn. I believe you have valuable qualifications for the Secret Service."

The Spy School

Antwerp was surrendered on October 9, 1914; and the victorious Von Beseler kept his word. *Fräulein Doktor* Schragmüller was relieved of duty at the bureau of censorship and vanished upon a mysterious errand. The *Nachrichtendienst* was already using three academies for the education of spies and counter-spies. One of these flourished at Lörrach, where the spy-master, Friedrich Grüber, had his private seminary and espionage bureau, not far away from *Doktor* Elsbeth's beloved Freiburg. Another was at Wesel and in contact with such widely divergent conspirators as Lieutenant Colonel von Ostertag, Consul Gneist and the agents Wangenheim, Van der Kolk and Flores. The third, at Baden-Baden, in charge of the sagacious Major Joseph Salonek, was an institution designed to co-ordinate both the methods and the schooling of agents of the German and Austro-Hungarian military secret services.[4]

Fräulein Schragmüller may in time have visited all three, while studying the variations of short-course, intensive training technique. There is naturally no available record of her own classroom work nor of her "graduation"; but it is said that her trained mind and limitless zeal accepted all that average candidates found so rigorous as a tonic of mental stimulation.

Rigorous was what the training of secret-service operatives had to be. As a candidate, Elsbeth Schragmüller simply ceased to exist. She was assigned a number, an obscure, pleasant lodging and given a sum of money to cover modest weekly expenditures. She had to report at eight o'clock each morning to a private residence in a quiet street, and spend a long day indoors, either attending lectures on technical military subjects, writing reports, or passing stiff examinations, both oral and written.

It was all severely Spartan—or Prussian. The career of an agent of espionage was made to seem honorable and important; but none of its perils or hardships was glossed over with patriotic or romantic persuasions. Tests in secret inks, in reading or drawing maps and plans, were frequent. There were charts to be committed to memory, depicting every uniform of the armies opposed to the Central Powers, with unit designations and badges of rank. No doubt

Fräulein Elsbeth already could distinguish the French or Belgians from troops of the British Empire; but how long did it take her to learn to detect the differences between Seaforth and Gordon Highlanders, or Welsh Guards and Royal Welch Fusiliers?

The student spies, women as well as men, were subject to military discipline. Concentration upon all the pursuits of espionage were rigidly prescribed. They were not allowed to get acquainted with each other—a necessary precaution against accidental or deliberate betrayals in future months of hazardous service. At Baden-Baden, for example, when one of the classes assembled in the improvised lecture hall, every candidate sat alone at his small writing table and wore a mask covering the upper part of the face. In the anteroom where these masks were put on and taken off, each of the prospective spies was required to stand facing a wall. Anyone unmasked who passed through the room was not to be identified.

To that same end, nobody was ever permitted to linger near the door or wait in the street outside the school. Departures at the close of a day's grind could only be made at three-minute intervals. And after intensive study hours and upon returning to his room the student need not suppose himself to be free or unsupervised. Detective officers assigned to the institution were drifting about the town, keeping a close watch upon every lodging. From their reports were the character and inclinations of each individual largely determined; and nothing could be so trivial they would not carry it to headquarters—a tendency to wink or nod to a pretty fräulein, a habit of drinking past the second, third or fourth stein of beer, or even so mild a dissipation as excessive smoking.

Fräulein Schragmüller's diligence, however it delighted her instructors, must have given the secret watchers a thoroughly dull time. No doubt that, too, was noted upon her record when she received orders to report back to headquarters. The young lady had disclosed no talent for dissipation. Here was no potential siren-spy.

"You seem to master difficult subjects with gratifying rapidity," said her chief. "All training of civilian candidates for military secret service in time of war is largely by what scientists call 'trial and error.' But with us every error may mean a fatal loss. We thought it important to discover what a highly educated person of penetrating intellect would make of our system of schooling.

"You are now equipped for active service, Fräulein. But we are not sending you to England, France, or even a neutral country. Qualifications like yours are not to be hazarded—unless upon the most vital emergency mission."

"And until then, Herr Oberstleutnant?"

"Antwerp," he said; and when she seemed crestfallen: "You will teach there, and you may count it a promotion. It has been decided to develop our principal spy school there—and only very capable agents and Intelligence officers will be assigned to the directorial staff."

The Blonde Woman of Antwerp

Of the secret-service "expeditions" supported by Germany in foreign lands before the outbreak of hostilities, the bureau at Brussels had flourished most importantly, owing to the resourceful management of Richard Cuers. His successors, such as Peter Theisen, had endeavored to imitate him; but now that war had come and Belgium lay prostrate, Brussels was like a provincial capital of the empire, and changing the location of the espionage office was seen as an urgent need. The strongest possible secret-service enterprise must be developed and brought to bear upon Great Britain, the Channel ports of France, and also upon neutral Holland where the services of the Entente allies might firmly entrench themselves.

Antwerp offered peculiar advantages and had straightway been chosen. In establishing their new spy school the Germans selected a fine old mansion in the heart of one of the best residential quarters of the city. The address was 10 Rue de la Pepinière; and the dwelling afforded that necessary convenience, a side entrance at 33 Rue de l'Harmonie. A shell fired on the second day of the siege had burst against a corner of the building, leaving a scar which remained to the end as a symbol of the city's violent subjugation.

When Elsbeth Schragmüller arrived at her new post, this house was already notorious. Belgians having to pass that way seldom paused to study its exterior. They were curious, but wise enough to hide their interest in an enemy who kept the sinister pursuits of his spy incubator so well hidden from them. Patrols of military police had a way of descending very sharply upon anyone who appeared to linger near the entrance of No. 10 or No. 33; and these Teutonic interlopers seemed never to have heard of an Innocent Bystander but went about making arrests and ordering internments upon the slightest pretext.

Major Groos, a veteran Intelligence officer, had been appointed to the Antwerp command. And he had brought with him as fine a technical staff of instructors as the German Secret Service could assemble. It was a bold and curious venture, planting that espionage headquarters in a hostile city like Antwerp; and one might argue without excess that the added weight of *Fräulein Doktor's* keen intellect and uncompromising ardor alone retarded an inevitable breakdown.

It has been said—by Entente propagandists or those victimized by their propaganda—that this woman came to be a savage tyrant, intimidating her masculine colleagues, some of them officers of the Prussian ruling caste, others favored by influential connections with Potsdam. At the heavy cost of diluting some future dramatist's material, *that* must be rejected as preposterous. Doubtless she frequently scored over the men because she is known to have held herself aloof from pettiness, from cliques, rivalries, and the internal politics of military rule. Twenty hours a day on duty, proof enough of her passionate dedication to the struggle of the fatherland, rather than her sex or alleged ferocity, gave her the last word.

Greater severity of discipline applied at the Antwerp school for spies is no doubt rightly attributable to her. As a graduate of the censorship bureau, she understood the depths and tenacity of the Belgian hatred surrounding them. It seems that she voluntarily made herself responsible for discipline; and neutral recruits who fled from their espionage schooling, or graduated spies who were caught and questioned, spoke of her harshly, with the poor restraint of a deserter's grievances or the unfettered imagination of the condemned. Within a very few months she was notorious: "the Terrible Doctor Elizabeth" —"the Beautiful Blonde Woman of Antwerp," whose baleful, burning gaze also earned her the nickname of "Tiger Eyes."

One interrogated violator of British law declared that she was not beautiful, or at least he could not be sure. But her eyes! He had been able to see nothing else, those intense blue eyes that projected such dynamic voltage they seemed to dissolve his will. It was as if a camera shutter clicked, and his soul lay exposed and shivering. Making such a start, it is not surprising that published accounts of her accumulating since the war unveil a woman blending the mental or physical characteristics of Mesmer, Machiavelli, Martin Luther and Maria Jeritza with Simon Legree and homicide.

The real *Fräulein Doktor,* while attending to the work in hand, surely cultivated this protective coloration of stained and striped malignance. It had all the confusing variety of a fatal accident depicted under oath by a crowd of eyewitnesses. And the more serpentine and sinister she became, the more cruel, cunning and incredible, the less trouble she had in dealing with subordinates, or the rabble of hirelings, renegades and malcontents forwarded to Antwerp, to be taught, blackmailed or bribed to risk their lives for German espionage.

Her largely self-inflicted reputation was not only a club and a sword for each hand, but a shield and suit of armor also, concealing the woman scientist from startled, inquisitive foes.

There were fruitful days during the long struggle whereon Entente counter-spies filed as many as six conflicting reports, exposing "Mademoiselle le Docteur" in as many different pursuits and places. And after the United States government came in with a vast retinue of semiprofessional informers, another "Blonde Woman of Antwerp" was detected in America. Every blonde suspect was *the* blonde sorceress of the Scheldt. Gertrud Würtz, whose duplicities were, in truth, endowed by Major Groos' establishment, procured the betrayal of some of Joseph Crozier's agents and, as the fiendish Woman of the Antwerp school, was thereafter enabled to vanish forever.[6] Felice Schmidt, a pretty little thing who even entertained ideas of compromising Lord Kitchener, was another probationary *Fräulein Doktor* when misfortune overtook her. While a clever operative of the Antwerp brand, Fräulein Anna-Marie Lesser, having replaced the excitements of espionage with a post-Armistice narcotic addiction, was finally stimulated to assert that she *was* the "notorious spy, Miss Doctor."

As rapidly as the blonde pupils of Antwerp were schooled and dispersed, to be mistaken for their teacher, none seems to have turned up in Russia or Roumania. Women agents covering those war sectors were clever enough to develop individualities of their own. Italy, too, unmasked its own romantic specialty, known to some as "The Beautiful Spy" and to the entertaining Charles Lucieto[6] as "Irma Staub", noblewoman and patriot adventuress. Fräulein "Irma" popped in and out of Switzerland, while plotting against the Allies, and chose her commonplace pseudonym to spare eminent relatives the mortification of sharing her patriotic notoriety.[7]

Speaking for America, however, the cipher expert, Major Herbert O. Yardley, in his interesting autobiography, *The American Black Chamber,* calls attention to the success of his Secret-Ink Bureau of MI-8 which finally proved the Nemesis of "the famous German spy, Madame Maria de Victorica, alias Marie de Vussière, the 'beautiful blonde woman of Antwerp.' " She had been sought, according to this authority, by the British Secret Service since 1914. And he thanks the British officials who gave their American allies, on November 5, 1917, "information which, though it had no direct bearing on Madame Victorica, finally led indirectly to her identity." If it had no "direct bearing" on this woman spy—who was neither a former student nor member of the teaching staff of the Antwerp school[8]—that may have been due to the now acknowledged failure of the British to identify Elsbeth Schragmüller during the years of the war. To them the "woman of Antwerp" was never "Mademoiselle le Docteur." They called her "Frau Captain Henrichsen", which curious label derived from her known collaboration with Henrichsen of the German Secret Service, a capable officer and dangerous espionage enemy.

Chapter Seventy-five

RIGORS OF THE ANTWERP SCHOOL

IN THE DEATH STRUGGLE of the giants, introducing such pleasantries as torpedo attacks upon unwarned and unarmed merchant ships, blistering gases and suffocating gases, air raids upon unfortified cities, and many repugnant forms of sabotage and propaganda, it seemed necessary to extend this frightfulness to espionage and secret service—in short, to the "terrible woman of Antwerp." The young directress of a secret agents' school has been charged with the pitiless innovation of the "fool spy": a cowardly, mistrusted, or palpably treacherous spy whose life is deliberately thrown away! The Antwerp headquarters found occasion to engineer several ruthless fool-spy "dismissals"; but Elsbeth Schragmüller had no more to do with the invention of this hateful practice than she had to do with the conquest of Belgium.

A Dutch traveler named Hoegnagel, for example, was sent from Antwerp and sacrificed to the French, reputedly to create a "diversion" and thus help to screen certain Parisian activities of Henrichsen and the devious Greek agent, Coudyanis. Hoegnagel was a pathetic blunderer who never should have been enlisted in any form of secret service. But if her recruiting agents insisted on inflicting the Hollander upon her, *Fräulein Doktor* simply did the best she could with him. His file card might have recorded "Hoegnagel—unsuited to espionage or counter-espionage; probably useful as a dupe." And it was only to play the dupe that she paid his expenses to Paris.

Innocent and clumsy, Hoegnagel had accomplished nothing in the French capital, but he attempted to communicate in a code provided him, which was already well known to the counter-spies of France. His writings on the margin of a newspaper were detected at once; and he was arrested, condemned and shot. His punishment seems rather vindictive under the circumstances, since he had never operated against the French in France. The more valued agents out of Antwerp drifted away like smoke; and the French who had executed Hoegnagel made much of his having been deliberately "sacrificed"—not because of their desperate exasperation, but because *Fräulein Doktor* was an unspeakable sadist.

Even if that propaganda were true, this record absolves her from having originated the device of the "fool spy." We have seen this sacrificing of an unconsidered accomplice employed by the Russian *Ochrana* and by Azeff when he sought to convince some *Ochrana* chief of his increasing worth as a police informer. And we have discovered Colonel Redl's treason indulging in a few variations of this dastardly technique at a time when Fräulein Schragmüller was immersed in her studies at Freiburg. Long before the outbreak of the World War the immolation of the "fool spy" was already an old Continental custom.

The lapses or limitations of Elsbeth Schragmüller as an innovator are hardly at issue here; but whatever contributions she did make to the science of foul play would seem rather to have been eclipsed by the nature and the novelty of her executive activities. Only an enemy propagandist would be so absurd as to insinuate—as Entente propagandists are known to have done—that a young woman of her experience could improve upon Stieber; the more likely and more remarkable thing being her feminine equivalent of that Prussian spymaster's demonic zest and untiring Teutonic intensity.

Perhaps, as her detractors have sought to believe, her patriotic obsession led to extremities of sadism. Perhaps she alone initiated the disciplinary and training rigors of the Antwerp institute. But the Prussian instinct for discipline was something too deeply rooted for her to alter in any degree; and if there were Prussian officers at Antwerp, it remains very doubtful whether she was even made responsible for enforcing discipline. However, the process of spy manufacture at Antwerp belongs to this history, not only on account of *Fräulein Doktor*, but also because, together with so much that was typical of the subterranean combat until 1918, there was much else wholly unique.

Education of a Spy

The military secret service of Belgium, like King Albert and his fragment of an army, had been forced to find refuge in a neighboring land. Yet already within the conquered country an impromptu counter-spying organization was working for the ultimate reward of national liberation. This rapidly improvised civilian secret service had begun employing children to keep watch upon the house at No. 10 Rue de la Pepinière soon after Fräulein Schragmüller reported there. In London, Paris and other centers the officers whose duty it was to detect and uproot Germany's spy system were eager to acquire descriptions of everybody entering the Antwerp school; and small groups of boys who seemed to play innocent, complicated games in the streets adjacent to No. 10 or No. 33 were the unsuspected eyes and ears that recorded what facts were obtained.

Anyone sent to Antwerp for secret-service training came either by automobile or, if by railroad, was met at the station and conveyed thence in a limousine with the shades lowered. Motorcars nearly always stopped at the Rue de l'Harmonie entrance. And even as the car slowed down, the house door would swing open. When the car stopped, the new arrival was whisked from it and into the house with unceremonious haste. Never for more than a second or two would a newcomer be visible to passers-by; so the boy watchers had to look sharp.

Once indoors a probationary pupil only found that furtive arrival duplicated in his reserved welcome and austere surroundings. Escorted through dim halls and past closed doors, he was assigned to a comfortable bedroom—and locked in. Windows on the street side would be shuttered and barred, the sole ventilation and meager exterior view coming from another window looking out upon a court. These isolating arrangements came as a result of Fräulein Schragmüller's inspection of other spy schools. She had given her colleagues a convincing demonstration that masks worn by students, as insurance against treachery should a "double spy" or potential informer invade the school, were inadequate to save them from future recognition.

The novices of Antwerp were sequestered, therefore, to live and work alone in rooms which were only more commodious than punishment cells. None lodged elsewhere in the captured city; and so no detectives had to be taken away from counter-espionage to observe future spies' habits or strength of character. Local animosity eddied about the school like an invisible poisonous mist. The trustworthy agent in training seemed too valuable to expose to profitless risks; whereas a more dubious article, if let to go about the city alone after hours, was little improved by being subjected to the temptations of hostile Belgians.

Names were entirely discarded. A white card bearing the student's code designation was affixed to the panel of his door. At regular intervals a soldier servant knocked at the door, unlocked it and served an ample, appetizing meal on a tray. Technical instructors came there to start the various courses; and for a probationary term of at least three weeks the candidate was given to understand that he must do all his work in his room and take what exercise he could in its limited area. Only after a recruit's zeal and capabilities had been solidly established would he be allowed a few privileges, but strictly within the confines of the school until the end of period of training.

When at length one proved his right to visit other parts of the mysteriously active institution, he was permitted to study all the intriguing equipment that an up-to-date spy school required. At Antwerp, it appears, were the finest available collections of models and maps, charts and photographs; by such means it was possible to explore all the cities, seas, harbors and countries of the world—likewise all types of war vessels, submarines, transports and merchant ships, aircraft, siege and field artillery, shore batteries and fortifications, as well as innumerable smaller weapons and articles devoted to warfare.

These informative treasures were always in process of revision or elaboration. Originally the result of careful study and selection by experts, the progress of the war added almost daily some new naval or military refinement or substitution, and reports upon these things were received from a variety of trustworthy informants. The school also boasted a fine library of technical and scientific works, including handsome volumes of colored plates exhibiting the uniforms and field equipment of all combatant armies, regimental and divisional designations, and badges of rank from lance corporal to field marshal.

Having gradually mastered this wealth of visual information, the hard-driven spy recruit came at last to the inner mysteries of his calling and was now generally taken in charge by *Fräulein Doktor* herself. Codes, ciphers and unique communicative dodges were among the last subjects of a bulging curriculum. With them were included study of chemical and "invisible" inks, their use and manufacture, and all the rest of the ingenuities, tricks and resources comprising offensive or defensive strategy of wartime military secret service.

Rival Firms and Relative Failure

It took from ten to fifteen weeks to bring the average candidate to a boil according to the Antwerp standards of spy competence. Toward the end of each student's training period *Fräulein Doktor* seems to have turned upon him the full blast of her volcanic patriotism. If he were German, she sought to infuse him with her own thirst for annihilating victory; if a hireling neutral or renegade, she endeavored to stir in him enough sporting instinct to play the greatest game devised by man. Yet her parting admonitions, a veritable decalogue of good conduct in an evil world of intrigue—repeated in the confessions made by certain matriculates of Antwerp who had failed to follow her advice, with consequent disaster—were mainly the common-sense rules of offensive secret service the world over, a cogent expression of her quick intelligence resolving the problems of the spy. To quote one of her precepts:

Conceal whatever linguistic gifts you have, to encourage others to talk more freely in your hearing; and remember, no German agent speaks or writes a word of German while on duty abroad, and this applies, even if German is manifestly not your native tongue.

And another:

When obtaining information by direct bargaining, make your informant travel as far as possible away from his home—and away from your immediate field of operations as well. Try to have him travel the distance by a tedious route, preferably at night. A tired informer is less cautious or suspicious, more relaxed and expansive, less disposed to lie, or to bargain with you shrewdly—all advantages in the transaction which you reserve to yourself.

Thus she originated no profound science of espionage; but her academic approach to the subject absorbing her for four years was scientific—modern—strangely new. With solid, humorless Germanic scholarship she studied, weighed and restated even the simplest exercises in furtiveness and guile[1] which had hitherto been left, by the hit-or-miss training methods before 1914, to the elementary resources of animal cunning.

It is significant that *Fräulein Doktor's* opponents were her only imitators. The French spy school located at Dijon, whence its graduates were sent through Switzerland into Germany, developed thorough and elaborate training courses which a De Batz or Schulmeister might have admired but would hardly have been able to pass. This institute, however, suffered a fundamental weakness in its recruiting methods. A high premium was paid to alien decoys for every potential spy enlisted. And as the integrity and natural aptitude of Dijon recruits were largely decided by those who stood to gain financially with each candidate enrolled, the whole undertaking was impaired by low standards of selection.

In London an Anglo-French training school was organized, chiefly under the supervision of the British, who laid great stress upon the thorough education of spies. This was particularly the case with agents destined to investigate naval affairs, either for the Intelligence Department directed by Sir Reginald Hall and the industrious Sir Alfred Ewing, or the far-famed division of Secret Service whose guiding genius was Captain Mansfield Cumming. The London school —according to a supposedly impersonal report upon it recorded at Antwerp—was an effective and admirable instrument of its kind, "run on a German plan, by which the 'scholars' are divided into five classes" and familiarized with all the details of espionage duty.[2]

During the war years the British would hardly have returned that compliment. Antwerp, being judged only by its alumni who were caught and convicted—which is like judging a business community by its bankrupts—never was highly regarded. There was Joseph Marks, a great billow of a man, ingenuous, craven and preposterous as a spy, who came into a certain renown as the first to bring out of Belgium authentic tidings of the "terrible Doctor Elizabeth." Marks, like the other Antwerp spies, in order to get out of the country, past the field gendarmerie and frontier guards, had to carry as a form of service identification a bank note marked with code signs on one margin.[3] He was face to face with his perilous career in espionage when he landed at Tilbury; and the British customs, the port control officers, policemen, all reminded him that he was alone in the midst of a numerous foe, including the counter-spies of New Scotland Yard.

There was nothing in his luggage to excite curiosity, unless it proved to be the stamp album which Elsbeth Schragmüller had provided, not invariably a part of the travel burden of rotund business men from Holland or, in fact, from anywhere else. Marks did not wait, however, to see how the officials at Tilbury would take it. As he waited in line he was blocking the path of other incoming passengers. Somebody spoke to him curtly: "Stand aside, please—your turn will come!" The spy misunderstood a gruff tone, assumed that "they" already were suspicious of him. And when "they" laid eyes on that stamp album . . . Now Fräulein Elsbeth had created this dodge expressly for his sort of naval mission. The album was well stocked, and sets of stamps which he was to post to "cover" addresses in the Netherlands from various British seaports would indicate that, on the date of the postmark, so many different types of war vessels were in harbor, according to the number of each variety of stamp he enclosed. Battleships were represented by European countries; while African stamps stood for battle cruisers, South American for heavy cruisers, Australian stamps light or scout cruisers, North American meant destroyers, and Asiatic countries denoted large naval auxiliary craft. But Joseph Marks, gross and palpitant, never gave himself a chance to test this novel and deceptive contrivance. Setting foot on English soil finished him as a spy. All his schooling went overboard, literally, at Tilbury dock; for he sought the nearest police official, and, to that busy Britisher's astonishment, confessed on what errand he had come ashore and surrendered.

Later he answered the questions put to him at Scotland Yard in manifest anxiety to please. He had been a reputable business man of Aix-la-Chapelle; but there German agents had taken him into custody three times, continually professing an absurd suspicion that he was acting for the French Intelligence. To convince them of his loyalty—being physically unfitted for army service—he had agreed to enter the school at Antwerp and learn to be a spy.

Marks was tried on the less serious charge of having come to England after being in communication with a secret-service agent of the enemy; and tears of gratitude actually ran down his bulging cheeks when he was sentenced to five years' imprisonment. Only if securely locked up for the duration of the war, he assured his jailers, would he feel safe from that "dreadful woman" at Antwerp.

Other naval spies whom she helped to educate and direct did the school more credit. Even those who sacrificed their lives—like the agent Müller, whose tragic misadventure in Newcastle via Deptford is related elsewhere—were not detected before they managed, thanks to one or another of her suggested stratagems, to transmit valuable diagrams or code reports. It was seldom much exertion for her graduates to compete with the troupe of more or less inexperienced practitioners sent out by rival spy-masters in Switzerland or Spain. Acute military minds ticked feverishly in Washington so long as America was neutral ground; but of the spies, near spies, crooked informers and clumsy amateurs enrolled by the Kaiser's attachés, Colonel von Papen and Naval Captain Boy-Ed, few matched the Antwerp brand. Anton Küpferle was a typical specimen sent to England to pose as a business man from Brooklyn. Küpferle had lived in Brooklyn, and right there the deception ended. This spy spoke English with a thick Teutonic rather than a "Brooklyn" accent. He dressed as no metropolitan American ever had dressed and owned the stiffly starched bearing and abrupt manners of a Prussian sergeant, which, indeed, was just what he formerly had been. No coward like Marks, he was even easier to detect; after a few sharp glances, bulky Joseph gave himself up; but one glance saw through Küpferle.

Until the Evacuation of Belgium

Because it is defensive, counter-espionage may be fairly appraised and publicly appreciated at the conclusion of hostilities; and even in defeat it has been acknowledged that the counter-spying organization of Germany was incorruptible, wide awake and courageous. Antwerp, playing but a minor part on the defense, had little to earn but silence or blame as the gradual diminution of German power in the field made the whole enterprise of offensive secret service emerge as a costly blunder.

In consequence the great notoriety of "the ravishing blonde super-spy, Mademoiselle le Docteur" has been nourished upon extravagant canard. Blasco y Ibañez, in his propagandic war novel *Mare Nostrum*, first introduced her as a repellent "heavy" character; and from that calculated beginning she was promoted overnight to the company both of spy-masters and master spies, even though there was no evidence whatever to support the latter label. A teacher of spies she certainly was, the first of her sex to be given high rank at a training school under regular army direction and discipline, the first ever to distinguish herself by helping to organize and control an espionage bureau in time of war.

The school was her pride, and she *was* the school. Its widespread fame, its successes and ultimate failure are her story—and so given here, but only to the limited degree that authentication permits.

She is alleged to have made secret journeys to Paris and other areas watched over by Entente counter-espionage to convey personal instructions to key agents or to gather intelligence on her own account. Who knows? Her value as an executive and her inexperience as a spy suggest instead that she was seldom encouraged, if not actually forbidden, to venture abroad from the espionage citadel at Antwerp.

Two attempts are known to have been made to dynamite her office. Certain Belgians were vindictive. There is, however, no proof that she ever shot any intruding foe—Nos. 10 and 33 were well guarded—nor any that there were intruders at whom to shoot. It seems, too, extremely improbable that the lady sent a revolver to an army officer who served as her technical adviser, recommending the patriotic expiation of suicide. He had willfully declined to notice the combat utility of the tanks, predicted in reports from one of her best spies whose warning was substantiated no later than September 15, 1916. But every general staff in the war had the honor to underrate that promising weapon of attack, including the colleagues of its British originators. Even conceding Elsbeth Schragmüller's remorseless patriotism, if she was allowed to adjudge the miscalculation of staff officers a capital offense, the carnage around her must have been frightful.

In similar vein, she has been charged with procuring the assassination of her own agent, Van Kaarbeck, a Dutchman who had relapsed into drunken indiscretions while spying for Antwerp in Paris. This man was of a reckless levity that would have made his nomination for a "fool spy" practically unanimous. The French only complained of the assassin's stroke because they had Van Kaarbeck already marked and measured for a stake at Vincennes. Doubtless *Fräulein Doktor* was eager to have him silenced before his arrest; the evidence against her as regards this homicide is its obvious expediency.

So much for her voyages in the canard line!

Colonel Nicolai, who was her chief, has written with baffling brevity: "It is remarkable that in the German I.S. [Intelligence Service] it was a cavalry officer of an old family and an unusually well-educated woman who knew best how to deal with the agents, even the most difficult and crafty of them."[4]

In a war game of studied ruthlessness, the Antwerp headquarters had in her a curiously "different" mentality and a player bound to score heavily against her diverse opponents. The Allies—British, French, Belgians and, finally, Americans—compounded all their arts of guile and vigilance to blind the spy system she inflicted upon them. After America entered the war, advancing billions in loans, the British who had hitherto carried that banker's burden could expend more money on secret-service missions. Antwerp, like other German combatants as the tide of victory turned, was gradually beaten down, suffocated with gold, overwhelmed by sheer weight of numbers.

When inevitable defeat and the Armistice came, mobs raided every structure in Belgium that had been used by the German police or secret service. But before the house in Antwerp was invaded, *Fräulein Doktor* and the permanent staff—lately much reduced, according to observers—had taken warning and retreated across the Rhine. The education of spies, at best a thankless task for civilian or soldier, had reached its ungrateful conclusion; and the records of her work, compromising to so many, were either removed in secret or burned.[5]

CHAPTER SEVENTY-SIX

THE SPY "SCHOOL" OF ALICE DUBOIS

ON THE ALLIES' SIDE there was no young woman engaged in spying or in the schooling of spies who, in point of qualifications and power or wartime notoriety, may be compared to "Mademoiselle le Docteur." There was, however, another secret-service patriot, who also had a *nom de guerre,* "Alice Dubois", who served the British and French with the utmost heroism, who made them a present of a formidable espionage system which, almost singlehanded, she organized *behind the German lines.*

The spy "school" of Alice Dubois was the war itself and the rigors of invasion. She conducted her impromptu operations with shrewd, unflagging ardor. She did much of the hazardous spying and the even more hazardous communicating herself—all this under conditions far more intensified and threatful than anything Fräulein Elsbeth Schragmüller, with some of the finest troops in Europe between her and the enemy, could possibly have had to overcome.

As the battalions of General von Kluck drove forward on the extreme right flank of the invading group of German armies in August 1914, they swept before them nearly half a million refugees. Thousands of these stricken, bewildered noncombatants managed to cross to England. Slim gray destroyers carried some; so did trawlers, navy tugs and private yachts. Many others came swarming ashore from barges, fishing craft, motor launches and even rowboats. British port authorities were swamped by these crowds. They had to take charge of them and shelter and feed them; but also they suspected that, screened by such wholesale panic, the German *Nachrichtendienst* would introduce spies into England. There were, moreover, many genuine refugees with military matters they gladly related. Pieced together, these details would form a comprehensive report to be transmitted to the expeditionary headquarters in France.

Intelligence officers went patiently to work, questioning the Belgian throngs. And it was presently the good fortune of one of them to encounter an eager young Frenchwoman who gave her name—"Louise de Bettignies." Her home—"Lille." Most recent occupation—"Governess." Attractive, intelligent, with chestnut hair and flashing brown eyes, she was well educated and of aristocratic birth, though admittedly poor in purse. She spoke unaccented English, answering candidly each question, and, besides showing herself a linguist—with flawless command of German and Italian—she proved to have much to tell.

Several messages of practical military consequence had been intrusted to her by local officials of the districts whence she had fled. Delivering them accurately, she revealed herself as one who had been keenly observant of the German forces and chaotic circumstances of invasion. Here, it became quickly apparent, was a secret-service agent of unusual promise, providing she could be recruited for other journeys even more adventurous than that which she had just accomplished. Louise de Bettignies was invited to London, where Major Edward Cameron[1] discussed the war situation with her pleasantly, until he got around to urging that she join in the struggle. "Gladly, but how?" How could she serve her country and his?

"By returning to France, mademoiselle, and organizing a system of espionage." In the now-occupied departments from which she had accounted herself lucky to escape!

She thought it over, then answered simply: "I am ready to undertake it." Thus the recruiting and almost simultaneous christening of "Alice Dubois". The name was fastened upon Louise in falsified identification papers provided her by the department of Special Intelligence at the British War Office. In them she was described as a "maker and seller of laces", a modest employment expected to allow her to travel about without rousing suspicion.

She at once set to work—as an amateur invited to help professionals. But secret service in time of war is a great game for amateurs. They outnumber and surpass the professionally trained contingent by a ratio of eight or ten to one.[2] For more than fifteen months in 1914-15 Alice was as destructive an individual adversary of the Germans as any of the Allies' commanders in the field. And she was much *less* destructive *to* the Allies than many of those generals who wasted lives upon such adventures as that of the French in their Champagne offensive—September to November 1915—where 400,000 casualties earned a total advance of less than *five* miles.

Alice had expected to join her mother at St Omer. The persuasive Major Cameron directed her to return to Lille. Arriving there without mishap, she began to consider first her need of getting together a not too-numerous but diversified, intelligent and absolutely reliable band of conspirators. Because of her birth she, as Louise de Bettignies, had always been accepted on terms of social equality by wealthy families employing her and had made many friends. She soon found some of the more rebellious of these ardently seeking a chance to work and plot against their common foe.

She enlisted a chemist, M. de Geyter, and his wife. In a little while from the private laboratory of this ingenious man came the invisible inks and the altered, forged or counterfeit passports which could only have been brought over from London at grave risk. Next she enlisted a manufacturer, Louis Sion, and his son, Etienne, who contributed services and also a fast motorcar—until the invaders remembered to confiscate it. She found a mapmaker who said modestly that he believed he might be of some help. His name was Paul Bernard. And it was ultimately one of his more impressive feats to write in a coded shorthand, with a fine-pointed calligraphic pen and the aid of a magnifying glass, a sixteen-hundred-word spy report on a picture post card *underneath the postage stamp*.

Charlotte

Then, in a small shop in the old town of Roubaix, Alice discovered a girl who was to prove as a spy hardly second to herself in pluck and deceptive range. This was Marie-Léonie Vanhoutte, who became "Charlotte", itinerant peddler of cheeses. Marie-Léonie specialized in looking so wholesome, so untroubled and harmless, it was difficult to believe that she even had heard of the war. With cheese and lace she and Alice patrolled the danger zones of armed invasion, either commodity excusing the almost continuous journeying about of the two young allies. And together the peasant-born shopkeeper and cultivated descendant of Crusaders combined the enduring great qualities of the French race.

The first six confederates of Alice Dubois grew to be twelve, then two dozen, then two score. Their skill and courage, their homes and all they possessed were placed at her disposal. Military intelligence—carefully sifted from a cataract of rumor, gossip, and furtive misinformation—became a continuous, regulated flow of facts. And the time arrived when Alice, always reserving to herself the most venturesome missions, had to evade enemy patrols and cross into Holland once a week to forward reports to her superior officers in London.

By degrees the German frontier control increased in effectiveness. Even the smartest of ruses no longer guaranteed safe passage of the border by day; and by night both Alice and her friend, Charlotte, had to surmount innumerable new hardships and dangers. Several times, as a last resort, Alice was forced to swim a canal. For this exploit she designed herself a special costume of knickers, blouse and skirt, made of a fabric dark in color but very light in weight. A strong swimmer, she was undaunted by icy canal water; but for such crossings Char-

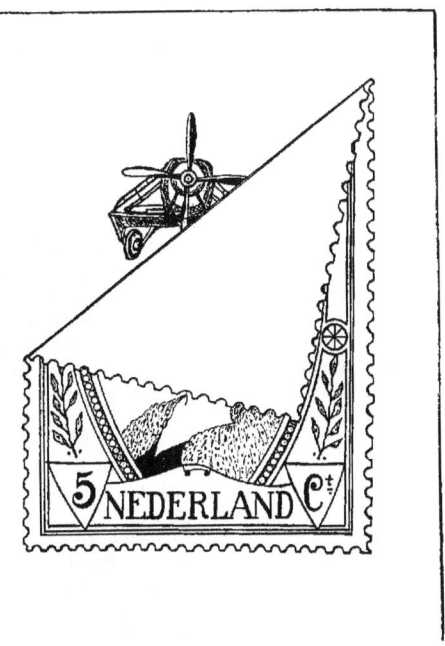

Spy sketch of an aviation improvement transmitted in chemical ink underneath the postage stamp of an "innocent" letter.

lotte, unable to swim, had to crouch in a large kneading trough which a Belgian baker had contributed to the cause, while Alice propelled it ahead of her.

She possessed from first to last seemingly inexhaustible reserves of wit and imagination and put to emergency use many articles never before associated with espionage. She instigated signaling with carillon bells, it is said; while cakes of chocolate, toys, umbrellas and even an elderly cripple's wooden leg served her as hiding places for minutely inscribed messages. Balls of knitting wool conveyed a simple code; and once when halted unexpectedly by a German patrol, Alice cast a ball of yarn into some bushes, to return an hour later and find the discarded "report" and hurry on her way. There was one famous little map she contrived to transmit to England inserted in the rim of a pair of spectacles. It located fourteen of the German heavy batteries or ammunition dumps in the vicinity of Lille. Some of her followers had been complaining that, while they risked their lives obtaining vital information, the reports submitting it were seldom appreciated or acted upon; and so, shortly afterward, when the fourteen batteries and dumps were all destroyed by the Allies' gunfire or bombs, Alice had an answer to stiffen the morale of the waverers.

Her own high spirits, manifested frequently in a reckless sense of humor, never failed her. She brazenly offered a bit of sausage to a counter-spy, who refused it, convinced that the papers sought could not be imbedded in the very food this flippant girl was eating. It was, again, her privilege and delight to stand by while a bleak Prussian sergeant major stamped the imperial eagle on the photograph attached to her latest identification card. The photograph was not only a good likeness, but also had an extraordinary glossy surface. And this gloss could, had her enemy's thumbnail scraped across it, have been exposed as a film of transparent paper on which, with invisible ink, the deft Paul Bernard had written a 3,000-word spy summary, covering the latest movements of enemy reserves.

Only after some months of this dynamic enterprise was Alice Dubois suspected. She was traced, halted, subjected to questioning and search. Yet even in the thick of traps and dangers there was her gift as a linguist and her incorrigible spirit of mischief. She often would pretend to be Teutonic herself, a German aristocrat. Of all soldiers the Prussian was the most easily dragooned by caste; and many an officious underling, whose questions threatened her safety, Alice managed to discomfit with her fine Mecklenburg accent and crushing, haughty air.

The Counter-Spying Cordon

German counter-spies in the sectors covered by Alice and her partisans had known from the beginning that a very superior brand of opponent was defying their measures of defense. Much more rigid restrictions upon noncombatant travel had been their first attempt to curb the menacing unknown. This vigilance became so acute that a train on which Alice and Charlotte were riding was flagged between stations by a patrol of field gendarmes. Interrogation and search of every passenger began.

What were the spies to do? Luckily they had taken seats in the last car. Whereas the uniformed searchers, keeping together with invincible stupidity, started at the first car to work back to the end of the train.

"We'll get out," Alice decided. And acting immediately, with Charlotte following, she not only left the coach but crept under it. Working their way forward, the girls began a slow, always endangered progress under the entire train. The first car, even before they arrived beneath it, had been visited by the military police.

"We'll take seats here," they decided coolly, locating themselves to resume their journey. In another quarter of an hour the train was allowed to proceed. Alice and her accomplice had once more avoided a trap.

Women adversaries, however, they found more difficult to deceive. German police matrons of a notoriously vindictive or "rough-neck" type were brought into Belgium to deal with its insurgent civil population. One of these creatures her antagonists called The Frog—with apologies to frogs—and during her first encounter with Alice she examined the spy so thoroughly, she even stripped her and treated her skin with harmful chemicals, endeavoring to develop invisible ink writing. All the while Alice held under her tongue a pellet of rice paper, which was one of Bernard's infinitely compact reports. The conspirators always made duplicates; and, feeling certain of ultimate detection unless she sacrificed it, Alice now gulped it down.

"Stop! What are you swallowing?" cried the vigilant police matron. "Give it to me!"

"It is nothing," said the spy. "I'm cold, that's all. And, naturally, a bit tired and nervous."

"Put on your clothes, then," The Frog advised, turning suddenly amiable. "We're finished with you here." She left Alice alone in the room for a few minutes but returned carrying a cup of milk. "Drink this," she invited. "You don't look any too well nourished."

The French girl was not to be taken in by this seeming change of heart. "You are very kind," said she, "but really, I detest milk."

"Drink it, I tell you," the German woman insisted, relapsing to her normal domineering tone.

Alice Dubois felt sure that the cup of milk contained an emetic. It would make her deathly sick and enable the paper pellet to be recovered. Accepting the glass, smiling ruefully, with many grimaces she pretended to start drinking. Then she gagged, began choking and coughing. The cup slipped from her quivering fingers and fell to the floor with a splash.

This was accomplished so realistically, The Frog could not be sure that the mishap was intentional. There was no use bringing in any more cups of doctored milk; by the time she had prepared another and forced this girl to drink it, normal processes of digestion would have defeated her purpose.

One more enemy trap yawned in back of Alice as she hurried away from the police post; but for leagues around now the counter-spying cordon was slowly closing her last avenues of escape. Warned of this, told to rest or go to England secretly and enjoy a well earned vacation, she ridiculed the anxieties of her well-wishers. All they could do, then, was redouble their own plotting to shield her from harm.

Children in the Service

In the espionage system she had built up around her adventurous leadership the intrepid spy even employed a band of clever and mischievous urchins. These boys were of enormous help to her as the German measures of counter-spying grew more oppressive. Among her fellow agents, who had to retain a certain degree of mobility even in dangerous districts close to the enemy's combat zone, all sorts of passports, identity cards, visas and acknowledgments of police registration were in constant demand. The supply available for secret agents was generally insufficient, even though *Messrs* Bernard and De Geyter kept up their steady output of ingenious fakes and forgeries.

By means of her squad of boys, Alice found it possible to extend the usefulness of one precious pass—whether genuine or forged—so that the leader herself, her dependable Charlotte, and probably several other active spies, could get by widely separated military control posts in a single day. The boys of her squad were allowed to play about pretty much as they pleased. They were seldom stopped or questioned. All of them managed to look so ragged and homeless, no Prussian sergeant ever hazarded his dignity by ordering one of them searched. This was a priceless immunity, for a youngster could swiftly carry a permission to travel back to another waiting adult as soon as it had been used to take some agent past the sentries.

At a certain Belgian inn where Alice or Charlotte repeatedly came for a few hours of exhausted sleep, there were three small children who helped protect the spies from arrest. At this haven Alice always occupied the same bedroom. Alarms and police visitations were frequent.

Police! There would be a loud knock upon the inn door—a peremptory summons to open. The proprietress, whose husband was away in the army, was particularly alert with a woman agent resting under her roof. At the first sound of enemy visitors she ran to Alice's door and aroused her. "They have come, mademoiselle!" No need to amplify just who *they* might be.

The spy, moving quickly, but with the precision of one accustomed to broken rest and unceasing dangers, leaped out of bed and wrapped herself in a heavy dark cloak. Then up the attic stairs to a window leading out upon the roof! Her few belongings she carried with her to an ultimate place of refuge in back of a big brick chimney. There she was sheltered to a degree from the weather and always well concealed.

Below, in a room adjoining that which she had just vacated, three children who had been put to sleep that night in one big bed were being roused. The oldest of them had to change at once to the bed Alice had occupied. Each of them was trained to pretend to be asleep until police searchers actually invaded their part of the inn. They were even then to make no outcry, but, if asked a question, to seem frightened and duck down under the bedcovers.

The Germans, with electric torches flashing, progressed from room to room, making themselves a terror and a nuisance, without regard for sleep or privacy. But they could discover no suspects. Every bed showing evidences of having been sleep in still had an available occupant. "Just another spy scare!" the visitors growled and after a while retreated angrily. When the coast seemed clear, the plucky Belgian mother put all three youngsters together again and brought Alice Dubois down from the roof to resume her fitful rest in a warm bed.

It was inevitable that this young genius of artful patriotism should find the nerve strain beginning to wear her down. She had risked pneumonia in icy canals and relentlessly overtaxed her physical—though never her mental—resources. No "front line" tour of professional secret service would ever have been permitted to last so long. Yet Alice herself had encouraged her superiors to place more and more reliance upon her organization, with consequent steady increase of responsibility, hardship and peril for her, its dynamo and chief engineer. Military trials, raids and arrests, widely advertised executions of convicted spies, persuaded a number of her minor allies that the right moment had come to dissolve. But though her espionage service might lose its earliest dash and effectiveness, she tried—and Charlotte tried—all the harder to make up for others' deficiencies.

Until one fateful day Charlotte received two messages. The first was authentically from Alice, who had just crossed into Holland, reporting by a simple code device that she was once more safe beyond the German barriers; but the second, in a strange handwriting—and warning the girl to hasten at once to an out of the way inn "on account of Alice!"

In the Net

Charlotte felt her heart skip a beat as she read that last menacing phrase. What could it mean? Only that enemy counter-spying operatives at last had penetrated so deeply, they comprehended the close relationship and identities of the two principal agents of the Dubois organization. Charlotte, however, went straight to the inn, afraid to seem wary or timid. The stranger who greeted her there, professing to be a Belgian refugee, was neither an imperiled Belgian nor a very subtle German. The girl's refusal to chat with him indiscreetly left him about where he began—in the dark. Yet he persisted in plying her with questions.

"But I have never known anybody named Alice Dubois," she stolidly maintained. After an hour of the informer's company Charlotte permitted herself a decent display of temper. "I know nothing about any of this," she exclaimed. "You have mistaken me for somebody else. I'm tired of talking to you—I have to go home." And home she went.

The German Secret Service was to have the last word, however; and at an early hour next morning three agents with drawn revolvers broke into Charlotte's house as though she harbored a criminal gang. They searched it with their practiced thoroughness; and even when they found nothing incriminating, they told the girl to clothe herself warmly, and marched her off to jail.

News of this arrest spread swiftly from one to another of Alice Dubois' confederates. A warning was dispatched to Holland. Alice must remain there, her game was played out! The message never reached her. She had already started on the return trip. And she was later to tell her colleagues that it would have made no difference, she would not have abandoned Charlotte to heed their well-meant alarm.

Her name, according to the record, had merely been mentioned at the examination of a spy suspect who formerly had occupied a very small place in her espionage organization. Yet this crumb of additional evidence—in view of the German counter-spies' prolonged doubt about the two young women—practically closed the case.

"The woman Dubois has reappeared!" German officers were not surprised to hear it, for no want of audacity had ever been mentioned in the copious reports bearing upon the activities of this suspect. "Allow her a few more days of liberty," was the decision at headquarters, "but have her shadowed. There is proof enough against her. But it will do no harm if she further incriminates herself."

Unable to communicate with her imprisoned lieutenant, even indirectly, Alice behaved with uncommon circumspection for several days. A great battle was in progress, however, and the spying must not be suspended. From France and England came the usual driving inquiries. She set forth at last on an inconspicuous journey to Tournai; but there a patrol stopped her and she was put under arrest.[3]

Alice and Charlotte were brought to trial under their real names. The German Secret Service knew all about them, it appeared, and what defense could they offer? Both were convicted, both condemned to death. Whereupon each rose to ask clemency for the other. Partners for so long, each sought to go alone into the last great adventure.

Owing to the world outcry occasioned by the shooting of Nurse Cavell, the German authorities had grown suddenly sensitive on the score of executing their feminine foes. Alice, the leader, and Charlotte, her chief of staff, were veritable spies, with only their intense patriotism to mitigate a capital offense. However, their death sentences were on the last day reprieved to twenty-seven and fifteen years' imprisonment, respectively; and they accepted these penalties with reviving spirit, confident that both would "outlive this dreadful war."

Charlotte or Marie-Léonie Vanhoutte did outlive it, and received honors and decorations on her release from an enemy cell. But Louise de Bettignies died at Cologne—as a result of the special hardships inflicted upon her in a German prison[4]—on September 27, 1918, only forty-five days before the Armistice which would have set her free.[5]

CHAPTER SEVENTY-SEVEN

LIQUIDATION OF A LUXURY

MARGARET GERTRUD MACLEOD née Zelle owed her stage presence and her stage name, Mata Hari—Eye of the Morning—to the East; and her notoriety as a spy in the World War was mainly an outgrowth of the theatrical fame of the "Javanese temple dancer." For her experiments in espionage she is scarcely a footnote to the history of military secret service, but she became an important pawn in a typical sordid intrigue of French civil and army politicians in 1915–16. And to that she adds such undeniable personal glamor as will outlive the fine patriotic services of other spies of her time.

Whatever this woman's deficiencies as a secret agent, she continues to excel all records as an inspiration of romantic nonsense. It has never been difficult in her case to sift out the facts from the persevering legends. Yet whole volumes have been devoted to her exploits with such comprehensive suppression of the truth, it would seem the biographers had never heard of her prewar reputation and were chivalrously bent on saving a wife and mother from a malicious canard.

Mata Hari was a picturesque celebrity of the Continental demimonde. She was never a great spy, never an effectual operative of the German Intelligence service. Before a French court-martial—at that time leading its field as producer of stereotyped verdicts decided in advance—she made out a strong case for herself. She had not been an active spy at all, but the courtesan-confidante of certain German officials. We shall see that some of these gentlemen had hit upon the thrifty scheme of paying for their recreation out of secret-service funds. But when that subterfuge was detected, the luxury had to be liquidated; and the dancer was transmitted with a blessing into the toils of the French.

She was born in Leeuwarden, Holland, on August 7, 1876, and was therefore past forty when her fatal charm convinced the counter-spies of Paris that she menaced the Republic. Her parents were worthy Netherlanders, Adam Zelle and Antje van der Meulen. In the great years of her stage success, her exotic dancing and muscular bravura, she cultivated a popular belief that she had been born in Java and was a half-caste with a Javanese mother; but also that she had served her apprenticeship as a temple dancer in Malabar with what resulting artistry she displayed to the audiences of Europe. Her knowledge of things Javanese was the result of careful first-hand study, for she had been married in March 1895 to a captain of the Dutch colonial forces, who soon afterward left Holland for Java and took his bride with him.

His name, MacLeod, and his ancestry were Scotch; and he appears to a surpassing degree to have been arrogant, brutal and besotted. Mata Hari never had a valid reason for her pirouette into the vortex of espionage, but through the best years of her life she ignored a prepossessing motive for murder. Why she refrained from killing MacLeod, who beat her when he was drunk and was seldom sober, and dragged her about by the hair when inclined toward domesticity, will not be found in the resolute character she later on discovered.

At length—in 1901—after six degenerating years in the tropics, she returned to Amsterdam with a daughter, Marie Louise, and her unbearable spouse. A son, Norman, had also been born to them in Demarang, and this child, it was said, had been poisoned in infancy by a native servant revenging himself upon MacLeod. Mata Hari was even alleged to have taken the law into her own hands and killed the murderer; but that is not the sort of act to be attributed to the woman she was in Java.

There she submitted to the odious mastery of MacLeod, and in such numerous intervals of neglect as his infidelities or drunken stupors conferred, she seems to have devoted herself to the erotic manuals and ritualistic dances of the East. The performances of Javanese dancing girls she must have repeatedly attended, and not only witnessed but studied and practiced them as a kind of spiritual anodyne. And to such good effect, when she came to the moment of her own stage debut, she was skillful enough to convince Paris—including persons familiar with the Orient—of her childhood dedication as a temple dancer and sacred courtesan of Siva.

Meanwhile, from 1901 to 1905 her personality was altering; and the transformation from Dutch to Javanese was no more remarkable than her change from weakness to strength, from tears to triumphs and good fortune of a kind. Bitter loneliness of spirit and desperate longing were the solvents in which Margaret Zelle vanished and from which the Java-born artiste, Mata Hari, emerged.

She had made several attempts to separate from MacLeod. In August of 1902 the heroic captain had thrashed her once more and left her, taking with him the six-year-old Marie Louise. Giving almost her first exhibition of spirit and energy, she obtained a court order restoring the child to her care and requiring MacLeod to support them both. He countered with calumnies. Her aunt, who had come to her aid, for he had left her penniless, believed the husband and turned her out. Her father, who had prospered from his shopkeeping days, tried to help her; yet he also stood somewhat in awe of MacLeod, his social background and army prestige. And so, all legend to the contrary, it was wholly by her own initiative that she at last cut loose from the—to her—intolerable boredom of Dutch village life and journeyed to Paris seeking a theatrical engagement.

Celebrated performers have failed to recapture their public or their best artistry after a professional suspension of four years. It is all the more notable, then, that this woman, at twenty-nine, who by her own acknowledgment had never before appeared on the stage—and who since 1901 had been remote from all things Javanese, save her bitter memories—could be presented at the Musée Guimet in 1905 and score an instantaneous hit.

Eye of the Morning, Star of the Evening

Imagination, defiant resolve and an instinct for showmanship—witness the name she chose, the stories she helped to circulate about her birth and romantic upbringing—were true causes of her challenging metamorphosis. She became a courtesan, which would seem to have been almost obligatory in a career like hers. Without sentiment or apology, it may be presumed that MacLeod had schooled her well for this easy step from the drab world of an abandoned wife in Amsterdam to the gay half-world of an abandoned woman in Paris.

Her husband, however, if deserving her damnation, achieved a pleasant enough role in the legends: he was the handsome young Scots officer of the British Indian Army who had found her sequestered in the temple, had helped her to escape, married her and cherished her bravely, until his sudden death from fever required her to escape again—from a meager widowhood—by dancing nude at the most fashionable parties in France. MacLeod had, by his example and cruelty, prepared her for anything, including prostitution; but it was once more her own clever initiative that made her for a decade the leading courtesan of Europe.

She exacted immense fees and, though she is reputed to have collected as a spy after 1914 well over a hundred thousand marks, she was fascinating to men until the day of her death and had therefore no diminishing access to her former, and far safer, livelihood. French counter-espionage officers allege that her secret-service code number was H.21, and that no German spies were assigned the letter H after the outbreak of the war. She professed no patriotic inclination toward the Netherlands, or France—even though her success had been founded there—or any other land. She was Javanese; it was both her chief stock-in-trade and her obsession. If she spied for Germany, perhaps her German admirers were the first who thought to ask her to work for them. She would personally have inclined toward the secret service whose opponent had the more agreeable capital.

Berlin had been no less hospitable to her than Paris; however, the British blockade caused the former metropolis to lose much of its prewar luxury and charm. On the day of the declaration of hostilities she was seen by French agents in Berlin, driving through the streets thronged with cheering, excited crowds, in company with Von Jagow, the chief of police. But that event hardly holds the sinister importance which some thereafter sought to attach to it. The Prussian official was an old friend. At the time of her first engagement in Berlin he had called on Mata Hari, acting upon a published complaint that in her Eastern dances she wore no costume; and, finding this to be true, he had remained to suggest how she might accommodate the law.

Mata Hari was an obliging person; it was her specialty to enchant distinguished audiences and cater to distinguished men; and accepting an offer from the German Intelligence would have seemed perfectly logical to one having her catholic tastes for adventure. She had many of the qualifications which go to make a valuable spy; but she had one uncompromising fault—she was too conspicuous, too easily noticed wherever she went. Even siren spies are better off without bells and headlights.

Enlisting her for any form of clandestine endeavor, the manipulators of German secret service may well have congratulated themselves. But could they congratulate her? She knew scores of affluent and influential men and had a limitless basic commodity to offer in exchange for their secrets. Even so, if her German employers gave these matters any objective consideration—which, to judge by some of their results, they seldom did—they must have recognized from the first that the dancer could never work for them or with them and come through the war alive.

If, as the French have claimed, H.21 was the enemy code designation of Mata Hari *before* August 1914, how shall we explain her contradictory behavior in the opening months of hostilities? For nearly a year this H.21, this clever and formidably subsidized espionne remained a comfortable distance away from the war zone and every field of secret-service activity. Why? Merely to baffle the Allies when finally her spying should begin? Professional espionage is rarely as ponderous with guile as all that. When at length she returned to France in 1915, she arrived only a few days after the Italian Secret Service had telegraphed Paris:

> While examining the passenger list of a Japanese vessel at Naples we have recognized the name of a theatrical celebrity from Marseilles named Mata Hari, the famous Hindu dancer, who purports to reveal secret Hindu dances which demand nudity. She has, it seems, renounced her claim to Indian birth and become Berlinoise. She speaks German with a slight Eastern accent.[1]

That message, duplicates of which went to all the Entente allies, doomed the woman as an agent of offensive espionage. French counter-spies began to shadow her. She was also under suspicion at the Sûreté-Générale in Paris as a possible criminal of another nature. Her papers at the Prefecture of Police, where she had inaccurately described herself as having been born in Belgium, were endorsed: "To be watched."[2]

Despite the veritable spotlight of this double surveillance, she is supposed to have carried her performances to the dimly lit theater of military secret service. She was ultimately to be charged with many and grave violations of the martial law of France, all of which we are asked to believe occurred after not one but two different French agencies of detection and criminal investigation became convinced she was a spy and set their operatives continuously to shadow her, take note of her friends and visitors, and keep watch upon her mail.

Detection of a Dancer

One may pursue this doubt while studying the evidence presented at the trial of Mata Hari. That all too-effective surveillance obviously had handicapped her accusers up to the very hour of her final arrest. It would have been easier, according to the accepted procedure of French courts-martial, to try her and convict her had less been known about her movements.

Until 1916 the interested services were completely baffled by her ostentatious demeanor as a spy. She was an actress, yet seemed incapable of the role, never furtive, frightened or mysterious. But now at last their skies cleared a little. It was at this time that the French discovered how she was transmitting their war secrets which they were still unable to prove that she obtained. The dancer had many good friends in the diplomatic set, including Swedish, Dutch and Spanish attachés. Diplomatic pouches of neutral states did not have to be passed by the censor; and it now became obvious that Mata Hari regularly communicated abroad without submitting to censorship.

If this kind of dodge had only been the resort of enemy conspirators, counter-spying problems would have been fundamentally simplified. Throughout the war, however, in a Europe thronging with influential families, with scions of noble houses, and the lady friends of scions, with politicians, diplomats, special couriers, ranking officers and their wives or friends, with all sorts of elegant folk accustomed from birth to deference and special privileges—and to spying—use of diplomatic pouches when transacting the most innocent private matters was a commonplace.[3] By international usage and agreement, those pouches were inviolate. But once convinced of Mata Hari's guilty seduction of neutral attachés, the French—who were saying at Verdun "they shall not pass"—resolved to violate the pouches. Evidence thus obtained from underneath the seals of Sweden and the Netherlands was to weigh enormously when she came to trial. But as yet, though her alleged secret-service communications had been read and photographed, she was not even arrested; and some have said that she wrote in cryptic phrases which remained an impenetrable code.

The best of French counter-espionage agents were taking up rapiers and joining in the unequal duel. But for some months its inequality favored the escape of the lone yet by no means friendless woman. Proofs against her impressive enough to satisfy a civil or military court had not been descried; and since she was so very well known, almost a personage—whose confidential relations with the Duke of Brunswick, the German crown prince, M. van der Linden, premier of the Netherlands, and others only a shade less exalted, were a matter of record—it remained peculiarly necessary to find something having the depth and metallic aspect of an ironclad case for her successful prosecution.

It was learned at length that she had applied for a pass to go to Vittel upon the pretext that one of her former lovers, Captain Maroff, permanently blinded in battle, needed her care. Her affection for this unfortunate Russian officer would not have been questioned, except that a very important aerodrome was just being established near Vittel, and the French had lately intercepted cipher instructions to other German spies directing them to get information about it. Expecting Mata Hari definitely to betray herself on this errand, the counter-spies saw to it that she obtained her pass. Whereupon she ungratefully conducted herself during her stay at Vittel with almost derisive circumspection.

The French authorities were exasperated beyond measure, certain of her menace, yet unable to convict her. Some acute brain suggested —why not deport her? And so it was decided. Her own reaction, when she was told of this banishment, is the one emphatic clue she was to give of having practiced in the field of international espionage; for she behaved like a professional spy, like the meanest hireling trapped during the war, vowing she never had worked for the Germans but gladly would enlist with the secret services of France. She even vaunted her influence over many powerful German leaders and offered to go to O. H. L., then at Stenay, and obtain any secret intelligence the French General Staff might require.

Captain Georges Ladoux of the French counter-espionage service was not surprised by her impudence and affected to trust her. Since she had said Governor General von Bissing would be her helpless victim at a glance, she was invited to go to Brussels and learn whatever she could; and she was given the names of six agents in Belgium with whom she might immediately co-operate. All of them were listed at Paris as dubious commodities, owing to the chronic exaggeration which afflicted their reports. And here again the guilt of the dancer seemed to grow less opaque, for one of the six Belgians whose identities had been confided to her was presently arrested by the Germans and shot.

His execution puzzled the French. They had never received anything from the man which they valued and had believed his reports were doctored by a Teutonic hand. If now, however, the Germans had convicted him of espionage, he must be a double spy, submitting accurate intelligence to some other belligerent. After a time the British confirmed this, saying that a resident spy of theirs had been mysteriously betrayed to the enemy by a woman. Their counter-spies even had obtained a description of her, but she herself already had slipped through their hands.

Mata Hari, quickly tiring of the thankless pretense of spying for one of the Allies, had set out for Spain via Holland and England. If, indeed, it was on her information that the British resident agent came to his death, her next move in hurling herself at the English port authorities is either a major stupidity of 1916 or its pre-eminent exhibition of valor.

She was allowed to land, it seems, and proceed to London, only upon the certainty that she would be interrogated at New Scotland Yard. And there, exceeding the effrontery of her interview with Ladoux, she admitted to Sir Basil Thomson that—yes, she was a spy, but she had come to spy in England, not for the German Intelligence, but for the ally of Britain, France! The chief of the Criminal Investigation Department chivalrously masked his skepticism, advised the lady to abandon her preoccupation with government intrigues, and allowed her to proceed to Spain.[4] She had thanked him for excellent advice; but Madrid soon saw her on intimate terms with Captain von Kalle, the German naval attaché, and the military attaché, Von Kron.

Retrenchment

German secret-service funds were running low, with even such formidable headquarters as those at Antwerp and Bern allowed to feel the pinch. It was not that so much gold had been wasted upon fruitless spying as that too many spy-masters had been simultaneously padding their expense accounts. Retrenchments being ordered all along the line, luxuries had to be liquidated; and the dazzling Mata Hari—now so generally suspected and hopelessly compromised—was a luxury the German service could not afford to confer on Von Kalle. Wireless instructions came to him, ordering H.21 to proceed into France; the code used being one already known to the French.

Von Kalle passed his orders on to her, adding—as a bait, it would seem—that she would receive an installment of fifteen thousand pesetas for her work in Spain, payable through a friend of hers in a neutral legation. And so Mata Hari re-entered France, a leaf turned, and the last chapter had been reached. She went directly to Paris and to the Hotel Plaza-Athenée in the Avenue Montaigne. There was no further need of subterranean methods; on the very next day she was arrested. She had not had time to cash her check and only a few *louis* were found in her possession.

After a preliminary hearing, distinguished by her protests and blank astonishment, she was removed to the prison of Saint-Lazare and assigned to a cell—in the national tradition of Sardou and Dumas *fils*—which formerly had been occupied by Mme Caillaux, who had shot a noted editor,[5] and Mme Steinheil, whose pistol extinguished a president of the Republic.[6]

In July, on the twenty-fourth and twenty-fifth, she appeared before a court-martial, not to be tried, but to be condemned. Colonel Semprou, president of the court, was a police officer, who commanded the Garde Républicaine. He was convinced of her guilt. Major Massard and Lieutenant Mornet entertained no doubts. Only one person present even thought of acquittal, her counsel, Maître Clunet. Chosen for her by the president of the Corporation of Barristers, the Solicitor-General, Henri Robert, this defender became her devoted friend and champion and is conceded to have led his forlorn hope magnificently.

Colonel Semprou opened with the charge of the dancer's intimacy with the Berlin chief of police and made a great deal of the payment of thirty thousand marks which she had received from Von Jagow shortly after the outbreak of war. Mata Hari could not know—and offer in defense—that Lieutenant Colonel Nicolai in August 1914 had been complaining about the inadequacy of the secret-service appropriation.[7] She merely asserted, with evident truth, that the payment was not official, but an admirer's gift. "He was my lover."

"We know that. But this amount seems rather large for a simple gift."

"Not to me," she retorted.

The president of the court opened a new line of attack. "From Berlin you came to Paris, passing through Holland, Belgium and England. What were you going to do in Paris?"

"My real reason was to keep a watch over the removal of my goods from my villa at Neuilly."

But what about her going to Vittel? Though the police reports recognized that she had nursed the blinded Captain Maroff "with affection",[8] she had also made the acquaintance of numerous flying officers.

"Men who were not in the army did not interest me at all," she answered. "My husband was a captain. An officer in my eyes is a superior being, a man who is always ready for any adventure, for any danger. When I loved it was always soldiers, and it did not matter what country they came from. To me a fighter belongs to a special race above civilians."

Without appearing to notice that this remark might have been aimed straight at him, Semprou resumed frigidly: "The flying officers also came after you, flattered you and courted you. How did you manage to get from them for nothing the secrets they had? It is certain that you told the enemy the places where our aeroplanes would put down our secret agents. Through this you have killed many men!"

"I do not deny that I continued, whilst I was with the Red Cross, writing to the head of the German Secret Service, who was in Holland.[9] It is not my fault that he had that appointment. But I wrote nothing about the War. He got no information from me."

She attributed her relations with soldiers to sympathy; while in other instances she had conferred her favors for money. "Harlot, yes—but traitress, never!"[10]

When confronted next with her offering to turn spy for France, she seemed to hesitate, then declared that she had been in need of money to begin a new life.

"How would you have been useful to France?"

"By using my connections for her! I have already told the chief of the Second Bureau the exact points in Morocco where German submarines have landed arms. It was interesting."

"Very interesting," put in Lieutenant Mornet, the commissioner for the government.[11] "But all these matters you have referred to could not have been known to you without your being in connection with Germany."

Taken aback for a moment, she then launched into rather a confused explanation—about confidences received at a certain diplomatic dinner—then broke off, exclaiming: "After all, I am not French. I have no *duty* towards this people. My services were useful—that is all I have to say. I am only a poor woman whom you are trying to entrap into a confession—a confession of faults she has not committed."

And as Mornet continued plying her with questions, she stretched out both her arms, pointing at him, and cried in a voice shrill with violence: *"That man is bad!"*

Semprou coldly passed on to the case of the agent in Belgium, for whom Mata Hari had received a letter, and who was subsequently executed by the Germans. The dancer insisted that she did not recollect this letter.

Being questioned at length about her stay in Madrid, and about the fifteen thousand pesetas which she was to have drawn in Paris upon the order of the German Intelligence, she used again the excuse already presented: she had been the mistress of the attaché in Spain who directed German espionage—and that this officer budgeted his love debts with the governmental expenses of spying.

The French counter-espionage service had contrived, as is elsewhere related, to place its agent, Marthe Richer, on the German Intelligence payroll in precisely this same relation. She was a patriot spy pretending to be what Mata Hari was professionally, a courtesan, and transferring her pesetas to Paris to help out the niggardly appropriations granted her chief, Ladoux. In no other way could she win the confidence of the enemy. Whereas Mata Hari, rather than pretending to love to get on the payroll, pretended espionage to obtain the best market price for her love. Nothing of which was allowed to intrude at her trial, interruptive to the orderly processes of dissecting and magnifying her guilt.

The Conviction of H.21

Whether the fees of a celebrated courtesan or the subsidies paid to a valued spy, Semprou persisted, all her remittances had been sent to the order of "H.21." A number on an intercepted list of German spies! "That is what you were known as."

"But that is not true. I—I am telling you that it was to pay me . . . pay for my nights of love. It is my—my price," she faltered. "Believe me, gentlemen."

Later, speaking more calmly, she made this final statement: "Please note that I am not French, and that I reserve the right to cultivate any relations that may please me. The War is not a sufficient reason to stop me from being a cosmopolitan. I am a neutral, but my sympathies are for France. If that does not satisfy you, do as you will."

Personal accounts of the testimony of witnesses describe them as moving and dramatic. Unlike Alfred Dreyfus, this prisoner was permitted to hear every syllable of evidence offered by the prosecution.[12] In one instance Mata Hari appeared to advantage, vigorously objecting when Mornet was about to read aloud a letter written to her by a married man whose family, she said, might thereby suffer needless mortification. But the letter was read at Semprou's command; and so, at long last, was the military verdict.

Against this Maître Clunet appealed in vain. Enormous private pressure was exerted in her behalf; but France at the time was still staggering from the blows of the defeatists, from the shocks and tremors of mutinies at the front, and execution of leading mutineers. Spies and all other subversive agents within the Republic were bound to be roughly handled.

Had it been otherwise, Mata Hari would have been let off with a prison sentence; for never did any condemned alien go to Vincennes with so many strong influences working to save her. President Poincaré declined to consider a pardon or reprieve. M. van der Linden, at The Hague, implored the queen to sign an appeal; but that lady, who had heard about the lovers so abundant, and the dance costumes so scant, firmly refused her prime minister's petition.[13]

On the morning of October 15, Mata Hari rose and dressed herself bravely. She had refused to gain a postponement of her execution by claiming, under a provision of the French law relating to capital punishment, that she was pregnant. The prison doctor offered her a glass of brandy, which she accepted; and she appears to have been more composed than Sister Léonide, the nun attending her. At this final moment she had again that steadfast courage which had suppressed the forsaken wife of MacLeod and produced the Javanese nautch girl.

It has been solemnly represented that she had been told only blank cartridges would be used, that she must act one more part, and that, alive, she would be smuggled out of France. But eyewitnesses discredit this nonsense, reporting no trace of a boldness or insolence of manner that morning which the comforting lie would have revived.[14] She was resigned and unafraid, and gently shook the weeping nun to quiet her. She placed herself against the stake whose cord was loosely knotted about her waist. Curtly refusing a bandage for her eyes, she faced the twelve riflemen.

Chapter Seventy-eight

WHO WAS GUILTY?

MATA HARI WAS DEAD, but the ghost of her personality still deluded the talebearers, and the ghost of her incrimination went on raising doubts of honor and patriotism. Nearly eight years after her execution—in the summer of 1925—two talented French writers, MM. Marcel Nadand and André Fage, published an article[1] which for the first time expressed bluntly that uneasiness as to the dancer's guilt which was troubling many persons. The record of the trial had thus far been kept entirely secret. Major Massard in 1922 had published his conclusions[2] as one who had gone through all the documents, had confronted the accused woman with unanswerable proofs, and was positive that justice and military duty demanded the death penalty in her case. But to impartial minds, even in France, the question was—and is still—an open one.

What if seven officers passed on "the evidence" and adjudged a volatile worldling guilty of espionage? How many court-martial verdicts have months or years later been proved by temperate judicial inquiry a noisome travesty upon justice? We have seen Alfred Dreyfus all but flayed alive by convinced and convincing military judges even at a time of purely trumped-up hysteria, when there was neither the nerve strain of war nor the wasting menace of invasion. Whether guilty or innocent, the dancer was condemned by methods which reeked of blundering. Whether just or unjust, her conviction cried to heaven for the traditional appeal to and searching review by unprejudiced civilian tribunals.

If so many influential and infatuated gentlemen had been induced by her charms to confide state secrets, where were these dupes and accomplices at the time of her trial? And what did any one of them suffer after her condemnation? The answers are: (1) that everybody was spared whom the army clique wished to spare, and (2) that none of her allegedly numerous informants has ever been honestly exposed as the accomplice of a convicted enemy spy. The inference is that no proofs were found which enabled the authorities to proceed against those who had been the dancer's careless or unwitting confederates in secret service. And yet, as we shall see, the French Intelligence secured before her death, and subsequently suppressed, the voluntary confession of Mata Hari. It has not been used either to substantiate the guilt of the woman or to incriminate her former protectors, lovers and accessories.

In pursuing the facts of this secret-service case, which really began after the spy had been escorted to the Polygone at Vincennes and shot, we must revert for a moment to Mata Hari's theatrical reputation. It helped not only to bring upon her the capital charge of espionage, and to impair her appeals for clemency after conviction, but also it has absurdly magnified her "menace" and importance as an alleged agent of the German Secret Service almost from the day of her death. Because she was exotic and fascinating in her individual way, and perhaps the most costly delicacy on the menu of Continental night life, Mata Hari was easily cast in the hallowed role of harlot-spy. Because she had been a noted theatrical personage, her photographs were distributed far and wide—and very captivating photographs some of them were! When she, a condemned German agent, was pierced by ten bullets at Vincennes, newspaper editors all over the world had pictures of her already at their disposal. No other spy, surviving, imprisoned or executed, enjoyed such advantages of prewar publicity. Pictures of bona fide secret-service operatives are difficult even for opposing governments to secure. And so, because the likenesses of great and authentic spies were hard to come by, every one of the countless articles, features and magazine stories written about espionage since her death has made some mention of the glamorous "Javanese" who could be counted on to add "sex appeal" to the illustrations.

Her convenience then as a figure of romance and melodrama has raised her to the heights of popular "secret service revelations", while the French authorities have naturally assisted by continuing to avow that they made no mistake in executing her as a dangerously capable espionne. Georges du Parcq tells in his book of reminiscences[3] of being asked by Mata Hari to write her memoirs. As a Parisian journalist he had known the dancer for years; but now he was visiting her in her cell as an old friend while himself enrolled as an officer of the *Deuxième Bureau de l'État-Major* or French Intelligence staff. He was no longer qualified for private literary undertakings; yet when he reported the condemned woman's desire to "tell everything", his superior officer, Comte de Lesdain, agreed that he should accept her offer. On the condition, however, that all his notes be submitted to the *Deuxième Bureau*, in case anything the dancer disclosed should prove of value to counter-espionage!

Du Parcq explains that for three hours Mata Hari dictated to him her "revelations ... in the main the story of the amours of a beautiful courtesan" yet an "indictment of many highly placed officers, both in the British and French Army." Whereupon the courtesan was extinguished by rifle fire and her *souvenirs* were suppressed by military bureaucrats. They lie today among the well-guarded archives of the Secret Service in Paris. Du Parcq is himself bound by his officer's oath of secrecy and his special connection with the ever more secretive Intelligence. The "confessions" of Mata Hari will, perhaps, remain unpublished for a century, until some Lenotre of the future uncovers them and resolves their historical interest.

The Love Letters of "M——y"

Meanwhile, in the case of Mata Hari the French army clique, cutting its usual capers on the bias, produced another of those shocking chicaneries, which not even the scandals and popular revulsions in the Dreyfus affair were able to eliminate. The French Secret Service —for reasons of its own, and shameful reasons of political intrigue— had given out a statement at the time of the dancer's trial, alleging that a member of the cabinet, signing himself "M——y" had written many letters to the notorious courtesan. General Nivelle and his colleagues needed an alibi for the failure of the Champagne offensive and other grotesqueries of the staff-college intellect. They appear to have deliberately chosen as their scapegoat Louis Malvy, then minister of the interior, with considerable authority of his own in matters of secret service, investigation and surveillance, exercised through the civilian bureau of political police. Possibly one of Malvy's own agents had come across a general whose relations to army contracts were rather more political than patriotic? And in seeming retaliation the French Secret Service permitted and encouraged the spreading of the rumor: Malvy is the rogue who has betrayed us to the Germans through the courtesan spy! ... Malvy is the only "M——y" in the cabinet!

As a result the minister of the interior was brought to trial. Four premiers of France were among his character witnesses. Each swore that Malvy had been a loyal and devoted servant of the Republic. The military camarilla demanded his conviction. France was at war; the army in the saddle; and the army clique had the last word in accomplishing the ruin of Malvy.

He was sentenced by the Senate to seven years' banishment from France. Considering the hysteria provoked by the war tension, defeatism and national exhaustion, Malvy was fortunate to escape the death penalty or a harsh sentence to Cayenne. However, when the Allies' final victory began to heal the more superficial of war wounds, Malvy's "treason" was forgotten and then Malvy was forgiven. Premier Edouard Herriot granted him amnesty, recalled him to public life, gave him a place in his cabinet.

The day came when Malvy was to face the Chamber of Deputies, a virtual ceremony of rehabilitation. But when he stood up to speak, hostile voices of the Opposition taunted and silenced him. "Mata Hari!" they jeered. "Mata Hari! . . . Mata Hari!" Malvy tried to speak. But the name of the woman shot as a spy rose in a ghostly rhythmic chorus. Malvy sought again and again to deny that he had ever had anything to do with Mata Hari. The cruelty of emotional partisans would not hear him. "Mata Hari! . . . Mata Hari!" they chanted.

Malvy's vitality had been weakened by the years of disgrace and injustice, and he suddenly pitched forward in a faint and lay slack and insensible upon the floor of the rostrum. He was carried by attendants to an anteroom and there revived, while the catcalls of the politicians who had baited him diminished to chuckles of contempt. Premier Herriot assured Malvy of his inflexible confidence. France needed his talents. But Malvy felt utterly beaten, and in despair he resigned.

Several years went by; and then came one more surprise illumination of the tyranny, petty hypocrisy and infamy of the French military clique in all its gangrenous, gold-braided grandeur. Another attractive woman had entered the Malvy-Mata Hari case, no dancer, courtesan or spy, but a clever and accomplished journalist. She had belatedly wormed a confession out of one of the very men who had blandly destroyed Minister of the Interior Malvy. Not from personal enmity, she uncovered scant proof of that, but destroyed him simply as a smoke screen of caste and because of the chance similarity of names.

It was the right "M——y" who confessed, it was that General Messimy who had been minister of war at the outbreak of hostilities in 1914; Messimy, an elderly fop and pretentious incompetent whom the strain of the invasion and first Marne had swept from his swivel chair and into the twilight of reviews and retirement. Messimy, with the conceit of the dandy, the arrogance of the "political general", and the exaggerated mustachios of a man not too sure of his manhood, had been Mata Hari's intimate friend. He was undoubtedly named and "exposed" in the *souvenirs* she had dictated to Du Parcq.

General Messimy thus at length exonerated Malvy by confessing to the adroit lady journalist that he had been the member of the cabinet who wrote those foolish and incriminating love letters to the courtesan-spy.

N.B. Messimy was not sent into exile or bidden to visit Vincennes.

CHAPTER SEVENTY-NINE

STRATAGEMS AFLOAT

NAVAL INTELLIGENCE during the World War attained its greatest reputation in the work of the code room at the British Admiralty, the celebrated "Room 40 O.B."; and behind that unfailing penetration of every enemy code device stands an enlisted man whose individual exploits were, very appropriately, performed afloat. In spite of his unique and important services, they have never received adequate recognition; but it is not too late to make the acquaintance of a proficient, indomitable Briton and decide what honors are his due.

Shipwright E. C. Miller was an expert deep-sea diver, so expert that in 1914 he was appointed diving instructor at the British naval training school. About a year later, with the war at full blast, Miller was ordered to descend to a German submarine which had just been sunk by shell fire off the Kentish coast. Its estimated position had been marked by a buoy. The diver was instructed to report upon the condition and internal design of the enemy's undersea craft, and he was told especially to look for certain new U-boat appliances.

"Find out all you can about these mechanisms and their installation," his commander said. "The Admiralty must have had some reports upon them from agents located near the German submarine bases. But not enough has been learned by our spies."

Miller went down and found the submarine with a great jagged gash in its hull where the shell had scored its annihilating bull's-eye. To enter the sunken enemy craft by that gash he had to risk fouling his air line. At even graver risk, he thoroughly investigated the whole length of the U-boat's complex interior. His powerful diver's lamp shed its cold white beam upon many a strange and many a gruesome object. Huge salt water eels and other voracious specimens of the deep were feasting upon the bodies of the German crew. Resenting the intrusion of the light, they turned upon the diver; but with the heavy tools for breaking and entering which he carried, Miller was able to beat off the fiercest scavengers.

He was not just a man-of-war's man doing his duty, but a great naval diver and an enterprising one. Still carefully protecting his air line, he forced his way aft and finally into the officers' quarters, into the captain's cabin. There, in a kind of strong room, he discovered a stout metal box, dragged it out of the hull and attached it to a line to be hauled to the surface. Miller himself ascended at once to help open this prize. He could describe all the up-to-date innovations aboard the U-boat; but from the captured strongbox came such unexpected treasures as the latest plans of enemy mine fields, two new code books of the German Navy, and another, a very precious code, used only to communicate with the Imperial High Seas Fleet. "Leave the marking bouy. Full speed ahead," said the officer in command. "These must be rushed to London."

Thus began, with Miller persevering in the foully choked and hazardous compartments of that lost submarine, the mystifying achievements of the British Naval Intelligence, wherein the celebrated code masters of "Room 40 O.B." played a momentous companion role. The diver's initial stroke was a complete surprise. But thereafter his extraordinary skill and daring, and his ability to break through steel barriers while enduring the pressure of great depths, was turned to all possible account by his superiors.[1] A special service unit was organized to rush Miller, his air pumps and other diving equipment to any point on the British coast where a German submarine was known to have gone down. In time he came to be as familiar with the structure and internal mechanisms of the formidable undersea raiders as any naval designer at Cuxhaven or Kiel.

Before the end of the war scores of U-boats were lying in known graves. All but a very few of these the crack diver contrived to explore. Mine fields, secret codes and special instructions to raiders at sea were repeatedly changed by the German Admiralty. Bulletins reporting upon all such alterations, however, were regularly circulated by British Naval Intelligence. Terrific losses were inflicted upon the merchant marine of the Allies by the German U-boats, but their own casualties were heavy. And whenever another of them came to grief, Miller would straightway be hurried to the spot where a buoy had been left by the craft that was the victor in this case.

In one of his ventures he found that he would have to use explosives to force an entrance. After blowing his way into the U-boat, he discovered that the hull was twisted, the compartment doors wedged hopelessly shut. "More dynamite," said Miller on rising to the surface. And after an interval he came up again, to demand laconically "More dynamite." Deep down on the ocean floor the diver was methodically taking apart one of the most complicated mechanisms ever devised by man. But at length up he came, bearing one more metal box holding the plans, maps and lead-weighted codebooks which the German captain, as defeat overwhelmed him, had not had time to dispose of in accordance with naval regulations.

Breaking the U-boat Blockade

Having to do battle with the swarming, savage creatures of the North Sea was not the most formidable of Miller's problems. He could never become so well acquainted with the congested interior of enemy submarines that his air line and passage aft would be entirely unimpeded. Each craft was populated with dead men; and the air in his diver's suit drew the bodies toward him as he worked his way from one compartment to the next. There were times when a group of enemy seamen with swinging arms and staring, sightless eyes appeared to gather deliberately and block his path to the strong room.

On one record occasion he invaded a U-boat which had been rammed and sunk, reaching its crew so soon after their tortured death that the bodies still were warm. And, as an odd footnote to the history of German naval discipline, Miller found the captain of the submarine huddled under the conning tower hatch, shot dead with a revolver bullet in his back. It was known that many of the German crews feared and despised their officers.[2] Sailors at Kiel were the first in November 1918 to raise the red flag of opposition to the war and the monarchy. The ace of British naval divers assumed at the time, from what he saw of the dead aboard that tragic craft, that as the U-boat had begun to go down, the German commander, being nearest the hatch, had started to open it with a split-second's chance of escape. But he alone would have been able to scramble out before the sea flooded in through the opened hatch, finishing the others aboard all the quicker; and so, upon what impulse we can only conjecture from later naval insurrections, one of the captain's subordinates had killed him.[3]

The codebooks which Miller dredged up from the depths of the sea were of more than general use in helping to "break" a variety of difficult German codes. They became a powerful defensive weapon in the mortal contest with the submarine blockade. Wireless orders from the German Admiralty to U-boats at sea were regularly intercepted, and the code messages read by the experts of "Room 40 O.B." Submarine captains went to their doom unaware of the ease with which their superiors' commands had been exposed to the enemy.

Because the Entente blockade was starving Germany, the U-boats in reprisal were ordered out to "blockade" Britain and sink defenseless ships "without a trace." Propagandists of the Allies found this a haphazard, unsportsmanlike way of inflicting slow starvation upon the English; but other bright minds, without raging against the morally degenerate "Huns", began devising traps and plots to combat the stalking undersea terrors. Depth bombs accomplished a good deal. Careful convoying of troop transports and supply ships in the war zone produced even better results. Naval planes discerned lurking German raiders fathoms below the surface of the sea. A marine variation of the microphone—or dictograph employed by civilian investigators—was attached to patrol vessels so that they might *listen* for the submerged vibration of U-boat motors. Restless fleets of armed trawlers, speedboats and swift destroyers added to the intensity of the savage ocean duel.

Cranks of the wide world bombarded the British Admiralty with schemes of prodigious antisubmarine experiment. Two uncommon suggestions which came from America were seriously considered. A noted zoologist wrote, advocating that sea lions be trained to follow British submersibles so that later they would follow German craft and disclose their position. Still another ingenious scientist proposed that submarines of the Allies cruise about and feed the sea gulls generously. Accustomed to this, the gulls would expect to be fed by all similar craft and would circle over German raiders wherever they appeared, virtually signaling to the Allies' patrol vessels or planes.

Of all this variety of defensive innovations, however, that which gave the dread U-boats the fight of their lives were the decoy or "mystery" ships, later designated as Q-boats—a jealously safeguarded secret and a masterly naval stratagem.

The Q-boat and Its Quarry

Decoy craft were known in the earlier days of sailing ships. Vessels then making long voyages through waters where enemy cruisers and privateers were likely to be met often were painted to look like frigates and fitted up with frowning broadsides of wooden guns. This disguise won many a cargo ship safely through, as smaller enemy men-of-war had not dared risk attacking. During the maritime struggle of the Napoleonic Wars a bold and resourceful Briton, Commodore Dance, in a great sailing ship, with three other merchantmen in company, made such a brave show in the Indian Ocean that an enemy squadron sighted them and sheered off, thinking them too strong.

In 1915 some energetic mind at the British Admiralty proposed that this system be tried in reverse. Ships now were sent out as apparently defenseless tramp steamers, plodding, nondescript and badly in need of paint. They were all close to being unseaworthy when the Admiralty took them over; but buoyant cargoes of wood and cork were put in their holds to keep them afloat even during a very unequal sea fight. Bridge, deck and superstructure were protected with well-masked armor plate. Naval guns and gun crews were hidden aboard each vessel.

Plying back and forth on the trade routes, the decoy or "mystery" ships invited the attack of enemy submarines. Torpedoes had begun to grow scarce in Germany; it was known that U-boat commanders had been ordered to conserve them. After firing one torpedo at a zigzagging merchant ship from close range in order to be sure of a hit, the enemy raider generally came to the surface to finish off the job of sinking the cargo carrier by shelling it with a deck gun. It was this moment of the submarine's venturing to break surface for which those counter-spies of the deep, the Q-boats, waited. Each Q-boat captain had to hold his fire, though his ship was sinking, until absolutely certain of point-blank range; for a submarine skipper was always ready to save his boat by performing a "crash dive", even when it meant the loss of some of his own men serving the deck gun, who might not have time to get below before the hatches were closed.

The first stratagem of the mystery ship's commander was to send off a "panic party"—a number of his crew in the attire of merchant seamen, one of them posing as the master of the torpedoed tramp steamer. They had to act up to their disguises, scramble into a lifeboat, each carrying a few of his possessions, and frantically row out of range. That was expected to lure the U-boat to the surface; and once the German started his shelling, he was bound to steer closer to shorten the range and dispatch the old tramp as quickly as possible.

Being aboard a Q-boat was rather like patrolling a dark alley, trying to catch a homicidal maniac by giving him first chance to spring out and stab you in the back. But at length the enemy presented himself as a fair target. Whereupon the Q-boat swung up a staff bearing its battle ensign—in accordance with the laws of war—at the same time sending from its hidden and powerful navel wireless a general alarm to neighboring warships, dropping its screens, exposing its concealed guns, and starting to fire them fast and accurately. There was never more than a lightning spread of seconds in which to give the U-boat a death stroke before its inevitable crash dive began; which necessitated aboard the mystery ships a great amount of drill and battle practice, a brave, intelligent crew and inflexible discipline.

Whenever in port the men of the Q-boat were ordered to conduct themselves like merchant seamen. "Stay at sailors' lodgings—loiter around waterfront pubs—but no talking about your ship or its adventures," they were warned, "and no going about with other naval ratings."

A spy or counter-spy on active service could not have been required to behave more circumspectly. All that smartness and precision which we associate with the modern man-of-war had to be cast aside to protect the Q-boat's masquerade; and because the crew had to appear slovenly, the difficulties of true discipline on board were all the

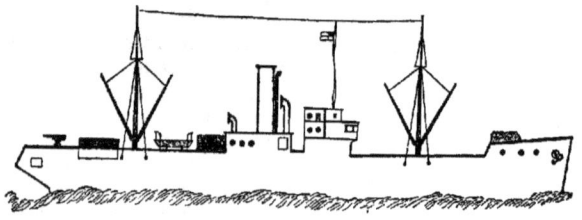

A Q-boat navigating the war zone in shabby disguise with a dummy naval gun mounted aft.

more acute. Yet if one of the officers or men made even a slight mistake when the battle crisis came, that meant giving the whole show away. The U-boat quarry would instantly submerge and then come back at the masked enemy with a second torpedo. Patience was ever at a premium aboard the Q-boats. Display of courage by members of their crews became almost a commonplace.[4]

Aboard the Q-5, when it had been struck by a torpedo, the engine-room watch remained at their posts to keep the dynamo running. Rising water finally drove them out. And thereafter, though several of the men were suffering from severe burns or wounds, they lay concealed on top of the cylinders—a supreme test of discipline! The attacking submarine, the U-83, had closed in meanwhile and was now exposed at almost point-blank range. The signal was given to open fire; and the first shot from the Q-5 beheaded the German captain as he was climbing out of the conning tower. Forty-five shells were fired in all, practically every one of them being a hit, so that the U-boat finally sank with its conning tower shattered and open, the crew pouring out as fast as they could.

All during the waiting, the decoying and the final, stabbing burst of gunfire, the Q-5 had been settling down by the stern. Gun crews had lain hidden and almost awash for twenty-five minutes while their craft sank beneath them. Yet there had been no trace of panic. Not a man stirred. A wireless message calling for help had been delayed until the sinking of the enemy raider was assured. But now all hands had to pitch in and try to keep their badly damaged vessel afloat. Luckily a destroyer and a sloop were not far off when the wireless began signaling its alarm. They came and took the Q-5 in tow, and that battered victor was successfully beached the following evening, February 18, 1917.

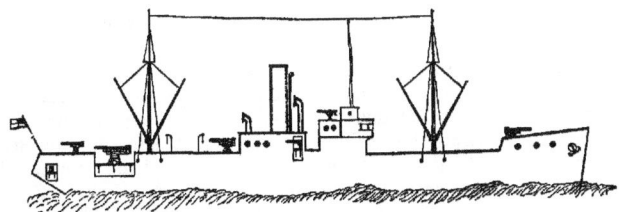

The decoy ship or Q-boat cleared for action, with its screens down, flagstaff with battle ensign exposed, and guns unmasked to open fire upon the enemy submarine.

Mystery V. C.

Cunningly disguised as an armed merchant vessel with a dummy gun mounted aft, HMS Pargust, another mystery ship, was torpedoed without warning on June 7, 1917. The boiler room, engine room, and No. 5 hold were immediately flooded.[5] The starboard lifeboat was blown to bits.

A "panic party" commanded by Lieutenant Francis R. Hereford, D.S.O., prepared to abandon ship. Hereford even carried conspicuously a stuffed parrot as a "pet" which he devotedly "rescued." And like the brave master of a merchantman he was ostensibly the last to leave his ship, except for the unfortunate firemen who crawled out at the last moment. The defensive dummy gun was likewise abandoned without firing a shot, after an effective pantomime of attempting to load it. As the boats with their "panic party" were pulling off the attacking submarine's periscope was observed some 400 yards away. Then it submerged, the periscope soon reappearing directly astern. Hereford, acting as a lure, ordered his boat's crew to pull around the stern. The enemy craft—the U.C.-29, one of the mine-layer class—breaking surface about fifty yards distant, followed closely.

Seeing that the U-boat was not yet in a position on which the Pargust's 4-inch gun would bear, Hereford, with magnificent disregard of the danger he incurred from the fire of his friends or the enemy submarine—which now had a Maxim gun trained on the lifeboat—continued to decoy the enemy within fifty yards of the Pargust. Then the mystery ship opened fire with all guns; and the U-boat, oil squirting from her side and crew pouring out of her conning tower, moved slowly across the bows with a heavy list.

Firing ceased when the German crew held up their hands in token of surrender. But the U.C.-29 began to glide away at gradually increasing speed, apparently expecting to escape in the mist. Fire was reopened then until the undersea raider sank, one man clinging to the bow. After a severe windward pull the British boats succeeded in rescuing two of the enemy, who were taken prisoner. American destroyers, newly arrived in the war zone at that date, came up just in time to save the Pargust from sinking. Because of the exceptional courage shown by the crew of this mystery ship, the Victoria Cross was bestowed upon all, one officer and one seaman being designated by ballot personally to accept the rare award.[6]

The Reckoning

The antisubmarine campaign of the Q-boats is not only an heroic and imperishable chapter of naval history, which has such a wealth of drama and heroism, but also a vital part of the secret-service combat of the World War. Like those other great instruments of surprise and potential victory, the tanks, the mystery and decoy ships were used too soon. They checked and discomfited the German foe in a small way when they might, in force, have overwhelmed an utterly unprepared adversary.

During the fifty-one months of the war only 200 German submarines were destroyed, and of these conquests 145 are claimed by the British. But more than 5,000 British auxiliary craft were assigned to this vast U-boat *battue,* together with miles of nets, thousands of mines, guns, depth charges and bombs, elaborate convoy systems, planes, a complex branch of Naval Intelligence, and all manner of traps, tricks and experimental contrivances. To dispose of 145 undersea adversaries!

Over 180 mystery ships of all types were commissioned, but only a very few were tried at first, and they were never employed in large numbers until the secret leaked out.[7] Yet they are known to have destroyed eleven German U-boats between July 1915 and November 1918,[8] or better than seven per cent of the authenticated sinkings. Nor did the achievements of the Q-boats end there. At least sixty submarines were damaged by them more or less seriously, putting the German craft out of action for considerable periods of time. And even more important was the decisive influence of the mystery ships upon the morale of U-boat crews. Manning a German submarine in the war zone was at best an unbearable strain upon the nerves; and when it came to pass that any harmless-looking tramp or sailing ship might abruptly change to a man-of-war, equipped with 18-inch torpedo tubes and booming 12-pounders, the German crews who had experienced months of "good hunting" suffered the icy death chill of the hunted.

CHAPTER EIGHTY

STRATAGEMS AFIELD

FOR EVERY CHANCE to outwit an enemy afloat, there are thirty subtle chances on land. And many of these stratagems afield, these furtive tricks and communicative ruses, however they violate civilian ethics, are noteworthy examples of combatant resourcefulness. They have to be unprincipled and often very cruel—yet hardly more so than waves of poison gas, shrapnel bursting in a schoolyard, or air bombs raining upon an unfortified town.

Refinements of cunning on which men and women must hazard their lives, in order to succeed and hold any degree of safety, must rely upon naturalness and extreme simplicity. In the region of the Vosges an agent is said to have signaled to a distant confederate by using a brightly polished spade as a heliograph. A Canadian artist in uniform sat down one day in a reserve area on the Flanders front to compose his war-worn spirit with a sketchbook. But presently he observed that the old windmill he was drawing had begun to turn *against* the wind. Counter-spies, being warned of the phenomenon, stole up at night to catch the enemy red-handed. What they found was a mechanism installed to control the windmill as a signaling device; but the perpetrator of this ingenuity is said to have escaped.

An incident of great cruelty, bearing some resemblance to the communicative dodge of the spy in Flanders, occurred during the Russian retreat from Lemberg. A rearguard of Russian cavalry seized a miller and bound him to an arm of his tall windmill. Then they turned it and lashed it fast, leaving their victim suspended head down on that arm of the mill now farthest from the ground. When hussars in the van of the Russians' pursuers rode into the mill yard, they discovered the plight of a harmless compatriot and hastened to release him, turning the arms of the windmill to bring him down within reach of the ground. As soon as the mill turned, distant Russian artillery observers recognized that their foes had arrived at that point; and the shelling which followed killed or wounded most of the troopers who had rescued the miller.

Stratagems of the secret-service conflict, whether East or West, were seldom as crudely merciless as that. The headquarters staff of the British Fourteenth Corps was amused one day when Intelligence officers exhibited a dead carrier pigeon which had been vividly daubed with paint to resemble a parrot.¹ The river Scarpe near by was then flowing past the British advance line at Arras and on to the enemy positions. One morning by chance a fish was discovered bearing a German agent's message. The spy had cut a slit in it, inserted the folded bit of paper, and floated the fish down the river. Whereupon luckless Tommies had to be assigned to "police the Scarpe", which meant netting or dredging up all sorts of tangled, pestilential refuse. But their noisome filtering of the French river recovered nothing more which had floated from the hands of a spy; and after a while the army command got around to forgetting all about it.

Belgium's Electrified Barriers

The frontier dividing the Netherlands from Belgium was the scene of a four years' campaign of wit and resource and unceasing danger. The German restrictions upon passage of the celebrated boundary became steadily more drastic, the vigilance of field gendarmes and counter-spies more formidable; but its importance and utility to the secret services and war conspirators of Belgium did not diminish. Refugees, contrabandists and agents of espionage regularly contrived to pass over the line and avoid hostile patrols. When at length the high voltage barriers of electric wire were put up to double the passers' risks, those graduate smugglers, poachers and inveterate plotters redoubled their ingenuity.²

Such a powerful current over a long transmission line was expensive, and so the German authorities did not keep it turned on all the time. There were various ways of trying to determine when the wire was live and when it was not; but after a few venturesome optimists had been electrocuted while making a wrong guess, it became a rule with the guides, passers and traveling spies always to assume the wire deadly and employ some artifice with that in mind. When the ground was dry and the weather fair, a barrel—which also must be dry and a nonconductor—could be driven in under the lowest wire after a bit of earth had been cautiously scooped out to make a sort of track for it. The barrel with both ends knocked out thus became a small insulating tunnel, through which one entering or leaving Belgium might stealthily crawl. Form-fitting suits of black rubber were tried with good result. They allowed the wearer a desirable freedom of movement as well as making him all the more difficult to see in the dark. But such suits were costly, hard to conceal when not in use, and dangerous to wear under street clothes. During a police search, if an espionage suspect were found wearing one of these garments, arrest and imprisonment would certainly overtake him. Moreover, there was the hazard that small rips in the insulated fabric might not be noticed, with death the price of the slightest oversight.

The German command brought many working parties of military prisoners into combat areas of the Western Front;[3] and often groups of these prisoners, who were chiefly Russians, broke out of their barbed-wire enclosures and made for Holland. Arriving at the electrified barriers, they of course lacked the co-operation of agents on the Dutch side of the border which the secret-service operatives enjoyed. Even so, a good number of prisoners luckily scraped through, others being turned back, and not a few electrocuted. The bodies of those who perished stayed on the wire for weeks thereafter, contorted and gruesomely blackened; no guard nor anyone else ventured to approach and remove them. Whenever the current was on, those symbols of the great war's pitiless compulsions would crackle in a ghostly way. So long as they drooped there it was an easy matter for guides and passers to be warned that the barriers were charged to kill.[4] In death the poor hunted Russians were still doing their bit for the Allies.

One night an intrepid French agent of espionage was returning in some haste from a tour of the industrial Rhineland and German chemical and munitions centers. He had been warned that a betrayer, a double spy, had denounced him; and that agents of the redoubtable Pinckoff, Germany's most feared counter-espionage chief, were trailing him to put a stop to his commercial pretenses and disguise. And then near the barrier—to add to his predicament—he encountered a dozen mud-stained Russian fugitives. He could not converse with them; but they all showed humbly that they saw in him a friend and ally and looked to him for leadership. He strove anxiously to make the group understand they must scatter, yet move in the direction that he indicated. Close to the wire a zone had been cleared by border guards; it provided no cover; and the only thing to do now was to run for it.

The spy gave the signal by starting, and the rest plunged after him. Instantly German patrols replied to the commotion by firing a volley. Bullets spattered among the escapers as they flung themselves down, flattened to the earth, the Russians instinctively pressing close to the foreign leader. A moving shaft of light suddenly illuminated the barbed and electrified wiring. A searchlight swept into action; and then a second, and a third. Groping white fingers spread right and left, reaching for the huddled group of men. The German rifle fire increased in volume as the powerful projectors combed over the ground. However, the French spy's confederates were battling for his safety from the Dutch side of the border; and there came to him distinctly the heartening report of a Winchester. A searchlight went out—one after another he extinguished them, that steady, invisible marksman with the fine American rifle.

A sound of shears clipping the wire could be heard as the firing died down. Alert passers, using shears with insulated glass handles, were cutting a path through the deadly barrier. Breaking the circuit thus set alarm gongs ringing in every post on the German side; but reserves could not be rushed to this point swiftly enough to close the gap and prevent the crossing. As he listened intently, the spy caught the direction of a signal he expected—the cry of the owl. Then up and away he bounded, closely followed by his devoted squad of Russians. Four of the latter were doomed to failure; German bullets laid them low. But the break-through of the eight others, conducted by the secret agent, when the whole frontier had been put on guard against him, is an excellent example of the audacity, co-operation and craft with which espionage operations of the Entente could be managed from the shelter of the neutral Netherlands.

By a kind of gentleman's agreement—in an underground duel unsuited to gentility—the Allies and the Germans were scrupulously careful to confine their espionage to each other. The least appearance of spying upon or intriguing against the Netherlands would have compromised the offending mission and presented its opponent with a long stride of unearned advantage.[5]

To make certain that their "neutrality" was at least maintained in this guise of private immunity, Intelligence officers of Holland set a close watch upon all of its country's conspiring visitors. They are even said to have kept themselves better informed about the machinations of British, French and German guests than any one of those belligerent camps was able to learn about its adversaries; which adroit referee supervision the intrigants of the warring great Powers seem at times to have welcomed, and to which they all very tamely submitted.

The vigilant German frontier guards and field police on the Belgian side of the border were strictly commanded not to violate the neutrality of the Netherlands; and many Belgians—though their fugitives, smugglers and secret operatives benefited from this—must often have wished the Teutonic lesson of respecting a small nation's sovereignty had been learned a little sooner.[6] Belgium, however, for all that it suffered the rigors of military occupation, was never really out of the fight and continued to hamper the Germans enormously as an observation ground for secret service behind the right flank of the German line in the West. Every conceivable stratagem was employed by the opposing forces, in moving or retarding the currents of combat intelligence. The tricks and artifices of "Alice Dubois" and her group had to be replaced as they became known; but a hundred boldly inventive successors kept raking the enemy from new and crafty ambuscades.

Let us turn back to the Dutch city of Maastricht in Limburg and see how its nearness to Belgium accommodated the espionage services of the Allies, how rigid German frontier regulations were simply and systematically flouted, and how the instrument of this defiance was an ordinary tramcar. Cars crossed the well-policed boundary there, rolling into Maastricht from various points in Belgium. And as soon as the first shock of invasion and conquest had passed, German officials began trying to promote an aspect of normalcy in what already seemed to them a permanently conquered province. They allowed the cars to resume their former international trips; and in the last two years of the war those cars regularly worked for the Allies' Intelligence. Belgian agents among the mechanics who kept the worn tramcars in running order attached tiny packets or summaries of spy reports to some hidden part of the mechanism. And in Maastricht a Dutch employee of the transit company was on the lookout for the packets. He received each week a substantial bonus for this slight extra labor, which broke the law of his own land and casually baffled the Germans.

A Partnership of Crime and Government

By their attitude of tolerance to both sides the Dutch authorities prevented many acts of provocation and violent crime which would have turned Holland into a secret-service battlefield. Burglary, kidnapping, blackmail and murder, instead of being the startling exception,[1] might have developed into a guerrilla conflict to change the course of events in northern Europe, divide the Netherlands, and add their rich colonies to the table stakes at Versailles.

This composed and rational state of affairs was not duplicated in Switzerland. There the warring espionage and counter-espionage services, French, British, Italian and, later, American against German and Austro-Hungarian, staged a melodrama that lacked nothing for operatic performance except a first-rate musical score. No holds were barred; and while regiments of agents and their hirelings seemed inextricably tangled in a night-and-day contest of gouging, throttling and stabbing in the back, more than a hundred on each side were arraigned by the Swiss, and either imprisoned or deported to the security of their own lands.

The higher military authorities of Switzerland were frankly pro-German,[8] which allowed most of the earlier conspiracies of the Entente a comfortable guise of counter-spying. The customary lavishness of secret-service expenditures was like a pulmotor to the war-afflicted hotel trade; and the majority of sane and thrifty Swiss were eager to hug the sidelines while rival spy teams followed the ball.

Some fear had been entertained from the days of the vast Teutonic preparations before Verdun that the conquerors of Belgium might grow desperate enough to try to turn the right flank of the French army at the price of an invasion of Switzerland. So perceptible after a while did this threat become that no less a strategist than Ferdinand Foch was assigned to work out a plan of mutual defense. The optimism of Foch and his virtual obsession for "attaque" had brought him into eclipse after the disastrous repulses of 1915 in Flanders; but in "Le plan H" this offensive fighter devised something "exquisite in its subtle simplicity"[9] for the sake of an elastic defensive.

When no German invasion concentrated upon Switzerland, "Le plan H"—more happily for the Germans even than the Swiss—went to waste. Perhaps some spy's report helped to discourage the staff strategists who thought the bracing tonic that the fatherland needed was another tough opponent. Whatever caused this sensible respect for Swiss neutrality or "Le plan H", the crisis inspiring that plan stemmed directly from a masterstroke of espionage—a raid upon the enemy conducted in behalf of Entente Intelligence with unbeatable underworld technique.

A notorious center of Austro-German conspiracy in Switzerland was burglarized by a Frenchman working for agents of Italy, with the primary result of safeguarding the Swiss, whose laws—like all laws—he cheerfully violated. The counter-spying raider was Baptistin Travail, a celebrity of Continental crime, who had even acquired a monarchical title after the fashion of leading industrialists in present-day republics. Europe's underworld knew him as "The King of the Alibis."

In 1911, having broken into the offices of the Messageries Maritimes and robbed the safe, he was able to establish in court that he had been playing billiards with a gendarme sergeant at the estimated hour of the crime. And after boarding and despoiling a locked car attached to the Calais-Brindisi express—and Baptistin is said to have *walked* the entire length of the railroad line from the French port to the Italian, selecting just the right point at which to perform his feat—he brazenly "proved" that he had been doctored that day in a clinic of Marseilles. King of the alibis—a major police problem of Western Europe in 1914—invaluable recruit of military secret service a year later!

The combatant governments without exception made use of known criminals or war-paroled convicts. How else could they maintain their output of forged passports and other counterfeit documents—including even prominent newspapers of an enemy country, as in the propaganda campaign before Caporetto—so necessary to the undercover pretenses of the struggle? But in the productive escapade of Baptistin Travail a criminal enterprise of greater violence and daring was turned loose upon an opponent.

While visiting his predatory talents upon Austria before the war Baptistin had become intimate with a shady individual keeping under cover, like himself, in the Viennese underworld. One day this comrade, an Italian, vanished abruptly; and the French craftsman lamented him briefly: "The *flics* must 've got hold of him!" However, their acquaintance was renewed unexpectedly late in 1915. The Italian was now wearing an officer's uniform with staff insigne; while Baptistin had come to Milan to avoid the double dragnets of police and compulsory military service, for which he had no appetite.

"So you were disguised in Vienna," he said.

The officer shrugged. "On duty. And I have not forgotten, Titin, how you helped me to hide. Now possibly I can make you some amende. These war times are bad for one in your line."

"I have not the capital to become a government contractor. That is the grand legal larceny."

"How would you like to come with me to Zurich?" the Italian Intelligence officer proposed. And over a bottle of wine the counterespionage transaction was concluded.

Baptistin and his friend went to Zurich, but only Baptistin went farther. It was he, this underworld magnifico, who contrived to break and enter, invading the headquarters of the notorious Herr Doktor Meyer, Teutonic propagandist and spy-master. Having boasted that he would break in and out with contemptuous ease, Baptistin took an artist's pains and jealously mantained his reputation and earned a handsome bonus. Avoiding the dangers of alarm bells and electrified door and floor traps, the intruder seems to have violated the desperate doctor's Swiss safe in nearly record time and swept it clean with the thundering finality of an avalanche. Except that Meyer and his conspirant accomplices in the house did not even catch an echo of the thunder! That was reserved for Austro-German espionage agents distributed over Italy.

It was rumored at the time that Meyer had kept such methodical lists of his budgeted disbursements, the Italian Secret Service came into sudden possession—through Baptistin's deftness—of a complete list of all the enemy spies on Italian soil. This no doubt may be suspended as the kind of thing war propagandists think up while falling asleep at night. Neither Meyer nor any other individual German or Austro-Hungarian spy-master harbored so comprehensive an espionage list in a single safe. Nevertheless, Baptistin's was obviously a grand coup, for we have this supporting testimony of Italian gratitude to prove the worth of his Zurich raid.

The story goes that this criminal's profitable engagement as an operative of counter-espionage did not induce him to reform; and yet that the military secret-service directors at Rome broke a record centuries old by generously remembering their obligation to the French rogue for his masterly crime. In 1923 Baptistin failed to clear himself with one more ingenious alibi. Being convicted at the Paris Assizes of a series of felonies, he was condemned to Cayenne for twenty years, a sentence carrying with it life exile from France. While he waited in the prison of St Martin-de-Ré for the ship that would remove him and other convicts to Guiana, an Italian officer of Intelligence learned of his disaster.

Urgent representations were made, so that presently the ambassador of Italy was appealing to the premier of France. Baptistin was pardoned because of notable "war-time services to an Ally"; which neighborly intervention came a few hours too late. The once invincible King of the Alibis had vowed never to suffer transportation to the penal rigors of Cayenne. And before the prison governor could send for him to tell him that again he was to go free, that his notorious luck still held, Baptistin assigned his debts to society by swallowing poison—a kind of ultimate alibi.

Fomenting Minorities

A favorite stratagem of the secret services during the World War was to try to stimulate rebellion in enemy areas known to have been restive or insurgent before the beginning of the conflict. Germany looked to the Irish for symptoms of civil war which, when it came, would have the menacing geographical relation to Britain of an ambuscade or stab in the back. Other Teutonic attempts of this nature were aimed far across the map, where Asiatic subjects of George V seemed ripe for a timely outbreak of imperial sabotage. Hindus and Moslems, however, were not lured very far along this chestnut-pulling path, even by the personal entreaties of Kaiser Wilhelm.

In the East there came into the possession of British Intelligence an autographed letter addressed by the Kaiser to the reigning princes of India. This urgent and incendiary document had been photographed down to a size not greatly larger than an ordinary postage stamp. It was carried inclosed in a tiny waterproof tube which could be concealed very easily; and it was expected to have a devastating effect. Persia would rise, and then the most barbaric of the Afghans, threatening India, raiding the outposts of the empire. But the letter is now only remembered because of the ingenuity of its transmission.

A backward glance with present-day perspective suggests that the German Secret Service missed its most propitious opportunity in Ireland. The Irish were seasoned shouters of "God strike England!" before either *Gott* or *Wotan* had to hearken to the phrase. The Irish had a political grievance that was old when the Hohenzollerns were mere robber barons, living up to their high-tariff cognomen. And the Irish were world-famous brawlers, rioters, mercenaries and soldiers of fortune, likewise possessing a stout tradition of rebellion from Tyrone, the great insurgent of Elizabeth's reign, through Drogheda, the Boyne, Robert Emmet and the Fenians. Germany had actually counted upon hostilities in Ireland to distract the British in July–August 1914, but when Ulster and the Catholic South suppressed their incipient civil war, the German General Staff and Secret Service allowed themselves—not unreasonably—to be distracted to other theaters where Albion-haters seemed more accessible.

The familiar, tragic story of Roger Casement need not be reported here, save as a prime example of the kind of secret service that *did not occur,* but which complacent members of the German General Staff mistook for aggressive fomentations. Casement, to his credit, perhaps, seems to have had little of that Irish aptitude for espionage, deception and betrayal which we have noted in Leonard MacNally and other Irishmen more profitably disposed to frustrate Irish rebellion. But even a more masterly intriguer could not have gone far along the road of German co-operation. Captain Nadolny and other General Staff and Intelligence officers with whom Casement negotiated were severely practical. Germany wanted a rebellion in Ireland but did not value it as highly as, for example, the sinking of the Lusitania. One cannot but reflect upon the relative impact on Great Britain of six months' unrestricted submarine warfare and the same amount of German expenditure in money, belligerent enthusiasm, discipline and technical experience conferred upon the insurgents of Ireland. A serious civil war in a hard-pressed combatant's back yard puts more instant pressure upon morale than isolated ship sinkings, however numerous.

Roger Casement appears to have nourished many delusions but never one which magnified the Irish "alliance" with Germany. When finally they got rid of him, and he was being put off from the submarine in a collapsible boat, the captain asked the conspirator what clothes he wanted; and Casement answered: "Only my shroud." The Germans were, of course, making a considerable show of keeping their engagements. The Aud, a small steamer, was at sea with 1400 tons of munitions hidden under a deck cargo of lumber. On being captured and while being escorted to Queenstown, the German naval ratings aboard the Aud blew up their craft and took to the boats. A British diver was sent down to investigate the character of this mysterious and sunken vessel, for the German Secret Service bargain with Casement was, of course, still unknown. The diver brought up half-a-dozen sample rifles from among those which were to have been bestowed upon the Irish insurrection. They seemed, apart from their recent brief emersion, "much the worse for wear," and they had Russian marks upon them. The German Secret Service was fomenting its greatest chance to stab Britain in the back by giving away the old Russian rifles captured at Tannenberg.

In not dissimilar circumstances the secret operations of the Allies met with uncommon success in lending aid to beleaguered Czech nationalism lodged though it was in a landlocked country, surrounded by Teutonic populations and involved in a desperate war. Those early agitations of the future Czechoslovakia were not promoted with venerable firearms. However, the Czech leaders—Professor Masaryk, Beneš, and their comrades—were the sort of insurgents any group or government honored itself by assisting. They were sincere and disinterested patriots, intellectuals yet of realistic persuasion, and they were men of sterling character.

CHAPTER EIGHTY-ONE

CAPORETTO: THE PERFECT SURPRISE ATTACK

AFTER SUCH GREAT VICTORIES in 1914 as Joffre's at the Marne, the Russians' before Lemberg, and the Germans' at Tannenberg, the various army leaders all began diligently organizing that dreadful business of wearing each other out. And what they produced was a hitherto impossible, oil-and-water mixture of massacre and stagnation, the development of the artillery barrage and a deep religious faith in frontal attack. The strategy of surprise was virtually discarded in the West until Caporetto, October 25, 1917. There were earlier surprises, but these were suffered by commanders in chief when their plans did not miscarry.

General Maximilian Ronge, director of the Austrian "K.S.", has written that every major attack in the World War was tipped off to the enemy well in advance by enterprising secret agents.[1] But what high command would condescend to heed a mere espionage operative? Intelligence itself was often treated as a stepchild at general headquarters; while spies and all their work were so consistently snubbed and mistrusted, no advance warning ever received in time was seriously acted upon. Ronge speaks with the authority of one whose spies' value must frequently have been questioned, yet he was also a chief beneficiary of this same obtuse attitude toward Intelligence reports when it afflicted his Italian foes. He has described the responsibilities and anxieties of his colleagues and himself at A.O.K.[2] in the days before Caporetto. It seemed that the Italian high command *must* have received innumerable warnings about the surprise assault which its opponent had in preparation.

Yet his own offensive espionage summaries told him nothing of any perceptible activity on the part of Count Cadorna or his generals. Capello, commanding the Second Army, had posted only two battalions to the mile on the fifteen-mile frontage of the Caporetto sector, compared with eight to the mile farther south. The very fact that this had long been such a quiet sector, where both sides sent divisions to "rest", ought to make the Italian chiefs suspicious. That thought danced before the eyes of Ronge and his aides. Not that there was anything more to be done about it. All possible secrecy had thus far been maintained by an ironclad framework of protective counter-spying. If any Italian agents were still getting through, what sublime affectation made Cadorna's headquarters so tranquil?

Every man who sets a cunning trap comes to that moment when he ponders deeply whether he himself may not get caught in it. Ronge drove his counter-spies hard; ever more urgent questionnaires were delivered to his agents lodged near the Italian zone of combat; if some defensive thrust were being arranged over there, where would it develop its strength? We know now that Cadorna had full warning of his enemies' intentions but did nothing. Agents of the Italian secret service reported the danger. And deserters—Czech and Transylvanian officers—delivered even more ample information. While from allies in France there came to Italy's commanding general a broad hint of the forces gathering to threaten his cloistered calm.

American agents in Switzerland at that time took note of how much they heard of the "coming German attack." Germans themselves were spreading these rumors; and confusion was clearly their aim. By careful checking it was discovered that there was just one vulnerable spot in all Europe to which no wild rumor assigned an impending attack: the Julian Alps front of the Italian Second Army. "Find out what it is they want us to think," an American staff colonel directed, "and find out why!" A few days later the Americans in Switzerland produced this bulletin—ultimately proved correct:

The Austrians are preparing with German help a great offensive against Italy. They will use propaganda to discourage the Italian troops, and expect the best results.

Entente Intelligence treated it as a very dubious commodity. The Americans were gullible amateurs and outsiders, inclined to spend money too freely in gathering information, while lacking the necessary tradition and experience for *European* secret-service work. Which did not prevent a second and more urgent bulletin speeding from Switzerland a day or two later:

The Germans and Austrians intend to prevent British, French, or American reserves being sent to the aid of Italy after their big attack. At the moment their offensive is launched, spies will blow up the Mt. Cenis tunnel through which troop trains would have to come to the Italian front from France.

For evident reasons American Intelligence has never elected to tell how its agents in Switzerland learned of these perils. However, the second bulletin, together with American officers' insistence that their informants were reliable, made the veteran partners shake their heads and wonder. Both French and Italian guards were doubled, tightening up the supervision of the Alpine railroad line. Then, in the thick mud of Flanders, while on patrol in no man's land, a British corporal spotted a picture post card. Being curious he picked it up, and being a good soldier, he turned it in. There was nothing much to see—a view of a quaint old town in the Austrian Alps, sent to a German private in the line in Flanders by another soldier, who wrote: "We are getting a much needed rest here in Austria." The sender signed himself only "Heinrich" but obliged by adding a military postal number.

British Intelligence readily identified "Heinrich" as belonging to the noted Alpine Corps of the German Army,[3] which had made such a splendid record in the annihilating campaign against Roumania under the command of General Krafft von Delmensingen. And why should these crack troops be resting *in Austria,* except by way of getting ready for the very offensive that Americans had been predicting via Lucerne? The Allies' whole system of Intelligence was now quick with alarm. Heinrich's postal, which was undated, must have been out there in the Flemish mud for days. By the time its import was generally conceded—October 23—it was too late to prepare Cadorna to withstand the onslaught. General Ronge had worried about being able to keep the secret from all the Allies; but on the morning of October 25 the Austro-German attack retained every attribute of a complete and overwhelming surprise.

Combatant Secret Service

The Italians had been attacking during August and September 1917, and, though the gain in grounds was not large, the influence upon the war-weariness of the Austro-Hungarian Empire was prodigious. General Ludendorff has written that the "responsible military and political authorities" of his tottering ally were convinced they could not sustain a continuation of the battle on the Isonzo. Therefore "in the middle of September it became necessary to decide for the attack on Italy in order to prevent the collapse of Austria-Hungary."[4]

On August 29 Waldstätten of the Austrian General Staff approached the German high command with a scheme for a break-through at Tolmino, to be followed moderately by "rolling up" the Italian front. Major Wetzell, Ludendorff's strategical adviser, was of the opinion that, though only the German army's general reserve—now but six divisions—could be spared for this enterprise, the forward thrust of even that comparatively small force at an ill-defended sector would suffice for a season to extinguish the Italian offensive.

General Krafft von Delmensingen, considered Germany's leading expert in mountain warfare, was now sent on a special mission of reconnaissance in the Julian Alps. He reported that the Austrians had contrived to hold on to a small bridgehead on the west bank of the Isonzo at Tolmino. This would provide the necessary jumping-off point for the projected surprise attack. Guns could be brought up mostly by hand and at night, and the infantry by seven night marches, taking no vehicles, but carrying their necessary ammunition, supplies and equipment on pack animals or on the men themselves.

Undiscovered by the Italians, twelve assault divisions—six Austrian in addition to the German reserves contributed by O.H.L.—and 300 batteries were thus concentrated under the command of General Otto von Below, with Krafft von Delmensingen as chief of staff and guiding genius. These troops were to drive against the mountain barrier while two Austrian armies, commanded by General Boroevic, were to advance along the stretch of lower ground near the Adriatic shore. The "soft spot" between Canale and Flitsch had only to give way before Von Below's assault to dislocate the whole Italian front.

Some military authorities have held that the German and Austro-Hungarian leaders were themselves surprised on the Isonzo by the extravagance of their success. This may well be; but every foot of the way leading to the pinnacle of victory had been brilliantly planned and prepared, and the resulting "knockout" was well deserved. There are many rival instances of the war's belatedly resurrected tactics of surprise—Riga, Cambrai or Rawlinson's superb stroke with the British Fourth Army on the eighth of August 1918, Germany's "black day"[3]—but Caporetto is included here as the most perfect modern example of surprise attack because more than any other it combined sound strategical judgment and thorough military preparations with an extraordinary application of combatant secret service.

In the offensive as well as the usual defensive branches, Intelligence made an invaluable contribution. Espionage and counter-espionage, censorship and propaganda, all were adroitly mobilized. Agents of the "K.S." for weeks prior to the battle had been gathering information about the critical state of affairs in northern Italy. Civil disturbances had broken out there; and the most severe rioting, in Turin, had not been suppressed until the populace was fired upon, with loss of life. Spies reported the names and addresses of those slain in the streets and collected such other details of the turbulence as would be unmistakably convincing to any resident of Turin or the neighboring districts of Piedmont.

Talented hands then set to work, manufacturing copies of several of the best-known Italian newspapers. Printed on Austrian presses, they were an artistic triumph of counterfeiting, carrying front-page stories of the recent collisions and bloodshed at Turin. No censor's pencil had cut across their blunt and terrible reality. Lists of the killed and injured were prominently set forth—the same lists that Italian papers had been refused the right to publish for home consumption. Editorial comment, caustic and uncensored, added to the reader's impression that virtual anarchy now reigned behind the Italian front.

No better soldiers than the Piedmontese were to be found in Italian uniform; they rated as shock troops and held many key positions which must be overwhelmed if the surprise of Caporetto was to attain enveloping dimensions. And so enemy battleplanes showered down bundles of the propaganda papers—apparently genuine, familiar type face, of recent issue, and utterly poisonous to morale. That matter of the date alone was a minor stroke of genius. General Ronge's lieutenants did not fall into the trap of dating the papers too recently, but so estimated it that they must appear to be the real article, just old enough to have been obtained in Italy and smuggled into Austria.

With naturally eager interest the fighting men of Piedmont read what was happening at home. The effect was electrical. While they were shedding their blood for Italy, it seemed that their kinsfolk were being ridden down, sabered and shot by stay-at-home Italians —mounted police and *carabinieri*—because the people were sick of the war, because they were hungry and in want, because they dared to protest. Most of this came to a head on the twenty-third and twenty-fourth, and next morning in a drizzle of snow and rain, after four hours' gas shell and one hour's general bombardment, Von Below's so-called Fourteenth German Army attacked.

General Capello had refused an appeal from the exposed left wing of his Second Army for reinforcements. He was sick in bed but would not yield to that threat, either, declining to go to a hospital and resign the command of his front until the day after it had ceased to exist. In spite of Von Below's spearhead of German reserves, the Italians still outnumbered their adversaries by seven to four; which superiority only made the narrow mountain roads the more impassably congested with troops who were beaten and ready to submit to it.[8] Count Cadorna lost nearly 600,000 men, about equally divided between casualties and prisoners. And for two critical days—October

30 and 31—even this appalling disaster seemed on the verge of being dwarfed. The Central Powers' drive attempted to capture the crossings of the Tagliamento; but this audacious effort suffered such hindrances as were bound to develop from the increasing friction between German and Austrian commanders.

Preceded by General Foch and Sir Henry Wilson, reluctantly spared French and British reserve divisions[7] began arriving behind the Italian defensive line which, on November 10, was fixed at the river Piave. The Austrian Tenth and Eleventh Armies, commanded by Conrad von Hötzendorf, now sought to move down from the Trentino upon the Italians' rear. But for this strategy Cadorna had been prepared; and when Ludendorff proved slow in deciding to transfer his German reinforcement to Conrad's front, the ultimate danger ebbed away. Diaz succeeded Cadorna;[8] the Italian army recovered from its panic; and the reforged defenses at the line of the Piave held firm.

Chapter Eighty-two

FRENCH OPERATIVES IN THE SECRET WAR

A CRIMINAL may be recruited for a secret-service mission when the exigencies of warfare or elastic morality of politics require an officer of government to resort to underworld practices. No espionage expert worth his weight in codebooks, however, will regularly employ underworld characters in gathering vital intelligence. Contrary, perhaps, to far-spread opinion, the genuine "ace" of espionage has to possess most, if not all, of the qualifications prerequisite to civilian or military eminence. If his courage and integrity are not above question, his chief dare not rely upon him in the midst of a national crisis.

The secret agent must not only be loyal but unselfish; he must refrain from boastful talk or any other form of intemperance. He must be as truthful and emotionally stable as he is resolute, resourceful or alert. And besides all that, the agent on active duty has to be able to sustain great loneliness of spirit. His is a peculiar calling. Though he may not trust anyone, he often must persuade individuals of no little shrewdness to have faith in him. He has constantly to exercise discretion while surmounting that most wearing test of the normal man or woman—physical, mental and spiritual isolation.

The secret agent has to do most of his work singlehanded. He is a combatant, risking his life repeatedly, yet he is no soldier. In the crisis of *his* battles he will seldom find himself fighting shoulder to shoulder with even one comrade—save infrequently in extended cases of counter-espionage—and never with a company, regiment or division to sustain him. After being given instructions, he is sent forth and is thereafter absolutely on his own. If he fails, his government must repudiate him. His colleagues are expected to deny that they ever have heard of him. If in time of war and he is caught, he is a spy and liable to be hanged or shot.

Balancing the risks, obscurity and want of fair rewards, the wide and contemptuous misunderstanding of the profession of espionage, against the undoubted talents and character which the true "ace" of military secret service must own, one well may ask why anybody having such prime qualifications elects to hazard his very life upon such an unfavored gamble? And may ask, again—why the neglect and frustrations are never wholly eliminated from the gamble, why these gifted operatives are enlisted only to be used ineffectually, out of all proportion to the overtaxing reliance upon other—and no more promising—combatant arms?

France, as we have noted, will yield to none in the severity of discipline, distortions of merit, or savage ingratitude which may be lavished upon the faithful secret agent. Yet when the World War pushed France toward the abyss, Military Intelligence at Paris and G.Q.G., Chantilly, could call upon such patriotic, masterly operatives as a Joseph Crozier,[1] Georges Ladoux,[2] Marthe Richer, Lucieto, Waegele and many more.

Charles Lucieto was successful as a practitioner of both spying and counter-spying; and it is probably on account of the comparative repute of the latter that he has been allowed a certain measure of credit for the former. At least one exploit of his in offensive secret service belongs among the distinguished annals of military espionage. This French agent, in Teutonic guise, was sent to study the making of German munitions, then largely concentrated in the industrial Rhineland. He found the great plant of Krupp at Essen a well-guarded city devoted to the manufacture of heavy ordnance, high-explosive shell, shrapnel and other basic war material. Elsewhere German chemical works were also running night and day. The *Badische Anilin und Soda Fabrik* of Mannheim was to chemical manufacture what Krupp was to cannon; and chemicals might mean a new poison gas.

Now at Ypres on April 22, 1915, the German command had instigated the suffocating novelty of chemical warfare—which in two decades has become a commonplace dread of Europeans. The first gas used, a chlorine compound, was ejected from metal tanks brought up with attempted secrecy to the Flanders front.[3] It drifted over to the line of the Allies in a cloud, and two French divisions gave way. As they broke before this unaccustomed offensive weapon, they left the Canadians with their flank "in the air." Gas choked Canadian and British throats also, but the courage and obstinacy of the empire's soldiers stopped the Prussian Guard and saved the front.

Belatedly improvised masks were issued to the troops. But subsequent attempts at gas-cloud surprise met with literally the reverse of success, the German innovators having neglected to note that westerly or southwesterly wind was most frequent in Flanders. When an abruptly shifting breeze turned pro-Ally, the awful opalescent mist eddied back upon the German attackers, leaving hundreds of the

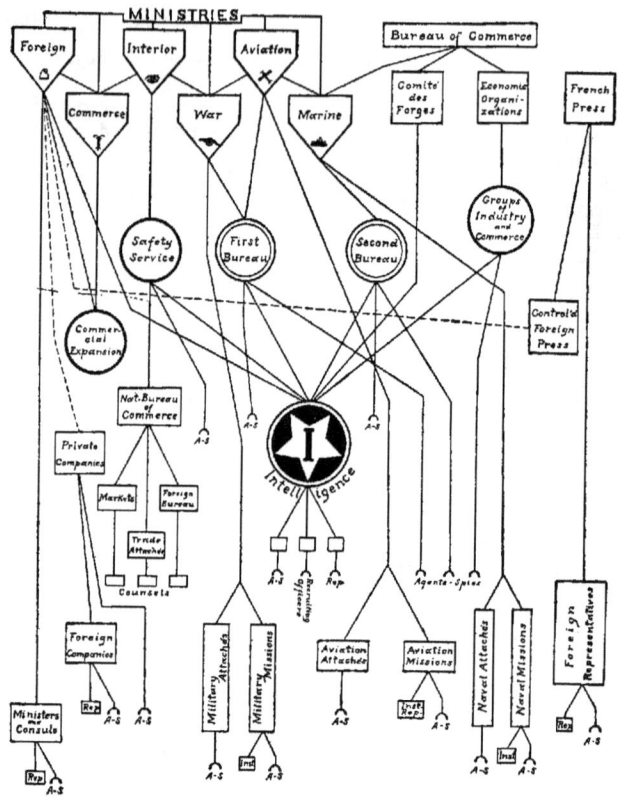

A German interpretation of the influence and operation of the French Intelligence in time of war. While this foreign design may seem to magnify the importance of government and military secret service in France, it is at least discreet in omitting reference to that bureau from which evidence condemning and disgracing innocent persons has in times past been put forth sensationally.

Kaiser's men to writhe and perish in agony, with foam-flecked, swollen lips and greenish, stricken faces.

Gas clouds soon went out of fashion as a serious menace. But what might come next in that line? Lucieto at Mannheim resolved to get his bureau chief an answer so definite, so conclusive that even a scientifically hidebound General Staff could not ignore its implications.

$$\frac{Service\ and}{Financial\ Dependence}$$

$$\frac{Financial}{Influence}$$

$$\frac{Official}{Positions}\ \square$$

$$\frac{Secret}{Positions}\ \complement$$

A - Agents

I - Instructors

R - Representatives

S - Spies

Key to design of French Intelligence organization

Gas Shells at Essen

A second visit to Mannheim convinced the Frenchman that neither chlorine nor any other asphyxiating gas was there being concentrated in tanks small enough for transport to the battle line. Yet he discovered many tank cars rolling away from the great chemical works. Where did they go, and why? No sooner had he satisfied himself on this score than his anxieties and peril increased. The tank cars went to the Krupp plant at Essen. And so the secret agent turned back to Essen, which was peculiarly dangerous ground for any operative of the Allies, for the Germans' counter-spying network was nowhere stronger than as a cordon on guard around Krupp's.

By hanging about the cafés where master mechanics of the famous arms factory spent much of their leisure, by treating to beer, the spy learned a good deal from the gossip of the Krupp workers. Then as a product of his luck and genius he seized an opportunity to make a friend of an elderly special policeman at the plant and displayed such enthusiasm for the old chap's tedious discourse, they spent long hours together. Thus in time Lucieto heard about a wonderful experiment impending—with the new gas shells. Poison gas in shells? To be discharged from an ordinary field gun? Impossible!

Affecting a blend of patriotic German hopes and thick-witted incredulity, the spy offered the policeman a bet at inviting odds. There *could* be gas loaded in regular Krupp shells—there soon would be gas shells, the policeman insisted, and he could prove it. How? Let him proceed to do so, and it would earn him a cool two thousand marks.

In order to win the money the policeman had to agree to take his friend, who posed as a commercial traveler, to witness with him the official testing of the remarkable new projectiles. The pair found an obscure but favorable point of observation and presently watched while a great fleet of military motorcars rolled up, delivering Kaiser Wilhelm himself, a glittering staff and many notables to the vast open field or artillery range where the exhibition was scheduled to occur.

A guard of honor presented arms, a band played, then a .77 field gun and a larger naval gun were prepared for the experiment. Their target was a flock of sheep, on a slope some twelve hundred meters distant. The field gun fired, its shell exploding with a light, thudding report, very different from the customary burst of shrapnel. Then the naval gun was discharged. Neither of the two shells exploded directly upon the grazing flock, but after each burst a cloud of yellow-green smoke arose and was blown toward the sheep. It seemed to cover them like a veil; and when it drifted away nothing alive remained near where they had been. Even the grass looked burnt, and the earth also, as if covered with rust.

"It's immense—it will win the war!" said the policeman, pocketing the wager the spy promptly handed him. "Isn't it colossal?"

"*Ja! Kolossal!*" murmured Lucieto.

Already the ornate throng of observers and invited guests was dispersing. And the French spy said:[4] "That's a lot of money for me to lose, but I'm not sorry! This great new invention of German science is going to finish the accursed French and English. But I still don't understand how they get the gas into the shells."

"No one knows that, except the special workmen who make them."

"Oh, of course not! But listen, old man, would you have any objection if I hunted around and found a piece of one of those shells, so I could keep it as a remembrance of this unforgettable day?"

"I don't see why you shouldn't. All the same I think it would be better if I went out there myself and picked it up," said the Krupp plant policeman; and that was what he was kind enough to do. A small fragment of one of the first gas shells ever loaded for use in battle was smuggled out of the Essen area by the secret agent and only three days later delivered by him to his superiors in Paris, who hurried it to the laboratory of a celebrated chemist.[5] The sole defense which could be made ready immediately was a greatly improved gas mask for the Allies' combat forces of the Western Front. But also—for that attack which is "the best defense"—the French and British bestirred themselves to manufacture gas shells of their own. And one more enormity, expressly forbidden by the Hague conventions and the so-called "laws" of civilized warfare, was added by general use to the legitimatized horrors of war.

Few espionage missions have illustrated so perfectly the threefold procedure of the spy: (1) to locate the most valued and reliable information; (2) to obtain it, and proofs if possible, without being discovered; and (3) to transmit quickly to a superior whatever has been obtained, while leaving the adversary in ignorance of his loss, so that what has been learned or secured will not be impaired by his alarmed alteration of his program.

Spying upon the Long-Range Gun

The complexity of the war in Europe—so many nations mobilized, so much propaganda and government intrigue, such variety of attack and defense—served to confuse the work of spy and counter-spy, often reversing their normal objectives. Spies on duty in an enemy's country were sometimes needed to help unmask particularly daring agents of that enemy; while operatives of counter-espionage were compelled by an emergency to go after information behind the enemy's front.

It was on Sunday, the twenty-fourth of March 1918, that the Germans opened fire on Paris with their long-range cannon. At once a wave of excitement spread over the city, for it seemed that the latest Teutonic offensive—uncomfortably close at sixty miles' distance the day before—had driven forward with such incredible velocity that heavy guns had now been brought up to within twelve or fifteen miles of the fortifications. An uncommonly candid statement from the government promptly dispelled that fear. Though one of its first shells registered upon a church filled with praying women and children, this biggest of all the Big Berthas, created at the Krupp plant, was described as purely an instrument of "frightfulness", typically German, but having no practical military value.

The French communiqué might have outranged all others in truthfulness by explaining that as long before as 1888 a French secret-service operative, stopping off at Essen, had come away with the original, primitive plan of such a long-range rifle. This ordnance expert's dream fantasy had been left neglected in a secret Intelligence file. Yet those shells which were dropping indiscriminately upon churches and hospitals, parks, public edifices, shops and dwellings not only traversed an unprecedented range of seventy miles from cannon to target but also had been thirty years on their way.

At G.Q.G. there were troubled experts swiftly mobilizing against Krupp's unbelievable monster. The *service de renseignement artillerie* was the agency responsible for combating ordnance innovations of the enemy, a new and special branch of the army devoted to both spying and counter-spying as each might relate to artillery. Volunteers were called for, and of more than seventy men who offered themselves five expert counter-spies were selected. Planes took them over the lines that night to land them by parachute in adjacent sectors forming an imaginary triangle, delimited by the towns La Fère, Coucy-le-Château and Anizy-le-Château. Within this triangle intermittent yet unmistakable detonations of the new cannon had been detected, partly by intensive aerial reconnaissance, partly by means of the latest sound-ranging devices.[6]

Anticipating these very measures, German artillerists were endeavoring to conceal the direction of Frau Bertha Krupp von Bohlen's far-crying namesake. At intervals they set off blanks, designed to reverberate like the real gun, but exploding miles away from its secret emplacement. Even so, a few hours after the first shells came crashing upon Paris, specialists had come to an agreement in plotting the suspected triangular zone. And now the five counter-spies were ready at dead of night to start closing in on the weapon. Two of the five returned successfully in a week's time. Another was shot and killed and the fourth wounded in an air raid, but without suffering detection as a spy. The fifth discovered that he could not meet the plane due to carry him back to Chantilly and so made his choice, escaping overland to the frontier of Holland, but not before he had submitted a complete report upon the long-range gun by carrier pigeon.

As soon as the gun's position at the edge of the forest of St Gobain was determined, and the five secret-service men accounted for, bombing planes and front-line batteries isolated the district in a hurricane of high explosives. That the gun could be moved was confirmed by the reports of the spies; and so heavy shell and bombs continually raked the triangular zone.

However, there were dummy guns implanted in the forest region, regularly camouflaged with nets and "foliage" to trick the air-camera's eye. And as several of the giant rifles had been manufactured at Essen, one of them could always maintain the harassing, long-range fire. It was never possible completely to silence Big Bertha, in spite of the combined efforts of gunners, observers, pilots of heavy bombers, sound-rangers and spies. The mighty Krupp had to be fired "off the map", or wholly by mathematical calculations. The Germans, when they discharged it, never knew what section, if any, of Paris they were registering upon; and days before the "Bertha" shells began dropping out of the sky, agents of Germany were organized to report daily upon the hits, casualties, property damage and impact on morale of the long-range bombardment.

After the defeatism and mutinies of 1917, the French were pardonably sensitive on the score of shaken morale; and they are, moreover, especially alert where the glamor and repute of Paris are at stake. Adding considerably, therefore, to the natural hazards of espionage in their capital, it was decided by the French government to recruit flying squads of repair men, who could be sent immediately to the scene of a shell burst, remove debris, relay paving, and do all else possible to erase the scars of the enemy's haphazard bull's-eye. Sometimes they completely restored a damaged street or building to its former outward appearance within five or six hours. Even so handicapped, the spies contrived to locate most of the hits scored from the distance of St Gobain. Colonel Nicolai relates that he was regularly in receipt of comprehensive intelligence covering the areas struck and all results of the indirect shelling; and a woman spy, Ida Kall, seems to have been chiefly credited with obtaining and transmitting this information.

A Headquarters Spy

The French do not trouble to deny her successes over a long and perilous tour of duty. They realized that all the spies could never be eliminated from a city so cosmopolitan as Paris and mainly strove to keep them away from confidential matters of military or political importance.

Not to be outdone, the French Intelligence was served by at least one eminently well-placed spy, stationed at German O.H.L.[7] right through the war. This agent acted as a commissioner of field police and gave such a good account of himself as a diligent, alert official, he was transferred each time that the headquarters *entourage* moved, from Charleville to Stenay, to Kreuznach and Pless. It was Waegele's ironic assignment to guard the Supreme Command from the plotting or mere observation of enemy agents. Now it is difficult to estimate the worth of a spy so located and impossible to imagine the tedious, subtle means by which he must have attained his position. On the way Herr—or Monsieur—Waegele could not afford to make even one slight blunder. He had to be more efficient than the ablest of his loyal German colleagues in the imperial police service. He had to observe the utmost caution in his personal life, being careful about the friendships he formed, and yet just as careful not to appear odd or unsociably inclined. He must have had to be extremely resourceful also in steering a course through the shoals and rapids of national or international politics. Conflicting German influences might entangle him; while enthusiasm for, or even unusual interest in, the affairs of France was likely to betray him.

At the same time, he dared not borrow the cheap mask of hostility toward France for his secret career in Germany as a French agent. Keen minds enlisted in counter-espionage are rightly disposed to mistrust fanatics. And a man like Waegele, rising steadily through every grade of the police service, who seemed rabidly anti-anything would have focused upon himself a searching investigation. Why did he hate the French?—what had they done to him?—had a French girl jilted him, a French firm cheated him?—had he ever lived in France, collided with the law there, or in a French colony, without having hitherto admitted it? Somewhere along these lines of inquiry the tiny clue or trace of espionage would have been found. Master spies never worry about big blunders, for history tells them it is small slips, the nearly unnoticeable flaws which lead to destruction.

As for the wartime accomplishments of Waegele at the German headquarters, not much is known save that he tipped off most of the major Teutonic offenses, both West and East. In all probability the total gains from his espionage would seem out of proportion to the danger and tension he endured or the apparent excellence of his opportunities. Communicative hazards were an habitual impediment; he could only be insured against certain death before a firing squad by screening his channels of communication with an intricate cunning bound to cause critical delays. In May 1918 when Hindenburg-Ludendorff and their specialist aides of the German General Staff were preparing the great thrust at Duchêne's Sixth French Army,[8] Waegele found out all about it, and did not underestimate the danger. "Big attack coming May 27 on the Chemin-des-Dames" was the accurate warning he sent through. But the Sixth Army was not saved, for the French Secret Service got the warning to Chantilly ten days too late.[9]

Chapter Eighty-three

THE CENSOR IN SECRET SERVICE

ONE GLOOMY DAY in the first winter of the war a British postal censor sat at his desk, examining papers and parcels going to neutral countries. He came to a newspaper bearing an Amsterdam address which he found on his up-to-date copy of the Suspect List. And when this paper had been closely inspected and revealed no perceptible ink or pencil mark of an enemy code or cipher, it was hurried off to undergo the usual tests for secret writing. Evidences of furtive communication at once developed. Written in the margin of the newspaper in an ordinary grade of chemical ink were a few words of English. The writer was seeking to report that "C" had gone "into the north" and that he was "sending from 201." The newspaper bore the postmark of Deptford.

Not much here to begin with, one might say—but no counter-spy would say it, for this case offers a perfect example of the censor as an agent of "front-line" counter-espionage. There was the location, Deptford, the number, "201", and "C" up in the north probably attempting to spy upon the Grand Fleet or the North Sea patrol. An inspector from New Scotland Yard, assigned to the case as though "C" were just any thief or forger, first rang up the police in Deptford. What about "201", he wanted to know; how many streets of the town reached that high a number on dwellings or places of business?

"Only one, Inspector," came the answer, "Deptford High Street." Visiting No. 201 High Street in Deptford practically solved the counter-spying problem. Deptford, where three hundred and twenty-two years before the fatal, mysterious stabbing of that great young poet and secret agent, Kit Marlowe, had occurred, was now to furnish the trap for a pair of German agents, one of them really dangerous.

At No. 201 detectives from the Yard found Peter Hahn, "baker and confectioner", a naturalized British subject. He assured them stolidly that—no, he never wrote anything on the margin of a newspaper, and, no, he positively never mailed anything to Amsterdam nor knew anybody who might be referred to as "C." When his shop was searched, however, an old shoe box turned up, harboring a vial of invisible ink and the necessary ball-pointed pen for writing with that kind of fluid. And since the rotund little baker still refused to confess, he was tucked away in a cell in London.

Inquiries in Deptford soon answered many of the questions Peter Hahn had greeted with obstinate silence. His neighbors remembered a friend who had often called upon him, a man of distinguished bearing, tall, well dressed, who had been thought to be a Russian. The district register of all of London's boardinghouses was now laboriously consulted. The determined counter-spies thus narrowed their hunt down to Bloomsbury where a troubled landlady, acknowledging the description of her guest, said that his name was Müller, that he was a Russian, and lately had gone on private business to Newcastle-on-Tyne. There had been no mistake—"C" *was* in the north.

Detectives were on watch in the Northumberland port when Müller boarded a train and easily recognized him from the description. Taken into custody and returned to London, he was discovered to be an accomplished secret agent with much technical naval information at his command. As he had traveled about Great Britain he had been picking up all manner of odds and ends of intelligence wanted by the German Admiralty. And since his trick of transmitting his findings was strikingly new, the spy might for months have remained at work and defied detection—but for the acuteness of that postal censor in spotting Peter Hahn's clumsy helpfulness. The newspaper detected, and many others dispatched by Müller himself, carried the spy's ingenious code. He merely inserted advertisements in British provincial papers—rooms to let, articles for sale, books wanted—according to a prearranged plan, and mailed the papers to various "cover" addresses in neutral cities.

Almost the standard type of professional international spy, Müller had been born in Libau and, before the outbreak of the World War, had been rover, speculator, glib promoter of abortive schemes and partnerships, as well as romantic but inconstant lover. His successes with impressionable young women were not hard to understand, for he was polished and well educated, speaking English without a trace of accent and five other languages as fluently. Owing to the place of his birth he could claim to be Russian. He was, however, a genuine cosmopolite; and his "looking" Russian was only the simple and useful disguise of strange aloofness. It probably spared him answering foolish questions, but at the end it helped the counter-spies to trace him.

Blundering Peter Hahn, regarded as Müller's dupe and tool, had agreed to help because of his dire need of money. Two years before the little Deptford baker had been bankrupt, with assets of three pounds and liabilities of eighteen hundred pounds. By aiding the German Secret Service he had prospered anew. As a naturalized British subject his crime was a form of high treason, and his sentence of seven years' imprisonment seems to have been uncommonly merciful.

Müller, treated as an agent of German espionage, was condemned at his trial and went to face a firing squad in the Tower of London. As for the codes so cleverly initiated in his newspaper advertising, they were finally determined by the craftsmen of "Room 40 O.B." at the Admiralty, where a solvent for all kinds of mystifying secrets was found. And after his execution officers of the Intelligence kept on inserting ads, composed according to the spy's various code terms, sending out false information to deceive the enemy, while collecting the sums of money forwarded to Müller from time to time.[1] About four hundred pounds in wages came to England before this new campaign of espionage was discovered to be worthless by the spy-masters of Antwerp, whereupon "Müller" was informed that he had been discharged from their service. By having dealt in Müller's stead with his methodical paymasters, British Intelligence could warn every censor to be on the lookout for similar sums of money at similar intervals coming to the same addressee from a neutral "firm" in some Dutch, Swiss, Danish or Spanish city.

The Unluckiest Spy

Their early success in the case of Hahn and Müller encouraged the censors of Great Britain to greater prodigies of industry and eyestrain —if that were possible—in pursuit of further intimations of espionage. And the only other instance of censorship allied to counter-spying which may be given here, while an equally important stroke of defensive secret service, is also a collector's item as an example of one man's unspeakable ill luck. No blunder of a dupe or clumsy accomplice laid this German spy by the heels. Robert Rosenthal was devoured by his own voracious destiny.

He had been born in Magdeburg twenty-two years before the outbreak of hostilities, had become a baker's apprentice and turned from that to forgery. A nondescript sort of semiprofessional crook and rolling stone, he had only been liberated from the German prison to take up espionage. And as we wade the length of this Mississippi, this Volga of a sewer, up to our necks in episodes of human frailty, corruption and deceit, it is cheering to distinguish the childlike faith of these German directors of secret service, who simply would not concede anyone such poor material but that a patriotic inoculation, combined with cold cash, would grind him or her out a dependable spy.

Rosenthal somehow connected himself with the American Relief Commission in Hamburg and then made a journey to Denmark. It was while in Copenhagen that he sat down and wrote, with no particular indiscretion, a letter to a pal of the Berlin underworld, reporting proudly that he was about to go to England to gather naval and military information, and would fool the enemy by pretending to be a commercial traveler offering a patent gas lighter. When some Danish postal clerk flipped that missive into the wrong pouch, the life of its author went with it.

Arriving not in Berlin but in London, it came to the desk of a British censor who handled matter written in German script. An enemy agent traveling with patent gas lighters! His letter, to be sure, was now several weeks old; yet the censor zealously rushed it to officers that might still be able to overtake a man whose "selling" masked his work as a spy. Though there seemed but a slender hope of tracing Rosenthal, the counter-spies picked up this chance alarm by the right end. Landing records at all British seaports were immediately checked. An alien business man claiming acquaintance with gas lighters was found among the lists of recent arrivals. Further rapid investigation discovered that this man—who, of course, had abandoned his right name—had been touring Scotland, selling little, but undoubtedly observing a great deal connected with British naval affairs in the north.

The pursuers came finally to that moment whereat the spy must either be arrested or found to have vanished from the land. Well, the luckless Rosenthal had gone—but he had not vanished. They located him aboard a vessel about to sail from Newcastle-on-Tyne. In about fifty minutes he would have stood safely upon a neutral deck beyond the three-mile limit and might have defied the British navy to apprehend him. Instead he journeyed to London, handcuffs replacing the gas lighters he had been carrying. Interrogated by Sir Basil Thomson at New Scotland Yard, he denied German birth or allegiance, denied Copenhagen, and willingly supplied the C.I.D. chief with a specimen of his handwriting.[2] It proved to be identical when compared to that of the letter missent from Denmark.

Whereupon the missent letter was read to him. And if he marveled at a counter-spying miracle, or cursed his own impudent fate, he did not show it, but at once sprang up, clicked his heels and remained standing to attention like a soldier. "I confess everything," he exclaimed. "I am a German soldier."

On sudden impulse he sought to dramatize his critical position; but actually he had never belonged for a day to any military force. He was convicted of espionage and after his condemnation became hysterical and twice tried to commit suicide. Instead of being shot he was hanged, for some reason that the responsible authorities never chose to divulge.

The Three Queens

The censor, engaged, as it were, behind the scenes of the war, not only had to be vigilant, but also could afford to be absolutely impartial. Wealth, titles, even royal blood made no difference to him; an imposing signature was not supposed to relax the severity of any bureau's regulations. Queen Sophie of Greece—"Madame Tino"—sister of the German Kaiser, the queen of Sweden, who was a princess of Baden, and the queen mother of Spain were all three intensely pro-German. Sophie, in particular, attempted so much artless plotting that she landed upon every suspect list of the Allies. Letters addressed to these ladies, or sent by them, were closely scrutinized, delayed if the circumstances required it, and often, in the case of the queen of Greece, refused further transmission.

The Spanish queen mother swayed the opinion of court circles in Spain to the German side, though Alfonso's queen was a British princess. It was even more apparent that the sister of Wilhelm in Athens collaborated with Baron Schenck and Colonel von Falkenhausen[3] in counteracting the normally pro-Ally majority sentiment throughout Greece. When it was discovered, however, that orders to German agents and German U-boats were going over the cables to South America in the Swedish government code, something had to be done. The British Intelligence allowed an exposure of this partisan practice to "leak out" in Stockholm, and a considerable scandal vibrated the Swedish capital.

British Intelligence, with the kind of shrewdness supposed to originate north of the Tweed, had arranged with its censors to close many channels of Teutonic propaganda but to keep others open for the thrifty purpose of distributing British propaganda in enemy covers on which the postage had been paid in Berlin. Furthermore, the industrious readers of stacks of foreign mail brought by every ship touching at a British port detected and helped to put a stop to the extensive German speculation in raw materials. According to a reputable authority,[4] this produced an important and calculable saving to the British Empire of not less than £100,000,000.

It was fairly easy, not to say entertaining and profitable, thus to tap the private correspondence of international celebrities, bankers, speculators and commercial organizations in search of clues to assist counter-espionage. But ploughing through the banal and multitudinous correspondence of plain folk was the herculean labor of the war censors. The mail of soldiers in training and in the field—who numbered millions—and the prisoners of war—who eventually numbered hundreds of thousands—had to be examined with as much assiduity as suspected messages and publications or the ostensibly "neutral" propaganda circulated by the enemy.

Censorship and the A.E.F.

There were disturbing possibilities for minor leaks of army information in the mail of the American Expeditionary Force, two million young men, representing many races and mostly inexperienced in war and European ways, who had come so far on such an unprecedented "crusading" errand. It was hard to make rational doughboys believe they were defending their homes, a mere three to six thousand miles distant, but it was natural that they should all want to write home and try to describe what they really were doing and seeing. And that was the very essence of military intelligence. As G.H.Q., Chaumont, patiently explained:

> Without intimate knowledge of the ingenuity with which seemingly trivial details, when assembled, furnish information of highest importance, no one can presume to say what is or what is not military information. Picture post-cards, poorly censored letters, found by Intelligence Officers, have furnished clues to puzzling problems, and have even eventually determined the results of battles.

Serious violations, involving deliberate betrayal, were feared by persons who instinctively mistrust alien names and "foreign" elements. But the A.E.F. proved itself the most loyal army in American history. The base censor detected in twenty months only one grave case of disloyalty, wherein a private soldier, Joseph Bentivoglio, had written secretly to relatives in Italy between the lines of two letters. Bentivoglio, who—luckily for him—seemed much too stupid to be in league with enemy propagandists, had crudely applied fruit juices to the furtive communication of such bulletins as this: "Things going bad with us here. The food is poor. Do not believe what is printed in the newspapers. We are all getting killed off." For which morbid choler he was court-martialed. American censorship in France in 1917–18 turned up but 141 other cases for disciplinary action, including a staff officer who had given a fascinating compatriot a whole box of official envelopes stamped in advance "Passed as Censored." With them she might have written any sort of indiscretion and sent it anywhere.[5]

With a vast army brought overseas, and soon wholly out of sympathy with its French and British allies, the American censor proved that, beside turning back forbidden military information, he could invaluably discover that which revealed army morale, soldiers' opinions on public questions, irregularities or abuses which they suffered, or suspicious persons with whom they might have become acquainted.[6]

The polyglot A.E.F. spread itself handsomely in using fifty-one languages, including American Indian dialects, Tagalog, Celtic and Esperanto. No wonder, even with 33 officers, 183 men and 27 civilian employees, the censorship bureau in France was continuously understaffed.[7] The average soldier's letter home in English could as a rule be censored by one of his own officers, marked and sent directly to a transport, without making a detour through the mountainous industry of censorship at the army base. But there another staggering cargo of packages and parcels was steadily unloaded to be censored as carefully as any of the first-class mail. A German agent had been detected writing secretly upon the tissue paper wrappings of fruit from southern France and Italy. The censor was charged with preventing such a practice from spreading dangerously to other areas.

CHAPTER EIGHTY-FOUR

THE BLUFF BARRAGE

NO GOVERNMENT dares to liberate the whole truth and nothing but the truth after the second or third day of a modern war. This rule of diminishing veracity is little altered by potential strength or weakness, by impending victory or defeat, and applies to all forms of government with nearly equal weight. It is evident that more pangs of doubt and resentment will be suffered by parliamentary democracies resigning themselves to the emergency Fascism of a general staff. Sudden censorship and the sugar pills of propaganda gag and nauseate those accustomed to a generous balanced diet. But what of the others whose last shred of liberty has long since been cut up into uniforms for infants or into military police brassards for organized gangster-guardians of the leader or supreme being? Where the people of democracies may be chafed and aggravated by palpable propagandic distortions, those who have hitherto been nourished on government handouts have learned to suspect everything bearing the imprint of the dominant faction. While submitting to oligarchy, these peoples grow to depend upon clandestine channels of gossip, rumor and canard. Unlike the theoretically free, they are inured to repressions of fact and are less shocked and much less influenced by the high-powered propagandists now invariably mobilized at the outbreak of war.

Propaganda was nothing new in the time of the World War, nor was it something inherently dishonorable. Anyone who tries to persuade is more or less a propagandist. The worst characteristic of propaganda after 1914 was its *volume,* and its worst ingredient a sickening pap of optimistic exaggeration which, in supplanting bitter truths about blunders, defeats and tragic failures, actually prolonged the war and protected the tenure of viciously incompetent leaders. It not only prolonged the war but made its mark upon the terms of peace. What people, what embattled nation, after great sacrifices is going to demand, or even concur in, a fair negotiated peace after being subtly assured for months that the final smashing victory is just on the point of being won? It was the same in buttressing the repute and power of many a stupid professional soldier; for how are abler men to rise to the top if everybody, even a badly beaten commander who has just thrown away a hundred thousand casualties, believes his own propaganda? Like the expansion of little ribbons on his chest, it assures him he is skillful, that his strategy is winning, exhausting the enemy, and all will be well if politicians—those blockheads, cowards, *civilians*—can be cajoled or coerced into leaving him and his clique in the hearse driver's seat at G.H.Q.

After a great war has passed into history the villain of the conflict is war itself; but while hostilities are actually in progress the "enemy" is the culprit, and every effort must be made to convince all the world of his guilt. This convincing process is not a recent innovation; nor is it a military or judicial one. It is a feat of strategic propaganda. The warrior Greeks, being blessed with imagination, are known to have excelled in it. But in the World War there was such wealth and novelty of *systematized* propaganda that the "Greeks bearing gifts" recede to the proportions of timid talebearers. Propaganda helped to win more than one great battle, and it ultimately disarmed a battle fleet. It demoralized whole nations and turned a dozen irresolute neutral states into energetic combatants. Its scientific manipulation absorbed the time of companies and battalions of individuals, who were required to possess every known trait from mere intellectual agility and talent for news distortion to imaginative genius and the persuasive resources of a founder of religion.

Propaganda gave so venerable a thing as falsehood a brand-new set of patriotic disguises. It spread to Oxford, Harvard and Heidelberg, and to Labrador, Tierra del Fuego and Tibet. Beginning as a solemn façade of Foreign Office apologetic, it became a tissue of deceptive transparencies and amazing elasticity and finally a blinding vapor that hung over Europe long after the smoke of the battles had drifted away. It not only deluded and discomfited its intended victims but also recoiled upon its own manufacturers and screened them from the truth. Like bombs of high explosive, propaganda was dropped upon camps and combat zones and unfortified cities, and like the bombs it exploded in millions of tormented minds. It consumed paper and ink as the guns consumed shells; it was packed with the sausages issued to troops in the line, pictured to multitudes unable to read, and played and sung to many who would rather listen than think. Propaganda in five years—1915 to 1920—surpassed all the lies ever told to ballot-bearing majorities or torch-bearing mobs, while also achieving the highest birthrate of misshapen facts and statistics on record. It came down on five continents as a creeping barrage of bluff and deceit, and the fragments of its most effective shells are still imbedded dangerously deep.

Mobilizing the Presses

Soon after the outbreak of the war in Europe the opposing groups of belligerents began to make a case for themselves, who were innocent and had suffered an outrageous "attack", by exposing the fomentations and intrigues of the enemy. A carefully compounded series of White, Green, Orange, Yellow and Blue "books" streamed from the presses, bearing the governmental imprimatur, exhibiting ostensibly undoctored telegrams and diplomatic dispatches, and proving in the main that very clever attorneys were at work. Since every combatant discharged itself of blame and disputed the evidence presented by the other side, a controversy developed that mere haphazard patriotism was not thought subtle enough to sustain. Gentlemen gifted in logic were called to the rhetorical front; but when a second class was called to the colors there was a marked emphasis upon other gifts. The heavy guns of diplomacy and international law were still pounding away. For the benefit of great masses of people whose young men were going to die in battle, however, and for the wavering populations of neutral neighbors, it now seemed desirable to employ spokesmen with journalistic experience who understood emotional appeal.

Very eminent authors were devoting themselves exclusively to propaganda before the end of the war. In America, for example, the shrewd selection of Sir Gilbert Parker as chief of the British propagandic organization produced the most gratifying results. Other novelists, editorial writers and dramatists lent their talents to the struggle of ideas. There was never the least doubt who would win *this* engagement, for what German propaganda was not infuriating was clumsy and grotesque.

The French also had a good deal to learn from their Anglo-Saxon colleagues, though where dear old Lafayette was concerned the French only had to rest on their oars and allow American sentiment to propel them. "Why do you trust your journalists?" General Petain is reputed to have said to an American staff colonel. "We use them, but we do not trust them." But the American attitude was better explained in the statement of General Pershing's chief of Intelligence, General Nolan: "You could not keep our people long supporting a war unless they knew what was happening." The most efficacious propaganda in 1918, the American, was largely dissemination of the simple truth. The American chief of staff, General P. C. March, regularly made public announcement of the number of American soldiers landed in France. It was expected to dishearten the Germans and stimulate the weary Entente, both of which it did. Teutonic leaders became justly enraged against the cruelly effective propagandic devices of their foes. A German staff announcement began: "The enemy has found a 'ministry for the destruction of German Confidence' at the head of which he has put the most thoroughgoing rascal in all the Entente—Lord Northcliffe." The British publisher is said to have relished the venomous compliment of the foes whose power he was insidiously engaged in amputating.

We hear today how the corrupt "Socialistic" morale of the German civil population robbed its gallant troops of their victory on land. It was, however, the *defeat* of the army that impaired the morale of the whole German nation. In an order issued by General Ludendorff himself, September 3, 1918, there is reference to the number of complaints received from Germany that men on leave from the front were creating an unfavorable impression by making statements which bordered on high treason and incitement to disobedience. Ludendorff added that "instances such as these drag the honor and respect of the individual as well as of the whole army into the mud, and have a *disastrous effect upon the morale of the people at home.*" So much for contemporary Nazi propaganda as to cowardly civilians who betrayed the heroic combatants!

CHAPTER EIGHTY-FIVE

SILBER AND ZIEVERT, THE CENSOR SPIES

JULES CRAWFORD SILBER and Karl Zievert were two other German secret agents who, like Wassmuss and Wolfgang Francks, had lived so long away from the fatherland that they could be passionately patriotic without the conventional Teutonic infirmities. Silber was in many respects the cleverest and most consistently successful German spy of the World War. Zievert, an Austrian agent, was as cunningly lodged in a confidential bureau of an enemy state—Russia—as Silber managed to be in England; but, though his espionage opportunities appear to have been really the better of the two, Zievert fell far behind Silber in total war-period accomplishment. Nothing interrupted the latter's hazardous tour of duty on British soil, and he "escaped" in his own good time, when the value of any German spy in Britain was becoming negligible. Whereas Zievert outstayed his usefulness in the empire of the tsar; and what we know about him comes from the record of his trial and condemnation.

The reader may be heartily recommended to Silber's own account of his secret-service exploits.[1] It is honest, unpretentious and so decently half ashamed and discreet, it could never be mistaken for the work of a "literary spy." It is, in fact, authentically unexciting—though its author's wartime tension and suspense must often have seemed unbearable—and it has never received the notice it deserves. Silber knew the British Empire well, had passed most of his adult years abroad, had contrived to obligate the English by services rendered during the South African War. When in 1914 the declarations of hostility began flying over the frontiers he discovered the typical wanderer's devotion to the land of his birth. There was no longer any chance to get home to fight; but one who spoke flawless English and looked and acted British could approach England disarmingly by way of America and Canada. Silber had papers of identification establishing his record of service against the Boers; and his want of a passport was not extraordinary at that early period of the conflict. England received him; English officials accepted his self-identification and welcomed his offer of linguistic gifts. He was marked for appointment to the rapidly expanding bureau of censorship; and it was as an English postal censor that this agent of Germany "fought" for his side throughout the remaining years of the war.

Silber's only ascertainable handicaps seem to have been his conscience and personal integrity and his manifest abilities—which won him promotion, the unwanted notice of superior officers, and transfer to duties assaying fewer chances for military or naval espionage. With a pleasing personality, it appears that he made friends readily, which added many crumbs of intelligence to his regular reports but also weighed upon his spare time; and Silber—an enemy alien busily occupied with his duties as a British government official—needed almost every minute of his spare time to train himself in the practices of secret service.

He was not a product of any of the Teutonic spy schools. From America he had communicated privately with the proper German authorities, and they had encouraged him to undertake his self-imposed mission. He did not try to operate with other spies, and the gravest of all the risks he ran seems to have sprung from the intermittent impulses of espionage chiefs to "help" him with active co-operation or advice. As a censor Silber could pass his own outgoing spy messages. In order to get the right postmark he sent himself letters from various points in London, using a commercial "window envelope" which allowed him to change the address—by inserting a new letter—after he had officially opened his envelope. Whereupon he marked it, resealed it with his censor's seal, and started it on its way to the Continent.

Communicating with his German chiefs, who were men he had never seen, who had let him recruit himself, and were not actually employing him—his British salary took care of expenses—Silber did not afflict himself with the amateur spy's hazard of aiming at a single address. He varied his correspondence expertly by consulting the Suspect List, always kept up to date at the censorship office, and taking from it promising neutral addresses of those whom the British Secret Service had discovered in league with Germany. In every instance his report was promptly forwarded to German O.H.L. by its suspected recipient. One of Silber's best "covers" was a nonexistent Belgian prisoner of war to whom he wrote for several months. Later, when he was transferred to the Liverpool bureau of censorship, he dispatched secret messages via New York in parcels that came to his desk on their way to important banking houses. It was easy to slip a letter marked "Please Forward" in with those which the bankers transmitted to accommodate favored customers; but Silber deemed it unsafe to make this ingenious experiment more than once with any one banking firm.

Caution, conservatism, diligent attention to detail and the finest zeal distinguished his subterranean conflict with the foes who surrounded but never suspected him. He had to sit by calmly as a censor and watch the British net slowly drawn around mobile German spies who had ventured into the United Kingdom and were now being allowed to incriminate themselves. There was no warning he could get to them, no rescue he dare hope to contrive. British spies in Germany also came to his attention; but to turn counter-spy and warn Nicolai and the *Nachrichtendienst* against them would have been only to risk compromising his exceptional espionage emplacement. Silber found that British agents abroad did not trouble about having a "cover" address but just wrote to somebody they knew or invented, being certain that their communications would come first to the censor and thence be routed to the proper department of Intelligence.

Silber inevitably secured a stupendous amount of banned information from the very correspondence he was engaged in censoring. But he could not sit at his table taking notes in the presence of other officials and had to tax his memory severely each day in carrying home the nuggets he had dredged from his share of the censors' mountain of mail.[2] He was shrewd enough never to work upon his espionage reports in the house where he lodged; but to account for the evening time he spent at another address, where his secret-service communications were made ready, he regularly bought theater and concert tickets and left the stubs lying around his lodgings. Many documents could be carried away from the government bureau overnight and photographed. Silber used hundreds of feet of film but was too cautious to be found buying it in quantities; which meant posing as a "kodak fiend" and buying his photographic supplies in shops all over metropolitan London.

As a monumental compliment to the amateur counter-spy, Silber confesses that the only person in England who ever seriously suspected him and gave him a real jolt of anxiety was a shopkeeper who became oversuspicious of some of his necessary purchases. This patriot, who by chance had picked up the trail of the ablest enemy hidden in England, began shadowing Silber but was discouraged from his pursuit when the spy cleverly explained the "nuisance" he was suffering to a superior officer, who promptly advised the amateur detective to mind his own business and leave a government censor alone.

The day came when Silber opened an envelope addressed in a

feminine hand and began reading into one of the great finds of his four years' intensive spying. The writer told of her pleasure in now having her brother—a naval officer—stationed at a port near their home. She was enabled to see him frequently, though he was working upon some mysterious undertaking of the navy having to do with

Secret agent's sketch of a naval base.

arming an old merchant craft. Silber did not recognize it at the moment, but here was the first news of the Q-boats or decoy ships which were to make the maritime raids of German submarines so much more hazardous. However, it seemed on sight a clue of prime import, and so he took the earliest opportunity to journey to the town where the writer lived, call upon her in his official capacity as a government censor and warn her of her dangerous indiscretion. The young English girl was sincerely contrite and implored Silber not to let the matter become known to her brother or to affect his career. In the course of their conversation he learned all he had come to find out about the Q-boats, for the brother had been more indiscreet at his own fireside than the sister had become when writing her schoolmate overseas. And that same evening the first detailed warning of the counter-attack of the Q-boats was made ready for its prompt dispatch to the Continent and Germany.

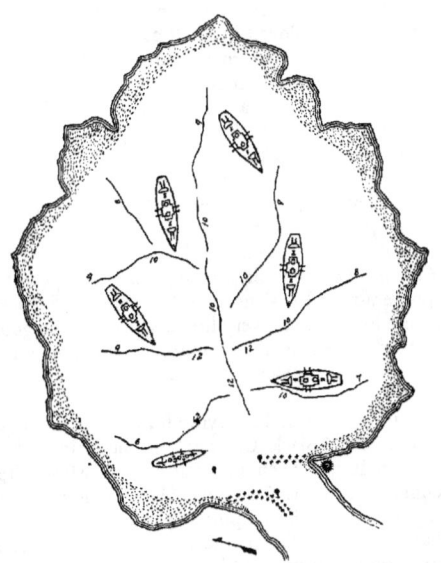

Espionage drawing of the naval base with mined channel and anchored warships developed after transmission of the sketch of "plant life" and insect colony.

Amid all the reminiscent blood and thunder, the witcheries of "Tiger Eyes", the personation of generals, and those spy sinkings of the cruiser with Kitchener aboard, this casual seduction of the British navy's special secret of the "mystery ships" is herewith proposed for a place among the ten authentic masterstrokes of World War secret service.

Zievert's Dark Deeds at the Cabinet Noir

No perfect immunity will ever be devised against the resident spy of conservative zeal and intellectual gifts. Karl Zievert was such an espionage operative. Drawing two salaries as a Russian official, another from Vienna, and a bonus from Berlin after war was declared, he had been living in Russia virtually all his life; and for more than forty years, with authority derived from the tsar's minister of the interior, he had been employed in Kieff as a secret postal censor. He was enabled thereby to open mail addressed to General Michael Alexeieff, chief of the Russian General Staff, to study letters written by Mme Brussiloff, wife of the army commander, to the wife of General Trotski, commandant of the Kieff district, and he even dipped into the official correspondence of the minister of war, Soukhomlinoff, and of Count Bobrinski, the Russian governor of occupied Austrian territory in Galicia. Zievert, a born bureaucrat, was only incidentally an Austro-German spy, since he had worked his way to the top in the Kieff division of postal espionage—the Romanoff imitation of the Bourbons' *Cabinet Noir*—by his prolonged and competent endeavors in spying upon eminent Russians for other eminent Russians. Epistolary secrets were his dish, in a very literal sense, and he gobbled them with relish and digested them in comfort, fashioning reports of the process which gave good value both to domestic and foreign customers.

Leaving him to his pleasurable prying for a moment we will look at the operation of the "Black Cabinet" in the principal centers of European Russia. It had been intermittently a Muscovite affliction since the reign of Catherine the Great. Hardy tendencies toward liberalism or revolution in the empire saw the office of censor firmly established as a private pillar of the throne; yet this Black Cabinet of the imperial secret service, unlike the *Ochrana* or political police, was never aimed at suppression of Nihilism, anarchy or the social unrest of the masses. It was reserved for far more notable espionage. To it came mainly the correspondence of nobles and men of large affairs, and their letters, being opened and read by an accomplished staff, were copied, or photographed in modern times, and preserved in a confidential file. Because of the relatively limited number of persons who were deemed important enough for this attention, the agents, comfortably housed in the post office, studied specimens of handwriting until they could recognize them at a glance. These agents were explorers of a special tribe, with such deftness and fidelity and taste for other people's confidences, they received an extra stipend of 350 roubles a month to add to the 150 roubles paid them as clerks of the post office. Several stars of the censorship staff could read twenty languages.

The Russians termed the work of the Black Cabinet *perlioustratzia*, and most of them in tsarist days seem to have accepted this perlustration, this tampering with the mail of distinguished, patriotic and law-abiding citizens, as an unavoidable abuse of paternalism in government. M. Ignatieff, while governor of Kieff, invariably sent his letters by the hands of trustworthy friends, as though he were involved in deep conspiracies. As celebrated a Russian statesman as Count Witte was, it is said, retarded at the beginning of his diplomatic career because an outspoken habit of mind, revealed in his written communications, exposed opinions on many public issues that were recorded against him. Public issue was the thematic test applied to every letter opened by the Black Cabinet. We may picture the busy censor at his work, searching for explicit treason, hunting a shadowy symptom of dissatisfaction with the existing authority; and after days and weeks of gorging upon dull, if intimate, private affairs, gossip and quite unrevolutionary interest in trifles, what a moment when a grand duke, a prince, or general was found unburdening himself of some thought deserving obsequies among the archives.

Members of the imperial family were not even immune from this postal spying. In Odessa—where a well-known general had shot himself on account of something he had penned unguardedly—there was a kind of "union rule" that the readers of the cabinet should receive double pay whenever an important relative of the tsar visited the city. The Black Cabinet had a branch in Moscow as well as in Odessa and Kieff, while its headquarters was located in St Petersburg. The Moscow branch was rather mystically designated the "secret expedition" and consisted of a chief and eight clerks, that in Kieff having a staff of similar size, probably the most efficient of all since its tireless censors were also Teutonic spies.

Except for the detection of this enemy espionage within the tsarist postal censorship, we should know a good deal less about its furtive administration. As the hour of the revolution struck, faithful employees destroyed by the sackful evidence of the unprincipled bureaucracy of the imperial government. Thousands of copies or photographs of letters secured by the Black Cabinet were included in that grand extermination of the proofs. However, the World War had wrought many changes in the tsardom before it provoked the uprisings which changed everything. And when spies were discovered in charge of the Black Cabinet at Kieff they were arrested and put on trial, much as though the rents in the ancient fabric of secrecies were already so wide, nothing was too damaging to be hidden hereafter from the public's view.

Both the prosecution and the defense made out a damning case against the Black Cabinet by way of arguing the guilt or innocence of the accused. The chief defendant was Zievert, shown to have been engaged in censoring or spying upon mail for nearly five decades. He had labored with uniform industry for two or more masters and shown himself remarkably impartial toward all political camps in Russia. His three chief assistants, Max Schultz, Eduard Hardack and Konrad Gusander, were like himself of Austrian or German birth but long resident in Russia.[3] It was offered in favor of the defendants that the notorious Plehve—he whose removal from the scene of his many cruelties was devised by one of Azeff's bombs—when at the head of the imperial police service had crushed a military conspiracy in Kieff, uncovered there by the Black Cabinet. Zievert and his accomplices at times seemed more disposed to excuse themselves as Russian spies than as German.

Their humorless spirit of research had made postal interception a mechanical art;[4] and Zievert argued with ingenuous logic that this work had been largely of benefit, not to the tsar or his ministers, but to obscure, ambitious and deserving Russians whose writings the Black Cabinet was able to bring to the attention of the most influential members of the government. According to Zievert, he never had failed to report any evidences of wisdom or patriotism that he chanced upon in a letter read by him and in this anonymous way had aided many a clever fellow in gaining some desired recognition or a better political post. Zievert had likewise helped a few incautious penmen to political oblivion and beyond, to Siberia. It developed that during the Beiliss trial the Black Cabinet had held up letters addressed to V. A. Maklakoff of defending counsel. At Kieff they even went so far as to read the mail of the local secret police, so that the *Ochrana* resolved to have a censorship bureau of its own, ostensibly to keep watch upon the mail of political refugees.

In 1911 Nicholas II had visited Kieff—it was during this visit that M. Stolypin was assassinated while in the theater and almost at the tsar's side—and General Kourloff, who had been charged with the safety of the imperial party, had commanded the Black Cabinet not to violate the letters of those ministers of state attending the tsar. This order Zievert did not obey, either owing to his intolerable thoroughness or because he was in foreign employ. One minor official, Varevoda by name, happened to work as a postal censor for the *Ochrana* as well as in the Black Cabinet, pocketing three salaries a month, from Zievert, from the post office, and from Colonel Kouliabko, chief of the secret police agency at Kieff. When this triplex functionary reported to Kourloff at the *Ochrana* office that Zievert was reading the ministerial correspondence, the general—a fairly able and powerful officer of the secret police—resolved to punish the too-officious censor. And the decision had a special tsarist tang about it, for Kourloff gave orders that the Black Cabinet of the *Ochrana* should hereafter read Zievert's mail.

That bureaucratic retaliation ought to have endangered Zievert the spy, yet he seems to have brought down upon himself the vindictive scrutiny of the secret police without disturbing his activities as censor or foreign secret agent. All of his subordinates at Kieff were Germans until the declaration of war, and even after that he managed to retain most of them. With their Teutonic diligence they packed the files with confidential matter. At the trial it was disclosed that they had even made photographic copies of letters from the dowager empress to noted admirals and army leaders. The French tutor of the tsar's children complained that his letters were all being opened and read; nor were members of the preponderant Rasputin camarilla able to exclude their correspondence from the attentions of Zievert and his kind,[5] whose power seemed more like an hereditary right than something bestowed upon clerks by a ministerial appointee.

The trial of Karl Zievert would have been either a profound mystery or a huge sensation in times of peace, but it was quickly obliterated by the excitements of the war. He and his confederates were convicted. It was shown that Russian military secrets of the Kieff district had been forwarded by him to Vienna even prior to the outbreak of hostilities. His son, Erich, a subaltern in the Russian infantry, had been taken prisoner by the Austrians, but, according to counterespionage reports, he was not being harshly restricted while "interned" in the enemy country. Zievert's own testimony about those deserving ones whom his keen eyesight had helped to promote failed to move the court, as it had been already definitely established that the Black Cabinet seldom troubled to pounce on and peruse letters exchanged by obscure members of the community. Zievert proudly admitted that the special electric kettle used in steaming open an ordinary envelope was of German make. He explained, too, that many letters had to be copied at least in part by hand; and if a word or signature proved to be illegible it would be photographed and its picture pasted on the file copy in the proper place. All the Russian censors' photographic apparatus, said he, was likewise "made in Germany."

CHAPTER EIGHTY-SIX

THE RESERVOIR OF VICTORY

AN HOUR CAME when the Entente Allies were barely holding their own in the West, while on the Eastern Front reverse after reverse and the revolutionary temper of Russia heaped up mountain high the presaging certainty of a separate peace. The Russians were justifiably tired of being slaughtered in ill-equipped droves to ease the pressure upon French, Italian or British lines. Serbia and Roumania had already gone the way of small nations that exhaust themselves kicking the shins of a giant. Italy, if not small, was something less than a martial steam roller and, after winning a dozen victories of the Isonzo, was still on the Isonzo.

This was not, however, the darkest hour for the Entente nor the brightest for victorious Germany. Neither side could win; an exhaustive stalemate was the most either had to look forward to, as the British navy was still formidably afloat. Admiral Jellicoe at Jutland had chosen to dodge rather than damn the torpedoes. The "only commander in chief who could have lost the War in an afternoon", he had preferred to secure the empire and its allies at a cost of easy popularity to be gained from the reckless expenditure of battle cruisers or a jaunty angle of the cap.

It was not the darkest hour, but it was a gloomy prospect, dismal, disillusioned and edged with despair. Yet it was at this very hour that some Entente statesmen and not a few military leaders began to lie down, roll over and cry "Uncle Sam!" Others echoed them, exclaiming "Santa Claus", for that hour of sunset was suddenly illumined by a Golden Angel rising in the West. It was an hour that extended almost to an era, and never to be forgotten in Europe, the hour of the great Blank Check.

Just by endorsing it you could get anything, anything you needed. Cash and material resources of every kind, presented to the stricken and nearly bankrupt! A gigantic, untapped reservoir of money, men and industrial equipment had been found to offset Germany's original preparedness, German war technique, staff work, transport and conservation of unbeaten fighting forces. With Russian morale shattered as a result of terrible losses and insufficiency of every kind, another ally one hundred million strong and incomparably stronger in "war potential" was ushered into the breach. Considering just what American help meant that spring of 1917 it is a sad thing that some Entente leaders have found time since then for churlish memoirs, shedding sneer by sneer a now-distorted recollection of the first aid they once uncovered with goggling, abject awe. American intervention just about saved their national solvency, their own reputations in history, their political parties, their jobs, their very hides; all of which is why they have gradually distilled in their minds more bitterness toward their rescuer than toward the German Empire that set out to crush them. American entry into the World War was a product of secret service as well as propaganda, and of the inevitable operations of a partisan law which still links the New World with certain lands of the Old, however much the intrigues of Europe may be exposed in warning. American secret service entry into the World War anticipated the army mobilization by about two years.

In its counter-spying activities America was actually not far behind the Entente Allies when it came to subterranean conflict with the secret agents and *sabotageurs* of Germany. On the "home front" of the United States there were frequently as many German and pro-German operatives to be shadowed and supervised as the combined counter-spying divisions of Great Britain and France were simultaneously pursuing. In our study of sabotage we have discerned an early inexperience and laxity that invited German agents to strike at the shipping of the Allies in the seaports of America. Gradually the loopholes in the law were closed and the vigilant eyes of government investigators opened.

The name of the American military secret service when war finally came to be declared was Colonel Ralph H. van Deman. This devoted and accomplished officer—"the father of American Military Intelligence"—had struggled long and vainly to have Intelligence recognized as a separate entity of the General Staff. In 1916, with Europe convulsed by war, there was only one American officer in Washington giving any thought to Intelligence and that was Van Deman, then a major. As a special concession to a time of world crisis he was allowed one clerk as an assistant. Weirdly neglectful as this may seem, it was but repeating the experience of the British at a much earlier date when Captain Hall was "Naval Intelligence" for the greatest navy afloat and Hozier "Army Intelligence" for an empire encircling the earth.

Van Deman and Lieutenant Colonel Alexander B. Coxe in 1917 were the entire Intelligence General Staff of the United States Army until, in imitation of the Allies and with the co-operation of foreign advisers, a vast and rapid expansion began. For thirty years Van Deman had been preparing for this very emergency, and, in spite of Washington's self-perpetuating inertia, he had contrived to gain experience in virtually every known branch of military secret-service work. He had begun as a member of the Ohio National Guard, and on the way—with that slight eccentricity identifying the born Intelligence officer—he had acquired his degree as a doctor of medicine. Having ready and waiting the ideal man for a chief of independent army secret service, the War Department characteristically called in "two other fellows"—Colonel, presently General, Dennis E. Nolan for chief at G.H.Q. in France, and Brigadier General Marlborough Churchill to take over Intelligence in Washington, supplanting its creator.

This was not supplanting Van Deman, for he was given other assignments of importance throughout the months of the war. General Nolan, a competent soldier enjoying the confidence of General Pershing, the commander in chief, happened to believe only in Combat Intelligence, which almost automatically ruled out espionage and secret service. Possibly, in view of the outcome of the 1918 campaign, General Nolan was neither biased nor mistaken. Before the Armistice Nolan had his ardent wish granted and was transferred to command a division at the front. Military secret service was beginning to lift its head in the A.E.F. before the termination of the war.

It is important to discover that the most effective counter-spying done by Americans in France took the form of spying upon other Americans. Every company in every battalion in every division that went overseas had its watcher or spy, responsible not to his commanding officer, but to another officer concerned with loyalty, morale, enemy espionage and kindred matters. It was not unreasonable to anticipate treachery, espionage and insubordination in a polyglot army thousands of miles from home and partially raised by conscription. Nothing very serious occurred, which reflects more credit on the character of the troops than the vigilance of the silent watchers. Their vigilance was scarcely strained. It is of interest, however, to reflect that the first army in Europe to copy the American scheme of internal espionage was the new Red Army of Soviet Russia.

Colonel Nicolai, the German chief of military secret service, has alleged that the opposing secret services of the Allies became immensely more aggressive under the combined influences of American gold and American competition. The story is also told of fifty American counter-spying agents landing in France with distinctive green and white hatcords. Considerably less ornamental than the lace and braid of Göring's secret police in Germany today, the counter-spies' hatcords were none the less absurd for secret-service duty and instantly and forever discarded. These operatives and others pursued "German" suspects wherever they found them but had more to do in helping to weed out malcontents and soldiers of inferior morale. One conscripted division had as many as eight hundred of its men sent home—not often for cause, but on account of their potentially depressive influence on the morale of their comrades.

Often no doubt such decisions were hasty and unjust. Suspicion, the very core of counter-espionage, was inevitably the keynote of American secret-service activities abroad. American Naval Intelligence raced Army Intelligence and the services of all Entente countries in that ingenious pastime of accumulating "Suspect Lists." There were more than one hundred and forty-five thousand names on one such list, proudly controlled in France by a division of counter-espionage responsible for port control. The American Navy list climbed gradually to an all-time peak for the Western hemisphere of one hundred and five thousand names. President Wilson ordered this mammoth record of indecisive suspicion destroyed after it had been printed at the government's expense. Whereupon a private citizen with a flair for patriotic repression contributed more than ten thousand dollars so that Naval Intelligence might have fourteen sets of cards typed by fifty girls duly sworn as secret operatives, thus preserving its precious list while disobeying a specific order of its commander in chief.

CHAPTER EIGHTY-SEVEN

AN AMERICAN SECRET-SERVICE STORY

THE AMERICANS throughout the eighteen-month period of their participating in the European conflict gave generous thanks to the Entente Allies for advice and help in training and material. With regard to the combat methods, training and material of the common enemy, however, it so happened that there were officers of the American Expeditionary Force more familiar with these things than most of the Entente officers, excepting only crack operatives of offensive secret service, either resident in Germany or safely returned from missions within the borders of the Central Empires.

Colonel Richard H. Williams, a captain of coast artillery when sent abroad with the group of American military observers in the summer of 1914, was one who not only experienced some of the hazards of a spy inside the enemy's lines—being repeatedly bathed in cold Teutonic suspicion—but who also was destined to take part in a striking and important—and officially authenticated[1]—secret-service exploit of the A.E.F. Williams observed the war for three years before becoming another of its multitude of combatants. His first duty, assisting Americans stranded in Europe, took him to Belgium and he was there when the steel-tipped tide of Von Kluck's and Von Bülow's armies inundated that land. Whereupon he was sent to Constantinople aboard the USS North Carolina to serve as military attaché under Ambassador Henry Morgenthau. He was the only attaché with the Turkish forces on the Gallipoli peninsula and the only American who saw, from the defenders' side, the desperate landings and attacks of the British and colonial troops of Sir Ian Hamilton.[2]

After the British, now commanded by Sir Charles Monro, effected their masterly evacuation of the peninsula,[3] Colonel Williams accompanied a Bulgarian army to the Dobrudja and watched Bulgars and Germans mopping up strong contingents of Roumanians and Russians. In January 1917 the War Department in Washington ordered its widely experienced attaché home. The German government already knew that the U-boat campaign would continue and President Wilson must ask for a declaration of war. Williams had been studying the troops of Germany and its allies under combat conditions;

and the Germans did not want to let him get away to use his information against them. Yet, still being at peace with America, they could not deny him the right to leave. As a substitute measure of counter-espionage, he was—unlawfully but firmly—required to depart from the Continent by way of Berlin, and there delayed "for eight days while secret agents did everything but X-ray him."[4]

When the American officer finally got to Copenhagen he found that no ships were sailing because of the submarine blockade. After waiting three months he booked passage on a Danish steamer bound for Sweden; but by this time the United States had declared war, and Williams was privately warned that a German destroyer had been ordered to intercept his ship and take him prisoner. A destroyer did stop the Danish vessel, and a boarding party searched it from bunkers to crow's-nest. The American, though not discovered aboard, presently turned up in Sweden without divulging the illusionist trick of his safe transport.[5] Eventually he reached America from Norway after making a detour by way of Iceland.

Colonel Williams' uncommon knowledge of the enemy was badly needed at American headquarters in France, whither he was immediately dispatched to join the Intelligence section of General Pershing's staff. In October 1917 he was still at Chaumont when the Germans prepared the greatest of their Zeppelin raids upon England. Thirteen of the big dirigibles set out from Belgium. Two had to turn back because of engine trouble; but eleven passed safely over English ports and industrial centers and scored a gratifying success of non-combatant deaths and demolition.

The victorious air fleet, when homeward bound, however, was scattered by a violent storm. Six of the raiders were able to reach Germany; five froze their motors in high altitudes over France and became the victims of planes, anti-aircraft guns, or their own helplessness. Two of these—the L-49 and the L-51—were driven down within forty miles of American G.H.Q. The L-49 was captured intact;[6] while the L-51 only bumped the earth with its forward gondola, or control car, bounced upward, struck again, and so pursued its wounded escape across country by bumps and bounces until finally the control car was torn loose in the top of a tree. Freed of that weight, the stricken aircraft drifted away to be lost, with most of its crew, in the Mediterranean.

Swamp Treasure

Colonel Williams was the first staff Intelligence officer to arrive at the spot where the L-49 had surrendered. Other officers, French and

American, were on the scene ahead of him; and he was informed that no maps or documents of any kind had been found aboard the L-49 or in the control car of L-51. The search was about to be abandoned when Williams suggested to a British colleague who had driven over with him from Chaumont that they traverse the clearly perceptible trail left by the damaged L-51 as far as it could be followed. This was done; but the trail soon ended without profit at the edge of a swamp. Williams, however, with what a superior[7] has termed his "characteristic doggedness", waded right into the swamp, was rewarded by coming upon a fragment of German map, and thereafter kept on wading and finding more fragments, until he had "explored the whole area of the swamp"—a mucky errand and rare doggedness, indeed, for any staff colonel.

When the American showed his fragments of map to the British officer, its acute significance was instantly apparent to him. Williams, still persisting, even climbed the tree which had torn off the L-51 gondola and found one more piece of the enemy map caught in its branches. Whereupon he worked all through the night at headquarters, in company with Captain S. T. Hubbard, Jr.,[8] and finally proved that his laboriously "captured" fragments formed a cross-section German code map of the North Sea, the Irish Sea, the Skagerrak and Kattegat, with only the English Channel missing. But, though it obviously related in some vital way to the enemy U-boat campaign, without the special German code the map's true import was indecipherable.

That morning another officer at American G.H.Q. mentioned having seen what he considered the most "interesting souvenir of the war" to date. Asked to give details, he told Williams that it was a "sort of album" containing some printed matter and many "photographs of all types of German naval vessels, heavier than air and lighter than air ships."[9] Colonel Williams suspected that the "souvenir" was the German codebook, with the photographs added to facilitate visual identification of German naval and aircraft, and he ordered his subordinate to find the souvenir hunter and have him report with his "album" immediately.

Two young American officers, it turned out, had caught up with the helpless L-49 soon after its surrender on French soil. They had clambered into the Zeppelin's cabin before any officers of the Intelligence arrived, and, when one of them uncovered the German book, he had instantly gathered it up as a striking oddity and the lawful loot of war. Running through the codebook, Williams now could determine the incredible value of his swamp treasure. He held the key to the current submarine operations of the enemy. And so Williams began cutting red tape with that same doggedness which had got him safely away from the shores of Scandinavia and had taken him through the swamp and up the tree only the day before. As acting G-2—chief of Intelligence—he saw Colonel W. D. Connor, acting chief of staff, who, in the absence of General Harbord, ordered the map and codebook to be carried at once to London and given to Admiral William S. Sims. Captain Hubbard was appointed messenger and provided a staff car to hurry him to British G.H.Q. at Montreuil.

There the American captain, after an all-night ride, was greatly assisted by General Macdonogh[10] and, thanks to the further travel facilities arranged, reached London no later than 11 P.M. Hubbard's orders were explicit: he must only deliver the map and codebook to Admiral Sims. But the admiral was attending a conference in Paris. Hubbard thereupon routed Sims' personal aide, Commander Babcock, from a sick bed, showed him the incomparable timeliness of the prize forwarded from Chaumont; and Babcock, forgetting his doctor's orders, sprang to the telephone and called British Naval Intelligence.

In the week following—before the German Admiralty grasped the awful truth that the German code and undersea operations map had fallen into the hands of the Allies—the British counter-submarine patrol scored its greatest "bag" of U-boats. British Naval Intelligence officers had been regularly intercepting German naval radio orders. With the codebook they could instantly decipher the orders and, by virtue of Williams' map, surprise many of the prowling raiders at their various designated rendezvous.

Not previously in the great war and, it would appear, never again before the Armistice was there to be so perfect and so fruitful an example of true *Allies* working in striking co-ordination. From the Frenchmen who compelled the submission of L-49 intact to the American Army Intelligence to the British army and then Naval Intelligence, on to the final effective counter-operation of the British men-of-war in the submarine zone, each partner helped as he could and contributed according to his special capacity.[11] Neither war nor secret service would be wholly "hell" if they gave us many such patterns of authentic teamwork; but let no despairing pacifist rise to this bait, for the anecdote of Colonel Williams and the Zeppelins' codes is the only one of its kind that we know.

CHAPTER EIGHTY-EIGHT

A WORLD MADE SAFE FOR DEATHS OF DEMOCRACY

ONE STRANGE, STILL NOONDAY of November 1918 the Entente Allies stood up in their trenches and looked around them and discovered that the long war was won. The governments behind the front had known for some weeks that it was going to be won, and so they were already mobilized to resume offensive operations in other theaters. With the Germans permanently out of their path—a permanency that went into Nazi receivership only fourteen years later —the chief conspirators of the Entente were accessible to a kind of "lost" feeling, and something had quickly to be done about it. Fortunately the spoils of war were lying all over the map, and also there was American intervention and President Wilson and his Fourteen Points, all of which had been hysterically inflated to represent gratitude. The inflation was dangerous. Wilson had too much power with the people. The American command over European affairs must be ingeniously reduced by pinpricks of statecraft and revised perspective.

The recently devoted Allies, who had been locked in the fond embrace of punch-drunk wretches able to make pretense of standing up together but not to be expected to proceed separately in any given direction, now fell joyously to work spying upon one another. This was a nuisance, and profitless save as a sort of childish release. It fostered incipient animosities but worked no actual harm. When an Englishman named Leather was convicted of espionage in France and sentenced to prison, we suspected that the honeymoon was over. And when, one after another, the great victors of the war suspended work upon their newly won or mandated territories to repudiate their American war debts, we knew it was over.

The first definitely postwar manifestations which concern this record were the sporadic White ventures and speculations splashing blood and counter-revolution over the map of Red Russia. A volume larger than this one might be compiled to cover the intrigues and conspiracies of that momentous struggle. It is well to remember that there was no *Cheka* in Lenin's original program; but the terrorist offensive of the Social Revolutionaries combined with the menace of

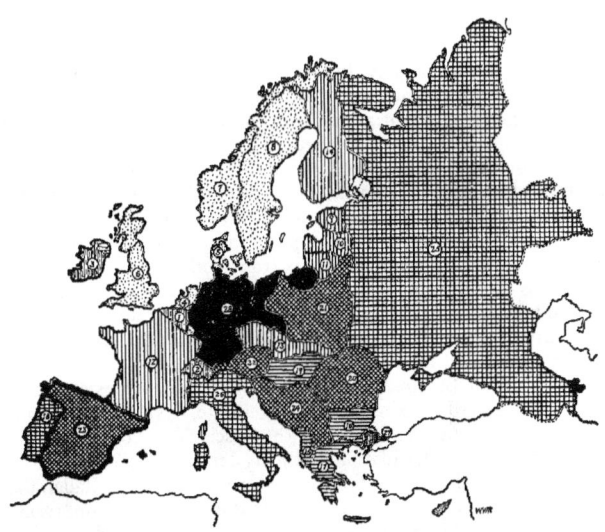

POLITICAL POLICE SUPERVISION, ESPIONAGE AND CENSORSHIP: EUROPE IN JANUARY 1937

Military counter-espionage; some police supervision and discreet control and censorship. *Great Britain* (6), *Netherlands* (4), *Denmark* (5), *Norway* (7), *Sweden* (8).

Moderate police supervision and censorship; some military secret service. *Belgium* (1), *Switzerland* (2), *Irish Free State* (3), *Northern Ireland* (3).

Political police supervision lawfully regulated; very active military secret service. *France* (12), *Czechoslavakia* (13), *Finland* (14).

Political police and military secret service, not strongly organized. *Hungary* (19), *Bulgaria* (16), *Greece* (17), *Albania* (15).

Political police and active military counter-espionage. *Esthonia* (9), *Latvia* (10), *Lithuania* (11).

Stringent police supervision, censorship, counter-espionage and military espionage. *Roumania* (20), *Poland* (21), *Yugoslavia* (24), *Austria* (22), **Spain* (23).

Dictatorial political police control; and military espionage and counter-espionage. *Italy* (26), *Portugal* (18), *European Turkey* (27), *Russia* (25).

Absolute censorship, frontier control and political police espionage, equivalent to martial law; military intelligence and secret service, all branches. *Germany* (28).

*Martial law in Spain owing to Fascist military insurrection.

counter-revolution—largely financed from London—persuaded the principal Bolshevist leaders that Russia could not be governed without secret police and that some organization resembling and superior to the hated tsarist *Ochrana* must be instituted.

The supreme *Chekist* of the revolution was Felix Djerzhinsky, a fanatic and incorruptible partisan who would have made his mark in any department of the newly founded Soviet state, but who was indispensable to the subterranean projects of police espionage and political repression. The Red baiters from Berlin to Tokyo, from San Simeon to the Vatican should face toward Moscow night and morning and hurl their anathemas upon the grave of Djerzhinsky. It was he who answered the White and Social Revolutionary terrors with a counter-terror, and he made his terror stick.

We learn that Benito Mussolini and his attendant obstetricians of Fascismo were ardent admirers of the resolute, devoted and resourceful Djerzhinsky. And so, as soon as the Fascist state could wean itself of government by intimidation and gangster violence, it flattered the *Cheka*—already changed to the *Ogpu*—by establishing an Italian *Ceca*, which force has come nowhere near executing, banishing, imprisoning or torturing the hundreds of thousands of foes marked up against the Russian model, but which has emphatically attended to all the foes it could find.

The respective secret services of Great Britain and France spent the five years following Versailles in active operation but with different objectives. Whereas the French staff decided, as one cynical observer remarked, that their language had no verb meaning "to overreach oneself" and tried to carve out the whole Continent as a rightful sphere, the British mainly devoted themselves to trying to hold what influence they already had. In this they failed. The Irish Revolution "degenerated" into a secret-service war, which was precisely what Britain had always preferred as less expensive and easier to win. However, the Irish—with only two hundred years of painful experience to turn to for a precedent—decided to win the English way; and so at last, to reverse the epigram, Britain had won every battle except the last one.

Michael Collins was the leader who learned to beat the British government on its own chosen field of intrigue and secret service. He had the customary plague of minor MacNallys to guard against, and he took another short cut and imported American gunmen with Irish names or sympathies who arranged the salutary extermination of double-dealers. Meanwhile, Collins was getting information right out of Dublin Castle and sending Irish agents and *sabotageurs* over

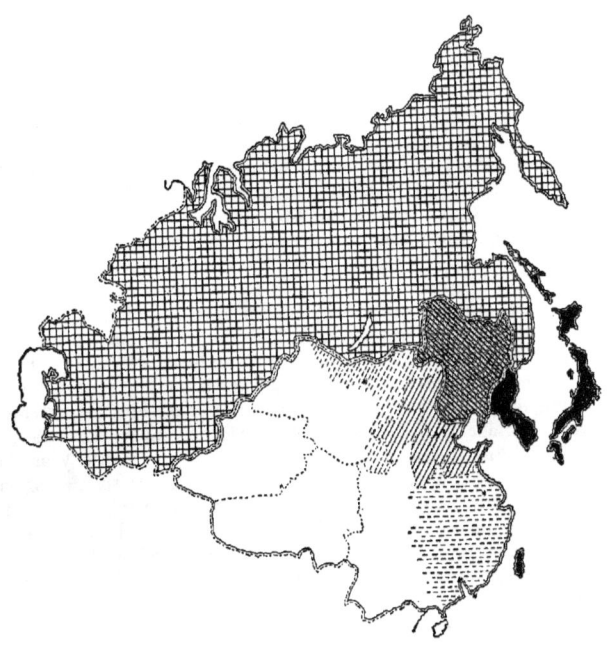

POLITICAL POLICE, CENSORSHIP AND MILITARY SECRET SERVICE IN THE FAR EAST, JANUARY 1937

 Zone of espionage and political secret-service "combat."
China and *Mongolia*.

 Secret-service zone, dominated by Japan.
North China and *Mongolia*.

 Zone of Russian political police and counter-espionage.
Siberia.

 Zone of secret-service "combat", Russia versus Japan.
Manchukuo.

 Zone of Japanese military and political secret service.
Japan and *Korea*.

into England as though he never had heard how the game hitherto had always been played. It was really no trouble at all after a few months of this hard-hitting guerrilla and undercover combat to induce London to do the civilized thing. Ireland became both a Free State, and virtually free, and Collins such an engaging national hero of world renown another Irishman had to assassinate him.

The British Secret Service, justly famous both for age, intelligence derivatives and consistent expenditure—about the same amount in buying power today as was expended by Secretary Thurloe in Cromwell's time—suffered another setback in Russia. Many sympathetic observers are still wondering why Britain felt inspired to save Russia its experiment in Communism, and why it chose such unsuitable ground to invite that spanking before an audience of Asiatics. Even the celebrated "Zinoviev letter", which managed to turn a Labor government out of office, itself turned out a cheap and preposterous forgery. The agents of the old lion have had no luck with Russia.

A skillful director of military secret service in the World War, the French General Dupont retained that post after the treaties of so-called peace and kept it even while serving as a member of an important interallied commission. Enabled thus to travel all over Germany as well as in the new states allied to France and bordering upon the beaten Reich, Dupont shrewdly laid out a network of "counterspies" extending from the Rhine frontier to the borders of Soviet Russia. German Intelligence officers have since complained that he bribed, intimidated or hired a number of their own countrymen to enlist in the work of internal supervision—mainly pertaining to the disarmament clauses of the Versailles Treaty—which were then the chief concern of the French government.

Moreover, the new states whose lands had been formerly German or Austro-Hungarian acknowledged both gratitude and a desire for continued subsidies by permitting their spy systems to be subordinate to the secret service of France, even as their army staffs were then dependent upon the French General Staff for advice and material bounties. Every Continental gain made by France through the peace settlements had agents placed to watch over it, a situation without German parallel even in Stieber's time, and one not far removed from the boundless mysteries and supervisions of Napoleon's imperial police service under Fouché and Savary. Such jealous concern for the metabolism of the status quo could not help but aggravate all the postwar tensions sprung from victory and defeat. Nazi Germany as it glowers and rattles the sword today is distinctly the product not of German but of French secret service. And this is true, without taking into account the number of present-day Nazi notables who were on Dupont's capacious payroll at one time or another following the collapse of the Hohenzollern and the mark.

Epilogue or Prologue?

Political police systems—the most offensive type of allegedly "defensive" secret service—are today the foundation and bulwark of thirteen "strong-arm" governments which were not even in existence twenty years ago. Of these the blatantly *Chekist* imitations of Italy and Germany provide us the most authentic "horrible" examples of the Fascist police state. The political police of Italy have a blunt instrument which they use to break a suspect's jaw, laying him up for a long painful period without fracturing the skull or otherwise gravely endangering his life. The political police of Nazi Germany, who seem to have practiced upon their own Nordic skulls, prefer a heavier, axlike blow, aimed from behind the victim and landing squarely on the back of the head. They persist in such crude technique even though the Semitic skull—and doubtless many a liberal or Roman Catholic skull—is designed to give better results when struck sharply just behind the ear. Apart from this and a few other administrative methods, there is little to choose between the existing control and efficiency of the Italian and German secret police.

The latter, the *Gestapo,* because of more recent origin, and, perhaps, because it is Teutonic, gives nearly all foreign observers a shuddering impression of ruthlessness, vigilance and excessive cunning. Most of this is sheer brutality. The German people are excessively docile; the great majority of them prefer to goose step through life on a plane of uniformed regimentation. Thus far the German secret police have encountered no opposition worthy of the name, and it is fairly obvious that there never will be any serious *Gestapo* opposition until the bellicose Nazi statesmen provoke a general war. It was, however, a strong and united opposition that produced the invincible and horrible *Cheka* of Djerzhinsky. The police organization which Himmler manages and Göring advertises is the first secret service in all history with an ornate uniform, quantities of braid, even its own publication or "house organ."

It has very recently added the old Mogul innovation of scavenger spies; but the German variety now peer into refuse cans and garbage pails to report those heedless or corrupt citizens who are wasting fats or bread. With the new dietetic theory of "let cannon fodder eat cannon" which Hitler appears to be inflicting on his subjects, it is to be expected that heavy-industry delicacies will be harder to throw away. And so no first-rate test of *Gestapo* efficiency has thus far developed—one of those penalties of peace!—and the thought persists that, had this Nazi secret service ever had to encounter the plutocratic coalition which for six years endeavored to unseat the Soviets, Hitler's regime today would still be a beer-cellar confederacy.

The recent adventure in Ethiopia disclosed the Italian *military* secret service in an interesting and impressive light. The returns from that front are still being counted, but the bribery of the Coptic priesthood seems to have been managed with about the same finesse developed by Cyrus in capturing Babylon with the connivance of the priests of Bel in 538 B.C. Meanwhile, actual warfare in Ethiopia has allegedly come to an end. Perhaps it is not really ended in Africa, but it ended in Europe as soon as the Italians captured the wireless and closed the frontiers.

And so down the centuries we have come all this way to find something really new in the fashions of international intrigue. The Spanish civil war—while as yet most of the facts have to be ascertained—provides one contemptible certainty. The liberal Powers of Europe, browbeaten by Fascist war gods and badgered by banking syndicates, consented to a purely theoretical embargo on all war supplies. For the first time in memory thus lowering a properly constituted government to the level of a treacherous military camarilla! And the embargo has been only a transparent farce, respected least of all by the partisan Fascists who exacted it to cover their aid to the Fascist rebels. After thirty-three centuries democracies win the booby prize as the dupes of blustering bankrupts! But war is at best a form of politico-economic receivership. War beckons today as the last recourse of the deflated and impoverished; and these our times, however painfully out of joint, seem better than ever for the new-old practices of secret service and the manipulations of spies and speculators.

NOTES

CHAPTER 1 *Thirty-three Centuries of Secret Service*
[1]Act V, Scene iv.
[2]E. S. Creasy, *The Fifteen Decisive Battles of the World*.
[3]Morgenthau, *Ambassador Morgenthau's Story*. (1919).

CHAPTER 2 *In the Shadows of Adventure*
[1]Mithridates the Great seems to have *almost* trusted the least trustworthy character with whom it is known he ever came in contact—Selencus, the archpirate. He appears to have had a greater love for pirates than for members of his own family; he infuriated the Romans, lately absorbed in the internecine struggle between Marius and Sulla, by taking the worst of the sea robbers, the Cilicians, under his wing. He allowed them entry to his ports and even the use of his war galleys; and on at least one occasion he accompanied the terrible raider Selencus on a devastating expedition that gained them a monument of plunder. The Aegean was now entirely in the hands of the pirates; Mithridates' allies were no longer an undisciplined mob of furtive cutthroats but "had grown into the semblance of a naval organization, attacking according to a considered strategy instead of, as hitherto, without order or unity of command." (Philip Gosse, *The History of Piracy*; Appendix I.)
[2]Edward Gibbon, *The Decline and Fall of the Roman Empire*.
[3]The Foley fortune soon raised itself to a place among the commercial monuments of eighteenth-century England, carrying the Foleys into the landed aristocracy. A younger son of the venturesome "Fiddler" Foley could afford to purchase Witley Court in Worcestershire, one of the very finest estates in England. The third Lord Foley became famous for his extravagances on the turf and at the gaming tables, causing the fourth Lord Foley, who was "land poor" even though possessed of an alleged income of £50,000 a year, to sell Witley to the Earl of Dudley for a sum reputedly in excess of £800,000.

CHAPTER 3 *The Cunning of Antiquity*
[1]In his very appropriately entitled work *Greater Than Napoleon*, Captain B. H. Liddell Hart proves Scipio Africanus a far greater man and greater general than Bonaparte and does it most entertainingly, in terms of modern military science. It would be better, one may submit, for education the world over if it taught us all to think of a soldier and true patriot of the caliber of Scipio as *greater* in every way than Napoleon.
[2]P. Cornelius Scipio was the father of that Roman general of the same name who, after his victory at Zama, was given the surname of Africanus. Father and son were born strategists; and it was the strategy of the father that saved Rome from siege and capture in the Second Punic War. At the outbreak of the war he had been sent with an army by sea but arrived three days too late to intercept Hannibal at Marseilles. Thereafter, instead of pursuing the invaders of his country, he in turn invaded Spain, effectually shutting off Hannibal's supplies and reinforcements. During all the fifteen years that Hannibal held out in Italy, this Roman army of Spain lay between him and his base. After annihilating Varro's army at Cannae—216 B.C.—Hannibal could not advance and capture Rome, for his siege engines had never come through from Spain.

CHAPTER 4 *Spies, Slaves, and a Fire Brigade*
[1]In 133 B.C. Tiberius Gracchus, the elder brother, had been beaten to death with the fragments of a broken bench by two senators; and twelve years later Caius Gracchus,

with about 3,000 of his followers, was massacred by the same champions of entrenched wealth and the status quo. The decapitated head of the younger of the Gracchi was carried to the Senate on the point of a pike. A reward of its weight in gold had been offered for this trophy, and one of the agents of law and order who had attended to the murder displayed the cunning of his type by filling the brain case with lead on its way to the scales.

[2] Sir Charles W. C. Oman, *Seven Roman Statesmen of the Later Republic*.
[3] H. G. Wells, *The Outline of History*.
[4] Oman.
[5] Plutarch.
[6] Ferdinand Mainzer, *Caesar's Mantle: The End of the Roman Republic*.
[7] The *Ochrana* or secret police of the Russian tsars derived its name from the Russian verb *ochranyát*, meaning to "ward" or "watch over." The Bolshevik government's substitute for, and improvement upon, this organization was known as the *Cheka*, or "Ch.K."—a contraction for *cherez-vicháika* or Commission Extraordinary. *Gestapo*, the common name of the secret police of Nazi Germany, is a contraction of *Geheime Staats Polizei*; while *Ovra* stands for *Opera Volontoria Repressione Anti-fascista*, or the Organization of Volunteers for the Repression of Anti-Fascism.
[8] *The Messiah Jesus and John the Baptist*, p. 470.

Chapter 5   Byzantium to Bagdad

[1] Gibbon offers Procopius as an eyewitness authority on the narrowness of the girdle; but the Byzantine chronicler appended other details which Gibbon prefers to leave "veiled in the obscurity of a learned language." Even while he adds with anti-clerical malice: "I have heard that a learned prelate, now deceased, was fond of quoting this passage in conversation." It seems hardly pertinent to our exploration of secret service to explore further the micrology of Byzantine theatrical costuming.
[2] Gibbon, *The Decline and Fall of the Roman Empire*.
[3] These prisons, "a labyrinth, a Tartarus," according to Gibbon, were located for exceptional convenience underneath the palace, which must either have improved upon ordinary penal standards of the age or lowered the sanitary conditions of the imperial edifice. "Darkness is propitious to cruelty," Gibbon adds in a footnote, "but it is likewise favourable to calumny and fiction."
[4] Queen Amalasontha not only "expressed herself with equal elegance and ease in the Greek, the Latin, and the Gothic tongue" (Gibbon), but also, according to other authorities, wrote to Justinian in a courtly fashion bordering upon excess. It was as good as a death warrant to tell Theodora's consort, as the Gothic queen did: "The friendship of Princes is comely, but your friendship absolutely ennobles me, since that person is exalted in dignity who is united by friendship to your glory." (C. Underhill, *Theodora*, p. 223.)
[5] *The Decline and Fall of the Roman Empire*.
Gibbon derived his "history and character" of John of Cappadocia from Procopius and accepts that chronicler's bias by noting that the "agreement of the history and the anecdotes is a mortal wound to the reputation of the præfect."
[6] P. W. Sergeant, *Dominant Women*.
[7] Gibbon.
[8] Gibbon.
[9] Gibbon.
[10] Compiled and translated into Spanish by Don José Antonio Conde (*Historia de la Dominacion de los Arabos en España;* Madrid, 1820); English quotation by E. S. Creasy.
[11] Sykes, *The Caliph's Last Heritage*.

Chapter 6   The Sect of the Assassins

[1] Maurice Hewlett's great historical adventure story, *Richard Yea-And-Nay*, more urbanely compares the Assassins with the greed, brutalities and intrigues of the Crusaders than any other description or document known to this writer.
[2] The Assassins of Syria, never more than 40,000 strong, but who exerted considerable

influence upon the Crusades from their ten castles in the hills above Tortosa, were extirpated—according to Gibbon—by the Mamelukes "about the year 1280."
³Thomas Keightley, *Secret Societies of the Middle Ages.*
⁴F. Stark, *The Valleys of the Assassins.*
⁵Jeremiah Curtin, *The Mongols.*
⁶The Templars were banned by Pope Clement V on March 22, 1313; but members of the order were safe wherever they happened to be beyond the reach of the avaricious king of France, Philippe le Bel. The order continued to flourish, though never again powerfully or arrogantly. Bertrand du Guesclin was, among others, grand master of the Templars later on.

CHAPTER 7 *Modern Spies from Medieval Asia*

¹This little-known military genius might well have been called "the Great", for compared to him the celebrated commanders of Western Europe, from Gustavus Adolphus, Turenne and Marlborough to Frederick of Prussia and even Napoleon Bonaparte, seem like cadets. Subutai, most widely ranging of Genghis' brilliant army chiefs, from China to the Danube "conquered thirty-two nations and won sixty-five pitched battles."
²Captain B. H. Liddell Hart, *Great Captains Unveiled.*
³Prince Ye Lui Chutsai, we are told, "labored with heroic fortitude to consolidate the empire" of the Mongols, while seeking to restrain them "from further annihilation of human beings." He even dared oppose Subutai "at a time when the Orkhon . . . wished to massacre the inhabitants of a great city. 'During all these years in Cathay,' the wise chancellor [Ye Lui Chutsai] argued, 'our armies have lived upon the crops and the riches of these people. If we destroy the men, what will the bare land avail us?' " (Harold Lamb, *Genghis Khan.*)
⁴*Great Captains Unveiled.*
⁵In the Hungarian campaign of 1241, before the battle of Mohi, Subutai forced the pass of Ruska on March 12 and advanced by the valley of the Theiss to the Danube near Gran, his vanguard arriving there on the fifteenth, and his main body on the seventeenth.
⁶While we find it hard to believe that even a medieval Mongol horseman could ride more than 400 miles in twenty-four hours, Marco Polo's claim that the Khan received "dispatches from places ten days' journey off in one day and night" seems much more credible. The celebrated "pony express" of America's Far West was a primitive enterprise compared to the Mongol *yam.* The pony express in California had only 190 stations and 400 horses, its riders averaging around thirty-three miles each trip. However, the dangers from Indians and highwaymen which they risked were far more serious than any afflicting the couriers traveling the well-policed roads of the Mongol empire; for it was said that "a virgin carrying a sack of gold" could ride unharmed from one end of that empire to the other.
⁷Jeremiah Curtin, *The Mongols.*
⁸Pètis de la Croix, *Histoire du Grand Genghizcan Premier Empereur des Anciens Mogols traduite de plusieurs Auteurs Orientaux & de Voyageurs Européens.*
⁹Sir Henry H. Howarth, *History of the Mongols.*

CHAPTER 8 *Treacheries, Sacred and Profane*

¹The Council of Constance, gathered to discuss the scandalous disorder of the Church, straightway condemned Wycliffe's bones to be dug up and burned, which did very little to reduce the scandals and infirmities that Wycliffe himself had discussed and deplored.
²G. F. Young, *The Medici.*

CHAPTER 9 *Church and State*

¹Mary I was the last *admittedly* Catholic ruler of England; but one hundred and twenty years later James II lost his throne because of his open espousal of the Church of Rome, among other affronts to the Protestant majority of his subjects.
²Frederick Chamberlin, *The Private Character of Queen Elizabeth.*

NOTES

[5] The very name Torquemada has been noted as an omen of the grand inquisitor's career. To a remarkable degree it suggests the terrible engine of fire and torture which he was destined to control. Compounded of the Latin *torque* and the Spanish *quemada* it forms a veritable *nom de guerre,* which many have suspected of being the implacable Dominican's own grim invention.

[4] Torquemada, despite his power and connections at court, could not grant his sister "an endowment suitable to her station", but barely enough to live as a nun "under the rule of the tertiary order of Saint Dominic."

[5] The excesses of the Spanish Inquisition have been the cause of the utmost exaggerations in print, ranging from the curious panegyric of Francisco X. Garcia Rodrigo —who as recently as 1877 lamented that the tribunal had become extinct—to the vehement denunciations of W. H. Rule. But in all the literature of the Inquisition there is nothing to compare with the comprehensive writings of Juan Antonio Llorente, to whom all scholars acknowledge boundless indebtedness. As one might suspect, Llorente paid the penalty of such candor and completeness.

His knowledge of Roman and canon law had enabled him to obtain a place among the lawyers of the Council of the Inquisition in Castile; he was vicar-general to the Bishop of Calahorra and later commissary of the Holy Office in Logroño, the place of his birth. In 1789 he was called to Madrid to assume the office of secretary-general of the Holy Office; he was in some trouble when the Liberal party fell, and was sent into retreat for a month as a penance. When Bonaparte's invasion of Spain took place, Llorente hailed the French as the saviors of his country. And in 1809, when the Inquisition was abolished, he accepted the important charge of going through its vast archives. He spent two years upon this task, employing a staff of research assistants to make the copies and extracts he required. Since he had been a member of the Assembly of Notables convoked by Marshal Murat to reform the government of Spain and had held other important offices under French patronage, when Napoleon's forces were compelled to evacuate Madrid, Llorente had to go also, and he found refuge in Paris, where he wrote his celebrated history of the Spanish Inquisition (*Historia Critica de la Inquisicion de España;* Madrid, 1822).

Royalist and clerical partisans now dominated the French government, and the historian was promptly punished. He was prohibited from hearing confessions or celebrating mass, which amounted to being unfrocked, and no longer permitted to teach Spanish (Castilian) in private schools. Llorente countered by issuing *The Political Portrait of the Popes;* and he was thereupon ordered to leave France without delay. In December of 1822 he set out to return to his native land—where two previous works of his authorship, *Anales de la Inquisicion de España* and *Memoria Historica,* had been published in 1812—but the hardships of his journey proved too much for the courageous old man, and he died a few days after arriving at Madrid.

[6] Rafael Sabatini, *Torquemada.*

[7] *Torquemada.*

[8] Nicolaus Eymericus, *Directorium Inquisitorum.*

[9] In his entertaining and exceptionally well-documented study of Torquemada and the Spanish Inquisition, the novelist Sabatini cites the punishment for "solicitation" of a Capuchin brother tried in the eighteenth century before the Grand Inquisitor Rubin de Cevallos. Being convicted of his sin, the friar was sentenced to go into retreat for five years in a convent of his order. Whereupon he startled the inquisitors by imploring them to permit him to serve out his sentence in one of the dungeons of the Inquisition. Asked the reason for his extraordinary petition, he said that he well knew the kind of burdens which the brothers of his order would impose upon a member penanced as he was; and when the grand inquisitor refused to change the sentence on such grounds, the Capuchin was sent to a convent where he died with two years of his sentence still to be served. There was evidently much torture in church penalties not inflicted in a torture chamber.

CHAPTER 10 *The Arts and Craft of the Jesuits*

[1] The Jesuits in France were declared primarily responsible for the assassination of King Henri III and two attempts upon the life of Henri IV, prior to his assassination

by Ravaillac. The murderer of Henri III was a young Dominican monk, Jacques Clément, yet Jesuit influences were blamed. And since Clément had been hastily slain directly after his deed, that impetuous vengefulness removed all chance of making him expose possible accomplices. The first attempt upon the celebrated Henri of Navarre—who, though he had found Paris "worth a Mass", retained all the enemies of a heretic ruler of a Catholic kingdom—was made by a soldier, Barrière, who was luckily arrested before getting in his death stroke. The second was the work of a nineteen-year-old youth named Chastel, who wounded Henri with a dagger. Now the Parlement and the reactionary Catholic University of Paris were by no means clear of blame where these plots were concerned. Before Henri of Navarre was definitely assured of victory, those two institutions had called down death and destruction upon his head. But a newly published work of the Jesuit, Mariana, gave the Parlement an opportunity of absolving itself and throwing upon the hated Jesuit fathers the sole responsibility for the attempts upon the life of the king.

Mariana, active at the court of Madrid as tutor to the future King Philip III, had written for his pupil a tract entitled *De rege et regis institutione*, which upheld the challenging theory that the power of the sovereign was delegated to him by the people, and that the sovereign was responsible to the people and must rule them justly. The Jesuit's tract went further and dared to advocate the "righteous" removal of the sovereign if he failed to respect this bargain, and therefore furnished a pretext in France for blaming the Society of Jesus for the killing of Henri III—whose Jesuit confessor, Father Augier, had called him "the best of penitents"—and for both attempts on the life of Henri IV. Chastel had studied in a Jesuit college; and two Jesuit fathers, who had been his instructors, Guéret and Guignard, were arrested. Guignard was hanged because found in possession of certain offending pamphlets. Chastel was cruelly executed, his dwelling razed to the ground, and a pillory was erected where the house had stood. The final result of all this was the expulsion of the Jesuits from the city of Paris.

²René Fülöp-Miller, *The Power and Secrets of the Jesuits*.
³Quoted by René Fülöp-Miller.

CHAPTER 11   *Police Espials, or the Kings' Evil*

¹Major Arthur Griffiths, *Mysteries of Police and Crime*, Vol I.
²This statute, known as 13 Edward I, was made chiefly for the maintenance of peace in the city of London. It recited how many "evils, as murders, robberies and manslaughters have been committed by night and by day, and people have been beaten and evilly entreated." It enjoined that "none be so hardy as to be found going or wandering about the streets of the city with sword or buckler after curfew" tolled at St Martin's Le Grand; and it further prescribed that as offenders against the law sought shelter in "taverns more than elsewhere, lying in wait and watching their time to do mischief", no tavern might remain open "for sale of ale or wine" after the tolling of curfew. Other matters affecting the peace of London were dealt with in the Act: "forasmuch as fools who delight in mischief do learn to fence with buckler," no school to teach the fencer's art was permitted within the city. Foreigners came in for special rules and admonitions. Those who "by reason of banishment out of their own country, or who, for great offence, have fled therefrom" were forbidden to become innkeepers unless "they have good report from the parts whence they cometh, or find safe pledges."
³M. G. Richings, *Espionage*.

CHAPTER 12   *Walsingham Sights the Armada*

¹Conyers Read, *Mr Secretary Walsingham and the Policy of Queen Elizabeth*.
²Read.
³Chamberlin, *The Private Character of Queen Elizabeth*.
⁴E. L. Taunton, *History of the Jesuits in England*.
⁵Quoted by Austin K. Gray, "Some Observations on Christopher Marlowe, Government Agent" (*Modern Language Association of America*, 1928; Vol. XLIII).

CHAPTER 13 *The Scavenger Spies of Mogul India*

[1] Dr Emil Schmit in Helmolt's *History of the World*.

[2] If Akbar had so many spies, it must be added that centuries earlier Asoka, an even greater ruler, appears to have had very few and possibly none at all. Asiatic countries under strong and stable governments—and for several reasons Russia might here be counted with the great empires of Asia—seldom have been able to get along without spies or the equivalent of our modern political police; and any exception seems worthy of note.

[3] With the help and under the direction of Faizi, the elder of the talented brothers, Akbar caused the most important of the Sanskrit works to be translated into Persian.

[4] The Mogul emperors gave this espionage permanent organization, but it was something they undoubtedly found in vogue upon establishing themselves as conquerors of India. The historical work of "Ferishta"—contemporary of Akbar—touches upon the subject, crediting Allauddin Khalji, an Indian Mohammedan king of the thirteenth century, with the introduction of espionage into his conquered kingdom. By means of it Allauddin controlled and finally suppressed the celebrated Fukhruddin, kotwal of Delhi; and yet he continued to be so apprehensive of conspiracies against his person that he repeatedly had nobles and people of importance summoned for questioning lest they know of any agitation which threatened his reign and failed to report it. His numerous spies procured him intelligence of all the "secret discourses of families of note" as well as news of transactions of every kind in the most distant provinces.

Under the Taghluk rulers of India this espionage grew more systematic, the name and occupation of every newcomer being registered, in anticipation of our present-day passport system. Ibn Batuta, renowned Moslem traveler of the fourteenth century, describes the conspiracy of Ain-ul-Mulk and tells by what means it was suppressed. This ambitious man was the governor of Oudh and had been ordered by the king, Mahomed Taghluk, to provide fodder for cattle, horses and elephants while the royal army remained encamped on the western side of the Ganges during a severe famine. The brothers of Ain-ul-Mulk began conspiring to steal the horses and elephants of the king and then raise the governor of Oudh to imperial rank. "The conspirators would have succeeded," Ibn Batuta explains, "but the Indian monarchs have a detective of their own in the house of all nobles, who regularly informs him of their doings and movements. In the same way the King has women-servants, who report all that they hear and see to female scavengers (*Bhangin*) who in return convey the message to the officer of detectives, and finally the report is sent to the King. Mahommed Taghlak had a detective of his own in the house of Ain-ul-Mulk, named Malik Shah, who informed him of his master's flight."

[5] "A sound mind in a sound body."

[6] W. Irvine, *The Army of the Indian Moguls*.

CHAPTER 14 *Father Joseph and the Cardinals' Spies*

[1] The adventures and intrigues of Marie de Rohan have attracted many writers, and the reader may be recommended to the accounts of her exploits by Victor Cousin, H. Noel Williams, Dorothy de Brissac Campbell and Louis Batiffol. A cleverly written and dramatic short description of her career will be found in the chapter "The Queen of Cabals" of Cameron Rogers' *Gallant Ladies*.

[2] B. H. Liddell Hart, *Great Captains Unveiled*.

CHAPTER 15 *Espionage and the Honors of War*

[1] In 1529 Pope Clement VII hired an imperial army "with 30,000 florins and the promise of the plunder of Florence", and we are told that the "ferocious ruffians of many nationalities" who composed this invading force were using the oath "By the glorious sack of Florence!" before they set out from Lombardy. Until King Louis XI of France created Europe's first standing army, as a regularly paid and professional instrument of warfare, it was the lavish custom of popes and monarchs to enlist their mercenaries with promises of pillage and booty.

[2] Winfried Lüdecke, *Behind the Scenes of Espionage*.

[2] John Lothrop Motley, *The Rise of the Dutch Republic.*
[3] Liddell Hart, *Great Captains Unveiled.*
[4] *Great Captains Unveiled.*
[5] "There is no doubt but that Wallenstein's curious mentality, his "many-sided genius" and unique career all contributed to his downfall. Oxenstierna, his contemporary, who has been called "the best-informed man and ablest judge of character of the time", confessed years after that he had never understood what object Wallenstein really had in view, or what plans were maturing in his acute, capacious mind. In the words of Schiller, his "character, obscured by faction's hatred and applause, still floats, unfixed and stationless in history."
[6] Georges Oudard, *The Amazing Life of John Law.* (Translated by G. E. C. Massé.)
Alberoni, the "arrogant cardinal—remarkable for his enormous head and unusually broad face—did not lack wit, but . . . possessed a low order of mind and a taste for political trickery . . . had compromised himself with that Swedish fool, Charles XII, as well as with some of the less reputable Jacobites . . . hated France and especially the Duke of Orléans." He was "an adept at assuming any kind of mask, even that of virtue, however little that might suit a cardinal who for a whole year had forgotten to be present at the celebration of the Mass and who shared his bed with a woman of the town."
[7] *Les Rêveries ou Mémoires sur l'Art de la Guerre,* first published at The Hague, 1756.
It is this work that only impressed Thomas Carlyle as "a strange military farrago, dictated, as I should think, under opium"—which may, perhaps, help to explain why so many of Carlyle's own works are sinking into the oblivion of required reading.

CHAPTER 16 *Mr Thurloe and Mr Pepys*

[1] Blake destroyed the Spanish Plate Fleet at Tenerife in an action of "almost incredible daring." He was the first naval commander to engage land batteries, the first "that brought ships to contemn castles on the shore." In fighting the Dutch, then the rulers of the sea, he prevailed against odds. He took an English fleet into the Mediterranean, the first English naval force to enter those waters, settled the grievances of English shippers with Tuscany and Malta, and then proceeded to Tunis. "Blake sailed boldly into Tunis harbour under the very guns of the port, burnt every ship there anchored, then sailed on to Algiers, whence he brought away all the English, Scotch, Irish and Channel Island slaves imprisoned there. The grim Protector and his heroic admiral had shown Europe what a strong ruler and an able sailor could do to the pests." That was in 1655. Cromwell gave Blake a sufficient force for such an eventful expedition. English ships had been "repaired and made seaworthy; even more important, consideration was shown to the hitherto abused seamen. They now received proper wages and were paid punctually; their food, although poor, was infinitely better in quality and quantity than under the previous government." (Gosse, *The History of Piracy.*)
Blake died in 1657 and was buried in Westminster Abbey; but after the restoration of the Stuarts the great admiral's bones were dug up by order of Charles II and removed to St Margaret's, Westminster.
[2] This and other Pepys quotations taken from the diary as transcribed from the shorthand manuscript in the Pepysian Library, Magdalene College, Cambridge, by the Reverend Mynors Bright, M.A.
[3] John De Witt was the celebrated grand pensionary of Holland. A few years afterward he and his brother Cornelius were massacred by the Dutch mob, enraged at their opposing the elevation of William of Orange to the stadtholdership when the states were overrun by French troops and the Dutch fleets beaten at sea by the English. The assassination of the De Witts provides one of the main incidents of *The Black Tulip* by Alexandre Dumas, *père.*
[4] John Buchan, *Oliver Cromwell.*
[5] Buchan.
[6] Looking backward from this age of machinal saturation, we see how far we have come from the time when "mechanic" was a synonym of "vulgar" and "common" and could be used to insult a Puritan "usurper."

⁷Of these Major General Worlsey in Manchester made himself particularly odious on account of his "corrupt informers" and his "pulling down of ale-houses."
⁸Only the plague of assassins' plots, as in Elizabeth's reign, justified the repressive measures introduced. But it was a time of petty tyrannies and petty espionage; with morals, with levity and pleasure continually under suspicion, it was probably the worst epidemic of domestic spying that England ever has suffered—not excepting the political or religious espionage of the reigns of Henry VII, Bloody Mary or Elizabeth, or of the generations of Jacobite agitation. "Both Royalists and Republicans, having no hope in open resistance," Macaulay observes, "began to evolve dark schemes of assassination; but the Protector's intelligence was good; his vigilance was unremitting and, whenever he moved beyond the walls of his palace, the drawn swords and cuirasses of his trusty bodyguard encompassed him thick on every side."
⁹Richings, *Espionage*.

CHAPTER 17 *Espionne of the Bedchamber*

¹The other spy who greatly enriched himself was the Emperor Napoleon's celebrated Alsatian agent and former smuggler, Karl Schulmeister. (See Chapter 34, page 226.) Joseph Fouché, while manipulating the police service of the empire, became the second richest man in France and, presumably, even wealthier than Louise de Kéroualle. Yet he can hardly be counted among professional spies or secret agents, for his rewards like his intrigues were on a far grander scale, and hundreds of spies, spy-masters and directors of police bureaus stood between him and the actual performances of surveillance and espionage. (Chapter 26, page 168.)
²*The Cambridge Modern History.*
³Sidney Dark, *Twelve More Ladies*.
⁴Richings, *Espionage*.

CHAPTER 18 *Defoe and the Jacobites*

¹Thomas Wright, *The Life of Daniel Defoe*. Defoe referred particularly to his mission to Scotland in 1706.
²Wright.
³While Jacobite conspiracies accomplished nothing conclusive or effective politically, much may be forgiven conspirators who enrich us with so many legends of courage, self-sacrifice and picturesque romance. There was Bonnie Prince Charlie's escape from Scotland after Culloden! Or earlier—the celebrated escape of the Earl of Nithsdale from the Tower of London. Captured during the insurrection of 1715, the stalwart Nithsdale had been condemned to die on February 24, 1716. Lady Nithsdale—"twenty-six, blue-eyed, childlike and slim"—coolly assisted by two tall friends, a Mrs Mills and a Miss Hilton, together with Evans, a Welsh serving-woman, contrived the whole affair, a classic of impromptu secret service. Nithsdale, big as he was, escaped from the Tower *in woman's attire*, without even troubling to shave off his beard. Lady Nithsdale's triumphant exploit won the applause of hundreds who were not Jacobites, but never found favor with Colonel d'Oyly, deputy of the Tower, who suspected that he had been outwitted.
⁴Compton Mackenzie, *Prince Charlie and His Ladies*.
⁵Colin, *Campagnes de Maréchal Saxe*.
⁶Records of this spy case become obscure as to its conclusion. French historians have thought Dr Hensey escaped; but British opinion holds that he was answered by the court with a throttling affirmative.

CHAPTER 19 *Bourbon Police Espionage*

¹Guignard.
²Upon being detected in her crimes the Marquise de Brinvilliers managed to escape into Germany, seeking asylum in the bishopric of Liége. There the multiple murderess entered a convent and gave herself up to devout religious exercises. But the French police were not to be cheated of their prey; and as extradition was virtually unknown in those days, they resolved to carry her off by a stratagem. One of the best secret

agents operating in Paris was François Degrais, described as "good looking, insinuating and of gentlemanly exterior." He was "without scruples" and so chosen to ensnare the fugitive marquise. Proceeding to Liége disguised as an abbé, Degrais readily obtained admission to the convent, and he was soon on good terms with the terrible Brinvilliers, no doubt bored by her enforced isolation and the strict routine of conventual existence. One day the genial abbé suggested to the marquise that they go for a drive in the country and breakfast at some rural inn. She eagerly agreed; and when the pair drove up to the inn in the carriage obtained by Degrais, a number of his fellow officers appeared and surrounded them, taking the lady into custody. Degrais now disclosed his identity; and the marquise was carried at once across the French frontier.

Degrais did not abate his cunning practices, and on the tedious journey to Paris—during which Brinvilliers made several desperate attempts to commit suicide, generally by swallowing pins or by acts of personal violence—he instructed one of his subordinates, Barbier, to profess secret sympathy for their prisoner. The marquise thereupon trusted this police spy and gave him letters to forward to her friends or presumed accomplices, all documents which later proved incriminating. For this effective pursuit and capture, which, in dealing today with an equally infamous creature—Brinvilliers ultimately confessed poisoning her elderly father and procuring the poisoning of her brothers—would win a detective wide acclaim as a G-man, Scotland Yard inspector, or luminary of the Sûreté-Générale, Degrais earned but a brief caustic mention in the writings of the celebrated Mme de Sevigné: "She [Brinvilliers] died as she had lived—resolutely . . . on her way to the scaffold she only asked that the executioners might walk between her and Degrais, the scoundrel who had betrayed her."

[3]Major Arthur Griffiths has observed: "In the very heart of Paris there was a deep gangrene, a sort of criminal Alsatia—the Cour des Miracles—where depredators and desperadoes gathered unchecked, and defied authority."

[4]"Many of the books suffering "perpetual imprisonment" in the Bastille and found there at the time of the revolution were utterly unimportant and inoffensive. And yet the incarceration of copies and the destruction of whole editions had been managed on such a grand scale, one papermaker on a single day of intellectual assizes hauled away 3,015 pounds of fragments. The selling of obscene works lawfully seized became a regular source of revenue at the police prefecture; and in the more spacious days of the empire it was observed with surprise that Comte Dubois, Napoleon's prefect, did not "sell the books seized by his officers, but gave them to his friends."

[5]The staff of the Bastille, besides the soldiers and officers in garrison—forty-seven men in all at the beginning of the eighteenth century—comprised a governor, a deputy governor, a major, "bound each day to report current prison facts" to the lieutenant general of police, an engineer responsible for the buildings, a surgeon in residence, and a doctor living in private and always at command, a secretary for the archives, a chaplain, a confessor, and two honorary ecclesiastical gentlemen, a police commissioner, four turnkeys, and a midwife, "whose functions were rarely exercised."

[6]It was possible "in lansquenet or hoca to win or lose sixty times in a quarter of an hour"; and the influence of gambling is revealed in the size of the fortunes which changed hands. Mme de Montespan, mistress of Louis XIV, wagered great sums with the same magnificent zest she brought to the Black Mass and other aggressive violations of the moral code. Frequently she lost 100,000 crowns; and one Christmas Day she elected to continue playing until she had lost seven times that much. On another occasion she laid 150,000 pistoles—equivalent to a million and a half dollars—on three cards and won. In a single night she was alleged to have won back five millions which she had previously lost. Monsieur, the king's brother, also gambled steadily and with seldom profitable result, a military campaign rarely costing him less than 100,000 francs, lost to other officers dissatisfied with risking merely their lives on the battlefield.

[7]D'Argenson's dwelling in the Rue des Bons Enfants was almost directly opposite the home of that Mme de Poisson whose daughter was Mme d'Étioles, destined to become the Marquise de Pompadour. In first calling upon the fascinating young married woman, Louis XV employed the subterfuge of "urgent business" requiring him to visit D'Argenson. Yet in spite of the admirable co-operation his residence had provided her in captivating the king, D'Argenson was feared and rejected by the new favorite as

soon as she became confident of her power, and he saw his command of the royal police tossed to the servile Berryer, who had little ability but was spared many failures by a talented subordinate, the detective Saint-Marc, whom D'Argenson had discovered and promoted.

[8]The *Convulsionnaires* were a sect of the Jansenists who met at the tomb of "Francis of Paris", where they preached and prophesied the downfall of the Church and the monarchy of France. Most of their ceremonies were extravagant and wild; they contorted their bodies violently and rolled upon the ground, imitating animals, birds and fishes, until these convulsions, from which they derived their name, ended in collapse and insensibility. French law dealt harshly with such fanaticism; yet the *Convulsionnaires* survived the most vindictive measures of repression. Two of their number were, in fact, discovered in the Conciergerie in 1775, where they had survived thirty-eight years' imprisonment.

[9]Griffiths, *Mysteries of Police and Crime*, Vol. I.

[10]From the time of Louis XIV it had been customary for the superintendent of the post office to know "the secrets contained in the diplomatic correspondence." And during the minority of Louis XV and the regency we find the financial wizard, John Law of Lauriston—who understood as many espionage and intelligence tricks as any banker of his day—gaining much advantage from his intimacy with the Marquis de Torcy, who as superintendent had access to diplomatic secrets and all other mail going abroad. It must, therefore, have been extending the work of the Cabinet Noir to a violation of the domestic correspondence of Frenchmen that made it seem so odious in the Pompadour's day. Record of a bold contemporary, Dr Quesnay, survives solely because he said with bitter candor that he would "sooner dine with the hangman than with the Intendant of Posts" who countenanced such base practices.

[11]Thérèse Louis Latour, *Princesses, Ladies and Salonnières of the Reign of Louis XV*.

[12]Soon after De Sartines' appointment a terrible crime seemed to have been committed in the neighborhood of the Jardin des Plantes. Five people had been murdered; and De Sartines ascertained that five large boxes of plunder had been removed from the dwelling where the five bodies were found. He likewise contrived with startling suddenness to detect the "murderers", who were thrown into jail. This was all very wonderful—except that the whole affair was a fabrication. The five bodies had been taken to the scene of the "crime" in the same boxes used to carry off the loot. De Sartines never told where he got the bodies; and nobody credited *his* confession, even when his prisoners were released without trial. So difficult was it to correct this sensational story once it got around that De Sartines was still believed to have operated against the multiple murderers with redoubtable astuteness.

CHAPTER 20   *The Bewitching Chevalier*

[1]It is even recorded that D'Éon's mother in a special ceremony consecrated the hapless four-year-old to the Sisterhood of the Virgin. Modern psychologists' opinions of the formative and lasting influence of the childhood years upon the character of the adult go a long way toward explaining D'Éon's talent and predilection for masquerading as a woman during his career in secret service.

[2]George Barton, *The World's Greatest Military Spies and Secret Service Agents*.

[3]*The Cambridge Modern History*, Vol. VI.

[4]Joseph Gollomb, *Spies*.

[5]Thérèse Louis Latour, *Princesses, Ladies and Salonnières of the Reign of Louis XV*. The king was known at the *Parc aux Cerfs* as a Polish count, distantly related to Queen Marie Leczinska, consort of the royal debauchee who posed as her relative.

CHAPTER 21   *Caron de Beaumarchais, Alias Norac*

[1]Henri Martin, quoted by Burton J. Hendrick.

[2]Louis XV ordered that a copy of Morande's pamphlet be brought to him before De Sartines had the whole edition privately destroyed, and the king is said to have enjoyed reading about his mistress' past, estimating that her amours had been about as numerous as his own.

NOTES 681

CHAPTER 22 *The Furtive Practice of Doctor Bancroft*
[1] Arthur Lee's journal, as quoted by Burton J. Hendrick in *The Lees of Virginia*.
[2] The Honorable William Eden, afterward Lord Auckland, lent his hand to some very profitable strokes of espionage and intrigue and his name to that huge collection of documents and manuscripts which the British government finally released in 1889 to F. B. Stevens, a famous American scholar residing in London. The Auckland manuscripts were thus made available to students of American history as the Stevens Facsimiles—twenty-five large volumes, which include all the reports that Eden received from informers, betrayers and British agents while serving under the colonial secretary, Suffolk, as the official specifically in charge of the Secret Service operating against the American colonies.
The Stevens Facsimiles and the published letters of King George III (the last edition in 1932) are the incontrovertible modern proofs of the treasons and espionage one hundred and sixty years old which are to be found in this chapter.
[3] Hendrick, *The Lees of Virginia*.
[4] Hendrick.
[5] The British Dictionary of National Biography.
[6] Hendrick.

CHAPTER 23 *Clandestine Spirit of '76*
[1] Hale, because such an appealing figure of noble young patriot and martyr, has remained virtually the best-known spy in American history, though it is not the American habit to concentrate upon the careers of those who fail. Yet in failing, as has lately been disclosed, Hale became a kind of "father" of American military secret service; and so there is that discoverable justification for the generations of schoolboys who, on being asked to name an American spy, have only been able to answer with the name of Nathan Hale.
[2] Morton Pennypacker, member of the New York State Historical Society, who has made a hobby of Long Island history, in *The Two Spies* discloses the tedious and persistent process of research which led him finally to identify the agents of secret intelligence whose devoted and hazardous services in the Revolutionary War earned them—as they desired—only the private gratitude of one man, George Washington.
[3] General Wolfe, while denied the advantages of an intelligence or espionage service as good as those serving his contemporaries in Europe, gained invaluable information from two deserters prior to his attack upon Quebec. The French garrison, they reported, was expecting a convoy of provisions. And so, at a critical hour—about 2 A.M.—when the flotilla of troop-laden boats was dropping silently downstream and French sentries twice challenged from the shore, a French-speaking officer was able to reply satisfactorily, and the surprise ascent to the Heights of Abraham proceeded without interruption.
[4] Hale, after he had paid with his life for his inexperience, ill luck or blunder was forgotten by the American public until Hannah Adams wrote her *History of New England* in 1799. "So far," that work explains, "Hale has remained unnoticed, and it is scarcely known such a character existed." Hale's fame thus began with legend born years after his death; for, though attempts have been made to trace every step in his career, there is much that still puzzles historical scholars. Nobody has been able to prove how he got to New York, and no one can say positively where he was captured.
[5] It is said that the spy passed in civilian disguise to Long Island, "examined every part of the British army, and obtained the best possible information respecting their situation and future operation." (H. Adams, *History of New England*.)
Other authorities allege that, when challenged and asked to give an account of himself, Hale explained that he was a schoolmaster, that he believed in law and obedience to law, and that having sworn allegiance to King George III he regarded it as his duty to keep that oath. And as the rebels would give him no peace, he had come to the encampment of the British in hopes of finding it there. There was no question about his studious appearance or obviously upright character, and the British, concerned with rebels in arms, allowed him to wander through all their camps on Long Island.

[6] The provost marshal denied the condemned spy both a clergyman and a Bible. He had written short simple notes of farewell to his mother, to his sisters, and to a Connecticut young woman whom he had expected to marry. These were destroyed before his eyes by Cunningham, who remarked that "the rebels ought not know they had a man in their army who could die with that much firmness."

[7] James Jay, the brother of John Jay, first chief justice of the United States, claimed the credit for the invention of the ink used in secret service by agents of the colonies. Jay was himself able to help the American cause by transmitting highly important news of events on the other side of the Atlantic. It was James Jay who forwarded to the Continental Congress the first authentic account of the determination of the British ministry to reduce the colonies to unconditional submission. King George's ministers were concealing this design at the time and proposing conciliatory measures. Describing his methods of secret communication, Jay wrote:

"To prevent the suspicion which might arise were I to write to my brother John only, who was a member of Congress, I writ with black ink a short letter to him and likewise to one or two other persons of the family, none exceeding three or four lines in black ink. The residue of the blank paper I filled up, invisibly, with such intelligence and matters as I thought would be useful to the American Cause. All these letters were left open."

[8] There are in existence no copies of the "stain" letters, those written in invisible ink, merely a few fragments. However, the invisible-ink letters reaching headquarters were, after being developed, copied by Alexander Hamilton and other trusted members of General Washington's staff, and these have been preserved among the Washington papers.

[9] Sargent, *Life and Career of Major John André*.

[10] Major André's trial and condemnation was not attended by the severity and vindictiveness which characterized the British provost's treatment of Nathan Hale. A military court, over which General Nathanael Greene presided, and which consisted of six major generals and eight brigadiers, tried André on September 29, 1780; he was hanged at Tappan, N. Y., on the second of October. It was General Greene who had announced the discovery of Benedict Arnold's treason on September 24 and stated: "The Providential Train of Circumstances which led to it affords the most convincing Proofs that the Liberties of America are the Object of Divine Protection."

[11] André was not only popular and capable, acting as Clinton's confidential agent and attending to most of the British commander's correspondence, but also was much admired for literary, musical and artistic talents. It was he who, when the British evacuated Philadelphia, took a fancy to and carried off the portrait found in Benjamin Franklin's home of that great American as a youth of twenty-four. This portrait, painted by Benjamin Wilson, was restored to the United States in 1906 by the gift of Earl Grey, whose ancestor had commanded the evacuating forces and seemingly inherited André's plunder after his execution. Whatever his military tradition or artistic tastes, John André died bravely. A monument honoring him was erected in Westminster Abbey; and in 1821 his body was brought from Tappan to a grave near the monument.

[12] Washington daily recorded with quill and ink his expenses as commander in chief, and with careful, explicit notations accounted for every expenditure. For the first two years he itemized his expenses in terms of pounds sterling; but after 1777 his accounts were in terms of both dollars and the English currency, the latter column being quaintly headed "Lawful Money." Washington was never extravagant and spent only $160,074 of public funds throughout the war. The cost of his secret-intelligence service was, therefore, 11 per cent of his total expenditures. Entries made for reconnoissances constitute a major item of $42,755. Unlike the modern commander in chief, George Washington employed no one to camouflage his reverses; and his ledger contains such entries as expenses "during the retreat through the Jerseys to Pennsylvania", and later that same year an item of $1,037 for expenses on the retreat from Germantown "until we hutted at Valley Forge for the winter."

[13] Pennypacker, *The Two Spies*.

[14] The limitations of space exclude many other espionage or secret-service activities

which influenced the conduct of the American War of Independence. We cannot tell at length of the Quakeress, Lydia Darrah, at whose home in Philadelphia the adjutant general of the British army was quartered, and who was able to transmit valuable information to General Elias Boudinot, who "questioned prisoners" and otherwise managed the primitive Intelligence of the Continental army.

Silas Town was an American officer who, at Washington's suggestion and under the command of General Philip Schuyler, obtained important intelligence disclosing the movements both of Burgoyne and St Leger. Town, at great risk in a hostile Indian country, "shadowed" St Leger's force moving upon Fort Stanwix. An island on which he hid is Spy Island to this day; and Town's warning to Schuyler is said to have resulted in the reinforcing of the garrison at Stanwix and brought General Herkimer to Oriskany.

A band of Rhode Island militiamen, led by Colonel Barton, disguised themselves, penetrated the British lines and made prisoner an English major general. Tory agents of equal audacity made war upon the "rebellious subjects of King George." And in the region visited by Silas Town there were the notorious "blue-eyed" Indians of the tribe of Walter Butler and his kind. Few white men disguised themselves as Indians for purposes of secret service, however, but rather to spread terror on the frontier and conceal the most fiendish depredations. Indians, even the very intelligent and largely pro-British Iroquois, were remarkably useful scouts but unwilling or incompetent spies.

On December 7, 1779, General Washington wrote to the Congress, telling of having received from one of his spies in New York City a letter describing the indefatigable efforts of the British authorities there to increase the depreciation of the Continental currency by increasing the quantity of counterfeits. The spy had made fruitless attempts to detect the persons concerned in its circulation but had written that—"Reams of paper made for the last emissions struck by Congress have been procured from Philadelphia." The Continental issues, first appearing in 1775, for a year had good standing until the counterfeits circulated by Tory agents began to appear. "A villain was taken at Peekskill, N. Y., with 28 counterfeit 40-shilling notes of Connecticut and one of $30 of Congress," was reported in a contemporary journal, which warned further that, though the "Congress note . . . was badly done", the product of an ordinary printing press, the Connecticut notes were "more deceptive, being genuine copperplate products well designed." Hugh Gaine, Tory publisher of the *Mercury* in New York, was a leading author of the counterfeit notes, and brazenly printed this notice:

"Persons going into the other colonies may be supplied with any number of counterfeited Congress notes for the price of paper per ream. They are so neatly and exactly executed that there is no risk in getting them off, it being impossible to discover that they are not genuine. This has been proved by bills to a very large amount which have been successfully circulated. Inquire for Q. E. D. at the Coffee house from eleven P.M. to four A.M. during the present month."

James Rivington, a New York bookseller, seemed as much of a Tory partisan as Gaine, yet he was also one of Washington's spies. Rivington kept his exact state of mind so fluid that we may suspect, had the British forces prevailed, he would have *remained* a Tory of deepest dye. There is no record that connects him with the Townsend chain; but he is said to have proved his value in helping to mask General Washington's descent upon Cornwallis at Yorktown. The British in New York were kept in readiness for an attack and so sent no aid to the harassed colleague in Virginia; and Rivington and others helped to build up the positive anticipations of the move against New York, which Washington never seriously considered as a substitute for Yorktown.

CHAPTER 24 *Liberty, Equality, Fraternity—Intrigue*

[1] Jean-Guillaume Hyde de Neuville, *Souvenirs.*
[2] G. Lenotre, *A Gascon Royalist in Revolutionary Paris.*
[3] *Mémoires de Sénar.*
[4] Sénar.

CHAPTER 25 *De Batz, the Gascon Wizard*
[1]Lenotre, *A Gascon Royalist in Revolutionary Paris.*
[2]Louis Madelin, *La Révolution.*
[3]As persistent a searcher as Lenotre found no special explanation of De Batz's undisciplined transfer to the army of Spain lodged anywhere in the military archives of the Bourbon monarchy. The future conspirator's restlessness must remain the most logical excuse for his vagaries as a dragoon officer. As for the significance of his being promoted to the rank of colonel upon his return, that suggests family influence had been at work during his absence, all the plums of army, church and state falling invariably to scions of noble houses. His almost instantaneous retirement on half pay shows that the Royal army, while subject to patrician pressure, was determined to protect itself from further neglect.

CHAPTER 26 *Fouché Facing Four Ways*
[1]It is more than a striking coincidence that the three great diplomatists of the French Revolutionary epoch—Talleyrand, Sieyès and Fouché—all studied in the "university" of the Roman Catholic Church and were graduate "masters in the knowledge of human beings before coming to play their part in public life." Fouché humbly taught Latin, mathematics and physics and maintained discipline in the boys' dormitory while teaching himself that inflexible self-discipline which was to make him the invincible politician, the unbeatable intriguer, and the most formidable director of police ever known to the Continent. It was his Church training also which undoubtedly gave him that "constitutional antipathy to luxury and display, and an exceptional capacity for concealing his private life and his personal sentiments."
[2]The impoverished lawyer and future Incorruptible had not yet dropped the "de" from his name for political reasons.
[3]This curiously fateful friendship struck up between Fouché and Robespierre also included the latter's sister, Charlotte. She seems to have become interested in Fouché's having abstained from vows of celibacy and to have considered liberating the "tonsured clerk" from his bondage as an Oratorian. In his study of Fouché, Stefan Zweig observes: "We do not know why the affair fell through in the end, but if we did it is not unlikely that we should discover the root of the fierce enmity which subsequently raged between Robespierre and Fouché, an enmity which has become historical, and which led to a life-and-death struggle between the sometime friends." (*Joseph Fouché: The Portrait of a Politician.*)
[4]Zweig.

CHAPTER 27 *Montgalliard the Unmitigated*
[1]Only one of many dissections of Comte de Montgalliard need be offered in support of this biographical unanimity, and it is given here because it is the most arresting short description of a master intriguer with which the writer is familiar: ". . . and if ever the muse of History were to own herself at a loss, it would be in the presence of this terrible Protean spy, who appears, disappears, and appears again, now coaxing and seductive, now cynical and merciless, selling those who buy him and surviving forty years of revolution, having always retained the favor, not only of every Government, but also of its most persistent enemies; trafficking in his sworn word, brilliantly witty, skillful in persuasion, specious, brutal, insinuating, authoritative, obsequious, arrogant, and blessed with a faculty of undaunted assurance calculated to disarm and baffle honest folks." (Lenotre, *Two Royalist Spies of The French Revolution;* translation by Bernard Miall.)
[2]Fauche-Borel, *Mémoires.*
[3]Archives of the prefecture of police: *Registres du Temple.*
[4]Montgalliard's sons were born respectively in 1786 and 1790; both entered the French army and died in the wars of the Empire.
[5]*État de la France au Mois de Mai,* 1794.
[6]The German population could not understand why "these crazy French gentlemen, the owners of country houses, castles, large incomes, and lucrative offices, should resign

NOTES

themselves so cheerfully, for the sake of a futile point of honor, to marching . . . with empty bellies, against the bitter north wind." They were unable at that time to comprehend the warfare between Royalists and Republicans. Long after, says Puymaigre (*Souvenirs*), at Oberkamlach, one of the battlefields of this fratricidal conflict, there was still to be seen a cenotaph bearing this inscription: *Here several thousand Frenchmen cut one another's throats without our understanding precisely why.*

[7] Lenotre.
[8] Lenotre.
[9] Caudrillier, *La Trahison de Pichegru.*
[10] Caudrillier.
[11] Clément de Lacroix, *Souvenirs du Comte de Montgalliard.*
[12] Lenotre.
[13] Montgalliard, *Mémoire concernant la Trahison de Pichegru.*
[14] Fauche made "little gifts of money" and "watches, stockings, body linen" to the unfortunate Republican officers who were drawing only eight livres a month in cash. Adjutant General Badouville, "the aide-de-camp and confidant of Pichegru—otherwise known as *Coco* or *Cupidon*—dogged the steps of the wealthy Swiss, would not be parted from him . . . and when he wrote to him signed himself: 'Your friend for life.'" The bookseller "adroitly distributed books, shoes and silver crowns" to the half-starved soldiery. "A distribution," he wrote, "which I seemed to make purely out of compassion, while exclaiming at the sins of the Convention in leaving them thus destitute." Properly to "enlighten" the troops he gave them pamphlets, as well as paying the editor of the *Gazette de Deux Ponts* one hundred louis annually, says Caudrillier, (Pichegru) "for editing his sheet 'in the most fitting spirit.'"
[15] Nodier, *Souvenirs de la Révolution.*
[16] Lenotre.
[17] Quoted by Clément de Lacroix from the *Archives nationales.*
[18] Lenotre.
[19] *Histoire secrète du Directoire.*
[20] Lenotre.
[21] Marengo and Hohenlinden occurred in the same year, 1800. At Marengo Bonaparte was already beaten when Desaix, with the intuition of military genius, came to his aid and converted defeat into a great triumph. Moreau and his troops the following December, "in the midst of snow, mud, and altogether abominable weather, inflicted an overwhelming defeat upon the Austrian army at Hohenlinden. If Napoleon had gained this battle, it would have counted among his most characteristic and brilliant exploits." (Wells, *Outline of History.*)
[22] Among this crowd of prisoners "packed together in the four storeys of the Tower" were men of every sort: peasants from the Morbihan, British naval officers, Norman fishermen, French gentlemen, *ci-devant* great nobles, generals, men of the people, even two children of nine or ten years, "cabin-boys, members of the crew of Captain Wright, and captured with him, who drew with charcoal, on the walls of the courtyard, gallows from which Bonaparte hung suspended." Georges Cadoudal's companions-in-arms used to "gather together under the trees to recite their rosary or to sing hymns; others played games . . . resigned to death, but fearing the 'examinations', from which some returned with fingers mutilated by the thumbscrews of the police." (Lenotre.)

CHAPTER 28 *Imperial Secret Police*

[1] Nodier, *Souvenirs de la Révolution.*
[2] Of Fouché's uncelebrated predecessors, Sotin was minister of police from July 26, 1797 to February 12, 1798; Dondeau was minister from February 17 to May 15, 1798; while Duval was minister from October 29, 1796 to June 22, 1799—Fouché taking control of the Ministry less than a month later, 2 Thermidor, year VII, or July 20, 1799.
[3] Lenotre, *Two Royalist Spies of the French Revolution.*
[4] Fauriel, *Les derniers Jours du Consulat.*
[5] Pasquier, *Mémoires.*
[6] *Souvenirs de la Révolution.*

⁷*Histoire secrète du Directoire.*
⁸Madelin, *Fouché.*
⁹Quoted from *Le Globe,* April 20, 1833, by A. Savine in the preface to *Quinze Ans de haute Police.*
¹⁰Lenotre (translation by Bernard Miall).
¹¹*Two Royalist Spies of the French Revolution.*
¹²Desmarest, *Quinze Ans de haute Police,* with a preface by Albert Savine, who deals at some length with the exploits of Dupéron.
¹³Lenotre.

CHAPTER 29 *Dublin Castle's Corps of Double-Dealers*

¹William McFee, reviewing *Dear Robert Emmet* by Raymond W. Postgate.
²Henri le Caron, *Twenty-five Years in the Secret Service.*
³Dr W. J. Fitzpatrick, *Secret Service under Pitt.*
⁴The noted conspirator, Hamilton Rowan, was one who met with this sort of suspicious reception upon reaching the haven of the French Republic. Rowan, though brilliantly defended by John Philpot Curran, had been convicted of sedition, fined and committed to Newgate. The accused had wanted to offer proof that two of his jurors had been heard to declare that "Ireland would never be quiet until Rowan and Napper Tandy were hanged"; but this challenge had been disallowed by the court. Rowan contrived his romantic escape from Newgate on May 4, 1797, and finally got away to France aboard a fisherman's boat, though the two men manning it had been shown the English proclamation offering a reward of £1,000 for his recapture. And no sooner was he safely landed on the coast of France than he was mistaken for a British secret agent, sent under strong guard to Brest, and there lodged among galley slaves, who at that time must have included the great convict-escaper and future detective, Eugène Vidocq.
⁵That Turner was unknown even to Newell is made evident by the *Life and Confessions of Newell the Informer,* which was published by the author (London, 1798).

CHAPTER 30 *Britain Leads with a Cuckold*

¹Holland Rose, quoting Thiers.
²According to the recollections of the Duchesse d'Abrantès; Vol. III, p. 63.
³Paul et Suzanne Lanoir, *Les grands espions.*

CHAPTER 31 *The Continental Blockade*

¹November 11, 1807.
²Daudet, *Émigration.*
³Lenotre, *Two Royalist Spies of the French Revolution.*
⁴D'Hauterive; Police Report.
⁵Police Report of June 6, 1805; D'Hauterive.
⁶D'Hauterive.
⁷Madelin, *Fouché.*
⁸Hyde de Neuville, *Mémoires.*
⁹Lenotre.
¹⁰Abbé Ratel frequently had occasion to congratulate his colleague in the name of the British government, only to draw Leclerc's modest reply: "The majority of those who assist us in our work do so merely because of their zealous spirit, their enthusiasm for the Royalist cause, and their desire to contribute to the restoration of order in Europe. Great and small alike help us by every means at their disposal." Such statements helped foreigners to their erroneous belief that Napoleon was execrated by the majority of Frenchmen. "The whole *émigré* world," Lenotre observes, "beheld the tyrant . . . through the wall-eye of the Abbé Leclerc."
¹¹He gave them a dark lantern and complete instructions. "Go down to the water's edge with your lantern lit—show a light three times at intervals of half an hour, and then hide it. The English boats, which will be tacking to and fro along the coast, and which are in the secret, will then come inshore." As for the English signals: "A flag at half-mast, hoisted and lowered three times, means that there will be a letter to be

forwarded on the following night." An excise officer prowling about the neighborhood called for the "hopeless" signal to be given the English—" a fire on the cliffs by day, or a rocket at night."

[12] The whole enterprise of communication between England and France, whether the exchange of letters or the smuggling of passengers across the Channel, was described by the comprehensive term, *La Correspondence*.

[13] Trafalgar was decidedly an "imprudent" engagement, and the imprudence was entirely Napoleon's. Admiral Villeneuve knew that his fleet was inferior and unready. Press gangs had recently supplied him with raw and reluctant levies, which could not possibly prove a match for the well-drilled crews of Nelson's ships. Villeneuve, according to authorities like Lanfrey, put to sea, obeying Napoleon's explicit orders, only because he knew that Admiral Rosily was en route to enforce those orders or to supersede him. And yet, in spite of their palpable inferiority in combat, both French and Spanish fought magnificently. Southey's and other contemporary accounts of the momentous sea fight pay such lavish tribute to Nelson, his officers and men, that they ignore the gallantry of the foe. Investigations by the British Admiralty as recently as 1912 correct this error of fact and good sportsmanship. As for the fighting qualities of Nelson's crews, there seems to have been no injustices or indignities that could knock the fight out of British seamen. More than half of them were victims of the abominable "recruiting" practices of the press gang. They suffered abusive treatment, the worst living conditions, bad rations, poor pay; and yet *they* fought magnificently.

[14] H. G. Wells, *Outline of History*.

[15] Lenotre.

[16] A pension on which she "lived wretchedly enough"; according to a French police report—*Archives des Affaires étrangères*—she "bitterly deplored her fate."

[17] Leclerc in Münster was on the direct route taken by spies proceeding from the port of Hamburg, a kind of secret-service base, to the frontier of France. Counter-espionage agents reported to Marshal Moncey in 1805 that agents of the British government were traveling on foot or on horseback over a route impracticable for wheeled traffic which led by way of Münster, Turnhout and Nymegen to Bois-le-Duc. Shelter was provided them in Trappist and Capuchin monasteries, which favored the cause of Bonaparte's implacable adversary.

CHAPTER 32   *The Powerful Impact of Pounds Sterling*

[1] The French, to judge from the reports lodged in their police archives (D'Hauterive, Vol. I, 1456) were convinced that this American consular official of rather indistinct allegiance ran the craft Jungfrau Elizabeth between Dunkirk and Calais, one of those vessels with specially constructed hiding places aboard for letters and parcels.

[2] Though Leclerc only turned aside his lines of communication to the island of Jersey after the dislocation of his chain by the Tréport-Abbeville raids, the Channel Islands, especially Jersey and Guernsey, had been used in secret-service enterprises from the earliest months of the French Revolution. These convenient bases, from the wars of the revolution until 1814, are said to have been in constant touch with espionage bureaus in Cherbourg and St Malo which had early been established by British Intelligence officers who visited those ports ostensibly for the purpose of arranging for the exchange of prisoners.

[3] Newspapers crossed the Channel without interruption throughout the term of the Continental Blockade. Both the *Moniteur* and the *Journal de l'Empire* were punctually received in London "a week or ten or twelve days after the date of their publication." (Lenotre.)

CHAPTER 33   *A Crackpot's Coup*

[1] Rovigo, *Mémoires*.
[2] Madelin, *Fouché*.
[3] The chief emissaries were Rovigo himself and the Duc de Massa.
[4] "If he refuses," were Napoleon's final words to Dubois, (Stefan Zweig, *Joseph Fouché*) "if he refuses, send along ten gendarmes immediately to take him to the

Abbaye prison, and then, by God, I will show him how quickly a trial can be put through."

⁶It was in one of these epistles that Fouché solemnly wrote of himself: "Il n'est pas de mon caractère de changer."
⁶Madelin, *Fouché.*
⁷Rovigo, *Mémoires.*
⁸General Lamothe for a time seemed gravely compromised by the Malet misadventure. The minister of war sent for him, but none of the garrison of Paris recognized him. Only when the soldiers saw Malet they exclaimed: "This is the General Lamothe who came to call us out and whose orders we obeyed." The minister of war still considered the real Lamothe under a cloud, for certain passes issued by the conspirators had been stamped with the initial "L"; but luckily for the innocent officer, Savary saw in the "L" the first letter of the word *Liberté*, and General Lamothe was saved from imprisonment and a military trial.
⁹Owing to his great distance from Paris, Napoleon heard about the conspiracy at the same time that he learned all the conspirators had been arrested and brought to trial. Even so, "the daring of the attempt, carried out at the very seat of government, made a remarkable impression upon him and he was not reassured until three or four more dispatches had come in," according to his aide and confidant, General de Caulaincourt. He was deeply concerned about the inevitable effect of the affair in Europe and feared that it might mean further attempts on the part of a few hotheads in the pay of England. Caulaincourt in his fascinating *Memoirs* of such curiously recent issue seems to hold that, whereas the emperor at Paris would have forgotten the Malet plot "in a day—at 600 leagues distance and the world without news of him or of his army", such an event was bound to cause anxiety. Napoleon kept thinking that others might try Malet's grand stratagem of imposture with better luck.
¹⁰The Malet incident is said to have made all Paris roar with laughter; and Napoleon knew well that ridicule can be more unsettling to those in authority than their own mistakes. However, he commended Savary and did not dismiss him, believing it best not to make arrests in the "Malet incident", at least not of any prominent persons or those known to have been his adherents. In the eyes of Europe and of France he wanted the whole conspiracy dismissed as nothing "more formidable than a madman's escapade." "—To ensure that the thing shall be unravelled I have not even changed the Minister of Police," the emperor explained to Caulaincourt, "for he is more concerned than anyone else in repairing the harm brought about by his lack of foresight. Savary clings to his ministry and salary. He is afraid of losing his post, although so far as that goes, he no longer needs it, as I have given him plenty of money. He has at least five or six millions. . . ."
¹¹Napoleon finally got around to discovering the scapegoat in M. Frochot, prefect of the Seine, who ranked as a counselor of state. The emperor had hitherto considered Frochot extremely efficient, which only added to his rancor in discovering the luckless prefect more guilty than any other official in failing to expose Malet's imposture on sight. All sections of the Council of State adjudged Frochot as having "failed in firmness and decision in carrying out the responsibilities entrusted to him." Napoleon thereupon made an example of him, depriving him of his functions as counselor and prefect.

CHAPTER 34 *An Emperor of Espions*

¹Documents found in the Austrian military archives at Vienna covering the courtmartial of Mack, together with a memorial later written by him during his imprisonment and addressed to the Emperor Francis, disclose how gradually the truth about his own betrayal had dawned upon him. Faulty intelligence made the Austrian commander irresolute, but all his bad generalship cannot be blamed upon—or credited to—Schulmeister and his bribed accomplices. Mack's measures of defense at Ulm were hopelessly confused. Within a single day he would issue a set of instructions, change them radically an hour afterward, and contradict his earlier contradiction before nightfall. The marshal was obviously no match for such opponents as Lannes, Ney or Soult, and it is clear that he welcomed the discovery of "the spy" who had made a fool of him.

Schulmeister the Alibi not only opened the door of Mack's prison but also masked his congenital inferiority to the best strategic brains of France.
²The reader acquainted with Sir Arthur Conan Doyle's unforgettable Brigadier Gerard will wonder why a braggart attracted any particular attention in Napoleon's armies; the conquest of the Continent had not promoted military modesty or been achieved with corps of shrinking violets. But, according to Diffenbach, Schulmeister gave offense mainly because he gloried more in his ill-gotten gains than in the stratagems he had contrived as a spy or the risks of detection he had incurred.
³Schulmeister is reputed to have been several times wounded in battle. A shrapnel bullet injured him seriously at Friedland, which may account for the "deep scars" observed by De Gassicourt two years later. Bravery was rather at a discount in the armies of Napoleon, but one has to reflect that Schulmeister's bravery was unusual in a spy at that time. The very word "spy" during and after the French Revolution suggested only that which was skulking, cowardly and infernal to the mind of a soldier. Small wonder then that Schulmeister was so eager to shine as a man of action and physical courage.
⁴Taking the name of an estate obtained by purchase rather than patrician inheritance was not uncommon, even in the days of the Bourbons. The watchmaker Caron became Caron de Beaumarchais by way of a deed admitting him to the landowning class. The confiscation or abandonment of fine properties due to the Terror and the emigration brought many upon the market at bargain prices; and as the mushroom aristocracy of the Empire sprouted beside every rut made by Napoleon's gun carriages, this polishing up of plebian names grew to be a much derided but everyday occurrence.
⁵Nothing would seem more clearly to expose Napoleon as an upstart and parvenu himself than this excuse offered to one whose duplicities he had been guiding and handsomely profiting from ever since the D'Enghien murder. Fouché and Savary were dukes. And far greater scoundrels, like Radet, flaunted the bit of ribbon which Schulmeister, even on a field of battle, was denied.
⁶Another Bonaparte, Prince Louis Napoleon, who elevated himself to power as Napoleon III, had a keen politician's eye for neglected henchmen of his illustrious uncle, and in 1850 when making a tour as President of France he sought out the former secret-service agent and warmly offered him his hand.

CHAPTER 35 *Napoleonic Adversaries*

¹L. Diffenbach, *Schulmeister*.
²Winfried Lüdecke, *Behind the Scenes of Espionage*.
³Lüdecke.

CHAPTER 36 *High Priestess of Holy Peace*

¹Clément de Lacroix, *Souvenirs du Comte de Montgalliard*.
²Encyclopædia Britannica.
³Lenotre.
⁴*De la Restoration de la Monarchie des Bourbons et du Retour à l'Ordre*, 1814.
⁵Lenotre.
⁶Lenotre, *A Gascon Royalist in Revolutionary Paris*.
⁷Lenotre.

CHAPTER 37 *Carbonari and Camorra*

¹The name was derived from the Italian word meaning "charcoal burners."
²A celebrated account of the ruthless suppression of Capobianco's movement and the fate that overtook him is to be found in Greco's *Intorno al tentativo dei Carbonari di Citeriore Calabria nel 1813*.
³Encyclopædia Britannica.

CHAPTER 38 *Prologue to Secession*

¹R. K. Wyllys, "The East Florida Revolution of 1812–1814" (*Hispanic American Historical Review*, 1929.)

[2]C. M. Brevard, *A History of Florida.*
[3]A. J. Pickett, *History of Alabama.*
[4]A number of Georgian frontiersmen, preparing for a descent upon Florida, assembled on the opposite bank of the St Marys River. Uniting with the border settlers on the Spanish side, they proceeded to organize an independent "Republic of Florida", with Colonel John McIntosh as president and a Colonel Ashley as military chief. Fernandina, on Amelia Island, had become in 1808 a port of free entry for foreign vessels. On the excuse of protecting American shipping interests, General Matthews determined to occupy Fernandina and Amelia Island, and to that end sent nine armed vessels into the harbor. Forces of the "Republic of Florida" he enlisted in his project, and, commanded by Ashley, they approached Fernandina by water and summoned the Spanish commander, Don José Lopez, to surrender. Lopez was forced to sign articles of capitulation March 17, 1812, possibly a delicate compliment to the Irishman, Matthews. These articles—which added to the political apoplexy of the Spanish minister in Washington—provided that Fernandina should remain a free port, but in case of war between Britain and the United States, British ships could not enter the harbor after May 1, 1813.
[5]Wyllys.
[6]*Documents from Henry, the British Spy!!* (Boston: Munroe & French Patriot Office, 1812.)
[7]It was on August 24, 1814, that Ross and Cockburn and their "barbarians" marched into Washington. As E. Benjamin Andrews observes in his *History of the United States*, Alaric had led his better-controlled pagan barbarians into defenseless Rome through the Porta Salaria on the twenty-fourth of August, 410 A.D.—just 1404 years earlier. Only a few days after writing Major Reed, early in September, 1814, Jackson appealed to the Secretary of War, General Armstrong—being evidently still unaware of the burning of the national capital—urging that the militia be called out at once and reduce Pensacola, used by the British as a base for war operations.
[8]This rare Jackson letter was acquired by Mr John J. Madigan, well-known dealer in autographs, from a direct descendant of President Zachary Taylor. The text given here is that which Mr Madigan released for publication in the New York *Times*, January 25, 1935.
[9]Political press correspondence by Drew Pearson and Robert S. Allen.
[10]Philip Gosse, *The History of Piracy.*
[11]*The History of Piracy.*
[12]T. R. Ybarra, *Bolívar the Passionate Warrior.*
[13]Ybarra.
[14]Marshall, on his way to Richmond to preside over Aaron Burr's treason trial, did not think it amiss to be a fellow dinner guest of the accused politician. He subsequently distorted his own words, on which "the ink was hardly dry", to favor Burr and excluded much evidence that might have convicted him. (Claude G. Bowers, *Jefferson in Power.*)
[15]Walton, *A History of the Detection, Conviction, Life and Designs of John A. Murrel, the Great Western Land Pirate.*

CHAPTER 39 *The Baltimore Conspirators*

[1]Some time after publication of the proofs had ceased to endanger Pinkerton operatives in Maryland a lively dispute persisted as to certain individuals' extraneous share in the preparation, protection and management of President Lincoln's momentous journey to Washington for his first inauguration. The written recollections of Samuel M. Felton—which are relied upon here—were among those then made public.
[2]Allan Pinkerton, *The Spy of the Rebellion.*
[3]Baltimore, subsequently garrisoned by Federal troops, under the successive command of General Butler, General Banks and General Dix, saw Police Marshal Kane removed from office and held under close arrest at Fort McHenry. But not too close—for in 1863 Kane managed to escape to the more stirring duties of an officer of Confederate infantry.

⁴Judge Davis afterward became an associate justice of the United States Supreme Court; while Colonel Sumner, Major Hunter and Captain Pope arrived uniformly at the more exalted rank of major general in the ensuing War of Secession.
⁵The questions here attributed to President Lincoln conform to the written recollections of Messrs Felton, Lamon and Judd.
⁶Pinkerton's report of the episode, accepted as authoritative by Nicolay and Hay.
⁷Asked to vouch for the integrity of his operatives, Pinkerton did so with complete and persuasive conviction.
⁸In July 1863, during the terrible Draft Riots which beset the city of New York, Superintendent Kennedy walked into a mob of infuriated Irish at Forty-Sixth Street and Lexington Avenue. He was recognized and attempted to stand against a hundred assailants, armed only with a bamboo cane. He was viciously mauled. Knocked down again and again, he got up each time and fought back in spite of the blows pelting upon him; until at last he was swept off his feet and beaten insensible. He would undoubtedly have been dispatched on the spot had not a venturesome bystander, John Eagan, who knew him, stood over his body and convinced the nearest ruffians that the superintendent of police was, in fact, already dead. Pursuing this stratagem when the rioters had turned aside to another chore of violence and looting, Eagan loaded the supposed corpse into a wagon, covered it with sacks and drove to police headquarters, where a surgeon found Kennedy suffering from twenty-one cuts and seventy-two bruises.
⁹The New York detectives were David S. Bookstaver, Sampson and De Voe.
¹⁰As the dispute over the questions—was Abraham Lincoln gravely endangered by the Baltimore conspirators?—and who did the most to protect him?—did not subside, statements supporting the recollections of Felton, Judd, Lamon and Pinkerton were obtained from Governor Andrew Curtin and from participating employees of the railroad and telegraph companies, Messrs Kenney, Franciscus, Stearns, Lewis, Thayer, Dunn, Wynne and John Pitcairn, Jr.
¹¹Mrs Warne was the first woman in America, and, very likely anywhere else, professionally employed as a private detective and then as supervisor of other operatives of her sex.
¹²Sampson and De Voe. In his *Recollections of a New York Chief of Police*, George Washington Walling has Sampson say: "We should have been murdered in Washington but for the good head and great heart of Timothy Webster, the bravest, coolest man, I think, that ever lived."

CHAPTER 40 *Agents Blue and Gray*

¹John G. Nicolay.
²The wording is not Abraham Lincoln's, but, presumably, Allan Pinkerton's, or that of some anonymous collaborator of his who assisted in writing the account of his Civil War services to the Federal government, *The Spy of the Rebellion*, published in 1883.
³"Major E. J. Allen" was Detective Pinkerton's chosen *nom de guerre*. It was a mysterious and masking touch, unhappily not otherwise duplicated in the inexperienced operations of espionage while he commanded the new Federal Secret Service. He neglected to provide an equal degree of "camouflage" or protection for even his best offensive secret agent, Webster. The name "Allen" seems to have been chosen for him by Major General McClellan who, in a letter dated April 24, 1861, advised: "Whenever you telegraph me, better use only your first name." But Pinkerton's own published statements make it Allen—not Allan, as so many military authorities and writers of magazine articles appear to have taken for granted.
⁴Pinkerton, *The Spy of the Rebellion*.
⁵Mrs Greenhow escaped Federal penalties but was overtaken at the height of her career as a Southern agent by the worst of hostile fortunes. After her release from the Washington prison she continued to serve the Confederacy and made at least one voyage to England as a special emissary and propagandist. Still later, running the Union blockade outside Wilmington, N. C., the ship Condor which transported her on a second journey abroad ran aground on the New Inlet bar. The Condor was commanded by that Captain Augustus Charles Hobart-Hampden, a veteran of the

Crimean War, on a year's leave of absence from the British navy to engage in some profitable blockade-running adventures under the *nom de guerre* of Captain Roberts or Hewett or Gulick. Mrs Greenhow, too impatient to wait for the Condor to be floated, was determined not to risk capture. She insisted on being taken ashore immediately; and her boat overturned in the surf. All the others were saved, but she perished—it was said, because of the weight of her heavy silk dress and the many gold sovereigns she carried in a belt around her waist.

⁶The Baltimore *American* of November 23, 1861, had condemned Timothy Webster's effrontery in this loyal paragraph:

ESCAPE OF A STATE PRISONER

"It was rumored yesterday that the man Webster, who was arrested, stopping at the hotel of Messrs McGee, upon the charge of being concerned in the regular transportation of letters between Baltimore and the seceded States, had succeeded in making his escape. It is learned upon the best authority that during a late hour of the night he was removed from the western police station and placed in a carriage under the charge of a special detective officer. The wagon was driven towards Fort McHenry, he having been previously ordered to that post, but while the vehicle was in motion, he gave a sudden bound from his seat, and before the officer could seize him he was beyond his grasp. It is not known which direction he took, but he will scarcely be able to escape from the city."

But the camp of the Secessionists had already chuckled over the news in the *Gazette* of November 22, which inspired account concluded:

"We have learned from an entirely reliable source that Mr Webster was arrested in endeavoring to procure replies to a number of letters which he had delivered from Marylanders now residing in Virginia to friends at home. A fact which, in view of the hazards of such an attempt, should content the unfortunate exiles from Maryland with the gratification of communication with their friends there and without the reciprocal joy of hearing from the latter in return. We have reason to believe that Webster is beyond the reach of the Yankees."

CHAPTER 41   *Lafayette Baker and Belle Boyd*

¹Timothy Webster was convicted on April 18, 1862, and his execution was set for the twenty-ninth—because, said Mr Pinkerton, he was still so ill and weak, the rebels feared he would die if they were not unduly prompt about hanging him. Until almost his last hour he was attended in prison by Mrs Lawton, who might long ago have fled but had stayed and suffered arrest as a concomitant of her splendid devotedness. Webster's only petition, addressed to General Winder, was that as a Union secret agent he be allowed to face a firing squad and die a soldier's death. This privilege was straightway denied him. The capital penalty still hung as a threat over those two subjects of Queen Victoria, Lewis and Scully; but after a term of imprisonment the unfortunate men, together with Carrie Lawton, were returned to the North.

²Jacob R. Perkins, *Trails, Rails and War; the Life of General Grenville M. Dodge.*
³Perkins.
⁴The Federal Quartermaster General Meigs complained: "No government can keep 120 regiments of cavalry mounted while such a system is tolerated. They have killed off ten times as many horses for us as for the Rebels." And Sherman said: "They will bankrupt the Government," agreeing with Meigs that "30,000 horses had perished in the Western armies during the winter of 1863–64." Sherman particularly resented his cavalry's "refusal to destroy railroads", observing that the mounted raiders did not have "the industry to damage a railroad seriously." J. E. B. Stuart's fondness for brilliant raids brought General Lee to a "rare outburst of anger" at Gettysburg. The Union General Jacob D. Cox, "that judicious observer," declared that the cavalry's fondness for raids was "never worth the candle." While General Hooker, "believed by many Northern critics to have suffered seriously at Chancellorsville because General Stoneman's cavalry was away on a fruitless raid when needed on the battlefield,"

NOTES 693

was said to be "the author of that popular epigram, 'Who ever saw a dead cavalryman?'" (Lloyd Lewis, *Sherman, Fighting Prophet*.)
[5] Charles A. Dana, *Recollections of the Civil War*.
[6] Baker, *History of the United States Secret Service*.
[7] Hergesheimer, *Swords and Roses*.
[8] *Belle Boyd in Camp and Prison, written by Herself* (New York, 1865).

CHAPTER 42 *Crazy Bet and Other Ladies*

[1] Elizabeth van Lew died in 1900. Having remained to the end unwilling to boast, or even to talk, about her great and hazardous services to the cause of the Union, she would have continued to be passed over and forgotten but for the investigations of historical societies interested in the records of feminine partisans of the American Civil War.

[2] More than a century before the outbreak of the War of Secession, a Virginian of distinction, Richard Henry Lee—then only twenty-seven years old—disturbed the House of Burgesses with a famous speech against slavery, urging that some means be sought to end the evil in the colony, not because it was an injury to the blacks, but to the whites—one of the most conspicuous instances of farseeing statesmanship in the colonial era. Many famous Virginians of the Revolution, Washington, Jefferson, Patrick Henry, George Mason and others, left written records disclosing their abhorrence of slavery. And Richard Henry Lee was no more strongly opposed to the evil on economic grounds in 1759 than a greater Virginian, General Robert E. Lee, in 1861.

[3] Elizabeth van Lew appears to have kept a diary throughout the most perilous months of her secret-service operations but to have prevented its discovery by burying it in the ground. When subsequently found and examined, many pages proved to have been mutilated by its author, who no doubt considered their content too dangerous ever to be made public.

[4] We must note here the striking resemblance of Miss van Lew to that "Miss Dix" named by Samuel M. Felton and Allan Pinkerton, whose warning corroborated the report of the detectives upon the Baltimore conspirators' plan to prevent the inauguration of Abraham Lincoln. At the time Pinkerton published his *Spy of the Rebellion* (1883) there was, however, no reason to protect Miss van Lew with a pseudonym. She was not then in danger of being exposed, for she had long since been denounced in the South as a "spy" and "traitor" and socially ostracized in Richmond. Assuming that a genuine Miss Dix, or some other Southern gentlewoman favoring law and order, communicated with Mr Felton, it is probable that Elizabeth van Lew was a source of the political warnings received by General Scott and Colonel Stone in Washington. Throughout her partisan career she showed instinctive preference for communicating secret intelligence to military authorities.

[5] The Northern prisoners suffered severely in Southern camps and barracks of detention—which were, often of war necessity, as foully inhospitable as the peacetime concentration camps of Germany today. But the belligerents exchanged their prisoners every few months, and this fairly rapid "turnover" not only improved the captured soldiers' chances of gathering information but provided a succession of observers to report upon changing conditions within the enemy's lines.

[6] S. Emma E. Edmonds, *Nurse and Spy in the Union Army* (Hartford, 1865).
[7] Elizabeth van Lew and her secret-service collaborators had enlisted the raiders' guide by paying him $1,000 in Confederate money. With the cash in his pocket there was every temptation to desert a hazardous enterprise, which he did—with a coward's unerring instinct—at the most critical moment of the raid.

CHAPTER 43 *Rebels of the North*

[1] It was Booth's original plan to assassinate not alone President Lincoln, but General Grant, Vice-President Johnson and Secretary of War Stanton. Booth was a pathetic megalomaniac who, in his constant dream of self-exaltation, saw himself always as the great hero destined to avenge the sufferings and humiliation of the South. His accomplices were men of insignificant caliber, typical malcontents, the backwash of four

years of civil war. Having been in happier days a well-known actor, Booth could enter Ford's Theatre without credentials. At the last moment General Grant had decided to spend the week end with his daughter Nellie, then at school in New Jersey. Lincoln, though he had seen the play, *Our American Cousin*, once before and is said not to have been eager about sitting through it again, attended the performance without the general, after having been told that many people were going that evening simply for the pleasure of being in the same theater with the President.

A single bodyguard, one John Parker, was on duty outside the door that gave entrance to the presidential box. The conspirators had been careless enough to make no plan for disposing of any such barrier. But Parker was one of those shiftless mortals destined to "dispose" of himself. Suffering such want of discipline as would, in almost any other country, have made his choice seem prearranged, Parker left his post almost immediately, found himself a seat in the theater gallery, and sat down to enjoy an evening at the play.

Booth rode up to the stage door at 9:45 and boldly asked to have someone hold his horse. Captain Williams of the mounted police force of Washington, who knew him, invited him to come to a near-by saloon for a drink. Unluckily Booth resisted that fateful hospitality. It had been rumored that the President would leave after the second act, and a throng stood around Mr Lincoln's carriage, eager to see him and cheer him. Booth attached himself to that crowd but was so visibly unnerved, he caught the eye of Sergeant Dye of the military police—the only *vigilant* man in that part of Washington. Dye motioned to a fellow officer to watch Booth; but nearly everybody knew the actor, and after Dye had been told who his suspect was he seems to have paid no further attention to him. Booth now entered the saloon he had avoided before; and a policeman said: "He is probably drunk again." Booth came out, went to the stage door and made some jesting reference to his lack of a ticket. The doorman naturally laughed at that one. Booth strolled in.

It is said that he came out once more; there was still time for somebody to become aware of the President's danger. Booth borrowed a chew of tobacco from the stage-door keeper and then disappeared into the shadows "behind the scenes", humming a popular air. He went directly to the presidential box, believing he had a guard to dispose of; but Parker was not waiting for spies or conspirators that evening. And so the archplotter proceeded, aware for the second time that evening how strongly Providence favored his just and noble "cause." Stealing into the President's box, he gently closed the door behind him and made it fast with a kind of bolt he had fashioned that afternoon from an old music stand. He drew his small pistol, held it close to President Lincoln's head and squeezed the trigger. It was so small a weapon, nobody in the audience heard the report. Everyone present—Parker doubtless included—was laughing uproariously at the hardly immortal comedy line: "Well, I guess I know enough to turn you wrong side out, you darned old sock-dolaging man-trap!"

²Lieutenant Colonel Green of the Thirteenth New York Cavalry had detailed Lieutenant Edward A. Dougherty and fifty men to pursue Booth. They located him with Harriott and other conspirators in a log cabin, and in forcing the assassin's surrender, one of the detail, Sergeant Boston Corbett, shot him. Booth died as a result of the wound.

³Hamil Grant, *Spies and Secret Service*.

⁴It was Becker who drew a pension from banking firms to keep him out of mischief and yet out of prison. In no other way was it found possible to prevent the circulation of his masterly forgeries. Becker won a $50 wager in the bar of the Palmer House, Chicago, by *painting* a two-cent postage stamp upon an envelope and having it accepted as genuine in the mails.

⁵Allan Pinkerton, *The Molly Maguires and the Detectives*.

⁶Claude G. Bowers, *The Tragic Era*.

CHAPTER 44 *Before the Deluge*

¹Griffiths, *Mysteries of Police and Crime*, Vol. I.

²Vidocq, master conspirator, was himself the victim of conspiracy. M. Delavau, the new prefect in 1832, was so much under priestly influence that he had resolved to dis-

NOTES 695

miss the celebrated ex-convict detective. He was wholly out of sympathy, or so he said, with Vidocq and his methods, successful though they had proved in practice. Vidocq got wind of the sanctimonious intrigue and resigned to establish a *bureau de renseignements*, forerunner of the private detective agency. As for the sincerity of Delavau, he chose as Vidocq's successor the detective's former comrade and chief rival, imitator and detractor, another ex-convict, Coco-Lacour, who merely perpetuated all of Vidocq's methods of crime detection.

[3] Guedalla, *The Second Empire*.
[4] Guedalla.
[5] M. Claude was promoted chief of the Sûreté on account of his work in the Orsini affair.
[6] Mazzini was too circumspect for Orsini, who was resolved to move heaven and earth to bring about the liberation and unity of Italy. And he later said at his trial that he believed the only way to secure his great aims was by revolution. He reasoned that revolution in France would surely produce one in Italy; and to promote the first he felt he only need assassinate the emperor. Orsini was typically the reckless and baffled conspirator. He had tried to organize a revolt in Mantua; and the Austrians had retaliated by sentencing him to death. This sentence was at the last moment commuted to imprisonment for life in a fortress. Orsini, however, was not satisfied with half a martyrdom. Escaping, he took part in the revolution in Rome, where he became a member of the constituent government. In 1853 he made his way to Vienna and instantly became involved in a plot to instigate mutinies among the Austrian troops. Again caught, again condemned to perpetual punishment in Mantua, he was aided in making a second sensational escape. And so on to France, the bombs, the Opéra, detection, trial and the "chopper!"
[7] MM. Canler, Goron and Gustav Macé are commonly listed among the ten most celebrated and accomplished detective officers of the nineteenth century. Their reputations are not, however, a part of the annals of secret service, for though each of them would undoubtedly have proved effective in counter-espionage, the writer has no record of their ever having engaged in the detection or pursuit of spies.
[8] Niebuhr and Von Gerlach were the leaders of what was then known as the *Kreuzzeitung* party.

CHAPTER 45 *Stieber the Spy-Master*

[1] It was Prince Otto von Bismarck himself who gave Stieber this formidable title.
[2] The reader will note that the mental attitude and cynical practices of Wilhelm Stieber, reprehended by so many Germans in his own time, are merely commonplaces of the National Socialist philosophy of misgovernment and repression fastened upon Germany today.
[3] Wermuth und Stieber, *Die Communisten-verschwörungen des neunzehnten Jahrhunderts*.
[4] The military minds of Vienna, doubtless inspired by the political turbulence of 1848, established only two years later a permanent service of special intelligence, the *Evidenzburös*, whose first chief was Anton Ritter von Kalik. This officer rose to the rank of major general and was in charge of the Austrian Intelligence department until 1864. It is probably no more than a coincidence that the capable and experienced Ritter von Kalik retired just as Stieber was about to drive across the frontier of Austria with his wagon load of sacred images and pornography.
[5] Stieber shut out the powerful Reuters telegraphic agency, and he quickly detected the subterfuge when a Reuters subsidiary began to flourish in Berlin. This he also excluded, inviting Dr B. W. Wolff to start the semiofficial Wolff bureau as a German competitor of Reuters.
[6] Auerbach, *Denkwürdigkeiten des Geheimen Regierungsrathes Dr Stieber, aus seinen hinterlassenen Papieren bearbeitet*.

CHAPTER 46 *King of Sleuthhounds*

[1] Stoffel, *Rapports militaires écrits de Berlin: 1866–1870* (Garnier Frères, 1871).
[2] An anecdote persists about the smoldering feud between espionage and military

operations—between Stieber and aristocratic Prussian officers—and how it finally flared up in the presence of Prince Bismarck. It placed him in a predicament that even he, the accomplished diplomatist, did not relish. The feud must be composed for the sake of winning the war with France. If he took sides against Stieber, his spy-master would lose heart; if he sided with Stieber, his general officers would sulk. Bismarck was the host, had been serving coffee to his guests—it was up to him. And he is said to have dealt with the situation in this characteristic manner:

A frigid silence had greeted some angry, bombastic remark of Stieber's. Bismarck, holding a tray of coffee cups in his right hand, broke the tension by striding over to the spy and extending his free hand, the left. Grateful for such a public show of confidence, Stieber eagerly grasped the chancellor's hand in both of his. The military onlookers saw, however, it was Bismarck's left hand that he offered to the spy, which mollified them. Whereas we have been asked to believe that Stieber never noticed the difference. But he had smarted too long under the contempt of the officer caste; and keen and socially hypersensitive as he was, he would have been blind indeed to have overlooked his chief's imperfectly partisan gesture. And even if the inference had escaped him, would not some enemy have quickly circulated a tale of the left-handed "affront", gossip certain to have reached the spy-master from one of his spies?

[3]The incompetents never were replaced. At the crisis of the Franco-Prussian War, when General Trouchu was speeding to Paris as the newly nominated military governor expected to prepare the capital to withstand a siege, his special train was blocked for hours on a main line near Épernay by trains loaded with material for the projected *siege of Mainz*. Louis Napoleon's military advisers all spent themselves upon such preparations and plans for grandiose conquest and had nothing left in the way of ideas when it came to defending France from the conqueror.

[4]Hamil Grant, *Spies and Secret Service*.

[5]Since Stieber's death German apologists for him have attempted to include systematic counter-espionage among his numerous elaborations or inventions of military secret service. But to the busy Dr Stieber counter-spying was never more than a by-product or interesting sideline, even in 1870–71. His spies and secret agents in France were so numerous and widely scattered, now and again some of them were bound to stumble over a hapless member of the adversary's inadequate secret corps. And that was Stieber's great spy-proof "innovation" of counter-espionage.

Throughout the war with France it was Stieber's artful contention that the badge of the Red Cross was being abused by French agents engaged in espionage. And also according to General Prince Hohenlohe, after the battle of St Privat "a Frenchman was observed galloping about the bivouac. In the prevailing state of exhaustion . . . our men had merely noted that he was unarmed and wore a white brassard with the red cross of the Geneva Convention. But when, for a third time, he circled round our guards, we thought it suspicious, and Major von Roon was instructed to question him. During the interrogation he was insolent and yet, at the same time, nervous. . . . His armlet was found to bear the depot stamp of a regiment of fusilier guards. He was a French staff-captain, and . . . he might have been shot at once. The Prince of Württemberg, however, being forbearing and good-natured, had him handed over to the civil authorities."

If Stieber attended the battle of St Privat, *he* would have been the chief civil authority in the field, since he never attained military rank. Even if the staff captain luckily escaped Stieber's attentions, the spy-master learned of his offense and thereafter harried and suspected every Red Cross worker that he met.

[6]Paul et Suzanne Lanoir, *Les grands espions*.

[7]The Baroness de Kaulla was a Jewess and her notoriety did much to nourish the anti-Semitic suspicions, complicated by fear of a new and more powerful Germany, by counter-espionage and General Staff intrigues, which boiled to a culmination with the arrest of Alfred Dreyfus. Stieber had died before the misfortunes of Captain Dreyfus overtook him. (See Chapter 52.) Yet the shadow of the Prussian spy-master lay darkly upon the famous treason trials.

[8]As an example, before 1914 the "Viktoria Insurance Company of Berlin" had what was called a "special bureau" in Paris on the Avenue de l'Opéra, and all clerks and

agents of this branch of the concern were Prussian reserve officers. An entirely new staff appeared about every six months in Paris; and no employee went back to Berlin without being granted a vacation which he spent in touring the eastern departments of France.

[5] Bismarck would not permit him to dispose of German hostilities with the same harsh measures he had taken against the French noncombatants. However, he proudly records having received from the chancellor a bonus of two hundred thalers for having managed to suppress a bitterly anti-Prussian article before it sprang from the Hanoverian press.

CHAPTER 47 *Lessons from a School of Hard Knocks*

[1] After 1884, when Ratchkovsky was appointed head of the Russian secret police service abroad, the French influence became predominant in the operations of the *Ochrana*. Ratchkovsky—who was a more notorious character in every respect than Wilhelm Stieber, and who was graciously thanked both by Tsar Alexander III and his successor, Nicholas II, for various acts of provocation—in his police work adopted those methods hallowed in France even after the fall of the Second Empire. And it was Ratchkovsky who carried home the French theory of provocation, which did not recoil even from bomb-throwing or the planting of infernal machines when such acts, or threats, of violence would discredit revolutionary exiles, intimidate the law-abiding citizen, or create, as his French instructors put it, "a public opinion."

[2] The Board of Regents of the Bank of France had financed the coup d'état and plebiscite that elevated Prince Louis Napoleon to the imperial throne as Napoleon III. The sum involved was 25,000,000 francs, "paid out under the pretext of a long-since outlawed agreement." Napoleon repaid the debt by the convenient method of extending the privileges of the bank to the year 1897. The bank financed the Franco-Prussian War up to the battle of Sedan and the proclamation of the Republic; but thereafter the regents sabotaged all patriotic efforts of national defense. This so infuriated Gambetta that he threatened to create a new central bank. The regents at length gave in and agreed to provide the Government of National Defense with the necessary funds; but their capitulation had been neither prompt nor graceful, and by the time they decided to yield it was too late.

During the Commune of 1871 the laboring masses had the bank in their power. Two and a half billion francs—at that time wealth inconceivable—might have been "borrowed" to fight their reactionary enemies. But the average Frenchman's "holy respect for property" kept the workers from employing such a mighty weapon. They withdrew but 16,000,000 francs, of which 9,000,000 belonged to the city of Paris, throughout the historic three months of the Commune. And in that same period the bank advanced 365,000,000 francs to Thiers and his reactionaries, who, with the powerful assistance of the German army, finally brought about the liquidation of the people's government. (These facts offered upon the authority of the noted French economist, Francis Delaisi, in his recent *La Banque de France aux mains des 200 Familles*, published by *Le Comité de Vigilance des Intellectuels Anti-Fascistes*.)

[3] J. P. T. Bury, *Gambetta and the National Defense*.

[4] Though the imperial secret-service agencies failed both in estimating the Prussian strength and in defending France from Stieber's espionage system, and though the French people showed less enthusiasm for a defeated emperor than for the defense of their own homes, many heroic risks were taken and many ungrateful rewards given before the Bonapartist collapse at Sedan. One important dispatch of MacMahon's was carried through the lines by *twenty* different secret-intelligence volunteers. A courageous young woman, Mlle Louise Imbert, disguising herself as a man, rode from Metz to Thionville in the midst of the invading armies, with dispatches concealed in her hair. A policeman, Flauhaut, was sent on the twentieth of August from Thionville to Metz with two vital messages MacMahon had addressed to Bazaine. On his return journey he was discovered and pursued by a Prussian cavalry patrol. He leaped out of the vehicle in which he was riding and dived into the Moselle, swam four kilometers, eluded his enemies, and arrived on schedule with Bazaine's reply at Thionville. For his fidelity and daring he was rewarded with a gift of fifty francs, which hardly com-

pares with the sum of 4,000 francs paid to the secret agent, Héron, for his hazardous ride from Metz to Verdun after the battle of St Privat.

[6] The record of the Bazaine trial shows that a peasant courier "who returned from Saarbrücken"—a really dangerous mission—on September 24, 1870, was paid five francs. Next day the rate jumped, for an item emerges: "To a peasant from Donchéry, 50 francs." Secret-service costs rose as Bazaine's fortunes ebbed. On October 22, a week before the capitulation of the fortress and Army of the Rhine, these expenditures were recorded:

> To Valcour, Interpreter, Special Mission, 300 francs.
> To Prieskewitsch, Interpreter, Special Mission, 300 francs.
> To Vernet, Interpreter, Special Mission, 300 francs.

A Sergeant Courtial of the Twenty-fourth Regiment also received 300 francs for some sort of counter-spying assignment. While the agent, Anthermet, and his wife stand forth thriftily as a couple who collected 1,100 francs—200 to buy the man civilian attire, 400 francs for a horse and carriage, and 500 francs for personal expenses and, we may assume, salary for both. Not all "special missions" in the time of the Franco-Prussian War involved colliding with German counter-espionage and a possible death sentence; and yet, owing to the sweep of the invasion, a great number of non-combatant arrests led to espionage trials and another excuse for a hanging or shooting.

CHAPTER 48 *Private Patrons of Intelligence*

[1] According to the estimates of Professor Villari, quoted by Colonel G. F. Young.

[2] A Fugger *Letter* from Piadena in Italy, May 26, 1601, describes the sensational case of a Lansquenet named Daniel Burghammer having given birth to a child, a matter of medical inquiry and clerical concern. There was no passing event, however slight its political significance, that the Fugger correspondents ignored. The more usual communication, however, was in the nature of political or diplomatic intelligence, as for example this note sent from Paris, August 15, 1581: "An English Envoy Extraordinary named Walsingham has arrived here. He has requested free passage from the King and has gone on at once to the Duke of Alençon."

[3] Baron de Hirsch, noted European speculator and philanthropist, was reputed in his day to have added enormously to his large fortune by means of a well-organized private intelligence service supplying him exclusively with advance information, diplomatic secrets, etc. This financier was clever enough to have manipulated such a system for speculative purposes; and yet other great fortunes were accumulated in late Victorian and Edwardian times by stock exchange forays unaccompanied by professional espionage or more than the usual intrigue. It is not improbable that Baron de Hirsch was but another target for the rabid anti-Semitism of the French public at the time of the Dreyfus case.

[4] Mr H. Ashton-Wolfe, who can find the most uncommon revelations in the dustiest archives of the French monarchical police, gives in his *True Stories of Immortal Crimes* a very romantic account of a patrician young lady, the Marquise Ivonne de Kergolese, daughter of a duke, whose devotion and adventurous nature also strongly influenced the career of this celebrated outlaw leader.

[5] One of Cartouche's most cunning assistants, the pickpocket known to his fellow outlaws as "La Magdalene", was of special interest to his distinguished English contemporary, Daniel Defoe. One understands why the creator of Moll Flanders and the resourceful Crusoe was impressed by this rogue, whose particular stratagem it was to hold up wax hands, neatly gloved, in an attitude of prayer while with a free hand he picked the pockets of kneeling neighbors in the various congregations of Paris, who constituted his special prey. This "Cartouchien" was finally caught and put to death by the torture of the "water-ruff." And his last contribution to crime annals was the "record" of swallowing eight pints of water poured into the leathern ruff strapped around his neck and head before he succumbed to the law's prescribed torment of suffocation.

[6] The jeweled sword-hilts of the time were especially attractive to the Cartouche

band; and the Prince Regent had more than once found his scabbard empty. Both the regent's eyes had been injured, one by a ball when playing fives, the other by the blow of a lady's fan, or, some said, by "her little round heel", and he was, in any throng, an easy victim for thieves. The constant theft of swords on account of their jewel-studded hilts caused wrought-steel hilts to be imported from England for the first time, so that the courtiers might retain their swords.

[7] Pêcome, an aide-major of the Paris Guards, was the junior officer who had sworn to make an end of Cartouche, and who disconcerted his superiors by arranging the transaction of betrayal with Duchatelet. Pêcome at first had organized a body of eighty comrades who patrolled the streets of Paris in disguise, heavily armed, searching for Cartouche. But this enterprise was discouraged when it became known to higher authorities, as it did through the arrest of several of his operatives as suspicious characters. It was even feared that Pêcome was in league with Cartouche and an auxiliary of the outlaw band; and it was thought too dangerous to allow bodies of armed men "to roam thus at large under the flimsy pretense of thief-catching." That Pêcome and his allies were honest in their intentions was proved when the young aide-major arranged Cartouche's downfall. Duchatelet, the informer, seems to have been granted a kind of immunity, a primitive form of turning king's evidence, for it is recorded that he "escaped" into Germany and served as a soldier. Yet Vidocq, in his memoirs, declares that he discovered an underground cell at Bicêtre prison, in which this very Duchatelet had been confined for forty-three years.

[8] Griffiths, *Mysteries of Police and Crime*, Vol. II.

[9] Of the capture of Euroa, which was held for many hours, Major Arthur Griffiths wrote: "It was a masterly operation, conducted from first to last with cool judgment and the most determined strength of purpose. Ned Kelly . . . had planned the whole affair with all the foresight and precision of a general in the field; every detail was executed by his well-disciplined followers with the unhesitating exactitude of soldiers implicitly obeying the orders of their chief. Only by perfect submission to a single resolute will . . . could this audacious outrage have been made possible."

[10] Griffiths.

[11] Philip Gosse, *The History of Piracy*.

[12] Aleko E. Lilius, *I Sailed with Chinese Pirates*.

CHAPTER 49 *De Blowitz at Berlin*

[1] A contemporary and colleague, Sir William Howard Russell of *The Times* was, perhaps, equally famous as a war correspondent.

[2] *Memoirs of M. de Blowitz*.

[3] Five years later this masterstroke of journalism was still perplexing Prince Bismarck. Upon meeting the famous correspondent in 1883 he endeavored to persuade him to tell by what means and through whose connivance he had illuminated the dark and mysterious Congress of Berlin.

CHAPTER 50 *The Ochrana*

[1] Even in espionage of a military or diplomatic nature within the boundaries of Russia, the tsarist agents appear to have done better when their work was closely akin to police supervision. From 1859 to 1863 Bismarck was the Prussian ambassador to St Petersburg, and in his *Thoughts and Recollections* he recorded his curious encounters with the tsar's system of espionage. One Russian diplomat said to him: "My first indiscretion compels me to perpetrate a second. You will, of course, report . . . to Berlin, but do not make use of your cipher-number—for this purpose. That one has been in our possession for years, and as things are at present, our people would at once conclude that I had been the source of your information. Further, will you, please, do me the favor of not suddenly giving up the cipher in question completely. Employ it for a few months yet, when you happen to be sending telegrams of no special import." And Bismarck observes: "For my own peace of mind at the time I thought I was justified in the belief that, in all probability, only that particular one of our ciphers was known to the Russians. It was an extremely difficult business

in St Petersburg to be sure of the secrecy of any cipher, because every embassy was inevitably obliged to employ Russian servants and subordinates in the domestic affairs of the house, and it was an easy matter for the secret police to obtain agents among their number."

²Pokrovsky, *History of Russia*.

³Tsar Nicholas was not without his romantic recreations. Catherine, daughter of Russia's most celebrated poet, Pushkin, was unhappily married to Prince Sergius Troubyetskoi and the object of such undisguised admiration on the part of Nicholas I that, when her daughter Sophie was born, the child's paternity was ascribed to the tsar. Color was lent to this supposition in 1857, upon Sophie Troubyetskoi's marriage to the Duc de Morny, half brother of Napoleon III, for she received a dowry of two million roubles from Tsar Alexander II, supposedly her half brother. This union is a particularly distinguished example of one form of diplomatic secret service to which little space can be given—that "secret service" of backstairs negotiations and clandestine compensation which pertains to births, marriages, deaths, financial provision and all other matters relating to imperial, royal and other eminent illegitimacies. Sophie's husband, the Duc de Morny, was the natural son of Hortense Bonaparte *née* Beauharnais, queen of Holland and the Emperor Napoleon's vivacious stepdaughter and sister-in-law, and of her lover and chamberlain, General Comte de Flahaut, noted as the handsomest man of his day. De Flahaut's mother was, in turn, an illegitimate daughter of King Louis XV of France, known as Adelaide Filleule. Born and reared in the notorious *Parc aux Cerfs*, it was not to be expected that she would take conjugal vows too seriously; and despite her respectable alliance with Comte Charles de Flahaut, her handsome son—father of the future Duc de Morny—was himself illegitimate, it being no contemporary secret that *his* father was the former Bishop of Autun who became the brilliant statesman, wit, multimillionaire and unscrupulous intriguer, Prince de Talleyrand-Périgord.

⁴René Fülöp-Miller, Introduction to *The Ochrana* by A. T. Vassilyev.

⁵From the days of the Decembrist or Dekabrist revolt, the actual or supposed ringleaders of revolutionary movements were kept in the Bastion behind iron-bound doors, guarded by jailers and double sentries with fixed bayonets. There, it is said, suspects were shut in cells separated from each other by walls a yard thick, and often after many years they had not yet been put on trial because the authorities did not know what charges to bring against them.

CHAPTER 51   Agent Provocateur

¹Colonel Victor K. Kaledin of the Russian Military Intelligence during the World War, who served as a "double spy", ostensibly betraying his country to the German *Nachrichtendienst* for pay, defines an *agent provocateur* as "a police agent who is introduced into any political organization with instructions to foment discontent against a government, or to fake a case in order to give his employers the right to act against the organization in question." Such an agent, he adds, is "held in the greatest contempt in Service circles, and is generally chosen from the lowest types." In his opinion Azeff was a "noticeable exception", in that he was a "genuine revolutionary, and in his work fulfilled more the rôle of a double spy."

This is an interesting deviation from the customarily rabid denunciation of Azeff by tsarists and revolutionists alike. The defect in it would seem to be that, whereas the military agent doubles his own value as a spy, literally, by becoming a double spy, representing to an enemy that he is betraying the side he actually is serving, Azeff gained little *information* from his *Ochrana* connection that assisted him or his fellow revolutionaries. He certainly deceived both sides, but what he chiefly doubled was his personal income, an all-important accomplishment to him. Had Azeff anticipated the French spy, Marthe Richer, and turned over to the cause of revolution his earnings from the secret police—an unthinkable gesture—that would have made him more truly a double spy, as Colonel Kaledin suggests.

The latter's generous attitude does him credit as a former officer of rank in the Russian Imperial Army who can speak of a revolutionist without screaming "Criminal!"

Murderer!" and foaming in print. The reader hunting amusement will find the perfect opposite of Colonel Kaledin's urbane attitude by reading about "Azef" in A. T. Vassilyev's *The Ochrana*, or any other part of that comically solemn apologetic. To Vassilyev, palpably, everyone in Russia was out of step but a holy trinity of God, the tsar, and the Spirit of Political Police. And sometimes the S.O.P.P. seems to have had to be pretty patient with God and the tsar.

[2]Police archives of Rostov, made public after the conquest of that region by the Bolshevik Red Army, show that the *Ochrana* with actuarial thoroughness had the Azeffs listed as "A poor family" in 1894—twenty years after their arrival in Rostov.

[3]The newspaper was the *Donskaya Ptchela* [The Don Bee].

[4]Azeff wrote: "I have the honor to inform Your Highness that two months ago a circle of revolutionaries was formed here whose aim is . . ." and there followed, besides a list of student names, certain facts cited to show that the writer was in a position to report upon the temper of revolutionary-minded Russian students abroad and also reveal much about the propaganda going on in Rostov.

[5]Boris Nikolajewsky, *Azeff the Spy*.

[6]Ratayeff, *The History of Aseff's Treachery*.

[7]Nikolajewsky.

[8]This act of terrorism occurred in the spring of 1901. Karpovitch, the assassin, was caught and sentenced to prison, but after a few years he escaped and, "anxious to resume terrorist work", rejoined the Battle Organization and came to be Azeff's right-hand man.

CHAPTER 52 *The Degradation of Alfred Dreyfus*

[1]M. Gribelin, an official of the Archives Department, and the secretary of M. Cochefert were also present. An order to the director of the military prison had already been drawn, and in Du Paty de Clam's portfolio was an unconditional warrant, signed by the minister of war.

[2]Walther Steinthal, *Dreyfus*.

[3]Steinthal, *Dreyfus*.

[4]M. Bertillon one would rather expect to have been discredited utterly by his negligence—or worse—in this celebrated case. However, the blunder seems to have cost him no particle of reputation, which, as has been said, is much harder to win than to lose in bureaucratic France. Handwriting experts appear something of a tribe apart, forgiven every fantasy of professional judgment. If this were not so, there could never be experts on both sides of practically every case involving handwriting identifications.

[5]Colonel Walter Nicolai, chief of the German military secret service during the World War, has stated that these differing explanations were offered to interested German officials.

[6]The same General Mercier whose coachman had been Stieber's clever agent, Ludwig Windell.

[7]Steinthal, *Dreyfus*.

[8]Some of the evidence given by staff officers during the Dreyfus trial, and made public long afterward, exposes certain aspects and methods of French counterespionage which continued to the outbreak of the war in 1914 and abound in all parts of Europe today. Lieutenant Colonel Cordier, one of the court-martial witnesses, testifying as to the character and ability of a counter-spying agent, explained: "I have said that this agent had certain little faults. He had affairs with women, and particularly one that I do not need to retail here. In consequence of this particular affair, a lady named Madame Millescamp thought it appropriate to have her revenge by informing the German Embassy that certain work was afoot. At once we ordered our agent to break off all relations and to be very circumspect. Then Mme Millescamp was arrested and sentenced to five years' imprisonment. We were thus assured of *her* silence.

"Our next business was to find out how the Germans were taking the affair. We learned that they were laying a trap for a *lady*. This lady was in correspondence with our agent. It was *she* who had been securing the bits of paper; he had been receiving them from her. His meetings with her, which, because of her employment, took place generally at night, and often in churches, were arranged by postcard whenever she had anything to hand over."

[9]It developed that treason was of more concern to the Intelligence bureau than espionage, the witnesses before the court-martial describing some of the extraordinary means applied to test the loyalty of French officers. Colonel Sandherr, the chief of Intelligence, had ordered the fitting up of a complete observation post, for example, in a house opposite the German Embassy in the Rue de Lille. A flat had been rented there in which a counter-spy permanently resided. In the window shutters openings were made, through which, as Lieutenant Colonel Picquart disclosed, everyone who visited the German Embassy was photographed.

General Gonse stated in his testimony before the court: "Immediately below that flat the officers attached to the embassy had hired the rooms on the ground-floor, where the unmarried men took their lunch every day, the wife of the *concierge* doing the cooking for them. There was a dining-room and a smoking-room, in which coffee was taken. Right over this room Colonel Picquart had things arranged so that anyone sitting near a certain piece of furniture was able, by means of speaking tubes which he had fitted in the chimney, to overhear all the conversation that went on below. An agent, who was personally unknown to me, was sent to this upper room daily, and had to report every evening to Colonel Picquart."

[10]The isle has an area of about twenty-five acres; its greatest altitude is fifty feet and its temperature ranges from seventy-six to eighty-eight degrees the year round, modified at night by easterly winds. But from December to March it is drenched with rains and becomes a hotbed of fever and insects.

[11]Alfred Dreyfus, *Cinq Années de ma Vie.*

CHAPTER 53   *Picquart and Zola: The Counter-Detection*

[1]Colonel von Schwartzkoppen, though he appears to have observed all the rules of discretion—codes, ciphers and secrecy—prescribed for one of "the accredited spies", otherwise known as military attachés, was evidently left unperturbed by the French counter-spies who dogged his steps, put him to bed and got him up, swept out his flat and read his mail before he did.

[2]Steinthal, *Dreyfus.*

[3]The intention and circumstances of this meeting have been much distorted by controversy. The version given here is that of a former chief of the German Secret Service, whose impartiality need not be taken for granted.

[4]Esterhazy, unencumbered by principles or the slightest extenuation of his treachery, wrote a book, *Les Dessous de l'Affaire Dreyfus*, published by Fayard Frères in 1898.

[5]Clemenceau held that all the accumulating evils of the Dreyfus case should be attributed to the passion or the indifference of the sovereign people. In a final eloquent summary, the moral of which is pointed by some European nations in our own day, he wrote:

"No better lesson than the Dreyfus affair will ever be shown to the people; they have to make the effort to distinguish between liars and truthful men. They have to read, question, compare, verify, think. . . . Presently illumination will come. It will be understood that a country without justice is a mere enclosure of animals designed for the butcher."

[6]Henry's camouflage of photography was one of his few really ingenious secret-service dodges, the more so because it was perfectly normal and legitimate in safeguarding a valued evidential document to lock the original away in a vault and present attested photographic copies to the various interested tribunals. When the "faux Panizzardi" was read aloud in the Chamber by the minister of war in 1898, it provoked a storm of applause. Yet a young Englishman, Mr L. J. Maxse, is said to have been able to detect the fraud at once and to have denounced its perpetrator. His coup—England being very generally pro-Dreyfus—was but one more hammer stroke upon the weakening barricade at the portal of French justice. However, the reader may reflect that, had Henry not been overzealous in his perfidy, had he chosen to destroy the evidence against himself as soon as it had served its purpose in

damaging the cause of Dreyfus, all the counter-spying crimes committed might never have been explicitly brought to book, and their victims hence left to die in disgrace.

[7]It is of record that participants in the case as little alike as General Picquart and Esterhazy both believed that Henry's death was not a suicide.

[8]Lemercier-Picard was a tool of Henry's who, upon being implicated by the confession of the chief of Intelligence, confessed to having forged anti-Dreyfus documents.

[9]Only a French military court of that period could have solemnly connected "extenuating circumstances" with the crime of treason. France, a republic of some radical pretensions, was defended by an army still largely Royalist—or Bonapartist—and spiritually influenced by a reactionary Church.

[10]The very day of Dreyfus' presidential pardon was the day of the death of Senator Scheurer-Kestner, one of the noblest of his champions.

[11]Picquart, for reasons implicit in his character, is said ardently to have opposed acceptance of this kind of pardon. And he and his devoted ally, Mathieu Dreyfus, were estranged on account of it.

[12]Mme Zola at the time of her famous husband's funeral in October, 1902, had urged that Dreyfus deny himself the privilege of attending, so many were the threats of a violent outbreak or warnings of an attempt upon the officer's life.

[13]After the sale of the factory at Mülhausen in 1897 to raise funds for continuing the family's attempts to reverse the conviction of Alfred, Jacques Dreyfus took up residence in Belfort and became a French citizen.

[14]His son, Pierre, was twice cited for bravery.

[15]In 1902 General von Schwartzkoppen had married Luise, Countess von Wedel.

[16]When Dreyfus was seeking to have the *Cour de Cassation* revise his case in 1903, Von Schwartzkoppen had written a memorandum on it which was found among his papers. This was published, together with pertinent correspondence, in Berlin in 1930, a translation being printed by *L'Oeuvre* of Paris. Dreyfus was then making his first visit to Berlin as the guest of Dr Bruno Weil, his German biographer, who found him "a friendly old officer, optimistic, and with no sign of bitterness." Upon returning to Paris, Colonel Dreyfus wrote to the editor of *L'Oeuvre*:

"The papers of General Schwartzkoppen make me live again with painful intensity and with such physical and moral sufferings that the years between have not been able to soften the memory of them. They confirm in irrefutable fashion the facts established by the masterly inquiry of the *Cour de Cassation* which resulted in the revision of 1906.

"General von Schwartzkoppen acted like an honest man in revealing all he knew; it is, however, profoundly regrettable that he did not feel it his duty to do so the day he understood that a judicial error had been committed."

Georges Clemenceau, one of the first to rally to the defense of Dreyfus, often said that the victim never discovered what "l'affaire Dreyfus" was about. It is true that he would never permit his defenders to pose him as a martyr, and, as far as he could, he prevented them from making political capital out of his case, whose political significance he would no more admit than its ethnic impulsion. Only when informed in 1933 of the treatment of his co-religionists in Germany he exclaimed, as though realizing a mistake for the first time—"And so my sufferings appear to have been all in vain."

During the last months of his life he had been nearly blind and found his chief pleasure in being with his children, his grandchildren and his wonderfully devoted wife and in charitable works. His wife during the summer of 1934 was the sole support of 350 indigent families. He died in Paris on July 12, 1935, in his seventy-sixth year.

Chapter 54 *The French Reaction*

[1]Sir John French's public rebuff and virtual exclusion from command of the capable General Sir Horace Smith-Dorrien, in 1915, is the best example of this communicated "infection."

[2]Major Rollin, one of the witnesses in the Dreyfus case—but not habitually untrust-

worthy—wrote of Lajoux: "He was a bold, intelligent agent, rather difficult to deal with and touchy. He rendered us very great service. During the time I was in the Intelligence, out of fifteen cases of treason and espionage that led to arrests, we owed four to Lajoux."

[3]We observe how carefully Intelligence protected itself in making such a doubtful investment—a spy promising to trick Richard Cuers. The chief of the General Staff was General de Mirabel, the immediate predecessor of De Boisdeffre.

[4]From the statement by Major Rollin.

[5]Lajoux was so successful in espionage, he was no doubt difficult and inclined to invite suspicion. An even more abysmal specimen of the corrupt practices of French Intelligence at this time concerned an agent named Corninge. For ten years this man had been employed by a fire insurance company of Paris, was in receipt of a fair salary, and assured of a pension after twenty-five years' faithful service. But in 1891 he was persuaded to resign his insurance career and join the Second Bureau as an agent. According to his own subsequent statement, Intelligence officers like Sandherr, Cordier, Rollin and Burckhardt by turns appealed to his patriotism and held out to him dazzling prospects of a distinguished future in government secret service.

His first mission took him to Geneva, and for eight years he worked for the French Intelligence and was particularly successful in exploits of counter-espionage. Relations that he was able to establish with Italian military officers in Paris proved peculiarly fortunate for his superiors, who, however, came around in time to that routine suspicion of this valuable operative, and for the routine reason that he had learned more about their activities than it was safe for any "outsider"—a mere patriotic French citizen, not of the officer caste—to know. And so, very abruptly in April of 1899, he was advised that he need expect nothing more: since "the Second Bureau was in liquidation" and he "the unfortunate victim of an act resolved upon by higher powers." Thus M. Corninge, who had twice been engaged with the guaranteed reward of an honorable, pensioned retirement, found his eighteen years' diligence had earned him no prospect of a pension nor further employment.

[6]Picquart would never have gained his appointment as chief of Intelligence without very special qualifications. Lest this record, in its admiration for his self-sacrificial fortitude in the Dreyfus affair, seem to make him out a bit angelic, we had best consider Picquart as a director of espionage and counter-espionage, quite apart from the Esterhazy-Dreyfus-Henry-Zola imbroglio. Picquart was not above instructing a subordinate to make use of an *agent provocateur*, common to political police work but unusual in military secret service. Galanti, a spy and smuggler—suspected of being a double spy by the police of Belfort—was taken into the French service as an agent by Captain Maréchal, who acted upon orders from Picquart. On May 19, 1896, Galanti reported to Maréchal that he had met near Fort Bessoncourt a foreign agent named Caïnelli and had won his confidence by pretending to be a confederate. Caïnelli told the smuggler that he had been commissioned "by a certain power" to make his way into one of the outer batteries of Fort Bessoncourt, measure the caliber of the guns, and also to obtain photographs of five of the batteries.

Caïnelli said he already had invaded one of the batteries but found the gun muzzles covered with caps chained fast. As he had no implement with him for cutting chains, he had failed in his undertaking. Galanti helped him secure a file; and when Caïnelli ran short of money and was ready to leave Belfort, Galanti—regularly in touch with the French Intelligence—came to his rescue with money so that he might continue his espionage project. Instructed by his superiors, Galanti played the *provocateur*, arranging with Caïnelli to make his next attempt on the night of May 31, 1896. Hidden patrols of soldiers surrounded Fort Bessoncourt and the trap was all in readiness. Promptly at midnight Caïnelli drew near the guns. He was arrested, subsequently convicted as a spy, and sent to prison for three years. Immediately after his arrest Colonel Picquart had ordered Galanti to take a quiet vacation in Switzerland.

CHAPTER 56 *Messengers to Garcia and Aguinaldo*

[1]Since the writer happens neither to be related to, nor even acquainted with, this intrepid officer, the account of his exploit given here is wholly disinterested. A mere

twenty-four years after successfully completing his Cuban mission, Lieutenant Colonel Rowan, retired, was awarded the Distinguished Service Cross, its citation crediting his achievement with having had a vital bearing upon the victory of the United States over Spain. Rowan was unique in the Spanish-American War in that he faced serious opposition and had long odds against him. In most other actions or operations of the conflict, the Spaniards found themselves in his position; and since in a war which was an American "walk over", real heroes ought to be scarce, it is all the more astonishing to learn how Rowan became overshadowed by the pumped-up or puffed-up, manufactured article.

[2] Much of Rowan's later acclaim was distorted, quite without his participation or consent, by incredible "ballyhoo" and bad taste. The late Elbert Hubbard was the chief offender, with his millions and millions of copies of a sublimated advertising tract exploiting *The Message to Garcia*. Only recently Hollywood discovered this quaint publicity "release" and was straightway inspired to produce a motion picture which, like all of its kind put through the cinema filter marked "Military Spies, Plot A to Z", left everything to be desired.

[3] Fitzhugh Lee, a nephew of General Robert E. Lee, had been one of the most effective of Confederate cavalry leaders. When the Maine was sunk—"by the tact, conciliation and good sense" which he manifested, he "upheld the best standards of his clan," according to Burton J. Hendrick, "and won national renown." When, soon afterward, war broke out between the United States and Spain, Fitzhugh Lee put on a blue uniform, receiving a commission as major general of volunteers; and by both North and South, this action was accepted, thirty-three years after Appomattox, "as the symbol of a united country."

[4] Señor Polo y Bernabe.

[5] The functions of the Secret Service of the United States Treasury Department, under John N. Bell, Wilkie and other chief operatives, were very strictly defined, American Congressmen and politicians living in unholy dread of anything which might resemble a political police service left at the disposal of the President. But in times of war restrictions upon that detective bureau—which alone bears the designation of United States Secret Service—are sufficiently relaxed from protecting the currency and safeguarding the life of the President and members of his family to permit it to take some part in general or military secret service.

[6] In June 1898 the USS Charleston sailed into the harbor at Apra, Guam, and began firing at an old dismantled fort. The Spanish governor, who had received no mail for months and did not know that his country and the United States had gone to war, sent out word politely that, since all his gunpowder was spoiled, he would be unable to reply to the salute of the visiting American warship.

[7] Though so easily traced, trapped and arrested, this man was not insignificant as a spy. His message of May 7—but six days after Dewey's victory at Manila, and with the Spaniards still holding the land defenses—was a genuine espionage coup. The information which Downing obtained was more valuable than the average spy would secure directly after reaching an "enemy" capital.

[8] Don Wilkie, *American Secret Service Agent* (as told to Mark Lee Luther).

[9] This talented secret agent has never yet been identified; but one may remark his noticeable resemblance to that Lieutenant Colonel Aristides Moreno, an American Intelligence officer of Spanish descent, who was in charge of counter-espionage on General Pershing's staff at Chaumont, France, 1917-18.

[10] Don Wilkie.

[11] Funston's stocky figure, aggressive leadership and florid, bearded countenance reminded many a veteran of the great U. S. Grant. Having overcome his seeming handicap, the lack of a formal military education at West Point, Funston not only deserved promotion but had earned the confidence of President Wilson, Secretary of War Baker, and General Scott and General Bliss. Pershing on the Mexican border was then a brigadier and his subordinate. Funston, whose energy had always been thought inexhaustible, was suddenly stricken and died. Had he lived it appears certain that the year following would have seen this Kansas volunteer at the head of the greatest force of American troops ever to take the field. And that supreme honor as commander in

chief of the A. E. F. in France would have come to Frederick Funston, who won his spurs in tropic Luzon by a daring feat of military secret service.

[12]A future President of the United States, Herbert Hoover, was among the Occidental refugees who found shelter in the British Legation. As a Quaker he was ineligible to join the legations' combatants employing every man, woman and child for the salvation of their lives; but British and American (marine) officers still recall his accurate report as a mining man upon the dangers which he had observed in fleeing to Peking.

CHAPTER 57 *The South African War*

[1]Douglas Blackburn and W. W. Caddell, *Secret Service in South Africa.*

[2]Edward Marjoribanks in his *Life of Sir Edward Marshall Hall* relates that, except Seddon, Bennett was the coolest and cleverest man whom Marshall Hall ever defended on the capital charge. The noted barrister was convinced that Bennett's "visit to South Africa, his employment at Woolwich [England's great arsenal] and his tour in Ireland, together with the revolver and the disguises found in his possession, were only consistent with his having been employed as a Boer spy."

CHAPTER 58 *Spies of the Rising Sun*

[1]The Japanese code of morals and honorable living, known as *bushido*, permits espionage practiced in the service of the sovereign and the state. It is recognized as necessary and "fair"; it calls for courage and audacity, two of the virtues highly prized according to the *samurai* code.

[2]The detection of these well-placed Japanese agents has been ascribed variously, to sentiment—in that the documents incriminating them were discovered by *Ochrana* agents in the dwelling of the Russian woman who was to be married to one of them; to the woman herself—who was alleged by some believers in the omnipotence of the *Ochrana* to have been a fascinating counter-spy, employed by Colonel Gerassimoff, chief of the St Petersburg branch of the secret police, to "investigate" the affections of the Japanese and win their confidence; and, finally, to the police interception of indiscreet communication with other naval officers of Japan on espionage assignment in European countries—which seems the most probable explanation.

[3]M. Manasevitch-Manoiloff was not only a police agent but a popular journalist and also "in the secret service of Count Witte", according to Boris Nikolajewsky. It was Manasevitch-Manoiloff's considerable achievement in the encyclopedic chronicles of Russian political police intrigue to arrange the "recruiting" of that "heroic priest", Gapon, who on "Bloody Sunday" in St Petersburg, January 22, 1905, with cross in hand had led the masses to the tsar's palace in search of justice and freedom. Gapon escaped death or injury from the blast of rifle fire which was the typically tsarist answer; and he then managed to flee in disguise to Geneva. Fame and money, however, were soon to work his ruin. When the shrewder Social Revolutionary exiles began to give the priest a wide berth, he became leader of his own independent party.

He was this party's sole member; and the generous contributions which his reputation enabled him to collect from liberal-minded Russians and others were spent in debauchery at the smart cafés or gambling resorts of Paris and the Riviera. He completely lost touch with revolutionary plans and ideals; and the *Ochrana* decided he was ripe for the plucking. Through Manasevitch-Manoiloff he met Lopuhin, who, though in retirement, was making great efforts to re-establish himself in the Police Department; and later he met Ratchkovsky, Azeff's notorious collaborator. Gapon's all too-obvious selling out to the authorities frustrated the betrayals and denunciations he was paid to engineer; yet he stood for the menace of treachery now that the police had brought him back to Russia; and so a committee of revolutionaries "tried" and condemned the renegade priest and appointed an implacable subcommittee which attended to his execution.

[4]The chivalrous praising of enemy spies—after killing them—became less unusual in the World War; as, for example, the general British commendation of Carl Hans Lody and Fernando Buschman; or the Germans' comments in praise of "Alice Dubois" and Gabrielle Petit.

NOTES 707

⁵The secret-police system of the formidable Yuan Shi Kai, while co-operating to a degree with the Russians in counter-espionage, was also a grim and hopeful bystander —hoping without doubt that *both* combatants wear themselves out, so that China might regain full authority over the coveted Manchurian provinces.

⁶Winfried Lüdecke, *Behind the Scenes of Espionage.*

⁷Lieutenant Alexander Bauermeister, celebrated German Secret-Service officer, tells of General Kuropatkin in the war with Japan frustrating a victory by General Grippenberg "out of sheer jealousy."

⁸The depth of the Russian front ranged from fifty-five to sixty *versts,* or an average of approximately thirty-eight miles.

⁹General Rafael de Nogales, *Memoirs of a Soldier of Fortune.*

¹⁰*Memoirs of a Soldier of Fortune.*

¹¹Joseph Pilsudski, one day to rule his native Poland as military hero and dictator, was at this time a violent revolutionist. He had suffered exile to Siberia and had taken part in every sort of conspiracy, founding in 1894 the Socialist newspaper *Robotnik,* which he edited and printed—and, of course, distributed—secretly, first in Wilno and then in other Polish or Russian towns. For such a "crime" he was again arrested, this time in Lodz, in the secret offices of the very secret *Robotnik,* and he was thrown into the dreaded tenth pavilion of the Warsaw citadel, from which, so it was said, no political prisoner ever had escaped alive. Pilsudski "escaped" by cleverly feigning insanity, and, upon being transferred to a St Petersburg hospital, escaped from there with the help of a medical certificate forged by a patriotic Polish physician. After 1902 he established his headquarters in Cracow, which was under more "liberal" Austro-Hungarian rule. And there he resumed and expanded his earlier revolutionary dream of armed resistance and a "private Polish army", and from there he set out for Japan. The "private army" never really materialized—though he was in the field as an insurrectionist, striking at Russia, in 1905-06—until "Pilsudski's Legion" fought in the World War.

CHAPTER 59 *Watchdogs of Dictatordom*

¹Quotation from the New York *Times,* December 19, 1935.

CHAPTER 60 *Trapping an Archtraitor*

¹It was by means of this newly organized censorship that—during the critical Bosnia-Herzegovina "annexation period"—the tsar's military attaché in Vienna, Colonel Zantiewitsch, was discovered to be engaged in espionage. His exposure and the misadventures of other attachés, mostly Russian, who compromised themselves appear in Chapter 55, page 413.

²The acute nature of these precautions show that the best minds of Austrian counter-espionage realized they had cut across the trail of a master operative, presumably one in the pay of their great potential enemy, Russia. The substantial amounts of cash negligently dispatched in care of "General Delivery", the sending address of Eydtkuhnen, were enough to warn a practitioner like Ronge that symptoms of a major treason case were being held as "bait" in the trap prepared at the post office.

³A. Redl, *Organisation der Auskundschaftung fremder Militärverhältnisse und die Abwehr fremder Spionage im Inlande.*

⁴The address upon one of Alfred Redl's registered-letter receipts was that of the joint headquarters in Brussels of the French and Russian Intelligence departments. The Lausanne receipt carried the address of a foreign bureau of the Italian Secret Service, one subsequently distinguished by the wartime operations of General Zupelli and Professor Borghese. While the Warsaw address was probably that of Dr Katz, a notably energetic Russian spy-master stationed in Poland who removed his headquarters to Copenhagen at the outbreak of the great war.

⁵The best account of the detection of Colonel Redl available to the English reader is that by George Renwick, F.R.G.S., originally published in the *Sunday News* of London and included in Nicolai's *The German Secret Service,* translated into English by Mr Renwick. It is chiefly upon his authority that the dialogue of this chapter is offered as authentic.

NOTES

⁰These four officers were among the most talented of the Austrian Intelligence Service, August Urbanski von Ostromiccz and Ronge commanding it in succession. Of Wenzel Vorlicek, Colonel Victor K. Kaledin, who was operative K. 14 of the Seventh Section of the Russian General Staff, has written "the sad-looking, very shy Wentzel Vorlicek, who had cost Russia two million gold roubles in counter-espionage." That large sum may seem an overgenerous compliment to an able enemy officer; but at least the Russian military secret service *had* 2,000,000 gold roubles to spend and was unfailingly lavish in its struggle with the aces of the Austro-Hungarian service.

⁹Redl's remarks and air of resignation, as reported by the officers who visited him, would seem further to discredit the suggestion that he plotted to escape on the "escorted" return journey to Prague.

CHAPTER 61   *The Costly Treason of Alfred Redl*

¹There was evidently no concern about Redl being able to escape from the Hotel Klomser by a trick, or agents of the secret service would have been stationed to cover every possible means of exit.

²Redl's body was removed a few hours after discovery, burial occurring on Tuesday (May 27) with only one witness present, in the Central Cemetery in Vienna, grave 38, row 29, group 79.

³George Renwick, *The Story of Colonel Redl.*

⁴The ferment in Bohemia seemed so gravely to threaten the stability of the Habsburg empire that severe repressive measures had been put into effect, including every form of police spying and censorship. Redl undoubtedly knew of the political police supervision of Prague, and possibly because of it he continued to receive payments from Russia in care of the general post office at Vienna.

⁵Plan Three is said to have fixed every detail of the offensive campaign, down to the last man, gun and wagon. It arranged how all the necessary forces should be assembled and moved, and the points at which Serbia would be attacked. All these technical matters were outlined in written detail, fully illustrated with maps, charts and statistical tables. Plan Three was a potential masterpiece, and, as Redl proved, in its own field a *best seller.*

⁶Winston Churchill in *The Unknown War* indicates that, not only were the Austro-Hungarian casualties heavy, but also the abortive attempts to conquer the "hated pig-farmers of Serbia" cost the Austrians their best chance to avoid the destructive Russian invasion of Galicia by winning a decisive battle in the first two months of the great war.

⁷The Austro-Hungarian attempts in August and September of 1914, and a third in November of that year, were all repulsed in such derisory and ignominious fashion that the High Command of the Dual Monarchy could never leave off planning a fourth, and overwhelming, stroke.

This invasion was not accomplished for many months; but, starting on October 6, 1915, it finally was begun, with Kövess' Third Austrian Army strongly re-enforced by Gallwitz's Eleventh Army brought from the Russian front. Bulgaria by this time had been enticed into the struggle on the side of the Teutonic allies and Turkey, the traditional Bulgar foe. Therefore, General von Falkenhayn had two additional Bulgarian armies which he could throw into the balance against Putnik and his gallant but depleted Serbian forces. The Bulgars now struck westwards into southern Serbia across the rear of the main Serbian army, driving a deep wedge between Serbia and the Entente Allies, based upon Salonika, which proved the decisive factor in clearing the path of the long-delayed Austro-German-Bulgar Juggernaut.

⁸Putnik made such good—and even devastating—use of an enemy plan sent him by the Russian General Staff, one might rashly assume that mere possession of such military documents confers success automatically upon the thief or borrower. Much additional skill and brainwork is necessary, as the Serbs' commander in chief made clear. His Russian benefactors, though so deft with their bribery, were much less agile on the intellectual side. Having purchased Plan Three and many another, they came close to ruining themselves by miscalculating the Austrian reaction to Redl's wholesale iniquities, as the reader will discover in Chapter 67, page 502.

⁹A special verbatim report of this espionage trial was prepared for Franz Josef, who was not ordinarily encouraged by his courtiers to scrutinize affairs pertaining to the secret service.

¹⁰The Russians appear never to have noticed that executions for espionage or even high treason were no longer the judicial practice of Western Europe in time of peace. It was perhaps necessary to extinguish utterly any Russian, regardless of his rank, who had dealt with Alfred Redl and been betrayed by him. Russian Intelligence, considering Redl, for obvious reasons, a precious commodity, took no chances on a man sent to prison getting word out to some friend or accomplice who might vindictively denounce the Austro-Hungarian traitor to his own government. Immediate hangings sealed the lips of those who were the victims of his double- and even triple-dealing.

CHAPTER 62 *Secret Committees of Macedonia*

¹The collapse of Samuel's effort to restore the empire of Simeon the Great was typical of Balkan warfare down to modern times. At the battle of Petrich—which occurred near where the frontiers of Greece, Bulgaria and Jugoslavia now meet—Samuel was defeated by the Emperor Basil II, "surnamed the Slayer of the Bulgarians," according to Gibbon. However, when Basil at Petrich captured 15,000 of Samuel's Bulgars, he did not kill them but gouged out their eyes, leaving one soldier in every hundred with a single eye so that he might guide his companions back to their king. And Samuel, on beholding this groping army of blinded men, fell dead from grief. Basil died in his sixty-eighth year when about to "embark in person for a holy war against the Saracens of Sicily" and "his martial spirit . . . was dismissed from the world with the blessings of the clergy and the curses of the people." (Gibbon)

²It was difficult during the Russo-Turkish War of 1877-78 for the Russians to find reliable spies among the Turkish population. However, the capture of the fortress of Plevna—despite Osman Pasha's heroic defense—was attributed in great measure to the daring and effective operations of one Russian agent, whose achievements were subsequently acknowledged in published statements of the Russian chief of staff. This agent had come as a volunteer into the Greek Legion of the tsar. And the record is that he swam across a river, concealed himself for a time, donned a Turkish uniform and made his way into Plevna with a contingent of the sultan's reserve troops. Thereafter he delivered personally, or dispatched by means of a cleverly arranged messenger service, almost daily reports upon new Turkish batteries, their exact location and the weight of their guns, also reports upon the location of powder magazines and lines of communication leading to the batteries, the strength and morale of the garrison, and the number of recent casualties suffered by the Turks. And when the crisis came, though Osman Pasha had doubled his outposts, this spy crept through the lines and brought word to the Russians of the Turkish commander's decision to force his way out by the Sofia road.

³In addition to that objective of independence, Imro is said to have had the more immediate and vital mission of preserving the concept of the very existence of Macedonia, which was disappearing, leaving Macedonia "a mere historical conception, something that existed . . . two thousand years ago, like Cappadocia, or Moesia."

⁴Albert Londres, *Les Comitadjis; ou, Le terrorisme dans les Balkans.*

⁵Stoyanoff was kept locked standing in a cage for days, besides enduring inquisitorial persuasions applied with ropes, whips, pincers, hot irons and other forms of Turkish delight, such as will be found in the note following.

⁶Says Stoyan Christowe in *Heroes and Assassins* (p. 53): "Heads were compressed with wet ropes, priests and school masters were debased by perverted soldiers and gendarmes, hot irons were inserted in anuses, finger-nails were extracted, tongues were pinched with heated fire tongs. For two months the hellish scenes continued and were terminated only as the result of work done by British news correspondents and special investigators of the British embassy at Constantinople. The number of those tortured, jailed, and killed reached thousands."

⁷The word *comitadji* means, literally, committeeman; and the armed agents of Imro were first called *comitadjis* by their Turkish foes. The Bulgarian form of the word is

comita; but in the ranks of Imro, it is said, a *comitadji* is known as a *tchetnik,* while the band to which he belongs is a *tcheta.*

[8] Deltcheff, "father" of the *comitadjis,* their chief organizer and "inspector general", was on the point of graduating from a military school in Sofia when he learned that Damian Grueff was laying the foundations of a revolutionary society. He straightway contrived to get himself expelled from school, so that he might hurry back to Macedonia and take part in this movement.

[9] The *haiduks* were the heroes of Balkan folklore and the intrepid ancestors of every Balkan insurgent. A great many of these formidable Turk-baiters have been immortalized in the histories of the different Balkan peoples. Greek *haiduks,* it is said, were struggling against Turkish rule before the general rebellion to which Lord Byron lent his aid and prestige.

[10] Melnik, founded in the twelfth century by Byzantine nobles exiled from the imperial court, lies in ruins today because in 1913 the Greco-Bulgarian boundary cut it off from Salonika.

[11] The Macedonian revolutionary leader, Zandansky, got the idea that this "romantic knight-errant" Saraffoff was a secret agent working only for Ferdinand of Bulgaria, and so he ordered his friend and henchman, Todor Panitsa, to shoot him. Panitsa, being of the thorough school of Balkan assassins, shot and killed both Saraffoff and Ivan Garvanoff as they were leaving the royal palace after a conference with Ferdinand.

[12] Christowe, *Heroes and Assassins.*

[13] The revolutionary kidnapers disguised themselves as a band of robbers, dressing in a variety of costumes, including Turkish. But they thoughtfully provided a chaperon for Miss Stone of Boston—a Mme Tsilka, who added some complications of her own by giving birth to a baby that had to be added to the "robber" band as it moved from one mountain hiding place to another. Boris Bakmetieff, then the Russian minister to Sofia, and afterward the last tsarist ambassador to the United States, played an important part in negotiating payment of ransom and the liberation of the American missionary.

[14] Macedonia got the worst of it, for in suppressing the revolt the Turks burned 201 villages with a total of 12,440 houses. Some 4,690 inhabitants were slain or burned alive; 3,122 women and girls were dishonored, 176 of the youngest and most attractive being carried away into the Turkish harems. More than 100,000 people were made homeless by this counter-revolutionary vigor, and 30,000 took refuge across the frontier in Bulgaria. Yet as the sultan's commanders were destroying his subjects and their property, both sides felt severely the economic impact of the insurrection.

CHAPTER 63 *Black Hand in the Balkans*

[1] Colonel Walther Nicolai, *The German Secret Service.*

[2] Russian agents and agitators are said to have traveled all over Galicia and throughout the other Slav sections of Austria-Hungary. Distinguished personages from these regions—living in St Petersburg or Moscow—volunteered their services. And these same people are alleged to have sabotaged war loans after the outbreak of hostilities, to have encouraged the activities of revolutionary committees, and "represented military service for Austria as degrading." Nearly 150 death sentences were passed upon Russian spies caught in the interior of the Dual Monarchy during the first two years of the war, according to General Maximilian Ronge, chief of the Austro-Hungarian "K. S." at the close of the war and author of *Kriegs- und industrie-spionage.* While his German colleague, Nicolai, laments that political leaders "like Kramarsch and Raschin, were condemned to death, but received pardon through an amnesty."

[3] It was the sincere, if prejudiced, opinion of the Russian government that, but for Article 29, the tsar's Black Sea Fleet might have sailed out to join Admiral Rozhestvenski in his voyage of doom to the Far East, and that thus reinforced his conquest of Togo in the Straits of Tsu-shima would have been certain.

[4] King Milan of Serbia had divorced Queen Natalie in 1886. Upon his voluntary abdication, his son, Alexander Obrenovitch, was proclaimed king on March 6, 1889, the government being placed in the hands of a regency. King Alexander and his queen,

Draga, were not happy, though their union had begun with many of the romantic flourishes of the best Viennese operettas. Alexander, it is said, was planning to divorce Draga when, on the fateful night of June 11, 1903, the conspirators of *Narodna Odbrana*, led by her brother-in-law, forced an entrance into the palace.

[5]Potiorek was, after Conrad von Hötzendrof, the most eminent military personage of old Franz Josef's empire. When Conrad had been invited to become chief of the General Staff in 1908, it is said that he modestly proposed Potiorek in his stead. It was this general, a fatuous fire-eater, who wrote: "But in God's name anyhow no rotten peace! Better a defeat on the battlefield in a struggle with a Great Power than that." Potiorek, as governor of Bosnia and the great soldier entrusted with the conquest of Serbia, was given his fill of defeats by Putnik, without encountering the Great Power.

[6]Princip, a high-school student, seems also to have been a psychopathic case, and certainly the typical dupe of patriotic agitations. On that account he was not condemned to death for his crimes, but he might as well have been, since he died in prison during the war, a victim of brutal treatment and neglect, but also of his own physical and mental infirmities. He has been honored with a monument since the establishment of the Kingdom of the Serbs, Croats and Slovenes.

[7]The Archduke Franz Ferdinand died at 11 A.M. There is no certainty, of course, that —even if he wore the shirt of mail—an assassin of Princip's amateurish or fanatic stamp would have been sufficiently clearheaded and a good enough marksman only to aim at the head or throat. Orders from Vienna had unquestionably come to Serajevo that the heir's morganatic wife—who was a charming woman, a particular favorite of the German Kaiser, but anathema to Habsburg orthodoxy—was not to be "exalted", which to a degree explains the inadequate police and military protection, and which is confirmed by the want of respect shown the assassinated couple when their coffins were returned to Vienna.

[8]Kaiser Wilhelm was justified in remarking to Admiral von Capelle—who recorded it—that he "did not believe that a great war would develop." In his opinion "the Tsar would not associate himself with the murderers of princes." However, owing to the prolonged influence of Imro and the Turks, terror had become a commonplace of Balkan politics; and the Russian government was confronted with the much more serious issue of racial sympathies fiercely astir in all classes at home, coupled with the rankling loss of prestige which had resulted from the Bosnian affront of 1909 and the growing demands of that prime chancellery sport of face-saving.

[9]When told by Count Paar of the double assassination, old Franz Josef could only exclaim: "Horrible! The Almighty does not allow Himself to be challenged with impunity. . . . A higher Power has restored the old order, which I unfortunately was unable to uphold." To the subtle brain of the monarch who had ruled one of the world's great empires for sixty-six years, death was the penalty inflicted by a God jealous of the purity of the Habsburg line upon Franz Ferdinand, the heir-apparent, and Sophie Chotek, his morganatic wife, because Sophie's wholesome body was not dutifully diluted with royal blood.

CHAPTER 64 *The Coming of World Catastrophe*

[1]The little-known engagement at Custozza in June 1866 was the last Austrian victory until 1915. The army of the Archduke Albert routed the Italians, but it has been said that two more Austrian corps in the north with Von Benedek might have prevented Sadowa. It was George Meredith who, as special correspondent of the London *Morning Post* at Italian headquarters, demonstrated, according to Philip Guedalla, that the reverse at Custozza "was a moral and almost a physical victory."

[2]The German Kaiser did not believe that the tsar "would associate himself with the murderers of princes," according to Admiral von Capelle. Baron Krupp on July 17 informed a colleague on his board of directors that "the Emperor had spoken to him on the conversation with the Austrians, but had characterized the affair as so secret that he [Krupp] would not have ventured to communicate it even to his board of directors. . . . The Emperor had told him personally that he would declare war immedi-

ately if Russia mobilized. The Emperor's repeated insistence that in this matter no one would be able to reproach him again with want of resolution had produced an almost comic effect."
[3]Conrad von Hötzendorf, *Aus meiner Dienstzeit*, 1906–1918.
[4]Conrad von Hötzendorf.
[5]Churchill, *The Unknown War*.
[6]Franz Josef was intimately associated with only an elderly trio of officers. Not only Count Paar but also his other aide-de-camp, Baron Bolfras, was a septuagenarian, and the invaluable Count Beck, perhaps the emperor's one trusted male friend, had been seventy years of age in 1906, when he already had served Franz Josef for fifty years.

CHAPTER 65 *The Sheep's Clothing of Wilhelm Stieber*
[1]Nicolai, *The German Secret Service*. (Translated by George Renwick, F.R.G.S.)
[2]A caste-conscious reference to Ludendorff attributed, on the best authority, to Wilhelm Hohenzollern.
[3]*The German Secret Service*.
[4]Walther Nicolai was a General Staff major when appointed to the command of the military secret-service organization of the German Empire; and through the greater part of the war, despite the heavy responsibilities, far-reaching influence and superior importance of his position, he ranked as a lieutenant colonel.
[5]*Nachrichtendienst* was the designation either of an elite Intelligence Corps of the Imperial German Army or else of the whole intelligence and secret-service department of Germany. It would seem to have been the equivalent of the "K. S." or *Kundschafts Stelle* of the Austro-Hungarian army; and yet we find a star of the Russian military secret service, Colonel Victor K. Kaledin, describing it in this fashion: "From that moment . . . I became part and parcel of a select corps known as the *Kontrazviedka Generalnago Schtaba* (Russian) and *Nachrichtendienst* (German); with two secret ciphers"—but if Kaledin was thus enlisted in it at a price, while posing as a treacherous Russian willing to sell his espionage services to the Germans, it would hardly seem that *Nachrichtendienst* was a "select" corps.
[6]Yet the German government seems to have been politically cautious about Great Britain in the summer of 1914. In Darrell Figgis' *Recollections of the Irish War* one comes with surprise upon this evidence (p. 29), ". . . a few weeks before this, Carson had run his cargo of rifles at Larne, and these rifles had been bought in Hamburg. Germany, I was told, believed that Britain was looking for a cause of war, and the German Government had therefore warned all firms that they must under no circumstances sell arms to Ireland. Another affair such as Larne, with its noise and alarm, might bring serious consequences that Germany was anxious to avert. This, be it remembered, was told me before our affair at Howth, and two months before the European war. I thought it fantastic then, though I soon had cause to know that the fear was genuine."
[7]This scooping up of a chain of spies happened repeatedly on the Continent after the outbreak of hostilities; and, to do justice to the Germans' counter-espionage, they profited from one bitter experience and thereafter scored the greatest hauls. The sixty-six agents of the Frankignoul chain in Belgium and the occupied departments of France were probably a wartime world's record.
[8]Captain Tappken was the chief of German Naval Intelligence at the time of this momentous blunder. However, so much has been done to disguise the identity of the blunderer, it seems very possible that some other "acting chief" of the German Admiralty's espionage service led the British counter-spies to the barber, Ernst.
[9]Three of these German agents the reader will come upon elsewhere in the chapters covering the World War. Heinrich Schtaub was a "parachute spy" on the Eastern Front, having been landed more than twenty times behind the Russian lines, according to his adversary, Colonel Kaledin. Bartels, for some rather vague reason, was known to the Russian secret service as "the good angel of the German Petrograd 'I' " and does appear to have played an influential part in maintaining clandestine bases in or near the tsar's capital.
[10]For Von Tausch it appears that Steinhauer exposed the unfortunate Captain

Scholtz, who had become entangled in the feminine snare known to her French employers as Jane Durieux. In the town of Appenweier the German agent was enterprising enough to crawl under a bed presently to be occupied by Jane and the infatuated Scholtz; and he records with humorless naïveté how disgusted he became that night when neither the man nor the woman said anything incriminating about military or political secrets. But on the basis of evidence subsequently collected by Steinhauer, the French enchantress was banished from Germany, while Scholtz, her dupe, suffered six years' imprisonment in a fortress and the loss of his army rank.

[11] Gustav Steinhauer and S. T. Felstead, *Steinhauer: The Kaiser's Master Spy.*

[12] Steinhauer claims that one or two of the postmen had warned the spy, thinking he conducted a secret betting business: "Be careful, your letters are being opened."

[13] Gustav Steinhauer.

[14] Graves, in or out of prison, had one quality of the effective espionage agent, *luck!* The completed manuscript of his book, written in collaboration with Edward Lyell Fox, was delivered to his American publishers on June 1, 1914, more than three weeks before the event at Serajevo.

CHAPTER 66 *The Drama Begins: Down with the Curtain*

[1] Ernst is reputed to have urged that his wages be increased to thirty shillings a month as the "danger" became more apparent to him. His various correspondents were paid according to the estimated worth of each, but none seems to have earned better than a pound a week, making German espionage in the United Kingdom—the greatest naval and commercial rival of Germany—a curiously cheap undertaking.

[2] As late as August 21 the German high command had no idea of the dispatch or movement of the British Expeditionary Force, which is proved conclusively by an army order issued on that date.

[3] Steinhauer and Felstead, *Steinhauer: The Kaiser's Master Spy.*

[4] As widely accepted a military critic as Frank H. Simonds helped to circulate this report of great Russian forces being transferred to the French front via Archangel and Scotland. The German General Staff appears to have swallowed it like so much *Würzburger* bock. On September 5 the representative of German O.H.L., Colonel Hentsch, told General von Kluck: "The news is bad. . . . The English are disembarking fresh troops continuously on the Belgian coast. There are reports of a Russian expeditionary force in the same parts. A withdrawal is becoming inevitable." Mr Winston Churchill, whose audacity and inspiration were generally leagues ahead of "wiser" professional managers of the war, had actually proposed to bring a Russian expeditionary force to the Western Front in such a way. While this proposal may have leaked out and become magnified into a current reality, the helpful legend of the visiting Russian contingent has more often been ascribed to the wishful, excited imagination of a railway porter, "working," says Captain Liddell Hart, "on the simple fact of the night passage of troop trains with Gaelic-speaking occupants."

[5] During a period of fifteen days in May and June 1915 seven authentic enemy spies were detected and arrested in Britain. Each of them had received more training than Lody was given time to ingest. None represented as good material for espionage assignments as Lody had done; and, since all seven blundered, all would have been caught —regardless of the earlier British apprehension of Lody.

[6] This protean agent of German Intelligence—who seems a mere "cover" in the Lody case—turns up as the dangerous Captain Stammer of the German Admiralty Intelligence Staff in the book by Steinhauer and Felstead; whereas in the even more ingenuous master-spying of Armgaard Karl Graves he frightens us as the "very astute and calculating" Herr *von* Stammer, confidential secretary to the chief of Naval Intelligence at Königergratzerstrasse 70. At least we may safely assume that Stammer was connected with the German Intelligence. And it is interesting to note that all the excellent advice which Graves confesses receiving from the "astute" Stammer was just the sort of thing which, if observed, would have prevented Lody's giving the English that evidence which convicted him.

[7] Lüdecke, *Behind the Scenes of Espionage.*

⁸Steinhauer alleges that Lody had "already done a certain amount of secret-service work in America", but even if he had thus practiced spying in a country innocent of counter-espionage, it was no preparation for the wartime supervision he encountered in Great Britain.

⁹Sir Basil Thomson in *My Experiences at Scotland Yard* gives the text of two letters written by Lody just before his execution, one to relatives in Stuttgart, the other to the commanding officer at Wellington Barracks where he had been held prior to being removed to the Tower. We regret lack of space to reprint them here; but both are commended to the reader's attention for their simplicity and admirable tone. Lody left a ring which he asked to have forwarded to a lady in America, and this was done. It was said that the German government had insured his life for 60,000 marks in favor of his relatives, and that when his death became known in Germany, "the people of his native village planted an oak to be known evermore by his name."

CHAPTER 67 *Intelligence and Secret Service*

¹The reader may consult a now forgotten but important and arresting work, *German Atrocities*, by J. H. Morgan, professor of constitutional law in the University of London. The diary of a German officer, which the author examined, recorded the "undiscriminating butchery" of civilians and concluded: "In future there ought to be an inquiry into their guilt instead of shooting them." A soldier wrote: "Befehl ergangen sämtliche männliche Personen zu erschiessen . . . Ein schrecklicher Sonntag [Order passed to shoot all the male inhabitants . . . A frightful Sunday!]." The incredible present-day behavior of the Nazi government and its secret police, the *Gestapo*, will come with something less of a shock to anti-Fascist sensibilities after a study of Mr Morgan's carefully documented exposure of the authorized German conduct in the field during the invasion of Belgium and the early months of the World War. Or as Arnold Zweig's Catholic chaplain in *Education before Verdun* is moved to observe: "I was with our Rhinelanders in Belgium. What I saw, and what our men proudly did, as being the whole duty of a soldier, was murder, robbery, outrage, arson, sacrifice—every crime that can burden the soul of man."

²Captain B. H. Liddell Hart, *The Real War*.

³Graf Schlieffen was chief of the German General Staff from 1891 to 1906, and it was he who developed the famous plan of campaign by which the armies of France were to be rapidly enveloped and decisively defeated. So accurate of vision was this remarkable military scientist that he even allowed for British intervention in a general war, estimating that a force of 100,000 regulars would immediately begin "operating in conjunction with the French." He is credited with planning first to use Landwehr and Ersatz troops in front operations; he proposed, too, that all the resources of Germany must be fused into the army. And, though his dying words are said to have been: "It must come to a fight. Only make the right wing strong!"—the actual battle plan of Von Moltke absurdly violated the most obvious fundamentals of Schlieffen's masterly conception.

⁴It is known, however, that Schlieffen did not personally wish to violate either Dutch or Belgian neutrality if he could contrive to "avoid the moral reproach." Such was the cunning of the old German strategist, he counted upon deployment of his force to draw French troops across the frontier of Belgium first. They would seek, he believed, the best natural defensive position in the valley of the Meuse, south of Namur, and thus supply him his pretext for invading a neutral land.

⁵Winston S. Churchill.

⁶B. H. Liddell Hart.

⁷These plans may have been radically altered, since the Germans knew, with the conviction of Wolkerling, that they were in the hands of the Russians; but changes would never have *weakened* Lötzen, and there was no reason for the Russian high command to assume the fortress could be taken without the use of siege ordnance.

⁸The Austrian official history, *Oesterreich-Ungarns letzter Krieg*, states with slightly oblique candor: "The Russians did not exaggerate when they claimed in their message

of victory that the enemy had lost 250,000 dead and wounded and 100,000 taken prisoners."
[9]Hoffmann, *War Diaries and Other Papers*.
[10]During the Manchurian war Rennenkampf and Samsonoff had distinguished themselves in a typically Russian manner as "dashing cavalry commanders"; but the latter had become convinced that Rennenkampf deliberately failed to support him when he was threatened by a superior force of Japanese. This grievance had boiled into a public encounter when blows were struck on the railroad platform at Mukden. Hoffmann, a German military observer in Manchuria, knew all about the origin and endurance of the Rennenkampf-Samsonoff feud, and he has even been said to have counted on it in his conception of East Prussian defensive strategy which was so fortunately appropriated by Ludendorff. Disregarding that, however, as well as the uncoded radio dispatches, we may marvel at Russian staff minds that would place those two generals to command armies, virtually side by side, which of simple necessity must co-operate.

CHAPTER 68   *The Quicksands of Tsardom*

[1]Lieutenant Alexander Bauermeister ["Agricola"] in his *Spione durchbrechen die Front* describes a German secret-service attempt to bribe the Russian Lieutenant General Schulmann, commandant of the fortress of Ossowiecz, alleging that Schulmann in negotiation with R., a remarkably audacious secret agent, agreed to surrender the fortress, but that the intervention of a Russion corps commander, Irmanoff, caused the removal and "disappearance" of Schulmann and the court-martial and execution of R. While in his *Memoirs of a Spy* Nicholas Snowden [Miklós Soltész] gives a very convincing account of his mission that led to the acceptance of an Austrian bribe of 30,000 roubles by a Russian staff colonel, who—with a view also of buying the liberation of his brother, a war prisoner in Austria—handed over a copy of the Russian defense plans which proved of substantial value in facilitating the great Gorlice offensive of the Austro-German armies in May 1915. It was during this operation that the Grand Duke Nicholas, then the Russian commander in chief, is said to have arrived at the front "and horse-whipped the Russian general commanding, in the presence of many of his own officers, blaming the general for the terrible disaster."
[2]A. T. Vassilyev, *The Ochrana*.
[3]Churchill, *The Unknown War*.
[4]A statement made by George Renwick in a translator's note to Chapter II of Nicolai's *The German Secret Service*, and upon the authority of No. 14 of the *Archives of the Russian Revolution*.

CHAPTER 69   *Sabotage*

[1]B. E. Palat, *La Ruée sur Verdun*.
[2]Mackenzie, *Athenian Memories*.
[3]Lüdecke, *Behind the Scenes of Espionage*.
[4]Rintelen, *The Dark Invader*.
[5]Mrs Vorse further relates that, when she returned to America, she was unable to sell a magazine article on how Germany talked the day after the sinking of the Lusitania. Some American editors believed the public had had its fill of war literature and wanted to forget all about it. Others thought the war would soon be over and scouted the suggestion that the United States might be drawn into it.
[6]A well-documented and entertaining account of this prewar endeavor to suppress the German Secret-Service activities in North America will be found by the reader in the late French Strother's *Fighting Germany's Spies*.
[7]In the light of Von Papen's important, if transitory, influence on the imposition of Nazi absolutism upon the German Republic and the German people, it is interesting to discover how many of his fellow Germans in able memoirs have nominated him for the Pig-Iron Cross as Champion Teutonic Blunderer of the World War. To give but three of many citations seconding this popular nomination:

(A) Captain von Papen had made the German reservists of America afraid to "serve" under him after the episode of the unfortunate Werner Horn. He gave "this fellow, a fine and most patriotic man . . . a badge—black, white and red . . . to wear on his sleeve." Horn was told by Von Papen that he was now a soldier; "evidently," Rintelen observes, "an 'Enlistment Act' of Papen's own!" Yet Horn swallowed the military attaché's "creed" with such relish that in 1916 he tried singlehanded "to blow up a bridge connecting Canada and the United States." (Horn also aimed at the Welland Canal with its vital flow of imperial traffic!) His "bomb did not go off", however, and the failure cost him his liberty and afterward his sanity. Having suffered imprisonment both in the United States and Canada, he returned to Germany about 1924, "a completely broken man, whose mind had given way."

(B) Captain von Papen himself set out for Germany early in 1917, his luggage crammed with confidential documents incriminating to many persons who did not enjoy his diplomatic immunity. The attaché's person was inviolate since the United States government had invited him to go home and provided him with the customary safe conduct. But that eviction, occasioned by the breaking off of diplomatic relations with Germany some weeks prior to the American declaration of war, did not safeguard Von Papen's trunks. British authorities at Falmouth seized the lot and were "unkind enough" to forward to Naval "I" all the codes, letters, copies, counterfoils and secret documents "the enlightened diplomat saw fit to carry across the seas. The results were: a trail of ruin and misery for dozens . . . of Germans and others in America sympathetic to the German cause." At Donington Hall an interned Bavarian colonel, "a Front Officer", asked Rintelen with justifiable heat:

"What regiment does that fool come from?"
"First Regiment of Uhlans of the Guard, sir."
"That explains everything," said the colonel.

(C) By the time the discomfited Rintelen was lodged among criminals at Atlanta, Von Papen was on duty in Palestine. When General Allenby rolled up the Turkish Front in the autumn of 1918, British cavalrymen found a German staff officer's tent from which the occupant, it was clear, had fled recently and with undignified haste. All of his confidential documents that Von Papen had not lost at Falmouth were discovered in the tent, for, such was the "calm" of that Front, the ex-attaché had been catching up on his reading and filing. A wire sent to London provoked this alleged historic reply: "Forward papers. If Papen captured, do not intern; send him to lunatic asylum." One of the captured documents, forwarded to New York, caused a new indictment to be drawn against Rintelen, but "the American authorities had a sense of humor too," the master of sabotage has written, "and amidst the derisory laughter over the ill-fated German officer's retreat in Palestine, the charge against the German officer in residence at Atlanta was dropped." (*The Dark Invader.*)

⁸Captain Franz von Rintelen was very faithfully defended by a noted member of the New York bar, Mr George Gordon Battle. He appears to have been accorded a fair trial; and, considering his guilt as an alien enemy—and the punishments which were inflicted upon *American* radicals, pacifists and many a dissenter in those intemperate times—the German leader's four-year sentence was a light one. Rintelen is hardly on secure ground when he objects that the British Admiralty and Foreign Office acted "contrary to all law and to International agreements" (*The Dark Invader;* p. 270), since his own admittedly unlawful acts were flagrant violations of a nation's neutrality, that very special concern of international agreements and the laws of war. Earlier (pp. 98–99) Rintelen justifies his violation—the proposed sabotage campaign —by quoting an official telegram sent from London to a timid naval commander who had located the German light cruiser Dresden in December 1914 but required a "sop for his conscience which was still trained to peacetime considerations."

The Admiralty had wired him: "You sink the Dresden, and we shall attend to the diplomatic side." If that want of respect for international law on the part of the British justifies Rintelen and his agents in their sabotage attacks, why should he expect the same British to forget wartime expediency and not oblige the American courts at the expense of his discomfiture?

Exclusive "credit" for the exposure of the whole German corps of *sabotageurs* must not be strictly reserved to the inept Von Papen. American counter-espionage came of age in this undercover conflict; and such operatives as Paul Altendorf—who posed for months in Mexico as a German agent or sympathizer, or even as a Mexican, and whose investigations compare with the best counter-spying exploits of modern times—obtained a surprising amount of conclusive evidence. Some of it has only been made public in the course of the prolonged litigations based upon the alleged sabotage that caused the ruinous "Black Tom" and Kingsland munitions disasters.

⁹Alfred Louis Moreau Gottschalk, a member of a noted family of New Orleans, bearing the name of a distinguished pianist and composer, and the descendant of a great French general, may not have been directly warned, but a curious allegation holds that two weeks before the Cyclops left port, and a long time before the collier was reported missing, an advertisement appeared in a Portuguese newspaper announcing that a requiem mass would be celebrated for the American consul general "lost when the Cyclops was sunk at sea." This announcement is said to have born the signatures of prominent citizens of Rio de Janeiro; but they disclaimed responsibility for it, and its insertion thus added to the mystery. Was the advertisement the work of some isolated German fanatic or of vainglorious German agents, of whom the war produced a bumptious bumper crop? And why did a Spaniard in New York write to a German in South America, asking: "Where is the Cyclops?" American postal censors acknowledge having seen the inquiry and mark it down as something nearly as mysterious as the collier's being utterly blotted from the surface of the sea. No wreckage, lifeboats nor bodies were ever picked up; and a complement of fifteen officers and 221 men, besides the fifteen passengers, went without a trace to some unknown oceanic fate.

CHAPTER 70   *Special Missions*

¹Lieutenant Bert Hall had an adventure-seeking tradition to live up to, inasmuch as his father, George Hall, had survived four years of fighting in the American Civil War, and then, when nothing more could be done for the Confederacy, had joined the ill-starred Maximilian and Carlotta, and even had managed to survive as a minor member of the cast of that imperial tragedy.

²Hall was one of *two survivors* of the original seven American members of the Lafayette Escadrille. Besides Captain Georges Thénault, the commanding officer, and Lieutenant de Laage de Meux, his second in command, the Americans were: Victor Chapman, Elliot Cowdin, Hall, James McConnell, Norman Prince, Kiffen Rockwell and William Thaw.

³The French directors of espionage were curiously addicted to landing spies near Rocroi, though they ought to have known that German vigilance would be acute in that area at the time. German O. H. L. or general headquarters had moved to Charleville on September 28, 1914, and a report had come in warning Colonel Nicolai and the secret-service corps that an entire regiment of French Zouaves was to be found in the Rocroi woods, and that it was foraging and requisitioning in and around the neighboring villages. As the Kaiser was in the habit of motoring through those woods, a good deal of tension and staff excitement developed. Not until November was it possible to round up the isolated enemy troops. It was not a regiment which finally surrendered at Signy-le-Petit but a French company at full war strength—two officers and 223 men, together with four English soldiers, all in uniform and with complete equipment. Pending their capture, Kaiser Wilhelm had shown imperial obstinacy and continued his motoring, and the vicinity of Rocroi—scene of a famous French victory in the Thirty Years' War—had been made unhealthful for the Allies, whether soldiers or secret agents.

⁴Bert Hall's narrow escape at the Rocroi field only convinced the French command that other missions should be submitted to the same hazard. Bach and Mangot were, therefore, ordered to land their spies at Rocroi; and they set out with some misgiving. Other fliers, including Hall, considered the proposed exploit suicidal. The two airmen approached the point of greatest danger and went about their mission in an intrepid yet methodical manner. They had agreed that Mangot should descend with his spy first; then Bach would drop down and do the same, while Mangot took off again as quickly as possible. Thus they hoped that only one plane would be apparent at a time, with the other on watch for German aircraft, planted machine gunners, or counter-spying lookouts.

Mangot made his landing according to plan, and his spy darted away toward the woods. The aviator taxied around to take off, but met with misfortune and turned over, wrecking his plane. Bach landed at once, unloaded his agent, and, seeing that his comrade could not extricate himself, ran to his assistance. Badly as he had smashed his machine, the Frenchman was himself unhurt; and Bach managed to lift the wreck and help him scramble out. Having left his motor running so as not to be "caught with a dead stick", Bach hurried Mangot into the observer's cockpit vacated by the spy and started. He was skimming along, almost leaving the ground, when suddenly the propeller struck a stump that had been hidden by the tall grass. For a moment it held, and Bach hung on, hoping he might still get home with "the tip knocked off his prop." But then, with a loud report, the propeller flew apart, splinters spreading out in a wide circle; the plane rolled to a stop; and the two pilots were marooned inside the German lines.

[5]According to Colonel Walther Nicolai, chief of the German Secret Service, during the first twelve months of this air-spy innovation, nine such spies just landed behind the combat zone, four of whom were in uniform, together with five planes, fell into German hands. In cases where the spy was taken after the pilot had set out for home, attempts to pick up the captured spy again were carefully watched. The French planes at the appointed time circled over the landing places, while under close observation from well-hidden counter-spies. But the airmen—with the exception of Bert Hall, whose precipitate climb out of a machine-gun trap has been described elsewhere—stayed at a considerable height and ultimately gave up the mission and zoomed away. The German secret-service operatives had not been able to extort from the captured spies the sign or signal agreed upon as showing conditions were safe for a landing.

[6]Many pigeon baskets, for example, carried this appeal:

"The resistance of the Boche is being exhausted by the Allied attacks, which have already freed a part of French soil. In order to maintain the advance, it is necessary that the Allies should be well informed regarding the position of the enemy and his intentions. It is your duty, as good patriots who are in the midst of the enemy troops, to render this service to the Allies. The means of doing so are here at hand.

"You may risk your life, but think of the Allied soldiers who give theirs so gallantly to set you free. By sending information you will be doing your country an incalculable service and you will hasten the end of the War.

"We shall know how to reward you when peace comes, and you will always have the satisfaction of knowing that you acted as a good patriot."

And again:

"The Germans will not succeed in breaking the power of the Allies. They cannot prevent us from achieving victory and from annihilating for ever that vile people which is the enemy of the human race."

[7]In December 1917, sixty-three baskets of pigeons were found behind one German army, and that same area yielded forty-one in January and forty-five in May 1918.

[8]One of them persuaded the inhabitants in this fashion:

"Attention!

"Are you a good patriot? Will you help the Allies to beat back the enemy?

"Yes.

"Then take this packet; take it, unobserved, to your home; open it in the evening when you are alone and act according to the instructions which you will find in it.

"If you are observed, let the packet lie. Note the spot and come back by night and get the packet. See that you destroy the parachute immediately; it can be of no use to you.

"If you carry out these instructions carefully, you will have acted as a good patriot, done a great service to the Allies, and helped to hasten the hour of final victory.

"Patience and courage!

"Long live France! Long live Belgium! Long live the Allies!

"For our native land!

"In order to hasten the hour of your delivery, which is certain, take special care in filling in, on the form, the desired information. Ask reliable friends, should there be anything you do not know. To establish your identity give the names and addresses of two persons in unoccupied territory. This will serve to identify you after the Delivery, so that you may be rewarded.

"Every soldier of France and Belgium is at one with you. Support them in their duty and show them once more that the courage of the oppressed is no less than theirs.

"Long live the Allies!"

[9] An appeal to the people residing close to the Franco-German border promised:

"To every patriot of Lorraine!

"By providing the news we ask for, you will perform an invaluable service and hasten the end of the War.

"When peace comes, France will know how to reward you and you will be proud that you have acted as a good patriot."

CHAPTER 71 *Genius in the Near East*

[1] Ferdinand Tuohy, *The Secret Corps.*
[2] Joseph Gollomb, *Spies.*
[3] Ashton, *Secret Service.*
[4] *The Secret Corps.*
[5] F. Tuohy, *The Crater of Mars.*
[6] When Wassmuss had refused to leave, he was taken into custody as an enemy alien not to be allowed at large in Persia, seeing that its unrecognized or "neutral" war had been made an *ex post facto* fragment of the mighty struggle in the West. His personal belongings were likewise held subject to seizure and were to be removed with him to British headquarters. But the night before that transfer was scheduled to occur, Wassmuss—whose acknowledged talent for intrigue had earned him a guard of four British sentries—became suddenly stricken with restless concern for the welfare of his mount. He seemed to his guards a genial fellow, resigned to his captivity; yet when he discovered these symptoms of a peculiar native sickness, he began making trip after trip, accompanied by two of the sentries, down the stairs to the stable to see how his treatments were combating the indisposition of his favorite pony. All through a sleepless night the tender-hearted consul trudged, armed men going with him; until, near dawn, he made one trip alone. The pony was doing well enough. The British soldiers were drowsy, bored by such Teutonic diligence, caught off their guard. Wassmuss had come back to his bed each time—but this was the last time. And so off he rode on the entirely sound and refreshed Persian pony, to be seen no more, but heard of with regrettable regularity.

[7] The Swedish doctor, projecting all the righteous indignation of a "neutral" caught while accepting pay from the other side, denounced his arrest in Bushire as an indefensible breach of neutrality. He then perplexed his captors by taking off his breeches in the center of the city and refusing to put them on again. Had this resource occurred to Lindberg in some war-convulsed area, he might have been summarily bayoneted or treated as a dangerous lunatic. But in the East there was that almost universally respected "law" decreeing that no white *sahib* must ever be subjected to native ridicule. All sorts of concessions and inducements were therefore held out to the Swede, who had to be escorted to an internment camp, which, in his undraped condition, meant a humiliating pilgrimage with a swarm of Persian riffraff following the spectacle. Finally a subaltern was inspired to remind the prisoner that "going down to the base camp" would necessitate marching him "past the home of Frau X." Lindberg had been paying that lady marked attention and he hastily changed his mind about the breeches. He had hoped to embarrass the overbearing British, but found himself beaten by a youngster's ruse.

[8] The British, in spite of the promised large reward of rupees, were disposed to respect Wassmuss also as a determined and resourceful antagonist. Referring to the German consul, a British Intelligence officer has written: "And through all this tense period of strife it is in his favor that we only had cause to chalk up one bad mark against him. This had to do with his descent upon, and capture of the small British

community at Shiraz, including Consul O'Connor. The Persians let everyone go later, in return for ransom, but the unpleasant circumstance remained that Wassmuss had tried hard to persuade the locals to hand him over one of the English girl captives. When long after—in 1920—Wassmuss was taxed with this, he did not deny it, merely confining himself to the observation that life was very dull and crude in Persia at that time, without feminine society from the West." (F. Tuohy, *The Crater of Mars*.)

CHAPTER 73 *The Martyrdom of Edith Cavell*

[1] Addressing a group of army officers in London as recently as February 2, 1934, Captain Alfred Duff-Cooper, Financial Secretary of the War Office, revived the case of Edith Cavell when he observed that she "was a noble and courageous woman whom the Germans were entitled to execute according to the rules of warfare. But any politician could have told them the execution was going to arm 100,000 men against Germany." Statistics given out at the time, and probably exaggerated to stimulate further recruiting, claimed an increase of 30,000 enlistments the fortnight after Nurse Cavell's execution, by comparison with the average of preceding weeks in 1915.

[2] Lord Kitchener exerted himself for the strategical preservation of Antwerp, sending the last available British regular division—the Seventh—collected from the fortresses of the Empire, to Zeebrugge. Commanded by General Rawlinson, it marched toward Ghent, only to retire upon Thielt and Roulers when Antwerp surrendered. Rawlinson was supported by the Third Cavalry Division, coming from Ostend, by a territorial division borrowed from the French, and by Admiral Ronarc'h and his brigade of *Fusiliers Marins*, later to stand so gallantly beside the Belgians along the line of the Yser.

[3] Dr Bull was not wholly in sympathy with the clandestine endeavors of some Belgian civilian committees; and his loyalty to Miss Cavell caused him to view with a jaundiced eye the commitments and inept maneuvers of some of her non-British confederates. Undoubtedly the Thuliez notebook and M. Baucq's zeal in behalf of *La Libre Belgique* were veritable buoys and beacons to guide the German counter-spies.

[4] Quien was condemned to death by a court-martial at Paris in 1919, but his sentence was commuted to a long term of imprisonment. He was released in January 1936 after serving seventeen years of his twenty-year term in Clairvaux Penitentiary. He denies that he denounced Nurse Cavell to the German authorities at Brussels or was a secret agent for them, insisting that it was a case of mistaken identity. Having inherited a sizable fortune while imprisoned, he is now bending every effort to have his case reopened. At a new trial he insists that he can prove his innocence. Louis Bril did not survive to be condemned by court-martial—or to prove his innocence—for his ill repute and obvious pro-German activities resulted in his being assassinated at Scharbeek in 1916.

[5] Sadi Kirschen was so severely criticized by some Belgians for his conduct of Edith Cavell's defense that he was passed over when awards and decorations were being distributed after the Armistice. This criticism was mainly founded upon his failure to co-operate with M. de Leval, the attorney of the American Legation. Kirschen kept De Leval away from the trial, pleading that his presence would only prejudice the German court. It was also alleged that before the trial he neither talked with Miss Cavell nor examined the documents presented by the prosecution, and that he was not to be reached when De Leval tried to get in contact with him on the three days preceding the fateful eleventh. However that may be, it was Brand Whitlock's opinion that Kirschen defended the English nurse well. Kirschen claimed that the Germans refused him permission to see Miss Cavell or examine any of the documents prior to the convening of the court.

[6] That General von Bissing was not indifferent to all forms of feminine appeal will be made clear to the reader by the exploit of the seductive Mlle Angèle, related in Chapter 72.

[7] Philippe Baucq, with but a night to live, sat down in his cell and wrote letters to his wife, dating all of them save one weeks and months ahead. They were given to a priest, who could not disapprove this well-meant deception. In the letter dated October

12, a few hours before his execution, Baucq told his wife that he had been "let off" with a prison sentence of fifteen years and gave both instructions about winding up his business affairs and many thoughtful suggestions as to the upbringing of their young children.
²Joseph Crozier, *In the Enemy's Country*.

CHAPTER 74 *The Real Fräulein Doktor*
¹The writer has to acknowledge with regret having published a number of inaccurate and even grotesquely exaggerated statements about this German operative and her record in the World War. He did so in 1928 (*Spy and Counter-Spy: the Development of Modern Espionage*) upon the authority of an Intelligence officer whose imagination, he then believed, would be professionally held in check. The misinformation thus obtained has been given an unfortunate currency abroad, reproduced not only in the British edition and French translation of *Spy and Counter-Spy*, but also quoted by Sir George Aston in his book, *Secret Service*, and in other works, and accepted as the result of the writer's personal investigation of Fräulein Doktor's character and career. Only now, eight years afterward, it is possible to assume this blame and to correct the canards reported by one who professed to have known her, and which were published in good faith.
²The complete title of this work is:
Die Bruderschaft der Borer und Balierer von Freiburg und Waldkirch, Beitrag zur Gewerbegeschichte des Oberrheins von Dr Elsbeth Schragmüller: Karlsruhe, G. Braunsche Hofbuchdruckerei und Verlag; 1914.
³This dialogue given on the authority of Lieutenant-General Paul von Lettow-Vorbeck and associates, *Die Weltkriegsspionage*.
⁴Probably the best available account of the discipline and training methods of the secret service at Baden-Baden is to be found in the war reminiscences of Nicholas Snowden [Miklós Soltész] *Memoirs of a Spy* (New York, 1933).
⁵Crozier refers to "Gertrud Würtz, a ravishing blonde who seldom showed herself," but who "was not, however, a supernumerary figure. . . . Her whole being seemed to mirror only innocent sentimentality, yet she was "destined soon to demonstrate to us her resources of spirit and her personal attraction." Later, after she had cost him the lives and services of several of his best agents, Crozier tells how members of his mission "had first seen to it swiftly and secretly that she received all the travel facilities she desired. She embarked at a time and place actually chosen by us. We had warned the English secret service. The reception that we had arranged for her would avoid the necessity of our ever having to see her again." Crozier is generally so dependable in his narrative, it is strange to find him confidently suggesting here that the beauteous Gertrud was either executed in England or imprisoned for a term of years, whereas no English authority describing the superlative effectiveness of British counter-espionage during the war so much as mentions the arrest of Gertrud Würtz, or any other ravishing blonde creature of her type sent from Antwerp via Holland.
⁶Lucieto, *On Special Missions*.
⁷"Irma Staub", according to Charles Lucieto, on more than one occasion chose the pseudonym, Countess of Louvain, a singular selection in view of the conduct of German troops when invading Louvain. Lucieto's almost lyrical account of his protracted "duel" with "The Beautiful Spy" is akin to the palpable misrepresentations of his description of *Fräulein Doktor*—but in both instances we venture to detect the work of some collaborator, editorial assistant or publisher, who believed devoutly, in 1926, that no book of secret-service adventures was worth issuing until a veteran hand had touched up the Sex Appeal.
⁸Madame de Victorica flirted with a career in the German Intelligence or political secret service as early as 1910, when Elsbeth Schragmüller was twenty-three years old and in the midst of her studies at Freiburg. Major Yardley in his *The American Black Chamber* commits himself to the fascinating observation (p. 119): "Like so many other successful spies, Madame Victorica was of necessity a drug addict." The reader who has come this far through the history of secret service may be able to decide for him-

self what "of necessity" means or may note that from Walsingham's men and Father Joseph, from Louise de Kéroualle, D'Éon, Baron de Batz and Karl Schulmeister to Miss Elizabeth van Lew, Timothy Webster, Stieber, Zernicki, Azeff, Cuers, Baden-Powell and Frederick Funston, none of these notably different yet uniformly successful agents of espionage was addicted to drugs, or overindulgent in alcoholics, or even, in many cases, addicted to nicotine. We know from Joseph Crozier that the concealed drug addiction of one of the minor members of his French espionage mission nearly ruined all his work, cost him his life, and upset the careful calculations of months. It is hard to imagine any human failing which "of necessity" would prove a more malignant handicap to professional or amateur operatives of espionage or counter-espionage.

CHAPTER 75 *Rigors of the Antwerp School*

[1]Information about the school and the methods of training practiced there has been obtained from a variety of reasonably reliable sources, including persons who were actually admitted to the institution as secret-service pupils. After one experience of bland or witless misrepresentation, such as the writer acknowledges in note 1 of the preceding chapter, he feels obliged to warn the reader of the improbability of any informant telling the exact and unvarnished truth about so romantic a character as "Mademoiselle le Docteur." But what is given here is the result of prolonged personal investigation and as much careful checking of facts as the circumstances of World War secret service have made possible.

Elsbeth Schragmüller may not even have been the best of teachers, on both sides of the conflict, or on the Germanic side. Her rules and precepts are mainly a distillation of the best that anyone might compile after a few months' intensive experience of, or concentration upon, the working problems of the spy. In addition to those given on page 569, other rules attributed to her are:

"Collect every available bit of information, but without showing interest in any of it. Never fasten upon some item of intelligence you think you can or you *must* obtain, and so go about pursuing that single fact, making conspicuous inquiries, exposing your determination to learn a particular thing.

"Always record your findings in terms of absolute innocence. Figures or dimensions you have to report may best be remembered as items of personal expenditure. In Portsmouth you have seen ten heavy naval guns on trucks, ready for mounting. But you remember that excellent dinner of sea food you enjoyed at Portsmouth, costing you *ten* shillings.

"Do not burn a letter or other paper and treat the charred or ashen fragments as unreadable. Microscopic examination can do a great deal with paper ash. Tearing up papers and throwing them away, in secret service, does not destroy them. Paper scraps are never disposed of with absolute security even in lavatories.

"Never talk or behave mysteriously, except in this one instance: a communicative person with matters of genuine value to impart will often yield them the more readily if he, or she, has been told something—perhaps wholly fictitious—in a flattering and confiding way, with a slightly mysterious air.

"Avoid every temptation to show off, to be clever, or too original and inventive about communicating tricks or other secret-service dodges, unless you are positive your invention is really *new*. In a contest of wits the spy on duty abroad is bound to find himself working against enormous odds."

[2]Sir Paul Dukes in *Red Dusk and the Morrow*, his narrative of personal adventures as chief of the British Secret Intelligence Service in Bolshevik Russia, gives the impression that he was schooled in the laboratory "inks" and "put through the ciphers" in about three weeks' time. And he states this with no obvious intent to boast of his own remarkable talent for mastering espionage intricacies rapidly or to emphasize his superior officers' flattering concentration upon his training. Dukes, however, appears to have been an exceptional spy as well as a modest one, and the only British agent to be awarded a knighthood for espionage achievements during the postwar turbulence of the Russian Revolution. He would, presumably, take about a fifth of the time required by the average recruit in learning what was obligatory. He was enlisted to go to Russia, and only expected to undertake that one perilous mission; and he was al-

ready more familiar with the country than anybody who might train him at the British Intelligence "school."

³Other agents were given a cigarette paper marked with the necessary code signs, which they concealed in a tuft of cotton carried in the ear.

⁴Nicolai, *The German Secret Service*.

⁵The celebrated woman spy-master of Antwerp, having fought the Allies to the bitter end, seemed suddenly never to have lived. Fräulein Elsbeth contrived to disappear; and where next she might emerge in secret-service work, no man was able to determine. However, the years passed and she was still among the missing. Then a secret agent—one she herself had helped to educate—was committed to a Swiss sanatorium as an incurable narcotic addict. Here, exclaimed the European press, was the last tragic chapter of the life story of a remarkable German "adventuress." Loss of power she had enjoyed, lack of excitements which had stimulated taut nerves, had eventually caused this breakdown. To ease the pain of Teutonic defeat, the embittering circumstances of peace, she had begun taking morphine. And so this "Mademoiselle le Docteur"—whose name was given as Anna-Marie Lesser—had come to the utter ruin of her health.

That news dispatch, cabled around the globe, was just a bit too thick for Elsbeth Schragmüller. Whereupon she consented at last to acknowledge her wartime identity and to defend, if not her clandestine activities in Antwerp, her present temperate life. In so doing she revealed herself finally to her mystified former adversaries, with the substantiation of Colonel Walther Nicolai, today connected with the Nazi secret police service or *Gestapo*, but then conducting a private detective agency in Berlin.

Still the doctor of philosophy, Elsbeth Schragmüller chooses today a life of studious retirement in a quiet street of Munich. Her mother survives and is said to be her only companion. *Doktor* Elsbeth has avoided every form of self-exploitation, or she might have become the most famous surviving woman partisan of the World War. But she has declined to profit from her secret-service "reputation" by writing her memoirs, has claimed neither rewards nor honors for four years of unsparing vigilance and devotion. She has complained, however, that the French Secret Service, once its operatives discovered her residence—which seems to have occurred even before the Anna-Marie Lesser episode—refused to believe that she had really retired at the close of the war. French spies continued to spy upon her, which is not surprising, for the French not only felt the sharpest impact of her plots and counter-plots, but also have distinguished themselves in misinterpreting her character or confusing her identity.

It is surprising to find even fewer traces of accuracy about her in the writings of Major Massard, Charles Lucieto, and other Frenchmen than in the works of Thomas Coulson, who seems to have once been a major in the British Intelligence. Captain Landau, whose Belgian agents were her local adversaries in Antwerp, calls her "Frau Doktor . . . Chief of the German Secret Service in Belgium" and curiously puts his trust in the rogue's-gallery portrait by Blasco y Ibañez out of Lucieto and other imaginations of the French Secret Service. Landau, however, has admitted to the writer that his description (*All's Fair;* p. 165) of the "good-looking, buxom, middle-aged" *Frau Doktor* was mainly the figment of a subordinate's melodramatic brain.

If Elsbeth Schragmüller will not publish any memoirs of secret service—a modern oddity of real psychological significance—we had best rely on Walther Nicolai's limited published praise of her. He does not say she was the equal of two divisions of the Prussian Guard, for he knows the hitting power of even *one* division. She was not a morphine addict, or anything else pitiful, nerve shattered, bloodstained or intellectually weak. She was the equal of a patrician cavalry officer, says Nicolai, and her superiors were proud of her: high praise from a Nazi spy-master, trained in the traditions of the German General Staff.

CHAPTER 76 *The Spy "School" of Alice Dubois*

¹Major Cameron was one of the most capable and talented officers of the British Intelligence. Like others of his calling, when the tensions and nerve strain subsided, he appears to have found his recollections of the long secret-service combat unbearable. He committed suicide.

[2] This ratio is not the exaggeration it may appear. For example, scarcely 2,000 persons were professionally engaged in espionage at the outbreak of the World War; and, omitting all the frauds and pretenders, not less than 50,000 persons had some active connection with espionage or counter-espionage before November 11, 1918. Only a small proportion of these had any considerable training before setting to work; at least 40,000 were amateurs in every sense of the word.

[3] It has been alleged that Alice Dubois, on her last journey to Tournai, was careless enough to bring with her several new and fraudulent passports to be distributed among her still-numerous followers. And when interrogated she is said to have made one blunder against which she had repeatedly warned the others—"if questioned, never admit knowing any one who has been unfortunate enough to be caught." In naming those who might vouch for her, or help her arrange a bail bond, she mentioned several persons already under suspicion like herself or actually in jail like Charlotte. But even without such admissions, the German counter-espionage officers had all the incriminating proofs that a court required.

[4] M. Antoine Redier, biographer of Louise de Bettignies, furnishes a convincing account of the punishment of the famous spy which resulted in her death. She had incited other prisoners against working upon munitions for the German army, which was contrary to the laws of war. As a retaliation the prison governor, Durr, ordered that she be deprived of her warm woolen clothing and compelled to wear a prison uniform of cotton. "I will see that she dies of cold," this furious official is alleged to have promised.

Freezing weather, cold stone walls, little nourishment and no room for exercise combined to punish Louise de Bettignies, who had refused, and inspired others to refuse, to work on enemy grenades. Pneumonia with a temperature running above 104° was the result; and because of subsequent medical neglect, even after her period of special incarceration had ended, purulent pleurisy developed.

A pleural abscess which grew from day to day finally caused the prison doctor to order an operation. Louise asked to have it performed in Cologne or Bonn. But at length it was performed in the prison hospital at Siegburg by a young surgeon from Bonn, assisted by the prison physician and two nuns. The room, according to surviving prisoners who experienced its surgical horrors, was unheated and badly lighted. Louise had received no attention preliminary to operating. Her wound did not heal; the Bonn surgeon never visited Siegburg again; and the prison doctor gave the spy little consideration. Only when a fatal infection developed was the prisoner removed to the Hospital Sainte-Marie in Cologne.

[5] Victorious British troops marched into Cologne, and officers of the Intelligence found a white cross lying on the ground which bore the name of their daring espionne:

Louise de Bettignies
gest.
27/9/18

Subsequently France and her native city of Lille accorded Louise the tribute of a public funeral with full military honors. Four medals, two British, two French, were pinned on a white silk cushion that lay upon her coffin. The citation with which this plucky young amateur of secret service was awarded the *croix de guerre* read in part:

"For having voluntarily devoted herself to the service of her country; for having affronted, with inflexible courage, the perils and difficulties of this great work; for having surmounted, thanks to her exceptional abilities, the greatest obstacles, risking her life continually, and assuming during the whole of her services tremendous responsibilities; *a heroism which has rarely been surpassed.*"

CHAPTER 77 *Liquidation of a Luxury*

[1] Alfred Morain, *The Underworld of Paris.*
[2] Morain.
[3] Compton Mackenzie, the novelist, who held a responsible post as an officer of the British Intelligence during the World War, has published his mildly ironic recollections of king's messengers traveling dangerously on ships liable to be torpedoed by

NOTES

German submarines and bringing safely to Athens and the British Legation, at the risk of their lives—tennis balls.

⁴Sir Basil Thomson confesses to such a gallant excess in *My Experiences at Scotland Yard* as having said to the forty-year-old "Javanese" dancer: "Madame . . . if you will take the word of one nearly twice your age, give up what you have been doing." Perhaps the most delicate counter-espionage technique in the history of the war!

⁵The wife of Joseph Caillaux shot and killed Gaston Calmette, editor of *Le Figaro*, and was acquitted after a sensational trial at which her chief counsel, Maître Labori—one of those we have seen fighting to save Alfred Dreyfus—proved that Calmette had threatened to publish letters compromising M. Caillaux because they had been written to his present wife, the accused, before his divorce from his first wife.

The cell, No. 12, had also been occupied by the condemned spy, Marguerite Francillard.

⁶President François Félix Faure.

⁷If Herr von Jagow of the Berlin police had 30,000 marks to pay Mata Hari as an espionage retainer, that appears rather a heavy deduction from the total German secret-service allowance of 450,000 marks. Every budget in Europe had its nooks and crannies where extra sums needed for espionage might be carried to passage in the national parliament, and the Berlin police budget would have been an excellent hiding place for such funds. However, it still seems the more probable that Von Jagow had nothing whatever to do with external military espionage and that like the German attachés and others intimate with the dancer after the outbreak of war, he padded his accounts with a courtesan.

⁸The dancer was genuinely devoted to the blinded Russian captain, and one of the last letters which she wrote at Saint-Lazare, just before being taken to Vincennes to be shot, was addressed to him.

⁹Mata Hari appears to have communicated with a German Intelligence officer in Amsterdam, Major Specht—not, as we know, the "head of the German Secret Service", but one of Nicolai's energetic subordinates.

¹⁰This dialogue is taken from the official record, as quoted by M. Alfred Morain, former head of the French Department of Criminal Investigation.

¹¹Mornet's position at the trial of the alleged spy was that of Judge Advocate General.

¹²It is one thing, however, to hear the evidence offered to a military court implicating a prisoner accused of espionage and quite another to assemble on very short notice rebuttal testimony which will be so overwhelming as to persuade judges in whose minds the guilt of the accused is already an established fact.

¹³Sir Basil Thomson observes that Mata Hari had "a reputation in Holland, where people were proud of her success and, so cynics said, of her graceful carriage, which was rare in that country." But naturally a prime minister's arguments in favor of rescuing the Dutch woman who had developed a graceful carriage could not be presented to Queen Wilhelmina.

¹⁴The French journalist, Georges du Parcq, in his interesting reminiscences, *Crime Reporter*, has told of his last interview with Mata Hari, whom he had known for years. "You have been a good friend to me," the dancer said, continuing with painful hesitancy, "I have a child . . . a little girl. She is in a convent in Holland . . . and of course I shall never see her again, Georges, and I wonder . . . when the war is over . . . you would go and see her and be a friend to her?" Du Parcq answered: "Willingly. You have my word of honor. I will do everything I can." And then Mata Hari, who all too evidently had *no* hope of escaping execution, gave him, says the journalist, a miniature of herself "in a frame of small pearls . . . just head and shoulders, and executed by Fossard, the famous Swiss miniaturist," and asked him to give it to her daughter.

CHAPTER 78 *Who Was Guilty?*

¹*Le Petit Journal*, Paris; issue of July 16, 1925.
²E. N. Massard, *Les Espionnes à Paris*.
³Du Parcq, *Crime Reporter*.

NOTES

CHAPTER 79 *Stratagems Afloat*

[1] The undersea career of this submarine investigator was varied and thrilling enough to add a volume to the already extensive and dramatic library of naval memoirs of the great war; but Shipwright Miller, modest and reticent, chose, when the conflict with the U-boats ended, to retire into the comparative obscurity of a veteran naval rating aboard a British man-of-war. He had been promoted to the highest noncommissioned rank and, so far as is known, neither expected nor received any other reward or recognition.

[2] *The Kaiser's Coolies* by Theodor Plivier will inform any reader not already familiar with that compelling book just *why* the common seamen of the Imperial German Navy developed their revolutionary impulses from an intense hatred of so many of their superior officers.

[3] In locating one submarine Miller found it lying squarely across the hulk of the very trawler which had produced sensational headlines in an earlier war. During the Russo-Japanese War, after calamitous reverses on sea and land, the military minds of St Petersburg decided to restore the prestige of the tsar's government by sending the Baltic Fleet to the Asiatic theater of war. Passage through the Suez Canal was refused as a violation of neutrality; the fleet must go around Africa.

The Japanese were in no danger of being taken by surprise. Even so, the Suez rankled in Russian minds, and when the Baltic Fleet steamed out into the North Sea and headed southward, it passed close to British fishing craft and fired upon one venturesome trawler, sinking it with loss of life. That aroused the whole British Empire. But the tsar's diplomats hastened to make amends, explaining that a battle fleet in time of war can not permit foreign vessels to crowd its course—that the trawler might even have been chartered by Japanese spies. And there the incident ended.

Miller's light, more than ten years later, by an incredible coincidence played upon that sunken trawler as it lay beneath the U-boat. And the diver must have remembered grimly that the battleship which had fired upon the fishing boat had not long afterward joined it in "Davy Jones' locker." The Russian Baltic Fleet, commanded by Admiral Rozhestvenski, having steamed so many thousands of miles to the war zone, met the full weight of the confident Japanese Navy in the Straits of Tsu-shima and was utterly destroyed.

[4] Scores were decorated for extraordinary heroism; the crews were awarded sums of "prize money"; and many were promoted. Commander [later Rear Admiral] Gordon Campbell, most celebrated of Q-boat captains, Lieutenant Commander Harold Auten of the Stockforce, Lieutenant Charles G. Bonner and Lieutenant Ronald Neil Stuart, Petty Officer Ernest Pitcher and Seaman William Williams received the Victoria Cross.

[5] The Q-boats developed largely from practical experience in decoying German submarines, and many were later designed so that steam might be turned on from the bridge. By enveloping the center part of the ship in steam, it was made to seem to have been badly hit in the boiler and engine rooms. Often, as in the case of the Pargust, no such stricken masquerade was necessary. A U-boat would sometimes pump out oil as it submerged and endeavored to escape, oil being the equivalent of steam as proof of a mortal wound in the hull of an undersea raider.

[6] Lieutenant R. N. Stuart and Seaman W. Williams were the representatives chosen. These and other heroes of the crew of the Pargust were aboard the mystery ship Dunraven, Captain Gordon Campbell, V.C., D.S.O., commanding, in its never-to-be-forgotten duel with the U.C.-71, a great undersea cruiser of the latest, armored class. Since the Dunraven was disguised as an armed merchant vessel, it put up a fight—three brave men exposing themselves to the distant U-boat's shell fire while staging an "act" of mishandling the 2½-pounder aft. Leading Seaman Cooper, Seaman Williams, V.C., and Wireless Operator Statham conducted themselves as awkward, frightened amateur gunners, making all their puny shots fall short to lure the enemy nearer.

Shell bursts set the Dunraven on fire. After the first "panic party" had pulled away, a second was allowed visibly to abandon ship, hoping to reassure a wary German commander. Meanwhile, the fire grew worse. Wireless signals had to be sent out warning men-of-war to divert all traffic below the horizon so that nothing should interrupt the final phase of the action. Smoke from the burning vessel prevented its own gun crews from getting in a fair shot at the enemy on the surface. Until at last, being equipped with torpedo tubes, the Dunraven tried to blow up its adversary. But the two torpedoes discharged failed to score a hit.

Waiting and hoping for their turn at the Q-boat's guns, seamen sat on deck when it was growing red hot; and knowing the magazines were underneath, one young fellow, Martindale, who was badly wounded, tore up his shirt to stuff into their mouths to keep out the fumes. Others lifted off the deck onto their laps the ready-use boxes of cordite to delay their exploding. Every minute they expected to be blown up, yet they knew if they moved, all chance of bagging the submarine would be lost. And so none moved until given permission to do so!

Later, in tow, the Dunraven sank lower and lower until its fire was extinguished and its deck awash. Then word was regretfully passed to abandon ship. Its crew had failed to destroy the enemy, but failed heroically, and, as the American Admiral William S. Sims wrote to Gordon Campbell:

"It is purely incidental that the submarine escaped: that was simply due to an unfortunate piece of bad luck. . . . According to my idea of such matters, the standard of conduct set by you and your crew is worth infinitely more than the destruction of a submarine. Long after we are dust and ashes, the story of this fight will be an invaluable inspiration to British and American naval officers and men—a demonstration of the extraordinary degree to which the patriotism, loyalty, personal devotion, and bravery of a crew may be inspired."

[7]For an account of how one skillful German secret agent obtained an early warning of the development of the British Q-boats, the reader may consult Chapter 85, page 647.

[8]On July 24, 1915, came the first Q-boat victory when the Prince Charles, a coastal steam collier of 400 tons with an armament of two 6-pounders and two 3-pounders, under the command of Lieutenant Mark Wardlaw, D.S.O., sank the U-36. The final decisive Q-boat triumph was the sinking on November 9, 1918, of the U-34 by the Privet or Q-19, under Lieutenant Commander Matheson, R.N.R., who with the same mystery ship had accounted for the formidable U-85 on March 12 of the preceding year.

Chapter 80 *Stratagems Afield*

[1]Ferdinand Tuohy, *The Secret Corps.*

[2]No professional smuggler since Karl Schulmeister has become a celebrated agent of espionage. Yet war, the old outlaw, seems to change other outlaws into honest, useful men. One ventures to believe that no class of individuals active during the World War proved more valuable partners in secret service or tools of the belligerent governments than the smugglers on every frontier. Joseph Crozier and Henry Landau, two spy-masters who employed them regularly on the Belgo-Netherlands boundary, grow lyrical about their utility, courage and resourcefulness, and what is more, seem to have paid their smuggler *passeurs* accordingly.

[3]Conducting prisoners of war, in working parties or any other formation, into battle areas was, of course, expressly forbidden by the Hague conventions and all other acknowledged laws of "civilized warfare."

[4]A live mouse or sparrow was also used to detect whether the current was turned on along the electrified barriers.

[5]Landau of the British Secret Service, in charge of offensive espionage in the Netherlands, tells in his book *All's Fair* of an amiable brother and sister, White Russian refugees, who offered him "for thirty thousand gulden . . . a copy of the Dutch Army mobilization plans." Fearing that they were being used to compromise him, he dropped the engaging pair like the proverbial red-hot stove. "Hat in hand, I expressed regret that a wonderful friendship had come to an end." After warning them, "for their own good, not to have anything more to do with the matter", the

British captain abruptly took leave of the friends he had hitherto prized. But with the live-and-let-live attitude of the opposing secret services in "neutral" Holland, he did not report Tania and Sergei, who might be innocent, to the Dutch authorities.

⁶The French agents, Fouquenot and Creusen, were seized by the Germans on Dutch soil, a few meters from the electrified barriers and dragged into Belgium. The Dutch were powerless in the face of the German bluff—that agents of the secret police had made the "arrests" on Belgian soil. There were no eyewitnesses; it was simply the prisoners' word against their captors' sworn testimony. Fouquenot and Creusen were convicted in Liége, but the Germans had not quite enough brazen nerve to execute them; and so they spent three years in prison, being liberated at the time of the Armistice. According to Captain Landau, it was Creusen who later made friends with the Kaiser's cook at Amerongen and hatched a plot to poison the All Highest Fugitive, after he had found refuge on Dutch soil. The British Secret Service was not interested in this harebrained stroke of vengeance, and Creusen, duped by the cook, was ultimately denounced to the Dutch police, who avoided making the affair public by deporting Creusen to Belgium.

⁷Landau and Crozier, perhaps owing to differences in racial temperament rather than to divergent conceptions of veracity, give strangely opposite views of the dangers and tensions of the secret service "duel" waged on Dutch soil. The interested reader should compare Landau's—"Instead, the greatest tranquillity reigned. Our codes were left unguarded at night in an ordinary safe, an easy mark for any cracksman; our couriers came and went unprotected" (*All's Fair*, pp. 131–132)—with Joseph Crozier's remarkably candid account of "The Expiation of a Coward", or the violent removal of the informer, Devos of Baarle. (*In the Enemy's Country*, pp. 187–191.)

⁸General Wille, chief of staff of the Swiss army adorned every suspect list of the Allies, and no wonder in view of his consistent attitude throughout the war. An amusing *gaffe* attributed to Wille had for its scene the Bellevue Palace Hotel in Bern. The last great drive of the German armies in the West had begun, shattering the British Fifth Army and threatening the whole line of the Western Front. Wille and his adjutant entered an elevator, in which they found the American secretary of legation, Hugh Wilson, who slightly resembled one of the Austrian attachés. Seeing him in a dim light, Wille saluted, bowed, beamed, waxed eloquent. "Isn't it splendid?" he cried. "What a glorious victory! Thousands of prisoners, hundreds of guns!" Then the adjutant whispered something to him, and the Swiss general abruptly had the elevator stopped and got out.

⁹Captain Peter E. Wright, *At the Supreme War Council*.

According to Foch's Plan H, the troops of the Swiss confederation, "after acting as covering troops, would have retired to the central, inexpugnable *massif* of their country, while fifty French divisions would have caught in flank the German armies pouring through the flat corridor of the Aar Valley, too narrow for them either to deploy or retreat, while the Swiss army hung on the other flank."

Chapter 81 *Caporetto: The Perfect Surprise Attack*

¹General Maximilian Ronge, *Kriegs- und industrie-spionage*.
²Armee-Ober-Kommando: the Austro-Hungarian G.H.Q.
³Captain Henry Landau has told in his book, *All's Fair*, how he was stricken with "blank amazement" when a deserter offered to sell him an authentic copy of the latest edition of the German Field Post Directory, stolen but two days before from the Düsseldorf Post Office. "An army of spies could not have gathered the data it contained. It made our Brown Book look silly, and yet the Brown Book represented the sum total of our information about the German Army gained during more than three years of spy activity, and from the interrogation of several hundred thousand German prisoners of war captured by both the French and the British armies. By adroit negotiation and by handing us for examination a torn-out page instead of the whole directory, the deserter could have demanded and received a fabulous sum for it; instead, he meekly accepted a hundred pounds, the first sum I offered him."
⁴Erich Ludendorff, *My War Memories*.

NOTES 729

⁵The new German "infiltration" tactics distinguished the great surprise offensives of General von Hutier at Riga and Von der Marwitz at Cambrai, both of which were tactically on a par with the Caporetto triumph. The surprise attack of Rawlinson's Fourth British Army on August 8, 1918 was tactically and in point of secretive preparation an even more brilliant stroke. According to Captain Liddell Hart, even "the War Cabinet in London was kept in the dark, and in that august assembly the Australian Prime Minister, Mr Hughes, was in course of a vehement demand that the Australians should be taken out of the line when a telegram brought the undreamt of news that the Australians were far on the other side of the line." But for the story of secret service, Caporetto—with its preliminary surprise assault upon the morale of the Italian forces—has an obviously special significance.

⁶In view of the Italians' more recent conception of themselves as great African conquerors and invincible soldiers with a national past of glorious victories, it would be wholesome and chastening for them frequently to remember Caporetto. But instead they are bent on obliterating it. The power of Italian propaganda was able to command the removal of scenes of the terrible retreat from a motion picture version of Ernest Hemingway's *Farewell to Arms*, not only from prints to be exhibited in Italy or Italian colonies, but from *all* prints, thus distorting history with Fascist abandon as well as a masterpiece of truth-telling about the European war.

⁷J. C. Silber, the German spy who "spent the war" as a British postal censor, tells in *The Invisible Weapons* of having read that only British drums and music could at first be sent to stiffen the morale of the Italians. Haig had just finished squandering at Passchendaele *one fourth* of all British effectives, a force of veteran troops strong enough to have knocked over Boroevic and reached Trieste if transferred in time to counter-attack the Austrians on the shore of the Adriatic.

⁸Cadorna was characteristically "promoted" to membership in the Supreme War Council at Versailles, while Badoglio, whose troops were of all those in the line the most terribly shattered, made that defeat the foundation for the military renown which would lead him to Addis Ababa.

Chapter 82 *French Operatives in the Secret War*

¹Joseph Crozier, who was also Lieutenant Pierre Desgranges of the Second Bureau de l'État-Major, has told (*In the Eenemy's Country*) of the continual friction between his secret-service mission and the more hidebound elements of the French army command, as represented by General Boucabeille, military attaché at The Hague. Crozier was recalled and ordered to report to his regiment—but not to go to the front, lest he be captured and executed by the Germans as a former spy. What really mattered to him, however, was the ruin of the painstaking work of months; and, thanks to the persistence and loyalty of his chief, the able Colonel Wallner, Crozier (and his other self, the elusive Desgranges) were restored to secret-service duty at the one point where "they" could render the best service to France.

²Commandant—then Captain—Georges Ladoux, in charge of a vital branch of French counter-espionage, endured much the same want of professional appreciation. In his case this came to a boil only after the war had ended, when he suffered the public humiliation of being tried upon technical charges relating to passport control and the misuse of passports by his agents. Ladoux was acquitted but did not long survive the unhappy termination of brilliant confidential services. And, as is customary, news of his exoneration received much less public notice than the original accusations.

³The Allies had a number of credible warnings from spies and other sources concerning the novel menace of the gas-cloud attack. The only French general who took the danger seriously, and warned the neighboring British, was General Ferry commanding the Eleventh Division. A German deserter who gave himself up near Langemarck on April 13 was even found to have on him a primitive respirator, which he said had been issued as a safeguard to all the attackers. But Ferry's superiors reproved him, especially for having warned the British direct, instead of through the usual liaison channels via Joffre's headquarters. And after the German success with

the chlorine cloud—which their own supreme command was also too "scientifically hidebound" to exploit—Ferry was punished, as was repeatedly the custom in the French army during the war, by being removed *for having been right.*

[4]Lucieto, *On Special Missions.*

[5]M. Edmond Bayle. He found that the shells had been charged with phosgene and chloroformiat of trichloromethyl, a suffocating gas of great power.

[6]Sound-ranging was one more of the new partners of Intelligence or military secret service brought to a high average of effectiveness and utility during the Great War. By means of sound-ranging devices—including very often a keenly attuned human ear —it was possible to determine the approximate position and caliber of the Germans' heavy ordnance on the Western Front. Ferdinand Tuohy has written (*The Secret Corps*) that one of the very best amateur sound-rangers he encountered in the war zone was a girl employed in an estaminet close to the British lines, who knew the sound of each of the "big ones" and could detect a newcomer among the enemy howitzers or great rifles the first time she heard it discharged.

[7]Oberste Heeres-Leitung: German G.H.Q.

[8]Duchêne was, it appears, a perfect example of the professional stuffed shirt or inflated uniform. He rebuffed junior British commanders who appealed to him to be warned of coming dangers with a curt "J'ai dit." And he ignored other warnings forwarded from American headquarters with the endorsement of Colonel de Cointet, chief of the French Intelligence.

[9]The secret agent's warning, dated May 25, about the attack coming on May 27 was not received, it is said, until June 6, on which date the German advance had penetrated the Chemin-des-Dames line to a maximum depth of more than thirty miles. But even if it had traveled its roundabout course more swiftly, Waegele's warning would never have influenced a commander as stupid and obstinate as General Duchêne.

CHAPTER 83 *The Censor in Secret Service*

[1]A motorcar is said to have been bought with this money, christened "The Müller", and used to the end of the war by junior officers of the Intelligence on duty in England.

[2]Thomson, *My Experiences at Scotland Yard.*

[3]Colonel von Falkenhausen was the German military attaché at Athens; Baron Schenck von Schweinsberg was in charge of German espionage and special propaganda in Greece and the Aegean Islands. The German minister, Count von Mirbach-Harff, was frequently embarrassed by the activities of his colleagues, though he himself and the naval attaché, Baron de Grancy, were also actively in league with the powerful pro-German elements of the court party headed by Tino and Sophie.

[4]Brigadier-General G. K. Cockerill, director of Special Intelligence at the British War Office in his final summary of the activities of his department during the World War.

[5]T. M. Johnson in *Our Secret War* tells of another American officer who wrote abusively about a censor with whom he had already experienced certain difficulties, referring to him as "that poor slacker" who "had to do something to justify his existence." But it chanced that the "poor slacker" came from a combat unit and was just then censoring mail while recovering from serious wounds. He had been decorated for gallantry in action; and when the offensive letter was found to violate several strict army regulations, the writer, according to Johnson, "got what was coming to him."

[6]When General Pershing told the French soon after the Armistice that he knew his troops were anxious to be sent home, it was a base censor's report which had informed him. And when officers from Pershing's staff investigated and stamped out the abuses in military prisons, such as that one near Paris where ex-Lieutenant "Hard-Boiled" Smith and his uniformed thugs held sway in the best manner of political police in a European autocracy, news of the oppressors had first come from those overworked, unknown men who read soldiers' mail.

[7]The base censor received 30,846,630 letters and 6,335,645 of them were actually examined, according to the statistics published by T. M. Johnson. Not until July 1918 was a chemical laboratory set up; and thereafter it examined 53,658 suspicious documents for traces of secret ink.

NOTES

Chapter 85 Silber and Zievert, the Censor Spies

[1] J. C. Silber, *The Invisible Weapons*.

[2] The British department of censorship grew under the pressure of its own successful operation into a huge organization that moved successively from the General Post Office in Mt Pleasant to Salisbury House, from there in 1915 to "York" and "Imperial" Houses in Kingsway, and a year after that to a block of buildings in Carey Street. A staff of 3,700 persons was employed in the London department, with an additional 1,500 engaged in the censorship branch at Liverpool. There were other branches at Folkestone, Gibraltar and Alexandria. In view of this vast organization it is not surprising that J. C. Silber could conceal his enemy espionage sideline, but rather more to his credit that he made his mark in the extensive work of the bureau and gathered for his share much important reading to do.

[3] One of the curiosities of this espionage trial was the discovery in court that these Zievert subordinates had applied themselves so faithfully to their secluded form of secret service, living apart from their Russian neighbors, they had never learned to speak Russian fluently or without a strong German accent.

[4] Zievert in attacking heavily sealed letters, for example, had found that lifting off the wax seals with a heated blade or hot wire was unworthy of his perlustrating genius. Sometimes, however careful one might be, the blade or wire slightly scorched the envelope, and notable Russians were too accustomed to spies not to recognize what that meant. Zievert therefore had invented a device he is said to have been able to use with unique and incredible dexterity. It consisted only of a thin, round, polished and flexible stick about the size and diameter of a knitting needle. This was slit along half its length. It could be inserted under the flap of a sealed envelope at the corner, pushed nearly across to the opposite corner, until the letter caught in the slit and was then gripped by a swift turn. Next came a delicate move: to wind the letter slowly and carefully around the stick without so distending the envelope at the top that the flap would be strained and the seal or seals upon it cracked or marred. Once the letter had been furled tightly around the stick, it could be withdrawn from under the envelope flap at the corner. And having been read and recorded, it then must be rewound about the stick, inserted under the flap again, very gently unwound, loosened from the slit in the stick, and the stick finally withdrawn with care from the envelope, which, being no doubt a bit bulged at the top by its recent invasion, had to be pressed flat by hand before being sent on its way. If, as was alleged at the time, Zievert mastered this dexterous feat so that it served him regularly in Black Cabinet investigations, we must number him among the most talented of his curious calling.

[5] Only Nihilists, Social Revolutionaries, Bolsheviki and such political refugees or agitators avoided the discernments of the Russian *Cabinet Noir* by the simple process of putting no trust in the imperial post office. Russia's liberals and radicals developed an underground courier system of their own, largely contrived through the revolutionary sympathies of workers in the imperial railway and express services.

Chapter 87 An American Secret-Service Story

[1] Lieutenant-General Hunter Liggett and Wesley W. Stout, *A. E. F., Ten Years Ago in France*.

[2] A German officer attached to the Turkish army was so unnerved by his remembrance of the slaughter of the British that he committed suicide aboard one of the German vessels in the Bosphorus. Colonel Williams, aboard the same ship at the time, had noticed the German's gloomy state of mind and, on inquiring about it, was told: "I can't sleep. I keep seeing those Englishmen piling up in front of our guns."

[3] The tragedy and waste of Gallipoli was lightened by this remarkably ingenious evacuation, without the loss of a single man after he left the trenches. The chief stratagem devised was like, yet a substantial improvement upon, the device applied in that same quarter of the world by the Persian conqueror, Darius, some twenty-four hundred and thirty-five years earlier. About 520 B.C. Darius was compelled to cross the Danube by stealth to withdraw his army from its punishing contact with a plague of more mobile Scythian horsemen. He accomplished this by deliberately sacrificing his

wounded and sick; after telling them he meant to launch a surprise attack against the Scythians at nightfall, he stole away with all his able-bodied troops, leaving his camp fires blazing and the customary noises and movements of the camp behind him.

The British evacuation was more humanely conducted, with extraordinary skill and complete deception of the enemy. While the front trenches were kept fully manned, other troops were withdrawn and embarked each night. There were some 80,000 Turks entrenched before the Anzac and Suvla lines, at a distance of from twenty yards to half a mile. But to prevent discovery, when the night came to leave even the forward trenches, rifles were arranged with water dripping into tins which were attached to the triggers, so that when the tin became heavy enough it would pull the trigger. Shots thus were intermittently discharged from the evacuated trenches long after the last British soldier had put to sea. The withdrawal was completed at 3:30 A.M. on December 21, 1915; and Sir Charles Monro issued a Special Order of the Day, congratulating all ranks justifiably on "an achievement without parallel in the annals of war."

[5] Liggett.

[6] T. M. Johnson, in *Our Secret War*, says that Colonel Williams was "nicknamed 'Houdini' because he liked the mystic." It would seem more than probable that this officer appropriately earned the nickname of the world-famous escape artist by the ingenious manner of his own escape from the German destroyer's searching party and on past the U-boat blockade.

[6] The grounded Zeppelin, L-49, was triumphantly captured by a party of Frenchmen too old for military service—which was pretty old in the battle-worn France of 1917—who were out on a boar hunt. Being armed, the hunters were able to prevent the German crew from firing a Very pistol into the envelope of the airship and destroying it by fire.

[7] Lieutenant-General Hunter Liggett.

[8] When mentioning this talented American Intelligence officer, every commentator—with the exception of Captain Liddell Hart—feels obliged to add with a kind of astonishment that in civil life Captain (afterward Major) Samuel T. Hubbard, Jr. had been a cotton broker in New York City. It is perhaps surprising to learn of a cotton broker who found in himself notable capacity for the intricate work of the Intelligence; yet it is really no more astonishing than the number of professional soldiers found in these annals who were unsuited to Intelligence duty and even totally incompetent soldiers.

[9] *A. E. F., Ten Years Ago in France.*

[10] Macdonogh, as a colonel and the successor to Colonel Edmonds as chief of military espionage and secret service, was attached to the staff of Sir John French in the opening months of the war. By October 1917 he was chief of Intelligence of the British War Office.

[11] A letter, dated October 25, 1917, came to the chief of the Intelligence section, General Staff, United States army headquarters in France from Rear-Admiral W. R. Hall—the now-celebrated Sir Reginald Hall of the British Naval Intelligence—who wrote:

"Commander Babcock, Admiral Sims' aide, has handed to me the important documents which you were good enough to send to Admiral Sims.

"I hasten to express to you my most grateful thanks for your kindness and promptitude in sending me this most valuable document, which I assure you will be of the greatest value. You may rely that any information contained therein which will be of value to the United States forces will be at once communicated to them."

www.ingramcontent.com/pod-product-compliance
Lightning Source LLC
Chambersburg PA
CBHW070831160426
43192CB00012B/2170